COUNTER THE COUNTERFEIT & BUILD A STRONG FOUNDATION FOR SUCCESS

Books are our best friends, is the adage we have grown up with. However, the pirates of piracy are continuously forging 'our best friends'. Our books and their supplementary online resources are copyrighted, and we don't lend any right-to-copy. Piracy is synonymous to stealing books.

Knowledge comes real, let's not encourage its counterfeit. Therefore, we appeal all our readers to discourage pirated books and **choose authentic ones**.

HOW TO IDENTIFY THE PIRATED BOOKS?

1 COVER AND SPINE

- Look and feel (new or used book)
- Blurred images on the cover
- Hologram pasted on front
- Defective spine (wrinkles) or air pocket at its bottom
- Unclear ISBN/bar codes
- Missing/non-operational Unique Coupon Code for exclusive access to **McGraw Hill** Edge

2 TEXT/PRINTING/BINDING

- Uneven inking of pages
- Poor quality or blurred photographs/images/charts
- Substandard paper quality and opacity
- Misaligned pages
- Missing pages
- Inferior binding quality

You can further watch this video on How to identify a pirated book

For more information about identifying piracy, visit **https://www.mheducation.co.in/piracy**

To report a pirated book, send 'Hi' on WhatsApp code given on the back cover or write to us at **support.india@mheducation.com**.

Reported pirated books are examined to combat their piracy.

Let's fight the Pirates of Piracy and resolve to go for original!

About the Author

M Karthikeyan holds a Commerce degree from the University of Madras and a Law degree from Dr. Ambedkar Government Law College, Chennai. A seasoned legal professional with nearly two decades of experience, he currently serves as the Senior Central Government Panel Counsel at the Madras High Court.

Previously, as Special Government Pleader and Additional Government Pleader, he represented the Government of Tamil Nadu in numerous writ petitions and appeals before the Honourable Madras High Court. He has also been empaneled with major financial institutions and government entities, specialising in diverse legal domains, including constitutional and taxation law, where he has served as Amicus Curiae in critical cases.

With extensive experience in representing government bodies and prestigious organisations, he has developed expertise in arbitration, banking claims, and legal documentation. Beyond his legal practice, he is deeply committed to academia, imparting knowledge on Ethics, Integrity, and Aptitude, as well as Governance and Internal Security for Civil Services Main Examination aspirants.

Ethics, Integrity and Aptitude

For Civil Services and Other State Services Examination

5e

M Karthikeyan

McGraw Hill Education (India) Private Limited

Published by McGraw Hill Education (India) Private Limited
Registered Office: Anjana Complex No: 5/90 A, Butt Road, St. Thomas Mount,
Chennai – 600016

Ethics, Integrity and Aptitude, 5e

Print Edition
ISBN-13: 978-93-6444-648-8
ISBN-10: 93-6444-648-8

E-Book
ISBN-13: 978-93-6444-402-6
ISBN-10: 93-6444-402-7

1 2 3 4 5 6 7 8 9 7091297 29 28 27 26 25

Printed and bound in India.

Typeset at Pee-Gee Graphics, A-6/95, Sector 15, Rohini, Delhi-110089 and printed at
Magic International Pvt. Ltd., Plot No. 26E, Sector-31, (Industrial), Site-IV, Greater Noida 201306
Cover Designer: Anita Kanojia
Cover Image Source: Shutterstock

Visit us at: www.mheducation.co.in
Write to us at: support.india@mheducation.com
CIN: U80302TN2010PTC111532
Toll Free Number: 1800 103 5875

This book is dedicated to my mentors

Shri Justice P. D. Audikesavalu

Judge, Madras High Court

Chennai

Shri Saidai Duraisamy

Chairman

Manidhanaeyam Charitable Trust

Chennai

Preface

I am delighted to present the thoroughly revised and updated edition of my widely acclaimed book -Ethics, Integrity, and Aptitude. This edition features a comprehensive revision to enhance students' and general readers' understanding of the subject.

Given the UPSC's increasing focus on case laws based on real-life scenarios in the Mains examination, this edition includes a substantial number of such case laws for practice.

To align with the evolving nature of General Studies Paper-IV, new chapters have been added, anticipating potential future questions. These additions aim to better equip aspirants for the exam.

Key Additions in the Fifth Edition

- New chapters on Applied Ethics and Case Studies
- More success stories on the Right to Information (RTI)
- Inclusion of recent e-Governance schemes
- A glossary for better understanding of key terms

Additionally, on EDGE there would be –

- Solved previous years' questions from 2013 onwards with model answers
- Additional learning resources on Indian Thinkers, Philosophers, Leaders and Reformers
- Exam-oriented videos explaining the strategy/tips to prepare paper IV

Structure of This Edition Resonates with the Syllabus

The book has been structured to align seamlessly with each topic in the Ethics syllabus for the Civil Services Main Examination. Since this paper was introduced in 2013, relevant content cannot be found in a single source or even multiple sources collectively. Recognising this challenge, I set out to create a comprehensive, one-stop reference that provides candidates with a clear and complete understanding of the syllabus.

Given the generalist nature of the examination, I can confidently say that after reading this book, you will be well-equipped to tackle almost all the questions in the Ethics paper with ease. To ensure relevance to the evolving UPSC pattern, additional chapters have been included to enhance conceptual clarity and broaden understanding of key topics.

I sincerely hope readers find this book valuable and effective in their preparation. Your feedback and suggestions for improving content and accuracy are always welcome, as they will contribute to making future editions even better.

All the Best!

M Karthikeyan

Acknowledgements

I sincerely express my deepest gratitude to everyone who supported me throughout the creation of this book. A special thanks to those who provided unwavering assistance in editing, proofreading, and designing.

I am especially grateful to Mr. S. Girissh, Mr. M. Senthil Kumar, Ms. P. Manaswini, and Mrs. P. Suriya, whose contributions played a vital role in the successful publication of this book.

Finally, I extend my heartfelt appreciation to my students—your curiosity and insightful questions inspired me to bring this compilation to life.

I extend my sincere gratitude to McGraw Hill Education, India for their support. A special thanks to Tanweer Ahmad, Nikhil Wadhera, Rahul Banerjee, Mausumi Mukherjee, and Pratiti Ghosh for their encouragement, invaluable assistance and support throughout this project for bringing the 5th edition.

Wishing all readers the very best on their journey of learning and growth.

M Karthikeyan

Contents

Essence, Determinants and Consequences of Ethics

1

1. INTRODUCTION

Can you respond to the following questions instantly?

1. Is abortion morally right or wrong? If considered wrong, what should be the stance for a girl, who becomes pregnant because of a group assault?
2. Should we award the death penalty to those who murder?
3. Can we go for euthanasia just because the chances of someone's survival are less?
4. How far is it justified to fatten a hen or a goat or a cow to provide us with nutrition?
5. How will you justify telling white lies to your friends, parents and your loved ones?

LEARNING OBJECTIVES

1. Understanding the concept of ethics, its distinction from morality, and its evolution
2. Comprehending the essence and foundational principles of ethics in human behaviour
3. Identifying the determinants of ethics, including religion, law, culture, morals, time, knowledge, and personal experiences, and analysing their influence on ethical decision-making
4. Evaluating the consequences of ethical behaviour on individuals and society, recognising its role in fostering personal integrity and social harmony

Do we have any standard ethical principle to answer all these questions? If yes, then what are the ethical standards that we can use to answer such questions where you need to make decisions? Do they emerge from societal norms, religious teachings, or from divine command? Are they secular, rooted in rationality and logic?

Maybe ethical standards have evolved from human nature and have been shaped by thousands of years of civilisation. The attempt to answer the above questions, logically, will result in a new branch of philosophy–Ethics. Ethics are a system of moral principles that define what is good for individuals and society. Ethics affect how people make decisions and lead their lives.

1.1 What is Ethics?

Ethics is a branch of **Axiology**[1] that is a field within Philosophy. It is mainly concerned with 'defending, systematising, and recommending concepts of right and wrong behaviour'.

Ethics covers the following dilemmas:

- How to live a good life
- Our rights and responsibilities
- The language of right and wrong
- Moral decisions – what is good and what is bad?

Our concepts of ethics have been derived from religions, philosophies and cultures. They infuse debates on topics like euthanasia, abortion, human rights, and professional conduct.

The word 'Ethics' is derived from the Greek word *ethikos,* which is further derived from *ethos,* meaning customs, usages or habits. Ethics can also be termed as 'Moral Philosophy'.

FAMOUS QUOTES ON ETHICS

"Ethics is the science of judging specifically human ends and the relationship of means to those ends. In some way it is also the art of controlling means so that they will serve human ends.

Thomas Garret

'Ethics' is the discipline that examines one's moral standard or moral standards of society. It asks how those standards apply to our life and whether these standards are reasonable or unreasonable — that is, whether these are supported by good reason or poor one. **Manuel G. Velasquez**

Ethics refer to a set of moral principles which should play a very significant role in guiding the conduct of managers and employees in the operation of any enterprise. **Dale S. Beach**

Ethics is that discipline which deals with what is good and bad and also deal with moral duty and obligation. Ethics are set of moral principles or values. **Carol Buchholtz**

Ethics is a conception of right and wrong conduct. Ethics tell us when our behaviour is moral and when it is moral. Ethics deal with fundamental human relationship how we think and behave towards others and how we want them to think and behave towards us. **Post, Frederick, and Lawrence**

Ethics are formalised principles derived from social value. These are moral principle which originate from social value and represent rules for moral behaviour and conduct of individuals or groups thereof carrying on business.

Webster's Directory"

[1]**Axiology:** It is a branch of philosophy, derived from the Greek word */axios/*, which means worth or value of something and */logos/* signifies the logic or thesis

Ethics is the science of the habitual conduct of human beings. Habits are the expression of settled disposition of the will or character. Character is the permanent habit of willing, the inner bent of the mind, which is expressed in habitual conduct. Character is the inner counterpart of conduct, which is outer expression.

Thus, ethics is the science of character and conduct. It evaluates the voluntary and habitual actions of people and considers their rightness and wrongness. It also evaluates the character of a person and considers their **virtuousness**[2] or **viciousness**[3]. Ethics is not concerned with the origin and growth of conduct such as psychology, rather, it is more concerned with the evaluation of conduct with reference to an ideal.

1.2 What Ethics is Not?

• Ethics is Not Same as Law

While there is a significant overlap between ethics and areas of law, such as human rights, they are not the same. Some frameworks of 'law' have resulted in discrimination, and even genocide (for example, **Apartheid**[4] in South Africa and Nazi Law).

Laws are rules and regulations that create a minimum set of standards with specific punishments for violations. Many people equate abiding by the law with ethics, a concept known as **'ethical legalism'**[5]. In other words, if an action is legal, it is, therefore, ethical. But law cannot cover every situation, so an ethical person will often try to go beyond what the law requires. For example, lying or betraying the confidence of a friend is not prohibited by laws, but it is considered unethical.

• Ethics is Not Same as Religion

An individual's religious background can influence their approach to ethics; for example, they may draw upon Islamic ethics, Christian ethics, or Sikh ethics.

However, most commonly, ethics is underpinned by approaches that are non-religious. Perspectives that are pluralist, secular, or perhaps described as humanist, are familiar in applied ethics. Sometimes, the approaches to applied ethics are not incompatible with their religious values.

Ethics is also not completely the purview of a religion or religious beliefs and ethical principles apply to everyone regardless of religious affiliation.

---

[2] **Virtuousness:** The quality of doing what is right and avoiding what is wrong

[3] **Viciousness:** Doing brutal things on purpose, out of ill-will

[4] **Apartheid:** A racial segregation that existed in South Africa from 1948 to 1990s. It was dismantled by Nelson Mandela in 1990

[5] **Ethical legalism:** Ethical legalism is the principle that legal regulations and disputes should be governed by clear, general, and predetermined rules

- **Ethics is Not Same as Economics**

By attempting to respond to resource challenges, an economic formula to work out value for money was raised. Value for money is an important consideration, but it is important to consider ethical issues such as distributive justice, as well as the benefits and harms of treatment and care interventions.

- **Ethics is Not Same as Opinion**

Ethics is not just a matter of opinion. There are many issues on which people commonly disagree, yet, there are also areas of widespread agreement, such as the condemnation of rape, torture, and genocide.

Ethics is not just based on what we feel is right or wrong. Sometimes, our feelings convey to us that we are facing an ethical dilemma, and we want to only act in the right way, but feelings and opinions may prevent us from behaving ethically, perhaps out of conflicting desires.

1.3 Ethics vs Morals

When discussing ethical behaviour, it is important to understand the differences between ethics and morals. Ethics are a set of rules that govern behaviour based on principles of right and wrong. Morals, on the other hand, refer to a person's personal beliefs and values.

The main difference between morals and ethics comes down to the level of social acceptance. Ethics are generally more broadly accepted and are shared by most of society. Conversely, morals are more subjective and personal, and may not be shared by everyone in the society.

By understanding the distinctions between ethics and morals, we can make better decisions. Knowing the way of differentiating between the two can help us act responsibly and adhere to a moral code. This course of action will be more consistent with our personal beliefs, and this will also promote an understanding of the rules and standards of behaviour expected by our communities.

At its core, morality is based on beliefs about what is right and wrong in terms of how people should act and treat each other. Morality can be influenced by personal convictions, cultural norms, and religious teachings.

Ethics is a branch of philosophy that examines questions of morality in a structured and systematic way. It attempts to determine criteria for evaluating moral judgements by understanding the nature of those moral judgements.

? Thought Box

A doctor working in a conflict zone is faced with a dilemma whether to follow hospital policy (ethics) and treat patients in the order of severity or prioritise a child whose parents are begging for help (morality).

How should the doctor navigate this situation, and what does this choice reveal about the tension between ethics and morality in real-life decisions?

1.4 Origin of Ethics

Ethics is thought to have emerged independently across different cultures and contexts.

In the Western philosophical tradition, many trace its roots to the ethical frameworks of the Ancient Greeks, beginning with thinkers like Socrates, Plato, and Aristotle.

Greek philosophy explored questions such as, 'What is the best way to live?', 'How can one live a fulfilling life?' et al. Greek thinkers believed that the aim of human life was to achieve a 'good life', which they equated with 'happiness'. For the Greeks, happiness went beyond mere pleasure or satisfaction. It meant attaining a life of excellence or virtue. This concept of virtue became central to ethics, the branch of philosophy focused on how people should live and what constitutes 'right' or 'wrong' action.

A central aspect of human experience is moral consciousness, and for a harmonious society, moral sensibility is essential. If we consider the Indian context, throughout Indian history, many religious teachers and philosophers have emphasised the rational foundations of morality. The duties outlined in the Dharmasastras are carefully structured guidelines intended to govern community life.

In India, ethical ideals and principles are largely drawn from the *Vedas*, as well as epics like *The Ramayana* and *The Mahabharata*, along with teachings from various Indian religions. This makes Indian ethics an essential component of religions that originated in India.

1.5 Origin of Ethics in India

Religion and ethics are deeply intertwined, with each religion offering a moral framework to guide its followers.

The moral behaviour of man is the foundation on which ethics, as a speculative science, is based. A substantial portion of the moral codes are also based on social customs, religious beliefs and traditions. In Indian ethics, morality is very much based on certain beliefs, customs and traditions of Indian religions. It should also be mentioned that the foundations of Indian ethics can be sought in the theological and metaphysical beliefs in the form of prayers, worship, and in the form of principles and ideals that direct man's life in society. When we speak of Indian ethics, we cannot deny the intimate relationship that prevails between ethics and religion.

Morality means living consciously within the framework of certain principles of conduct laid down by those regarded as authorities. Morality in general as an institution of life lies in the awareness of an important distinction between what is and what ought to be. Morality is basically the way of living with awareness based on a distinction between our animalistic demands, and the demands of the higher faculties of human life; and this makes the human distinct from animals. As the ancestors of Hindus in India were more spiritual in nature, they fixed their focus and attention on a life beyond death.

According to them, the human soul (inner being) is regarded as an eternal entity that co-exists with the Supreme Being. They strongly believed that every human soul goes to the round of births and rebirths, and reaps the fruits of the performed actions. When a soul comes to be associated with the human body, it is bound to perform certain actions and deeds in conformity with laws divine and therefore reap the fruits thereof. Hence, it is believed that if good deeds are performed, happiness results and if evil deeds are performed, misery falls to the lot of the doer.

The human soul is immortal and continuously engaged in action, bound to experience the results of its deeds—it reaps what it sows. Since every person ultimately seeks happiness, the fruit of karma, it is essential to distinguish between good and bad actions. Ancient Indian lawgivers and thinkers recognised the need to establish rules of conduct to guide human life toward its highest purpose.

The primary source of morality in India is often considered the authority of the scriptures, particularly the *Vedas*. Following the *Vedas*, the *Smritis* are widely accepted as a moral authority. Together, the *Vedas* (Srutis) and the *Smritis* (such as the Dharmashastras of Manu) are regarded as foundational sources of morality in India. In cases of conflict between the two, the authority of the *Vedas* takes precedence. Additionally, conscience and reason play key roles in guiding moral decisions.

Indian morality is rooted in both authority and social reasoning, with Buddhism and Jainism valuing 'reason' highly. Jainism emphasises 'right faith' among its three jewels—Right Knowledge, Right Faith, and Right Conduct—with ethics grounded in the '*panchamahavrtas*' and '*triratnas*'. Followers are encouraged to use 'reason' to evaluate the precepts before accepting them.

In Buddhism, 'reason' is also respected, and followers are urged to question to resolve doubts, especially concerning the noble truths. Modern Hindu thinkers like Vivekananda and Gandhi likewise valued reason in moral matters, seeing it as a guide, though not the sole source of moral ideas.

The Indian term for ethics and morality is '*dharma*'. *Dharma* comes from the root '*dhr*', which means 'to hold together'. Thus, the primary function of dharma is to hold human society together for its growth and stability. For human society to survive, right conduct is the most essential one, where the dharma is always coextensive with morality.

2. ESSENCE OF ETHICS

The essence of ethics means the intrinsic properties and features that characterise ethics. It elaborates on what ethics is.

(i) Ethics is a set of moral standards and values acceptable in a society. Ethics checks people from making decisions and actions which are harmful to society.

(ii) Ethical principles prescribe obligations and virtues for everybody in a society. Ethics is important in every human endeavour.

(iii) Ethical standards differ from society to society. An ethical behaviour in one society might be considered unethical in another society.
For example, practices like abortion and artificial birth control are unethical in most of the Islamic countries. But these practices are ethical in countries like China, Russia, Japan and many other countries.

(iv) Ethics is normative or prescriptive in nature. It focuses on what ought to be rather than what is. It does not rest on feelings of approval or disapproval, but on principles.
For example, it may be unpleasant to fire an employee but morality may require to do so.

(v) Ethical norms might not be legally binding. But these have the sanction from society and are more powerful than law. A person is said to be unethical, when his/her behaviour is inconsistent with the prevailing values and norms.

(vi) Ethics are not hard and fast rules. Ethics are subjective to time and frame of reference. There is always an element of discretion and society's attitudes and beliefs are expressed through ethics.

(vii) There exist no sharp boundaries between ethical and non-ethical. Therefore, making a clear choice is mostly difficult and ethical dilemmas are often faced by people.

(viii) Ethics aims at perfection in human conduct. Ethics helps lawmakers in framing proper laws and can effectively regulate the behaviour of citizens.

(ix) The concepts of equity and justice are implicit in ethics. Its primary objective is to ensure fair and equitable treatment to all.

(x) Understanding ethics as the science of morality, criticises vague and sometimes inaccurate, popular notions of right and wrong, vice or virtue.

(xi) The study of ethics exposes the defects and inconsistencies of customs and usages of social, political and religious institutions, and gives us a real insight into the nature of the moral ideal.

(xii) Studying ethics helps in removing erroneous notions and inconsistencies prevalent in popular beliefs. This exposure and criticism slowly help the readers to give up the wrong moral authority and moral sanctions which they previously believed to be correct.

(xiii) Studying ethics teaches us how important morality is, not only by exposing errors but also by criticising those erroneous notions. It also prepares oneself to move forward constructively; it helps us to separate essential from non-essential, the spirit from the form, constant from temporary, and thereby helps us to distinguish right from wrong, vice from virtue, and the benefit from harm.

(xiv) Studying ethics indirectly makes its influence felt in all walks of life of any individual who has a basic understanding of ethical theories and attempts to practice them. One of the unique aspects of ethics is that ethical theories inevitably act on practice. Understanding theoretical ethics is the prerequisite for applied ethics.

(xv) The proper solution for real problems of politics, governance, economics and religion, all depends on a clear understanding of the principles which distinguish right from wrong, vice from virtue, benefit from harm, and good from bad.

(xvi) To raise humanity to its highest level–the might should be based on the right virtues. Politics should have the foundation of ethics, religion should have a strong footing on ethics, and economics should also secure ethical principles.

The essence of ethics is to do the right things. Choices are not based on personal gains and are based on values. Ethical people show concern for the common good, rather than satisfying their personal interests or they go for balancing both. Ethical behaviour requires courage, which is the ability to stand up for what is right, even when it is difficult to do so. For example, refusing an order of a superior, that would require unethical action, could take a lot of courage.

3. DETERMINANTS OF ETHICS

There is no one-size-fits-all approach to defining ethics. Everyone's ethical decision-making process is shaped by their own set of beliefs and values.

However, there are some common elements like religion, culture, law, morals and personal experiences that many people consider when determining what is right or wrong action.

3.1 Religion

Religion plays an important role in determining ethics. Distinct sets of beliefs and values held by different religious traditions are used to guide ethical decisions. Religious teachings often contribute to the ethical framework of societies.

For instance, the Bible is often seen as the ultimate source of morality for Christians, while Islamic tradition emphasises certain values from the Quran and Hindus believe in the Bhagavad Gita.

The Five Pillars of Islam offer a code of conduct that governs the behaviour of Muslims. The Buddha taught ten meritorious deeds for us to perform to gain a happy and peaceful life as well as to develop knowledge and understanding. The *panchamahavrtas* and *triratnas* form the ethics of the Jain tradition.

In all the major religious traditions, there is the principle of reciprocity, i.e. the golden rule, the idea that one should treat others as one would like to be treated.

- **Religion and Ethical Behaviour**

Religion is important to ethics because our actions are, in many cases, governed by religious doctrines or 'divine commands' as they may sometimes be called. All religions fundamentally and inherently speak or proclaim ethical conduct in the same way. There is probably no religion that has doctrines conflicting with fundamental ethical principles.

It will be easy to follow our faith and, at the same time, be ethical in our actions after understanding this aspect of religion.

From an ethical point of view, symbolism and practices can have their place, but it is more important to understand the unifying and exalted principles associated with religious beliefs. One can appreciate other religions and their practices only with this clarity. Understanding our religion in its true perspective is important in formulating our ethical standards and resolving ethical conflicts.

- **Influence of Religion**

Religion has a more positive influence in shaping our ethical behaviour. Almost all religions have influenced the ethical thinking and standards followed by individuals and societies for the past centuries. Following a religion helps us in forming moral standards and benchmarks.

Religious faith also has a psychological impact on our moral conduct. The other aspect of religion is the self-realisation of the right moral stand in accordance with religious beliefs. It is, however, necessary to understand the basic tenets of the religion and not be governed by the trivialities of rituals and external symbolisms.

Following one's faith is a good practice, but understanding its cardinal principles and tenets is very crucial. That alone can give balance to our social and religious lives and guide us towards morally correct behaviour.

3.2 Law

Law is a set of rules prescribed by a country or community to regulate the actions of its members. In other words, it is a code of conduct given by a governing authority to an individual or to a society to maintain order in the society. It may be enforced by punishments.

In a democratic society, the law is passed by the legislature. Laws are written in a specific code, to interpret when they are required. It sets out standards, procedures and principles that must be followed. It is enforceable by a judicial system or police machinery, with an understanding that breaking a law is a crime or unacceptable behaviour.

Ethics and law are closely related to each other, especially in some cases where the law mandates ethical conduct. After all, law and ethics are derived from the society and for the society, and there is no surprise that there is a common area where law and ethics meet.

Law plays a greater role in ethical decision-making. Ethics involve a choice to follow or not, whereas making them enforceable requires the authority of law. Moreover, it is difficult to quote morality or ethics to punish an individual for their wrongdoings, because it differs from person to person, and from society to society. Law provides a common set of rules and thus, and helps to achieve fraternity among the citizens of a nation. For a country to achieve a nation-state status, it primarily follows the path of law.

Though there have been differences of opinion regarding the fundamental nature of law, it is to be regarded as a source of ethics. The law reflects the customs of society. If moral principles and ethics are to be followed effectively by society, then there must be high, reasonable and authoritative laws which should command an individual.

The institutions in a state might have different obligations to serve but they should be in consistence with the law, to bring uniformity to the system. Laws and regulations set the minimum standards of conduct to ensure fairness, safety, and justice within the society. This type of arrangement will strengthen the unity and integrity of a nation-state.

For example, the idea that everyone is equal before the law (equality before the law guaranteed by Article 14 of the Indian Constitution) determines the value that all humans are born equal. The abolition of untouchability guaranteed by Article 17 of the Indian Constitution determines the ethical quality of avoiding discrimination among people.

3.3 Culture

Culture refers to the outlook, values and practices shared by a group or society. Interpretation of what is ethical is mostly influenced by cultural norms. The theory of cultural relativism says that interpretations of truth are influenced by cultures and there is no singular truth on which ethical or moral behaviour is based.

In the Indian Culture, there is a harmonious blend of art, religion and philosophy. Culture gives meaning and coherence to life and acts as a prescription for correct and moral behaviour. Culture provides a means for achieving a sense of integrity, safety, and belonging. Life appears chaotic and unpredictable, without cultural values and normative beliefs that bring a sense of order and control over aspects of life.

For example, collectivism is reflected in the joint family culture of Indian families. Cultural relativism is best explained in the way, the French and the Americans have different views on whistleblowing. American companies consider it to be a natural part of business. The French, on the other hand, tend to view whistleblowing as undermining solidarity among coworkers.

3.4 Morals

Individual morals are also key determinants of ethics. An Individual's set of morals and values guides ethical decisions as they play a crucial role in determining what is right or wrong.

For example, sharing your lunch with your friend, who didn't bring any, reflects the moral values you practice. You do this because you believe it's kind and generous to share with others. This choice represents your personal commitment to doing the right thing and fosters ethical qualities like compassion, empathy, and generosity.

3.5 Time Factor

Ethical standards seem to be fluid. This fluidity reflects the shifts in both collective and individual perspectives as time progresses. Thus, what was considered to be ethical and right, say 50 years back, will become unethical and wrong over a period of time. This time gap could be a few years, decades or centuries. Time does not determine ethics directly, in conjunction with religion and society, it changes ethical standards. Thus, the time factor plays an important role in determining ethics.

For example, *Sati* or self-immolation was a common day practice once, and today, it is a crime. Widow remarriage is being promoted; caste identities have given way to class identities to some extent, especially in urban areas and this is reflected in increasing inter-caste marriages in urban middle-class families; and increasing secular attitudes among individuals.

3.6 Knowledge

When the ethical standards evolve, we ask how and why. We begin to question the previously established ethical standards. Today's generation even challenges the logic behind previous and today's ethical ideas. In such a scenario, knowledge plays an important role in identifying the demerits of a standard and helps to find better alternatives. Without the input of knowledge, one would stick to the age-old customs and traditions. Knowledge is a sign of progress, when one starts to question the established system; it paves the way for others to think about the possible changes. The questioning ability of Socrates changed the face of Athens, though only after his death. Knowledge could pave the way for the enlightenment of a particular society. The time factor, too, plays a role in determining the knowledge foundation of the society.

3.7 Personal Experiences

Personal experience also shapes a person's ethics. Past experiences can influence a person's outlook on ethical behaviour, and those experiences may be either positive or negative.

The way an individual's behaviour is dealt with in real-life situations also affects his ethics. If his behaviour (right or wrong) is reprimanded by his elders, he tends to avoid repeating it in the future thinking that it is unethical and vice-versa. A person who speaks harshly, if not objected to by his parents, will form a habit of speaking in that manner and will not feel unethical about it.

Individuals, as children, develop ethical standards if other family members are engaged in ethical behaviour. The children, when growing up, are also influenced by the behaviour of their friends and peer group.

4. CONSEQUENCES OF ETHICAL BEHAVIOUR

Ethics provide good tools for thinking about moral issues. Navigating through ethical dilemmas and arriving at an ethical decision becomes easy by developing a personal code of ethics. Implementing ethical guidelines in decision-making really helps. Ethical decision-making profoundly impacts personal growth and society as a whole as it goes beyond fulfilling individual responsibilities.

4.1 Impact of Ethical Behaviour on Individuals

- **Ethical decisions at every stage foster personal growth and development:** Making decisions after understanding ethics enhances our ability to think critically, evaluate different options and perspectives and then act with integrity. Individuals cultivate moral character and become better individuals by consistently making ethical decisions.
- When a particular set of ethical behaviours is manifested or practised, it will get strengthened. Ethics will get entrenched within the individual; and thus, will be ingrained. Values, such as honesty, integrity, hard work, etc. will get strengthened and reinforced when they are practised in everyday life.
- **Brings good people as well as good actions:** Ethics is not just about the morality of particular courses of action, it is more about the means to live a good life and to bring out the goodness of individuals. Virtue ethics is more concerned about a moral character that decides the right actions and nice human beings.
- **Ethics helps in building and maintaining relationships:** Developing trust and mutual respect are key in building and maintaining relationships. This is more effectively done by understanding ethics. Prioritising ethics by individuals and organisations helps in establishing a reputation for integrity. This will, in turn, increase credibility and opportunities to flourish.
- **Ethics eliminate confusion:** Ethics does not always provide the correct answer to moral problems. And for many ethical issues, ethics does not provide a single right answer, it only gives a set of principles that can be applied to arrive at ethical choices and decisions. Ethics plays a crucial role in eliminating confusion and clarifying the issues. After understanding this, it is up to the individuals to arrive at conclusions. Ethics leads people not to conclusions but to 'decisions'.
- **Ethics provides a moral map:** Many ethical issues are connected to emotions. While dealing with issues like euthanasia and abortion, our brains will go with the flow even when our hearts continue to argue. In tackling such issues,

> **? Thought Box**
>
> A company decides to prioritise ethical sourcing of raw materials, even if it increases costs. How might this decision impact its relationships with customers, suppliers, and competitors in the long term?

the role of ethical theories and philosophers comes into the picture. The ethical principles and rules offered by them help us to take a clear view of moral issues. So, understanding ethics provides us with a moral map and a framework that helps us to navigate through difficult issues.

- **Ethics can pinpoint a disagreement:** Studying and understanding ethics plays a crucial role in removing erroneous notions and inconsistencies prevalent in popular beliefs. In debates over ethical issues, understanding the framework of ethics can help identify the specific points of disagreement and the reasons behind them. This clarity often reduces the intensity of the argument and can provide valuable insights for resolving the issue effectively.

4.2 Impact of Ethical Behaviour on Society

Ethical actions bear consequences, which are not just good for the individual but also the society at large. To raise humanity to its highest level, politics should have the foundation of ethics, religion should have a strong footing on ethics, and economics should also secure ethical principles. Here, we can consider society to be a large, breathing organism which follows ethical values:

- **Ethical action leads to continuance of the society:** Any ethical action, which describes our doing as correct, will help the society to survive. In an immoral society, anything can happen, and it can lead to chaos. Ethical society survives, and people practice ethics so that future generations can enjoy an ordered and disciplined world in the coming years.
- **Survival of societies:** A society needs to project itself as virtuous to ensure its survival. By imbibing and following ethical principles and values, their sustenance becomes easy. Historically, societies whose ethics degenerated were gradually destroyed and vanished from the earth.
- **Nurturing ethical leaders:** An ethical society is one, which has the capacity to engage in continuous discussion as to what its beliefs and values are, and where boundaries of behaviour should be drawn. Such a society will be led by an ethical leader. It is not just that individual who creates an ethical society, vice versa is also true; a good society too creates ethical individuals and leaders.
- **Impact on family:** The society is made of a number of individual units. One of the important units among them is the family. Values of the family flow to the society and the society's values are imbibed by them. Moreover, we can consider the society to be a large family. Thus, an ethical society changes the conditioning and thinking of the individuals in the family.
- **Impact on international affairs:** In the international arena, an ethical society is held in high esteem. Other societies try to emulate the practices of such a society. An ethical society's views are highly respected, and are given the highest positions in international organisations. Also, ethical societies try to prevent the escalation of any issues, wars and

other unethical acts that can be nipped in the bud. Thus, an ethical society not only helps its own people, but it also plays a vital role in the survival of humans.

- **Impact on sustainable development:** Understanding ethics and being ethical are crucial for sustainable development. Ethics help in an in-depth consideration of the environmental and social impacts of choices we make. By doing this, individuals can contribute to the well-being of future generations and preserve natural resources.

The fabric of society is shaped by the collective impact of ethical decisions. Individuals, who prioritise ethics in their decision-making contribute effectively to a more just and equitable world. Ethical choices inspire others to follow suit and ripple through communities. This, in turn, creates a positive domino effect on society.

Thus, an ethical society is not the one which accepts ethical values. It practices these ethical values with full vigour. It helps individuals in society to accept and follow ethics, it helps in the survival of the human race, and it shines as a beacon for other societies to follow, and not just humans it protects and preserves its environment with all the trees, plants, animals, birds, etc., in it.

Quick decision-making is possible when one follows ethics, because it provides a credible set of choices. We can, thus, differentiate between each choice based on the values. Decisions already made and also subjected to ethical analysis help to identify its value premises. Ethics, thus, play an important role for the administrators, who can now arrive at better judgements, which are loaded with value and also help them to defend such decisions when questioned in society. Therefore, such decisions help in the continuance and survival of the society.

It is always essential and desirable to do the right thing and engage in ethical decision-making, though it is not very easy. By understanding the ethical decision-making process, recognising the challenges that may arise in the process, employing effective strategies, and considering the impact of choices, one can navigate moral complexities with integrity and contribute to a better world.

In the present times, the significance of ethics has increased manifold. This is because the present conditions offer numerous opportunities to indulge in corrupt practices. New market-based approaches and increased private sector participation have paved the way for unethical values to climb up. Thus, in recent times we can witness corrupt practices being followed and adopted right from the peon to the head of a department, government or private sector. Values, such as honesty, and integrity, et al., have taken a back seat over new values such as efficiency, result orientation, customer satisfaction, etc. The end is now considered to be more important than the means to achieve them. Thus, there is a need for ethical practices to be followed and accepted in the system. The significance of ethics has thus now grown and is considered to be more important and any absence of ethical practice might lead to further deterioration of the society.

5. RECLAIMING 'THE GOLDEN RULE'

Acting ethically has become a lost art. Many people fail to pause and consider whether their actions align with what is 'right' when faced with conflicting interests. The Golden Rule is the basis for modern ethics. It emphasises the importance of understanding how our actions impact others, urging us to put ourselves in the shoes of those on the receiving end. The Golden Rule is the principle of treating others as we would want to be treated. —'Do not do to others what you do not want them to do to you.'

SUMMARY

- The word Ethics is derived from the Greek word *ethikos,* which comes from the substantive *ethos*. Ethos means customs usages or habits. Ethics can also be termed as 'Moral Philosophy'.
- Ethics is the science of the habitual conduct of human beings. Habits are the expression of settled disposition of the will or character. Character is the permanent habit of willing, the inner bent of the mind, which is expressed in the habitual conduct.
- Ethics exposes the defects and inconsistencies of customs and usages of social, political and religious institutions, and gives us a real insight into the nature of the moral ideal.
- Ethics help in removing erroneous notions and inconsistencies prevalent in popular beliefs. These exposure and criticism slowly help individuals to give up the wrong.
- Ethics raise the humanity to its highest level-the might should be based on the right virtues. Ethics is more simply about 'fixed, universal rules of right conduct that are contingent neither on time, nor on culture or circumstance'.
- There are multiple factors, which determine ethics. Determinants are nothing, but the source from which the ethical standard arises. The determinants of ethics are viz Religion, Law, Culture, Morals, Time factor, Knowledge and Personal experiences.
- Consequences are the outcome of any act that we carry out. Some of the consequences of our actions cannot be predicted.
- Some of the expected consequences of ethical behaviour or being ethical in action are Strengthening of Values, Feeling Good and Continuance of Society. There is also crucial impact of ethical decision making on individual and society.

PREVIOUS YEARS' QUESTIONS

1. It is believed that adherence to ethics in human actions would ensure in smooth functioning of an organization/system. If so, what does ethics seek to promote in human life? How do ethical values assist in the resolution of conflicts faced by him in his day-to-day functioning. *UPSC CSE Mains 2022*
2. Ethics is knowing the difference between what you have the right to do and what is right to do." – Potter Stewart *UPSC CSE Mains 2022*
3. Distinguish between laws and rules. Discuss the role of ethics in formulating them. *UPSC CSE Mains 2020*
4. What is meant by 'crisis of conscience'? How does it manifest itself in the public domain? *UPSC CSE Mains 2019*
5. With regard to morality of action, one view is that means are not of paramount importance and the other view is that the ends justify the means. Which view do you think is more appropriate? Justify your answer. *UPSC CSE Mains 2018*
6. Increased national wealth did not result in equitable distribution of its benefits. It has created only some "enclaves of modernity and prosperity for a small minority at the cost of the majority". Justify. *UPSC CSE Mains 2017*
7. The crisis of ethical values in modern times is traced to a narrow perception of the good life. Discuss. *UPSC CSE Mains 2017*
8. Explain how ethics contributes to social and human well-being. *UPSC CSE Mains 2016*
9. All human beings aspire for happiness. Do you agree? What does happiness mean to you? Explain with examples. *UPSC CSE Mains 2014*

Human Values

2

1. INTRODUCTION TO HUMAN VALUES

Before exploring the concept of values from an academic perspective, consider the following situations:

1. After working for seven consecutive days, tirelessly, during rescue operations in a flood-hit village, you have sent an application for two days of leave for some rest. Your boss rejected your application without citing any reason. What would you do?
2. You are working under a knowledgeable and intelligent person. He is impressed with your inclination to learn and excel. He has further ensured that you always work on different projects and learn from them. This helped you grow professionally. You have developed faith in him. He also ensured that you are transferred along with him to every place he is transferred to. A few months before his retirement, it came to light that he is cleverly committing several frauds by taking advantage of your blind faith in him.

   Without knowing his actual intentions, you are involved in some of them. What would you do?

   (a) Expose his misdeeds and prove that you have worked in good faith.

LEARNING OBJECTIVES

1. Comprehending the concept of human values and their significance in individual and social contexts
2. Exploring different types of values, including intrinsic, extrinsic, terminal, institutional, and individual
3. Differentiating between morals, values, and ethics, and understanding their interrelationship
4. Recognising human beings as creators and fulfillers of values
5. Appreciating the importance of values in fostering ethical and harmonious living
6. Examining the mechanisms through which values influence thoughts, actions, and decisions
7. Analysing the factors that affect human behaviour and their interplay with values
8. Identifying the role of family, society, and educational institutions in nurturing and inculcating values
9. Familiarising oneself with some prominent human values
10. Reflecting on the essential values every human being must possess for personal and societal well-being

(b) Do not disclose anything as you may get into trouble too.
(c) Do not disclose anything because you are sure that you have evidence to prove that you worked without any mala fide intentions.
(d) Expose his misdeeds but help him at personal level.
(e) Maintain it as a secret, since he would retire soon.
(f) Ask for your share of the misdeeds.
(g) Leave the organisation.

3. You are responsible for managing traffic at one of the four road junctions along the route the country's president will take to a meeting. You are supposed to stop the traffic on all the roads five minutes before the president's convoy reaches that junction. A few seconds before the convoy reaches the junction, an ambulance with a critically ill person emerges from one of the by-lanes close to the junction. The ambulance must cross the junction on its way to the hospital.
Which of the following is the most appropriate step that you would take in this situation?
(a) Stop the ambulance till the president's convoy passes by.
(b) Stop the president's convoy and make way for the ambulance.
(c) Ask the ambulance driver to drive very fast and clear the road before the convoy arrives.
(d) Ask the ambulance driver to take by-lanes and not to touch the main road by which the convoy passes.

The answers for these questions show definite patterns of reaction from you. In all these circumstances, you would decide based on your judgement. It is also certain that your decision would likely differ from those of your friends, if they were asked to answer the same questions. This is because every individual is unique. The primary reason for these differences lies in the values that each person holds as a member of society. The term 'value' carries different meanings across various disciplines, yet it remains central to the functioning of society and the existence of individuals. Values form the foundation of any culture or individual identity. To know further about values, let us delve into the chapter.

2. DEFINING VALUES

Defining 'value' is one of the most difficult tasks in ethics, because it can be defined from various perspectives—philosophical, sociological, psychological and so on. Though values are indefinable, they are not **unintelligible**[1]. It can be defined by pointing out an instance or it can be with regards to an object of interest, it can be seen as a process of realisation, it can also be seen as judgements on objects which are verifiable by experience. Though values lack a universal definition, we can refer to Rokeach's perspective: 'Values are beliefs about how one ought or ought not to behave, or about some state of existence worth or not worth attaining.'

[1] **Unintelligible:** Impossible to understand

Values are abstract ideals, positive or negative, that represent a person's belief about ideal modes of conduct and ideal terminal goals. A value is a concept of the desirable with a motivating force. According to Hodgkinson, values are generally learnt in the process of socialisation right from the childhood. While the internalisation of values continues throughout life, it occurs most rapidly during the early stages of development. The experience one gains transforms into values. Values are important because an individual's behaviour is definitely conditioned largely by the values they have internalised.

Values help determine whether an employee is passionate about work and the workplace, which in turn can lead to above-average returns, high employee satisfaction, strong team dynamics, and synergy. Values are usually shaped by many different internal and external influences, including family, traditions, culture, and more recently, media and the Internet. Values are principles guiding decisions on right and wrong, helping prioritise and determine what is most important.

3. TYPES OF VALUES

(a) Terminal Values and Instrumental Values

Terminal Values

Terminal values are the goals that a person would like to achieve during their lifetime. These represent the highest values within a person's value system—those deemed most important or desirable. They are typically the ultimate goals individuals strive to achieve, and often remain steadfast. Such values include happiness, self-respect, recognition, inner harmony, professional excellence, and a prosperous life.

Instrumental Values

Instrumental values are the preferred modes of behaviour to achieve the terminal values. These are the most often used values. They are means to achieving the terminal values, that is, they are the instruments used to achieve the desired goal. These values including honesty, sincerity, being ethical, etc. keep changing based on the situation.

(b) Mainstream Values

These values are accepted by the community at large; this varies from culture to culture, time to time, and more.

Example:

1. System of dowry during the early 1900s.
2. *Varnashrama dharma* in ancient India.

(c) Institutional Values

They are determined by particular institutions. These values are propagated by the institutions so that one can imbibe and inculcate them.

Example:

1. Patriarchal system of family makes the male as head of the family.
2. Democracy as value in free India.

(d) Individual Values

It corresponds to both intrinsic and extrinsic values. It represents those values which are considered important by the individual and which help to achieve one's desire.

Example: Honesty, courage and self-esteem.

(e) Intrinsic versus Extrinsic Value

Intrinsic value is closely associated with ethics. It refers to something that holds value in itself, possessing an inherent meaning that can be recognised. In contrast, extrinsic value refers to values that are not intrinsic. Intrinsic values are fundamental in making moral judgements, particularly in **consequentialism**[2], where decisions are made about what is right or wrong. In such cases, intrinsic value helps guide individuals toward the right path by identifying the appropriate consequences. Thus, intrinsic value serves as the foundation of ethical consequentialism. Additionally, intrinsic value plays a crucial role in determining whether justice is morally right or wrong, particularly when justice is denied. This forms the basis of moral justice. Furthermore, intrinsic value helps in distinguishing between moral virtue and vice, guiding ethical choices.

See Table 2.1 regarding the values and their corresponding examples.

Table 2.1 Values and Examples

Values	Examples
Intrinsic Values That are inherently rewarding to purpose	Affiliation to friends and family, connection with nature, concern for others, self-acceptance, social justice and creativity
Extrinsic Values That are centred on external approval or rewards	Wealth, material success, concern about image, social status, prestige, social power and authority

[2] **Consequentialism:** A moral philosophy that judges actions based on their consequences

4. MORALS, VALUES, AND ETHICS

"Morality describes what is. Ethics describes what ought to be." **Charles Colson**

The word morality is derived from Latin word '*moralis*', meaning 'traditional customs or proper behaviour'. These morals are given out by the society at large, or a particular community, or might have religious sanction, or even exist within one's family. Thus, these morals judge the actions of individuals whether they are right or wrong, and if it goes against the existing morals, it is termed as immoral.

Values are guides which help an individual choose between right or wrong. It does not have confirmation with the society. It can be called as an element of belief, which helps the individual in taking the right decision. Values refer to the relative worth of a quality or object. Value is what makes something desirable or undesirable.

Ethics are the standards by which behaviours are evaluated for their morality – their rightness or wrongness. Imagine a person who has a strong value of achievement and success. Knowing only that this value is important to them gives us a general expectation of their behaviour, that is, we would expect them to be goal-oriented, gaining the skills necessary to get what they want. However, we cannot know whether they will cheat to get what they want or 'do an honest day's work each day'.

5. FEATURES OF VALUES

Values have the following features:

1. Values are way of life.
2. Values are stimulus to good behaviour.
3. Values are broad and go beyond the given situation.
4. Values help in identifying and appraising an action.
5. Values are a mix of information and conviction.
6. Values are learnt.
7. Values are steady, lasting and permanent.
8. Values are based on a particular purpose.
9. Values are not subjective creations of the individual minds.
10. Values are over-individual and ultra-personal.
11. Modern philosophers hold that moral and aesthetic values are products of creative evolution, which is a process of realisation.
12. Value propositions are not assertions, but merely emotive expressions and social commands.

6. HUMAN BEINGS: CREATORS AND FULFILLERS OF VALUES

Human beings are value-creating animals and they not only create values, but also fulfil them. Thus, humans are not only the source of values, but also those who judge the behaviour involved in day-to-day functioning of the society. This ability of man has its role in formation of his or her personality, formation of groups, formation of social institution and more.

Though there is a claim of difference between personal and social values, there is not much difference between them because personal values are also conditioned by the society and surroundings. In fact, personal values would have been acquired from society only. The process of socialisation helps in inculcating values in an infant, only then he or she becomes a complete person or a social being. Internalisation of the values is a key and fundamental part of the socialisation process.

7. HIERARCHY OF VALUES

All values are not given equal preference by an individual. There is a hierarchy of values. When confronted, higher values take precedence over lower values. Everyone faces this 'conflict of values' situation. In those circumstances, the conflict is resolved or minimised only because of the hierarchical arrangement of values. In the absence of this hierarchy, the individual will suffer seriously in terms of his or her personality. Arrangement of the sociocultural system is determined by values as well, and the hierarchical arrangement ensures coherence among its numerous values. Values involved in various setups, such as economy, politics, religion and so on, form a network.

The values of these groups interact, and in that process, affect and overlap with each other. Some researchers have arranged values by their height. Honesty, integrity, love for neighbours, unconditional faith, compassion for people in remote places, and the virtue of giving are virtues that can be prioritised in a hierarchy based on their significance. Honesty is the lowest among these and the virtue of giving is the highest. Furthermore, the anti-values corresponding to these values can be illustrated as: dishonesty (e.g. theft), lies, lack of love for neighbours, inability for unconditional faith, lack of love for people in remote places, and the lack of the virtue of giving.

The strength is in the same order. That is, dishonesty is the strongest anti-value, while the lack of virtue of giving is the weakest. Theft as dishonesty is a crime and the lowest anti-value. A lie is not a crime but related to honour, while the lack of love is not a matter of honour. Inability for unconditional faith is just a moral defect, and the lack of love for remote people, or the lack of the virtue of giving is not a defect at all.

8. VALUES: CORE OF CULTURE-INDIVIDUALITY

The values that form the core of a culture and society often become internalised, shaping an individual's personality, which can make people unaware of these values. A normal person is one who balances the conflicting values successfully and proceeds with his or her goals in life. If not managed properly, conflicting values create severe stress and mental strain, which may eventually result in personality disorders.

9. HOW ARE VALUES ACQUIRED?

The socialisation process is the foundation for acquiring values. Each society practices different cultures, and this change is reflected in one's values. Culture plays an important part in the socialisation process.

There are a number of situations based on the ecological perspective also. When a child grows up, the immediate and the smallest contexts are the immediate family, friends and peer group. There are other numbers of contexts when the child moves out into the society, and therefore, contexts exist as layers. Outside, the child is exposed to school, teachers, shopkeepers, and so on. There are some broader contexts also, such as mass media, society, and more, which play an important role in the socialisation process, but their impact cannot be seen directly. Moreover, each of these layers are not separate, they interact with each other to form a much more complex system.

As people affect the child, the child too affects the people interacting with him or her. As the child grows up, his or her behaviour and personality develop and gets conditioned with its interaction with these multiple layers. Learning about values and learning values start quite early in life, starting with simple commands from parents and family members. For a child, prohibition and parental guidance are the source of values.

Consider an 18-month-old child who grabs a bowl lid and is startled by a strong 'no.' The child hides behind the lid, the mother retrieves it, scolds the child, and tantrums follow. These tantrums subside when the mother reaccepts the child. At this stage, the child experiences emotions like anger, frustration, and fear, but doesn't understand their behaviour, only sensing the emotions.

Now, take the example of a 3-year-old instructed by her father to stay in bed until seven. While she stays in bed, she engages in distracting activities, leading to her father's scolding, after which she remains quiet for a while.

After similar incidents, the child learns to stay in bed quietly until seven, influenced by her father's authority. Through such experiences, children understand which behaviours are approved or disapproved, leading to rewards or punishments. They begin associating behaviours with concepts of good and bad, right and wrong, reinforcing positive and negative actions. Rewards and approval act as positive reinforcements, while disapproval and punishment serve as negative reinforcements. Positive feelings arise from appreciation, while punishment creates negative associations, discouraging certain behaviours. Over time, behaviours leading to positive outcomes become habitual and deeply ingrained.

Values become truly internalised when they transition from the fear of reprimand to a sense of commitment or obligation rooted in personal experience. This involves moving from a 'must consciousness' to an 'ought or should consciousness.' In 'must consciousness,' actions feel compelled, while 'ought or should consciousness' reflects a sense of duty or moral obligation.

For example, saying 'I must be honest' implies compulsion, whereas 'I ought to be honest' conveys a voluntary sense of responsibility. The experience of 'ought' in decision-making shapes an individual's self-image, and violating this sense of duty can diminish their self-perception.

When changing from 'must' to 'ought', the following changes occur:

- From experiences of reprimand, fear of punishment to experience of choice and feeling of self-respect.
- From certain values of conformity towards self-guidance and broad availability of values which guides one's behaviour.
- From external or outside sanctions to internal or inside sanction.

Students are taught values by fostering rational decision-making, critical thinking, and responsible behaviour. Through this education, they develop the ability to think critically, question, empathise, reason, reflect, and act accordingly. Hence, during the process of socialisation at home and school, conscious attempts are made to inculcate understanding, awareness, sensitivity, reflection, appreciation and so on as per the thought process of the person. Thus, decision-making, choosing an alternative should come naturally, which shows ingrained values. When these are not carried out, the individual might consider taking the shortcut, leading to immoral and unethical behaviour.

Therefore, deeply ingrained values of right and wrong help us make correct decisions. These decisions are not only good for us but have a benefit for others involved too. Questions are raised about an adult's involvement in inculcating values in a child. Some argue that value inculcation should be a natural process, children acquire values when they mature, there should be no outside involvement. Some argue that adult intervention is necessary to guide a child's behaviour; the child might not know the difference between right and wrong, hence adult intervention is necessary to teach values. Finally, few others ask adults to be guides in helping the child choose the right path. The adult here needs to create opportunities for the child to develop his or her values.

Thus, value development involves the stages where a child's maturity develops, the cultural context where the child grows, beliefs and understandings of child's development and growth and finally, the involvement of an adult in value inculcating process. Only if individuals accept and imbibe, these values can these be internalised and turned into habits and ultimately as one's behaviour. Hence, the individual will act responsibly and respectfully.

10. WHY DO VALUES MATTER?

Values shape basic character of an individual. It determines the choices one makes; it motivates one towards achieving, and helps in taking decisions.

1. Values influence our behaviour.
2. Value is the foundation for understanding the level of motivation.
3. It helps in interpreting what is right or wrong.
4. It influences attitude and behaviour. Each value corresponds to a particular behaviour. Being a spendthrift means their value is based on hedonism, while celebrating Independence Day corresponds to patriotism. Thus, each behaviour is based on an underlying value.
5. It implies that outcomes of certain behaviour are preferred over others.
6. It allows members of an organisation to interact harmoniously. It thus helps achieve goals which would have not been possible individually.
7. They act as guideposts of lives of individuals, they direct towards who they want to be.
8. Values also help in making judgements. Though taking judgements is dependent on various factors, values do also play an important role.

11. HOW DO VALUES CHANGE?

Each of us holds some values. But the strength of it differs from individual to individual; this can be related to the exposure of the individual to that value. Repeated practice strengthens the value. The most likely the place from where the lessons of value can be learnt is one's home, or his or her school. A fair amount of independence in the classroom inculcates the value of questioning and intuitiveness, whereas authoritative classroom generates obedience and **conformity**[3] within the individuals. What a person experiences in their day-to-day life is entrenched as value. One is likely to shape values in his or her neighbourhood, market, religious place, work place, leisure place, and each of these places strengthen a particular value, such as a religious place evokes obedience and good nature, workplace evokes competitiveness and achievement, media might evoke mixed response to state activities such as national security concern, patriotism, and altruism.

---

[3] **Conformity:** accordance with

Moreover, each value gets shaped when new experiences are faced in various social settings. Thus, we need to understand what is possible in a particular situation, what is pleasing and what would be the usual behaviour in that situation.

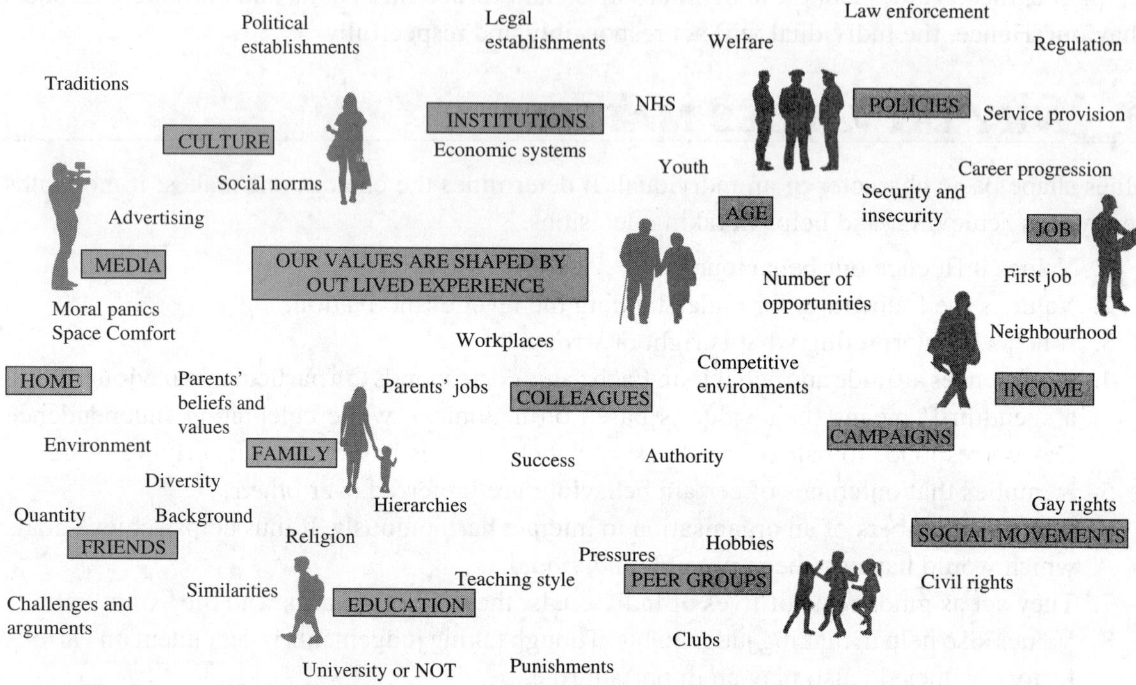

Fig. 2.1 Factors Affecting Values

12. ROLE OF FAMILY, SOCIETY AND EDUCATIONAL INSTITUTIONS IN INCULCATING VALUES

Values drive our behaviour and action in our everyday life. Values determine what words we use, what dress we wear, our perceptions and our understandings of others, and so on. Values are formed on the basis of our desires, inclination, needs, choices, interests and likings. These are the core of value formulation. Values have certain directional quality, it determines what choices we make, the path we choose, the direction we take. If preferences harden, become concrete and definite, they become the basis for taking decision, our choices and action. Knowing and understanding one's feelings is a part of value formulation. A deep liking of something involves values too. Thus, people's actions, as well ass reactions towards something can make us understand what kind of values they have. Also noticing one's behaviour, their activities in their leisure time, will help us identify their values.

12.1 Family Values

The family is the smallest and the most secure of all social institutions. Confucius, the Chinese sage of the ancient world, says that the family is the foundation of the state. In fact, the family has been the fundamental unit from which have sprung the finest sentiments known to mankind. It is the nursery at which the seedlings, the young ones, receive the best nourishment for their souls. The elder members of the family do not simply preach but practice whatever they value most. Whatever be the structure and size of the family, there are certain values that families cherish and practice. The family is the source for emotional support, economic independence, education, recreation and the right care of the young and the aged. The members of the family with varying relationships such as husband/wife, father/mother, son/daughter, and brother/sister try to understand each other well.

The family continues to be the cornerstone of stability in society. The relationships promoted inside a family are the most enduring. Unfortunately, in modern times, the family is seen more as a functional unit. In modern urban societies, individuals are free from most kinship responsibilities, and so they try to create their own world of existence. Isolation and the breaking up of families leading to alienation is the price to pay for individual-oriented growth. Except for immediate members of the family, cohesion is absent among relatives in urban societies. On the other hand, in rural areas, cohesion is still visible, and people are able to relate to each other quickly, connect, and correlate with them.

> **? Thought Box**
>
> In a rapidly changing world, how can the family remain a cornerstone in imparting values, and what balance should it strike between preserving tradition and encouraging independent thought in younger generations?

It is from the family that most individuals inherit personal, cultural, moral, and spiritual values. Such inheritance is far more valuable and enduring than any property that one may inherit. Will Durrant, a famous historian, traveller and writer, says that he searched for happiness in knowledge but was disillusioned. He searched for happiness in travel but became tired. He sought happiness in wealth but found only dispute and discard. He looked for happiness in writing but was fatigued.

One evening, he saw a woman with a sleeping child waiting in a car in the parking lot of a railway station. A man came out of a train, went near the car, kissed the lady and the child gently, got into the driver's seat and drove off. Obviously, he was her husband returning from work. Will Durrant says that he was stunned by the realisation. He says, 'Every normal function of the family holds great delight for its members.'

Tommy, a third-grader was struggling academically and exhibiting disruptive behaviour. His parents had recently separated, which seemed to affect him deeply. As a teacher and counsellor, Jane invited both parents to a meeting, though neither knew the other would be present.

The mother arrived first, followed by the father, and their irritation was evident. However, their mutual concern for Tommy brought them to the table. Jane discussed Tommy's declining performance, delicately pointing out that their strained relationship was likely the cause.

To convey the impact on Tommy, Jane retrieved a crumpled paper from his desk, smoothed it out, and handed it to his mother. She read it silently, then passed it to his father, who frowned, but read it as well. The note said: "Dear Mother...Dear Daddy—I love you; I love you; I love you."

The father gently helped the mother with her coat as they left together, thanking Jane for her efforts. Family values bring people together even if for a short period. Individual aberrations may appear to destroy them.

Jack Welch, the former CEO of General Electric and a dynamic management guru, offers an insightful glimpse into the importance of family values through an anecdote from his youth.

During the final hockey game of a challenging season in his senior year at Salem High School, Jack's team had to win against Beverley Hills to salvage their record. Despite an early lead, the game went into overtime tied at 1-1. Beverley Hills scored, and Jack's team lost. Frustrated, Jack, the vice-captain, stormed into the locker room, angrily throwing his hockey stick.

Moments later, the locker room door opened, and Jack's mother entered. Without hesitation, she grabbed his collar and sternly said, "You punk! If you don't know how to lose, you'll never know how to win. If you can't understand that, you shouldn't be playing."

This moment underscores how families are the foundation of great values, passed down through generations. Some family members not only uphold these values but also establish newer and nobler ones, exemplifying their enduring importance.

Irrespective of the size of the family or its structure as nuclear family, joint family or extended family, there are bound to be some factors that lead to frustration, anger, dissension and dispute. Failure to appreciate the role of each member in the family, their relationship with each other, and the generation gap leading to variant perceptions are the main contributors to the breakup of the families' estrangement and alienation. What is needed is an understanding attitude of the other's perception. This is achieved by mutual love and respect. When understanding is practiced proactively, all differences will vanish into thin air. The aged will not feel neglected. The children will not get frustrated. Siblings will not quarrel and fight. The young ones will not get alienated. Relationships within the family and outside will flourish on an even keel. Empowerment of women in society can succeed and become meaningful only if women are empowered by the family.

12.2 Values Inculcated in Educational Institutions

(i) Value Concerns at the School Stage

A key debate in value education is determining which values students should learn. Value education cannot occur in isolation, it must align with the world we live in. Core values, such as honesty, truthfulness, love, and loyalty, should be nurtured to promote peace and goodness in society. These universal, timeless values transcend regional, religious, social, and cultural boundaries, fostering harmony and peaceful coexistence.

Value development must occur within the societal context, addressing both local and global values. In today's interconnected world, understanding and integrating global values alongside local ones is essential for holistic growth.

(ii) Value-Inculcating Techniques through Education

Values learnt from the lives of great leaders – lives of great people from India and around the world – provide insight into what values one needs to develop. Lives of leaders such as Gandhiji, Nehru, Sardar Patel, S. C. Bose, and other great freedom fighters and people such as Martin Luther King Jr., Nelson Mandela, Abraham Lincoln, and several other world leaders guide individuals to the path to lead value-laden and purpose-filled life.

(a) Examples of life lessons: Mahatma Gandhi's Life Story Teaches Leadership (Compared with Traits)

Trait: Self-confidence

Example: Salt March – where he marched 388 km towards the sea at Dandi, Gujarat, and made salt for himself. Emotionally stable, Mahatma Gandhi was cordial with the people of all religions and understood their feelings. The British government influenced him in a number of ways to stop the campaign, but he was very determined in his goal.

Traits: Extraversion, Humility, Courage

Examples: Gandhi first implemented his philosophy of non-violence in South Africa, where Indians embraced and adapted it. Later, in India, his teachings on non-violence were widely adopted without hesitation. In South Africa, he stood up for the rights of Indians and, upon returning to India, he led the movement demanding independence from British rule.

One notable incident in South Africa occurred when Gandhi, traveling in a stagecoach, asserted his rights and refused to give up his seat for a European passenger. As a result, he was beaten by the driver. Despite being jailed numerous times, Gandhi remained steadfast in his mission, continuing his fight for justice and equality.

(b) Values learnt from poems

There are several great poets in India and around the world whose poems can provide insight into value-laden life. Great poets of India such as Tagore and Bharathi as well as other medieval and ancient poets such as Kabir, Tulsidas, Thiruvalluvar, Manikavasagar have given us a rich heritage of poems, which should be read in every home and their meanings should be understood by every heart. Other internationally renowned poets, such as Keats, Tennyson, Robert Frost, Browning,

Wordsworth, and others have been credited with numerous poems which too, deal with value development in individuals.

Keats with his powerful words writes about the intrinsic value of truth and beauty: "Beauty is truth, truth beauty, that is all ye know on earth, and all ye need to know." These feelings refine the hearts, elevate sensitivity, and develop love for one and all. Thus, overflowing love, sympathy, and kindness replace hatred, jealousy, animosity, and violence. The lines of Robert Frost motivate to work incessantly: "The woods are lovely dark and deep, But I have promises to keep, and miles to go before I sleep, and miles to go before I sleep."

The poems of Tennyson and Browning have the power to create an inspiring atmosphere and encourage learners to remain active and optimistic. Lines such as, "I was ever a fighter, so one fight more" and "How dull it is to pause, to make an end, to rust unburnished, not to shine in use" resonate deeply, motivating individuals to **persevere**[4] and embrace a life with purpose.

(c) Values learnt from stories

Ancient Indian books such as the *Jataka* tales, *Panchatantra*, and *Hitopdesa* have value-laden stories. These stories guide how an individual should behave. Indian writers such as Prem Chand, Bhagwati Sharan Verma, Sharat Chandra Bose, Mahashweta Devi, Bankim Chandra Chattopadhyay, Bharathi, and Rabindranath Tagore, and contemporary greats such as R. K. Narayanan, Amitav Ghosh, Arundhati Roy, Jhumpa Lahiri, and numerous others have given extraordinary works of art, which guide individuals on their quest to live a peaceful and happy life.

A Story Illustrating the Consequences of Greed

One day, King Butcher gave a large bone to a hungry dog. The dog eagerly grabbed the bone in his mouth and headed across a stream, intending to enjoy it in solitude. While crossing the bridge, he glanced into the water and saw what appeared to be another dog holding a large bone. Unaware it was his own reflection, he thought, "What a juicy bone that dog has! If I take it, I'll have two bones to eat. I'm so hungry!"

Convinced of his plan, the dog barked loudly to scare the 'other' dog away. However, his bark startled no one but himself. Instead, his bone slipped from his mouth, splashing into the stream and sinking out of reach. Disappointed and still hungry, the dog learned a hard lesson.

Moral of the Story

1. Greed leads to loss.
2. Don't overreach what you can hold or manage.

[4] **Persevere:** To achieve something that is difficult

Values can also be developed through numerous other ways. Some other important ways are through sports. Sports develop discipline in and inculcates values such as team spirit, supportiveness, and competitiveness, and helps individuals function together as a cohesive whole. Other areas such as fine arts, and visual and performing media, which can help individuals to develop values.

Inculcating values through continuous and comprehensive activities at educational institutions.

Step 1: The schools must identify suitable values for primary, middle, and secondary grade students.

Step 2: Activities must be chosen in such a way that they act as an instrument of inculcation of such values.

Step 3: School environment and educational ambience should be adapted in such a fashion so that the children get a rich experience while acquiring values.

Step 4: The textbook material should be correlated with the learning of values by identifying areas in which the desired values may be promoted.

Through all academic programmes, the following are important for inculcation of values by suitably introducing the element of values in every step:

1. **Knowing:** The children must be made to understand the values and ethical issues associated with a particular topic.
2. **Making judgements:** Conflicting situations must be created while teaching/learning so that the child can evaluate the implications of the decision regarding values.
3. **Believing:** Stress should be given to develop faith in those targeted values so that it will create a scope for internalisation of values.
4. **Action:** The children should be motivated to practice those values in real-life situations.
5. **Internalisation:** Through constant emphasis on such relevant ideas, thoughts and actions.

The children should be led to a stage where the practice of acquired values may be spontaneous and immediate leading to acquired positive behavioural patterns and outcomes. It should be noted that values cannot be taught like a subject (i.e. Languages, History, Science or Mathematics). They can only be inculcated through the situations deliberately planned while teaching various school subjects. A values-centred approach in the classroom will add meaning to each class. Moreover, as students engage creatively in the classroom, lesson objectives will be realised effectively.

Teaching Methods

Teaching methods for value education should involve a variety of ways that blend the formal and the informal instructional processes. The success of value education and development in students substantially depends on the vision, motivation, skills, attitudes, values, and behaviour of the teacher. Teaching methods should inculcate values in children which will further positively aid in their overall development in the future.

13. HUMAN VALUES FROM INDIVIDUAL TO UNIVERSAL PERSPECTIVES

Human values as a concept can be interpreted from different individual perspectives as it has multiple nodes of origin. For instance, in the case of India, the very notion of human values can be understood from four '*purusartha*' which identify '*Artha*', '*Kama*', '*Dharma*' and '*Moksha*' as fundamental human values. These values have been defined among others by Kautilya and Vatsayana.

According to these scholars, '*Artha*' has been interpreted as the value of existence and maintenance of human life. It emphasises on material gain and physical well-being. '*Kama*' has been defined as the pleasure resulting from satisfaction of desires. The sensuous desires have been interpreted in the form of gratification which is necessary for human well-being. '*Dharma*' has been interpreted as the law or principles of integration and maintenance of things. Lastly, '*Mokhsa*' reflects the supreme goal of human life which is liberation or salvation from the effects of '*Karma*'. Similarly, from Buddhist perspectives, human values have been defined based on four eternal truths. These truths have been identified as '*Shashwat Satya*'. The truths are as under:

(a) Life is not devoid of sorrows, suffering and anguish, etc.
(b) The anguish and suffering have a cause.
(c) The suffering that an individual faces can be put to an end.
(d) There are many ways and means through which pain and suffering can be overcome in life.

Buddhism, in this regard, has also elaborated that if a person is unable to define the real vs. unreal, due to ignorance, then that person is bound to suffer. As a result, the ultimate goal of the individual is to make himself or herself self-aware about his or her surroundings that can help him or her to achieve true knowledge for liberation. Buddhism has recommended the eight-fold path that can help an individual to lead a balanced life and well-being. These are as under:

(a) Right Perception (*Samyak Drishti*)
(b) Right Determination (*Samyak Samkalpa*)
(c) Right Speech (*Samyak Vaka*)
(d) Right Conduct (*Samyak Karma*)
(e) Right Vocation (*Samyak Ajivika*)
(f) Right Exercise (*Samyak Vijayama*)
(g) Right Memory (*Samyak Smriti*)
(h) Right Meditation (*Samyak Samadhi*)

Human values ultimately take a universal shape if they are similar in practice among different cultures throughout the world. The meaning behind each value is uniform and universally accepted across different social and cultural spaces. Some of the human values which have gained a universal acceptance are:

1. Un-Biasness 2. Loyalty 3. Cooperation 4. Transparency 5. Objectivity 6. Discipline 7. Inspiration 8. Social Responsibility 9. Managing Conflict

The presence of universal human values in any organisation or society can help in enhancing the credibility among the stakeholders, facilitating decision-making choices in a rational way, promoting self-discipline, encouraging objectivity in life, and most importantly, ensuring trust and balance among the individuals in a larger setup. One of the stark differences that can be seen between individual and universal human values is that individual human values are directly concerned with the development of human personality.

It focuses on reshaping the individual's norms and outlook towards honesty, loyalty, and honour. On the other hand, universal human values are those which have a greater social and cultural acceptance, and these values are oriented towards human growth and development. Despite the difference between the two, universal human values take shape only when individual human values gradually take shape into a collective and gain a mass acceptance from different socio-cultural spaces of society.

14. SOME PROMINENT HUMAN VALUES

1. Truth

Truth is the foundation of integrity and ethical conduct, guiding an individual's conscience to uphold honesty in thoughts, words, and actions. It is not merely about stating facts, but aligning one's behaviour with principles of fairness, transparency, and authenticity. Truth can be context-dependent, yet its universal essence lies in fostering trust, credibility, and accountability in personal and professional relationships.

Example: Despite facing frequent transfers and professional challenges, Ashok Khemka, an ICS bureaucrat and an IAS officer since 1991, remained steadfast in his commitment to truth and integrity. His courage to act against unethical practices exemplifies ethical governance and inspires others to prioritise truth over personal convenience.

"Three things cannot be long hidden: the sun, the moon, and the truth." **Buddha**

"In a time of deceit, telling the truth is a revolutionary act." **George Orwell**

2. Love

Love is a profound, selfless, and enduring sentiment that fosters empathy, compassion, and a deep connection among individuals. Unlike fleeting emotions, love is a conscious and intentional force that nurtures care and sensitivity towards the well-being and happiness of others. It transcends personal boundaries, inspiring acts of kindness and service that strengthen communal bonds and collective harmony.

Example: During the COVID-19 pandemic, actor Sonu Sood exemplified love and compassion by assisting thousands of migrant workers.

> "Love is not only something you feel, it is something you do." **David Wilkerson**

> "Love and compassion are necessities, not luxuries. Without them, humanity cannot survive."
> **Dalai Lama**

3. Peace

Peace is a state of inner tranquillity and harmony, achieved by freeing oneself from excessive desires, superficial attachments, and external disturbances. It reflects an individual's ability to prioritise balance, contentment, and emotional stability over material pursuits or conflicts. Peace is not merely the absence of discord but a proactive condition of well-being that fosters personal growth and societal harmony. Practices such as meditation, mindfulness, and empathetic dialogue are instrumental in cultivating peace, reducing stress, and nurturing collective understanding.

Example: The resolution of the decades-long Bru-Reang refugee issue in the Northeastern states of India through negotiation and cooperation underscores the transformative power of peace.

> "Peace begins with a smile." **Mother Teresa**

> "You cannot find peace by avoiding life." **Virginia Woolf**

4. Non-Violence

Non-violence is the principle of achieving objectives and resolving conflicts without resorting to harm, coercion, or aggression. It is rooted in promoting harmony, mutual respect, and understanding among individuals and communities. Non-violence requires love, compassion, and self-restraint to ensure that actions are constructive rather than destructive, fostering peace and unity. This principle advocates that true power lies not in the use of force but in the ability to influence change through peaceful means.

Example: Mahatma Gandhi's leadership in India's struggle for independence through non-violent resistance is a prime example of the transformative power of non-violence.

> "Non-violence is the weapon of the strong." **Mahatma Gandhi**

5. Righteous Conduct

Righteous conduct is the practice of acting in accordance with principles of fairness, integrity, and moral uprightness. It involves making decisions that are free from bias, selfish interests, or unjust influence, ensuring that actions contribute to the greater good and uphold ethical standards. Righteous conduct calls for a commitment to justice, honesty, and accountability in all aspects of life, promoting societal harmony and individual well-being. It encourages individuals to base their actions on reason and virtue, fostering trust and cooperation in both personal and public spheres.

Example: Dr Varghese Kurien, through his ethical leadership, prioritised the collective well-being of dairy farmers by founding the Amul cooperative. His commitment to fairness and social justice ensured fair compensation for farmers, transforming India's dairy industry and empowering millions.

"The time is always right to do what is right." **Martin Luther King, Jr.**

"The highest form of morality is not to do what is wrong, but to do what is right."
Khalil Gibran

6. Compassion

Compassion is the ability to understand others' suffering and take proactive steps to alleviate it. It transcends cultural, religious, and geographical boundaries, fostering empathy, selflessness, and action-oriented kindness. Unlike empathy, which focuses on understanding emotions, compassion emphasises action to reduce suffering and promote collective well-being. Key characteristics of compassion include empathy in action, where one actively works to alleviate distress, selflessness, which prioritises others' needs over personal gains, and universal relevance, as it encourages harmony and inclusivity across diverse communities.

Example: Mother Teresa's lifelong dedication to serving the sick and destitute in Kolkata highlights selfless humanitarianism. At an institutional level, the *Ayushman Bharat Yojana* embodies compassion by providing free healthcare to economically weaker sections of society.

"Compassion is the basis of morality." **Arthur Schopenhauer**

"Nobody cares how much you know until they know how much you care."
Theodore Roosevelt

7. Discipline

Discipline is the ability to control one's behaviour, actions, and thoughts in pursuit of a goal. It involves maintaining focus, adhering to a set of rules or principles, and managing time effectively. As a human value, discipline enables individuals to stay organised, work diligently, and achieve their objectives with consistency and perseverance. It fosters self-control, responsibility, and efficiency, making it essential for personal and professional growth.

Example: M.S. Dhoni, former captain of the Indian cricket team, is known for his discipline both on and off the field. His calm demeanour, strategic thinking, and focus on continuous improvement made him one of the most successful cricketers.

"Discipline is the bridge between goals and accomplishment." **Jim Rohn**

"The cost of discipline is always less than the cost of regret." **Nido Qubein**

8. Genuineness

Genuineness refers to the authenticity and sincerity of one's feelings and actions, where kindness, care, and concern are expressed in a truly heartfelt manner. It is about being transparent, honest, and real in interactions, which fosters trust and deepens connections with others. When individuals display genuine behaviour, they create an environment of mutual respect and trust, making relationships more meaningful and lasting.

Example: Dr A.P.J. Abdul Kalam, former President of India, exemplified genuineness through his unwavering commitment to students. His authentic engagement with young minds, coupled with his genuine interest in their development, inspired millions.

9. Modesty

Modesty is the quality of being humble and unassuming, marked by a lack of arrogance or self-importance. It allows individuals to appreciate the worth and contributions of others without feeling the need to elevate themselves. Modest individuals are not driven by the desire to dominate conversations or situations, but instead, they listen attentively, learn continuously, and contribute thoughtfully.

Example: Sundar Pichai, the CEO of Alphabet (Google), is a prime example of modesty in leadership. Despite his extraordinary success, Pichai remains grounded and approachable, consistently demonstrating humility in both his personal and professional life.

"Modesty is the art of enhancing your charm by pretending not to be aware of it."
Oliver Herford

"True humility is not thinking less of yourself; it is thinking of yourself less." **C.S. Lewis**

10. Self-Respect

Self-respect is the steadfast commitment to one's dignity, principles, and values, regardless of external pressures or temptations. It involves upholding personal integrity and ethical conduct, even when faced with challenges. A person with self-respect remains true to their core beliefs, earning the admiration and trust of others through consistent, principled actions.

Example: Ratan Tata, the former chairman of the Tata Group, is a prime example of self-respect in action. Throughout his leadership, he refused to compromise on ethics, even in the face of significant challenges.

"Self-respect is the cornerstone of all virtue." **John Herschel**

"Respect yourself and others will respect you." **Confucius**

11. Rationality

Rationality is the capacity to think logically, make decisions grounded in reason, and approach situations with objectivity, free from emotional bias or pre-conceived notions. It involves analysing facts, weighing evidence, and considering various perspectives to arrive at balanced, well-informed decisions. Rational thinking enables individuals to solve problems effectively, make sound judgements, and achieve optimal outcomes in both personal and professional settings.

Example: A powerful example of rationality in practice is Dr. Manohar B. B. V. N. R., an Indian scientist and engineer, who played a pivotal role in the development of cost-effective solutions for India's Mars Orbiter Mission (*Mangalyaan*).

"The first step in the evolution of ethics is a sense of solidarity with other human beings."
Albert Schweitzer

"Rationality is the recognition of the fact that the unreal is unreal, and the real is real."
Ayn Rand

12. Courtesy

Courtesy is the practice of demonstrating respect, kindness, and politeness in all interactions, regardless of the behaviour or status of others. It involves treating every individual with dignity and consideration, contributing to a harmonious and inclusive environment. Courtesy is not just about superficial manners but reflects an underlying respect for others that fosters mutual understanding and positive relationships.

Example: A remarkable example of courtesy is Indra Nooyi, the former CEO of PepsiCo. During her tenure, she consistently demonstrated exceptional respect and thoughtfulness toward others, whether interacting with employees, business partners, or competitors.

"Courtesy is the one coin you can never have too much of or be stingy with."
John Wanamaker

"Politeness costs nothing, and gains everything" **Lady Mary Montagu**

13. Incorruptibility

Incorruptibility refers to the unwavering commitment to one's moral principles, despite external pressures or temptations. It involves steadfastly resisting the allure of personal gain, bribery, or unethical shortcuts, and maintaining the highest standards of integrity. An incorruptible individual remains true to their values, regardless of the challenges or incentives to compromise.

Example: Kiran Bedi, India's first woman officer in the Indian Police Service, is a prime example of incorruptibility. Throughout her career, particularly during her tenure at Tihar Jail in Delhi, she refused to be swayed by corruption, choosing instead to implement reforms that prioritised transparency and fairness.

"Incorruptibility is the true test of moral leadership."

"A man is not honest simply because he follows the rules. He is honest when his actions are aligned with his moral values, even in the absence of rules."

14. Civility

Civility is the practice of showing respect, politeness, and consideration toward others, particularly in public and social interactions. It is an essential aspect of social harmony, helping to maintain peaceful coexistence in diverse communities. Civility goes beyond mere politeness; it reflects an individual's commitment to creating an environment of mutual respect, fostering understanding, and promoting positive relationships among people.

Example: Dr Abdul Kalam, former President of India, was a shining example of civility throughout his career. Known for his humility and grace, he engaged with citizens from all walks of life with genuine respect and warmth.

"Civility costs nothing, and buys everything." **Lady Mary Wortley Montagu**

"Civility is the art of living together with respect, kindness, and understanding."

15. Wisdom

Wisdom is the ability to make sound, thoughtful decisions based on knowledge, experience, and a deep understanding of life. It involves looking at the bigger picture and considering the long-term consequences, often guided by ethical principles. Wisdom is not just about intelligence, but also about exercising judgment with compassion and foresight.

Example: Dr B.R. Ambedkar, a pivotal figure in India's history, exemplified wisdom through his leadership in drafting the Indian Constitution.

"Wisdom is not a product of schooling, but of the lifelong attempt to acquire it."
Albert Einstein

"The only true wisdom is in knowing you know nothing." **Socrates**

16. Wholesomeness

Wholesomeness refers to a balanced state of well-being that integrates physical, psychological, emotional, and spiritual health. A wholesome individual tends to their own needs while also nurturing the well-being of others, creating harmony within themselves and their environment. This holistic approach fosters a sense of complete fulfilment, contributing to both personal growth and collective well-being. A wholesome person practices self-care, cultivates mental clarity, and maintains a strong ethical foundation that guides their actions.

Example: Mahatma Gandhi exemplified wholesomeness through his approach to life, which emphasised the interconnectedness of body, mind, and spirit. He advocated for physical fitness, mental discipline, and spiritual purity.

17. Charity

Charity is the act of giving selflessly to others, driven by empathy, compassion, and a desire to alleviate their suffering. It is an expression of kindness that transcends expectations of **reciprocity**[5], focusing solely on improving the lives of others. True charity embodies the spirit of generosity, whether through financial support, time, or resources.

Example: Sonu Sood, during the COVID-19 pandemic, embodied the spirit of charity through his tireless efforts to help migrant workers stranded across India.

"Charity begins at home, but should not end there." **Thomas Fuller**

"No one has ever become poor by giving." **Anne Frank**

18. Affection

Affection is the emotional bond that forms when we recognise our shared humanity with others and care for their well-being as much as our own. It is a deep sense of warmth and connection, rooted in mutual understanding and care. Affection fosters strong relationships, promoting love and empathy, and helps build trust and emotional security.

Example: Atal Bihari Vajpayee, former Prime Minister of India, demonstrated affection for the nation through his diplomatic approach and commitment to national unity, peace, and

[5] **Reciprocity:** The practice of exchanging things with others for mutual benefit

development. His leadership during the Kargil War and India's 1998 nuclear tests reflected his deep care for the country's welfare and its security.

> "Affection is responsible for nine-tenths of whatever solid and durable happiness there is in our lives."
> **C.S. Lewis**

19. Care

Care is the genuine concern for the well-being of others, demonstrated through nurturing actions and emotional support. It goes beyond surface-level empathy to proactive and thoughtful engagement with the needs of others, aiming to alleviate their suffering and promote their happiness. Care involves a sense of responsibility and compassion, often requiring personal sacrifice for the benefit of others.

Example: Mahatma Jyotirao Phule demonstrated care through his social reform efforts, especially for the marginalised communities.

> "Too often we underestimate the power of a touch, a smile, a kind word, a listening ear, an honest compliment, or the smallest act of caring."
> **Leo Buscaglia**

> "Take care to get what you like, or you will be forced to like what you get."
> **George Bernard Shaw**

20. Reverence

Reverence is a deep respect and admiration for individuals who exemplify wisdom, integrity, and excellence in their actions. It involves recognising and honouring their contributions to society, particularly in areas like morality, self-discipline, leadership, and the promotion of harmony. Reverence is not about idolising individuals but about valuing their commitment to upholding higher principles and inspiring others through their actions.

Example: Revered for his leadership in unifying India post-independence, Sardar Vallabhbhai Patel's role in integrating over 500 princely states into the Indian Union demonstrates his wisdom and commitment to national unity.

21. Gratitude

Gratitude is the heartfelt appreciation for the help and kindness extended by others, recognising their contributions to our growth, success, and well-being. It fosters strong relationships by nurturing a sense of connectedness and mutual respect. Gratitude involves acknowledging the impact others have on our lives, which can inspire a cycle of generosity, kindness, and shared prosperity. It is both a reflection of **humility**[6] and an expression of respect for the efforts of others.

Example: Eklavya, a figure from the Mahabharata, embodies gratitude through his dedication to mastering archery, despite being denied formal training by his teacher, Drona. Eklavya's gratitude for the knowledge he had received from his teacher led him to self-train with a statue of Drona and become an extraordinary archer.

"Gratitude is not only the greatest of virtues, but the parent of all others."
Marcus Tullius Cicero

"Gratitude is the sign of noble souls." **Aesop**

22. Co-operation

Co-operation involves working together towards a common goal by sharing responsibilities, communicating openly, and respecting one another's strengths. It fosters unity, teamwork, and the collective power of diverse perspectives, leading to effective problem-solving and achieving success. In both personal and professional contexts, co-operation builds trust and promotes a sense of shared responsibility.

Example: ISRO's Mars Orbiter Mission (*Mangalyaan*) is a prime example of co-operation. Engineers, scientists, and administrators from diverse backgrounds worked together, overcoming resource constraints to achieve a significant scientific milestone, demonstrating the power of teamwork in accomplishing national goals.

"Alone we can do so little; together we can do so much." **Helen Keller**

"The strength of the team is each individual member. The strength of each member is the team."
Phil Jackson

23. Honesty

Honesty is being truthful, transparent, and sincere in words, actions, and intentions. It involves integrity, accountability, and adhering to ethical principles, even in difficult situations. Honesty fosters trust and respect in relationships and encourages personal and professional growth through self-reflection and learning from mistakes.

Example: Dr M. S. Swaminathan, known for his role in India's Green Revolution, exemplified honesty in his commitment to agricultural development. Despite challenges, he remained true to sustainable farming practices, building trust and credibility among farmers and colleagues through his integrity.

---

[6] **Humility:** Lack of pride

"Honesty is the best policy, but insanity is a better defence." **Steve Landesberg**

"No legacy is so rich as honesty." **William Shakespeare**

24. Kindness

Kindness is a type of behaviour marked by acts of generosity, consideration, rendering assistance, or concern for others, without expecting praise or reward in return. Affection, gentleness, warmth, concern, and care are words that are associated with kindness. Kindness is an interpersonal skill which often requires great courage and strength.

Kindness is also something you can show yourself. Being kind to your mind with positive self-talk, being kind to your body in how you listen to your body and what you put in it, and being kind to yourself especially when you are struggling mentally, physically, and emotionally is all equally as important as it is to be kind to others.

Examples:

1. During Wayanad landslides, two children from nearby Kakkanad reached the Infopark Police Station and handed over ₹2,500 to the Station House Officer donating their small savings to the Chief Minister's Distress Relief Fund. This reflects the kindness of those two children.
2. After the devastating earthquake that struck Turkey, India demonstrated its global solidarity and kindness through **Operation Dost** which involved relief operations, aid from medical personnel, etc.

"Kindness in words creates confidence. Kindness in thinking creates profoundness. Kindness in giving creates love." **Mother Teresa**

25. Consistency

Consistency is having a long-term commitment, and involves sustained effort in doing actions repeatedly until you achieve your target. It is 'the absence of contradictions'. It is the harmony of conduct or practice with profession. Moral consistency is the ability to preserve non-contradictory moral values across different types of situations, and is often considered the hallmark of ethics.

Example:

1. Usain Bolt is one of the most iconic athletes of all time, with a record of eight Olympic gold medals and world records in both the 100m and 200m races. His journey to becoming a world-class athlete was not an easy one. One of his biggest hurdles was his tendency to start races slowly, which often put him behind. Bolt knew he needed to improve his starts in order to reach his full potential. He spent countless hours practicing his starts and perfecting his form. Bolt's success can be attributed not only to his natural talent but also

to his dedication, discipline, and hard work. He has consistently pushed himself to be the best, both on and off the track.

2. Mahatma Gandhi, advocate of "*Satyagraha* and non-violence", stood by the principle, in spite of various obstacles and confronting ideologies of the same time.

"Arise, awake, and stop not till the goal is reached." **Swami Vivekananda**

"Winners are not those who never fail but never quit." **Dr APJ Abdul Kalam**

"Our greatest weakness lies in giving up. The most certain way to succeed is always to try just one more time." **Thomas A. Edison**

15. A FEW ESSENTIAL HUMAN VALUES

1. Temper

Temper refers to the quality of self-control, moderation, and balance in one's actions, emotions, or desires. It acts as a driving force that distinguishes the strong from the weak, providing energy, determination, and resilience. Temper is not inherently negative, rather, it is a gift that must be appreciated and controlled. Unchecked temper can lead to destructive consequences, but when harnessed effectively, it becomes a powerful tool for personal growth and achievement. Like gasoline, temper can fuel progress or cause harm, depending on how it is managed.

Significance of Temperance

Temperance, as the moderation and control of temper, plays a vital role in various aspects of life:

Personal Growth: Temperance ensures balance and equilibrium, preventing excessive indulgence or emotional outbursts. It allows individuals to make thoughtful decisions, maintain a calm **demeanour**[7] under pressure, and build a strong moral character.

Effective Leadership and Efficient Governance: Leaders who embody temperance exhibit patience, fairness, and restraint. These qualities lead to effective policy-making, equitable resource allocation, and the ability to navigate complex situations without succumbing to short-term pressures or emotions. Temperance in governance ensures integrity, fosters public trust, and promotes sustainable practices.

Promotes an Ethical and Philosophical Way of Life: Temperance aligns with Aristotle's doctrine of the mean, advocating a balance between excess and deficiency. It is a cardinal virtue alongside prudence, justice, and fortitude, forming the foundation of ethical behaviour.

- **Deontological Perspective:** Temperance is seen as a duty to oneself and society.

---

[7] **Demeanour:** The way a person behaves

- **Utilitarian Perspective:** It contributes to the greatest good by promoting responsible and sustainable actions.

Improves Physical and Mental Health: Temperance encourages moderation in habits, work-life balance, and lifestyle choices. By avoiding extremes, it helps prevent burnout, stress, and health issues, leading to a more fulfilling life.

For example -

Narendra Kumar, an IPS officer known for his fight against the mining mafia in Madhya Pradesh, exemplified temperance. He approached law enforcement with a balance between dialogue and action, aiming for reform rather than punishment. His ability to remain composed under pressure demonstrated the strength of temperance in leadership.

QUOTES ON TEMPERANCE

"The measure of a man is what he does with power. — **Plato**

Moderation in all things. — **Ancient Greek maxim**"

Temper, when managed through temperance, is a valuable asset. It provides the energy and drive necessary for success while promoting balance and restraint. Temperance enhances decision-making, strengthens relationships, and ensures ethical behaviour. In governance, it fosters sustainable policies, equitable leadership, and public trust. Ultimately, temperance transforms personal virtues into a collective good, ensuring harmony and progress in both personal and societal contexts.

2. Piety

Piety refers to a deep and sincere devotion to religious principles or spiritual beliefs, often manifesting through acts of reverence, worship, and adherence to moral obligations. It encompasses a profound respect for the divine, as well as for one's ancestors, family, and community. This value is universally acknowledged across different cultures and religions, although its expression may vary. At its core, piety emphasises the harmony between personal devotion and ethical conduct, inspiring individuals to live with humility, compassion, and integrity.

Piety is not just a personal virtue but a powerful social force that influences the moral fabric of the society. When individuals live piously, they contribute to the creation of just, compassionate, and ethical communities. By embodying virtues like charity, humility, and justice, pious individuals set an example for others, fostering an environment where people support one another and work toward the common good. Piety also contributes to emotional well-being and social stability by offering individuals a sense of purpose and community, reducing isolation, and fostering mutual support networks. In this way, piety plays a key role in building societies grounded in ethical living and social responsibility.

Significance of Piety

Piety carries profound significance in shaping individual character, fostering community unity, and enhancing societal well-being:

- **Moral and Ethical Compass:** Piety offers individuals a clear framework of spiritual and ethical guidelines drawn from religious teachings, that influence decision-making, behaviour, and personal growth. It serves as a moral compass, helping one navigate life in alignment with higher principles and values.
- **Community and Social Cohesion:** Piety strengthens social bonds by fostering shared beliefs, values, and rituals. It cultivates a sense of collective identity and belonging, creating unity among people who follow similar spiritual or moral codes.
- **Self-Discipline and Growth:** Engaging in religious practices such as prayer, fasting, or meditation, which are integral to piety, encourages personal discipline and resilience. These practices promote emotional stability, inner peace, and the development of virtues like patience, humility, and self-control.
- **Spiritual Fulfilment and Purpose:** Piety provides individuals with a sense of connection to something greater than themselves, offering spiritual fulfilment. It imbues life with meaning and purpose, especially when individuals dedicate themselves to serving others or seeking divine guidance.
- **Mental and Emotional Well-being:** Spiritual practices linked to piety, such as prayer or meditation, can help reduce stress, anxiety, and depression, by providing emotional support, a sense of community, and hope. This sense of spiritual connection fosters resilience, peace, and a deeper sense of calm. **Cultural and Religious Continuity:** Through piety, individuals contribute to the preservation of cultural and religious traditions, passing them down through generations. This fosters a sense of shared heritage and continuity, allowing traditions to evolve while maintaining their essential values.
- **Social Responsibility and Advocacy:** Piety often inspires individuals to act for the greater good, engaging in acts of charity, community service, and advocacy for justice. Many religious teachings emphasise helping the less fortunate, which motivates pious individuals to contribute positively to their communities and beyond.

For example -

Malala Yousafzai: Guided by her Islamic faith, Malala has dedicated her life to advocating for girls' education, reflecting a deep commitment to both her religious beliefs and social justice. Her actions demonstrate how piety can inspire one to fight for the betterment of others. "I don't want to be thought of as the 'girl who was shot by the Taliban' but the 'girl who fought for education.' This is the cause to which I want to devote my life."

Dalai Lama: The Dalai Lama's life of prayer, meditation, and compassionate leadership exemplifies Buddhist piety. His teachings emphasise kindness, compassion, and mindfulness, demonstrating how piety can guide one's interactions with others. "My religion is very simple. My religion is kindness."

QUOTES ON PIETY

"The highest form of piety towards God is to do justice to men. **Immanuel Kant**

True piety does not mean walking around with downcast eyes or with a gloomy face. It means having the courage to look at reality with open eyes. **Pope Francis**

Piety is not only the virtue of the pious, but also the charm of the virtuous. **Joseph Joubert**"

Piety is a deeply transformative value that shapes both personal and collective life. Through a commitment to religious or spiritual practices, piety nurtures ethical behaviour, strengthens community bonds, and provides individuals with a profound sense of purpose and meaning. The benefits of piety are far-reaching, encompassing emotional well-being, cultural continuity, and social justice. By living with devotion and humility, individuals and communities alike can experience the lasting impact of piety, creating a more compassionate, ethical, and harmonious world.

3. Beneficence

Beneficence is the ethical principle of doing good and actively contributing to the welfare of others. It involves not only refraining from harm but also taking deliberate actions to promote the well-being of others, alleviate suffering, and improve the quality of life. Beneficence goes beyond passive non-maleficence (the avoidance of harm) and requires active engagement in acts of kindness, support, care, and charity. It is central to many ethical systems, particularly in medicine, social work, law, and personal conduct, where it serves as a moral compass for actions that benefit others.

Significance of Beneficence

Beneficence plays a vital role in the ethical frameworks of various disciplines and in the fabric of society:

- **Moral Foundation:** Beneficence is foundational to ethics, offering a guiding principle for individuals and institutions to take actions that improve the lives of others. It emphasises the importance of altruism, compassion, and selflessness in moral decision-making.
- **Human Connection:** Beneficent acts foster empathy and compassion, which strengthen social bonds and promote a sense of community. It encourages individuals to look beyond

themselves and connect with others in meaningful ways, building a foundation of trust and mutual care.

- **Healthcare Ethics:** In medicine, beneficence is a core ethical principle that directs healthcare providers to prioritise the well-being of their patients, ensuring that actions are taken to heal, support, and improve patients' lives.
- **Legal and Social Policy:** Laws and policies that reflect beneficence aim to improve the overall welfare of society. They work toward reducing inequalities and ensuring that vulnerable groups are protected and cared for, thereby promoting the collective well-being.

For example -

Bill and Melinda Gates: Through their foundation, the Gates have committed significant resources to global health, education, and poverty alleviation, embodying the principle of beneficence on a global scale. Their philanthropy reflects a commitment to improving the well-being of millions.

Nelson Mandela: After his release from prison, Mandela dedicated his life to promoting reconciliation, justice, and equality in South Africa, showing how beneficence in leadership can create lasting change for the greater good.

QUOTES ON BENEFICENCE

"What counts in life is not the mere fact that we have lived. It is what difference we have made to the lives of others that will determine the significance of the life we lead. **Nelson Mandela**

Success is a lousy teacher. It seduces smart people into thinking they can't lose. And it's an unreliable guide to the future. **Bill Gates**

The purpose of human life is to serve, and to show compassion, and the will to help others. **Albert Schweitzer**

We make a living by what we get, but we make a life by what we give. **Winston Churchill**"

Beneficence, then, is not merely an ethical principle but a way of life that promotes mutual well-being, encourages acts of kindness, and builds a society where everyone's welfare is considered. Its benefits are manifold, impacting both the giver and the receiver positively, fostering a more compassionate and equitable world.

4. Abstinence: The Value of Self-Restraint and Discipline

Abstinence is the voluntary practice of refraining from certain activities, particularly those associated with indulgence or excess. While commonly linked to avoiding sexual activity, alcohol, drugs, or addictive behaviours, abstinence can also extend to other forms of restraint, such as abstaining from food, luxury, or speech. Often rooted in spiritual or personal discipline, abstinence serves as a means of exercising self-control and promoting a lifestyle of moderation and intentional living.

Significance of Abstinence

Abstinence plays a crucial role in fostering personal growth, health, and moral integrity:

- **Self-Control:** By practicing abstinence, individuals cultivate the ability to master their impulses and desires, fostering discipline and emotional stability. This self-restraint empowers individuals to act with intention and focus, avoiding distractions or harmful behaviours.
- **Spiritual Growth:** In many religious traditions, abstinence is considered a vital practice for spiritual purification and growth. By abstaining from worldly pleasures, individuals are believed to elevate their spiritual connection and focus more fully on their faith.
- **Health Benefits:** Abstaining from harmful substances, such as alcohol or drugs, or from excess in any form, promotes physical health and well-being. It also contributes to mental clarity and emotional resilience, improving one's overall quality of life.
- **Moral and Ethical Living:** Abstinence can reflect a commitment to higher moral standards and integrity. It is often viewed as a conscious choice to refrain from actions that could undermine one's values, contributing to ethical living and personal dignity.
- **Enhanced Focus:** Abstaining from distractions, such as indulgence in pleasures or excessive consumption, can improve concentration and focus. Whether for academic success, career advancement, or personal growth, abstinence enables individuals to dedicate their energy to meaningful pursuits.
- **Relationship Building:** In contexts like sexual abstinence before marriage or abstaining from distractions in relationships, individuals can build stronger emotional connections based on trust, respect, and deeper understanding.

? Thought Box

In a world that celebrates instant gratification and abundance, how can practicing abstinence and self-restraint enrich our lives, and where should we draw the line between discipline that empowers us, and deprivation that limits us?

For example -

1. **Mahatma Gandhi:** Gandhi practiced *brahmacharya* (celibacy) as a central part of his spiritual discipline, believing that control over physical desires was key to moral clarity and inner strength. He says "*Brahmacharya* means control of the senses in thought, word and deed. Every day I have to take a fresh vow because every day I find myself assailed by fresh temptations of the flesh."

2. **Digital Detox:** People might abstain from using digital devices like smartphones or social media for periods to reduce stress or improve mental health.

QUOTES ON ABSTINENCE

> "The only way to get rid of a temptation is to yield to it. Resist it, and your soul grows sick with longing for the things it has forbidden to itself. **Oscar Wilde**
>
> Abstinence is the surety of temperance. **Plato**"

Abstinence is not simply about restriction; it is about creating space for more meaningful pursuits and building a life based on discipline, integrity, and spiritual growth.

Abstinence as a Path to Personal Mastery

Abstinence is more than simply denying oneself; it is a path to personal mastery, growth, and purpose. By choosing restraint, individuals gain greater awareness of their desires, better control over their impulses, and the ability to make deliberate, thoughtful choices. Whether in spiritual practices, health goals, or personal development, abstinence serves as a powerful tool for self-improvement and moral living.

Abstinence fosters a sense of agency and intentionality, allowing individuals to align their actions with their values and long-term objectives. It encourages people to pause, reflect, and choose actions that nurture their well-being, and the well-being of others.

Abstinence is a value rooted in self-control, discipline, and intentional living. It is a practice that transcends mere denial, and instead becomes a vehicle for spiritual growth, personal development, and moral living. Whether used to foster health, deepen relationships, or strengthen faith, abstinence empowers individuals to take charge of their desires and choose a path of greater integrity and fulfilment.

5. Endurance of Labour

Endurance of labour refers to the capacity to sustain prolonged physical, mental, or emotional effort while working toward a goal or overcoming challenges. It embodies resilience, perseverance, and the ability to maintain focus and productivity despite fatigue, obstacles, or discouragement. This quality is essential for personal success, societal advancement, and collective achievements.

Significance of Endurance of Labour

1. **Personal Growth:** Endurance cultivates discipline and adaptability, enabling individuals to face challenges with confidence. Overcoming hardships builds self-belief, fostering personal development.

2. **Enhanced Productivity:** Sustained effort leads to consistent output and higher-quality results, whether in personal, educational, or professional pursuits.
3. **Improved Problem-Solving Skills:** Challenges encountered during labour foster perseverance, creativity, and critical thinking, equipping individuals to tackle future obstacles effectively.
4. **Stronger Relationships:** Endurance in relationships—familial, professional, or social—builds trust, loyalty, and mutual respect over time.
5. **Physical and Mental Health:** Endurance fosters stamina and reduces the likelihood of burnout, promoting resilience, and an improved capacity to manage stress.
6. **Legacy of Inspiration:** Acts of endurance inspire others to emulate perseverance and contribute to larger causes.

For example -

Thomas Edison (Invention of the Light Bulb) – Edison failed over 1,000 times before creating a functional light bulb, showcasing the power of persistence and experimentation.

PV Sindhu (Badminton) – Years of rigorous training and mental toughness propelled Sindhu to consistent success in international tournaments.

Indra Nooyi (Former CEO of PepsiCo) – Overcoming challenges in a male-dominated corporate world, Nooyi transformed PepsiCo and became a role model for aspiring leaders.

QUOTES ON ENDURANCE

"Endurance is one of the most difficult disciplines, but it is to the one who endures that the final victory comes.

Buddha

The difference between a successful person and others is not a lack of strength, not a lack of knowledge, but rather a lack of will.

Vince Lombardi

The best way out is always through.

Robert Frost

Success is stumbling from failure to failure with no loss of enthusiasm.

Winston Churchill

The difference between the impossible and the possible lies in a person's determination.

Tommy Lasorda"

Endurance of labour is a cornerstone of personal and societal progress. It fosters resilience, creativity, and sustained effort, driving long-term success and achievement. From historical innovators to everyday workers, examples of endurance remind us that consistent effort and perseverance can turn aspirations into reality.

6. Want Little

The value of "Want little" embodies the conscious choice to limit one's desires and material needs, focusing on essentials rather than excess. It emphasises simplicity, contentment, and mindful living, encouraging individuals to find fulfilment in non-material aspects of life. Rooted in minimalism and self-restraint, this philosophy promotes appreciating what one already has, while fostering inner peace, sustainability, and purposeful living. By choosing to live with less—not out of necessity but as a deliberate practice—it nurtures a deeper connection to personal values and the world around us.

Significance of Wanting Little:

1. **Fosters Contentment:** Reducing excessive desires enhances satisfaction and gratitude for existing possessions, creating inner peace and emotional well-being.
2. **Supports Sustainability:** Minimal consumption lowers waste, conserves resources, and contributes to environmental preservation.
3. **Enhances Focus:** Avoiding distractions from material pursuits enables individuals to concentrate on meaningful relationships, goals, and personal growth.
4. **Builds Self-Control:** Practicing restraint cultivates discipline and mindfulness, essential traits for success in personal and professional life.
5. **Encourages Ethical Living:** Limiting wants fosters fairness and equity, enabling more equitable resource distribution and reducing societal disparities.
6. **Long-Term Happiness:** Emphasising intrinsic fulfilment over material gratification nurtures lasting joy and emotional resilience.

For example -

Steve Jobs – Known for his focus on essentials, Jobs often avoided unnecessary distractions to prioritise creativity and innovation.

The Dalai Lama – His teachings emphasise mindfulness and contentment, underscoring the spiritual richness of wanting less.

Leo Tolstoy – Tolstoy renounced his wealth and embraced simplicity, advocating for a life focused on moral and spiritual growth rather than material desires.

The value of 'Want Little' invites individuals to seek happiness and fulfilment beyond material possessions. By embracing simplicity, cultivating gratitude, and reducing excess, one can lead a life of balance, sustainability, and profound contentment, benefiting both oneself and the society at large.

QUOTES ON 'WANT LITTLE' APPROACH

"The world has enough for everyone's needs, but not enough for everyone's greed.
Mahatma Gandhi

Simplicity is the ultimate sophistication. **Leonardo da Vinci**

Contentment is the greatest wealth. **Buddha**

A simple life is a happy life. **Albert Einstein**

He who is contented is rich. **Lao Tzu**"

7. Steadiness of Purpose

Steadiness of purpose is the unwavering commitment to one's long-term goals, values, and ideals, even in the face of challenges, distractions, or setbacks. It embodies resilience, perseverance, and a clear sense of direction, ensuring consistent progress toward achieving meaningful objectives. This value emphasises the importance of maintaining focus and dedication over time, rather than being swayed by short-term obstacles or immediate rewards.

Significance of Steadiness of Purpose

1. **Achievement of Long-term Goals:** Steadiness helps individuals stay on track toward their long-term objectives, ensuring consistent effort and focus despite challenges or setbacks.
2. **Resilience in Adversity:** This value strengthens one's ability to navigate difficulties without losing sight of the ultimate goal, fostering emotional and mental resilience.
3. **Credibility and Trust:** Consistent commitment to a clear purpose builds trust and credibility, as people admire and respect those who honour their goals and promises.
4. **Personal Growth:** The journey of staying true to a steady purpose cultivates valuable qualities like patience, discipline, and the ability to delay gratification, all of which contribute to personal growth.
5. **Motivation and Inspiration:** A steady purpose not only drives the individual but also inspires others, fostering motivation within teams and communities.
6. **Emotional Stability:** A steady purpose provides individuals with direction and reduces feelings of anxiety or uncertainty, promoting emotional well-being and stability.
7. **Improved Decision-Making:** Steadiness of purpose helps to align decisions with long-term objectives, minimising impulsive or short-term choices in favour of strategic, thoughtful actions.

For example -

1. The story of Elon Musk with Tesla and SpaceX, where despite numerous financial and technical challenges, his purpose to advance sustainable energy and space exploration has remained constant.
2. J.K. Rowling faced multiple rejections before publishing the first *Harry Potter* book. Her persistence and belief in her story were key to her eventual success.

QUOTES ON STEADINESS OF PURPOSE

"The path from dreams to success does exist. May you have the vision to find it, the courage to get on to it, and the perseverance to follow it. **Kalpana Chawla**

Success is not final, failure is not fatal: It is the courage to continue that counts. **Winston Churchill**

Perseverance is not a long race; it is many short races one after the other. **Walter Elliot**

Success is the sum of small efforts, repeated day in and day out. **Robert Collier**

If you are persistent, you will get it. If you are consistent, you will keep it. **Harvey Mackay**"

Steadiness of purpose is the foundation of long-term success and fulfilment. It requires focus, resilience, and commitment, empowering individuals to achieve greatness while building valuable personal and professional traits. This value not only drives personal growth but also inspires others to remain steadfast in the pursuit of their own dreams and aspirations.

8. Freedom of Will

Freedom of will refers to the inherent ability of individuals to make choices and decisions without being unduly influenced or constrained by external forces. It is the capacity to act in accordance with one's own beliefs, desires, and values, allowing individuals to shape their lives and actions based on their personal convictions. This concept is often associated with autonomy, self-determination, and personal accountability, emphasising that individuals possess the power to steer their own lives through their decisions.

In essence, freedom of will—often referred to as free will—is the idea that human beings are capable of making choices that are not preordained by natural laws, fate, or divine forces. It suggests that individuals have the autonomy to act according to their own reasoning, desires, and moral judgements, independent of external constraints or predetermined outcomes.

Significance:

1. **Promotes Moral Autonomy:** Free will empowers individuals to act based on their own judgement, ensuring they are morally accountable for their actions. This autonomy reinforces ethical decision-making and the understanding that we are responsible for the consequences of our choices.
2. **Personal Evolution:** The liberty to choose shapes individual growth. By making independent decisions, individuals cultivate resilience, learn from mistakes, and chart their path to self-improvement and personal transformation.
3. **Improves Innovation and Originality:** Free will fosters an environment for creative exploration. It enables individuals to break away from conventional constraints, thinking and acting freely to innovate and create novel solutions.
4. **Promotes Justice and Accountability:** Societal systems, including legal and ethical frameworks, are grounded in the assumption that individuals possess free will. This allows for personal responsibility, where actions are evaluated based on the autonomy of decision-making, ensuring fair justice.
5. **Enhances Intrinsic Dignity:** Belief in free will upholds human dignity by affirming that individuals are autonomous agents capable of determining their own paths in life, fostering respect for personal choices and self-governance.
6. **Empowerment and Self-Reliance:** Freedom of will enhances personal empowerment, equipping individuals with the confidence to navigate life's challenges, assert their rights, and make decisions aligned with their core values and purpose.

For example -

1. Leonardo da Vinci, through his numerous inventions, artwork, and scientific discoveries, exemplified freedom of will in choosing his own paths of intellectual and creative exploration.
2. Anna Hazare's decision to lead a nationwide anti-corruption movement through peaceful means highlighted his freedom of will.
3. P.T. Usha, often referred to as the 'Queen of Indian track and field', followed her will to become one of India's most celebrated athletes.
4. M.S. Swaminathan exercised his freedom of will in choosing to improve Indian agriculture through the Green Revolution. His dedication to improving food security led to groundbreaking changes in Indian farming techniques, ensuring greater self-sufficiency.

QUOTES ON FREEDOM OF WILL

"The only real prison is fear, and the only real freedom is freedom from fear. **Aung San Suu Kyi**

To be free is not merely to cast off one's chains, but to live in a way that respects and enhances the freedom of others. **Nelson Mandela**

The best way to predict your future is to create it. **Abraham Lincoln**"

Freedom of will is a foundational value that empowers individuals to live authentically, make meaningful choices, and shape their own paths. It is tied to self-determination, creativity, and responsibility, leading to personal fulfilment and growth.

9. Dignity

Dignity is the intrinsic value and respect owed to every individual, simply by virtue of their humanity. It signifies the acknowledgement of each person's worth and the moral imperative to treat them with honour and fairness, irrespective of their social standing, achievements, or background. Dignity safeguards individuals from humiliation, oppression, or exploitation, ensuring that their fundamental rights and humanity are upheld. It serves as the bedrock of human rights and is universally recognised, transcending cultural, social, and political boundaries.

Significance of Dignity:

- **Cornerstone of Human Rights:** Dignity forms the very foundation of human rights, serving as the essential principle behind equality, justice, and freedom. It provides the ethical framework for ensuring that every individual is granted respect and fundamental rights.
- **Fosters Social Unity:** Upholding dignity creates an environment of mutual respect and empathy, where individuals recognise the inherent worth of others, leading to stronger bonds, reduced conflict, and social cohesion.
- **Empowerment and Self-Respect:** When individuals are treated with dignity, it boosts their self-worth, fosters a sense of pride, and empowers them to take ownership of their lives. It promotes mental resilience and a sense of personal agency.
- **Ethical Integrity:** Dignity serves as a guiding principle for ethical behaviour, shaping individual actions, societal norms, and legal frameworks towards justice, fairness, and respect for others.
- **Inclusivity and Equality:** Dignity promotes inclusiveness by affirming that everyone, irrespective of race, gender, socio-economic status, or background, is deserving of respect. It fosters a society that celebrates diversity and rejects discrimination.

- **Personal Growth and Motivation:** Experiencing dignity leads to greater self-confidence and motivation, driving individuals to pursue their potential, set ambitious goals, and achieve personal fulfilment.

For example -

1. As India's first President, Dr Rajendra Prasad demonstrated the dignity of individuals, regardless of their caste or social status. His simplicity, humility, and respect for all people, regardless of their backgrounds, promoted a strong sense of dignity for the people of India.
2. Lal Bahadur Shastri, India's second Prime Minister, led with simplicity, honesty, and dignity. His leadership during the 1965 India-Pakistan war, along with his focus on the welfare of the common man, earned him immense respect.

QUOTES ON DIGNITY

"The dignity of man is inviolable. To respect and protect it is the duty of all government.
International Covenant on Civil and Political Rights

Injustice anywhere is a threat to justice everywhere. We are caught in an inescapable network of mutuality, tied in a single garment of destiny. **Martin Luther King, Jr.**

Dignity does not consist in possessing honours, but in deserving them. **Aristotle**"

Dignity is an essential value that underpins human rights, justice, and equality. It is a universal principle that affirms the inherent worth of every individual, promoting respect, empathy, and fairness. Upholding dignity is vital for building a compassionate and inclusive society, where individuals are empowered to thrive and contribute meaningfully to the collective good. By respecting the dignity of all, we foster an environment that values humanity, embraces diversity, and champions equality for all.

10. Simplicity

Simplicity refers to the essence of being clear, straightforward, and free from unnecessary complexity or excess. It involves focusing on what truly matters, minimising desires, and embracing a life that is purposeful and uncluttered. In a broader sense, simplicity encourages living intentionally—whether in thoughts, actions, possessions, or systems—by stripping away distractions and reducing life's intricacies to the essentials. It fosters a mindset of appreciating life's unadorned truths and encourages peace through clarity.

Significance of Simplicity:

- **Mental Clarity:** Simplicity reduces cognitive overload, enhancing decision-making and problem-solving, leading to improved focus and reduced mental fatigue.
- **Stress Relief:** By eliminating unnecessary complexities, simplicity reduces distractions, alleviating stress and contributing to better emotional well-being.
- **Financial Stability:** A simple lifestyle reduces material desires, leading to lower expenses, increased savings, and greater financial independence.
- **Environmental Impact:** Embracing simplicity promotes mindful consumption, reducing waste and one's ecological footprint, encouraging sustainability.
- **Time Efficiency:** Simplifying life frees up time for meaningful activities like personal growth and relationships, enhancing overall productivity.
- **Gratitude and Contentment:** Focusing on life's essentials fosters a deeper appreciation for what one already has, leading to greater satisfaction and happiness.
- **Personal Growth:** Simplicity creates space for introspection, self-awareness, and emotional development, driving personal progress.

For example -

1. Ratan Tata, known for his humble and simple lifestyle despite being one of India's wealthiest industrialists, embodies simplicity in leadership.
2. Sardar Patel, a key figure in India's post-independence integration, lived humbly, renouncing materialism and luxury. His simplicity reflected his dedication to the nation and the unification of India.
3. Kasturba Gandhi, wife of Mahatma Gandhi, embraced a life of simplicity and selfless service. Committed to social causes like women's empowerment, education, and health, she lived modestly and played a significant role in the independence movement and rural development.

QUOTES ON SIMPLICITY

"Simplicity is the ultimate sophistication. — **Leonardo da Vinci**

The art of being wise is the art of knowing what to overlook. — **William James**

Life is really simple, but we insist on making it complicated. — **Confucius**

Simplicity is the key to brilliance. — **Bruce Lee**"

Simplicity is more than just a lifestyle choice—it's a mindset that allows individuals to focus on what truly matters. By eliminating unnecessary complexity, individuals can create a life that is purposeful, focused, and fulfilling. Embracing simplicity leads to greater clarity, enhanced well-being, and deeper appreciation for the essentials of life. Whether through minimalist living, streamlined thinking, or a focus on what adds true value, simplicity has the power to transform how we experience and engage with the world.

SUMMARY

- While values may be indefinable, they are inherently intelligible.
- Values are vital because an individual's behaviour is largely shaped by the values they have internalised.
- Terminal values are core and enduring, representing fundamental personal character traits.
- Intrinsic values are the most desirable and serve as goals to strive for. These values are widely accepted by communities, although they may vary across cultures and over time.
- Institutional values are those defined and propagated by specific institutions, encouraging individuals to adopt and internalise them.
- Individual values encompass both intrinsic and extrinsic values, reflecting what an individual considers significant to achieve personal desires and goals.
- Intrinsic values form the foundation for moral judgements, particularly under consequentialism, where decisions about right and wrong depend on identifying the appropriate outcomes. These values guide individuals toward ethical choices and are central to ethical consequentialism.
- The term 'morality' originates from the Latin word '*moralis*', meaning 'traditional customs' or 'proper behaviour'. Morals are shaped by society, specific communities, religious teachings, or even family traditions.
- Family values are transmitted from one generation to the next. However, some family members go beyond preserving inherited values to establish newer and nobler ones, exemplifying the dynamic evolution of values within families.
- Values cannot develop in isolation, but must evolve within the societal context. Individuals must be educated about both local and global values, as these overlap and interact in today's interconnected world.
- Value education is essential for instilling proper values in the next generation, ensuring they contribute to a harmonious and ethical society.

PREVIOUS YEARS' QUESTIONS

1. "Do not hate anybody, because that hatred that comes out from you must, in the long run, come back to you. If you love, that love will come back to you, completing the circle." — Swami Vivekananda *UPSC CSE Mains 2023*
2. "The simplest acts of kindness are by far more powerful than a thousand heads bowing in prayer." — Mahatma Gandhi *UPSC CSE Mains 2023*
3. "Corruption is the manifestation of the failure of core values in the society." In your opinion, what measures can be adopted to uplift the core values in the society? *UPSC CSE Mains 2023*
4. "Life doesn't make any sense without interdependence. We need each other, and the sooner we learn that, it is better for us all." — Erik Erikson *UPSC CSE Mains 2021*
5. "We can never obtain peace in the outer world until and unless we obtain peace within ourselves." — Dalai Lama *UPSC CSE Mains 2021*
6. The current Internet expansion has instilled a different set of cultural values which are in conflict with traditional values. Discuss. *UPSC CSE Mains 2020*
7. Discuss the role of ethics and values in enhancing the following three major components of Comprehensive National Power (CNP) viz. human capital, soft power (culture and policies), and social harmony. *UPSC CSE Mains 2020*
8. "Where there is righteousness in the heart, there is beauty in the character. When there is beauty in the character, there is harmony in the home. When there is harmony in the home, there is order in the nation. When there is order in the nation, there is peace in the world" — A.P.J. Abdul Kalam *UPSC CSE Mains 2019*
9. State the three basic values, universal in nature, in the context of Civil Services and bring out their importance. *UPSC CSE Mains 2018*
10. The crisis of ethical values in modern times is traced to a narrow perception of the good life. Discuss. *UPSC CSE Mains 2017*
11. Without commonly shared and widely entrenched moral values and obligations, neither the law, nor democratic government, nor even the market economy will function properly. What do you understand by this statement? Explain with illustration in the contemporary times. *UPSC CSE Mains 2017*
12. Social values are more important than economic values. Discuss this statement with examples in the context of inclusive growth of a nation. *UPSC CSE Mains 2015*
13. "There is enough on this earth for every one's need but for no one's greed." — Mahatma Gandhi *UPSC CSE Mains 2013*
14. Some people feel that values keep changing with time and situation, while others strongly believe that there are certain universal and eternal human values. Give your perception in this regard with due justification. *UPSC CSE Mains 2013*
15. What do you understand by 'values' and 'ethics'? In what way is it important to be ethical along with being professionally competent? *UPSC CSE Mains 2013*

Sensitive Parenting

3

LEARNING OBJECTIVES

1. Understanding Parenting From Philosophical Perspectives
2. Exploring the Family's Role in Value Development of a Child
3. Differentiating between General and Sensitive Parenting approaches
4. Recognising multifaceted responsibilities of parents in fostering a nurturing environment for their children
5. Understanding Children's Needs
6. Evolving from Good to Great Parenting
7. Navigate Parenting Teenagers and addressing their unique challenges and needs
8. Ensuring Cyber Safety
9. Embracing valuable lessons from children that can strengthen the parent-child relationship

1. PHILOSOPHER'S VIEW ON PARENTING

Philosophers have long explored the ethical and practical dimensions of parenting, viewing it as a vital role in shaping both individuals and society. From Buddha to Aristotle, philosophical perspectives on parenting focus on fostering moral, intellectual, and emotional growth in children. Let's explore in detail:

1.1 Buddha

In his *Samyutta Nikaya,* Buddha asserts that parents play the primary role in a child's physical, mental, and spiritual growth. Parents teach their children to speak, walk, and eat and they also provide essential moral guidance. Children should remember that parents are their first teachers, whom Buddha refers to as the *brahma* of the household.

1.2 Seneca

Seneca was a Stoic philosopher of Ancient Rome. In Roman civilization, fathers, or paterfamilias, held a significant authority. They were expected to play a key role in their sons' moral development, while mothers were responsible for maintaining discipline and supporting their children's ambitions. Seneca advised encouraging individuals to aspire to greatness while restraining them from arrogance. He emphasised allowing them to enjoy some comforts of wealth without succumbing to indulgence, teaching them resilience in the face of failure, and focusing on instruction rather than mere punishment. He also suggested offering praise, but with moderation.

1.3 Plato

Plato, an ancient Greek philosopher said, "***Let parents bequeath to their children not riches, but the spirit of reverence***[1]." The idea of the individual is eliminated in Plato's Republic, and children are instead taught the importance of collectivity, community, and solidarity with the state. Plato believed in the importance of education and the state's role in raising children. He argued that children should be educated in a way that fosters virtue and prepares them to be just citizens.

1.4 Aristotle

Aristotelian ethics enriches our understanding of the value of parenting and caring, as a part of intelligent virtue. Chosen on the basis of sound reasoning, it constitutes an achievement in the sense of the production of something good, another human to flourish in the next generation. Achieving this goal counts as part of the producer's well-lived life. Aristotle viewed childhood as a crucial period for moral and intellectual development. He believed that parents should model virtuous behaviour, as children learn through imitation.

1.5 Jean-Jacques Rousseau

During the eighteenth century, Jean-Jacques Rousseau's views started to change parenting practices. Children, according to Rousseau, were inherently innocent, weak, and easily tempted. Given that children are basically virtuous from birth, it is the duty of their parents to protect them against people who might corrupt their innocent minds. He believed in allowing children to explore and learn from their experiences rather than imposing strict rules.

1.6 Confucius

In Confucianism, 'filial piety' developed as a system of inheritance between children and their parents. A virtue involving a child's obedience to their parents is termed as 'filial piety'. Confucius considered this virtue, in addition to reverence for one's parents, to be the foundation of goodness. He calls filial piety the basis of love for other people and the community. It is also deeply traditional, a ritual form of behaviour, which creates strong family connections. Cultivating it also helps maintain political stability, as it prevents children from rebelling against their parents and creating disorder in society.

---

[1]**Reverence:** A feeling or sense of respect

1.7 Simone de Beauvoir

French philosopher Beauvoir discussed the impact of societal norms on gender roles and the upbringing of children. Rather, the objective should be to create a child who is capable of establishing and achieving personal goals, developing unique projects, and utilising this capacity for the rest of their lives. Raising a person who is autonomous is, in essence, the aim of parenting.

QUOTATIONS ON PARENTING

"All that I am, or hope to be, I owe to my mother. **Abraham Lincoln**

There is no school equal to a decent home and no teacher equal to a virtuous parent. **Mahatma Gandhi**

The children of today will make the India of tomorrow. The way we bring them up will determine the future of our country. **Jawaharlal Nehru**

The way you help heal the world is that you start with your own family. **Mother Teresa**

We can give our children only two things in life—strong roots and powerful wings. Then they may fly anywhere and live independently. **Sudha Murthy**

Don't educate your children to be rich. Educate them to be happy, so they know the value of things, not the price. **Victor Hugo**

Don't worry that children never listen to you; worry that they are always watching you. **Robert Fulghum**

Raise your words, not your voice. It is rain that grows flowers, not thunder. **Rumi, poet**

There's no way to be a perfect mother and a million ways to be a good one. **Jill Churchill**

The Golden Rule of Parenting is do unto your children as you wish your parents had done unto you! **Louise Hart**

The best inheritance a parent can give his children is a few minutes of his time each day. **O. A. Battista**

Kids are like a mirror, what they see and hear they do. Be a good reflection for them. **K Heath**

Child is the father of Man. **William Wordsworth**"

2. ROLE OF FAMILY IN VALUE DEVELOPMENT OF CHILD

Family plays a crucial role in the value development of a child, serving as the primary environment where foundational beliefs, attitudes, and behaviours are formed. Supportive family dynamics foster emotional security and encourage moral growth, helping children internalise values that guide their future decisions and social relationships.

As per Ralph Waldo Emerson,

"Cause and effect, means and ends, seed and fruit, cannot be severed; for the effect already blooms in the cause, the end pre-exists in the means, the fruit is the seed. Thus, the happiness and the fruit of fulfilment are in the seed of clear, unambiguous, strong moral values."

The pertinent question that arises is, why should we teach moral values to children?

- ✓ Is it because our parents taught them to us?
- ✓ Is it because they make society safer?
- ✓ Is it because they are simply the 'right' thing to do?
- ✓ Is it because they are a part of tradition? or,
- ✓ Is it because research shows that moral and value-oriented behaviour helps a child develop autonomy, confidence and independence?

Values should be taught to children because it is the most significant and effective thing that we can do for their happiness.

The age-old wisdom and our own experience teach that both individual and collective happiness is connected to behaviour which is governed by moral values. The same basic moral values have been taught by the seers and sages across continents and this is not a coincidence..

Children often learn the connection between living by values and achieving personal happiness through trial and error. Failures and the unhappiness that come from amoral choices can prompt them to change, teaching them morality through experience. However, a single lifetime isn't long enough to independently discover all the links between values and happiness. Therefore, it is the responsibility of parents to share what they've learned, passing on both values and their significance to their children.

2.1 Why Teach Values to Children?

Moral values are an essential part of a child's upbringing. Lessons in moral values can encourage them to develop into responsible and compassionate adults. Also, when families' values align, they typically have stronger bonds and more successful relationships. By contrast, a lack of family values can cause discord and dysfunction. Teaching moral values is about more than just imparting a set of rules for right and wrong, it's about nurturing the character and conscience of a child. True moral value inculcation involves helping children develop a deep understanding of the principles that guide ethical behaviours. It aims to foster critical thinking in children and make them more mindful. We can help children integrate moral principles into everyday life and shape them into compassionate, responsible, and moral people by incorporating moral values into everyday experiences with appropriate guidance and acting as role models.

2.2 When to Teach Values to Children?

The answer to the question is: NOW and ALWAYS.

Childhood is the best time to introduce moral values to children because they just start learning things in life and it's important to build their character. In early childhood, children learn values through interacting with their parents, so it's important to focus on encouraging your child to live by the right values and guiding their moral development. Socially acceptable behaviour, good manners, social etiquette and essential values amongst others are things that need to be actively taught to the child on a day-to-day basis and over a period of time. It is better to begin training and teaching your child at a young age as they are quick to learn and pick up things easily. With getting older, it is more difficult as they must unlearn the undesirable behaviour and then re-learn the appropriate expected behaviour, this requires a lot more effort.

The children with or without the help of their parents will develop both conscious and subconscious values during their preschool years. They learn this mostly from their friends, television, and their family. These values are tested, developed, and sometimes altered as they enter the school. As they begin to approach their adolescence, they struggle for independence and start to formulate their own value system, which is generally different from that of their parents. And if the parents fail to teach them about the values, they end up thinking that values are not important. If the parents focus on the values and consciously try to teach, develop and set examples, it helps in the process of personal value development of the children.

2.3 Where Should the Value Inculcation Begin?

It is often said that home is the first school and parents are the first teachers. Whatever is taught at home, in either a positive or negative sense, can be far more influential on children than what is taught in school or any other institution. Parents have at least a three to five-year head start ahead of schools, also parents have the potential to be, during at least the first eighteen years of life, a drastically more influential force on their children than any other person, factor, element or group.

The family is the basic institution. Parents have a basic responsibility.

2.4 Who Should Teach Values to Children?

Parents are a child's first teachers and role models. They are responsible for shaping the child's behaviour and implementing positive values. Children listen, observe, and imitate their parents. So, it is important that they should be good role models the kids would want to follow. To create an environment for their child to follow their lead, parents—whether they are mothers or fathers—must do what they teach. Parenting is without a doubt one of the hardest and most demanding jobs there is. Being a good parent involves sacrifice and ongoing learning. Raising well-mannered and responsible children requires an immense commitment of time, patience, and energy. Instilling and inculcating good values in a child will make him/her a good person and a better citizen in the future.

2.5 How to Teach Values to Children?

There is a great deal of assortment among families when it comes to parenting. Every parent has a different approach to interacting and guiding their children. A child's conduct, morals, and principles are generally established through this bond. There are generally four parenting categories: **authoritarian, authoritative, permissive,** and **uninvolved**. Every category employs a distinct approach to how parents raise their children. Parenting style can also be situation-dependent.

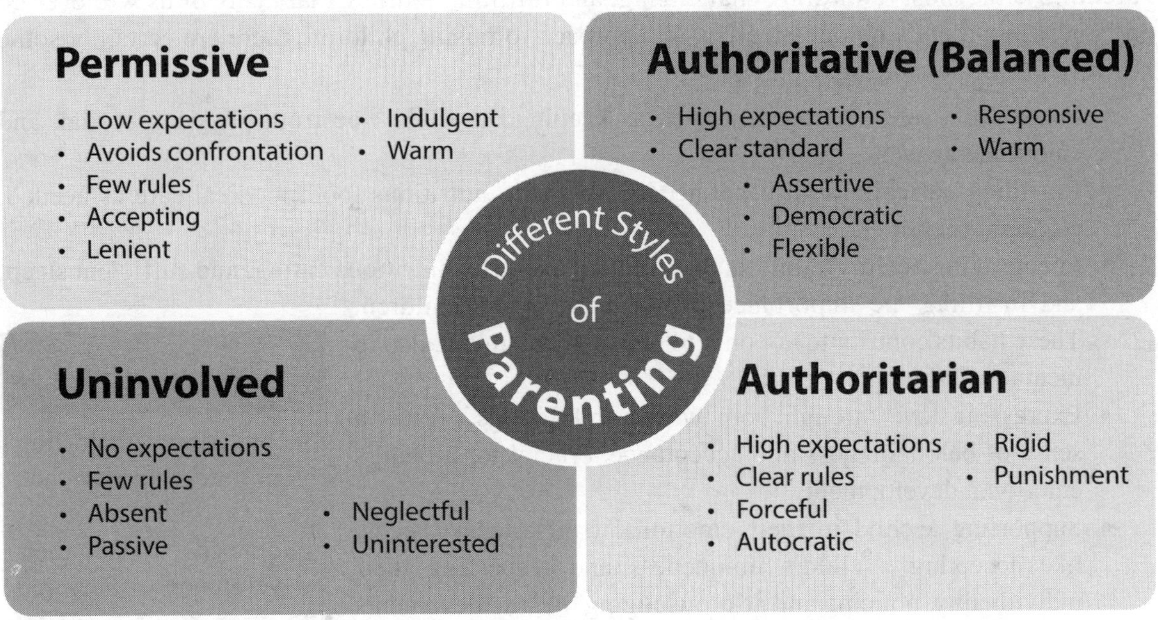

Fig. 3.1 Different styles of parenting

Authoritative (balanced) parenting is generally regarded as the most effective style because it provides kids with both security and support. However, incorporating permissive or authoritarian principles into a balanced approach can be useful when parenting a child with typical needs.

3. WHAT IS PARENTING?

Parenting is a process of raising, promoting, and supporting the physical, emotional, social, and cognitive development of a child to adulthood and across the lifespan.

In an ever-changing world, parenting can be subject to fads and changes, and parenting in some privileged circles has become a competitive sport. But the needs of child development as delineated by science remain relatively stable: safety, structure, support, and love.

3.1 What is Sensitive Parenting?

Sensitive parenting refers to family interactions in which parents are aware of their children's emotional and physical needs and respond appropriately and consistently. Sensitive parents are 'in tune' with their children. This type of parenting is also known as 'Responsive Parenting'.

3.2 Essential Responsibilities of a Parent

Parenting is the most rewarding, challenging, and fulfilling journey that many of us will ever go on. And while there's no one-size-fits-all approach to raising children, there are certainly some key responsibilities for every parent.

- Providing a safe environment such as keeping our child free from physical, sexual, and emotional abuse.
- Providing our child with basic needs like water, nutritious food, medical care as needed, clothing, shelter etc.
- Encouraging healthy habits such as regular exercise, nutritious eating, and sufficient sleep, and instilling the importance of self-care in the children. These habits contribute not only to physical health but also to mental well-being.
- Expressing love through both words and actions creates a sense of belongingness and acceptance, crucial for a child's emotional development.
- Supporting a child in their emotional (self-esteem) needs, like accepting a child's uniqueness and respecting their individuality, noticing and acknowledging their achievements and pro-social behaviour, and not criticising or ridiculing them when they misbehave.

? Thought Box

How does adjusting your parenting approach to your child's emotions and needs impact their development compared to using a one-size-fits-all method?

- Teaching them morals and values, such as honesty, respect, responsibility, compassion, patience, forgiveness and generosity.
- Advocating the importance of education instils a love for learning, and actively supports the child's academic journey, and creates a positive attitude towards education.
- Developing mutual respect with the child by using respectful language, and respecting his/her feelings, opinions, privacy, and individuality.
- Providing discipline, which is effective, appropriate, structured, consistent, predictable, and fair.
- Involvement in a child's education by doing things like communicating regularly with our child's teachers, assisting the child with his/her homework, and talking to the child each day about school.
- Teaching the child age-appropriate skills to allow them to become more and more independent.
- Getting to know a child by spending quality time together; being approachable to the child, asking questions and most importantly communicating continuously.
- Most importantly, we should not hold the child accountable for their behaviour and actions.

4. WHAT KIDS REALLY WANT?

Understanding what kids really want involves delving into their fundamental needs and desires, which often encompass a mix of emotional, social, and developmental factors. By examining these core aspects, we can gain insights into how to support their growth and happiness more effectively. Whether it's through playful activities, meaningful interactions, or fostering independence, recognising these needs can help us better nurture and guide their development.

- **Time and Attention**: Children value time and attention from the people in their lives. They feel most loved by their parents when they truly listen. However, parents often find themselves juggling work, home responsibilities, community obligations, extended family, and other things, and eventually are unable to dedicate enough time to their kids. Over the past decade, many parents have become increasingly aware of this challenge and are making commendable efforts to spend more time with their children.
- **Feeling of Togetherness**: Authentic, focused, and sincere togetherness is what kids crave. Parents don't have to do anything but provide only that warm feeling of togetherness. When parents work long hours, consistent communication and expressions of love help children feel valued and understood. Establishing a child-centred routine and making the most of vacations by prioritising quality time together can make a significant difference in meeting their emotional needs.
- **Leisure time**: Kids need more time to simply be kids. Play is essential for exploration and learning, but electronic entertainment has replaced much of their unstructured leisure time.

This shift has increased pressure on children, limiting their ability to express emotions like frustration, joy, or resilience through play. Today, kids are often taught orderliness over spontaneity, stifling their creativity.

- **Friendship**: Every child needs someone to share their journey. Building friendships is harder today due to large schools, busy schedules, and security concerns. Friendship involves caring, sharing, and trust, which develop through time spent together. Child psychologists emphasise that having one or two close friends during adolescence is vital, as supportive friendships help teenagers resist negative peer pressure.
- **Acceptance and respect**: All humans crave acceptance, especially kids and teens, who seek belonging, self-confidence, and respect. True connection and recognition for achievements or character help them feel valued. This reduces the focus on appearances and discourages harmful stereotypes like 'nerds', 'freaks', 'jocks' or 'preppies'.

5. FROM BEING A GOOD PARENT TO A GREAT PARENT

Transitioning from being a good parent to a great parent involves more than just fulfilling basic responsibilities. It requires a deep commitment to understanding and nurturing a child's emotional, social, and developmental needs. While good parenting lays a solid foundation of love, support, and guidance, great parenting transcends these basics by actively engaging with a child's unique needs and potential.

- **Being a good role model**: Parents are a child's first role models, with children instinctively observing and imitating them—a process called 'modelling'. Kids learn language, behaviour, and life skills by watching their parents. When parents admit mistakes and discuss how to correct them, they teach accountability and resilience. Demonstrating respect and resolving conflicts calmly shows children the value of respect and effective problem-solving.
- **Spending quality time with children**: Meaningful connections are about quality, not quantity. Simple, consistent interactions tailored to a parent's lifestyle can have a lasting impact on the child. Setting aside daily 'connect' time, like sharing a bedtime story, enjoying meals together, or playing during bath time proves helpful. Show love and appreciation daily and create special rituals that reinforce your bond. Laugh, be silly, and prioritise face-to-face moments by turning off technology during these times. Even small efforts make a big difference.
- **Appreciating the child's efforts**: Everyone likes to be complimented. It has been found in numerous studies that

> **? Thought Box**
>
> What specific actions can you take today to better understand your child's unique needs and strengthen your bond with them?

humans respond positively to approval. Craving for appreciation is as strong as craving for food. Children do small things to grab the attention of their parents and an appreciation by parents helps build a healthy self-image.

When a child approaches with some drawing, the parent should look at it and ask questions, should find something to say it is awesome. The child will come back with numerous such drawings, the parent should just play along and point out something that can be improved. It can be seen that the child will put in more and more effort learning indirectly that practice makes perfect.

And if the child is **snubbed**[2] at the first instance, the child will never draw again or even if he does, he will hesitate to share it. And, as the child grows older, he will be hesitant to share other aspects of his life, and the parent will wonder why the child is not sharing anything with them.

The best way to make a child enthusiastic about something is through encouragement and appreciation by the parents for their child's effort in that area.

- **Instilling discipline**: All children need discipline which means learning self-control and following social norms. They develop this through positive and negative feedback from adults, with parental acceptance and appreciation as key tools.

  Punishments like **spanking**[3] or shaming may temporarily change behaviour but can lead to fear, resentment, or withdrawal over time. Effective discipline focuses on teaching self-control rather than imposing external control. For example, redirecting a tantrum by calmly setting expectations, like asking politely, helps children learn acceptable ways to express their needs. This requires patience, consistency, and commitment.

- **Teaching the child about responsibility**: No child is born responsible. Responsibility isn't innate; it's taught through proper guidance and support. Teaching responsibility involves holding children accountable, such as denying TV time if they don't clean their room, and helping them understand actions have consequences. However, consequences should be gentle yet firm, not severe or traumatic. Positive reinforcement is equally important—praising children for responsible behaviour, like making their bed, motivates them to continue and reinforces good habits.

- **Catering to the emotional needs of the child**: A child's physical needs are easy to identify, but their mental and emotional needs can be less obvious. Good emotional health helps children build social skills, confidence, and a positive outlook, supported by friendships and encouragement from adults.

  In early development, children rely on home for trust and acceptance. Parents should love their children unconditionally, avoiding conditional love tied to achievements like grades

---

[2]**Snub:** To treat someone rudely, to ignore deliberately

[3]**Spank:** To strike especially on the buttocks with the open hand

or competitions. While setting high expectations is fine, success or failure should never determine parental love. Children should feel valued as individuals, not as a doctor, an engineer or a gold-medallist, knowing their parents support and love them regardless of outcomes.

- **Encouraging social intelligence**: Raising children with **social intelligence**[4] is a crucial task for any parent. In today's digital world, it's essential to be mindful of how our children interact and communicate with others. Teaching kids social intelligence is equally crucial because the majority of them grew up with digital technology and the internet. Teaching your children good manners and etiquette will help ensure they make a good impression on their peers and adults. This includes essential things like introducing themselves when meeting someone new, making eye contact while talking, using polite words such as 'please' and 'thank you', and being respectful of other people's feelings.

  Encourage your child to make choices, set goals, and take responsibility for their actions to foster self-confidence and self-awareness. Support their relationship-building skills by providing opportunities to interact with others, such as through playdates, extracurricular activities, or engaging conversations at home.

- **Teaching body boundaries**: By teaching children about body safety, you can help prevent child abuse and create a safe and respectful environment for a child at every age. Teaching kids how to defend themselves against unwanted conduct or inappropriate touch is a crucial part of teaching them about body safety. It involves educating kids on how to convey their boundaries to others and about body autonomy. Children must be taught about personal boundaries, appropriate touch, and private areas.

  There are three types of touches which include **Safe touches** that keep children safe and are good for them, and that make children feel cared for and important. Safe touches can include hugging, pats on the back, and an arm around the shoulder. **Unsafe touches** are touches that hurt children's bodies (for example, hitting, pushing, pinching, and kicking).

  Teaching children about body safety is essential to preventing abuse and fostering a safe, respectful environment. This includes helping them understand body autonomy, personal boundaries, and appropriate touch. Children should learn to communicate their boundaries and recognise the three types of touch:

  1. **Safe touches**: These promote well-being and show care, such as hugs, pats on the back, or a hand on the shoulder.
  2. **Unsafe touches**: These cause harm, like hitting, pushing, or pinching.
  3. **Unwanted touches**: These are any touches a child does not want at a given moment.

---

[4]**Social Intelligence:** The ability to understand one's own and others' actions

Teach children to confidently say 'no' to any touch that makes them uncomfortable and to set clear boundaries. Foster open communication, assuring your child they can approach you with any questions or concerns, no matter how awkward or frightening they may seem.

- **Developing gender sensitivity**: Gender biases are evident from birth, reflected in toys, clothes, and decor. Parents can encourage neutrality by choosing items that avoid reinforcing stereotypes while allowing kids the freedom to play, wear, or read what they like. Toys and books play a significant role in shaping gender perceptions, so selecting ones that avoid stereotypes is the key.

  By ensuring a gender-neutral mindset in the kids, they can be open to accepting and understanding different perceptions of who they are, what they like, and much more. Parents should model inclusive behaviour, as children learn by observing. For example, discouraging boys from expressing emotions or interacting equally with girls can lead to confusion and suppressed feelings, potentially fostering frustration or anger.

6. PARENTING TEENAGE CHILDREN

The teen years pose some of the most difficult challenges for families. Teenagers, dealing with hormone changes and an ever-complex world, may feel that no one can understand their feelings, especially parents. As a result, the teen may feel angry, alone, and confused. To bring the children to their wavelength, the parents have to enter the world of their children and offer support. And one important support is psychosocial. **Psychosocial**[5] support refers to the ongoing process of meeting emotional, social, mental, and spiritual needs, all of which are considered essential elements for positive and meaningful human development. Here are some tips for parents:

6.1 Children Dislike Being Told What to Do

Globally, people dislike being told what to do, and children are no exception, especially when instructed in front of others. As children grow, they want to assert independence, signalling to parents: Please don't treat us like kids anymore.

6.2 Effective Parenting Makes Children Independent

Independence doesn't mean children can do anything they want. Offering suggestions instead of instructions allows them to feel valued and capable of making decisions. For example, instead of forbidding bad friendships, parents can explain the potential consequences. While children may not grasp it immediately, they often understand over time.

[5]**Psychosocial:** Having both psychological and social parts

6.3 Understanding Children's Psychology and Needs

Parents don't usually intend to hurt their children's feelings but may do so by prioritising their own perspectives over the child's. For instance, parents may prefer traditional styles (be it attire, be it hairdo), while children lean toward modern trends, leading to mutual misunderstandings. Children often focus on peer approval, overlooking parental preferences. Parents should guide them on the downsides of certain trends, fostering understanding and balance.

6.4 Sharing Problems and Mistakes

Sharing their own mistakes helps parents show children they are human, fostering trust and understanding. Benefits include:

- Children understand parents have challenges too.
- They feel safe sharing their own mistakes.
- Trust replaces fear of punishment.
- Kids are more open to guidance.
- Parents can more effectively correct and support their children.

6.5 Making the Children Feel More Important Than Anything Else

Punishing children for not meeting parents' expectations, such as poor grades despite their efforts, can harm their self-esteem. Parents should prioritise their child's well-being over performance. While it's important to encourage improvement, children should feel valued for who they are, not just their achievements. Parents are responsible for their child's growth, but this should not come at the cost of their emotional health. Support and encouragement should be given equally to both their efforts and their existence.

6.6 Do not Correct but Direct

Everyone wants to do what they enjoy, both children and parents. Problems arise when children act inappropriately or fail to meet their parents' expectations. It's common for children to fall short, and it's the parents' responsibility to guide and shape them. The key is to change how parents communicate and approach their children. Instead of being critical, parents should direct children on what they need to do. Simply saying 'you're wrong' doesn't solve the problem. For example, if a child struggles in math, showing anger won't help. Parents should actively engage and guide their children to improve.

7. PROTECTING CHILDREN FROM CYBERSPACE IN THE CYBER AGE

Children must be educated about the dangers of cyberspace, including **cyberbullying**[6] and online predators. Parents should teach kids to recognise potential risks and understand that not everyone online has good intentions. They should be encouraged to report any concerns to parents or teachers. These lessons are simply traditional advice, updated for the digital age.

7.1 Nothing should be Accepted from or Discussed with Strangers

The basic rule applies to all situations: everyone online is a stranger. It's important for children to avoid talking to or accepting anything from strangers, but this can be hard for them to remember. Cyber predators often convince children that they are not strangers. Therefore, parents must consistently remind their children that these individuals are strangers and that the standard rules of safety always apply.

7.2 The Child's Friends should be Known by the Parents

Just as parents get to know their children's friends in real life, they should also be aware of the people their children interact with online. It's important to assess whether these online friendships are appropriate and if the people involved influence them positively. Unlike in real life, it's difficult for children to identify adults online, as cyber predators can easily pretend to be peers. Parents, however, may be better at spotting adults posing as children. Therefore, parents should stay informed about who their children are communicating with online.

7.3 After School, Students should Directly be Home

Just as parents warn children not to wander aimlessly after school, the same approach should apply online. Children shouldn't be allowed to surf the internet without purpose. Instead, they should have specific tasks to accomplish within a set time limit for browsing. There should always be a clear reason for their online activity, and parents can establish time limits to help manage it.

7.4 Avoid Saying Harsh About Others

Children should be taught that anonymity online doesn't give them the right to be disrespectful or say hurtful things about others. Just like in real life, they should always be polite and respectful.

[6]**Cyberbullying:** Bullying with the use of digital technologies. It can include sharing personal or private information about someone else causing embarrassment or humiliation

If they encounter harmful content about themselves or their friends, they should be encouraged to immediately inform their parents.

7.5 Do not Take What does not Belong to You

Children should be encouraged to use the internet for research while completing their homework and projects, but they should avoid copying content directly from websites. Taking images, text, or other materials without proper attribution is still considered plagiarism. Just as in real life, they should be taught not to copy, even if the material is freely available online.

7.6 Personal Things About Oneself should not be Shared with Others

Children should be taught not to share personal information about their families online. They need to understand that they can never be certain who they're actually communicating with, even if the person seems familiar. Others may be observing the conversation and could misuse the information shared. Therefore, it's safer for them to avoid sharing personal details online altogether.

7.7 The Basic Rules – Quick and Simple

- **Screen-free times and places**: Set consistent routines and screen time limits, and use 'do-not-disturb' on phones when seeking undistracted time.
- **Regular discussions about online activities**: Talk openly about new discoveries, fun, and challenges to encourage communication about tough topics. Make sure children feel comfortable approaching you with concerns, no matter how embarrassing.
- **Open talk about social media:** Have regular conversations about their social media use. Ask questions like, 'What do you enjoy about it?' and 'Have you seen anything concerning?'
- **Educating on digital usage**: Teach children to recognise what's real versus edited, how to spot ads, and identify authentic influencers. Help them decide what content deserves their attention.
- **Setting limits:** Parents should set a boundary line between real and digital life, encouraging friendships with people, not screens.
- **Setting a good example**: Model responsible social media use and be mindful of your own screen habits.
- **Control settings**: Set parental controls and privacy settings to the highest level when children start using new platforms. Discuss safety rules for online interactions and purchases.
- **Watch for signs of problems**: In teens, look for withdrawal from friendships or hobbies. Younger kids may argue about media use and lose interest in other activities.

8. LESSONS TO LEARN FROM CHILDREN

Children, with their innocent eyes and boundless energy, often offer invaluable lessons that can enrich the lives of adults. Their unique perspectives, unburdened by societal expectations and preconceived notions, can provide fresh insights into the world.

- **Power of Observation**: Children often ask questions like, 'Why is the sky blue?' or 'Why do birds fly?' These may seem annoying, but they reflect a child's natural curiosity and mindfulness—qualities we often overlook as adults. In our fast-paced world, we tend to miss the small details around us. Children, with their questions and observations, remind us to slow down, stay present, and focus on the simple things in our daily lives.

  "*Seeing the small in the big and the big in the small*" **Zen Buddhism**

- **Curiosity**: Nothing is more adorable than the face of a curious child because they see something interesting and new even though it appears very routine. They look up to the extraordinary in 'ordinary' things. Kids are naturally curious about the world around them. They embrace randomness and an open mind of a curious generalist showing an inclination to explore out of their comfort zone which people need to imbibe in their lifestyle.

  "*Be a lifelong student, Never lose the curiosity of a child*"

  Indira Nooyi, Former CEO of PepsiCo

- **Power of Questioning**: Children explore the world through constant questioning, much like the ancient principle of 'Neti Neti' from the Upanishads, which means 'Not this, Not this' — a method of negation to reach the supreme truth. This process of continuous inquiry helps children delve into the root causes, a skill that adults can learn to apply when addressing real-world challenges.
- **Art of Disruption**: Children may break toys, but they also try to rebuild them, often dismantling things constructively. They embrace the unknown with a sense of freedom, much like natural philosophers, unbound by what is familiar. To create, they must first break, a lesson adults often forget. Sometimes, to learn more, we must unlearn what we know.

  "*You don't learn to walk by following rules. You learn by doing, and by falling over*"

  Richard Branson

- **Art of letting go**: Children are incredibly forgiving, quickly moving from fighting to hugging. Loving and forgiving come more naturally than holding grudges. Like children, learning to let go brings inner peace and lightness. Forgiveness erases negativity and fosters positivity. Sometimes, it starts with being gentle with yourself and practising self-forgiveness too.

  "*The more you let go, the more you control*" **Buddhism**

- **Having it and giving it**: Children naturally ask for things and are generous in sharing. Wanting material possessions isn't wrong; many ancient scriptures acknowledge the role of money and material wealth. They only caution against letting them become obsessions. Moderation is key to finding peace and happiness, even in the pursuit of success. For example, during India's economic crisis in 2013, 5th grader Laila Indira Alva wrote to RBI Governor Raghuram Rajan, offering her savings of 20 dollars to help the country, showing that even children understand the value of moderation and selflessness.
- **Tolerant attitude**: Children make friends with people effortlessly. They are at ease even with perfect strangers and are not confined by social boundaries. This is because they have no hidden agenda when they reach out to make friends. We adults have a lot of mental blocks like gender, colour, economic status, race and religion to name a few, before accepting someone as a friend. As adults, we must learn to accept differences. Where all think alike no one thinks much, like children do, leaders must encourage and enjoy individuality and difference.

Life is all about learning, and age is not a limiting factor for growth.

Many valuable lessons come when we humbly accept that our adult adaptations to the social world can sometimes block the fresh perspectives children naturally offer. Reconnecting with our inner child opens the door to deeper insight and true happiness. Let children guide us.

SUMMARY

- Family plays a key role in teaching values, and it's important to teach them at every age for a child's happiness.
- Parents have a 3–5 year head start over pre-schools and influence their children's values for 17–18 years, more than any other factor.
- Parents are the primary source for teaching values, and the best method is through their own example, supported by storytelling, role-playing, and imagination.
- Parenting supports the physical, emotional, social, and cognitive development of children, with sensitive parenting responding to their needs consistently.
- Parents must understand what children really want: time, attention, togetherness, friendship, respect, and acceptance.
- Great parenting includes being a role model, spending quality time, appreciating efforts, instilling discipline, teaching responsibility, and addressing emotional needs.
- While parenting teens, it's essential to avoid commanding, share problems, make them feel valued, direct rather than correct, and involve them in decision-making.
- Protecting children from cyberspace involves teaching them not to talk to strangers, share personal info, or engage in harmful online behaviours.

- Parents can learn valuable lessons from children, including curiosity, the power of questioning, disruption, letting go, and tolerance.

PREVIOUS YEARS' QUESTIONS

1. "If a country is to be corruption-free and become a nation of beautiful minds, I strongly feel there are three key societal members who can make a difference. They are father, mother and the teacher." A.P.J. Abdul Kalam. Analyse. *UPSC CSE Mains 2022, 2017*
2. "Life doesn't make any sense without interdependence. We need each other, and the sooner we learn that, it is better for us all." Erik Erikson. Analyse *UPSC CSE Mains 2021*
3. "Where there is righteousness in the heart, there is beauty in the character. When there is beauty in the character, there is harmony in the home. When there is harmony in the home, there is order in the nation. When there is order in the nation, there is peace in the world." Analyse. A.P.J. Abdul Kalam *UPSC CSE Mains 2019*
4. We are witnessing increasing instances of sexual violence against women in the country. Despite existing legal provisions against it, the number of such incidences is on the rise. Suggest some innovative measures to tackle this menace. *UPSC CSE Mains 2014*

Value Education

4

1. INTRODUCTION

LEARNING OBJECTIVES

1. Understanding the Need and Objectives for Value Education
2. Recognising the Importance of Value-Based Education
3. Comprehending the Role of Value Education
4. Learning Methods to Inculcate Values into daily life and educational practices
5. Examining Value Education in Modern India

The true perspective of development of any society or nation is observed from its values, and it tells us the extent to which it has developed. People generally worry about the declining values of the younger generation but forget how and why it happens. Values are mostly learned and not inherited. It is well known that today's children are tomorrow's citizens; thus, if we provide quality education to the present-day children, they will lead us to a better future. It has to be realised that today's value education will be an invaluable solution to resolve tomorrow's problems.

We are living in a modern society, where science and technology cannot be relied on for solving problems that are non-moral and value related. Education today is said to be solely for the purpose of 'earning bread and butter'.

What is needed in this era is education that focuses on building character, shaping lives, and fostering the development of well-rounded individuals. Providing just academic knowledge without teaching human values will lead to defective personalities, who may become rich in material possessions but poor in social concern, self-understanding and peace.

Swami Vivekananda rightly said, "Excess of knowledge and power, without holiness, makes human beings devils." Mahatma Gandhi expressed that it is sinful to have wealth without effort, pleasure without conscience, knowledge without character, commerce without morality, science without humanity, worship without sacrifice, and politics without principle. Therefore, to achieve the goal of raising a valuable human capital, it is important to give them good value education and instruction.

Education as an organised social institution has been considered as an important tool for nurturing values. Conceptually, objective of education encompasses the objective of value education.

Practically we can define value education to be a 'deliberate planned education, which is aimed to develop values, emotions, proper attitudes, skills etc. for holistic development of the student. Education should ultimately teach various aspects of life including intellectual, civic, spiritual and moral.

QUOTES ON VALUE EDUCATION

"True knowledge is not attained by thinking. It is what you are, it is what you become.
Sri Aurobindo

We want that education by which character is formed, strength of mind is increased, the intellect is expanded, and by which one can stand on one's own feet. **Swami Vivekananda**

Real education enhances the dignity of a human being and increases his or her self-respect.
Dr. A.P.J. Abdul Kalam

Value education is not just about imparting knowledge, but about shaping character and creating responsible citizens. **Kailash Satyarthi**

To educate a man in mind and not in morals is to educate a menace to society. **T. Roosevelt**

Education without values, as useful as it is, seems rather to make man a more clever devil.
C.S. Lewis

Education is not the learning of facts, but the training of the mind to think. **Albert Einstein**

Values are the building blocks of our character and our character is the foundation of our life.
John Wooden

The function of education is to teach one to think intensively and to think critically. Intelligence plus character – that is the goal of true education. **Martin Luther King Jr**

Education is not only about acquiring knowledge, but also about acquiring values that will guide us in life. **Nelson Mandela**

Open your arms to change but don't let go of your values. **Dalai Lama**

The highest function of education is to bring about an integrated individual who is capable of dealing with life as a whole. **Jiddu Krishnamurti**

Educationists should build the capacities of the spirit of inquiry, creativity, entrepreneurial and moral leadership among students and become their role model. **Dr. A.P.J. Abdul Kalam**

Education need not only be a tool for survival but for enhancing perception. The children must blossom and flower into great human beings. **Isha Sadhguru**

Education is the kindling of a flame, not the filling of a vessel. **Socrates**"

This approach fosters balanced individuals by meeting the needs of both society and the individual. Educators must ensure equal opportunities for all children to access quality education. Value education, essential for shaping lives, is now more crucial than ever for parents, teachers, and students alike.

2. NEED AND OBJECTIVES OF VALUE EDUCATION

In today's complex world, qualities like resilience, integrity, and humility are crucial for professionals and leaders. Education should not only prepare youth for the workforce, but also instil values that foster responsible and compassionate citizenship. Research shows that value-based education not only enhances academic achievement, but also improves social skills and relationship-building abilities. Children, who learn values early, are more confident, competent, and effective learners. Real-life scenarios should be used to teach values like loyalty, kindness, integrity, compassion, and selflessness. Connecting learning experiences to the real-world help students find purpose and retain the teachings. Whether it's Math, Science, or History, values can be integrated into various subjects to teach important themes such as equality, liberty, patriotism, and respect for other cultures. A value-driven education system produces globally minded individuals, who are empathetic, collaborative, and resilient in the face of life's uncertainties.

> "What is wrong is wrong, even if everyone is doing it. Right is right if no one else is doing it."
>
> **William Penn**

Moral values, essential for distinguishing right from wrong, are eroding in a materialistic society marked by rising violence and selfishness. The decline in discipline and respect highlights the need for renewed focus on ethical principles to secure a better future for the next generation.

Following are a few examples which influence moral values:

- Peer group influence plays a crucial role in shaping the moral concepts of adolescents as they spend more time with their peers, seek advice, and readily accept their views.
- Childhood experiences also influence the development of self-regulation during adolescence, with rules being shaped by reactions to childhood environments.
- Changes in moral principles occur as adolescents come in new social contacts outside their homes, leading to adjustments and shifts in their values.
- Gender-based moral standards set by society can contribute to the erosion of moral values among youth, reinforcing harmful behaviours based on gender stereotypes.
- Youth in adolescence often exhibit a willingness to question norms, analyse situations, and develop their own viewpoints, which can sometimes lead to engagement in criminal or immoral behaviours.

- Factors such as coming from a nuclear family with materialistic attitudes, parental behaviour, and lack of strict control can also impact morality development.
- Socialisation plays a significant role in shaping individuals' personalities, with an emphasis on instilling moral and ethical values in children. However, contemporary society often falls short in actively socialising these values.
- Technological advancements, while offering numerous benefits, can also have a negative influence on youth's moral and ethical behaviour. Mobile phones, internet, and other technologies have been observed to contribute to a decline in ethical values among young people.
- Various stimulating factors, such as exposure to unhealthy entertainment, pornography, substance abuse, a desire for quick wealth and instant gratification can accelerate moral decay among youth. These factors, combined with societal influences, peer pressure, and family dynamics, contribute to shaping the moral development of adolescents.

Value education plays a crucial role in facing these societal influences. It aims to instil moral standards for enhancing civil and democratic societies by promoting tolerance and understanding beyond political, cultural, and religious differences. It emphasises defending human rights, protecting ethnic minorities and vulnerable groups, and conserving the environment. It is a collective responsibility not just limited to schools but also includes families, universities, businesses, and sports as ideal platforms for teaching ethical principles. Following are some of the objectives of value education:

- Inculcating humanistic attitude in students.
- Educating students on the importance and role of values in life.
- Guiding students to identify and develop personal, moral, social, and spiritual values as global citizens.
- Encouraging pride in India's heritage by linking ancient wisdom with modern scientific principles.
- Building a foundation for ethical reasoning based on integrity, objectivity, and independence.
- Teaching societal ethical rules, personal accountability, and constitutional values like socialism, secularism, justice, and democracy.
- Helping students discern right from wrong and cultivate wisdom for ethical decision-making.
- Empowering teachers to model professional and ethical behaviour for students to emulate.
- To help students distinguish between right and wrong, good and bad and help them achieve the intellectual disposition and wisdom to do what is ethically right.

3. IMPORTANCE OF VALUE BASED EDUCATION

Value education is crucial for well-rounded development, emphasising moral principles and ethics from an early age. In today's fast-paced world filled with cultural and social challenges, its significance is undeniable. It moulds character, nurtures good citizenship, and enhances emotional intelligence. By encouraging critical thinking and self-awareness, it equips individuals to make ethical choices and positively impact society, fostering a fair and harmonious community.

- Value-based education is crucial in today's diverse society to **instil human values** in the younger generation amidst changing social norms and globalisation.
- Values serve as **guiding principles that shape behaviours** and beliefs, contributing to the development of individuals, families, societies, and nations and give meaning to our existence.
- The rapid advancement of science and technology has accelerated social change and highlighted the **importance of fostering universal and eternal values** for unity and integration.
- Value education **promotes basic values of humanism and socialism.**
- The idea of **'simple living and high thinking'** needs to be reintroduced **to combat the erosion of values in society** and prepare future generations for a better future.
- Good values are the spontaneous manifestations of **a sound character,** and it serves as the central pole around which our actions, desires and ambitions are organised.
- Values assist us to take **right decisions and make choices.**
- Values **give direction and firmness to life** and help us to be **morally sound.**
- Values **set goals for achievements**, motivate, define and colour all our activities in cognitive, affective, and conative domains.

4. DIFFERENT APPROACHES TO VALUE EDUCATION

Value education plays a vital role in shaping individual's moral and ethical frameworks, guiding them to navigate the complexities of life with integrity and responsibility. In modern educational contexts, a variety of approaches have emerged to effectively impart values to students, each offering unique methodologies and insights.

1. **Evocation Approach:** The students are encouraged to make spontaneously free, non-rational choices, without thought or hesitation. It provides an environment which allows maximum freedom for students.
2. **Awareness Approach:** In this approach the teacher presents value-laden situations or dilemmas through readings, films, role-playing, small group discussions and simulation.
3. **Inculcation Approach:** A positive and negative reinforcement of rewards and punishments by the teacher helps value inculcation.

4. **Moral Reasoning Approach:** Kohlberg's theory of six stages of moral development is the framework most frequently used in this approach. The teachers set up learning experiences which facilitate moral development. It consists of students discussing a dilemma and by reasoning they attain a higher level of knowledge.
5. **Analysis approach:** The group or individuals are encouraged to study the social value problems. They are encouraged to determine the truth and evidence of purported facts and arrive at value decision, applying analogous cases and testing value principles underlying the decision.
6. **Commitment approach:** It enables students to perceive themselves not merely as passive reactors or as free individuals but as inner relative members of a social group and system.
7. **The Union Approach:** The purpose is to help students to perceive themselves and act not as separate egos but as part of a larger interrelated whole.

Kohlberg's Theory of Moral Development

Kohlberg's Theory of Moral Development explains how individuals progress in their moral reasoning through six stages which are divided into Preconventional, Conventional, and Postconventional levels. This theory is crucial for understanding human morality and ethical decision-making, offering insights for promoting moral growth in areas like parenting and education. Despite receiving criticism, Kohlberg's theory remains influential in depicting the development of moral thinking and its impact on psychology and education.

Stages of Development

- Preconventional Morality: Focuses on self-interest and obedience to avoid punishment or gain rewards.
- Conventional Morality: Centers on maintaining social order and gaining approval from others.
- Postconventional Morality: Involves adherence to universal principles and a sense of justice.

Preconventional Level (Stages 1 and 2)

According to Kohlberg's Theory of Moral Development, moral thinking is self-centered at the Preconventional level, the earliest stage, when people, usually youngsters, are primarily concerned with their own needs and desires. These phases represent a stage in moral growth when the individual's interest is prioritised over the sentiments of others and social standards. Up to the age of nine, this stage of development is common. It paves the way for later, more sophisticated phases of moral reasoning that take into account larger social and ethical concepts.

Conventional Level (Stages 3 and 4)

Moving on to the Conventional Level, which includes Stages 3 and 4, Kohlberg's Theory of Moral Development digs more into the social components of moral reasoning that are common among adolescents and adults. This stage is distinguished by a shift away from self-centredness and toward accepting society's norms and expectations. At the Conventional Level, people manage the complexity of social connections and societal standards while balancing their personal desires. This level emphasises the shift from individualistic concerns to a more comprehensive awareness of social responsibility and the common good.

Postconventional Level (Stages 5 and 6)

Kohlberg's Theory of Moral Development offers Postconventional levels that represent the greatest kinds of moral reasoning, stressing the importance of principled conscience and universal ethical principles.

Knowing these stages helps one to appreciate the intricacy of moral growth and the path towards moral reasoning that is more complicated and guided by principles.

5. THE ROLE OF VALUE EDUCATION

Value education is a crucial component of addressing social evils in society. It serves as a proactive and preventive measure to instil positive values and attitudes in individuals from a young age.

The following are the ways in which value education plays a key role:

1. **Nurturing Empathy:** Empathy is central to being human, fostering ethical behaviour, healthy relationships, love, and professional success. It helps prevent bullying and cruelty. Value education promotes empathy, encouraging action to address societal issues like poverty, inequality, and violence.
2. **Moral Compass:** Moral principles like accountability, honesty, and integrity are taught via value education. These principles work as a moral compass, assisting people in acting morally and discouraging unethical behaviour.
3. **Promoting Social Responsibility:** Successful people have a social responsibility to make the world a better place and not just take from it. Value education highlights the importance of being law-abiding citizens who contribute meaningfully to society. It inspires individuals to address social issues and advocate for positive change.
4. **Character Building:** Character is defined by values, not academic expertise. Ravana's downfall in the *Ramayana* illustrates the importance of moral values. A strong value system is key to personal and professional success, with value education fostering traits like resilience, perseverance, and humility.

5. **Encouraging Critical Thinking:**

   "Critical thinking requires us to use our imagination, seeing things from perspectives other than our own and envisioning the likely consequences of our position."

   Bell Hooks

   Value education gives people the critical thinking abilities they need to confront social injustices and challenge cultural conventions. It gives individuals the freedom to think for themselves and strive for improvement.
6. **Fostering Inclusivity:** Value education fosters the ideals of inclusion and equality, helping build a society that embraces diversity and rejects **prejudice**[1]. Achieving inclusive education requires equipping educators with the training, flexibility, and resources to address diverse needs and learning styles. For instance, teaching the values underlying reservations, social justice, and affirmative action fosters social sensitivity and reduces envy among students.
7. **Conflict Resolution:** Value education teaches individuals how to resolve disagreements peacefully and productively, minimising violence and aggressiveness in society. It creates a tolerant mind to arrive at win-win solutions
8. **Raising Awareness:** Value education informs people on the effects of social problems and the need of solving them. It enables people to become change agents and raise awareness in their communities.
9. **Encouraging Responsible Consumption:** The impact of environmental deterioration is lessened by value education, which instils principles of environmental care and responsible consumerism. Behavourial changes among students to use Zero-mile products that avoid emissions from refrigeration or transportation has ripple effect on families too.
10. **Leadership Skills:** Leaders with a strong value system are better equipped to inspire and guide others. Value education nurtures qualities like fairness, accountability, vision, which are crucial for effective leadership.

6. VARIOUS COMMITTEES ON VALUE EDUCATION

The promotion of value education within the Indian education system has gained significant attention over the years, reflecting a growing recognition of its importance for holistic development. As society faces various challenges, the integration of ethical values into the curriculum has become essential to foster responsible citizenship and social cohesion. Various commissions and organisations have advocated for this integration, emphasising that values should not only be taught as standalone subjects but embedded across all levels of education.

---

[1]**Prejudice:** An irrational or hostile attitude towards a person, group, or race, often without grounds or enough knowledge

Radhakrishnan Commission: It was appointed in 1948. It gave importance to inculcation of ethical values among students not only in colleges but also in universities. Based on the recommendation made by this Commission, provision was made for moral teaching in colleges and universities.

Kothari Commission: Appointed in 1965, the commission stressed that knowledge without values is dangerous, and it emphasised instilling the right values at all stages of education, including higher education.

UNESCO (Promoting Value education through Higher Education): The 1998 International Conference on Higher Education, with participants from over 180 countries, emphasised promoting values like equality, justice, and freedom through higher education. It called for engaging students in social service and reaffirmed higher education's role in addressing poverty, intolerance, violence, illiteracy, hunger, environmental degradation, and disease.

National Council for Educational Research and Training (NCERT): Educationists strongly believe that values can be effectively taught with due care and caution. The NCERT, in its 1979 publication on *Social, Moral and Spiritual values in Education*, identified 84 teachable values. Cultural values, such as caring for the unprivileged, respecting the elderly, and fostering tolerance should be integrated into the national curriculum.

National Policy on Education-1986: It had laid emphasis on value education by indicating the need to make education a powerful tool for cultivation of social and moral values. Keeping in mind the pluralistic base of our society, the education system apart from preserving the cultural heritage, should also nurture our youth to be more adaptable to life in changing situations. An important interlinking of education and culture has also been indicated by the Programme of Action (POA) of 1992 for implementation of National Policy on Education.

National Education Policy (NEP-2020): The National Education Policy (NEP-2020) aims to instil ethical, human, and constitutional values among youth and citizens through education reforms. NEP-2020 recognises the importance of value-based learning and social responsibility in education. It emphasises integrating values into the curriculum at all levels, including subjects like maths and science. The policy also aims to train teachers in delivering value-based education, including human rights and gender equality. NEP-2020 highlights the vital role of education in promoting ethical values and creating responsible citizens who positively contribute to society.

7. VALUE DEVELOPMENT TECHNIQUES

Values are shaped by both genetics and environmental influences, as humans are partly defined by nature and partly by nurture. Key environmental factors, such as family, peers, and situational contexts, play a significant role in shaping an individual's ethical beliefs and attitudes.

Here are some techniques for developing values:

S. no	Technique	Description
1	Precept – ideal	Presentation of the ideal behaviours of parents and teachers
2	Influence	Use of approval and disapproval of acts, humour
3	Identification	Identification with a child hero from a story, novel, scripture or identification with a desirable group or individual
4	Association and conditioning	Creating situations of enjoyment: satisfaction in various co-curricular and curricular programmes
5	Ventilation	Providing an outlet through verbal and written statements on controversial issues
6	Parable and allegory	Short stories, songs, poems, depicting healthy attitudes
7	Psycho drama	Creating artificial situations to affect children's minds positively
8	Role playing and social drama	Acting out certain situations by taking various roles and looking at solutions of value problems

8. WAYS TO INCULCATE VALUE EDUCATION

Educational institutions play a crucial role in value education, which involves teaching students about core values, ethics, and moral principles that help shape their character and guide their behaviour. Here are some ways in which educational institutions can inculcate values:

1. **Integrating Ethics and Moral Philosophy in Curriculum:** Schools must integrate ethics and moral philosophy into their curricula, helping students understand various ethical theories and moral dilemmas. This can be taught through subjects like social studies, history, or dedicated ethics courses.

   Example: Schools like the International School of Geneva offer courses in ethical philosophy and critical thinking as part of their curriculum. These courses help students grapple with complex moral issues and develop their own ethical frameworks.

   NCERT has introduced a Value Education Framework titled 'Education for Values in Schools – A Framework', which offers schools guidelines to identify their core values and plan their actions accordingly.
2. **Diversity and Inclusion:** Schools that actively promote diversity and inclusion help students appreciate different cultures, perspectives, and experiences. This often includes anti-bullying programmes, cultural competency training, and celebrating diverse holidays and traditions.

   Example: The curriculum at the US schools like the KIPP (Knowledge Is Power Program) network includes elements that address social justice and cultural competence, fostering an inclusive environment.

3. **Extracurricular Activities:** Extracurricular activities such as debate clubs, student government, and community service organisations provide students with opportunities to practice and reflect on values like leadership, teamwork, and social responsibility.
   Example: International Baccalaureate (IB) programme requires students to complete community service as part of their Diploma Programme, reinforcing values like empathy and social responsibility.
4. **Assessment and Reflection:** Schools may encourage students to reflect on their own behaviour and values through self-assessment tools and reflective exercises. Regular feedback from teachers, peers, and self-assessments helps students understand their progress in embodying the values taught.
   Example: Tools such as the 'Social-Emotional Learning (SEL) Assessment' are used in schools to evaluate students' emotional intelligence and character development, helping tailor educational strategies to individual needs.
5. **Develop Character Education Programmes:** Schools should have specific programmes designed to teach character traits such as honesty, responsibility, empathy, and respect. These programmes can include structured lessons, discussions, and activities focused on developing good character.
   Example: Character education, a well-established concept, is increasingly being implemented by schools worldwide. Organisations like International Baccalaureate (IB) are promoting it to motivate students to excel academically and personally. Today, character education is recognised as essential in both academic and non-academic aspects of education, starting from primary school.
6. **Cross-Curricular Values:** Values are often taught indirectly through other subjects. For instance, literature classes might explore themes of justice, integrity, and human rights through novels and stories, while history classes might examine the moral implications of historical events.
   For example, if you are running an art lesson you could work on the tessellation of shapes when creating a mosaic as it incorporates both maths and art.
7. **Serving as Role Models:** Educators serve as role models for students. By demonstrating ethical behaviour, respect, and professionalism, teachers help students learn how to act in various situations. The most important talents of a role model and a successful leader are effective communication skills. If we can teach our children to listen to understand others and then effectively express their emotions and sentiments, we will be providing them with some of the most important life skills.
8. **Discipline and Conflict Resolution:** How a school handles discipline and conflict resolution can teach students about fairness, justice, and the importance of resolving disputes in a constructive manner.

9. **Cultural and Artistic Expression:** Activities such as drama, music, and art projects often explore moral and ethical themes. For example, plays and films may address social justice issues, encouraging students to think critically about their values and societal impact.
10. **Positive Behavioural Interventions and Supports (PBIS):** This framework helps create a positive school environment by setting clear expectations for behaviour, recognising and rewarding positive behaviour, and addressing behavioural issues in a constructive manner.
11. **Ethics in Education:** Training in educational ethics helps teachers understand their responsibilities in promoting values, maintaining fairness, and addressing issues like academic dishonesty or discrimination.
12. **Restorative Practices:** Implementing restorative justice practices focuses on repairing harm and restoring relationships rather than merely punishing misbehaviour. This approach teaches students about empathy, responsibility, and the impact of their actions on others.

To summarise, educational institutions play a multifaceted role in value education by integrating values into curricula, modelling ethical behaviour, involving students in extracurricular activities, fostering a supportive environment, engaging families and communities, and providing reflective and developmental opportunities.

8.1 Role of Teachers

Teachers are important in teaching values, modeling ethical behaviour, creating a supportive environment and embedding values in the curriculum. They teach respect, love, and honesty, and encourage critical thinking and discussion of ethical dilemmas. By participating in community activities and working with parents, teachers help students develop their value systems and ensure they become responsible and caring members of society.

- **Teacher as a facilitator:** The teacher should act as a facilitator to inspire, motivate, inform, and educate students based on real life situations. The teacher should think about the activities and projects of the people through the participation of the students in discussions and activities.
- **Educate high values:** The teacher should also expose students to works of art, beauty in nature and in human relationships, actions of moral worth, and develop their moral sensibilities. They should help in creating an atmosphere of love, trust, cooperation, and security in the school, conducive to the development of high ideals and values.
- **Self-possession towards learning:** Teachers should possess the right qualities of mind and heart necessary for the pursuit of knowledge—love for knowledge, curiosity and desire to know, sincere desire to keep on learning and updating knowledge. They should have a

sound social philosophy, characterised by social sensitivity, concern for social justice and human rights.

- **Fostering nationalistic sentiment and social responsibility:** National sentiment should be created among the students. Create awareness of future problems, especially problems related to food, water, energy, environment, pollution, health and population. Give equal importance to all students regardless of caste, creed, gender and income.

  The institutional processes in the training institution should help teachers acquire these capabilities by providing concrete situations and opportunities and actively involve them in appropriate learning experiences.

8.2 Role of Parents

Parents play a key role in teaching values and serve as the first role models for their children, demonstrating love, respect, honesty, and responsibility. Their actions shape their children's moral direction and prepare them for life's challenges. Parents should inculcate the values in following ways:

- **Foundation of good manners:** Child behaviour forms the foundation of good manners. Children should be taught to show respect to elders and learn basic courtesies such as saying hello, sorry, thank you and welcome. Honesty is also essential, parents should avoid telling harmless lies that might cause problems later. Additionally, children should be kind not only to their elders, but also to their peers.
- **Teaching good etiquettes:** Children should practice good behaviour and develop proper table manners, such as knowing how to hold a spoon and fork. To instil these habits, parents can take children out for lunch or dinner, teaching them not to overload their plates and encouraging mindful eating.
- **Life skills education:** Children learn a lot while playing on the ground. The qualities of giving and receiving, playfulness, friendship and consideration for others are acquired during play.
- **Cultivating affection and alleviating jealousy:** When the mother is expecting a child, it's important to ensure that the elder sibling is ready to share the mother's love with the new one. In this regard, parents should be mindful of potential jealousy from the older sibling, which can persist throughout their lives if not addressed thoughtfully.
- **Nurturing individuality and emotional resilience:** Parents should respect their children's feelings and individuality. They should never humiliate their child in front of friends and outsiders. A child should learn not to throw tantrums. Make it clear to them that their **obstinacy**[2] will not be tolerated.

[2]**Obstinacy:** Stubbornness

8.3 Role of Sports

Incorporating sports in the school curriculum sends a powerful message about the importance of sports in the development of young individuals, especially those dealing with challenges.

Sports inculcates life skills among young leaners. It also leads to the following:

- **Emotional Control:** Learning to balance all types of emotions and maintaining a calm mind.
- **Teamwork:** Working and collaborating with others to achieve a goal.
- **Perseverance:** Persisting towards the goal with patience and determination.
- **Respect:** Valuing other people and oneself by showing consideration and kindness.
- **Honesty:** Being truthful to oneself and the others.

Some of the key benefits of inculcating the habits of sports include:

Goal Setting and body language: Breaking down goals into achievable steps is essential for success. Students not only learn teamwork and innovation but also develop a positive body language, reflecting trust and leadership qualities. The ability to work together with a team, think creatively, and adapt to different situations are crucial skills for success.

Knowing strengths and weaknesses: Self-evaluation promotes holistic growth and an open mind set by recognising strengths and weaknesses within oneself and others. This fosters strong bonds and enable teams to address issues effectively, driving positive change and efforts to improve shortcomings.

The value of discipline and hard work: Success and growth, both personally and professionally, necessitate dedication to hard work and discipline. Maintaining a schedule and sticking to it is vital. A well-coordinated team that plans meticulously and executes tasks with discipline can conquer any obstacle by learning from it. When encountering challenges, it's essential to acknowledge that there are no quick fixes. Additionally, listening to others and considering various solutions is crucial.

Balancing success and failure: Balancing success and failure is essential for growth. While failure can trigger negative emotions like anxiety and stress, it can also unite people to take collective responsibility for decisions. Embracing failures as learning opportunities, rather than setbacks, fosters **resilience**[3] and determination. In sports, students are taught to persevere through failures on their path to success. By tackling challenges with a positive attitude, individuals can navigate through life's obstacles and emerge stronger and more resilient.

Therefore, sports not only lead to characterbuilding and creating a strong emotional and physical well- being, but it also sets habits for life which are based on social skills and life skills.

---

[3]**Resilience:** The ability to withstand adversity

8.4 Role of Media

The evolving media landscape greatly impacts how we socialise. From traditional screen media to digital platforms, media shapes our beliefs, attitudes, and behaviours. It influences our political views, opinions on popular culture, and perceptions of various social groups. The importance of media was highlighted during recent years, particularly during the COVID-19 pandemic, when reliance on technology for information, socialisation, and remote learning became crucial. Digital media platforms served as a vital lifeline for sharing news and connecting the global community. This shift demonstrates the powerful role media plays in shaping society today.

Social Learning Theory: Values Through Movies

Bandura's Social Learning Theory discusses how media influences children, who often imitate, and role play what they see, particularly from prestigious models. This can have both positive and negative effects. For instance, watching 'Sesame Street-an American tv series' can teach valuable social skills, while engaging in violent video games can promote aggression. The movie 'Turbo' encourages children to believe in themselves and pursue their dreams despite doubt, while 'The Lion King' emphasises the importance of facing the truth and claiming one's rightful place. Both movies highlight themes of grit, honesty, and healing, illustrating the power of belief and imagination in achieving success. Through media, children can absorb important life lessons that shape their behaviour and values.

8.5 Role of the State

The state plays a crucial role in promoting value education for holistic development and nation-building by integrating ethical, moral, and civic values into the educational system. This commitment is reflected in policies, curriculum guidelines, and initiatives aimed at fostering respect, tolerance, and social responsibility among students. Value education in India focuses on cultivating character and promoting harmony in society through structured programmes, teacher training, and community engagement. This approach is essential in preparing future generations to navigate the complexities of a diverse and rapidly changing society with a strong moral compass.

- **Integrating Value Education in the National Curriculum Framework:** The National Curriculum Framework (NCF) 2005, developed by the National Council of Educational Research and Training (NCERT), which sets the guidelines and direction for the development of syllabus and textbooks at all the school stages, emphasises on ethical development, inculcating the values, attitudes and skills required for living in harmony with oneself and with others. The schools affiliated to the Central Board of Secondary Education (CBSE) have introduced Life-Skills education which promotes inculcation of Values.
- **Value Education Kit:** CBSE has brought out Values Education Manual and Value Education Kit for classes I-XII. The Board has brought out Teacher's Manual on Environmental

Education and Adolescent Education, which help to foster values in children. CBSE also organises Capacity Building Programmes in Values Education for teachers of its affiliated schools.

- **Integrating Experiential Learning:** Values and attitudes are acquired and are best nurtured through experiences. These experiences need to be consistent and inbuilt in the personal and social environment of the students. NCERT has, therefore, incorporated such concerns, wherever possible, in the textbooks developed for the various stages of school education. NCERT has also brought out a Value Education Framework entitled 'Education for Values in Schools – A Framework', which provides guidelines to schools to identify their priorities of values and plan their actions accordingly. NCERT has also developed a Resource Book for teachers called 'Ways to Peace'.

9. VALUE EDUCATION IN MODERN INDIAN EDUCATION SYSTEM: PHILOSOPHERS PERSPECTIVE

Value education in the modern Indian education system is increasingly recognised as essential for holistic development. Philosophers throughout history have emphasised the importance of integrating values into education to nurture well-rounded individuals. By integrating these philosophical perspectives, the modern Indian education system seeks to create a balanced framework that not only imparts knowledge but also instils essential values, preparing students to navigate the complexities of life with integrity and purpose.

Swami Vivekananda's view: Swami Vivekananda viewed education as a path to perfection, focusing on shaping individuals rather than just imparting knowledge. Today, however, the focus has shifted to materialism, diminishing the importance of values. It is vital to promote eternal values and create environments in schools that nurture character development. Vivekananda believed values should be central to education, forming the foundation for moral growth. Education should integrate intellect with intuition, science with spirituality, and living with learning for a balanced system. In light of current challenges, it's crucial to reassess educational practices for a better future.

Mahatma Gandhi's view: Mahatma Gandhi believed that the term 'value' encompasses not only material possessions but also emotions and compassion for others. It involves the development of the Hand, Heart, and Head, guided by values such as Truth, Non-violence, Self-control, Conscientiousness, and Renunciation. These values promote respect for all religions and advocate for a simple life. Gandhi's ultimate goal was to reform and rebuild rural, social, and political systems, emphasising equality, empowerment of the weak and oppressed, decentralisation, and fostering brotherhood among all.

S. Radhakrishnan's view: Dr. S. Radhakrishnan said, "Education is not limited to the imparting of information or the training in skills. It has to give the educated a proper sense of values." Human values and qualities that set a man apart are diminishing due to growing selfishness and materialistic desires. Preserving and enhancing these values is crucial for a fulfilling life. Teaching value education is the key to restoring and elevating human values, making it a vital remedy for societal progress.

Rabindranath Tagore's view: Rabindranath founded Santiniketan, an experimental institute with a unique approach to education. The institute sought to incorporate the beauty of nature in teaching, focusing on poetry, music, and art to nurture personality and encourage cultural exchange. This approach promoted internationalism, world citizenship, and universal fraternity beyond race and religion. The nationalist slogan *Vande Mataram* also emerged, inspiring the National System of Education movement. This movement aimed to revive the ancient Indian spirit, blending spirituality, intellectualism, science, art, and productivity, while integrating new ideas and creating innovative forms of expression by bridging the East and West.

Dr. B.R. Ambedkar's view: Dr Ambedkar was a revolutionary thinker, who believed in education as a tool for liberation and enlightenment. By promoting critical thinking and organising efforts, he aimed to elevate learners' intellectual capabilities and cultivate respect among them. He reintroduced Buddhist philosophy and spirituality in modern India, viewing education as a means to shape one's destiny and create a more enlightened society.

> **? Thought Box**
>
> Is value education in the modern Indian education system a priority or a formality?

10. THE ROLE OF VALUE EDUCATION IN PREVENTING SOCIAL EVILS

Value education plays a transformative role in shaping responsible individuals and addressing social evils by instilling moral and ethical principles. It equips individuals with the ability to make wise decisions, fosters empathy, and encourages a sense of belonging and responsibility toward society. Here's how value education tackles various social issues:

1. **Poverty:** Poverty deprives individuals of basic needs and opportunities, adversely affecting their well-being. Value education promotes compassion, encouraging individuals to work towards an equitable society by engaging in community service and supporting those in need.
2. **Corruption:** Corruption undermines fairness and trust in society. Value education instils honesty, integrity, and accountability, empowering individuals to resist corrupt practices and contribute to a just society.

3. **Discrimination:** Discrimination fosters inequality and division. Value education emphasises respect, inclusivity, and equality, fostering a more harmonious society.
4. **Violence:** Forms of violence, such as domestic abuse and terrorism, harm communities. Value education promotes non-violence, empathy, and peaceful conflict resolution.
5. **Drug Abuse:** Substance abuse destroys lives and families. Value education promotes healthy lifestyle, self-control, and resilience.
6. **Environmental Degradation:** Issues like pollution and deforestation threaten future generations. Value education fosters environmental responsibility and sustainability. Initiatives like School Nutrition (Kitchen) Gardens teach children to appreciate and care for nature through hands-on learning.
7. **Child Labour:** Child labour robs children of their rights and opportunities. Value education advocates for child rights, education, and justice.
8. **Gender Inequality:** Gender inequality limits opportunities and fosters discrimination. Value education challenges stereotypes and promotes equality.
9. **Substance Abuse:** Substance abuse harms individuals and families. Value education builds resilience and fosters a supportive environment for recovery.
10. **Cyberbullying:** Cyberbullying impacts mental health, especially among youth. Value education promotes responsible digital behaviour and empathy.

Value education is a powerful tool for addressing social evils and building a compassionate, equitable society. By instilling moral values, promoting ethical decision-making, and fostering empathy, it empowers individuals to combat societal challenges and contribute positively to their communities and the world.

? Thought Box

Can value education be the cornerstone in eradicating social evils, or is it merely a complementary tool?

How to instil values among young minds?

1. Integrating moral based stories and discussions in early education
2. Using role-play and simulation to teach empathy
3. Encouraging open conversation on equality and discrimination
4. Promoting gender-neutral language to foster inclusivity
5. Highlighting examples of successful non-violent leaders and women contributors
6. Encouraging peaceful approaches to resolving disagreements.
7. Encouraging participation in sports and creative activities
8. Keeping the students updated about health and nutrition to reduce susceptibility to drug use
9. Providing skill-based education to empower children and break cycles of poverty.
10. Empowering students with strategies to resist peer pressure and make positive choices

CASE STUDIES

1. **Akshar School in Assam:** India's education sector has turned into a profitable business, hindering access to quality education for low-income families. ASER 2022 reports that 32% of Indian children attend private schools with fees ranging from ₹20,000 to ₹2,00,000 per year. This has widened the gap between privileged and underprivileged families, making it difficult for economically disadvantaged families to afford education. However, Akshar School in Assam is a beacon of hope, offering a unique model that accepts plastic waste as fees, providing education and addressing environmental issues. Founded in 2016 by Mazin Mukhtar and Parmita Sarma, the school empowers underprivileged children by breaking financial barriers.

   Akshar School offers a holistic education approach focusing on sustainability and vocational training. Through courses like teaching, carpentry, and recycling, students are prepared for skilled careers with an environmental conscience. The school's recycling centre transforms waste plastic into eco-bricks, promoting a circular economy. By accepting plastic waste as 'school fees,' Akshar School empowers underprivileged children to access quality education. Over 80% of students come from low-income families, benefiting from practical skills and environmental awareness. This model ensures education is accessible and fosters a sense of responsibility towards the environment.
2. **Value Education Course in Nepal:** Nepal offers a dedicated value education course for grades 6 to 8, aimed at shaping students' personal behaviour. A study conducted in Dolkha, Kavre, and Chitwan, involving 600 students and teachers, used a quantitative approach to assess its impact. The findings highlighted that the course successfully imparted essential life values such as honesty, hard work, respect, cooperation, compassion, and forgiveness. While positive behavioural changes were noted among students, the study revealed a gap between the perceived importance and actual implementation of value education. Students expressed the need for improved teaching methods to better instil these values and enhance their personal growth. This underscores the importance of refining instructional practices to maximise the course's effectiveness.
3. **Eco-School Programme:** Bal Bharati Public School in Dwarka, a leading co-educational senior secondary institution, actively participates in the Eco-Schools Programme. Students enthusiastically engage in initiatives promoting environmental responsibility, such as 'A Day Without Any Waste,' where one student commits to a zero-waste lifestyle. Efforts include composting kitchen waste and adopting package-free hygiene products, showcasing dedication to reducing plastic use and transitioning to a sustainable lifestyle.

The Eco-Schools Programme fosters environmental awareness and responsibility through hands-on activities. By encouraging waste reduction, it helps students develop sustainable habits that extend beyond the school, inspiring broader environmental stewardship.

SUMMARY

- Value education fosters moral and ethical values, shaping responsible citizens and future leaders. It emphasises character-building, life skills, and universal values alongside academic knowledge, as advocated by Swami Vivekananda and Mahatma Gandhi.
- Value education promotes democratic societies through tolerance, human rights, minority protection, and environmental conservation. It nurtures humanistic attitudes, ethical reasoning, and pride in heritage, preparing individuals to make ethical decisions in a rapidly changing world.
- Educational institutions and sports play key roles in value education. Schools integrate ethics into curricula, foster diversity, and encourage reflection, while sports teach teamwork, perseverance, respect, and honesty. Parents and teachers act as role models, shaping values through actions and interactions.
- By instilling values like honesty, accountability, and equality, education combats social evils such as corruption, discrimination, violence, and environmental degradation. It empowers individuals, promotes community service, and encourages sustainable practices, fostering a harmonious and equitable society.
- In conclusion, value education is essential for personal growth and societal harmony, equipping individuals to make informed decisions, embrace diversity, and contribute positively to the world.

PREVIOUS YEARS' QUESTIONS

1. "If a country is to be corruption free and become a nation of beautiful minds, I strongly feel there are three key societal members who can make a difference. They are father, mother and the teacher." A.P.J. Abdul Kalam –Analyse. *UPSC CSE Mains 2022, 2017*
2. Discuss the role of ethics and values in enhancing the following three major components of Comprehensive National Power (CNP) viz. human capital, soft power (culture and policies) and social harmony. *UPSC CSE Mains 2020*
3. "Education is not an injunction; it is an effective and pervasive tool for all round development of an individual and social transformation." Examine the New Education Policy, 2020 (NEP, 2020) in light of the above statement. *UPSC CSE Mains 2020*
4. Our attitudes towards life, work, other people, and society are generally shaped unconsciously by the family and the social surroundings in which we grow up. Some of these unconsciously

acquired attitudes and values are often undesirable in the citizens of a modern democratic and egalitarian society.

(a) Discuss such undesirable values prevalent in today's educated Indians.

(b) How can such undesirable attitudes be changed and socio-ethical values considered necessary in public services be cultivated in the aspiring and serving civil servants?

UPSC CSE Mains 2016

5. "Integrity without knowledge is weak and useless, but knowledge without integrity is dangerous and dreadful." What do you understand by this statement? Explain your stand with illustrations from modern day context.

UPSC CSE Mains 2014

Dimensions of Ethics

5

1. UNDERSTANDING ETHICS

Ethics, as introduced earlier, revolves around distinguishing between right and wrong. Think of it as a compass that guides us through life's complexities, offering principles and values to make responsible choices. It shapes how we treat one another and influences our moral judgements.

Ethics is more than following traditions or customs—it requires critical analysis and reflection based on universal principles. As a branch of moral philosophy, it involves thinking deeply about morality, ethical dilemmas, and decision-making.

By exploring ethical theories and dimensions, we can better navigate dilemmas and balance conflicting interests, temptations, and compromises. Adopting an informed ethical framework prevents distorted thinking and empowers us to make sound decisions with integrity.

Understanding the various dimensions of ethics enables us to balance conflicting interests, resist temptations, and avoid unnecessary compromises. Compromising ethical standards can lead to distorted thinking and a loss of control over our decisions. However, a clear understanding of ethical principles empowers us to develop a personal code of ethics to which we can genuinely commit.

LEARNING OBJECTIVES

1. Understanding ethics and distinguishing it from morality, exploring non-moral, amoral, and immoral actions
2. Analysing ethical frameworks like Universal, Relative, and Cultural Ethics through examples, benefits, and drawbacks
3. Defining and evaluating key ethical theories, including virtue ethics, teleological ethics, and deontological ethics
4. Studying philosophers like Aristotle, Kant, Rawls, and Hume, examining concepts like the Golden Mean, Pauline Principle, and Kohlberg's Theory
5. Exploring Indian thinkers like Gandhi, Kautilya, Thiruvalluvar, and Basavanna to understand the influence of identity on ethics
6. Engaging critically with ethical and moral questions in contemporary socio-economic and political contexts, integrating personal, professional, and cultural perspectives

It helps us to:

- Recognise ethical dilemmas in sensitive situations
- Identify relevant ethical principles in advance
- Make decisions using clear ethical distinctions
- Explore and evaluate alternatives to resolve dilemmas
- Select the best course of action by applying sound ethical principles

To have a proper appreciation of dimensions of ethics we need to understand various theories of ethics. Theories of ethics are generally divided into four categories:

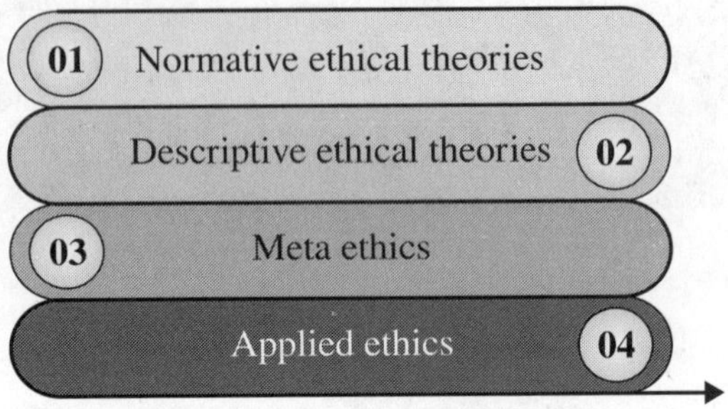

2. ETHICS Vs MORALITY

Both ethics and morality play crucial roles in shaping human society. In simple terms, ethics are more practical and based on community values and established on higher-order norms, whereas morals are a person's or society's ideas about what is right or wrong, especially regarding how a person should act and treat others.

Distinction Between Ethics and Morality

- Ethics represent a structured system of beliefs that guide behaviour, while morality is more personal and can differ from one individual to another.
- Ethics are typically founded on logical reasoning and a shared set of values, whereas morality often stems from intuition or religious convictions.
- Ethics are generally more objective, while morality tends to be subjective.
- Ethics aspire to universal application, while morality can be influenced by cultural contexts.
- Ethics are overarching and can govern all areas of life, while morality tends to focus on specific issues such as politics, economics, religion, and family matters. When someone acts immorally, it usually pertains to one of these areas. In contrast, unethical behaviour has broader implications that span various aspects of life.
- Ethics apply to groups and organisations, while morality pertains to individual conduct. Consequently, ethical practices may not always align well with the cultures of organisations and vice versa.
- Ethics encourage individuals to reflect on their actions before taking them, whereas morality prompts reflection afterward. For instance, a person might resist an opportunity for an extramarital affair because it would be unethical, rather than simply because it is wrong. Alternatively, someone might donate to charity out of a belief that it is the right thing to do, rather than from a fear of eternal punishment.

- In terms of decision-making, ethics guide how one should behave, while morality evaluates whether one has acted rightly after the fact.
- Ethics assist in assessing whether a behaviour is good or bad, while morality helps determine if intentions were good or bad.

3. NON-MORAL Vs AMORAL Vs IMMORAL

1. **Non-Moral Actions:** Non-moral actions are those where moral considerations of right or wrong do not apply. While most actions and behaviours are often evaluated within a moral framework, non-moral actions lack such debates and have no ethical implications in their typical context. These actions usually do not result in harm or benefit to oneself or others. For example, choosing to eat apples, selecting the colour of a shirt, or deciding on a hairstyle are generally considered non-moral actions since they do not involve moral judgments. However, in specific situations, even these seemingly neutral actions could carry moral implications depending on their broader context.
2. **Amoral Actions:** Amoral actions or events refer to areas of interest that show indifference and lack of sense thus not adhering to societal moral rules or codes. For example, sociopath persons with disorders are often described as someone lacking a conscience, and kids are considered 'amoral' because they do not possess an understanding or awareness of right and wrong.
3. **Immoral Actions:** Immoral actions are those actions that are deemed evil, sinful, or wrong according to a particular ethical code or theory. An immoral action can thus be defined as a breach of a rule or ethical guideline. Notably, an action may be viewed as immoral according to one set of rules, while being regarded as moral or even non-moral under another but can be laid that it is immoral. Such cases frequently arise within the framework of sociological or moral relativism. For example, killing someone is immoral as per the natural law of ethics.

> **? Thought Box**
>
> Why are children and sociopaths considered amoral with only sociopaths experiencing the social stigmatisation associated with it?

4. UNIVERSAL ETHICS

Universal ethics is a set of moral principles that apply to all people, regardless of their culture, religion, or other distinguishing features. Universalists say that there does exist a common thread of ethics between the different cultures and differing periods. Though ethics may not be similar across the nations, there exist some common ethical values that can be found among them. Example: Concept of universal human rights.

5. RELATIVE ETHICS

> "What is morality in any given time or place? It is what the majority then and there happen to like, and immorality is what they dislike."
> **Alfred North Whitehead**

Relative ethics holds that what is considered morally right or wrong is not absolute but depends on the customs, practices, traditions, and societal norms of a particular time and place. According to this view, ethical standards are flexible and evolve due to changes in social, cultural, and historical contexts. For relativists, there is no single concrete foundation for the development of ethics. The question of 'What is ethical?' seems to change from time to time, from nation to nation, from culture to culture.

Ethical relativism represents that morals are shaped by social roles, norms, experiences, emotions, and rules that aim to bring the most benefit to society. It rejects the idea of moral absolutes, asserting instead that ethics are fluid and adaptable.

Examples:

- **Practice of *Sati*:** Once considered a sacred duty for widows in India, the practice of *Sati* was gradually abolished after 1829, and is now recognised as a crime by both law and societal standards.
- **Family Structures:** In most parts of India, patriarchal family systems dominate, where women are often not treated equally to men. In contrast, regions like Kerala, the northeastern states, and Nicobar Islands follow matriarchal systems where women enjoy more prominent roles and better social positions.

This perspective highlights how societal norms and values shape what is considered ethical, demonstrating the evolving nature of morality across different cultures and contexts.

6. CULTURAL RELATIVISM Vs ETHICAL RELATIVISM

Ethical relativism says ethics are relative and does not accept that there are universal ethical values. Whereas cultural relativism says that values between cultures are only relative, it does not openly speak about the relative position of ethics, but it also does not dispute the claim of a universalist ethical standpoint. Cultural relativism believes that there always exist some universal values apart from societies. Cultural relativism emphasises the importance of understanding actions and practices within the specific values and norms of a particular culture. It suggests that we should not evaluate the behaviour or thought processes of individuals based on the standards of an outside culture.

7. UNIVERSALISM Vs CULTURAL RELATIVISM

Universal ethics asserts that there are fundamental, universal ethical principles that apply to all living beings, transcending cultural boundaries. Ethical universalists believe that while specific practices and interpretations may vary, certain core values are shared across all cultures. These universal values form the foundation of ethics, which is considered fixed and not dynamic. Universalists study different cultures to identify these common values.

While universalists acknowledge **cultural relativism**—the idea that cultural beliefs and practices must be understood within their context—they reject **ethical relativism**. They argue that ethical values remain constant, but their interpretation and application may differ among cultures. For example, while all societies protect infants, the methods and practices vary according to cultural contexts.

Universal values like 'do not steal' or 'do not murder' underpin societal existence, but their understanding and practice differ across cultures. Universal ethics thus emphasises the shared moral foundation while respecting cultural diversity in interpretation and application.

8. BRANCHES OF ETHICS

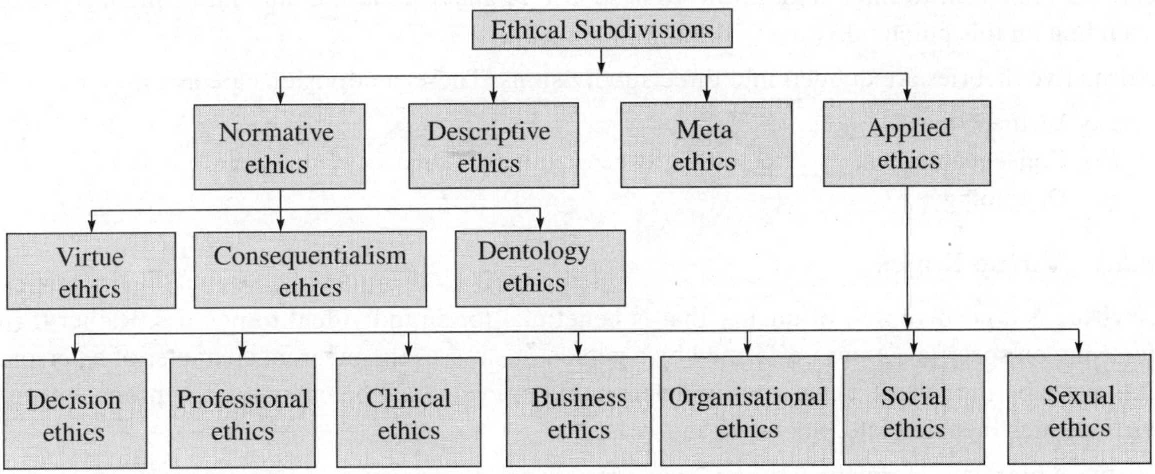

Fig. 5.1 Branches of Ethics

8.1 Meta Ethics

Meta ethics is a branch of philosophy that studies the nature of morality, including the meaning of moral terms, the logic of moral reasoning, and the assumptions underlying normative theories.

Meta ethics is considered a non-normative approach to ethics, along with descriptive ethics.

Meta ethics explores fundamental questions such as:

- What is the nature of goodness?
- How can we distinguish between good and bad? Are moral values objective or subjective? How do ethical attitudes influence or motivate us?

8.2 Normative or Prescriptive Ethics

Normative ethics formulates principles and standards for evaluating human conduct. It tells us what we ought to do or what we ought not to do. It discusses ways of deriving the principles as well as ways of justifying those. Normative is derived from the term 'norm'. It examines the standards of one's action from rightness or wrongness. Normative ethics includes the formulation of moral rules that have direct implications for what human actions, institutions, and ways of life should be like.

It is also known as perspective ethics, which emphasises the need to consider multiple viewpoints when making ethical decisions. This can be challenging because our personal biases and preferences often influence us. However, striving for objectivity is crucial when evaluating the potential consequences of our actions. For instance, if you're deciding whether to buy a new car, it's important to think about how your spouse might react to the amount of money you're spending on this purchase.

Normative theories are divided into three subdivisions. These subdivisions are as follows:

(a) Virtue Ethics
(b) Consequentialism
(c) Deontology

8.2.1 Virtue Ethics

A virtue is a positive trait or quality that is beneficial for an individual to possess. Rather than focusing on specific actions performed by a person, it stresses the inherent character of a person. It focuses on the role of a character in determining or evaluating behaviours. Key proponents of virtue ethics include Plato, Socrates, and Aristotle.

Virtue ethics is a normative theory that prioritises 'being' over 'doing'. According to this perspective, morality stems from an individual's character rather than their actions or the consequences of those actions.

For example, virtue ethics suggests that a person acts kindly not because it is their duty or because it maximises societal utility, but because they embody the virtue of kindness.

Some key ideas of Virtue Ethics:

- **Happiness Principle**

Aristotle, a key figure in virtue ethics, began his exploration of ethics by examining human nature and happiness rather than virtues. He observed that all individuals seek happiness, which he defined as the only inherently valuable pursuit. Happiness, according to Aristotle, lies in the full realisation of one's potential and is achieved through virtues, which he described as 'excellences' of character. Virtues are essential for leading a good and fulfilling life.

Aristotle emphasised that humans, as rational and social beings, must find satisfaction both rationally and socially to attain happiness. He highlighted the role of the rational soul in regulating emotions, enabling the development of virtues while keeping vices in check. By guiding emotions along a balanced path, individuals could cultivate virtues. This idea is exemplified in Aristotle's *Principle of the Golden Mean*, which advocates for moderation between extremes.

- **Principle of Golden Mean**

The Principle of the Golden Mean in ethics asserts that virtue lies between two extremes: deficiency and excess. For example, in the case of a warrior, cowardice (fleeing from battle) represents a deficiency, while recklessness (charging at 50 enemy soldiers alone) signifies excess. Virtue, therefore, exists in achieving a balanced state. This principle highlights the importance of balance in life, a concept echoed in Buddha's *Middle Path* in Indian philosophy.

According to Aristotle, emotions such as fear, confidence, anger, pleasure, and pain are natural, but experiencing them in excess or deficiency is undesirable. Virtue lies in feeling these emotions at the right time, in the right measure, directed towards the right people, for the right reasons, and in the right manner, achieving a balanced and optimal state.

- **Relativity of Golden Mean**

The Golden Mean is not a mathematical midpoint but a context-dependent balance that varies in real-life situations. Aristotle emphasises that emotions like anger are not inherently wrong; what matters is the degree of their expression—it should neither be excessive nor insufficient but proportionate to the situation. However, there is no universal 'middle' applicable to every scenario, as each context is distinct.

For example, consider the analogy of the 'sweet spot' on a cricket bat. The ideal place to hit the ball is not at the exact center of the bat, but slightly towards the thicker end, depending on the situation. Similarly, the Golden Mean is not always precisely centered; it shifts relative to what helps an individual thrive.

This relativity makes developing moral virtue a challenge. Virtue, as the Golden Mean, is not a one-size-fits-all concept—it adapts to the individual's context. Aristotle viewed ethics as an art of living rather than an exact science. Living a virtuous life is not about achieving perfection but navigating the complexities of life, often through a non-linear, zigzag journey rather than a straight path.

Aristotle's Developmental Model of Virtues

Aristotle asserts that moral virtues are not innate but are cultivated through habitual actions. Ethical standards are shaped by individuals and society, not external forces like religion. Virtues develop during socialisation, starting from family and friends, and are ingrained through consistent practice. Over time, these virtues, such as honesty and integrity, become part of one's character.

Potential → Repeated Actions → Habits → Character

Input/Output Dynamic

1. **Input Phase:** The stage of learning and acquiring virtues, often easier as it involves identifying and practicing good traits.
2. **Output Phase:** The application of virtues in real life, which reflects one's character and can be more challenging. Virtues, once ingrained, become habitual and subconscious, much like learning to ride a bicycle—once learned, it is hard to forget.

Role Models and Social Impact

- Role models, from national leaders to parents, play a vital role in shaping virtues. Observing and emulating their traits helps individuals internalise positive values.
- Social virtues, like honesty, tolerance, and generosity, extend their influence beyond the individual, fostering a positive environment. Conversely, associating with dishonest individuals can have a negative impact.

Aristotle's Perspective

As social beings, humans are deeply influenced by those around them. While some virtues, such as courage, are personal, others, like kindness and generosity, are inherently social, emphasising the collective nature of ethical development.

Benefits and Drawbacks of Virtue Ethics

Benefits

- **Focus on Character:** Virtue ethics emphasises personal character over rigid rules, making it an accessible and relatable moral framework.
- **Practical Application:** It is highly relevant to everyday situations, guiding individuals to act with integrity and make morally sound choices.

- **Cultivation of Virtues:** By promoting traits like kindness and honesty, virtue ethics fosters personal growth and inspires positive behaviour in others.
- **Context-Sensitive:** Unlike rule-based systems, it allows for flexibility and nuanced decision-making in complex moral dilemmas.
- **Continuous Growth:** Encourages lifelong self-improvement, prompting individuals to reflect on and refine their moral character.

Drawbacks

- **Uncertainty in Virtues:** It can be challenging to determine which virtues to cultivate, as individuals are not always rational.
- **Lack of Universal Rules:** The absence of a common ethical code can lead to inconsistent and subjective moral decisions.
- **Individual-Centric:** Over-reliance on personal character may cause variability in moral judgments based on individual experiences.
- **Circular Definition:** Virtue ethics can be vague, as it defines a 'right decision' as what a virtuous person would make, requiring prior knowledge of virtues.

8.2.2 Consequentialist Ethics

1. Utilitarianism

"The end may justify the means as long as there is something that justifies the end"

Leon Trotsky

Utilitarian ethics belong to the consequentialist school of ethics where the proponents focus on outcomes or consequences. It has its origin in the eighteenth century. To be precise, in utilitarian ethics, one will judge an action, law, or system as right or wrong, virtue or vice, only from the consequence or utility that causes it all.

The principle of utility means that one should always do something that has more utility or usefulness for all others concerned. It is also called the greatest happiness principle as one should always do something which benefits all the concerned. The interests of everyone affected by an act should be considered like any other or the interests of any other person.

David Hume on Utilitarianism

According to Hume, ethics cannot be based on reason and rationality. Ethics guides what one should do, that is direct the actions of the individuals. Since actions are motivated by feelings and sentiments, ethics too are guided by the same. Hence, Hume's theory goes against the long-established tradition of human rationality.

He argues that human reasoning alone lacks the power to motivate ethical actions. While reason can guide understanding of what is right, it often fails to inspire action. Instead, emotions, feelings, passions, and desires must work alongside reason to drive behaviour. Often, people know what they should do but struggle to act on it. For example, someone may recognise the need to lose weight but lack the motivation to follow through. This highlights how strong desires and emotions can either motivate or deter individuals from taking specific actions.

Thus, Hume sums up this concept that one cannot derive an 'OUGHT' from an 'IS.' IS means human reason, OUGHT is the way ethics is practiced. Thus, we cannot derive ethics from human reason. Reason alone does not determine what ethics are. For deriving ethics, one should feel something. According to Hume, logic and reason (IS) alone are not enough to understand the ethical (OUGHT) conclusions.

2. Hedonism

Bentham's utility concept is based on hedonism. It means pleasure, which can also mean that humans are generally pleasure seekers. They try to do acts that maximise their pleasure and minimise their pain. Utility or usefulness is also based on consequences. A particular law, act, or rule is good or bad based on its consequences. It is good if it has good consequences, which bring happiness and pleasure rather than pain. Thus, we can clearly distinguish between good and bad.

Early utilitarianism placed their theory on the hedonistic lines that are based on pleasure. Utilitarianism gives a simple conception that a happy life is filled with pleasure, while an unhappy or bad life is filled with pain and suffering. This happiness just does not belong to an individual, it is meant for everyone around him. Consequentialist ethics means that the consequence of an act, good or bad, should not just be for an individual, the good effect should be for everyone. We feel not only about ourselves; we do feel for others too.

Let us consider the Nirbhaya case; we anger have angry feelings towards the perpetrators. We empathise and feel sorry for the victim, their family and friends. This goes against the concept of psychological egoism, which states human think about themselves alone. Thus, utilitarians reject egoism, they state that humans have a natural tendency to sympathise with others.

The ancient Chinese scholar Mo Tzu criticised both war and funeral practices using utilitarian principles. He argued that war is inherently destructive, causing widespread harm, injury, and death, and ultimately offering no benefit to the people. Similarly, he opposed the traditional three-year mourning period in ancient China, viewing it as a waste of valuable resources that could be used more productively. Since neither war, nor extravagant funerals bring happiness to anyone involved, Mo Tzu advocated for their abolition.

3. Ethical Egoism

Ethical egoism is a philosophical theory that states that people should make moral decisions based on what is best for themselves. Ethical egoism, in philosophy, is an ethical theory according to which moral decision-making should be guided entirely by self-interest. What is good for an individual is good for society. Example – Sects like Protestants in the West, Sindhis, and Agarwals in India promote ethical egoism through entrepreneurship.

4. Ethical Altruism

Ethical altruism is a philosophy that states that the moral value of an action is based on its impact on others, regardless of the consequences for the actor. Ethical altruism emphasises selflessness while ensuring that one's actions do not harm others, maintaining a balance between personal satisfaction and the well-being of the community. For instance, donating a portion of one's wealth to charity without seeking recognition reflects this principle, as it prioritises the needs of others over personal gain.

5. Social Contract Theory

According to social contract theory, an act is moral if it is carried out based on an agreed contract and it is not, if it goes against the contract. When one agrees to enter a social contract, he or she would be giving up a degree of freedom he or she enjoys. An individual will agree to behave in a definite or a particular way and will agree not to breach the contract.

This behaviour of an individual is termed 'a strategy of cooperation' because here the core of the social contract is one's peace, stability, security, and comfort. Social contract theory states that the general nature of human society if not properly regulated, would result in a state of war. Because, people if they enjoy unlimited freedom will result in constant confusion and will create instability, uncomfort, and insecurity.

So, human beings as rational creatures will devise a system to escape from the evils of this natural order of existence. In furtherance of their self-interest, humans will enter mutually beneficial contracts with his or her fellow beings. The said contract may be with individuals, society, rulers, etc.

Thomas Hobbes builds his modern ethical theory of social contract on scientific principles. This theory is rooted in the concept of the *Principle of Self-Interest* or *Ethical Egoism.* According to social contract theory, humans, though rational, are inherently self-interested, which increases the likelihood of breaches in agreements. To address this, negative reinforcements are necessary to ensure adherence. As Hobbes famously stated, 'a covenant needs a sword', implying that mere words or promises are insufficient to secure compliance. Laws, therefore, play a crucial role in upholding ethics.

For a social contract to function effectively, it must meet the following conditions:

- It must involve rational individuals capable of fulfilling the agreement both mentally and physically.
- There must be a system in place to punish or penalise those who violate the contract.

Principles of social contract ethics

1. **Involves agreement**: Hobbes argues that life in the state of nature is chaotic and unstable, preventing people from achieving peace and comfort. Recognising this problem, humans, being rational, seek solutions through mutually agreeable contracts. These contracts are not born from natural cooperation but from self-interest, allowing individuals to gain what they want. Sometimes, this involves agreeing to give absolute power to a ruler.
2. **Contract sets up a boundary**: Acts within the boundaries that are agreed to be carried out. Hence, anything within the contract is right and others wrong. This constraint of boundary deprives the individuals of some of their freedom, they thus give up part of their freedom to agree to this contract.
3. **Involves rationality**: For a contract to work effectively it should be between rational beings who are capable of carrying it out with understanding and the ability to punish someone who violates the contract. With rational beings, the possibility of breaching a contract is negligible as they understand the system of rewards for their compliance and penalties for their violation. Thus, Hobbes is of the view that every agreement needs a sword.
4. **Common-sense morality**: Hobbes says that social contract theory is based on the principle of the golden rule, thus ingraining the principle of common-sense morality. The principle of the golden rule means that 'do not do to another that you would not want others to do to you.'
5. **Principle of self interest**: As per contractarians one should do good to others not because it is moral or right thing. It is for the benefit of their self, self-interest through which they can lead a happy life afterward. The concept of *karma* in Indian ethics too had egoism in it. According to the concept of karma, if you want to lead a good, happy life in your next birth you should do good and virtuous activities, or the suffering of the individuals is because of the bad deeds they committed in their previous birth.

6. John Rawls' Theory of Social Justice

John Rawls' theory of social justice, framed within the context of social contract theory, offers a foundational approach to understanding justice in a democratic society. Rawls proposes that principles of justice should be established through a hypothetical agreement among rational individuals in an original position. This scenario emphasises fairness, as individuals are stripped off knowledge about their own social status, abilities, or personal circumstances, ensuring that the chosen principles are impartial and just.

At the core of Rawls' theory is the 'original position,' where individuals come together to determine the rules governing their society. Under the 'veil of ignorance,' they are unaware of their future positions, which compels them to choose principles that safeguard basic rights and ensure equitable opportunities for all. This framework encourages participants to prioritise fairness and consider the implications of their choices on the most disadvantaged members of society, promoting a just and inclusive social contract.

Rawls articulates two primary principles of justice that emerge from this original position. The first principle ensures equal basic liberties for all individuals, such as freedom of speech and religion. The second principle, known as the difference principle, allows social and economic inequalities only if they benefit the least advantaged members of the society. This principle emphasises that any inequalities must serve to improve the situation of the most vulnerable, challenging utilitarian notions that prioritise overall happiness over individual rights.

In addition to these principles, Rawls stresses the significance of fair institutions in realising social justice. He argues that a just society must implement institutions that uphold the principles of justice, ensuring that they are not merely theoretical constructs but are actively applied in practice. This includes establishing fair political processes, equitable economic opportunities, and a robust social safety net to support those in need, thereby fostering a stable and just society.

Rawls' theory has significantly influenced contemporary discussions on justice and ethics, providing a compelling framework for evaluating social contracts in modern democracies. While it has faced critiques, particularly regarding its feasibility and the practical application of the difference principle, Rawls' emphasis on fairness, equality, and the moral obligation to support the least advantaged remains relevant, shaping debates on justice and guiding public policy efforts aimed at achieving a more equitable society.

> **? Thought Box**
>
> Do you think Rawl's Theory of Social Justice can be applied to any present-day situation in India? If yes, then justify how.

Benefits and drawbacks of Consequentialist Ethics

Benefits

- **Practical Approach:** Teleological ethics offers a pragmatic framework for resolving ethical dilemmas.
- **Encourages Altruism:** It inspires individuals to enhance the well-being of others.
- **Emphasis on Outcomes:** This ethical theory prioritises the observable outcomes of actions over the intentions behind them.

Drawbacks

- **Potential for Justifying Atrocities**: Teleological ethics may be used to rationalise extreme or abhorrent actions.

- **Challenges in Assessing Consequences**: Accurately gauging the full range of consequences from an action can be challenging.
- **Difficulty in Measuring Good and Evil**: It can be hard to quantify the extent to which good outweighs harm.
- **Neglect of Individual Rights**: This approach may overlook individual rights that should remain inviolable.
- **Uncertain Outcomes**: The consequences of actions can often be unpredictable.

8.2.3 Deontology Ethics

> "In law, a man is guilty when he violates the rights of others. In ethics he is guilty if he only thinks of doing so."
>
> **Immanuel Kant**

Deontology considers ethics as a duty, an obligation, and a principle on which one must take a stand. It is a non-consequentialist ethical concept, which focuses on the act itself rather than its consequence. It stresses the principle of not treating people as a means to an end. Deontology focuses on the intention rather than the consequence. It does not accept that the end justifies the means.

Everyone is bound to do some duty or the other. The duty arises from what we are, what we do, and what we have to do. And it goes by various names such as obligations, commitments, etc. We are bound to perform our duties as citizens of this country; we should perform our duty towards our parents, our friends, our siblings, our workplace, etc. We are thus bound by various duties.

Immanuel Kant is the first and foremost philosopher and theorist of deontology ethics. In this section, we will look into the theory given by Immanuel Kant otherwise known as the 'Theory of Categorical Imperative'.

- **Categorical imperative**

Kant introduced the 'categorical imperative', a moral law grounded in rationality. He argued that moral judgments are universally rational, with no grey areas—what is right is always right, and what is wrong is always wrong. Humans must follow this imperative unconditionally to be moral.

Kant rejected the notion that morality is derived from God's commands, asserting instead that rationality makes us moral beings. Rationality shapes our sense of duty, defines our freedom, and allows us to act independently of external influences. Unlike humans, animals act on instinct without rational thought and cannot be held morally accountable. For Kant, morality is based on reason, not feelings or emotions, and ethical duties are dictated by rationality rather than divine authority or others' opinions.

Kant identified two types of imperatives: categorical and hypothetical. Categorical imperatives are absolute, prescriptive commands that must be followed without exception. In contrast, hypothetical imperatives depend on specific circumstances and consequences, aligning with consequentialist ethics.

- **Principles of Deontology**
  1. **Principle of respect to autonomy:** Autonomy is based on the human capacity to direct one's life according to rational principles. The principle of autonomy is closely tied to independence, meaning individuals should not be bound by the views or interference of others. Without this independence, a person loses their autonomy, responsibility, and ultimately their dignity. This is exemplified by the concept of voluntary informed consent: individuals must act freely and without coercion, making choices based on accurate information. Failing to provide proper information is unethical, and forcing someone to act against their will is immoral. Example: Extreme cases like rape.
  2. **Principle of universality:** The principle of universality posits that individuals should act according to personal laws or moral beliefs that can be universally applied to all people. This means that one's actions should be guided by principles that could be accepted as moral laws for everyone, fostering a sense of shared ethical responsibility. Ultimately, this principle encourages individuals to reflect on their choices and consider the broader impact of their actions on society as a whole.
  3. **Principle of correspondence:** It is an understanding that what we know and experience, in our lives here on earth, can be used to understand both the finer and smaller as well as the larger and grosser. This translates to every aspect of life and is more than just something to understand. It is the ability to shift one's perspective to understand and see the correlation between the outside world and the inside world as well.

- **Natural Law of Ethics**

  "Natural law is the first principle of morality; it forbids evil and commands good."

  Martin Luther

Natural law is a theory in ethics that says that human beings possess intrinsic values that govern their reasoning and behaviour. According to natural law, rules of right and wrong are inherent in people and are not created by society or court judges. It guides us to the path of natural reason by which we know good from evil, virtue from vice, etc.

Natural law is not taught to human beings. We 'discover' it by continuously making choices for good instead of evil. It is also believed by some schools of thought that natural law is passed to humans through divine presence. Thus, natural law helps us to understand God's message (Eternal law). Natural law too follows the tradition of universal ethics.

For St Thomas Aquinas, natural law is inextricably connected with religion. He believed and stated that natural law 'participates' in the divine 'eternal' law. According to him, eternal law is a rational plan by which all creation is ordered, and natural law is the way that human beings participate in the eternal law. He further posited that the fundamental principle of natural law is that we should do good and avoid evil.

Pauline Principle

The Pauline Principle asserts that one must never do evil to achieve good; the end does not justify the means. It serves as a moral guide in ambiguous situations, emphasising that the morality of an action depends on its principle, not its outcomes.

For example, lying is generally impermissible under natural law as it opposes basic human nature. Even if lying seems necessary—such as to make someone happy or save a life—the Pauline Principle deems it wrong, as doing harm to achieve good violates moral integrity.

Consider a flood scenario where a small boat with a capacity of eight people must accommodate twenty, including the elderly and injured. Is it justifiable to leave behind the weaker individuals to save the stronger? According to the Pauline Principle, committing evil (letting some die) for a perceived greater good (saving others) is wrong. In such situations, natural law defers to divine intervention, trusting that God will provide a solution.

Ultimately, the principle emphasises that actions must align with moral integrity, regardless of the outcomes.

Principle of Double Effect

According to the principle of double effect, it is sometimes morally acceptable to cause harm as an unintended and merely foreseen side effect of achieving a good result, even though it would not be acceptable to cause the same harm as a direct means of attaining the same good outcome. The principle of Double Effect is an ethical principle that allows for an action to cause harm as a side effect of achieving a good end. Under this principle, it can be understood that there will always be some unintended externalities for any amount of good act.

It is moral for an act to have both positive and negative consequences if certain conditions are met.

- The act must be good in intention itself
- Should expect a good outcome and not a bad one
- It should not go against the Pauline Principle where means are good
- It should occur in a serious situation

Consider a scenario where you are physically attacked, and you attempt to defend yourself by retaliating. Self-preservation or self-defense is a natural human instinct. However, harming or killing others contradicts the natural law that one should not kill. This raises an ethical dilemma, what should one do in such a situation?

Thomas Aquinas, an Italian priest, addresses this issue under natural law. According to him, in the cases of self-defense, the primary intention should be to protect oneself, not to harm or kill the aggressor. Therefore, it is morally permissible to hurt or even kill someone if it is an unintended consequence of protecting oneself. However, if the intent is to harm or kill, the act violates the moral principles of natural law.

This reasoning aligns with the principle of double effect, which states that an action can have both positive and negative consequences. For the action to be morally justified, the intention behind it must be good, and the negative consequences, though unintended, must be acceptable and proportionate to the circumstances.

Benefits and Drawbacks of Deontological Ethics

Benefit

- **Consistency:** Deontological ethics can be consistently applied across a wide range of situations, as it imposes ethical duties on everyone in every context.
- **Emphasis on Intentions:** This approach prioritises intentions, which are within our control, over the unpredictable outcomes of actions.
- **Universality:** Deontological principles apply to all individuals, regardless of their race, age, or gender.
- **Encouragement of Virtues:** Deontology fosters virtues such as courage, justice, wisdom, and self-discipline.

Drawbacks

- **Rigidity:** Deontology can be seen as inflexible, often disregarding the consequences of actions. For instance, it would mandate telling the truth even if doing so could aid a murderer, which many find intuitively problematic.
- **Challenges in Business Contexts:** Applying deontological principles in business settings can be challenging, as decisions often rely on abstract notions like rights and duties.
- **Circular Reasoning:** Deontology can sometimes lead to circular reasoning, where a maxim must be ethical to begin with to be considered universalisable.

8.3 Descriptive Ethics

Descriptive ethics is a branch of philosophy that studies how people believe about morality and ethics. It's also known as comparative ethics. It documents the values, practices, and norms of a given cultural, social, or professional setting. Descriptive ethics is different from normative ethics, which judges moral claims. Descriptive ethics aims to understand ethical belief systems without making judgements.

1. Kohlberg's Theory of Moral Development

Kohlberg's theory explains how people develop moral reasoning and morality. It is a framework that outlines how individuals progress through different stages of moral reasoning. Developed by psychologist, Lawrence Kohlberg in the 1950s and 1960s, the theory is based on the idea that moral reasoning develops in stages as people mature.

Kohlberg's theory is a classic example of describing the essence of descriptive ethics where the ethical prepositions evolved over some time from conventions, descriptions, values, and morality.

The theory is broken down into three levels, with two stages at each level:

- **Preconventional morality:** The earliest period of moral development, lasting until around age nine.
- **Conventional morality:** Marked by the acceptance of social rules regarding what is good and moral.
- **Postconventional or principled level:** Individuals arrive at the highest moral tier of intrinsic moral principles.

Kohlberg's theory suggests that moral development begins with a desire to avoid punishment and may evolve into a desire to make the world a better place. He believed that individuals progress through these stages in a fixed order and that not everyone reaches the higher stages. His theory emphasises the development of moral reasoning rather than just the moral decisions themselves.

2. Gandhian Ethics

Mohandas Karamchand Gandhi, widely known as Mahatma Gandhi, stands as a timeless emblem of ethics and morality. Over his seventy-eight years, he embodied the principles of action, truthfulness, and nonviolence. Although he was inherently a leader, his ability to unite and guide a diverse nation was honed through profound interactions with individuals from various backgrounds.

Gandhi was not merely an intellectual confined to the halls of academia; he was a visionary who not just propounded ethical prepositions but walked the talk. He integrated nonviolence and peaceful protest into his leadership philosophy, using these tools to challenge injustice and oppression. For him, nonviolence was rooted in compassion, humility, forgiveness, and tolerance. He firmly believed that the strength of the human spirit surpasses that of weapons and fear. His unwavering commitment to truth, along with his conviction, courage, love, and sense of justice and sacrifice is a reverberating testimony to lead a life of morals.

- **God and Religion**

For Gandhi, God embodies both Truth and Love, and he believed that the closest path to understanding truth is through love. He sought to experience God through serving humanity, recognising that the divine resides within each individual, rather than in distant realms. Gandhi held a deep respect for the fundamental truths found in all major world religions, asserting that "Truth is God and God is Truth." While some may not believe in God, he argued that no one can deny the existence of truth, including atheists. He emphasised that religion and morality are inextricably linked, and for him, there is no higher principle than truth and righteousness.

- **Truth**

Truth is defined by the inner voice that guides each individual. It must resonate in our thoughts, words, and actions. While truth can be subjective—varying from one person to another—it shouldn't deter those on a quest for understanding. With sincere effort, one can come to realise that these differing perceptions of truth are akin to the countless leaves of a single tree. A person's character is built on virtuous actions, which are fundamentally rooted in Truth. Truth serves as the foundation for all that is noble and admirable.

One can attain Truth through dedicated practice (Abhyas) and a detachment from all other worldly pursuits (Vairagya). Gandhi believed that truth is synonymous with God and is a core principle of Satyagraha. His perspective on truth remained steadfast across various contexts, much like the ethical philosophy of Immanuel Kant.

- ***Satyagraha***

'Satyagraha is a relentless search for truth and a determination to pursue truth.'

Mahatma Gandhi

Satyagraha, as articulated by Mahatma Gandhi, embodies the purest form of soul force utilised against injustice, oppression, and exploitation. He believed that sacrifice, suffering, and trust are essential elements that empower this soul force. For Gandhi, self-sacrifice was fundamental to life, and he asserted that one cannot achieve anything meaningful without making sacrifices.

He coined the term *Satyagraha*, which is derived from two Sanskrit words: '*Satya*,' meaning truth, and '*Agraha*,' meaning 'polite resistance' or 'holding firm.' He applied *Satyagraha* during the Indian independence movement as well as in his fight against racism in South Africa. The concept proved so powerful that it inspired notable figures like Martin Luther King Jr, James Bevel, and Nelson Mandela in their respective civil rights movements.

- ***Sarvodaya***

> 'The greatness of a nation and its moral progress can be judged by the way its animals are treated.' **Mahatma Gandhi**

The term '*Sarvodaya*,' derived from Sanskrit, translates to 'Universal Uplift' or 'Progress for All.' Mahatma Gandhi introduced this concept when he named his translation of Ruskin Bond's work, '*Unto This Last*,' as '*Sarvodaya*.' He frequently referenced this ideal in his political philosophy, believing that the earth has enough resources to meet everyone's needs but not their greed. Gandhi envisioned a society where individuals are free from the desire for excessive material wealth and luxury, promoting the principle of 'Simple Living and High Thinking.' He firmly believed that inclusiveness could help eradicate many societal evils. His vision of a society grounded in *Sarvodaya* can be seen as a true form of socialism, where people embody love, fraternity, truth, non-violence, and self-sacrifice.

- **Ends and Means**

The connection between means and ends is fundamentally ethical rather than technical. It involves making choices that require an initial decision about the desired outcome, alongside an acknowledgment of the necessary steps to achieve it. Mahatma Gandhi consistently asserted that immoral means can never lead to good ends. He believed that noble goals cannot be realised through evil or unethical methods. Rooted in his understanding of the law of karma, Gandhi emphasised the intrinsic interdependence between means and ends. Importantly, he noted that while individuals have control over their means, they do not have control over the ultimate outcomes.

- **Gandhian Economy**

The Gandhian economy represents a unique school of thought rooted in spiritual and socio-economic principles. It emphasises values such as simplicity, decentralisation, self-sufficiency, cooperation, equality, non-violence, and human dignity. Key elements of this economic order include the establishment of self-sufficient village units, the nationalisation of essential industries, the promotion of *Swadeshi*, and adherence to the doctrine of trusteeship. These principles aim to address various challenges related to labour, capital, production, distribution, and profit.

- **Doctrine of Trusteeship**

The doctrine of trusteeship is a socio-economic philosophy proposed by Mahatma Gandhi. It suggests that affluent individuals should act as trustees, responsible for managing their wealth in a manner that benefits society at large. Gandhi argued that the rich ought to view their possessions as a divine trust, meant to serve the needs of the less fortunate and act as stewards.

This philosophy legitimised the status of wealthy individuals, provided they fulfilled their roles as responsible 'trustees.' For instance, J.R.D. Tata, the founder of the Tata Group, was deeply inspired by Gandhi's concept of trusteeship, which significantly shaped both his personal values and professional practices.

- **Seven Deadly Sins**

Mahatma Gandhi, a profound advocate for truth and morality, identified seven 'deadly sins' that he believed contributed to the moral decline of individuals and society. These sins encapsulate the ethical challenges faced by humanity, highlighting the behaviours and attitudes that lead to personal and communal degradation. Gandhi argued that recognising and addressing these sins is essential for fostering a just and harmonious society.

1. **Politics Without Principles**: This sin highlights the moral deficiencies of political leaders who prioritise their interests over ethical governance. It reflects a troubling trend where criminal behaviour among elected officials becomes normalised.
   Example: According to the Association for Democratic Reforms (ADR), 44% of sitting Members of Parliament (MPs) in the 17th Lok Sabha (2024) face criminal charges, highlighting a significant ethical concern within the political sphere.
2. **Wealth Without Work:** Gandhi warns against accumulating wealth without effort, which fosters inequality and social injustice. This pursuit often leads to a disconnect between economic gain and moral responsibility.
   Example: The soaring prices of cryptocurrencies and speculative practices at the stock market have created fortunes for some without corresponding labour or contribution.
3. **Pleasure Without Conscience:** This principle critiques the pursuit of personal pleasure at the expense of ethical considerations and the well-being of others. It reveals a societal neglect of moral values when gratification takes precedence over responsibility.
   Example: The ongoing issue of marital rape, indulgence in illicit substances particularly affecting adolescents, exemplifies this troubling trend.
4. **Knowledge Without Character**: Gandhi emphasises the importance of ethical integrity in applying knowledge responsibly. Misuse of knowledge can lead to significant harm, undermining societal well-being.
   Example: The 2021 Mumbai blackout, attributed to cyber disruptions, demonstrates the potential dangers of knowledge wielded without moral accountability.
5. **Science Without Humanity**: This sin addresses the misuse of scientific advancements for destructive purposes, often disregarding human impact. Such applications can lead to catastrophic consequences for society and the environment.
   Example: The recent missile bombardments between Israel and Gaza serve as a stark reminder of science being used without regard for humanity.

6. **Commerce Without Morality:** Gandhi critiques business practices that prioritise profit over ethical considerations and social responsibility. Such a mindset can lead to exploitation and harm in pursuit of financial gain.
   Example: Controversies surrounding privacy violations involving tech giants like Google and Facebook reveal the ethical dilemmas in modern commerce.
7. **Religion Without Sacrifice:** This principle warns against the superficial practice of religion that lacks genuine selflessness and commitment. It reflects a deviation from true spirituality when ritualistic observance overshadows meaningful actions.
   Example: The rise of religious fundamentalism, which has fuelled communal tensions in various parts of the world, including France, illustrates this disconnect.

9. INDIAN PHILOSOPHICAL SCHOOLS

What is the primary source of morality in India? The foundations of Indian ethics can be sought in the metaphysical and theological beliefs in the form of worship, prayers, and in the form of ideals and principles that direct man's life in society. When we speak of Indian ethics, we cannot deny the intimate relationship that prevails between ethics and Hinduism, Buddhism, and Jainism.

When discussing Indian ethics, it is impossible to overlook the close connection between ethics and the religions of Hinduism, Buddhism, and Jainism. Ethics and religion are deeply intertwined, and every religion, regardless of its nature, encompasses a system of morality to guide its followers. In this context, Indian ethics forms an essential part of Hinduism as well as other religions originating from India. The ethical ideals and principles of India are reflected in the Vedas, other Indian texts, and the teachings of these religious traditions. The authority of the scriptures, particularly the Vedas, is central to this, with the Smritis being accepted as authoritative after the Vedas.

9.1 Hinduism

Hinduism is not just a religion; it's a vibrant tapestry of beliefs and practices that have shaped the lives of millions for centuries. At its heart are some fascinating ethical concepts that guide how individuals navigate their responsibilities and relationships. Ideas like *dharma* (duty), *karma* (the law of cause and effect), and *moksha* (spiritual liberation) create a moral compass that encourages compassion, integrity, and balance in daily life. These principles not only inform personal choices but also foster a sense of community and interconnectedness. Let's dive into these rich ethical concepts and see how they continue to inspire and influence the way we live today.

- ***Dharma***

Dharma is a central concept in Hinduism that refers to a person's duty in life, and the moral code that Hindus are expected to follow. The Indian term for morality and ethics is *'dharma,'* which derives from the root *'dhr,'* meaning to uphold or sustain. Therefore, the role of *dharma* is to maintain social harmony, ensuring the stability and growth of human society, e.g. Ten cardinal virtues are known as *Sadharana Dharma* according to Manu; endurance, patience, self-control, integrity, purity, restraint of senses, wisdom, learning, truth, and absence of anger or non-violence.

- ***Karma***

Karma simply means action. *Karma* reminds us that what is often referred to as the consequence of an action is not something separate, but an integral part of the action itself. The consequence is the future outcome, yet it is inseparable from the present action. As the saying goes, 'Whatever a person sows, they shall reap.'

- **Supreme Goals (*Purusharthas*)**

The dominant interest of Indian thought is in the highest value of human life. There are four values, which give meaning to human life. They are called *Purusharthas*. They are as follows: (1) *Dharma* (2) *Artha* (3) *Kama* (4) *Moksa.*

1. *'Dharma'* is seen as a means to achieve integration of personality at the spiritual level, leading to liberation.
2. *'Artha'* generally refers to the pursuit of wealth, prosperity, and material success, including advantages and profits.
3. *'Kama'* is a broad term encompassing all desires, from physical cravings to spiritual longings. In Hindu philosophy, there is a clear emphasis on enjoying worldly pleasures while also seeking the realisation of spiritual values.
4. *'Moksha'*, also known as *'mukti,' 'apavarya,' 'kaivalya,'* and *'nirvana,'* represents the ultimate liberation.

In all Indian philosophical traditions, the first three *Purusharthas* are viewed as instrumental values that, either directly or indirectly, lead to the highest goal of human life, which is *moksha*.

- **Way of righteousness in *Bhagavad Gita***

The Gita outlines the path of disinterested action (*Nishkama Karma*) as the way to achieve *moksha*. To attain liberation, one must be freed from the bondage of their actions. Therefore, the Gita emphasises the importance of performing actions without attachment to their outcomes. Lord Krishna teaches that the focus should be on the righteousness of the action itself, not the results. He advises Arjuna to always act in alignment with *dharma* (ethical conduct). As the lawgiver, Krishna provides nine commandments to guide this ethical way of living:

- *Amanitva* – Absence of pride
- *Adambhitva* – Absence of deceit
- *Ahimsa* – Non-violence
- *Santi* – Patience
- *Arjava* – Uprightness
- *Acaryopāsāna* – Service to the teacher
- *Sauca* – Internal and external purity
- *Sthairya* – Steadfastness
- *Atmavinigraha* – Self-control

9.2 Buddhism

Many people view Buddhism primarily as a religion, which raises the question of why it appears in a philosophy textbook. In these traditions, religion and philosophy are not seen as separate disciplines. The Buddha's teachings, known as *'Dhamma,'* tackle essential questions about the self, the human experience, and the nature of existence—topics that are also fundamental to western philosophical discourse. Additionally, the Buddha placed significant emphasis on moral practice, suggesting that intellectual exploration and ethical conduct are both core components of his teachings. The teachings of Buddha in the form of the religion 'Buddhism', spread throughout Central and Southeast Asia through China, Korea, and Japan from India. Buddhism emphasises the importance of the mind, teaching that mental distress, such as remorse, anxiety, and guilt, should be avoided to cultivate a calm and peaceful state of mind.

- **Meritorious Deeds**

The Buddha taught ten virtuous actions that we should practice to attain a happy and peaceful life, as well as to cultivate knowledge and understanding. The ten meritorious deeds are: 1. Charity 2. Morality 3. Mental culture 4. Reverence or respect 5. Service in helping others 6. Sharing merits with others 7. Rejoicing in the merits of others 8. Preaching and teaching the *Dhamma* 9. Listening to *Dhamma* 10. Straightening one's views.

- ***Dhamma***

Moral conduct benefits all beings with whom one comes into contact. Mental culture brings peace to others and inspires them to practice *Dhamma*. Reverence gives rise to harmony in society. Service improves the lives of others. Sharing merits with others demonstrates a concern for their well-being. Rejoicing the merits of others motivates them to perform more good deeds.

Teaching and listening to the *Dhamma* are key to happiness for both the teacher and the listener. Correcting one's views allows a person to show others the beauty of the *Dhamma*.

- **Middle Path**

The Buddha instructed to avoid living life in either of the two extremes. The first is a life devoted to pleasures and desires—this lifestyle is degrading, sensual, vulgar, unworthy, and ultimately unproductive. The second extreme is a life of self-torture, which is painful, unworthy, and equally ineffective. Instead, the Buddha urged us to follow the Middle Path, 'which leads to insight, which leads to wisdom, which produces calm, knowledge, enlightenment, and *Nibbana*' (*Samyutta Nikaya* 56). His teachings emphasise the 'middle path' as a way to reject extremes and embrace a life of moderation.

- ***Karma***

Buddhists believe that their actions in the present will impact their happiness in the future. This principle, known as *karma*, encourages Buddhists to practice generosity, kindness, and compassion towards others. *Karma* influences a Buddhist's rebirth, as they strive to ensure their actions are right to break the cycle of *samsara* and be reborn in a higher realm. The outcome of an action (often referred to as *karma*) is determined more by the intention behind it than by the action itself.

> *'If one speaks or acts with a wicked mind, because of that, pain follows one. If one speaks or acts with a good mind, because of that, happiness follows one.'*
>
> **Pali Canon: The Dhammapada: Verses 1-2**

- ***Karuna***

Karuna is the Buddhist word for compassion. *Karuna* is a part of Buddhist's spiritual path, and they attempt to show compassion for everyone in the world who is suffering. Buddhists accept that there is suffering in the world and *Karuna* teaches that Buddhists should care for others even though they are also trying to overcome their suffering.

- ***Metta***

Metta is a state of loving kindness that involves developing pure, selfless, and unconditional love for all beings. *Metta* offers a more positive outlook on life compared to *karuna*, as it involves expressing love and kindness to others proactively, even before they require assistance. For example, giving a gift to a friend to bring them happiness reflects *metta*, whereas helping someone who has fallen demonstrates *karuna*.

- **The Five Moral Precepts**

The five moral precepts are the five principles that Buddhists follow to live ethically and morally good lives:

S. No	Precept	Ethical value of the precept
1	To refrain from taking life	Love
2	To refrain from taking what is not freely given	Generosity
3	To refrain from misuse of the senses or sexual misconduct	Contentment
4	To refrain from wrong speech	Truthfulness
5	To refrain from intoxicants that cloud the mind	Mindfulness

- **The Four Noble Truths**

The Buddha consistently sought to enlighten individuals on the key issues of suffering, its cause, its cessation, and the path to ending it. The answers to these four questions form the core of the Buddha's enlightenment, and they are known as the Four Noble Truths.

(a) **Life is full of suffering (*Duhkha*):** According to the first noble truth, all forms of existence are subject to suffering. For Buddha, it is a universal truth. All known and unknown facts and forms of life are associated with suffering.

(b) **There is a cause of this suffering: (*Dukkha-samudaya*):** Everything in this cosmos has a cause, and nothing exists and happens without a cause. Desire is all pervasive. The desire for possession, enjoyment, and a separate individual existence are some of the virulent forms of desire.

(c) **It is possible to stop suffering (*Duhkha-nirodha*):** *Nirvana* is the state of being without suffering. It is a state of supreme happiness and bliss which can be achieved.

(d) **There is a way to extinguish suffering (*Duhkha-nirodha-marga*):** The ways to destroy suffering consist of the practice of the eightfold virtues. In the practice of all these virtues, one has to avoid extremes and follow the middle path. He called it the Eightfold Path to liberation.

- ***Astangika Marga***

The eightfold path is the practical application of the four noble truths. They are also closely connected to the fourth noble truth to destroy suffering. The following are components of the eightfold path of Buddhism:

1. Right View (*Samyak-dristi*)
2. Right Aspirations (*Samyka-sankalpa*)
3. Right Speech (*Samyak-vac*)
4. Right Conduct (*Samyak-karma*)
5. Right Livelihood (*Samyag ajiva*)
6. Right Effort (*Samyak vyayama*)
7. Right Awareness (*Samyak smrti*)
8. Right Concentration (*Samyak samadhi*)

9.3 Jainism

Jainism is an ancient Indian religion known for its profound teachings on nonviolence, truth, and asceticism. Rooted in the belief that every living being possesses a soul and deserves respect, Jainism advocates for a life of compassion and ethical responsibility. In a world often marked by conflict and materialism, Jain teachings offer a refreshing perspective on how to navigate our relationships with others and the environment.

- **The Three Jewels (*Triratna*)**

    1. **Right Faith (*Samyag Darsana*):** This involves cultivating a genuine belief in the teachings of Jainism and recognising the inherent worth of all living beings. It encourages practitioners to develop a compassionate worldview.
    2. **Right Knowledge (*Samyag Jnana*):** This emphasises the importance of understanding the nature of reality, the self, and the principles of karma and rebirth. Gaining knowledge helps individuals make informed ethical choices.
    3. **Right Conduct (*Samyag Caritra*):** This refers to living by Jain ethics, particularly through the observance of nonviolence and truthfulness in daily life. It serves as a practical guide for ethical behaviour, fostering harmony in both personal and societal interactions.

- **The Five Great Vows (*Pancha Mahavratas*)**

In Jainism, moral conduct is primarily defined by the observance of the ***Pancha Mahavratas***, or Five Great Vows, which guide practitioners toward ethical living. These vows serve as essential components of right conduct and provide a framework for harmonious existence.

1. ***Ahimsa***: The principle of nonviolence entails refraining from causing harm to any living being, whether mobile (*trasa*) or immobile (*sthavara*). Jainism underscores the inherent equality of all life; thus, taking a life is considered a violent act. This vow extends beyond physical harm to include emotional and verbal injuries, such as intentional insults. While it is acknowledged that complete nonviolence may be challenging for householders, they

are encouraged to fulfill their worldly duties while minimising harm. Notably, the killing of animals for food is strictly forbidden.

2. ***Satyam***: This vow emphasises the commitment to truthfulness, which involves speaking only what is true, beneficial, and pleasant. Practitioners are encouraged to uphold the truth even in dire situations. However, if revealing the truth could cause unnecessary harm to others, it may be justifiable to withhold it for their well-being.
3. ***Asteyam***: The vow of non-stealing encompasses various forms of theft, including taking others' property, inciting others to steal, accepting stolen goods, or adhering to a 'finder's keepers' mentality. Practicing *asteyam* means respecting the rights of others and refraining from any form of dishonesty.
4. ***Brahmacharya***: This principle calls for the abstention from sensual pleasures and casual relationships. It promotes respect between genders, urging individuals to avoid any intentions that objectify others. Practicing brahmacharya fosters healthy and respectful interactions.
5. ***Aparigraha***: This vow advocates for the renunciation of greed and the avoidance of excessive attachment to material possessions. While financial stability is necessary for a decent life, the mindless accumulation of wealth can lead to suffering and dissatisfaction. Instead, practitioners are encouraged to cultivate contentment and live with a sense of purpose rather than attachment.

- **Other Ethical Values of Jainism**

***Anukampa* (Compassion):** *Anukampa*, or compassion, is a fundamental tenet of Jaina ethics. This principle highlights the importance of fostering empathy, kindness, and understanding toward all forms of life. Compassion transcends mere sympathy; it involves actively working to alleviate the suffering of others through selfless deeds. Jain teachings encourage individuals to be mindful of the feelings and needs of others, promoting acts of kindness, generosity, and support. *Anukampa* serves as a foundation for nurturing harmonious relationships, fostering social cohesion, and contributing to the well-being of all living beings.

***Anuvrata* of Limited Possession (*Aparigraha Anuvrata*):** The vow of limited possession inspires Jains to lessen their attachment to material goods and adopt a lifestyle characterised by simplicity and modesty. This practice cultivates a sense of contentment and encourages individuals to detach from worldly desires.

***Anuvrata* of Limiting Consumption (*Parigraha Parimana Anuvrata*):** This vow focuses on moderating consumption to include only what is essential. It urges individuals to avoid excess and embrace moderation in various aspects of life, such as food, clothing, and other personal needs.

9.4 Sikhism

Sikhism has evolved its philosophy, drawing on Hindu thought but offering creative interpretations and new concepts. As in the case of Hinduism, Sikh philosophy cannot be completely segregated from religious philosophy. Sikhism is idealistic because it starts with the inquiry of the nature of the ultimate reality i.e., *Ik*, and this inquiry is spiritual in nature. Sikhism believes that there is one God i.e. *Ek Onkar* (*'Ek'* is One and *'Onkar'* is God). Everyone's God is the same, regardless of their religion. Before the soul takes human form, it undergoes cycles of birth and death.

To unite with God, our lives should be lived with exemplary conduct. Sikhs are encouraged to continually remember God, live a moral and honest life, and maintain a balance between their worldly and spiritual duties. The true path to salvation and union with God does not require celibacy or renunciation, but rather living a householder's life, earning an honest living, and avoiding worldly temptations and sins. Sikhism rejects blind rituals such as fasting, pilgrimage, superstitions, and idol worship. It teaches that all people are created equal by God, regardless of their color, religion, or gender.

- **Ethical Principles**

Sikhism is fundamentally an ethical religion centered on three core principles:

1. **Work, worship, and charity** (*kirt karo*, *nam japo*, and *vand chako*) should guide one's life.
2. **God embodies all attributes, values, and virtues**, serving as the standard for moral values and ethical living.
3. **Self-reliance is the primary barrier to realising God**, often manifesting as lust, anger, greed, materialism, and pride. Guru Nanak emphasised that sweetness and humility are the essence of all virtues.

- **The Sikh Householder**

Guru Nanak completely rejected the *varnashrama dharma* system. He proposed that there is only one *varna*: humanity, encompassing both men and women. He emphasised the householder stage of life as the sole *ashrama* and identified one *dharma*, which is the worship of God and the service of humanity, applicable to everyone. He criticised renunciants, wandering ascetics, yogis, learned men, and celibates, arguing that they were destined to continue in the cycle of transmigration. In contrast, he praised the devoted householder as a necessity, affirming that the householder's life (*grihastha*) is divinely ordained and then only one can do *seva* after satisfying their basic needs. He believed it promotes social unity and coherence and envisioned it as a space where men and women, husbands and wives, have equal status. He says a Sikh Householder should pursue God-realisation while living as a householder, as 'the householder who generously gives to charity is as pure as the waters of the Ganges.'

- **Principle of 'Just War'**

The tenth guru, Gobind Singh, embraced the concept of a just war, stating, 'When all attempts to restore peace fails and words are ineffective, the flash of steel is lawful, and it is right to draw the sword.' However, he also reminded his followers that a Sikh should never be the first to draw the sword.

- ***Langars***

Sikh *langars* are places of serving free, vegetarian food to anyone in a Sikh temple, or gurdwara, regardless of their faith, gender, age, or status. *'Langar'* means 'eating together without discrimination', or 'free kitchen', and that is a place where anyone may come to be fed.

9.5 Tirukkural

The Tirukkural is a profound work of Tamil literature that addresses the fundamental aspects of life through its exploration of ethics, politics, love, and spirituality. Also known as 'Tamil Veda' or 'The Divine Book', it is widely acknowledged for its universality and secular nature. It is divided into three sections:

- ***Aram* (Virtue),**
- ***Porul* (Wealth), and**
- ***Inbam* (Love)**

As a comprehensive ethical guide, the Tirukkural prioritises key moral principles. Written on the ideas of *ahimsa*, it emphasises non-violence and righteousness as virtues for an individual. In addition, it highlights virtues such as truthfulness, self-restraint, gratitude, hospitality, kindness, goodness of spouse, duty, giving, and so forth, besides covering a wide range of social and political virtues. The Tirukkural covers a wide range of topics, including the roles of kings and ministers, taxes, justice, forts, war, the greatness of the army and soldiers' honour, the death sentence for the wicked, agriculture, education, and the avoidance of alcohol and intoxicants. It also addresses themes like friendship, love, sexual unions, and domestic life. The text effectively challenges the misconceptions prevalent during the *Sangam* era and reshapes the cultural values of society at the time. The values emphasised in the Tirukkural include:

The Concept of Virtue (*Aram*)

- **Moral Integrity:** The Tirukkural emphasises the importance of leading a life rooted in moral integrity. It advocates for honesty, humility, and the fulfillment of one's duties without attachment to the rewards. The text suggests that true virtue lies in the intent behind actions rather than the actions themselves.

Nayanotu Nandri Purindha Payanudaiyaar
Panpupaa Raattum Ulaku **(Kural 994)**

This couplet emphasises the virtue of wise and grateful giving. It suggests that the world applauds the conduct of those who help with impartiality and generosity.

- **Non-Violence (*Ahimsa*):** One of the central ethical ideas in the Tirukkural is non-violence. Thiruvalluvar highlights the significance of not causing harm to others, either through actions or words. Non-violence is not just physical but also mental and verbal, promoting kindness and compassion in all interactions.

Innaasey Thaarai Oruththal Avarnaana
Nannayanj Cheydhu Vital **(Kural 314)**

This couplet highlights a profound moral teaching about responding to harm or wrongdoing. It advises that the best way to deal with someone who has wronged you is not through retaliation or revenge, but rather by doing good in return. The poet Thiruvalluvar advocates for non-violence, forgiveness, and the idea of overcoming evil with good.

- **Righteousness (*Dharma*):** Righteousness, or *Dharma*, is presented as a guiding principle for ethical living. The Tirukkural advises adherence to moral laws and ethical duties, emphasising that righteousness should govern all aspects of life, from personal behaviour to societal responsibilities.

Azhukkaaru Avaavekuli Innaachchol Naankum
Izhukkaa Iyandradhu Aram **(Kural 35)**

This Kural emphasises that perseverance and steadfastness are integral to practising righteousness. It suggests that overcoming obstacles with determination is a key aspect of leading a virtuous life and fulfilling one's moral duties.

- **Self-Control:** The text places great importance on self-control, especially in managing one's desires, anger, and speech. Self-control is seen as essential for maintaining ethical behaviour and avoiding actions that lead to harm or moral corruption.

Atakkam Amararul Uykkum Atangaamai
Aarirul Uyththu Vitum **(Kural 121)**

This Kural teaches that self-control is a critical virtue that not only leads to personal and spiritual upliftment but also helps avoid the pitfalls of moral and ethical decay. It encourages individuals to cultivate self-restraint to achieve a higher, more enlightened state of existence.

- **Duty and Responsibility:** Thiruvalluvar underscores the significance of fulfilling one's duties responsibly, whether as a ruler, a householder, or a member of society. The concept of duty is closely linked to social ethics, where individuals are expected to contribute to the well-being of others and the community at large.

Kaimmaaru Ventaa Katappaatu Maarimaattu
EnAatrung Kollo Ulaku **(Kural 211)**

Thiruvalluvar draws an analogy with the natural world, which provides abundant resources (like sunlight, rain, and air) without expecting anything back from the beings that benefit from them. Similarly, the highest form of charity or good deed is one that is done without any thought of personal gain or reciprocation, as a duty. It calls for a selfless approach to helping others, where the act of giving is its reward, reflecting the ideal of true generosity and virtue.

Social Ethics

- **Justice and Fairness:** The Tirukkural advocates for justice and fairness in all dealings. It encourages rulers and leaders to be just and impartial, ensuring that their decisions benefit the greater good rather than serving personal interests.

  Orndhukan Notaadhu Iraipurindhu Yaarmaattum
  Therndhusey Vaqdhe Murai **(Kural 541)**

  This Kural advises that a just ruler should conduct thorough investigations impartially, uphold objectivity, refer to legal statutes, and deliver a fair judgment.
- **Charity and Benevolence:** The text emphasises the ethical duty of helping others, particularly those in need. Charity and benevolence are considered noble acts that not only benefit the recipients but also elevate the giver morally. Thiruvalluvar highlights that true charity is done without expectation of return.

  Variyaarkkondru Eevadhe Eekaimar Rellaam
  Kuriyedhirppai Neera Thutaiththu **(Kural 221)**

  This couplet focuses on the principle of effective giving or charity. The verse points out that charity should not be random or superficial but should aim at truly resolving the problem or difficulty faced by the person in need.
- **Community and Social Responsibility**: Thiruvalluvar places a strong emphasis on the importance of contributing positively to society. He suggests that individuals have a responsibility to their communities and that their actions should aim to promote social harmony and welfare.

  Kaimmaaru Ventaa Katappaatu Maarimaattu
  EnAatrung Kollo Ulaku **(Kural 211)**

  This reminds us that one must take up social responsibilities and act without any expectation of reciprocity.

Personal Ethics

- **Truthfulness:** Truth is one of the highest ethical values in the Tirukkural. It advocates that speaking the truth is foundational for both personal and societal well-being. However,

Thiruvalluvar adds nuance by stressing that truth must be spoken in ways that do not harm others. This balance between honesty and kindness highlights the idea that truth should be used to uplift, not hurt.

Vaaimai Enappatuvadhu Yaadhenin Yaadhondrum
Theemai Ilaadha Solal **(Kural 291)**

In this couplet, Thiruvalluvar defines truthfulness (*Vaaimai*) as more than just stating facts. It goes beyond factual accuracy to encompass speaking in a way that does not cause harm or contain any element of malice or evil.

- **Contentment:** The text advises cultivating contentment to maintain ethical integrity. Contentment helps in overcoming greed and envy, which are seen as obstacles to virtuous living.

Avaaillaark Killaakun Thunpam Aqdhuntel
Thavaaadhu Menmel Varum **(Kural 368)**

This couplet explains that contentment is the source of the highest form of joy. True happiness comes not from wealth or external possessions but from being satisfied with what one has. Contentment brings inner peace, making it the ultimate form of wealth.

- **Forgiveness:** The Tirukkural encourages forgiveness as an ethical response to wrongdoing. Thiruvalluvar suggests that forgiveness is a powerful virtue that can resolve conflicts and foster peace, both within oneself and in society.

Poruththal Irappinai Endrum Adhanai
Maraththal Adhaninum Nandru **(Kural 152)**

In this couplet, Thiruvalluvar emphasises the virtue of forbearance and forgiveness. He states that the ability to endure wrongs done to you (patience and tolerance) is a commendable quality. However, the greater virtue lies in completely forgetting the injury or harm, as it leads to true peace of mind and reconciliation.

Ethics in Governance

- **Just Leadership:** Thiruvalluvar discusses the ethical responsibilities of rulers and leaders. He stresses that a just ruler should govern with fairness, wisdom, and a commitment to the welfare of the people. Ethical leadership is marked by a balance of power and compassion.

Anjaamai Eekai Arivookkam Innaankum
Enjaamai Vendhark Kiyalpu **(Kural 382)**

In this couplet, Thiruvallar portrays a wise, fearless, generous, and energetic ruler as the ideal, highlighting how these virtues are crucial for leadership and governance.

- **Moral Governance:** The Tirukkural advocates for governance that is rooted in ethical principles, suggesting that rulers should prioritise justice, protect the vulnerable, and ensure the prosperity of the state through virtuous means.

Iyatralum Eettalung Kaaththalum Kaaththa
Vakuththalum Valla Tharasu **(Kural 385)**

Thiruvalluvar emphasises that a ruler's governance should be balanced and fair, encompassing four main actions:

- *Iyatral* (To acquire): A ruler should ensure the proper acquisition of wealth and resources for the state.
- *Eettal* (To give): The wealth should be shared with the people through acts of generosity, focusing on welfare and public good.
- *Kaaththal* (To protect): The ruler must protect the wealth and resources of the state from misuse or external threats.
- *Vakuththal* (To distribute justly): The wealth should be distributed in a fair and just manner, ensuring that everyone receives what is due.

The Tirukkural presents a comprehensive ethical framework that addresses both personal and social morality. Thiruvalluvar's teachings are timeless, offering guidance on how to live a virtuous life that contributes to personal fulfillment and the greater good of society. The text's emphasis on virtues such as truthfulness, non-violence, justice, and compassion reflects a universal moral philosophy that transcends cultural and temporal boundaries. Through its exploration of ethical conduct, the Tirukkural continues to inspire individuals to pursue righteousness in all aspects of life.

9.6 Kautilya on Ethics

Kautilya was one of the greatest ministers in the court of Chandragupta Maurya during 317-293 BCE. In his work *Arthashastra*, he shares his perspectives on the state, war, social structures, diplomacy, ethics, politics, and statecraft. Kautilya was known for his sharp opinion on each of the four-dimension frameworks of: war and peace, human rights, international economic justice, and world order. The *Arthashastra* is considered rooted in political realism, where the state is of utmost importance, and the king is obligated to fulfil his duties to safeguard it.

Kautilya emphasised that *dharma* and the state are interdependent, and achievable through the right means and outcomes. To some, Kautilya may appear amoral due to his unwavering focus on realism. As a consequentialist—one who believes that the ends justify the means—some of his recommendations may seem unethical, particularly to those who prioritise means over outcomes. However, Kautilya was, in many ways, a progressive thinker, aiming to create a better society. He did not eschew *dharma*:

'Sukhasya Mulam Dharmah
Dharmasya Mulam Arthah'

Instead, he believed that happiness stemmed from dharmic behaviour and that *dharma* could thrive only in a prosperous society. With a strong moral foundation, he proposed policies to promote prosperity, without constantly resorting to moral platitudes on every page.

- **Kautilya's Concept of *Rajrishi***

The concept of *Rajrishi* envisioned by Kautilya is crucial for an ideal king and closely resembles Plato's idea of the 'Philosopher King.' In this concept, Kautilya identifies several key principles of good governance, which include:

- ➢ An ideal king must integrate his identity with his duties.
- ➢ An effective administrator must provide proper guidance.
- ➢ A wise king should avoid extremes while staying focused on the goal.
- ➢ The king and public servants should receive fixed salaries and allowances.
- ➢ The primary responsibility of the king and his servants is to maintain law and order. Losses from theft or corruption should be deducted from their salaries.
- ➢ The king must take preventive and punitive actions against corrupt officials.
- ➢ The king must also ensure the replacement of ministers with competent individuals.
- ➢ Both the king and ministers must lead a disciplined life and adhere to a code of conduct.
- ➢ Kautilya emphasises the careful selection of *Amatyas* (high-ranking officials), who should be chosen based on merit.
- ➢ Administrative qualities, such as consistency in practice, competent ministers, and qualities of leadership, intelligence, moral integrity, and physical strength, should be emulated.

Kautilya asserts that the true source of a king's strength lies in the prosperity and loyalty of his subjects. He states that a king who is not rooted among his people is easy to overthrow. However, a just king, even when faced with calamity, will receive support from his subjects. In contrast, a king without the support of his people will be abandoned when attacked.

In this light, let us consider Kautilya's famous injunction, '*Yatha Raja Tatha Praja*.' This reflects the idea that 'As the king, so are the people.' The king's happiness lies in the happiness of his subjects, and his welfare is tied to their well-being. He should not regard only what pleases him as good but rather consider beneficial whatever brings happiness to his people.

Other Ideologies Propagated By Chanakya

- **Merit and virtues:**

'A man is great by deeds, not by birth.'

It emphasises that true greatness is earned through one's deeds, achievements, and character, rather than simply inheriting status or privilege. This concept inspires individuals to pursue excellence and make meaningful contributions to society, irrespective of their background or social status. It emphasises that true greatness is defined by one's merit and actions.

- **Mindfulness:** Chanakya advises that before beginning any task, you should ask yourself three crucial questions:
  Why am I doing it: This question encourages you to reflect on the purpose and motivation behind your actions.
  What might the results be: This prompts you to think about the potential outcomes and consequences of your actions.
  Will I be successful: This question urges you to evaluate your abilities and the likelihood of success.
  By considering these questions carefully, you promote thoughtful decision-making and improve the chances of achieving positive results.
- **Detached Efforts:**

  > **'Once you start working on something, don't be afraid of failure, and don't abandon it. People who work sincerely are the happiest.'**

  It highlights the significance of persistence and dedication in one's work. Chanakya asserts that once a task is begun, one should not fear failure or give up prematurely. He believes that true happiness comes to those who work diligently and sincerely. This quote encourages individuals to adopt a resilient mindset, embrace challenges, and remain committed to their goals, even in the face of obstacles. It suggests that genuine fulfillment and satisfaction are achieved through sincere effort and perseverance in the pursuit of one's objectives.
- **Amenable to correction:**

  > **'Learn from the mistakes of others; you cannot live long enough to make them all yourselves.'**

  Chanakya advises that it is unrealistic to live long enough to make every mistake on our own, so we should learn from the mistakes of others. By observing and understanding their errors, we can gain valuable wisdom without having to face the negative consequences ourselves. This encourages individuals to be observant and open to the lessons others' experiences offer, helping us make wiser decisions and avoid repeating the same mistakes.
- **Emotional Intelligence:**

  > **'Even if a snake is not poisonous, it should pretend to be venomous.'**

  It emphasises the value of projecting strength and deterrence, even when one may not have inherent power or advantage. This concept suggests that cultivating an image of strength and resilience can be beneficial, regardless of actual abilities. It serves as a reminder to project confidence and give the impression of power, thereby discouraging potential adversaries or threats.

- **Social Intelligence:**

  'A person should not be too honest. Straight trees are cut first and honest people are victimised first.'

  The saying implies that excessive honesty can make a person more susceptible to harm, likening honest individuals to straight trees that are often the first targets. While it acknowledges the challenges that honest people may face, it does not suggest that dishonesty is the answer. Rather, it serves as a reminder to exercise caution and tact in certain situations, while still maintaining one's values and integrity.

- **Attack as a Defense:**

  'As soon as the fear approaches, attack and destroy it.'

  Chanakya advises that when fear arises, one should immediately take action to confront and overcome it. Rather than letting fear control you or immobilise you, it is better to face it directly and conquer it. This quote encourages individuals to be proactive in addressing their fears, showing courage and determination when faced with challenges. By acting quickly and decisively, one can overcome fear and achieve personal growth and success.

Relevance of Chanakya's Teaching in Contemporary Times

- **Enduring Relevance of Education:** Chanakya emphasised the importance of education as a cornerstone for success. He advocated for a well-rounded education covering various fields, including economics and politics. Today, quality education remains essential for personal and professional development.
- **Human Nature in Leadership and Communication:** Chanakya's insights into human nature are crucial for effective leadership and communication. He highlighted the need to understand individuals' strengths and weaknesses. This knowledge is still vital for successful leaders today, who must grasp the motivations behind people's behaviours.
- **Strategic Thinking and Diplomacy:** Chanakya's teachings on strategic thinking and diplomacy are highly relevant in contemporary settings. He provided guidance on maintaining power and resolving conflicts through diplomacy. These principles apply to modern negotiations and power dynamics in business and politics.
- **Ethics and Morality in Leadership and Governance:** Chanakya stressed the necessity of ethics and morality in leadership. He believed that leaders must uphold moral values to gain public trust. This principle is essential in today's governance and corporate leadership, where ethical practices build credibility.
- **Role of Financial Stability and Wealth Management:** He highlighted the importance of financial stability for effective governance. A ruler needs a strong financial foundation to ensure state stability. This principle is also applicable to personal finance, where managing wealth is crucial for individual security.

- **Effective Leadership and Social Welfare:** Chanakya recognised the need for balancing economic growth with social justice. His ideas about good governance emphasised the welfare of the people. Implementing these principles today can enhance governance and ensure the well-being of society.

9.7 Basavanna

Basava (1131–1167), also called Basaveshwara and Basavanna, a prime leader of the '*Virashaiva* Movement', was an Indian philosopher, poet, *Lingayat* social reformer and statesman who attempted to create a casteless society and fought against caste and religious discrimination. He advocated for social equality, along with equality across caste, class, occupation, religion, and gender—principles that remain central to modern social philosophy. The primary aim of the *Vachana* movement, spearheaded by Basaveshwara in the 12th century, was the welfare of all. His *Vachanas* served as a powerful catalyst for social transformation.

1. **Philosophy propounded by Basavanna:** Basavanna's spiritual discipline was based on the principles of *Arivu* (true knowledge), *Achara* (right conduct), and *Anubhava* (divine experience) and it brought a social, religious, and economic revolution in the 12th century. This path emphasises a holistic approach known as *Lingangayoga* (union with the divine), which harmoniously integrates *bhakti* (devotion), *jnana* (knowledge), and *kriye* (action). Basaveshwara also introduced two significant socio-economic principles, one of which is:
   - ***Kayaka* (Divine Work):** Every individual in society is encouraged to choose a profession aligned with their interests and perform it with utmost sincerity and dedication. Thus, insisting on the honest discharge of occupational responsibilities.
   - ***Dasoha* (Equal distribution)**: There must be an equal income for equal work. The worker (*Kayakajeevi*) should sustain their daily life through their hard-earned income but must refrain from accumulating wealth or property for the future. He must utilise the surplus money for society and the poor.

   He preferred a peaceful method of persuasion, a non-violent method to achieve his goal of establishing a society based on social equality. He used the *Vachanas* to point out the deficiencies of the society and wanted to correct them. Through his constructive approach, he defined the good life as a sure way to God.
2. **Ethical Essence in *Vachanas*:**

   'Do not say "who is he," "who is he" and "who is he"?
   Say that he is ours, he is ours, and he is ours,'

   Interpretation: This teaches us to see every individual as part of one family, as children of God. We are called to embrace all human beings as our brothers and sisters, without discrimination or exclusion.

The *Vachanas* advocate for economic and social equality. They emphasise treating all individuals as equals, regardless of their social or economic status. Basavanna urged his followers to renounce attachment to wealth and to love and serve the poor. He asserted that poverty is not a sin, and a poor person is in no way inferior to others.

'I shall sheathe the Vedas, fetter the Shastras,
Put Tarka in tongs, deface the Agamas.
Look father, most generous Kudalasangamadeva,
I am a son of Madar Chennayy's family.'

Interpretation: Basavanna rejects the notion of occupations being tied to caste or hierarchy. He emphasises individual choice over hereditary roles, condemning caste-based divisions as unjust and fraudulent. His principle of *Kayakave Kailasa*—"Work is Worship"—promotes dignity and respect for all forms of labour.

3. **Gender equality:** Basaveshwara is revered as a champion of gender equality. In an era when women were often regarded as *'maya'* or embodiments of illusion, and unfairly labeled as the root of all evil, he challenged these stigmatising beliefs and advocated for a more equitable perspective on women's role in society. Basaveshwara with his followers protested against the injustice and declared that women should be equal to men. She should have the right to a good education, the right to express themselves freely, the right to participate in public discussions, and above all the right to take up spiritual practices. He encouraged women to pursue various occupations and to earn for their own families as men did. To him, man and woman were equal in the field of spiritual *sadhana*, and were equally beloved of God.
4. ***Anubhava Mantapa*—The First Parliament of the World:** In the 12th century, Basavanna's visionary ideas sparked a significant societal transformation. He established a forum known as *Anubhava Mantapa*, where individuals from all social backgrounds could openly share and discuss their real-life experiences. These discussions were documented in literary form, preserving their essence for posterity. The *Anubhava Mantapa* stood out not only for fostering dialogue but also for encouraging participants to actively implement these teachings in their daily lives. Remarkably, both men and women took part in these discussions, promoting inclusivity and collective deliberation. Their ideas revealed that women are also equal or even greater than men. Hence the principles and philosophy of *Shivasharanas* on the emancipation of women is much to be appreciated and such ideas are relevant for the present society.

9.7.1 Applied Ethics

Ethics serves both theoretical and practical purposes. Theoretically, it establishes the foundational principles that guide moral judgements. Practically, it focuses on achieving specific goals and determining the appropriate means to attain them. Through the frameworks of meta ethics and normative ethics, applied ethics seeks to address and resolve contentious real-world issues. It delves into specific controversial topics such as suicide, euthanasia, abortion, violence, and terrorism, which will be explored in detail in the chapters ahead.

SUMMARY

- Ethics is a branch of philosophy studying moral principles and how they could help improve the quality of life for an individual or a community. It is a system for distinguishing right from wrong, acting as a moral compass to guide decision-making. Ethics differ from morality, with the former being a structured, logical system of principles and the latter being personal or societal notions of right and wrong.
- There are four types of ethics namely, Meta Ethics, Normative Ethics, Descriptive Ethics, and Applied Ethics.
- Aristotle's concept of moderation between extremes in virtue ethics or the Golden Mean and Natural Law which is an ethical theory based on inherent human values guiding behaviour.
- There are four types of major schools of thought when it comes to learning about ethics, morality, and actions namely, Virtue Ethics, Utilitarianism, Social Contract Theory, and Deontology.
- Discussions of Kant, Hume, and Kohlberg's theories and frameworks describing stages of moral reasoning.
- Following Gandhian Ethics, the principles of nonviolence (*Ahimsa*), truth (*Satya*), Doctrine of Trusteeship, and social justice.
- Understanding the various ways in which religions like Hinduism, Buddhism, Jainism, and Sikhism have influenced Indian ethics and philosophy over the centuries and using these ethical frameworks, individuals can navigate dilemmas, make value-based decisions, and promote personal and societal integrity.

PREVIOUS YEARS' QUESTIONS

1. "The concept of Just and Unjust is contextual. What was just a year back, may turn out to be unjust in today's context. Changing context should be constantly under scrutiny to prevent miscarriage of justice." Examine the above statement with suitable examples. *UPSC CSE Mains 2024*
2. "In law, a man is guilty when he violates the rights of others. In ethics, he is guilty if he only thinks of doing so." —Immanuel Kant. Analyse *UPSC CSE Mains 2024*
3. "Ethics encompasses several key dimensions that are crucial in guiding individuals and organisations towards morally responsible behaviour." Explain the key dimensions of ethics that influence human actions. Discuss how these dimensions shape ethical decision-making in the professional context. *UPSC CSE Mains 2024*

4. What were the major teachings of Guru Nanak? Explain their relevance in the contemporary world. *UPSC CSE Mains 2023*
5. "The simplest acts of kindness are by far more powerful than a thousand heads bowing in prayer." —Mahatma Gandhi. Analyse *UPSC CSE Mains 2023*
6. "Ethics is knowing the difference between what you have the right to do and what is right to do." —Potter Stewart *UPSC CSE Mains 2022*
7. "The best way to find yourself is to lose yourself in the service of others." Mahatma Gandhi Analyse *UPSC CSE Mains 2020*
8. What teachings of Buddha are most relevant today and why? Discuss. *UPSC CSE Mains 2020*
9. "A man is but a product of his thoughts. What he thinks he becomes." —M. K. Gandhi. Analyse *UPSC CSE Mains 2019*
10. "Falsehood takes the place of truth when it results in unblemished common good." —Tirukkural. Analyse *UPSC CSE Mains 2018*
11. "Anger and intolerance are the enemies of correct understanding." —Mahatma Gandhi. Analyse *UPSC CSE Mains 2018*
12. About morality of actions, one view is that means are of paramount importance and the other view is that the ends justify the means. Which view do you think is more appropriate? Justify your answer. *UPSC CSE Mains 2018*
13. Analyse John Rawls' concept of social justice in the Indian context. *UPSC CSE Mains 2016*
14. Discuss Mahatma Gandhi's concept of Seven sins. *UPSC CSE Mains 2016*
15. "Human beings should always be treated as 'ends' in themselves and never as merely 'means'." Explain the meaning and significance of this statement, giving its implications in the modern techno-economic society. *UPSC CSE Mains 2014*
16. All human beings aspire for happiness. Do you agree? What does happiness mean to you? Explain with examples. *UPSC CSE Mains 2014*
17. The good of an individual is contained in the good of all." What do you understand by this statement? How can this principle be implemented in public life? *UPSC CSE Mains 2013*
18. "There is enough on this earth for everyone's need but for no one's greed." —Mahatma Gandhi. Analyse *UPSC CSE Mains 2013*
19. Some people feel that values keep changing with time and situation, while others strongly believe that there are certain universal and eternal human values. Give your perception in this regard with due justification. *UPSC CSE Mains 2013*

Applied Ethics

6

1. INTRODUCTION

LEARNING OBJECTIVES

1. Understanding applied ethics: Its significance and relevance as a branch of philosophy
2. Exploring key areas: Gaining insights into diverse domains like bioethics, media ethics, environmental ethics, Professional Ethics, Social Ethics, etc.
3. Framework to navigate through ethical dilemmas

Applied ethics is a philosophical quest into the process of making ethical judgements in many of the specialised provinces and situations that humans encounter. The uniqueness, complexity, novelty, and dilemmas associated with various aspects of social life could be better understood with the help of applied ethics.

The intent of such an enquiry is to understand and develop theoretical frameworks and guidelines that can form the foundation of ethical judgements in such domains of human enterprises. Ethical judgement, at the core of it, concerns with demarcating what constitutes right or morally permissible.

Essentially, applied ethics is an attempt to determine the interests that should be harboured for a harmonious societal order and the behaviours that should be exhibited to pursue the interests. It is, therefore, a question of value judgement where some interest, acts, and behaviours are accorded precedence over the other.

2. SIGNIFICANCE AND RELEVANCE

Applied ethics is a branch of philosophy which focuses on the application of moral rules, principles, or concepts to address persistent problems of the society, like euthanasia, abortion, privacy, and many others. The term 'applied ethics' gained prominence during the 1970s, when philosophers and academicians started using ethical theories and moral philosophy to address the social issues.

The interaction of philosophy with the professionals and field experts led to the generation of interest in professional ethics and related issues, leading to the development of fields such as medical ethics and business ethics. The intellectual stimulus for applied ethics is derived from moral philosophy with its objective to provide solutions for emerging moral problems in society. For example, the humanity has evolved with the acknowledgement of civil rights and human rights and have constantly resisted suppression. Eminent people in the fields of law, political theory, and professionals have made constant endeavour to incorporate ethical norms into their field.

A notable example is Justice V. R. Krishna Iyer, who pioneered the legal-aid movement in the country. There is a wide range of topics that falls into the subject matter of Applied Ethics.

3. AREAS OF APPLIED ETHICS

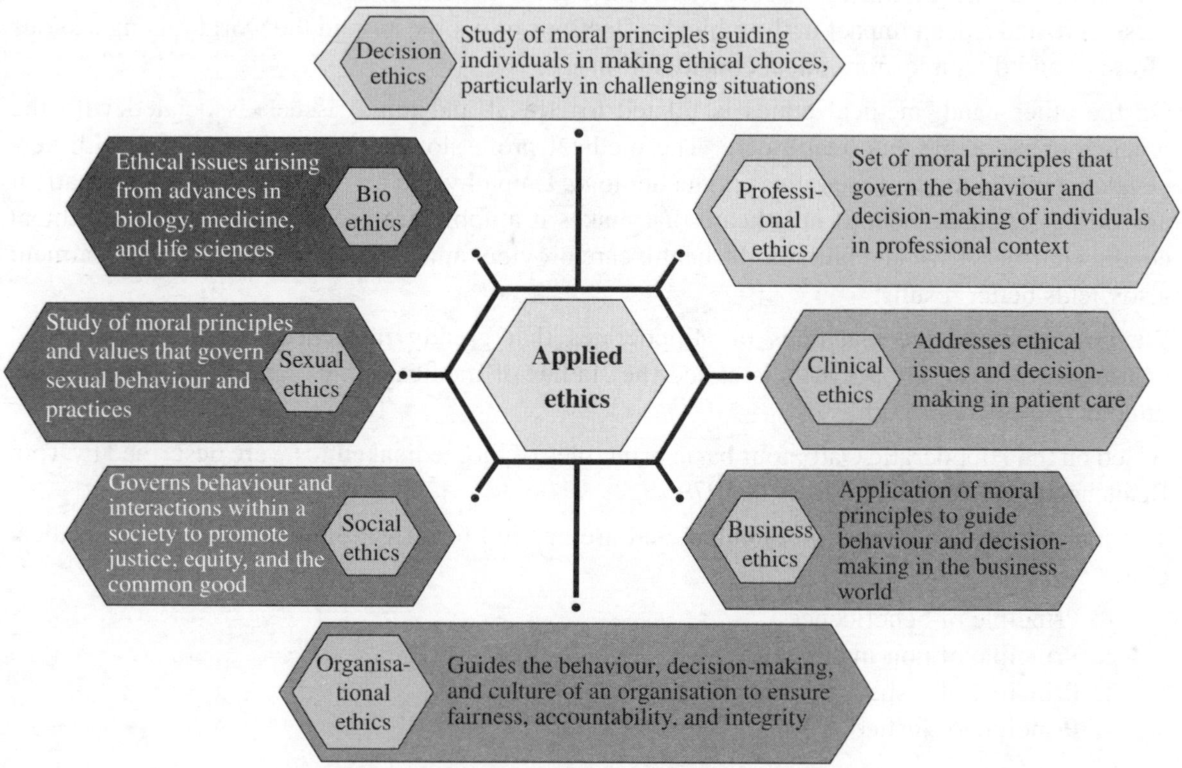

Fig. 6.1 Subsets of applied ethics

Applied ethics deals with the actions and their moral backing in the areas of public and private life. It discusses issues such as abortion, protection of human and animal subjects in clinical trial, affirmative action, privacy, moral issues in the workplace, right to information, **intergenerational**

and intragenerational[1] parity, intellectual property right, discrimination on any grounds, environmental sustainability, animal rights, and much more.

Dr Rajendra Prasad's *Applying Ethics: Modes, Motives and Levels of Commitment* discusses the significance of applying ethical principles, the motivation their application requires, as well as the levels of commitment involved in their application.

3.1 Bioethics

Bioethics is an interdisciplinary field, and various breakthrough research in the field of medicine, nursing, biomedical technology, and human sciences have framed the structure of bioethics from time to time. Developments such as, organ transplant, invention of dialysis machine, artificial ventilators, in-vitro fertilisation process, etc. have led to a sea of change in the world outlook. All these have had a deep impact in the ethical reflections of people around the world raising a series of issues and dilemmas for ethical consideration.

On the other hand, medical ethics is related to ethical and moral issues associated with the practice of medicine and health care. The medical profession is constantly engaged with new developments in modern medicine and technology. Empathy and compassion towards the patient are an important element of healthcare that makes it a noble profession. Having a good ethical conduct nurtures trust and faith for the health care provider and patient's response to the treatment also yields better results.

We now come to the teachings of Hippocrates that greatly influenced medical ethics and continues to do so. Hippocrates is called the 'father of medical ethics' and the founder of the famous 'Hippocratic Oath'.

Based on the Hippocratic Oath, four basic principles of biomedical ethics were described by Tom Beauchamp and James Childress in 1979.

The four principles are non-hierarchical and are applied to reflect ethical issues in biomedical ethics.

1. Principle of beneficence
2. Principle of non-maleficence
3. Principle of respect for autonomy
4. Principle of justice

- **Abortion**

Abortion means the 'termination of pregnancy', especially that of a human foetus. Here, the concern is about those cases where a conscious decision is taken to undergo abortion. In bioethics,

[1]**Intergenerational Parity** refers to fairness and equality between different generations.
Intragenerational Parity focuses on fairness and equality among individuals and groups within the same generation

the debate revolves around the issue of asserting a value of life to the foetus and the reproductive and bodily autonomy of the women involved. An ethical proposition that surrounds this issue is to perceive life as sacred in itself.

Pro-choice arguments: Uphold abortion in favour of the woman's rights to choose for herself in line with the fundamental right guaranteed under Article 21. The emphasis is on the autonomy and personal rights of the woman.

Pro-life groups: Those who believe that abortion is inherently immoral and are against its application at any stage of pregnancy are pro-life groups. The main contesting issue is regarding the moral status of the unborn foetus, and to consider whether the unborn foetus has a right to life or not?

Abortion as a Right

1. Gender justice
2. Welfare of the child
3. Health of the mother and the child
4. Economic hardships
5. Unsafe practices

Abortion as a Social Evil

1. Right to life of foetus
2. Erosion of cultural values

Indian approach to Abortion

In September 2021, the Medical Termination of Pregnancy (Amendment) Act of 2021 came into force, extending the upper gestational limit for abortion from 20 to 24 weeks.

The Supreme Court in 2022, in its judgement, held that the decision to carry a pregnancy to term or terminate it is firmly rooted in a woman's right to her bodily autonomy, and her ability to choose her path in life. It also recognised that an unwanted pregnancy can have serious negative effects on a woman's life, such as disrupting her education, career, and mental well-being.

Ethical approach to Abortion

1. Principle of natural justice – There is need to strike a balance between the rights of women and the rights of foetus. The other social factors must be considered before arriving at the decision in such cases.
2. Non-maleficence – The negative impact of unwanted pregnancies and the mental disturbance suffered by the mother should be duly considered.
3. Respect for autonomy – The bodily autonomy and reproductive rights of the women should be respected.

4. Beneficence – To do good and for the welfare of the society, by a holistic approach to the promotion of awareness regarding birth controls will help in reducing unwanted pregnancies in the society.

The ultimate goal of ethical norms is the goodness and welfare of the society. The mean path in the case of abortion could be arrived though the recognition of women's reproductive rights and by taking reasonable measure to avoid unwanted pregnancies in the country.

- **Euthanasia**

Euthanasia comes from the Greek word, '*eu*', meaning 'good', and '*thanatos*', meaning 'death', referred to as good death. It revolves around the issues of right to die, and physician assisted suicide. In euthanasia, deliberate action is carried by a medical practitioner to bring about the death of a person which is understood as 'mercy killing'. Oxford dictionary describes euthanasia as 'a gentle and easy death especially in case of an **irrevocable**[2] and irreversible painful disease'.

Types of Euthanasia

(a) **Voluntary Euthanasia** – It is a situation where the patient is conscious and can make a rational decision to end life. In some cases, the patient may have his living will, as a form of consent to terminate life, in case of an irreversible disease. The request may be of the nature to withhold treatment.

(b) **Involuntary Euthanasia** – It is a situation where the patient has not given his or her consent and euthanasia is administered for the benefit of the patient to end the suffering.

(c) **Non-Voluntary Euthanasia** – It is a term which is used when the patient is not in a situation to convey consent about ending his life. The patient's wishes are not known and thus it is usually a caretaker or a family member who may be consulted to make the decision. When a person is in coma, or brain damaged situation or in a neonate position, his wishes are not known. These cases not really against the will of the person.

(d) **Active Euthanasia** – It is sometimes referred to as 'killing' where some steps are taken to assist in one's death, for instance, by injecting a lethal injection. The purpose is to make death painless as much as possible.

(e) **Passive Euthanasia** – It is referred to as 'letting die'. There is no action or 'negative' action undertaken consciously to let someone die, the health care professional deliberately withholds the treatment, to let the patient die through the natural course of the illness.

The central question in Biomedical ethics revolves around legalising euthanasia. There are strong arguments from both the segments of people, for or against euthanasia.

---

[2] **Irrevocable:** Not able to be changed, recovered

VERSUS

Arguments against euthanasia

01 **Sanctity of life:** Those who are against it, argue from the perspective of the 'sanctity of life' principle. For them, life is sacred per se.

02 **Ethical codes:** Upholding the codes of medical ethics; principle of beneficence and nonmaleficence. These codes are binding on doctors, to do no harm to their patient and preserve their life.

03 **Devaluation of human life:** The fear of permitting euthanasia may lead to devaluation of human life leading to stigmatising and abusing chronically ill patients.

Arguments in favour of euthanasia

01 **Right to die:** Those who believe that it should be the right of an individual to decide when to end life. They argue for the inclusion of "right to die" as an extension to "right to life".

02 **Human dignity:** The right to life with dignity is the core of the entire debate. Being alive in a vegetative state is contrary to the very essence of "life with dignity".

03 **Quality of life:** Biological existence without any quality of life is contrary to having a good life.

04 **Against medical ethics:** If the person is unable to perform the basic biological functions and the illness is untreatable, irreversible, then merely prolonging the life is outrightly unacceptable to the principles of medical ethics.

These are some strong debates from both the segments. As we have observed, such issues are conflicting and overlapping and hence leads to ethical dilemmas.

Indian Perspective

The right to life and liberty, under Article 21 of the Indian Constitution is meaningful only when it protects human dignity. The Supreme Court, in *K.S. Puttaswamy v. Union of India*, affirmed that human dignity is an integral part of Article 21. This includes the right to live with dignity, which extends to facilitating a dignified death for terminally ill patients with no hope of recovery.

While the 'right to life' does not encompass the 'right to die,' the 'right to live with dignity' does include the 'right to die with dignity.' In *P. Rathinam v. Union of India*, petitioners challenged Section 309 of the Indian Penal Code (IPC), which criminalises attempted suicide, arguing it violated Articles 14 and 21. The Court ruled that the right to life includes the right not to live a forced life, deeming Section 309 unconstitutional.

The issue of euthanasia arose directly in *Aruna Shanbaugh v. Union of India*, where the Court permitted passive euthanasia under specific conditions for patients in a persistent vegetative state, but rejected active euthanasia, aligning with its earlier stance in *Gian Kaur v. State of Punjab*. Later, in *Common Cause v. Union of India*, a Constitution Bench clarified that passive euthanasia aligns with the right to live with dignity and need not rely solely on legislative enactments.

The legal and moral questions surrounding euthanasia are complex. Balancing safeguards and discretion while limiting euthanasia to well-defined situations remains a challenge. The moral dilemma is heightened by advances in medicine, which prolong life for patients in intolerable conditions, often placing emotional and financial burdens on families and society.

- **Surrogacy**

Surrogacy is a process where a woman, called the surrogate, carries and gives birth to a child for another person or couple, called the intended parents. Surrogacy can be a complex process that involves medical, emotional, financial, and legal considerations.

The surrogate is impregnated through in-vitro fertilisation (IVF) using eggs from the intended mother or an egg donor and sperm from the intended father or a sperm donor. The surrogate is not genetically related to the child because she doesn't provide the egg. Surrogacy can be an option for people who are unable to become pregnant or carry a pregnancy, or who have a health condition that makes pregnancy dangerous.

Legal Considerations

In India, surrogacy is regulated by the Assisted Reproductive Technology (Regulation) Act, 2021 and the Surrogacy (Regulation) Act, 2021. These legislations prohibit commercial surrogacy and only allows altruistic arrangements.

Ethical Issues Involved

1. Exploitation of a surrogate mother
2. Commercialisation – There is a connection between the surrogacy industry and the trafficking of young women and girls into the country
3. Child rights and legal repercussions
4. Means and end argument – The secrecy and anonymity of surrogacy can create a negative environment that affects human relations
5. Exclusion of unmarried and homosexual couples from accessing the surrogacy option
6. Underground market – the black market associated with the sale and purchase of children
7. Emotional impact in the part of the surrogate mother and biological parents

- **Clinical Trial**

According to the World Health Organisation, clinical trials are a type of research that study new tests and treatments and evaluate their effects on human health outcomes. People volunteer to take part in clinical trials to test medical interventions, including drugs, cells and other biological products, surgical procedures, radiological procedures, devices, behavioural treatments, and preventive care.

Clinical trials are carefully designed, reviewed, and completed, and need to be approved before they can start. People of all ages can take part in clinical trials, including children. The clinical trial must adhere to,

1. **Informed consent**: A legal requirement and a core ethical principle, informed consent is a way to respect the autonomy of participants and protect them from harm.
2. **Conflicts of interest**: Conflicts of interest can influence the conduct of research at any stage.
3. **Patient engagement**: Patient advocacy groups and communities can educate themselves about their condition, the experts, and the research.
4. **Access to post-trial benefits**: It's important to consider the level and nature of care available outside the research context.
5. **Patient privacy**: Clinical trials impact human rights, including the right to privacy.
6. **Administering interventions and measurements**: The appropriateness of the facilities and settings should be assessed, especially for studies involving young children.
7. **Unethical practices**: Unethical practices can put patients at risk of harm, compromise results, and create flaws in drug development.

Risk-benefit analysis is the main responsibility of ethics committees which give final approval for implementation of any research proposal, thereby taking care of the principles of non-maleficence and beneficence.

The concept of informed consent is a formal procedure whereby a patient's consent is taken before carrying forward any treatment or surgical procedure or clinical trial. Every patient has a right to be aware of, and at the same time be a stakeholder in the entire process of his/her treatment. In the light of this, informed consent is a value-oriented concept that revolves around the principle of autonomy of the patient.

A patient's autonomy is to be valued and respected. Under no circumstances it should be compromised. The patient is free to either accept the treatment proposed by the doctor, to look for an alternative procedure, or to completely call off the treatment. He/she has a free choice and violation of it may have some legal **repercussions.**[3]

- **Animal Rights**

The animal rights are significant to understand as the world belongs to all life form equally. Sometimes it is hard to comprehend that animals also have rights. There may exists differences between humans and animals, but does that mean that we can outrightly deny them any moral consideration? There are two approaches to understanding animal rights.

1. **Not Conscious, Hence No Rights:** The opinion that lack of conscious acting as the scale of accessing rights, there is no question of animals having rights. Modern western philosopher Rene Descartes famously argued that animals are like machines. Animals are passion driven and are devoid of consciousness. It implies that animals certainly lack the ability to suffer. Peter Singer, the most prominent thinker, argues that there is no rationality in discriminating against animals just because they are different or belong to different species.

   Mahatma Gandhi believed that non-violence meant more than just not hurting animals, it also meant showing love and compassion. He spent almost 30 years developing an animal husbandry system that was both economically viable and ethical.
2. **Experimentation on Animals:** Animals have been used for experimentations and research for discoveries and testing of various drugs. The main issue in bioethics is concerning the issue of justification of using animals for testing. Those who argue in favour of this view render animals as less valuable than human beings. The enlightenment philosopher, Immanuel Kant stated that the concept of morality cannot be extended to animals. His categorical imperative only applied to rational human beings and not to animals. He was of the opinion, since animals do not have any duties, they have no moral obligations. Animals stand outside the domain of morality.

   Those who argue against animal experimentation strongly put forward their belief that animals suffer pain. The limitation is that we do not understand their language and hence we feel that they do not feel pain. Further, many of the experiments are non-essential and thus could be avoided to be tested on animals.

[3] **Repercussions:** an unpleasant effect or result of something you do

3.2 Technological Ethics

Amid many technological breakthroughs in recent years, the importance of ethics and human values has been underemphasised. Information technology has grown rapidly due to its ability to capture and store a vast amount of personal data on the cloud, and display or auction it for public consumption. Some of the common issues in information technology, as an example are:

- **Privacy**

Privacy is a fundamental right of individuals and is an essential condition for the exercise of self-determination. The ability to control personal information is an important factor in sustaining privacy. Organisations are increasingly computerising the processing of personal information. This may be without the consent or knowledge of the individuals concerned. There has been a growth in databases holding personal and other sensitive information in multiple formats of text, pictures and sound. The scale and type of data collected, and the speed of data exchange have changed with the advent of computers.

- **Inappropriate Sharing of Information**

Every organisation stores vast amount of information that can describe individual employees' personal information, attendance, health records, salary, and performance ratings. Confidential information of the company including sales and promotion plans, staffing projects, manufacturing processes, product formulas, tactical strategic plans and research development. An employee or employer who shares such information with an unauthorised party violates someone's privacy and places the fortunes of company into the hands of competitors.

Exceptions: However, sometimes individuals have to compromise some of their personal privacy in order to achieve certain social benefit. For example, AADHAAR as a store house of information of citizens is a helpful tool to identify authentic beneficiaries of government schemes. Similarly, the sharing of data from educational index with the local education authority in the area might be considered morally justified even though it might breach individual privacy.

- **Digital Divide**

The digital divide refers to the gap between those with access to digital technologies, such as the internet, and those without, shaped by factors like income, geography, education, gender, and infrastructure. This disparity **exacerbates**[4] existing inequalities, particularly in education, healthcare, and employment, depriving marginalised groups—such as rural populations, women, and the elderly—of opportunities and essential services.

In an increasingly connected world, internet access is seen as a fundamental right. The digital divide violates this right, limiting participation in democracy, access to government services, and freedom of expression. Globally, the divide between developed and developing nations

[4] **Exacerbates:** to make something worse, especially a problem

perpetuates[5] inequalities, with many countries in the Global South lacking adequate digital infrastructure.

Addressing this issue requires policies promoting universal access, affordability, and digital literacy. A broader approach that moves beyond a narrow focus on distribution is necessary to tackle the deeper social justice challenges of the information age and ensure equitable technological inclusion.

3.3 Media Ethics

Media ethics is a vast subject. From understanding the world affairs for journalistic endeavour to production of news, and to the dissemination of news involves some pressing ethical concerns. Media people or communicators have to tackle many ethical concerns at different stages of content generation. Recently, the mass media has been looked up as a highly admired profession, and thus the incorporation of ethics in the entire functioning of media professionals can further advance authenticity, trustability, transparency, and integrity. Media ethics is vital to give moral judgement about the validity of the information being shared.

- **Print Media**

The print media was considered to be one of the strongest and most reliable means of communication. However, this reliability is tested by the challenges in the modern information era. Economic prospects in the media may hinder the authenticity and truth from becoming the main driver of its functioning. Journalists were expected to write in a manner that is transparent, objective, and unbiased. They must take the consent of the persons before getting their details to be published in a story, exempting the cases of exposing corruption and fraud.

- **Electronic (Television) Media**

Beyond print media, people increasingly rely on electronic media for regional, national, and international news. With faster information dissemination and accessibility to those who cannot read or write, electronic media serves as a powerful communication tool through its audio-visual format. However, it is often criticised for its bias and content manipulation, functioning at times as propaganda for governments, corporations, and bureaucracies. This has led to growing concerns about its transparency and societal commitment.

The commercialisation of media, driven by corporate investments, has transformed journalism into a profit-centric industry. Biased or misleading information compromises individual integrity and privacy, raising ethical concerns. Media must refrain from spreading fake news or serving monetary and political interests. Upholding journalistic standards requires fact verification and credible reporting.

---

[5] **Perpetuates:** to continue for a long time

For example, in the early 21st century, Wikileaks founder Julian Assange exposed hidden information about governments and corporations, sparking debates on transparency and the right to privacy. While some viewed these revelations as ethical activism, others questioned their impact on individual privacy.

Political propaganda and paid news further erode media integrity. Politicians and businesses manipulate content to sway public opinion, especially during elections, presenting biased information as factual news. Such practices compromise media credibility and deceive audiences, undermining its ethical responsibility to society.

- **Cyber Space**

In the digital age, the surge in information has overshadowed concerns about its quality. Cyberspace, once a hub for meaningful dialogue, is now influenced by profit-driven enterprises, compromising content standards. The internet permeates daily life, facilitating everything from news and entertainment to shopping, bill payments, and communication. Its transnational nature has reshaped perceptions of space and time, enabling global solidarity movements like *#BlackLivesMatter*.

Ethical issues in the cyberspace include hacking, piracy, copyright violations, and the spread of misinformation and fake news. These practices harm individuals, communities, and institutions, while hate speech, trolling, and online bullying exploit anonymity to provoke violence and division. Ensuring net neutrality and equitable access is essential for a fair society, but freedom of speech must not be misused for unethical or corporate interests.

Content promoting violence, discrimination, or immorality, including certain online games, should be regulated. Intellectual property rights must be respected, ensuring creators are recognised and fairly compensated for their work.

Press freedom, though vital, is not absolute. When it endangers individual dignity or national security, limited censorship may be warranted. The Press Council of India (2020) emphasised accuracy, fairness, and the exclusion of paid news. Media should serve the public good, promote justice, and uplift marginalised communities, aligning with the principles of equity and social responsibility.

> **? Thought Box**
>
> In an era, where artificial intelligence and data analytics are increasingly shaping decisions, how can we ensure that the use of technology aligns with ethical principles, respects privacy, and promotes fairness, while still fostering innovation?

3.4 Environmental Ethics

Environmental ethics emerged in the 1970s with the recognition that nature holds intrinsic value and its resources are finite. As a branch of applied ethics, it evaluates the morality of actions affecting the environment, providing principles, norms, and frameworks for decision-making on environmental issues.

Today, the planet faces severe environmental crises, including habitat destruction, biodiversity loss, and pollution. Climate change is evident through rising temperatures, extreme weather, and prolonged droughts. Natural resources are depleting—forests cleared for development have turned barren, rivers are drying up, cities face water shortages, and overfishing has depleted marine life. These challenges underscore the urgent need for sustainable practices and ethical approaches to protect the environment and ensure its future.

- **Development and Environmental Damage**

Ethical issues in development and environmental degradation arise from the conflict between economic progress and the responsibility to protect natural resources and ensure sustainability for future generations. These issues encompass various dimensions.

Development often prioritises immediate benefits at the cost of long-term environmental sustainability, burdening future generations with degraded ecosystems and climate challenges. It is unjust to compromise the ability of future generations to meet their needs for the sake of present gains.

Excessive extraction of natural resources, such as deforestation, mining, and overfishing depletes finite resources and disrupts ecosystems. The principle of stewardship dictates that humans have a duty to manage resources responsibly, preserving biodiversity and ecological balance.

Large-scale developmental projects, such as dams, mining, or industrial zones, often lead to the displacement of indigenous and marginalised communities. These projects frequently neglect the rights, livelihoods, and cultural heritage of these communities, violating principles of justice and equity.

Environmental degradation disproportionately impacts vulnerable populations, such as those living in poverty, who rely heavily on natural resources and have limited means to adapt to environmental changes. Fair distribution of environmental benefits and burdens is essential to prevent inequality and exploitation of weaker sections.

Environmental Accountability

Developed countries which burned the fossil fuel in the early 17th century have contributed the most to greenhouse gas emissions. The developing and small island nations are now facing severe climate impacts despite lower carbon footprints. This raises questions of global justice and responsibility, particularly in terms of who should bear the cost of mitigation and adaptation efforts.

Why is Climate Change a Moral Issue?

The climate change is traditionally considered as a matter of science and phenomena. However, there are significant reasons to show that climate change is equally a matter of moral values and responsibilities. If climate change is the result of human activities, then human beings should be responsible for it.

The connection between moral responsibility and climate change becomes evident when businesses and corporations engage in greenwashing, falsely or exaggeratedly promoting their environmental efforts to appear sustainable. Misrepresentation erodes trust and diverts attention from real solutions, undermining ethical accountability.

The socio-economic efforts, on the other hand, like the infrastructure and urbanisation projects often encroach on forests, wetlands, and wildlife habitats, leading to loss of biodiversity and increased human-wildlife conflict. Such actions challenge the intrinsic value of nature and the moral duty to coexist harmoniously with other species.

The consumer-driven development fuels unsustainable lifestyles that deplete resources and generate excessive waste. This reflects a disregard for the environment and prioritises individual **gratification**[6] over collective well-being.

The corruption and lack of accountability in enforcing environmental regulations allow unsustainable practices to persist, undermining both the environment and public trust. Effective governance is crucial to uphold ethical principles in development.

These flaws in the current global order significantly contribute to global warming and climate change. Addressing these challenges requires solutions that not only mitigate climate disasters but also promote moral responsibility and ensure long-term sustainability.

Adopting practices that balance economic growth with environmental preservation, such as promoting renewable energy and circular economies, is crucial. Implementing and enforcing strong environmental laws, alongside involving local communities in decision-making, can create an effective framework to combat climate change. Given the global nature of climate change, international collaboration is essential, with developed nations supporting developing ones to address shared challenges like climate extremes.

Beyond policies, fostering environmental ethics in individuals and organisations is vital to cultivating a culture of responsibility and sustainability. This shift can significantly reduce carbon footprints and promote eco-friendly lifestyles. India's 'Lifestyle for Environment' mission exemplifies this approach, encouraging harmony with nature. By integrating these strategies, development can align with ethical principles, ensuring a sustainable and equitable future for all.

---

[6] **Gratification:** pleasure, especially when gained from the satisfaction of a desire

- **Rights of Other Living Beings**

Anthropocentric ethics focuses on making decisions that prioritise the interests of human beings. Actions are considered right if they benefit humans; for example, consuming animal meat for its protein is deemed acceptable under this perspective. In contrast, animal-centered ethics extends moral consideration beyond humans to include all animals, emphasising their welfare and rights.

The number of animals in wilderness has seen a rapid decline as civilisation increases. Humans clear spaces of forest to settle and occupy the space. The competition between human beings and animals for resources and space leads to severe displacement and extinction of many wild animals, as seen in the case of the great Indian bustard. Furthermore, wild animals are hunted for entertainment, or for food or for resources such as ivory and bone, and are further threatened through such practices. The report of GEF highlight that the value of illegal trade has been estimated at between $7 and $23 billion per year, making wildlife crime one of the most lucrative illegal businesses.

Animals may be raised to be consumed, either in farms or in factory farms. The latter are industrial facilities (mostly seen in western countries) devoted to the production of meat and other animal products. These farms have become infamous for their treatment of animals. The animals in these farms are part of a mechanised process and are raised inhumanely and unnaturally.

The creation of zoological parks (zoos) is also considered as a form of cruelty by many, and once again moral arguments are offered against them. It is often said in support of zoos that they are entertainment and educational devices that may also be beneficial for the protection of endangered species.

Key Principles of Animal-Centric Ethics

1. **Intrinsic Value**: Animals could be seen as a being, with their own worth, independent of their utility or purpose they serve to human. This perspective asserts that animals have the right to live free from unnecessary harm or exploitation.
2. **Sufferer of pain**: Recognising animals as beings capable of experiencing pain and pleasure posts the ethical obligations to minimise suffering and ensure humane treatment.
3. **Rights-Based Approach**: Advocates for animal rights argue that animals deserve basic rights, such as the right to life and freedom from torture, aligning their treatment with principles of justice and equity. This ideal is same as the philosophy of Jainism which advocates that everything has a soul, and every soul must be respected.
4. **Environmental Interdependence**: Animals are integral part of the ecosystems. Ethical considerations must extend to preserve their habitats and ensure their survival, acknowledging their importance in maintaining ecological balance.

Applications of Ethical Values for Animal Welfare

1. **Animal Welfare Laws**: Legislation to prevent cruelty, promote humane farming practices, and regulate animal testing.
2. **Veganism and Ethical Consumption**: Advocating for plant-based diets and cruelty-free products.
3. **Conservation Efforts**: Protecting endangered species and biodiversity.

Animal-centric ethics calls for a shift in societal attitudes and practices, urging humans to coexist with animals in a respectful and sustainable manner.

- **Anthropocene**

The 'Anthropocene', a term used to describe the current geological age characterised by significant human impact on the Earth's ecosystems and geology, raises numerous ethical concerns. These issues stem from the transformative influence humans exert on the environment and their broader implications on Earth and its ecosystem.

The Anthropocene is often viewed through a human-centric lens, prioritising human needs over ecological balance. The long-term consequences of human activities, such as biodiversity loss, climate change, and pollution, will disproportionately affect future generations. The negative externalities of environmental degradation (e.g., rising sea levels, extreme weather, pollution) often impact the vulnerable and marginalised communities who are the least heard. Inhumane activities are driving a mass extinction of species, threatening ecosystems that support life on Earth, which is unpopularly called as the sixth-mass extinction.

Technological advancements such as geoengineering and genetic modification offer potential solutions to environmental problems, but raise ethical concerns about unintended consequences and human overreach. These changes that the humans are making to the planet like the concretisation could influence the evolution of future species in unpredictable ways. Global environmental challenges require collective action, but governance structures are often fragmented, leading to ineffective solutions.

Ethical Question Involved

The moral obligation to preserve the planet for the future generation and to ensure equitable distribution of environmental resources and risks across societies lies with the present generation. The responsibility for mitigating climate change and funding adaptation strategies lies with the human community as a whole. As stressed by Mahatma Gandhi, 'there is enough for everyone's need and none for anyone's greed.' The efforts should aim at controlling and manipulating the natural systems on a global scale so as to balance human needs and desires with the planet's finite resources. Beyond this, the development must respect the rights and traditions of indigenous people, thus establishing a fair and transparent system for managing global environmental crises.

Addressing Ethical Concerns

1. **Sustainability:** Adopting policies and lifestyles that prioritise long-term ecological balance over short-term gains.
2. **Global Cooperation:** Strengthening international agreements like the Paris Climate Accord to address shared responsibilities.
3. **Empowering Marginalised Groups:** Ensuring that vulnerable communities have a voice in decision-making processes.
4. **Education and Awareness:** Promoting understanding of the Anthropocene's ethical implications through environmental ethics education.
5. **Inclusive Development:** Balancing economic growth with ecological preservation and social equity.

These ethical considerations highlight the need for a paradigm shift that integrates environmental stewardship, justice, and equity into the Anthropocene's framework.

3.5 Professional Ethics

The term professionalism stands for the way one performs the actions in any profession. This may include a bundle of things in itself, such as the practices, standards, values, skills, education, and training. Professionalism requires mastery over the theoretical knowledge as mere theoretical competence is not enough, a professional should be able to implement the theory into practice.

> **? Thought Box**
>
> In professions where success often involves fierce competition, how can individuals balance the pressure to excel with the commitment to uphold ethical principles and integrity?

Professional ethics defines and codifies certain ethical norms necessary for all professions. It is the codes of conduct and the codes of ethics in professions. The codes of conduct may vary according to different professions. For instance, engineers will be having different codes of conducts from those of medical practitioners, but there are certain guiding moral principles in every profession that remain the same. These moral principles govern the behaviour of a professional in ethical decision-making, specifically in a situation of ethical dilemmas. Every organisation is committed to certain values, and it includes ethical responsibilities of on behalf of the profession.

Corporate Frauds

Corporate fraud refers to unethical actions carried out by a company or its employees. One notable example is the Satyam scam, a case involving a corporate computer services company. The company's founder fabricated multiple bank statements to inflate profits and revenues that were nonexistent. This practice of reporting false profit continued for nine years. Additionally, the fraud involved creating fake customer accounts to further exaggerate the company's profitability.

These kind of scams are clear example of conspiracy, forgery, and breach of trust that puts a question mark on the whole ethics of professionalism. It will also raise question on the disastrous system of accounting and accounting norms of a country. The increasing numbers of such frauds highlights the application of ethical codes and values, and make us think again and again about our blind dependency on such professions.

The ethical codes are devised keeping in mind the concepts of honesty, loyalty, thinking of maximising the betterment for all, to do the right thing and avoid the wrong, and raising voice against the wrong acts. The crucial questions are why there still exists a huge gap between what is conceptually accepted in all professions and what is practically implied, and why the adherence of virtues like truth, honesty, courage, temperance, modesty, righteousness, patience has become so difficult in our life.

- **Business Ethics**

Business ethics is a combination of two words- 'Ethics' and 'Business', which means application of ethics in business. It is the application of general ethical rules to business conduct and behaviour. These are the rules of business by which business activities are judged. Business ethics is the organised applications of value in business and industry. Business ethics focuses on moral standard as they apply to business policies, institutions and behaviour. It is the study of morally right or wrong action in business.

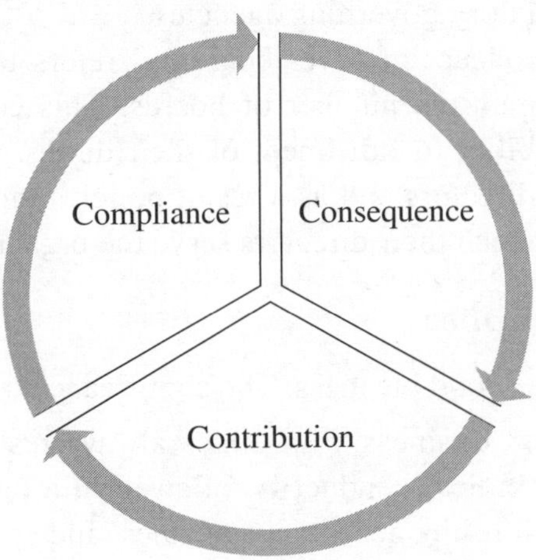

The three Cs of business ethics

Business ethics basically refer to the moral principles which are assumed to govern business activities. The purpose of business ethics is to lay down norms of behaviour by the business.

For example

1. To charge fair prices from the customers
2. To pay taxes to the government on time
3. To give fair treatment to the workers
4. To earn reasonable profits

Corporate Governance

It basically deals with how businesses are conducted. It is based on ethical policies that are an essential framework of a good, successful business.

Ethical Issues in Corporate Governance

Corporate governance is directly related and affects the market value and reputation of the company. So, if the company has a poor governance policy, then it may result in reputational damage, loss of capital investment, fines to the organisation. It is important that we avoid few common mistakes in corporate governance policies:

(a) Insider Trading: Insider trading occurs when shares are bought or sold on the basis of classified information. Insider trading is meant to buying or selling a security, based on non-public information about the security. Insiders have an advantage over other investors in market in terms of knowledge, information, a privilege that they could take to gain profits in business. A lack of transparency in business activities may expose the company to penalties from regulatory governing agencies.

(b) Over Boarding: The concept of 'over boarding' refers to a director or executive who sits and works for a multiple number of boards. This could lead to unrestricted time commitments and inability to fulfilment of their duties. Companies consider concerns about overcommitted directors and as a result policies must be adopted for limiting the number of boards on which their directors serve the organisation.

Significance of Business Ethics

Good business ethics promotes good business. The significance of business ethics are as follow:

(a) Positive Consequences: Business with ethics always results in positive consequences. This is because when ethical conduct is followed in a business, it builds mutual trust, confidence in the relationship, acceptance of rules, and approval of the society.

(b) Inner Satisfaction: In this world, all businessmen seek mental peace and self-satisfaction, free from tension and anxiety. So, it is believed that to attain mental satisfaction, only ethics can promote good business. It is also the social responsibility of the businessmen towards the society that they should not implement unethical conduct to earn profits in their businesses.

(C) Goodwill of the Business Organisation and Businessmen: Good ethical conduct will always promote the goodwill of both businesses as well as the businessmen. For a successful business, a good public image is important because once a business organisation's image is blemished, it directly affects the sales, profits, and the image of the business.

(D) Success and Development: An ethical environment in a business ultimately leads to the development and success of the business. It is because sincere work and honest effort of a person make them moral and help them to achieve success in their efforts in business.

(E) New Management: New ethical principles are needed in new management for overall development and honour of the organisation.

(F) Encouraging and Motivating Others: When a business achieves success by adhering to ethical principles, it inspires and motivates other entrepreneurs to follow the path of ethical conduct. Such examples set a positive precedent and encourage others to adopt similar practices.

• Corporate Social Responsibility (CSR)

Corporate social responsibility is basically related to operating a business in such a manner that accounts for the social and environmental impact created by the business. It is a commitment towards responsible business practices with their impact on the society, and to report on regular basis to show the progress made towards accomplishing business objectives. CSR reports cover a wide range of issues such as governance, worker safety and welfare, ethical conduct, purchase and supply chain operations, environmental impact, and energy audit. Today, CSR efforts also focus on social, economic, and environmental sustainability. It is a kind of international private business self-regulation which aims to work towards the societal goals of a philanthropic, activist, or charitable nature under ethically oriented practices and conduct. The types of Corporate Social Responsibility are as follows:

1. **Environmental Responsibility:** According to this, the organisation must work responsibly towards the environment following the principles of sustainable development. There are several ways to embrace this responsibility, like reducing pollution, greenhouse effects, increasing reliance on renewable energy, sustainable resources, etc.
2. **Ethical Responsibility:** The aim is to achieve fair treatment among all employees and stakeholders (includes leadership, suppliers, investors, manufacturers, and customers). There should not be any discrimination at the workplace on the basis of caste, creed, gender, religion, and nationality.
3. **Philanthropic Responsibility:** This responsibility aims to actively make the world and the society a better place to live in. It involves donating funds and good services to other organisations.

4. **Economic Responsibility:** It is the practice towards healthy finance of the organisation. The end goal is to earn profits without unethical conduct. Many industries all over the world are well-aware of the importance of CSR. Many organisations have shown commendable work in performing their duties towards the people, planet and profit.
5. **Community Investment:** Based on their heritage and business, a company focuses on the following major areas:
   - Strengthening communities
   - Improving opportunities for women and minorities
   - Helping children and youth to utilise their potential.

• Environmental, Social, and Governance (ESG) Index

The Environmental, Social, and Governance (ESG) Index is a set of criteria that businesses and organisations are evaluated on to assess their ethical performance in three key areas: environmental, social responsibility, and governance practices. ESG has become an essential measure of corporate responsibility, reflecting the growing emphasis on ethical and sustainable business practices.

Ethical Principles of ESG

1. **Environmental Responsibility**: Ethical companies strive to minimise their environmental impact. This includes reducing carbon emissions, ensuring sustainable resource use, and minimising waste. The principle here is that businesses should operate in a way that protects and preserves the planet for future generations.
2. **Social Responsibility**: The social aspect of ESG focuses on human rights, community impact, and worker welfare. Ethical businesses foster inclusive workplaces, prioritise fair labour practices, and contribute positively to the society through social development programs. They also respect diversity and promote equity in their interactions.
3. **Governance**: Governance relates to ethical leadership and decision-making. Companies must operate with transparency, accountability, and integrity. Ethical governance ensures that business practices are fair, legal, and aligned with the interests of all stakeholders, including employees, consumers, and shareholders.

Thus, the ESG index encourages businesses to align their actions with ethical values that support environmental sustainability, social equity, and good governance, leading to long-term positive impact for society and the planet.

• Polluter Pay Principle

The Polluter Pay Principle (PPP) is an ethical principle in environmental law that holds that those who cause environmental damage should bear the costs of mitigating or repairing the harm they have caused. This principle ensures that the responsibility for environmental protection is placed on those who are directly responsible for pollution, rather than on the public or taxpayers.

The ethical foundation of the PPP is rooted in justice and fairness. It argues that the costs of pollution should not be externalised to the society or future generations. Instead, the polluting entity is morally and legally obligated to internalise the environmental costs of its actions. By doing so, PPP aims to incentivise businesses and individuals to minimise their environmental impact and adopt more sustainable practices.

The principle's significance is in its role in addressing environmental harm and promoting accountability. It reinforces the idea that economic growth and industrial activities should not come at the expense of environmental degradation. For instance, a factory that emits pollutants into the air or water should be responsible for cleaning up the pollution, rather than shifting the burden to local communities or governments.

In practice, PPP is applied through pollution taxes, fines, and regulations that compel polluters to pay for the environmental damages they cause. This encourages both corporate responsibility and long-term ecological sustainability.

3.6 Social Ethics

Social Ethics refers to the principles and moral values that govern behaviour and relationships within a society. It emphasises collective well-being, justice, and harmony while promoting fairness, respect, and responsibility among individuals and groups. Social ethics addresses issues like equality, human rights, and environmental sustainability, guiding how societies balance individual freedoms with communal responsibilities.

In diverse societies, social ethics fosters inclusivity, tolerance, and empathy, ensuring marginalised voices are heard. It underpins frameworks for social justice, advocating equitable distribution of resources and opportunities. Environmental consciousness is also a vital aspect, emphasising the ethical duty to preserve nature for future generations.

Modern challenges, such as technological advancement, consumerism, and globalisation require an ethical approach to decision-making. By prioritising fairness and accountability, social ethics enables societies to navigate complex dilemmas, promoting a humane and sustainable coexistence. It is the foundation of a just and progressive society.

- **Distributive Justice**

Distributive Justice refers to the fair allocation of resources, wealth, and opportunities within a society. It ensures that benefits and burdens are shared equitably, addressing disparities and fostering social harmony. This concept is rooted in the principles of equality, need, and merit, aiming to balance individual rights with societal welfare.

For example, India's reservation policy exemplifies distributive justice. By reserving seats in education and government jobs for Scheduled Castes (SCs), Scheduled Tribes (STs), and Other Backward Classes (OBCs), the policy seeks to address historical, social, and economic inequities. It ensures these marginalised groups receive opportunities for advancement, promoting inclusive growth.

Another example is progressive taxation, where higher income groups pay proportionately more taxes to fund public services like healthcare, education, and welfare programs. This redistributes wealth to support underprivileged sections of society, ensuring fairness and reducing inequality. Such measures reflect the essence of distributive justice in action.

- **Refugee Crisis**

The refugee crisis in India raises several ethical issues rooted in human rights, national sovereignty, and humanitarian obligations. India, while being home to a large number of refugees from neighbouring countries, such as Afghanistan, Sri Lanka, Bangladesh, and Myanmar, faces complex challenges when addressing the rights and welfare of refugees.

One primary ethical concern is humanitarian responsibility. India is not a signatory to the 1951 Refugee Convention, and therefore does not have a legal framework to protect refugees. Despite this, the ethical obligation to provide asylum is a matter of global humanitarian standards. Denying refugees basic rights like shelter, food, and security conflicts with international norms.

Another issue is discrimination. Certain communities, particularly those from Muslim-majority nations, such as Rohingyas from Myanmar and Bangladesh, face exclusion and hostility in India. The government's Citizenship Amendment Act (CAA), which grants citizenship to non-Muslim refugees, has been criticised for discriminating against Muslim refugees and violating the principle of equality.

Additionally, the growing **xenophobia**[7] and social tensions associated with refugees also pose ethical challenges. Host communities often perceive refugees as a burden on resources and infrastructure, exacerbating issues like unemployment and strained public services. Balancing human rights protection with social cohesion remains a critical ethical dilemma in India's refugee crisis.

- **War Crime**

War crimes in the current context raise significant ethical issues that challenge global justice, human rights, and accountability. The modern landscape of warfare, marked by conflicts such as the Syrian Civil War, the Russian invasion of Ukraine, and the ongoing violence in Yemen, has witnessed widespread violations of international humanitarian law, particularly targeting civilians, women, and children.

[7] **Xenophobia:** a fear or hatred of foreign people and cultures

One key ethical issue is the disproportionate impact on civilians. Modern warfare often involves indiscriminate bombing, the use of chemical weapons, and targeted assassinations, which lead to massive civilian casualties. This raises questions about the morality of such actions and the extent to which they violate the principle of proportionality in armed conflict.

Another ethical dilemma is the accountability of leaders. Despite clear evidence of war crimes, political leaders and military officials often evade justice, either through lack of international will or by exploiting political power. The International Criminal Court (ICC) aims to prosecute such crimes, but geopolitical interests and selective justice undermine its effectiveness.

Additionally, the psychological trauma faced by war victims, particularly children and women, highlights the long-term consequences of war crimes, prompting ethical concerns about the responsibility of the international community to prevent and intervene in such violations. Addressing these issues requires a commitment to upholding human dignity and international law amidst global conflicts.

- **Gender Justice**

Gender justice refers to the fair and equal treatment of all genders, ensuring that individuals have the same rights, opportunities, and protections, regardless of their gender. In the contemporary world, gender justice is essential due to the historical and ongoing marginalisation of women, **LGBTQ+ individuals**,[8] and other gender minorities. Gender justice addresses issues of discrimination, inequality, and violence that arise due to societal norms and biases based on gender.

The need for gender justice is critical in combatting issues such as gender-based violence, pay disparity, unequal access to education, and healthcare disparities. Women and gender minorities often face systemic barriers in accessing opportunities, leading to economic and social exclusion. In countries like India, practices like female infanticide, dowry-related violence, and sexual harassment are prevalent, highlighting the urgent need for reform.

Significance of gender justice lies in its potential to create more equitable societies. By ensuring equal opportunities and protection for all genders, gender justice contributes to social stability and economic growth, as diverse perspectives are incorporated into decision-making. Moreover, it empowers individuals to live free from violence and discrimination, fostering a sense of dignity and respect.

Promoting gender justice is vital not only for protecting the rights of marginalised genders but also for creating a fair, progressive, and harmonious society.

---

[8]**LGBTQIA+** is an umbrella term that refers to lesbian, gay, bisexual, transgender, queer, intersex, asexual, and other identities. The "+" in LGBTQIA+ represents other identities that are not specified in the acronym, such as pansexual, gender fluid, nonbinary, and Two-Spirit

4. SPORTS ETHICS

Sports ethics[9], a branch of applied ethics, examines the moral and ethical issues inherent in sports. Fairness stands as a cornerstone of sports ethics, emphasising equal opportunities for participants, equitable rules, and impartial judgments. Adherence to the rules and regulations of a sport is essential to maintain fairness and ensure no participant gains an unfair advantage. Ethical concerns arise when these rules are bent or violated, such as in cases of cheating, doping, or match-fixing.

A crucial aspect of fairness is ensuring that all athletes—regardless of gender, race, socioeconomic background, or disability—have an equal chance to compete and succeed. This has driven significant efforts to combat discrimination in sports, promoting gender equality, racial inclusion, and access for athletes with disabilities.

Sportsmanship refers to the ethical conduct displayed by athletes, coaches, and teams both on and off the field. It involves respecting the rules of the game, accepting victories with humility, and handling defeats with grace. Integrity in sports emphasises honesty and transparency in all aspects of competition. A key element of sportsmanship is how athletes treat their opponents, balancing the desire to win with respect for the dignity of the competition and the rights of others.

Coaches have a vital ethical responsibility to set an example for their athletes by teaching values like respect, fairness, and integrity while ensuring their team's behaviour aligns with these standards.

As sports have become more commercialised, new ethical challenges have arisen due to financial pressures and media attention. Professional athletes, in particular, often face significant pressure from sponsors, teams, and the media.

The issue of sexual harassment and abuse in sports, especially in youth organisations and professional leagues, has gained increasing attention. Coaches, administrators, and organisations must ensure safe environments free from exploitation and abuse.

In conclusion, sports ethics involves principles of fairness, justice, respect, integrity, and responsibility. Ethical decisions in sports can impact not only athletes but society as a whole, requiring a balance between individual ambition and collective responsibility while addressing issues like inequality and harm.

4.1 Doping

Doping in sports refers to the use of prohibited substances or methods to enhance athletic performance. This practice raises a wide range of ethical issues, impacting not only the individual athletes involved but also the integrity of sports, the safety of competitors, and the broader cultural

[9]**Sports ethics** is a branch of applied ethics that explores the moral and ethical issues related to sports.

and societal implications of competitive athletics. Below are the key ethical issues surrounding doping in sports:

Doping undermines the principle of fairness, which is central to the idea of sports. Athletes who use performance-enhancing drugs (PEDs) gain an unfair advantage over those who follow the rules. This creates an uneven playing condition, making it difficult for athletes who choose not to dope to compete on equal terms.

Doping erodes public trust and undermines the integrity of sports, creating a perception that success is determined by who can cheat most effectively rather than by skill or dedication. Performance-enhancing drugs (PEDs) like anabolic steroids, stimulants, and blood doping can cause severe physical harm, including cardiovascular issues, liver damage, and psychological effects like aggression and depression.

Coaches, who play a critical role in an athlete's development, may encourage or administer doping, raising ethical questions about their responsibility to protect athlete health and uphold sports integrity.

Sports governing bodies, such as the IOC and WADA, have an ethical obligation to prevent doping, enforce policies, and maintain competition integrity. However, the effectiveness of these organisations in detecting and preventing doping has been contested, with calls for stronger enforcement and penalties.

Athletes caught doping face consequences like suspensions or bans, sparking debate over whether these punishments are just and proportional. Some argue that severe penalties are necessary to deter doping.

Doctors and medical professionals assisting with doping violate their ethical responsibility to 'do no harm' by enabling athletes to cheat or evade detection.

The ethical issues surrounding doping are complex, involving the responsibilities of athletes, coaches, organisations, and society in preserving the integrity of sport.

4.2 Betting and Gambling

Betting and gambling in sports raise ethical concerns that affect the integrity of the sport and the well-being of athletes, fans, and society. A key issue is match-fixing, where players, coaches, or officials manipulate outcomes for betting profits, undermining the core values of fair competition and athletic skill.

Another concern is gambling addiction, which can lead to financial ruin, mental health issues, and strained relationships. Gambling companies, through sponsorships and advertising, may exploit sports' popularity, prioritising profit over the well-being of vulnerable individuals.

Inadequate regulation of sports betting in many areas raises ethical questions about the ability to prevent match-fixing, illegal gambling, and exploitative practices. There is also concern about the effectiveness of existing regulations in preventing corruption and ensuring fair outcomes in sports.

The moral responsibility lies with athletes, coaches, sports organisations, betting companies, and governments to create an environment where gambling does not compromise fairness, health, or respect for competition.

- **Applied Ethics – Framework to Navigate Through Ethical Dilemmas**

Applied ethics guides our decisions in real-world contexts by bridging theoretical moral principles with practical challenges in areas like healthcare, business, environment, sports, and technology. It provides a framework for addressing dilemmas, promoting fairness, justice, and the common good. By encouraging critical reflection, applied ethics ensures that moral considerations shape our actions, fostering responsibility and positive change. In an evolving world, applied ethics helps align our choices with values of justice, compassion, and integrity, contributing to a more ethical and sustainable future.

SUMMARY

- Applied Ethics explores making ethical judgments in specialised human situations. It applies moral principles to societal issues like euthanasia, abortion, and privacy.
- Bioethics is an interdisciplinary field shaped by advances in medicine, nursing, biomedical technology, and human sciences.
- Abortion refers to the termination of pregnancy, raising bioethical debates on the value of foetal life versus women's autonomy, with life often seen as inherently sacred.
- Euthanasia, from Greek meaning 'good death,' involves ethical issues like the right to die and physician-assisted suicide.
- Surrogacy is when a surrogate carries a child for intended parents, involving medical, emotional, financial, and legal complexities.
- Animal Rights emphasise the equal value of all life and the recognition of animals' rights.
- Rapid technological breakthroughs have overshadowed ethics and human values, with IT enabling vast personal data collection, storage, and misuse.
- Media Ethics addresses ethical concerns in journalism, news production, and dissemination, requiring media professionals to navigate these challenges at every stage.
- Environmental Ethics emerged in the 1970s, recognising the nature's value and finite resources. It examines the rightness or wrongness of actions toward the environment.
- The Anthropocene describes the current geological age marked by significant human impact on Earth's ecosystems, raising ethical concerns about environmental transformation and its broader implications.

- Professional Ethics codifies ethical norms specific to professions, with varying codes of conduct (e.g., engineers vs. medical practitioners) but shared guiding moral principles.
- Business Ethics studies moral standards as they apply to business policies, behaviours, and institutions, focusing on right and wrong actions in business.
- ESG Index evaluates organisations on ethical performance in environmental, social, and governance practices.
- Social Ethics governs societal behaviour, emphasising collective well-being, justice, fairness, and responsibility in relationships.
- Distributive Justice ensures the fair allocation of resources, wealth, and opportunities, addressing disparities and promoting social harmony through the principles of equality, need, and merit.
- The refugee crisis in India involves ethical issues related to human rights, national sovereignty, and humanitarian obligations. India hosts refugees from countries like Afghanistan, Sri Lanka, Bangladesh, and Myanmar, facing challenges in addressing their rights and welfare.
- War crimes today highlight ethical concerns around global justice, human rights, and accountability, with conflicts like the Syrian Civil War, Russia's invasion of Ukraine, and violence in Yemen involving severe violations of international humanitarian law, particularly against civilians.

PREVIOUS YEARS' QUESTIONS

1. The application of Artificial Intelligence as a dependable source of input for administrative rational decision-making is a debatable issue. Critically examine the statement from the ethical point of view. *UPSC CSE Mains 2024*
2. Global warming and climate change are the outcomes of human greed in the name of development, indicating the direction in which extinction of organisms including human beings is heading towards loss of life on Earth. How do you put an end to this to protect life and bring equilibrium between the society and the environment? *UPSC CSE Mains 2024*
3. Online methodology is being used for day-to-day meetings, institutional approvals in the administration and for teaching and learning in the education sector to the extent telemedicine in the health sector is getting popular with the approvals of the competent authority. No doubt it has advantages and disadvantages for both the beneficiaries and the system at large. Describe and discuss the ethical issues involved in the use of online method particularly to vulnerable section of society. *UPSC CSE Mains 2022*
4. Impact of digital technology as reliable source of input for rational decision making is a debatable issue. Critically evaluate with suitable example. *UPSC CSE Mains 2021*
5. "Refugees should not be turned back to the country where they would face persecution or human right violation." Examine the statement with reference to ethical dimension being violated by the nation claiming to be democratic with open society. *UPSC CSE Mains 2021*

6. "The current internet expansion has instilled a different set of cultural values which are often in conflict with traditional values." Discuss. *UPSC CSE Mains 2020*
7. Suppose the Government of India is thinking of constructing a dam in a mountain valley bond by forests and inhabited by ethnic communities. What rational policy should it resort to in dealing with unforeseen contingencies? *UPSC CSE Mains 2018*
8. Increased national wealth did not result in equitable distribution of its benefits. It has created only some "enclaves of modernity and prosperity for a small minority at the cost of the majority." Justify. *UPSC CSE Mains 2017*
9. What is meant by 'environmental ethics'? Why is it important to study? Discuss any one environmental issue from the viewpoint of environmental ethics. *UPSC CSE Mains 2015*
10. It is often said that 'politics' and 'ethics' do not go together. What is your opinion in this regard? Justify your answer with illustrations. *UPSC CSE Mains 2013*

Attitude

7

1. UNDERSTANDING ATTITUDE

Attitude can be defined as evaluation-positive or negative regarding ideas, objects, actions, people, events, or concepts. The evaluation need not always be positive or negative, it can also be uncertain. We can like, dislike, or have mixed feelings toward any subject (living or non-living). We can have a good opinion, a bad opinion, or no opinion at all. We can be theist, atheist, or agnostic.

Attitude can also be looked at as an expression of favour or disfavour towards a person, place, thing, event, idea, or concept.

According to Alice H. Eagly and Shelly Chaiken, attitude is a psychological tendency that is expressed by evaluating a particular entity with some degree of favour or disfavour. The favour and disfavour are not poles apart but form a continuum. On one end, it is extremely favourable and on the other end, it is extremely unfavourable, and it can be moderate in the middle.

LEARNING OBJECTIVES

1. Understanding what constitutes an attitude and exploring various approaches to studying it
2. Learning about the process of attitude formation and the factors that influence it
3. Examining the functions of attitudes and their relationship with behaviour
4. Analysing the factors that enable attitudes to influence behaviour, with a focus on cognitive dissonance
5. Exploring the concept of attitude change and the factors that resist such change
6. Comparing and differentiating moral and political attitudes while developing an understanding of the importance of a positive attitude in civil servants

It is a manner that draws people to us or repels them. It is never content unless it is expressed. It is the librarian of our past, the speaker of our present, and the prophet of our future. Attitude is both our best friend and our worst enemy. It is more honest and more consistent than our words.

'Nothing can stop the man with the right mental attitude from achieving his goal, nothing on earth can help the man with the wrong mental attitude.' **Thomas Jefferson**

'Attitude is a little thing that makes a big difference.' **Winston Churchill**

2. THE ABC MODEL OF ATTITUDE

Modern psychologists, however, regard attitude as a complex and multidimensional construct. Social psychologist, Donelson R. Forsyth describes attitude as a combination of affective, behavioural, and **cognitive components**[1].

Every attitude has three components:

- beliefs, ideas, perceptions, or knowledge about the way things are or ought to be;
- action or response in a particular way, and
- feelings associated with such beliefs.

Attitude structure can be described in terms of three components. The three components also tell us about the body language of the person involved.

- Affective (A) – the emotional component,
- Behavioural (B) – the action component and
- Cognitive (C) – the mental component.

In the next sections, we will understand the components of attitude.

2.1 Affective Component

It refers to an emotional reaction towards an attitude object. The affective component is about how one feels emotionally about an object, person, issue, or event.

For example: Girish has acrophobia (fear of heights). Here 'heights' is an attitude object. Whenever Girish is exposed to heights, say a terrace, balcony, or when in an airplane, he feels extremely anxious, panics, and is scared. This is the affective component of his attitude. Many issues, such as politics, sex, caste, and religion, tend to be strongly rooted in affective components. They usually come from beliefs and value systems.

An individual's attitude towards an object cannot be determined by simply identifying their beliefs about it because emotion works simultaneously with the cognitive process about an attitude object. Therefore, affective components include our positive and negative feelings towards an object. Hence, the affective component of an attitude reflects how much we like or dislike an attitude object.

---

[1]**Cognitive Component:** It refers to the mental processes involved in acquiring knowledge and understanding, such as perception, memory, reasoning, and problem-solving.

2.2 Behavioural Component

It refers to the way one reacts, responds, or behaves towards an attitude object. The behavioural component is about how attitude influences behaviour. The behavioural component is a verbal or overt (nonverbal) behavioural tendency by an individual and it consists of actions or observable responses. It involves a person's response (favourable/ unfavourable) to do something regarding attitude object. Attitudinal responses are more or less consistent.

That is, a series of responses toward a given attitudinal stimulus is likely to show some degree of organisational structure or predictability. Behavioural component refers to our behavioural intentions or how we act according to the attitude that we have. Basically, it refers to how we are inclined to act towards an attitude object. The behavioural component of the attitude will determine how we act towards an attitude object.

For example: How would Girish behave when taken to a terrace or asked to go bungee jumping? He may scream, cry, faint, or run away! This is behavioural component of his attitude.

2.3 Cognitive Component

The cognitive component is about thoughts, beliefs, and knowledge about the object, person, issue, or event. The cognitive component refers to what our knowledge is about the attitude object. In other words, the cognitive component refers to what we know about the attitude object and the process that goes into forming and using an attitude. The cognitive component of an attitude includes our thoughts and ideas about the attitude object. The cognitive component is the storage section where an individual organises the information.

For example: What does Girish think about a helicopter ride? He thinks that they work against gravity and may fall anytime; he also thinks they are dangerous. This forms the cognitive component of his attitude. What will Girish think about bungee jumping? He may think bungee jumping is subject to manual errors.

Classical conditioning reflects the affective process assumption. Operant conditioning reflects the behavioural process assumption. Cognitive dissonance theory reflects the cognitive process assumption. (We will see all the theories in the sections to follow.)

These three components influence each other. Change in one component influences the entire attitude. Also, each component, apart from influencing attitude as a whole, influences each other. This makes the concept of attitude quite complex and dynamic. Though most attitudes have all three components they are strongly founded in the cognitive or the affective component.

3. ATTITUDE FORMATION

What are your thoughts on India's vote against Sri Lanka in the UNHCR (United Nations High Commissioner for Refugees), raising the age of consent for sexual activity, the decriminalisation of Section 377 of the IPC, Ram Gopal Varma's *Rakta Charitra*, body piercings and tattoos, public urination, communal speeches by politicians, Aamir Khan's *Satyameva Jayate*, moral policing, and Arnab Goswami's *News Hour*?

Everyone has a like or a dislike, an attraction or aversion, a favourable or an unfavourable opinion, or no opinions at all about all these issues. How does one acquire such an attitude precisely?

Attitude formation is not a simple or short process. It is a complex, dynamic, and long-term process. Attitudes are formed and developed from beliefs, feelings, and behaviour individually or in combination.

- **Social Learning**

Attitude formation happens through the process of social learning. A response to stimuli in a society is learned through experience and practice. When we say that response is learned through experience the response changes as a person matures. Most psychologists believe that attitudes are learned. This learning is either by an individual's interaction with others, observation of others' behaviour, or both. This process is called social learning and involves several methods namely:

1. Classical conditioning
2. Operant conditioning
3. Observational learning and
4. Social comparison

Social learning theory provides insight into two similar processes of conditioning that result in affective attitude formation. Specifically, the process of modelling is similar to classical conditioning and observational learning is similar to instrumental conditioning. In classical and instrumental conditioning, it is the person's actions that result in conditioned responses. In the social learning models, conditioning is the result of the observed or modelled behaviour of others.

For instance, a younger sibling observes the behaviour of an older sibling that results in rewards and punishments, thereby influencing (conditioning) their behaviour. The sibling learns what to do to achieve rewards versus what not to do to avoid punishment. In the sections coming up, we will study the methods involved in social learning.

- **Classical Conditioning**

It is a process by which two stimuli are used to elicit a strong, uncontrolled response that is not under the subject's control. One stimulus is succeeded by another stimulus to get the desired response. Initially, the response is for the second stimulus but when this process is consistently repeated an individual will learn that the second stimulus will automatically follow the first stimulus and over time the individual responds in the same fashion for the first stimulus itself.

Classical conditioning is a type of learning that has had a major influence on the school of thought in psychology known as behaviourism. It was discovered by Russian physiologist Ivan Pavlov. This conditioning is called Pavlovian conditioning after Ivan Pavlov who developed this method. In Pavlovian conditioning there are factors namely:

- Conditioned stimulus
- Unconditioned stimulus
- Unconditioned response and
- Conditioned response

Example I

- ➢ Conditioned stimulus (CS) – Bell
- ➢ Unconditioned stimulus (US) – Food
- ➢ Unconditioned response (UR) – Salivation
- ➢ Conditioned response (CR) – Salivation

When a dog is served with food (CS) it salivates (UR), which is quite natural. But making the dog salivate on striking a bell is called conditioning.

Initially, the bell (CS) is struck, followed by the presentation of food (US), which causes the dog to salivate (UR). At this stage, the salivation is still a response to the food (US), not the bell (CS).

After repeated pairings, the dog begins to salivate (CR) at the sound of the bell (CS) alone, even in the absence of food. This learned response, now a conditioned response (CR), demonstrates the process of classical conditioning.

Example II

Ram, a young kid, has formed a negative attitude towards a particular caste. He has had no exposure or contact with persons from that caste. This negative attitude is due to listening to his parent's abuse of the particular caste based on **prejudiced**[2] beliefs. Prejudiced beliefs, however, can be tackled with self-reflection, education, and a willingness to hear out others. For the sake of this example, we can understand the following components in these terms:

- Conditional Stimulus: Caste
- Unconditioned Stimulus: Prejudiced beliefs
- Unconditioned Response: Hostility
- Conditioned Response: Hostility

---

[2]**Prejudice:** A preconceived opinion or judgment about an individual or group that is not based on reason, experience, or factual evidence.

A naturally unconditioned response is turned into a conditioned response by pairing a conditioned stimulus with an unconditioned stimulus.

- **Conditioning on a Higher Order**

When a person comes pointing a gun or firing, people duck and lie on the ground. Here, the response is unconditioned to an unconditioned stimulus of gun firing. This is a brought response of any individual in the situation.

Also, we see people duck at the sound of a shot being fired. They may not see the shooter or even the gun, but their response is conditioned to the sound of a shot being fired. Even a tire going flat will make the same sound and elicit the same response. An individual is conditioned in several ways in real life. Our attitudes to several subjects are conditioned by society.

- **Operant Conditioning/Instrumental Conditioning**

According to instrumental conditioning, the likelihood of repetition of an action in the future depends on the reward or punishment that follows such an action. If the behaviour is accepted and rewarded, the behaviour gets strengthened and the probability of repetition is high. On the contrary, if the behaviour is unacceptable and punished, the probability of repetition is reduced. Unlike classical conditioning where the response is reflexive, in instrumental conditioning the response is voluntary and very much controlled by the individual. The response depends on the effect the response will have on the individual's environment. The effect can be favourable or unfavourable, advantageous or disadvantageous, and reward or punishment. The response and effect are bidirectional. The responses affect the individual's environment and in turn, the responses are reinforced by their effect.

B.F. Skinner is regarded as the father of operant conditioning. This means that behaviour that is reinforced tends to be repeated (i.e., strengthened); behaviour that is not reinforced tends to die out or be extinguished (i.e., weakened).

Example

When a person saves another life, he is praised and awarded. This is positive reinforcement. He would try to help others at every opportunity presented. On the contrary, taking a life will lead to punishment. This is negative reinforcement. It acts as a deterrent for the person to behave in the same way.

- **Observational Conditioning**

Attitudes can be formed not only through interaction but also simply through observation, even without direct engagement. Observational conditioning is learning through others' interaction with the attitude object.

Individuals learn by observing the behaviour of others and can develop attitudes. During the initial stages of growth, a child learns through the observational learning process. Through mass media and advertisements both children and adults learn attitudes.

Observational learning is sometimes also referred to as shaping, modelling, and vicarious reinforcement. While it can take place at any point in life, it tends to be the most common during childhood as children learn from the authority figures and peers in their lives. It also plays an important role in the socialisation process, as children learn how to behave and respond to others by observing how their parents and other caregivers interact with each other and with other people.

Example I

Young people attending camps often start smoking, inspired by the character Siddharth in the movie *Rang De Basanti*, who lights cigarettes using a cinder.

Example II

A child watching his/her father drive a car may try to imitate the action, jumping into the car seat and pretending to drive. In both classical and instrumental conditioning, the individual actively engages in the behaviour, while the secondary person influencing the behaviour may not even be aware of their impact.

Example III

Raheem had a scuba diving accident that left him hospitalised for three months, leading him to develop an aversion to scuba diving. His friend Ram, influenced by Raheem's experience, also forms a negative attitude toward scuba diving. Raheem's attitude stems from operant conditioning, while Ram's attitude arises from observational conditioning.

A person looks upon other individuals as role models. They imbibe their role model's beliefs and values. The individual's attitude is influenced by or the same as that of a role model. This is done by the process of observational conditioning. Children learn their roles to be played in family and society through observational conditioning. Role-choosing and role-playing, part of a child's growing up is by observational conditioning. In later stages, it is this observational conditioning that makes one choose a career and even the skill sets necessary for a successful career.

- **Social Comparison**

An individual is not a single animal. He or she is a social animal. He or she is both an individual and part of the social system. Being an active part of the social system; he or she tends to compare himself or herself with the other individuals in the society. He or she does so to check whether he or she is in sync with the social reality.

An individual compares his or her abilities and attitude with that of other people and alters his or her attitude in conformity to the socially established norms. When a child enters adolescence, their friends, peers, and others begin to influence the beliefs and actions of the individual. They compare themself with others in their group and change their attitude to get social acceptance and respect.

Example

While growing up Robert was averse to the idea of alcohol being consumed in his family. However, once he joined college, he started going out with friends and started partying. He looked at his friends, who smoked and drank. They were looked upon as cool suave guys. He slowly began to smoke and drink. This is an example of social comparison that is also known as 'peer pressure.'

4. FACTORS CONTRIBUTING TO FORMATION OF ATTITUDE

4.1 Culture

Culture exerts an enormous influence on an individual. Culture in itself includes religion, tradition, customs, prohibitions, rewards, and sanctions. Socialisation is the process by which culture shapes the attitudes of the people. Culture teaches individual beliefs, attitudes, and behaviour that are acceptable in one's life and society. This culture is not universal but rather diverse and localised. Each cultural group has its own set of do's and don'ts, practices, and customs. Therefore, each individual's attitude will be per his or her cultural group.

For the same attitude object, the response of two individuals belonging to different cultural groups will be different, e.g., kissing in public is acceptable in America while persecuted in Saudi Arabia. However, some customs and traditions could be cut across several cultural groups, several cultural groups throughout the world.

Example

Patriarchy is a pervasive cultural phenomenon that significantly shapes individuals. Its key features include male dominance in social hierarchies, a **hegemonic**[3] and fragile understanding of masculinity, and the oppression or delegitimisation of other genders, particularly through control over women. This is especially prevalent in many East and South Asian countries.

Cultural practices also manifest in rituals, customs, and norms. For instance, caste in India is a culturally learned system, while Japan emphasises privacy and courtesy. Similarly, India's spiritual identity and the classification of food as sacred or reflective of religious beliefs illustrate how culture is internalised and expressed in various societies.

[3]**hegemonic:** Leadership/dominance by one social state/social group over others.

- **Family**

Family is the most important and closest social group for a person. It is the nursery for attitudinal formation. Talcott Parsons considers that the important function of family lies in being the primary socialisation benchmark. In sociology, family is considered to be the distinct group of individuals connected by blood, adoption, marriage, or cohabitation and choice informed by various emotional and cultural factors. It is also the most fundamental unit of any economy.

Parents are more influential in the family system that structures and moulds the attitude of a child. Extended family and sibling relationships, in particular, play an important role in attitude formation. Parents are themselves products of the culture of their times. They teach the child about their family's and society's customs, traditions, beliefs, and practices. The influence of parents starts from the moment a child opens its eyes, and it continues all through the child's formative years. Because of this the attitude and beliefs of the individual will almost be a mirror image of the parent even in his or her adulthood. The child's political orientation, attitude towards race, gender, religion, caste, etc. largely reflect the family attitudes.

It should, however, be noted that this indoctrination is not rigid. Parents are not only products and participants of culture but also individuals. They selectively present their beliefs and values to the child which aids in attitude formation and development. This selectivity is based on experiences in their own lives.

4.2 Social Groups

Several social groups apart from family play an important role in attitude formation which includes friends, peers, colleagues, etc. The makeup of the social group itself shapes a person's attitude, beliefs, and behaviour. As the child grows, his or her family time comes down and he or she begins to spend more time with friends and other acquaintances. They gradually influence the attitudes of the child. They give advice and provide companionship and entertainment. Gradually, such social groups supplant the family. They aid in shaping the way an individual acts and thinks.

The very composition of the group itself determines one's attitude. When the group is diverse it brings a discriminatory attitude. Race, religion, caste, and gender discrimination get diluted or worn thin. The child develops a healthy attitude towards members of all races, colours, and creeds. Consider the voting pattern in India. Some people do not listen to candidate's speeches, read newspapers, or follow debates. They talk with friends, family, etc., and vote for a candidate. Families, friends, and other such social groups most definitely influence the choice of a candidate.

4.3 Institutions

A man is never alone. From cradle to grave he is under the influence of one institution or the other. In sociological terms, institutions are establishments with systematised regulated sets of norms and responsibilities that govern and shape specific areas of life. Institutions in the literature about humanities and outside include family, education, government, religion, the justice system, businesses, marriages, and many more. Since institutions are so intrinsically related to our lives, these dictate and often shape the culture thereby affecting the attitude of an individual or community.

Educational institutes act as repositories of knowledge, direct and shape the beliefs, and values of a person, and thus form attitudes. A modern school today imbibes creativity, accommodates diversity, and glorifies modern social values such as equality, freedom, and liberty. A child from such an institution will be liberal in mind and rational in decisions. **Ascriptive**[4] criteria do not influence such an individual.

On the contrary, a school that itself discriminates sows such seeds of hatred and animosity in the hearts of children. We often hear that caste-based discrimination exists in schools. A child studying in such an institution will develop unhealthy attitudes and mostly become caste chauvinist. Beyond educational institutions, religious institutions today are re-emerging in shaping a person's belief. Be it liberal and enlightening or fundamental, religious institutions not only form an individual's attitude but it creates a social attitude. The children are now part of sports clubs, the National Cadet Corps, scouts and guides, etc. These institutions help develop discipline, sportsmanship, and tolerance and teach children to face failures.

4.4 Familiarity

Familiarity breeds a positive attitude. Man generally has a fear of the unknown, so anything familiar might make him or her feel at peace. Familiarity and classical conditioning act on the emotions of an individual and therefore shape the affective component of attitudes.

Sociologists define familiarity as a dynamic relationship that grows over a period of time through interactions and engagement with the individual's surroundings. This can include a physical or psychological reaction which can be negative or positive given the context, and generating a sense of 'knowing' and 'comfort' in most cases. Familiarity is the specific sensation that is birthed after experiencing certain stimuli consistently.

Familiarity is key to forming connections and creating memories, which facilitate how we perceive and understand the world around us. It informs our responses and helps organise our feelings towards a particular thing, person, sensation, incident, or emotion. What feels familiar to an individual depends on the surroundings they are interacting with and this informs the attitude they grow to develop toward those things.

Example

An infant would cry when a new face takes him or her into their arms. He or she would only cling to those familiar persons. Advertisement is another form by which a product or a brand

[4]**Ascriptive:** (*adj.*) related to a belief that something is caused/created by someone/something

is made familiar to the public. Out of a million products a person chooses the most advertised product. Mere exposure and familiarity of an attitude object lead to the formation of a positive attitude towards it. This attitude is independent of the knowledge about the attitude object. One may possess zero knowledge about an object yet develop a positive attitude just because of his familiarity.

5. FUNCTIONS OF ATTITUDE

Familiarity and classical conditioning stress the affective component of attitude and operant conditioning. Observational conditioning stresses the behavioural component of attitude. The function that attitude serves helps us understand which component gains the upper hand over the rest in developing attitude. The functional view of attitudes (as opposed to the structural one) emphasises how attitudes might be useful to the people who hold them.

Generally, the functional view holds that the purpose of attitudes is to mediate between a person's internal needs (e.g., for safety, self-expression, etc.) and the external environment, full of people and information. Each attitude a person holds then can be expected to help that person meet their needs in some way or other.

Every individual responds to particular stimuli in a particular way to satisfy a particular need. The attitude of an individual is linked to his or her needs. When needs change so does his or her attitude? In a given situation, several people may express similar attitudes to an attitude object, but they will have different needs, and they satisfy different individual personal needs.

Example

A and B donate a part of their income to an orphanage. A donates because he is philanthropic and pro-social. B on the other hand donates to get tax concession. Here, the attitude is the same, but the reasons are different and satisfy different needs. When the government policy changes and does not give concessions anymore, B will stop donating but A will continue to donate.

5.1 The Identity Function

Attitude performs an important function in expressing one's beliefs and values. It is through these values and expressions that one establishes his or her identity.

Example

The Government of India is disinvesting public sector enterprises. Raheem voices his protest against this move. He claims that such a move would be anti-people and benefit only private industrialists. Clearly, this attitude shows that he is socialistic and establishes a leftist identity.

5.2 The Self-Esteem Function

An individual's attitude about an object helps him or her to develop confidence increase morale and enhance self-esteem. When he or she has a socially acceptable attitude and he or she realises that he or she has the right attitude then the person feels more confident and beams with pride which boosts his or her self-esteem.

Example

Ram and Raheem tease Ragini, who is shopping. Robert looks at it and immediately steps in and picks on Ram and Raheem. The onlookers too join Robert and eventually hand over Ram and Raheem to the cops. This attitude of Robert certainly enhances his self-esteem.

5.3 Knowledge Function

Attitudes aid in the accumulation of knowledge. They help an individual to interpret new information regarding the attitude object which would influence his or her response in the future. When a person has a positive attitude toward an object, he or she would seek more information that would help him or her reinforce and modify his or her attitude. A newborn child looks at the world in an amazed manner. As he or she grows, the world seems confused and chaotic. Attitude helps to organise and interpret the worldview. When new information is received, the person will be able to place it without much confusion because of attitude. An individual needs a structured, consistent, and stable world.

Proper **cognisance**[5] and understanding will make an individual look at the world in an orderly fashion. This need gives rise to acquiring knowledge we know so that we can predict. Prediction helps an individual to invest his or her physical and mental strength for his or her benefit and the benefit of others. It gives a sense of control over his or her life.

Example

Ram and Raheem are friends. Ram is a stockbroker, and Raheem is a white collared employee. Raheem has zero market knowledge as he has a negative attitude towards it. He wants to invest in stocks to become rich and because of this he has developed a positive attitude toward stocks and shares. He seeks knowledge about the stock market from Ram. He tries to construct an orderly and stable environment so that he can invest. This depicts that a change in attitude brings more knowledge about an attitude object. A person who has a positive attitude towards football will have more knowledge about it than those who have a neutral or negative attitude towards football.

5.4 Utilitarian Function

Every action concerning an attitude object is done with an expectancy to fulfil a psychological need. The operant conditioning principle emphasises this utilitarian aspect of an attitude. The

[5] **Cognisance:** (*noun*) Knowledge or awareness

outcome of an attitude may be in self-interest or public interest. Nevertheless, both serve as a utility. The self-interest or public interest is the reward or positive outcome that is associated with an attitude. An individual's attitude varies following the outcome, either positive or negative.

5.5 Ego-Defensive Function

Attitude helps an individual to protect one's ego, self-image, and self-esteem and cope with emotional conflicts. Attitudes serve as defensive mechanisms from crucifixion of one's ego thereby protecting them from psychological harm. The American Psychological Association (APA) defines the ego-defensive function of attitude as the active role attitude plays in maintaining or enhancing the self-perception of the individual. Studies highlight how defensiveness protects the ego (self-concept) and influences how people reject messages that challenge their strong opinions or values. When people are personally involved with an issue, they are more likely to respond defensively to opposing information. This helps us better understand why people resist changing their attitudes even when presented with strong arguments.

Example

Robert grew up in a predominantly conservative household where his father was the head, and his mother managed the household. He saw from a young age how his family gave more importance to and respected the labour of his father more than they did his mother's. When his mother expressed wanting to restart her education, Robert resisted the idea as he couldn't understand the need behind her decision. The ego-defensive function of attitude can be summed up as taking place through the following stages:

- Denial,
- Repression,
- Projection and
- Rationalisation

1. **Denial**

   Denial is a mechanism by which a person rejects information that is unfavourable for his or her ego. He or she rejects it as frivolous and untrue despite the presence of overwhelming evidence. Psychologically speaking, denial is a defense mechanism[6] where an individual feels like they have to reject facts, distort reality, or misconstrue information to avoid an uncomfortable truth. People usually deny reality due to shame, trauma, stressful situations, or extreme emotional discomfort.

   Example

   Raman is gay and is attracted to guys. Due to the social stigma surrounding queer relationships, he denies his sexuality fearing social repercussions and the possibility of

[6]**Defence Mechanism:** It refers to the psychological strategy an individual uses to cope or survive a traumatic or highly stressful event.

becoming estranged from his family and friends. Thus, he claims that he is straight and vocally expresses his denial.

2. **Repression**

An individual defends his or her emotional self by repressing or subduing his or her thoughts, feelings, and desires to the unconscious or subconscious level of the mind. Repressing any unacceptable thing to a conscious mind, which if allowed or recalled, creates unfavourable emotions which prevent it from resurfacing. Unlike denial which requires an active or conscious participation of the individual, repression is a subconscious defence mechanism to protect an individual's mind from expressing extreme forms of fear or anxiety.

Example

Rita suffers from a mental disorder called Dissociative Identity Disorder (DID) in which extreme childhood trauma resulting from consistent abuse leads the child to disassociate and repress those traumatic memories through the development of alters or different identities.

3. **Projection**

An individual defends his or her ego by denying the existence of feelings and impulses in himself and instead attributes such feelings and impulses to others.

Example

Unfaithful partners would often suspect their partner of being unfaithful in a projection of their guilt and insecurity. Arjun's accusations rang loud in their small apartment, his words sharp and unrelenting. Meera sat quietly at the dining table; her eyes fixed on the crumpled receipt she'd found in his jacket pocket—a hotel room booked in a city she'd never visited.

"You're always on your phone," he snapped, pacing the room. "Sneaking around, lying—what are you hiding, Meera?"

She finally looked up, her voice calm but heavy. "I'm hiding the truth, Arjun—the truth about you."

She slid the receipt across the table. The room fell silent, the weight of his guilt louder than her words ever could be.

4. **Rationalisation**

It is a defence mechanism by which an individual justifies his or her actions with a seemingly rational and logical explanation. Rationalisation includes minimising the gravity of a situation for one's benefit, making excuses, and blaming others for their failures, and refers to generally attributing their emotions and feelings to others. Rationalisation in this sense indicates an individual disavowing motivation from themselves. It differs from the projection in terms of the active misattribution of motives to others that happen in this case, which is usually absent from rationalisation.

Example

Robert applies for a job, and he does not land it. He says that it is better that he did not get the job as it was only a temporary job, and he would have quit it sooner or later.

Robert applied for a job but didn't get it. He rationalises the outcome by noting that the position was temporary and he would have left eventually.

6. ATTITUDE-BEHAVIOUR

Generally, it is assumed that attitude guides behaviour. Initially, Psychologists believed that by studying attitude one can explain behaviour. They were of the belief that an individual's behaviour is consistent with his or her attitude. Behaviour can be influenced by a number of factors beyond attitude, including preconceptions about self and others, monetary factors, social influences (what peers and community members are saying and doing), and convenience.

Someone may have strong convictions about improving the public school system in their town, but if it means a hefty increase to their property taxes, they may vote against any improvements due to the potential for monetary loss. Or, they may simply not vote at all because their polling place is too far from their home, or the weather is bad on election day.

Studies have demonstrated that, in some cases, pointing out inconsistencies between attitudes and behaviour can redirect the behaviour. However, later research led to the modification of this relationship between attitude and behaviour. Two famous studies by Richard LaPiere and Stephen M. Covey led to this modification.

6.1 Richard LaPiere-Classic Study (1934)

LaPiere spent two years travelling with a Chinese couple in America. Travelling required their stay in several hotels and dining in several resorts. Overall, they had 66 lodgings and were never refused services in all the 184 restaurants they dined. After completing his trip LaPiere mailed questionnaires to all the hotels and restaurants that the couple visited in their two years travels. He obtained 128 replies. In response to the critical question, 92% of the restaurants and 91% of the hotels/motels reported that they would not accept Chinese customers.

The majority of the remainder reported that they were uncertain whether they would and that it would depend on circumstances. LaPiere's study is often cited as evidence that there is little or no relationship between attitudes and behaviour. His study proved and explained that what people say they will do is often very different from how they behave!

LaPiere concluded that people responded more to appearance and self-confidence rather than race. It may seem strange that people claimed to be racist when they were not. Nowadays, we might be more concerned about the opposite pattern—people who claim not to be prejudiced, when their behaviour suggests otherwise. Either way, though, the key theoretical issue is that attitudes do not always match actions.

6.2 Stephen M. Covey: Professed Attitudes and Actual Behaviour (1937)

At the beginning of the semester, Covey gave a questionnaire and measured the attitude of students towards cheating in an examination. The measure showed that they were inclined to copy in the examination. In the semester examination, he allowed ample scope and gave opportunities to students to indulge in malpractices. However, he found that the students did not cheat despite being willing to do so. There was inconsistency between the professed attitudes and actual behaviour. It is quite natural for a person to think that an individual's attitudes and behaviour are directly related. However, it is not so, the attitude and actual working and behaviour are different. When someone says that he or she is not casteist, we expect him or her to act in conformity to his or her attitude. Yet we often find that the behaviour of such persons is not consistent with their attitude. He or she does not discriminate based on caste at his or her workplace, college, or among his or her friends. But when it comes to marriage the foremost criteria are that the spouse should be of the same caste. It is this irony that was made visible by LaPiere and Covey's studies.

7. FACTORS RESPONSIBLE FOR ATTITUDE BEHAVIOUR DISCREPANCY

7.1 Social Acceptance

Social norms and an individual's need to get socially accepted modify the individual's behaviour which would not be consistent with the individual's attitude. We often see this kind of behaviour exhibited by a politician while seeking votes. His attitude towards women and caste would be regressive. Yet in his public life and election meetings he talks about women empowerment, gender sensitisation, and anti-caste.

Example

Raheem has a negative attitude towards alcoholism. However, in college, he goes along with friends and indulges in alcohol consumption just to be accepted by his friends.

- **Social Bonding**

There is quite a lot of discrepancy when it comes to behaviour towards a friend, family, and others. The relationships that an individual has influenced the deviation of behaviour concerning attitude. Against the same attitude object, the individual will act differently who is closely related to the individual.

Example

Raheem has a negative attitude towards cheating in exams. He would definitely report any such instance happening in the examination hall to the invigilator. Ram, a close friend of Raheem indulges in copying and Raheem notices it. There is a huge probability that he would not report the issue to the invigilator.

7.2 Situation

Despite having an attitude towards an attitude object an individual's behaviour changes when the situation changes. Particularly, contingencies throw a person's response off balance.

Example

Raheem is an animal lover and a vegetarian. He goes for a trek into the forests. What will he do when a bear tries to attack him? He has lost his way. It has been three days and he's starving. All he could find were fish in a stream. Will he eat them to survive or starve to death?

7.3 Attitude Strength

The strength of one's attitude and resolve go a long way in maintaining the consistency between attitude and behaviour. A person with strong conviction and attitude towards attitude object behaves in a way that is consistent with his or her attitude. Mahatma Gandhi's strong attitude towards freedom and non-violence was manifested in the way he spoke and behaved. The *Chipko Movement* and *Jal Satyagraha* are examples of behaving in consistency with one's attitudes.

The strength of the attitude depends on the attitude extremity and personal experience.

1. **Attitude extremity**
   The extent to which an individual internalises beliefs about an attitude object determines the consistency between attitude and behaviour. Behaviour is consistent with attitude when the individual has a strong negative or positive attitude. An individual develops a strong attitude if the outcome of the attitude is about to have a greater impact on the individual. As the impact gets stronger, so will the influence of the attitude on behaviour.

> **? Thought Box**
>
> How does the strength of one's attitudes shape their ability to align actions with beliefs, even in the face of external challenges or societal pressures?

2. **Personal experience**

   When attitude is developed based on personal experience, the individual is more likely to behave by the attitude than an attitude formed indirectly.

   Example

   Ram uses a phone of a particular brand. Raheem, his friend, asks Ram about his experience. Ram says that he has had a nightmarish experience with the brand. Now, Raheem has a negative attitude towards that particular brand. Both Ram and Raheem go to the shop to buy mobiles for each other. Now in the most likely state who is more prone to rejecting that particular brand? Ram who has had personal experience or Raheem who has got the hearsay experience? Both have negative attitudes towards the brand. But it is a question of who will strongly behave in consistency with their attitude.

8. COGNITIVE DISSONANCE

As we have seen earlier, attitude and behaviour are not always directly related. There is a discrepancy between what one believes and how one acts. What happens in the mind of an individual when he behaves in contrast to a professed attitude? Certainly, an individual feels uneasy and uncomfortable while deciding against his or her beliefs. This negative feeling is called cognitive dissonance or an unpleasant state of mind. Cognitive dissonance may at times lead to attitude change.

Whenever there is an inconsistency between attitudes and behaviour, the individual will attempt to reduce the dissonance. When the inconsistency happens once or twice, the probability of attitude change is slim. However, when it becomes routine, cognitive dissonance becomes overwhelming; there is a high probability that the individual will change his or her attitude to match his or her behaviour. The amount of dissonance people experience can depend on a few different factors, including how highly we value a particular belief and the degree to which our beliefs are inconsistent. The overall strength of the dissonance can be influenced by several factors.

Ways of dissonance reduction:

1. An individual may change his or her attitude or behaviour to make them consistent.
2. By acquiring more knowledge or information about the attitude object that may support his or her attitude or behaviour. In other words, an individual attempts to justify his or her attitude or behaviour by gathering more information, thereby reducing cognitive dissonance.
3. By ignoring or downplaying, an individual reduces dissonance. He or she brushes aside the inconsistency as something unimportant and downplays the dissonance. He or she considers these issues as trivial and ignores them.

4. By self-consolation, it says that it was demanded by the situation and he or she was forced to act. He or she tries to reduce the dissonance by putting away his or her guilt consciousness. He or she thinks about all the good things he or she has done and slip ups are bound to happen now and then. By contemplating the good aspects, he or she reduces the unpleasant feeling in his or her mind.

9. ATTITUDE CHANGE

Attitude is based on cumulative experiences and practices and not on a single situation. Attitude is not necessarily permanent. It can be modified, discarded, or replaced. Several things lead to a change in attitude.

9.1 Persuasion

Sometimes individuals change their attitude upon persuasion by others. The importance of such a persuasion depends on the persuader and the message.

- **Persuader**

The source of the message is very important to cause attitude change. The persuader should be credible and trustworthy. Also, if the person perceives that the attitude of the persuader is similar to him or her then the attitude change will be successful.

- **Message**

The content is equally important in determining the quantity of attitude change. The message should be acceptable and elicit little counterargument. Only then will it be able to bring about attitude change?

9.2 Switching Groups

When a person switches his or her membership to a new group there is the likelihood that the new norms will bring about attitude change. This, however, depends on the individual's perception of the group and his or her position in it. If he or she perceives that he or she is in the core of the group then his or her attitude will in all likelihood be influenced by the group. On the flipside, if he or she feels that he or she is on the periphery of the group then he or she may resist change in his or her attitude.

9.3 Information

Ignorance breeds negative attitudes. New information about the attitude object either through education, media, observation, or experience dispels ignorance. The new information will lead to altering the response to the same stimuli, thus ushering in a new attitude.

10. RESISTANCE TO ATTITUDE CHANGE

Not every attempt to bring about attitude change yields results. Some attitudes can be changed easily, others with some or great difficulty or some are never possible. Some individuals resist change in attitude more vigorously than others. The ways by which individuals resist attitude change are:

(i) Avoidance,

(ii) Selective perception and

(iii) Group membership.

10.1 Avoidance

Every individual will have internalised his or her attitude by the time he or she becomes an adult. The person will search for information/evidence that would reinforce his or her attitude. He or she would also face evidence or information that would be in contradiction with his or her attitude. A conformist[7] or a conservative or status-quoist would feel uncomfortable with such information. Such an individual would conscientiously avoid such information or evidence whenever possible. Fundamentalism, patriarchy, and casteism are examples of avoidance.

10.2 Selective Perception

An individual's attitude will enable him or her to look at the world in a particular way. The individual's perception of the world may make him or her comfortable or uncomfortable. The world may be sane, insane, or even mundane to him or her. When he or she comes across a new piece of information, evidence, or experience about an attitude object, he or she seeks and selects those pieces that would help him or her reinforce their attitude.

Example

A person has been subjected to police brutality several times. He looks upon the police with antagonism. When he sees a cop, he will look for cold stares, aggressiveness, baton, and a tough

[7]**Conformist:** A conformist refers to an individual with a blasé attitude of remaining indifferent by behaving the way others in their group do instead of having contrary opinions.

tone that will help him confirm his beliefs. Finding none of these will not shake his belief rather finding one of these will reinforce his belief. Such selective perception causes resistance to change in attitude as it aids in reinforcing the internalised attitude.

10.3 Group Membership

A social group's survival rests on the conformity of members to its norms. Therefore, they try to curtail any attempts of deviance. An individual also prefers to go along with the group as it is comfortable and advantageous to him or her. Any individual expressing an attitude that contradicts the group norms will invite sanction, boycott, condemnation, and curtailment. The benefits of conformity and sanctions for deviance will cause strong resistance to an individual's attitude change.

Example

A parent refuses their ward's intercaste love marriage. This is mainly due to the consequences they will have to face within their caste group.

11. MORAL AND POLITICAL ATTITUDES

11.1 Moral Attitude

An attitude with a strong moral foundation is referred to as a moral attitude. Moral attitudes are deeply rooted in moral convictions. Morality refers to the set of principles that help individuals to identify between right and wrong.

Family, religion, culture, profession, and personal experiences determine individual moral attitudes as morality is shaped more by various social and environmental factors.

Moral attitude is more resistant to change than other attitudes as this forms a part of the character of the person having deep-seated moral beliefs. A moral attitude allows and encourages quick and intuitive social judgements.

Moral attitude often prevents an individual from acting 'immoral' as this is often rooted in conscience. However, attention should also be paid to acts that cause harm to the society and are justified by an individual morality. As moral attitudes are not easy to change, they may sometimes result in great harm becoming the negative implication of moral attitude.

Moral values are always supreme in the hierarchy of values. Values like truthfulness, humility, compassion, forgiveness, etc., are always considered superior to values like beauty or wealth. Moral attitudes are rooted in these values and have a crucial influence on individual actions.

11.2 Political Attitude

An attitude that someone holds towards a political ideology is referred to as a political attitude. Political attitude determines the outlook of an individual with respect to political parties, events, and issues.

One may be interested in contesting elections and the other may not even be interested in casting a vote, this likelihood of participating and showing interest arises from one's political attitude.

Family, society, education, exposure, social identity, geographical and historical factors, socioeconomic conditions, social media, etc play a significant role in shaping the political attitude of a person.

> **? Thought Box**
>
> How do you think an individual's internal perception of themselves can be vastly different than what others perceive them to be?

- **Radical, Liberal, and Conservative Attitudes**

Political ideology followed by a person directly affects the political attitude of that person. Political ideology ranges from extreme left to extreme right with liberal ideology in the centre. Radical attitude can be understood as a general outlook where individuals are rigorous and extreme about their ideological beliefs. These often correlate with politics. Political attitude is a topic of many contentions and is performed both in the private and public space of an individual's life. In lay terms, liberal ideology is a political and philosophical stance in favour of principles like equality, democracy, and individual rights. In modern connotation, liberalism is seen as a neutral or centrist approach to understanding politics.

People with the radical conceptualisation of equality, redistribution of wealth, power of the people, and various other aspects of individual identities are on the left of liberal ideology and are extremely dissatisfied with the existing **status quo**[8] and dominant capitalist institutions and systems in place. People who favour the status quo often doubt change in the existing political structure resulting in something better, favour capitalistic monopoly, and abide by conservative and patriarchal ideals lie on the right side of liberal attitude, which is conservatism.

12. ATTITUDE OF CIVIL SERVANTS

In a democratic country like India, the power lies with the people. People elect representatives, and these elected representatives exercise power and have the command to manage people for a specific period. The civil servants being the backbone of the country are expected to be partners

[8]**Status quo:** Equilibrium, current state of things

who will efficiently work and carry out the policies of the government. Their selection happens impartially through a competitive all-India test. Their administrative competence is developed through proper training. To evince a spirit of service to the community, they are given proper orientation to be politically neutral with the people. The right attitude of civil servants, who constitute the most vital pillar of good governance is very crucial for India to thrive as a healthy and vibrant democratic country.

Attitude is a learned tendency to evaluate issues, events, people, and situations in a particular way and determine individuals' behaviour and action towards them. Attitude is more associated with character or virtue. Attitude is an essential trait to succeed in any walk of life. However, it becomes more important in civil services for its impact on society.

As it is said by Winston Churchill, 'Attitude is a little thing that makes a big difference.' The government must proactively work towards building the right attitude in civil servants. Civil servants possessing attitudes aligning with traits like compassion towards people, tolerance, accountability, impartiality, fairness, dedication to public service, and a sense of engagement make a big difference in the lives of people and society.

Attitude of civil servants play a very crucial role in securing the confidence in the government of the country and poise and contentment of the people. The responsible officers of the government must realise that they are after all 'public servants' and that conciliation and cooperation should be the basic principle of the relationship between the rulers and the ruled.

'Dedication, professionalism, and diligence' the core values that civil servants are required to uphold. The civil service endeavours to serve the community and contribute to the effective governance as well as stability and prosperity of the nation.

With the community's rising expectations for public services, the civil service must continue to strive for excellence. Civil servants, charged with serving the interests and protecting the rights of the people and the country, are confronted with complex attitudinal problems involving conflicting values, preferences, unreliable information, and unintended negative consequences.

Civil servants must understand and accept that they are merely servants of people. Servant leadership can enhance service attitude in two ways: First, there is a direct effect, whereby leaders as role models inspire employees to engage in service. Leaders establish a common vision, thus promoting enhanced service awareness. Second, there is an indirect effect through intrinsic motivation, whereby basic psychological needs are satisfied based on reciprocity norms, which encourages civil servants to better perform their jobs.

Thus, it could be said that being equipped with a positive attitude towards leaders and the right attitude towards government enables civil servants to be highly engaged in the workplace. Reducing public spending without compromising on service quality, living affordability, public integrity, and economic growth matters requires a positive attitude and motivation of civil servants to share knowledge, ideas, and strategies.

12.1 Attitude Towards Leader

There is a relationship between attitude toward leaders and engagement among civil servants. The most significant factors that influence the performance of the public sector are management attitudes and administrative culture. In short, it can be said that the behaviours of civil servants in the workplace are strongly influenced by their attitude toward the leader. A positive attitude towards leaders makes them more dedicated and committed in the workplace and vice versa.

When undertaking tasks, the employees are emotionally inclined to the leader which results in the decision-making process becoming less influenced by cognition. Civil servants will accept the need and work to cut office expenditure if they have a positive perception towards the leader including the Prime Minister – the one that introduces cost reduction policy. Positive perception towards leaders inculcates a sense of engagement amongst civil servants and motivates them to take part in effective and efficient policy implementation.

12.2 Attitude Towards Government

A democratic system means that the government is elected by the people including civil servants during election day. In other words, civil servants favour one political party over other political party. This can bring out both the positive and negative outcomes. If the party that they support fails to form a government, those civil servants usually like to criticise and condemn the government in office.

This could lower productivity and performance eventually. Thus, managing political tension in the office healthily is crucial. In short, it can be said that the behaviours of civil servants in the workplace are strongly influenced by their attitude towards the government.

A positive attitude towards government makes them more committed to public service delivery in the workplace and vice versa. It is argued that a positive attitude towards government could make civil servants more engaged, in turn more willing to take part in the efficient delivery of services. Uncontrolled political differences in the workplace should be avoided as it will inhibit the unity amongst civil servants in the workplace which could reduce the quality of services given to the public.

13. BUREAUCRATIC AND DEMOCRATIC ATTITUDES

13.1 Bureaucratic Attitude[9]

The bureaucratic model is multidimensional, consisting of a formal structure like hierarchy and specialisation; administrative procedures and processes like compliance to formal rules and strong emphasis on law; and a personnel system like meritocratic recruitment, seniority, and tenure protection.

Bureaucratic attitude refers to the attitude possessed by the bureaucrats who roll out policies, and schemes keeping in focus the targeted section and once the law or rule is brought out, there is no flexibility in terms of relaxation in norms to anyone. There will be no scope for innovation and diverse ideas.

This bureaucratic attitude enables public servants to strictly follow the laid down rules and guidelines in decision-making processes. Objectivity, neutrality, secrecy, elite approach, etc are some basic attributes of this attitude.

Bureaucratic attitudes sometimes mar the spirit of democracy because of red tape, inspector raj, and corruption. It may also lead to apathy towards common people as rule is supreme and not citizens.

13.2 Democratic Attitude

The democratic model gives ultimate preference to citizens and encourages collaborative decision-making. There will be more scope for innovation and flexibility in operations. Those attitudes possessed by civil servants who promote the participation of people in decision-making are known as democratic attitudes.

Civil servants with a democratic attitude promote the delegation of authority. There is more focus on compassion, tolerance, and inclusiveness in place of rules and regulations. It promotes the active participation of people. This attitude strengthens the democratic institution at the grassroots level. It will make the governance system more transparent, and accountable and there will be efficient public service delivery.

As there is more participation of people in decision-making, the decision-making process will become slow and time-consuming. Sometimes, such an attitude becomes a hindrance to development as there will be difficulty in satisfying all the sections of society.

[9]**Bureaucratic Attitude:** Rigid compliance, An attitude that adheres to strict rules and procedures

13.3 Bureaucratic Leadership vs Democratic Leadership

Bureaucratic Leadership	Democratic Leadership
• Top-down decision-making	• Collaborative decision making
• Formal and one-way communication	• Open and two-way communication
• Limited involvement and participation of the public	• Encourages public participation
• Less flexibility and rigid adherence to rules	• High flexibility and more adaptability to changes
• Limited innovation	• Encourages diverse ideas
• Response to changes is slow due to hierarchical processes	• Response to changes is quick as there will be rapid adjustments

13.4 Balancing Bureaucratic and Democratic Attitudes

At higher levels of governance, there is a requirement for a bureaucratic attitude so that there is faster and more efficient decision-making. There should be provisions for flexibility and more focus on inclusive public service delivery at the micro level. At ground level, the democratic process has to be strengthened. In this way, to create a better administration for faster, equitable, and inclusive development of the country, both attitudes should be harmoniously balanced.

To create a more effective administration that is both efficient and responsive to the needs of the public, there should be a careful balance between both attitudes. A nuanced approach where the merits of each are leveraged and their demerits are mitigated is required. For example, for executing routine tasks, bureaucratic efficiency can be used, while a democratic approach can be adopted for policy formulation and areas requiring public input. This balance between bureaucratic and democratic attitudes ensures that the administration is not only fast and efficient but also inclusive and accountable.

14. FACTORS CONTRIBUTING TO FOSTERING POSITIVE ATTITUDE IN A CIVIL SERVANT

A positive attitude refers to an optimistic frame of mind. A positive attitude helps individuals to cope more easily with the daily affairs of life. People with this type of attitude are happier in life and are also more successful than those who do not.

A positive attitude is not merely a desirable trait but an indispensable asset for civil servants navigating the complexities of their roles, frequently amidst high-pressure situations. Their attitude towards the citizenry becomes a reflection of the state. Civil servants must possess a positive attitude in every action as administrative decision-making is becoming increasingly complicated by conflicting responsibilities that pressure the civil servants in different directions. Several factors contribute to fostering such a mindset in individuals.

Firstly, emotional intelligence and self-awareness play pivotal roles, aiding and enabling one to manage their own emotions and understand the emotions of others effectively. Additionally, resilience equips individuals with the mental fortitude to maintain optimism in adverse circumstances and this resilience is cultivated through experiences of overcoming challenges. Moreover, a positive outlook is fostered through a supportive work environment and healthy interpersonal relationships.

Furthermore, a sense of purpose and dedication to public service is still a deep-seated motivation to persevere and make meaningful contributions despite obstacles. With empathy, civil servants can comprehend and share the emotions of others, honour their viewpoints, and offer compassion. This can facilitate the development of a positive attitude, trust, rapport, and collaboration with others.

Lastly, civil servants view setbacks as opportunities for growth rather than insurmountable barriers only when they adopt a growth mindset that embraces learning and adaptation. In essence, a positive attitude emerges from a confluence of internal resilience, external support systems, and a commitment to purposeful action, essential for civil servants navigating the demands of their profession.

> **? Thought Box**
>
> Suppose you are working in the government, and you need support from your colleagues to fight for the cause you believe in. However, they do not share the same views as you. How would you convince them to care about a particular issue they are not interested in?

15. ROLE AND IMPORTANCE OF POSITIVE ATTITUDE IN THE CIVIL SERVANT

Civil servants will have a favourable perspective on themselves, others, and various circumstances with a positive mindset. Civil servants with positive attitudes easily manage obstacles, surmount challenges, and attain objectives. As civil servants engage with diverse stakeholders and navigate intricate issues, cultivating a positive attitude in them holds immense significance.

1. **Solution-driven Approach and Adaptability:** Civil servants possessing a positive attitude are more inclined to tackle issues and obstacles with a forward-thinking and solution-driven approach. A positive attitude gives them the ability to conceive innovative ideas and analyse alternate strategies resulting in more adept decision-making and resolution of problems.

2. **Collective Support and Collaboration:** Civil servants fostering a positive mindset tend to improve robust connections. A positive attitude enables them to proactively seek assistance and aid colleagues when needed. This establishes a framework to promote the exchange of insights and mutual aid.
3. **Communication and Leadership:** Civil servants can effectively convey messages even during high-pressure instances with an optimistic mindset. A positive attitude can cultivate a positive work atmosphere. They can actively listen and take constructive inputs, thereby efficiently leading the team and elevating overall efficiency.
4. **Building and Enhancing Resilience:** Civil servants with positive thinking build greater resilience. A positive attitude helps civil servants to quickly recover from emotional responses to failures and mistakes. It helps them to learn lessons and implement those corrections in subsequent actions.
5. **Improving Decision-Making Skills:** During adverse circumstances, maintaining a positive mindset and attitude results in better and more efficient decision-making. This positive frame of mind promotes constructive thinking and encourages to take calculated risks while making decisions.
6. **Positive Outlook towards Society:** Civil servants with positive attitudes are oriented towards the end. This attitude gives them motivation and energy to do things and accomplish goals. Civil Servants being the face of Government with a positive attitude contribute to the welfare of the people which is the ultimate aim and objective.

SUMMARY

- Attitude is defined as a positive, negative, or neutral evaluation of objects, actions, people, or concepts. It is often expressed on a continuum and contributes to shaping interpersonal relationships. The ABC Model of understanding attitude is the most commonly accepted one comprising of affective component, behavioural component, and cognitive component.
- Formation of attitude happens through certain mechanisms such as classical and operant conditioning, observational learning, and social comparison.
- Factors and functions of attitude inform a person's values and beliefs growing up, can influence their sense of self and how they relate to others, enable an individual to become organised and educated, provide the outlook needed to achieve one's goals and can also perpetuate defensive denial or deflection.
- Attitude and behaviour though are quite often used interchangeably in casual conversations, are distinct concepts academically. Early research suggested a direct relationship between the two; however, later studies, such as Richard LaPiere's 1934 study, revealed inconsistencies between expressed attitudes and actual behaviours. It is now commonly accepted that attitude refers

to a person's internal feelings or beliefs about objects, people, or concepts, while behaviour represents the external actions or responses to those beliefs.

- Cognitive Dissonance is characterised as an internalised psychological state in which an individual has conflicting and contrarian beliefs and the resulting confusion or discomfort that arises out of it. Best practices such as willingness to change, being more receptive to new knowledge, encouraging self-introspection, and gaining diversified knowledge coming from multi-cultural sources are some of how attitude change can be brought about for a positive change.
- Deeply rooted moral and political attitudes of different cultures are expressed on an individual and community level. Personal intuition of right and wrong coupled with radical, liberal, or conservative ideology forms the foundational blocks of a person's identity.
- A positive attitude beckons a healthy and well-functioning democracy and this is realised through the active participation of civil servants in the governance of a country.
- A balanced approach between bureaucratic and democratic attitudes ensures equitable, speedy, and inclusive governance.

PREVIOUS YEARS' QUESTIONS

1. Attitude is an important component that goes as input in the development of human beings. How to build a suitable attitude needed for a public servant? *UPSC CSE Mains 2021*
2. A positive attitude is considered to be an essential characteristic of a civil servant who is often required to function under extreme stress. What contributes to a positive attitude in a person? *UPSC CSE Mains 2020*
3. 'Hatred is destructive of a person's wisdom and conscience that can poison a Nation's spirit.' Do you agree with this view? Justify your answer. *UPSC CSE Mains 2020*
4. Young people with ethical conduct are not willing to come forward to join active politics. Suggest steps to motivate them to come forward. *UPSC CSE Mains 2017*
5. How could social influence and persuasion contribute to the success of Swachh Bharat Abhiyan? *UPSC CSE Mains 2016*
6. Our attitudes towards life, work, other people, and society are generally shaped unconsciously by the family and social surroundings in which we grow up. Some of these unconsciously acquired attitudes and values are often undesirable in the citizens of modern democratic and egalitarian societies. (a) Discuss such undesirable values prevalent in today's educated Indians. (b) How can such undesirable attitudes be changed and socio-ethical values be cultivated in the aspiring and serving civil servants? *UPSC CSE Mains 2016*
7. The current society is plagued with a widespread trust deficit. What are the consequences of this situation for personal well-being and societal well-being? What can you do at the personal level to make yourself trustworthy? *UPSC CSE Mains 2014*

8. What factors affect the formation of a person's attitude towards social problems? In our society, contrasting attitudes are prevalent about many social problems. What contrasting attitudes do you notice about the caste system in our society? How do you explain the existence of these contrasting attitudes? *UPSC CSE Mains 2014*
9. We are witnessing increasing instances of sexual violence against women in the country. Despite existing legal provisions against it, the number of such incidences is on the rise. Suggest some innovative measures to tackle this menace. *UPSC CSE Mains 2014*
10. In the context of defence services, "patriotism" demands readiness to even lay down one's life to protect the nation. According to you, what does patriotism imply in everyday civil life? Explain with illustrations and justify your answer. *UPSC CSE Mains 2014*
11. It is often said that 'politics' and 'ethics' do not go together. What is your opinion in this regard? Justify your answer with illustrations. *UPSC CSE Mains 2013*

Emotional Intelligence

8

1. INTRODUCTION

The Oxford English dictionary defines emotion by 'any agitation or disturbance of mind, feeling passion, any vehement or excited mental state'. Emotion can be referred to a feeling and its distinctive thoughts, psychological and biological states, and range of **propensities**[1] to act. There are hundreds of emotions, along with their blends, mutations, variations, and nuances. Indeed, there are many more variants of emotion than we have words for.

According to another perspective, emotions can be compared to an electromagnetic spectrum, encompassing anger, sadness, fear, shame, disgust, surprise, loneliness, and enjoyment, roughly in this sequence. These primary emotions blend with time and space to give rise to the new blended emotions.

An emotion is a strong instinctive feeling. Emotions per se are not harmful. It becomes a problem when they get extreme. The power of emotions has been recognised since time immemorial. That is why, societies have resorted to religious and ethical codes to subdue and harness emotions. Whether it is the code of Hammurabi, the Ten Commandments of the Hebrews, the *Manusmriti*, the *Vedas* of the Hindus, or

[1]**Propensities:** An inclination to behave in a particular way

LEARNING OBJECTIVES

1. Recognising the significance of emotions in shaping individual behaviour and decision-making
2. Understanding the concept of emotional intelligence and its practical applications
3. Exploring the types of intelligence and Howard Gardner's multiple intelligence theory
4. Gaining insights into Daniel Goleman's five domains of emotional intelligence
5. Analysing the development of emotional intelligence through key models, including Mayer and Salovey's model and the Pyramid of Emotional Intelligence
6. Understanding the family's pivotal role in nurturing emotional awareness and regulation
7. Highlighting the relevance of emotional intelligence in enhancing effectiveness within civil services
8. Learning about emotional resilience and the consequences of emotional illiteracy

the Edicts of Ashoka—all these texts include laws designed to regulate and restrain the intense emotions within individuals. It is contended that unchecked emotions can create havoc not just for individuals but for the social fabric at large, hence, the moral imperative is to curb them.

Scientific advancements of the present times, especially in the field of study of functioning of brain, have clarified the role and mechanism of emotions. Studies have made it clearer, as to how human brain changes in its rhythm while we think and feel, imagine and dream. This has enabled better understanding of emotions and EI. It can be stated that human beings have two minds – rational and emotional. This is akin to the popular distinction between the head and the heart. Usually, there is a balance between emotional and rational mind, with emotional feeds informing the operations of the rational mind, and the rational mind refining and sometimes, negating the inputs of the emotions. They are also semi-independent faculties, as each reflects the operation of distinct but interconnected circuitry of the brain. But when passions elevate, there is an imbalance, and the emotional mind dominates. Because of the way the brain is structured, emotional regions are deeply **ingrained**[2] in all thinking regions, giving them enormous influence on other regions of the brain. When and how that happens is important because it is at this junction that one takes decisions or acts in a manner, which is regretted later.

QUOTATIONS ON EMOTIONAL INTELLIGENCE

"Emotional intelligence is the ability to sense, understand, and effectively apply the power and acumen of emotions as a source of human energy, information, connection, and influence.

Robert K. Cooper

Emotional intelligence is what humans are good at and that's not a sideshow. That's the cutting edge of human intelligence.

Ray Kurzweil

It takes something more than intelligence to act intelligently.

Fyodor Dostoyevsky

What really matters for success, character, happiness, and lifelong achievements is a definite set of emotional skills—your EQ—not just purely cognitive abilities that are measured by conventional IQ tests.

Daniel Goleman

I've learned that people will forget what you said, people will forget what you did, but people will never forget how you made them feel.

Maya Angelou

I don't want to be at the mercy of my emotions. I want to use them, to enjoy them, and to dominate them.

Oscar Wilde"

---

[2]**Ingrained:** Firmly fixed

2. ROLE OF EMOTIONS IN AN INDIVIDUAL

The emotions prepare the body to act in a manner that may be beneficial/**detrimental**[3] to the situation. Emotions help to learn, enhance memory, and motivate one in achieving the best performance. Emotions give situations meaning. Without emotions, we would react spontaneously and robotically to events around us, with no control over our response. We would not be able to influence outcomes or achieve our goals or desires.

Experiencing emotions means that any new information we receive is interpreted and evaluated based on our past experiences, goals, and desires.

Emotions are crucial to learning and memory. They motivate us toward seeking new knowledge and achieving rewards. They also help us avoid harm and distress. Emotions provide information that helps us understand our relationship with the world.

3. TYPES OF INTELLIGENCE

Howard Gardner, one of the most acclaimed psychologists, questioned the traditional method of evaluating intelligence, as he was against the concept of understanding intelligence from limited perspective. He identified seven varieties of intelligence including the traditionally conceived intelligence. They are given in the tabulation below:

Table 8.1: Howard Gardner's multiple intelligences model

Intelligence	Related Activity	Great Practitioners
Logical-mathematical	Resolving the complex problems	Russell, Chandrasekhar, Newton, Venkatraman Rama Krishnan, Ramanujam
Musical	Great classical musical compositions from western and oriental countries	M S Subbulaxmi, Tansen, Rukmani Devi Arundale
Body-Kinesthetic	Elastic nature of physical body as in classical dance and gymnastics	Birju Maharaj, Padma Subrahmanyam, Mrunalini, Mallika Sarabhai
Visual-Spatial	Painting, architecture	Louis Corbusier, Renzo Piano, Frank Gehry
Linguistic-Verbal	Great writings	Amitava Ghosh, Anita Desai
Interpersonal	Public Relations	Winston Churchill, Mahatma Gandhi
Intrapersonal	Insights into human mind and conquering one's mind.	Aurobindo, Sigmund Freud, Gautam Buddha, Skinner, William James, Amit Abraham

[3]**Detrimental:** Tending to cause harm

4. WHAT IS EMOTIONAL INTELLIGENCE (EI)?

In 1990, Peter Salovey and Jack Meyer coined the term 'Emotion Intelligence' to describe the way of people's emotions. Later, Dr. Daniel Goleman had offered a definition for EI.

Emotional Intelligence (EI) is not one thing. It is about understanding emotions, impulses, and drivers, and intelligently handling these to enhance performance and relationships.

Our ability to act with EI depends on our level of emotional maturity. Maturity comes from wisdom gained through experience, combined with an increased understanding of ourself and an insight into how we may interact with others. This knowledge, gained along personal journey through life, explains why our EI increases with age and experience.

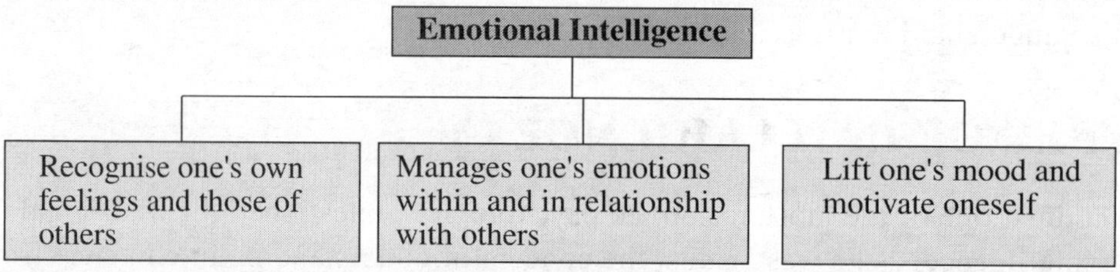

The fact remains, everyone is emotionally intelligent to some degree, but whether we choose to act with EI depends on whether we believe in and value our feelings, and on whether we understand the impact of EI has on our life today. Acting with EI is the way to enhance our personal performance and to succeed when working with others.

5. EMOTIONAL INTELLIGENCE Vs. INTELLIGENCE QUOTIENT

Historically, human intelligence is based on cognitive intelligence, and from the early 20th century onwards intelligence quotient, or Intelligence Quotient (IQ) tests have been available to measure cognitive ability and intellect. With school systems around the world geared towards valuing and developing the logical-mathematical and linguistic capabilities, IQ alone was widely believed to be the best predictor of success.

In recent years, research by various psychologists has suggested that qualities beyond IQ play a significant role in determining success. These qualities, often associated with the ability to interact effectively with others, are collectively referred to as Emotional Intelligence.

Research suggests a new approach to understanding and measuring human emotions through Emotional Intelligence (EI). It emphasises that a person's role in society is determined by 20% IQ and 80% other factors, including social institutions, culture, and, most prominently, EI.

IQ and EI are two different concepts, people with high IQ may have low EI, similarly, people with low IQ may have high EI. There is no tool to assess EI unlike IQ.

Men and Women with High IQ

- **Men**
  Ambitions, effective, productive, predictable, dogged, not bothering about others, concerned about himself.
- **Women**
  Fluent, expressive, valued, introspective, and prone to guilt rumination.

Men and Women with High EI

- **Men**
  Cheerful, socially poised outwards, friendly, confident, easy going, not tend to be depressive. They accommodate, assimilate the internal as well as external environment.
- **Women**
  Vivid, obvious, immutable, distinct, consistent, coherent, pragmatic, applied, exuberant. Gregarious respond well to stress they are resistant to guilty or depression.

Concluding with above characters of Men and Women, the EI takes larger part in shaping the progress of an individual in the personal and social life compared to IQ.

Table 8.2: Comparison between EQ and IQ

Emotional Quotient	Intelligence Quotient
EQ or EI is the ability to identify, assess, and control the emotions of oneself, of others, and of groups.	An IQ is a score derived from one of several standardised tests designed to assess intelligence.
It is the ability to identify, evaluate, control and express one's own emotions; perceive, and assess others' emotions; use emotions to facilitate thinking, understanding emotional meanings.	It is the ability to learn, understand and apply information to skills, logical reasoning, word comprehension, math skills, abstract and spatial thinking, filter irrelevant information.
It is expressed and enhances the teamwork, leadership, successful relations, service orientation, initiative, collaboration.	It improves the ability to analyse and connect the events and useful for the individual development.

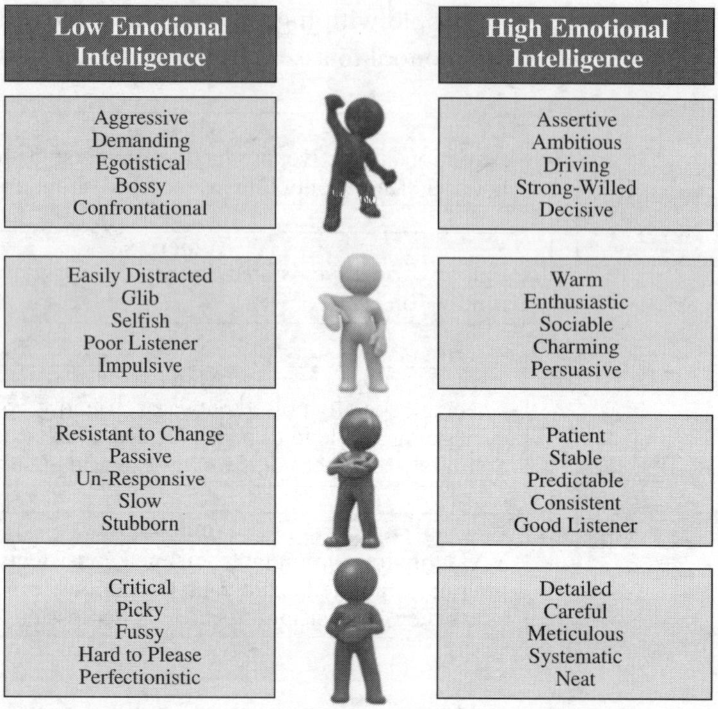

6. FIVE DOMAINS OF EMOTIONAL INTELLIGENCE

Daniel Goleman, an author, scientific journalist, and psychologist, developed a framework of five key domains that make up emotional intelligence. The five domains are as follows:

- **Being self-aware:** Recognising emotions as they occur is fundamental to EI. Without this awareness, emotions can overwhelm us, leaving us unable to respond effectively. Self-awareness helps us understand and manage our feelings rather than being controlled by them.
- **Managing emotions:** Building on self-awareness, emotional management involves maintaining balance—neither suppressing emotions nor being overwhelmed by them. It is an ongoing process, and individuals who can manage their emotions effectively are better equipped to handle life's challenges and recover from setbacks more quickly.
- **Having self-motivation:** Achieving any goal requires harnessing emotions to stay focused and motivated. For creative or challenging tasks, skills such as delaying gratification and regulating impulses are essential. Emotional control plays a crucial role in maintaining persistence and mastering complex tasks.

- **Recognising the emotions of others:** Empathy—the ability to tune into others' emotions—is at the heart of effective interpersonal relationships. Empathy fosters altruism and is essential in professions like teaching, management, and healthcare, where understanding and addressing others' emotions are key to success.
- **Handling relationships:** Effective interpersonal skills rely on managing the emotions of others, which is critical for teamwork, leadership, and collaboration. Many innovative ideas fail due to a lack of social competence or leadership ability. Developing these skills ensures better realisation of collective goals and fosters harmonious relationships.

To manage the emotions within, one need to identify what is going inside. This 'internal discovery' will help one control and manage emotions. Identifying others' emotions will enable one to make intelligent decisions while communicating with them and make others to get inspired of him.

6.1 Self-Awareness

Self-awareness is our ability to perceive and understand the things that make us who we are as an individual, including our personality, actions, values, beliefs, emotions, and thoughts. Essentially, it is a psychological state, where the 'self' becomes the focus of attention.

While self-awareness is central to our identity, it is not something we are acutely focused on at every moment of every day. Instead, self-awareness becomes intrinsic into the fabric of who we are and emerges at different layers depending on the situation and our personality.

Immanuel Kant described self-awareness not merely as the recognition of one's own existence but also as an understanding of the mental framework that enables knowledge.

- **Dimensions of Self-Awareness**
  i. **Internal Self-Awareness:** It involves introspection and reflection on one's thoughts, emotions, strengths, weaknesses, and values. Individuals with high internal self- awareness have a deep understanding of whether their own identity are in tune with their inner thoughts and feelings. Malala Yousafzai's autobiography *I Am Malala*, is a testament to her internal reflection of self-awareness.
  ii. **External Self-Awareness:** It involves understanding how one's action, behaviour, and words are perceived by others. It requires the ability to take perspectives outside of oneself and empathise with the perceptions and feelings of others. Ratan Tata's decision to turn the company's focus to its core values of ethics and social responsibility was influenced by his awareness of how the public and stakeholders perceived the Tata Group's image and impact.
- **Characteristics of Self-Awareness**
  i. **Introspection**: Self-awareness involves the ability to reflect on one's thoughts, feelings, emotions, behaviours and actions.

Example: Vipassana Meditation is a way of self-transformation through self-introspection.

ii. **Self-Compassion**: Being kind and understanding towards oneself, especially in times of failure or difficulty.
Example: Swami Vivekananda's teachings emphasise self-acceptance and self-compassion.

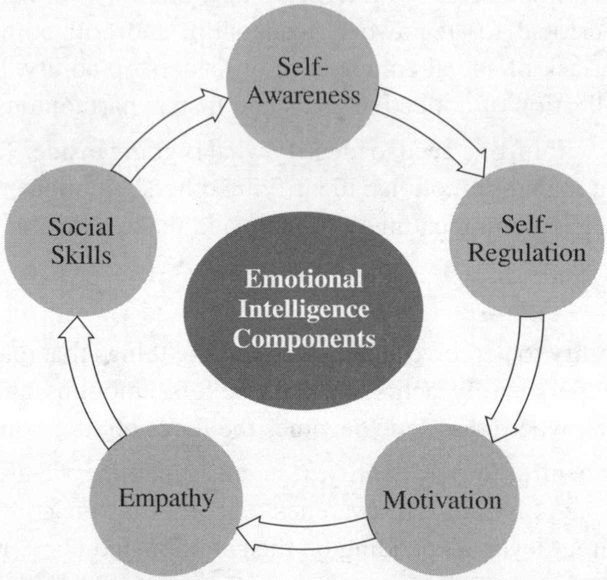

iii. **Empathy**: Self-aware individuals can understand and resonate with the emotions and experiences of others.
Example: Mother Teresa's selflessness and empathy.

iv. **Acceptance of Imperfection**: Self-awareness entails acknowledging one's flaws and limitations without being defensive.
Example: Stephen Hawking, after being diagnosed with Amyotrophic Lateral Sclerosis (ALS) and losing the ability to speak and move, adapted by utilising a speech-generating device to share his groundbreaking theories and ideas.

v. **Mindfulness**: Self-awareness involves being present in the moment and fully engaged with one's surroundings.
Example: The practice of Yoga, particularly the discipline of *Hatha Yoga*, emphasises mindfulness through physical postures (*asanas*) and breath control (*pranayama*).

vi. **Reflection**: Self-aware individuals regularly examine their beliefs, values, and behaviours to align them with their authentic selves.
Example: Gandhiji consistently practiced self-examination to ensure that his actions were aligned with his ethical and moral principles, including the renunciation of material wealth, adherence to vegetarianism, and commitment to celibacy.

vii. **Feedback**: By providing external perspectives, identifying strengths and weaknesses, feedback helps individuals gain a more comprehensive understanding of themselves.
Example: Steve Jobs said, *"Getting fired from Apple was the best thing that could have ever happened to me. The heaviness of being successful was replaced by the lightness of being a beginner again. It freed me to enter into one of the most creative periods of my life."*

- **Functions of Self-Awareness**

i. **Ethical Decision Making:** Self-awareness aids in making informed and rational decisions by understanding personal values, biases, and motivations.

ii. **Effective Leadership:** Self-aware leaders inspire trust and motivate others by understanding their own strengths, weaknesses, and impact on others.

iii. **Clear Communication:** Self-awareness helps to communicate with intention and clarity and understand the emotional triggers.

iv. **Strong Relationships:** Self-awareness enhances interpersonal relationships by fostering empathy, effective communication, and mutual understanding.

v. **Stress Management:** Self-awareness is crucial for effective stress management, as it helps individuals recognise and understand their stress triggers, emotional responses, and coping mechanisms.

vi. **Innovation and Creativity:** Self-awareness encourages innovation and creativity by embracing diverse perspectives, exploring new ideas, and challenging conventional thinking patterns.

vii. **Professional Development:** Self-awareness promotes continuous learning and growth by recognising areas for improvement, seeking feedback, and embracing challenges.

- **Philosopher's View on Self-Awareness**

i. **Socrates:** Socrates, the ancient Greek philosopher, famously stated, "*Know thyself.*" He emphasised the importance of self-awareness as the starting point for wisdom and virtuous living. According to Socrates, self-awareness involves introspection and self- examination to understand one's own beliefs, values, and limitations.

ii. **Rene Descartes:** Descartes, a 16th century French philosopher's famous dictum *"I think, therefore I am"* posited that the act of thinking is proof of one's own existence and consciousness. For Descartes, self-awareness is inherently tied to the capacity for self-reflection and rational thought.

iii. **Immanuel Kant:** Kant's concept of '*Transcedental Self-Awareness*' is that self-awareness is not just an empirical experience but involves a fundamental, a priori structure of consciousness. Knowledge is shaped by both the external world and the internal structures of the mind.

- **Roadblocks to Self-Awareness**
  i. **Denial:** Denial involves refusing to acknowledge or accept certain aspects of oneself, such as flaws, weaknesses, or negative emotions. This can hinder self-awareness by preventing individuals from confronting reality about oneself.
  ii. **Defensiveness:** When faced with criticism or feedback, defensive individuals may react with hostility or denial instead of engaging in self-reflection. This defensive stance impedes self-awareness by preventing individuals from considering alternative perspectives or acknowledging areas for growth.
  iii. **Fear of Vulnerability:** Fear of vulnerability can prevent individuals from being open and honest with themselves about their thoughts, feelings, and experiences. This fear may stem from concerns about judgement or rejection, leading individuals to suppress or ignore aspects of themselves that they perceive as weak or undesirable.
  iv. **Cognitive Biases:** Cognitive biases, such as confirmation bias or self-serving bias, distort individuals' perceptions of themselves and others. These biases can lead individuals to selectively interpret information in a way that confirms their existing beliefs or protects their self-esteem, hindering accurate self-awareness.
  v. **External Distractions:** External distractions, such as technology, social media, or busy schedules, can divert individual's attention away from self-awareness. Constant engagement with external stimuli may prevent individuals from tuning into their inner thoughts and emotions.
  vi. **Unhealthy Coping Mechanisms:** Engaging in unhealthy coping mechanisms, such as substance abuse, avoidance, or compulsive behaviours, can serve as a barrier to self-awareness. These behaviours may provide temporary relief from discomfort or stress but ultimately prevent individuals from addressing underlying issues.
  vii. **Social Comparison:** Constant comparison to others, whether in terms of achievements, appearance, or status, can undermine self-awareness by fostering feelings of inadequacy or superiority. Individuals may become preoccupied with external benchmarks of success rather than focusing on their own values and aspirations.

- **Ways to Develop Self-Awareness**
  i. **Practice Mindfulness:** Mindfulness is about being present in the moment and paying attention to ourselves, and our surroundings. One can practice mindfulness through meditation, deep breathing exercises, or yoga to cultivate present-moment awareness and observe our thoughts, emotions, and bodily sensations without judgement.
  ii. **Journaling:** Keeping a journal to record one's thoughts, feelings, and experiences on a regular basis. Writing can help us clarify our thoughts, identify patterns, and gain insights into our emotions and behaviours.

iii. **Seeking Feedback:** Solicit feedback from trusted friends, family members, mentors, or colleagues about our strengths, weaknesses, and areas for improvement. Be open about constructive criticism and use it as a tool for self-reflection and growth.

iv. **Reflect on Past Experiences:** Take time to reflect on past successes, failures, challenges, and significant life events. Consider how these experiences have shaped our beliefs, values, and identity, and what we have learned from them.

v. **Practice Self-Compassion:** Treat oneself with kindness and compassion, especially during difficult times or when facing setbacks. Practice self-compassionate self-talk and acknowledge that imperfection and vulnerability are part of the human experience.

vi. **Seeking Professional Help:** Seeking support from a therapist, counsellor, or coach who can provide guidance, insights, and tools like talk therapy, cognitive behavioural therapy for developing self-awareness.

vii. **Embrace Discomfort:** Be willing to step out of our comfort zone and confront difficult emotions, situations, or truths about oneself, which will give an opportunity for learning and self-discovery.

viii. **Self-Assessment Tools:** Using apps like Calm, Insight timer designed for self-assessment and personal growth, that offer mood tracking, goal setting, and reflection exercises. It provides structured and interactive ways to monitor and assess personal progress.

6.2 Self-Regulation

The American Psychological Association (APA) defines self-regulation as 'the control of one's behaviour through self-monitoring, self-evaluation, and self-reinforcement.'

Self-regulation is defined as the process by which individuals control their thoughts, emotions, and behaviours in order to achieve long-term goals. It involves managing one's internal states and responses to stay on track with personal or societal standards and objectives. Self-regulation is one of the five key components of emotional intelligence.

Self-Regulation vs. Self-Control

While self-control is about inhibiting strong impulses, self-regulation is about reducing the frequency and intensity of strong impulses by managing stress-load and recovery. In fact, self-regulation is what that makes self-control possible.

Self-regulation is a more automatic and subconscious process, while self-control is a set of active and purposeful decisions and behaviours.

- **Dimensions of Self-Regulation**

  i. **Behavioural self-regulation:** It encompasses the ability to respond to situations and how our actions align with our long-term best interests and deepest values.

For instance, we find it challenging to get up early in the morning to jog, but we do it anyway because we want to improve our fitness and health.

ii. **Emotional self-regulation:** It involves control of (or) influence over our emotions even when experiencing challenging situations.
For instance, If we had ever talked ourself out of a bad mood or calmed ourself down when we were angry, we were displaying effective emotional self-regulation.

- **Characteristics of Self-Regulation**

i. **Calm:** Self-regulation can help calm down after something exciting or upsetting and remain calm under pressure situations.

ii. **Focused:** Self-regulation can help focus on a task and stay on track to align with our goals.

iii. **Control of emotions:** Self-regulation can help control the reactions to strong emotions like anger, frustration, and embarrassment.

iv. **Confidence:** Self-regulated persons have confidence in their ability to achieve their goals.

v. **Adaptable:** People with self-regulation can adapt their responses and emotions to different situations. This helps them cope with change and consider issues from multiple perspectives.

vi. **Persistent:** They can continue to move forward toward their goals despite internal or external issues.

vii. **Strong relations:** Self-regulated persons behave in ways that help them get along with other people.

viii. **Self-efficacy:** Self-regulated persons do not need external motivation; they believe in their ability to succeed and take proactive steps to overcome challenges.

ix. **Optimism:** Constantly looking for positives enables self-regulators to improve their behaviours and actions continuously while remaining focused and motivated.

- **Functions of Self-Regulation**

i. **Emotional Control:** The ability to manage and respond to emotions in a healthy and constructive manner. This includes understanding one's emotional state and finding appropriate ways to cope with feelings like anger, frustration, or anxiety. Example, during 1893 train incident in South Africa, instead of reacting, Gandhi chose to remain composed. He decided to sit on a bench at the station and reflect on the situation. The incident became a catalyst for Gandhi's commitment to fight against racial discrimination and injustice.

ii. **Impulse Control:** The capacity to resist immediate temptations or distractions in favour of more valuable long-term rewards. It involves thinking before acting and making decisions that align with long-term goals rather than giving in to immediate desires.

iii. **Conflict Resolution:** Self-regulators can handle conflicts well because they can consider differing opinions and better empathise with coworkers and others in the workplace. Self-regulated persons address the cause of a conflict directly and avoid letting emotions guide their responses. Example, Sardar Vallabhbhai Patel approached the integration of princely states with a blend of firmness and patience. He understood the importance of diplomatic engagement and often used negotiation as a primary tool before resorting to more forceful measures. His approach to conflict resolution was deeply rooted in self-regulation.

iv. **Time Management:** Self-regulated persons can enhance their time management in the workplace by being accountable for deadlines. It helps in increasing productivity. Example, Mark Zuckerberg's decision of minimalism involves streamlining choices such as maintaining a consistent wardrobe and prioritising key strategic goals, to reduce decision fatigue and increase efficiency.

v. **Stress Management:** Recognising and validating our feelings rather than suppressing them can prevent emotional buildup and stress. Good self-regulation includes knowing how to manage stress in a way that doesn't negatively impact one's well-being or performance.

vi. **Goal Setting:** The ability to set clear, achievable goals and to create and follow a plan to achieve them. This includes breaking down large goals into manageable tasks and staying focused on the end result.

vii. **Continuous Learning:** The ability to reflect on past experiences, learn from mistakes, and apply that knowledge to improve future behaviour. This involves critical thinking and a willingness to adapt based on new insights. Example, the 22-year-old Manu Bhaker did not have the best of times in the Tokyo Olympics as she failed to qualify for the finals after her pistol malfunctioned. However, she made a strong comeback by becoming the second Indian to win multiple medals in a single edition of the Olympics in Paris, 2024.

viii. **Clarity in Communication:** Self-regulation improves the ability to listen actively and understand the environment better. So, it helps to better think before speaking or acting. Example, M. S. Dhoni is very clearheaded, and has a great clarity of thought in whatever he does. He is a very good communicator and has been successful in putting his views to fellow teammates, management and people.

ix. **Self-Monitoring:** The process of observing and evaluating one's own behaviour and performance. This includes being aware of how one's actions align with their goals and values, and making adjustments as needed.

x. **Self-Motivation:** The internal drive to persist in the face of challenges and setbacks. This involves maintaining enthusiasm and commitment to goals, even when faced with difficulties or lack of external rewards. Example: Dr A P J Abdul Kalam exemplified self-motivation through his quote, *"Believe in yourself and all that you are. Know that there is something inside you that is greater than any obstacle."*

- **Philosopher's View on Self-Regulation**

i. **Socrates:** Socrates believed that '*philosophy and wisdom*' could help people achieve self-control and do the right thing in their lives. He was known for his asceticism, or severe self-discipline, and for managing his own passions and appetites. Socrates believed that "*an unexamined life is not worth living*." This reflects the importance of constant self-reflection and critical thinking about one's actions and beliefs.

ii. **Plato:** Plato's theory divides the soul into three parts: the rational, the spirited, and the appetitive. In *Phaedrus*, Plato uses the allegory of the chariot to illustrate the dynamics of self-regulation. The chariot represents the soul, with the rational part as the charioteer, the spirited and the appetitive part as each horse. The rational part must guide the spirited and appetitive parts to ensure that the soul moves in a harmonious direction. Self-regulation, according to Plato, involves the rational part of the soul controlling the appetitive and spirited parts.

iii. **Aristotle:** Aristotle's concept of 'virtue ethics' is deeply tied to self-regulation. In his work, particularly the *Nicomachean Ethics*, Aristotle discusses the importance of developing virtuous habits through practice. For Aristotle, virtues are dispositions to act in ways that find a balance between excess and deficiency. Self-regulation is crucial for achieving this balance and living a virtuous life. For example, temperance is a virtue that involves self-regulating one's desires and pleasures.

iv. **Immanuel Kant:** Kant's moral philosophy also touches on self-regulation, especially in terms of autonomy and the moral law. In works like the *Groundwork for the Metaphysics of Morals*, Kant argues that rational agents must act according to moral laws that they prescribe to themselves, which requires a form of self-regulation. For Kant, the ability to regulate oneself according to rational principles is crucial for moral agency and respecting the autonomy of others.

v. **Epictetus:** Epictetus, a Stoic philosopher, emphasised self-regulation as central to living a good life. In his *Enchiridion* and other works, he teaches that one should focus on controlling what is within one's power (such as one's own actions and reactions) and accept what is outside of one's control. For the Stoics, self-regulation involves cultivating inner discipline to align one's behaviour with reason and virtue, regardless of external circumstances.

vi. **Michel Foucault:** Foucault's exploration of self-regulation can be found in his later works, such as *The History of Sexuality*. He examines how various institutions, and societal norms exert influence over individuals' self-regulation through techniques of normalisation and surveillance. Foucault's concept of 'bio-power' highlights how self-regulation is intertwined with social power structures and the way individuals internalise norms and expectations.

- **Roadblocks to Achieve Self-Regulation**

i. **Cognitive Biases:** Cognitive biases can undermine self-regulation by prioritising short-term gratification despite knowing it's detrimental to their long-term objectives.

ii. **Lack of Self-Awareness:** Difficulty in recognising one's own patterns of behaviour and triggers can hinder effective self-regulation. Without self-awareness, it's challenging to identify and address areas that need improvement.

iii. **Social Influence:** Social influences and peer pressure can lead individuals to act contrary to their own goals or values, impacting their ability to regulate their behaviour.

iv. **Procrastination: Procrastination**[4] is a common barrier to self-regulation. Delaying tasks or decisions can prevent individuals from achieving their long-term goals and disrupt their ability to manage their time and efforts effectively.

v. **Cultural Expectations:** Cultural norms and expectations can create pressure to conform, which may conflict with personal goals and values, making self-regulation harder.

vi. **Low Self-Efficacy:** Belief in one's own ability to succeed is crucial for self-regulation. If individuals lack confidence in their capacity to achieve goals or handle challenges, they might be less likely to attempt self-regulation.

vii. **Habit Formation:** Established habits, especially those formed over long periods, can be difficult to change. Once behaviours become habitual, they may operate automatically, making self-regulation challenging.

viii. **Emotional Regulation:** Difficulty in managing emotions like stress, anxiety, or anger can impact self-regulation. Strong emotional responses can lead to impulsive actions or difficulty in adhering to planned behaviours.

- **Ways to Develop Self-Regulation**

i. **Practice self-awareness:** An effective way to practice self-awareness is by checking in with yourself to identify areas of physical tension in your body. Pay attention to moments when you feel anxious and observe the physical signs that accompany these emotions. This practice allows for a deeper evaluation of both your physical state and your emotions.

ii. **Meditation:** It allows to reflect quietly and gain more control over our thoughts. Any amount of meditation, such as a daily, five-minute session, can have a positive impact on our self-regulation abilities.

iii. **Exercise:** Physical activity escalates endorphins, which can boost the mood and help counter stress. Regular exercise helps with focus and goal setting, and it gives us a sense of control over our body and our life.

iv. **Journaling:** It helps clear our mind and slow our thoughts. Writing can help us self-soothe as we process our day, regardless of whether our day has been positive or negative.

v. **Seeking feedback:** It can be challenging to look at ourselves objectively all the time. Asking for feedback from trusted colleagues or friends can help us incredibly when trying to improve our awareness and self-regulation.

[4]**Procrastination:** to be slow or late about doing something that should be done

vi. **Anger management:** Managing feelings of anger is paramount for maintaining a harmonious environment. Teaching self-regulation strategies such as deep breathing, counting to ten, or using 'I' statements can help them deal with anger constructively, thereby reducing instances of disruptive behaviour.

vii. **Being open to change:** Challenging ourselves to deal with changes in a straightforward and positive manner and working to improve our ability to adapt to different situations while staying positive.

viii. **Educate yourself:** Reading books and educational journals, listening to podcasts or taking an online course. As we learn more, we may become more observant, not just of ourselves but of the people and world around us, which is a great way to boost our overall emotional intelligence.

ix. **Self-rewarding:** Try implementing a reward system, such as taking a brief break after spending a long time working on a task or treating ourselves to a special dinner after we complete an important project. With this strategy, we can build a positive self-image over time, which can help us develop a more positive attitude.

6.3 Motivation

Motivation is derived from the word 'motive'. A state of mind that activates, directs, or encourages action in order to satisfy a need is referred to as the motive.

People who are emotionally intelligent are motivated by things beyond external rewards like fame, recognition, and money. Instead, they have a passion towards fulfilling their own inner needs and goals.

Those who are competent in motivation often tend to be action-oriented. They set goals, have a higher need for achievement, and always looking for ways to do better. They also tend to be more committed and good at taking initiative.

There are generally three major components of motivation: activation, persistence, and intensity.

- **Activation** is the decision to initiate a behaviour. An example of activation would be enrolling in UPSC coaching courses in order to get through Civil Service Examinations.
- **Persistence** is the continued effort towards a goal even though obstacles may exist. An example of persistence would be showing up for class every day, even though one is tired from staying up late the night before.
- **Intensity** is the concentration and vigour that goes into pursuing a goal. For example, one student might coast by without much effort (minimal intensity) while another student studies regularly, participates in classroom discussions, and takes regular tests putting much effort (greater intensity).

- **Dimensions of Motivation**

The two main dimensions of motivation are frequently described as being either extrinsic or intrinsic.

i. **Extrinsic motivation:** It arises from outside of the individual and often involves external rewards such as trophies, money, social recognition, or praise.
ii. **Intrinsic motivation:** It is internal and arises from within the individual, such as doing a complicated crossword puzzle purely for the gratification of solving a problem.

- **Characteristics of Motivation**

i. **Continuous Process:** Motivation is a continuous ever going process. It is because human needs, desires, wishes, or wants are endless. All of them can never be satisfied at a time. Satisfaction of one need, gives path to another need. Therefore, motivation is a process that goes on forever.
ii. **Dynamic Process:** Motivation is a dynamic and complex process. It is so because it is related to human behaviour which is never static but dynamic. It keeps on changing continuously.
iii. **Energising Force:** Motivation is the process that energises individuals to put in effort to achieve the set goals and to satisfy their needs.
iv. **Internal Feeling:** Motivation is the internal feeling of an individual. It is the energising force within an individual that directs or influences him to behave in a particular way.
v. **Willingness to Exert Effort:** Motivation is the willingness of an individual to exert effort in the pursuit of organisational goals and to satisfy some individual needs.
vi. **System-Oriented:** Motivation is the system that contains two main factors:
    ✓ Factors operating inside an individual i.e. his needs, aspirations, wants, wishes, values.
    ✓ Factors operating in external environment such as customs, norms of society, culture etc. Motivation is the result of interaction among these factors.
vii. **A Psychological Concept:** The concept of motivation is typically psychological. It relates to those forces operating within the individual employee which impels him to act or not to act in certain ways.

- **Functions of Motivation**

i. **Improved performance:** Motivation helps in satisfying needs of the individual in his capacity and providing them satisfaction, as it bridges the gap between the capacity and willingness.
ii. **Attitude change:** Positive attitude helps to achieve goals easily. Motivation helps to change this negative attitude to a positive attitude through suitable rewards, positive encouragement, and praise.

iii. **Introduce changes smoothly:** An individual can survive and grow only when he adapts himself to the dynamic environment. Changes are generally resisted, because of fear of adverse effects. This resistance can be overcome by motivation.

iv. **Well-being and Satisfaction:** Motivation provides a sense of purpose and meaning in life, contributing to overall well-being. Achieving goals through motivation can lead to feelings of accomplishment and satisfaction.

v. **Internal drive:** A passion to fulfil inner needs and goals, rather than being motivated by external rewards like money or recognition.

vi. **Commitment:** A commitment to goals and a higher need for achievement. Motivation and commitment are interdependent, with motivation fuelling commitment and commitment being the decision to act on that motivation.

vii. **Resilience:** Motivation helps to keep focus on the purpose and being able to bounce back from setbacks in challenging times.

- **Some Famous Views on Motivation**

i. **Aristotle:** Aristotle proposed that motivation arises from an 'appetitive' function, which always operates in connection with a specific goal or outcome. It is driven by the 'real or apparent good' of an anticipated result or an image of 'what is to come,' formed in relation to 'what is present.' This dynamic compels living organisms to either pursue a positive outcome or avoid a negative one.

ii. **Plato:** Human motivation arises from the tripartite soul, which consists of three parts: the rational, the spirited, and the appetitive. The rational part should govern the soul, guiding the spirited and appetitive aspects. Motivation, for Plato, stems from the balance of these parts, with reason leading to just and moral actions. When the appetitive (desires) dominates, it can lead to poor decision-making.

iii. **Immanuel Kant:** Kant believed that the highest form of motivation is acting out of duty, not out of desire or emotion. He argued that moral actions are motivated by adherence to universal moral laws, which he called 'categorical imperative'. According to Kant, an action is truly moral when it is done for the sake of duty, rather than for personal gain or desire.

iv. **Buddha:** One of the steps of the Noble Eightfold Path is 'Right Intention (*Samma Sankappa).*' This means having pure, wholesome motivations behind your actions. Buddha taught that our intentions should be based on renunciation, goodwill, and harmlessness. Acting with compassion and without attachment to the outcomes brings peace and leads to liberation.

- **Roadblocks to Motivation**

i. **Procrastination:** Procrastination is a classic example of how the pleasure unconscious can work against us. When we put off a task, we are avoiding short-term discomfort. But this often leads to greater stress and discomfort in the long run.

ii. **Addiction:** Addictive behaviours, whether to substances or activities like video games, can be major barriers to motivation. They provide immediate pleasure but often at the cost of long-term well-being and productivity.

iii. **Laziness:** What we often label as 'laziness' is usually a combination of low energy, lack of interest, or fear of failure. It's our pleasure unconscious telling us that rest is more appealing than action.

iv. **Emotional blockages:** These are obstacles that prevent us from doing what we want in life. They manifest through low self-esteem, depression, fear, and anger. These blockages are a result of the past, and will put a limit on our development no matter how talented or skilled we are.

v. **Lack of clarity:** Not knowing what needs to be done and when it should be done, can make it difficult to feel motivated.

- **Ways to Develop Motivation**

i. **Set specific and achievable goals:** Adopt the SMART (specific, measurable, achievable, relevant, and time-bound) technique to define goals clearly. This can help boost motivation by giving a clear path to achieving goals.

ii. **Create a supportive environment:** Surrounding ourselves with people, places, and habits that motivate us. For example, before exercising, a supportive environment might mean having your workout gear ready, finding a workout buddy, or creating a playlist of energising music to help set the tone.

iii. **Break down large goals:** Divide bigger goals into smaller, more manageable tasks. Setting fewer intimidating goals means we can appreciate our progress through smaller steps, and that helps maintain motivation towards the bigger picture.

iv. **Find sources of inspiration:** Inspiration can fuel motivation, making the journey towards goals feel more exciting and meaningful.

v. **Visualise the benefits:** Visualising the benefits of the goal we would like to achieve can drastically improve our motivation. Before diving into a work project or starting a workout session, for example, take a moment to visualise the benefits we'll gain. It could be the satisfaction of completing a difficult task, learning a new skill, or moving closer to a goal we have been working hard to achieve.

6.4 Empathy

Empathy, the ability to understand other people's feelings and see things from their point of view, is another critical emotional intelligence skill. It involves being able to recognise other person's emotional status and understand why they are experiencing them.

Empathy is an automatic response to our environment. Actually, we tend to unconsciously mimicry others' feelings. This comes from the most primitive parts of the brain and the aim is to enforce survival. For instance, when people that surround us, experience fear, then we will also feel and sense fear.

Being empathetic allows us to understand the power dynamics that can influence social relationships, such as those that exist between different communities and cultures. This is important for guiding the interactions with different people we encounter each day.

- **Dimensions of Empathy**
  i. **Affective Empathy:** Affective empathy involves the ability to understand another person's emotions and respond appropriately. Such emotional understanding may lead to one feeling concerned for other person's well-being, or it may lead to feelings of distress.
  ii. **Somatic Empathy:** People sometimes physically feel what other person is experiencing. When we see other person feeling embarrassed, we might feel awkward.
  iii. **Cognitive Empathy:** Cognitive empathy involves being able to understand another person's mental state and what they might be thinking in response to the situation. This is related to what psychologists refer to as the theory of mind or thinking about what other people are thinking.

- **Characteristics of Empathy**
  i. **Active listening:** Active listening is not just hearing; it's about engaging, responding, and showing that we care. When one actively listens, he/she is fully present, giving the other person undivided attention. This kind of listening instils a sense of worth in the speaker, making them feel valued and understood. It's one of the most outright yet powerful ways to show empathy.
  ii. **Open-mindedness:** Open-mindedness gives the willingness to consider what others are saying, even if it challenges our own beliefs or opinions. This willingness to give ears to different thoughts is a cornerstone of empathy.
  iii. **Non-judgemental attitude:** When it comes to empathy, a non-judgemental attitude is non-negotiable. Being non-judgemental means accepting others for who they are, not who we think they should be. It's like meeting someone at a crossroads and choosing to walk alongside them, without trying to steer them in the direction we think is right.
  iv. **Patience:** In our fast-paced world, patience often takes a back seat. But when it comes to empathy, patience is the main driver. It's giving people the space they need to express themselves, to process their emotions, or even to make some decisions. It's like planting a seed and awaiting to grow, without constantly digging it up to check if it's sprouted.
  v. **Humility:** Humility isn't about thinking less of oneself; it's about thinking of oneself less. It's putting others' needs and feelings before our own, not because we have to, but because we want to. And when we can put someone else's needs before our own, even if it's just for a moment, we are not just being humble, we are being empathetic.

vi. **Compassion:** If empathy is one thing to understand someone's pain, it's compassion to want to do something about it. Compassion aids us to act, to help, to make a difference. Example, holding the door for someone carrying a heavy load, making warm meal for a sick friend, or even the simple act of picking up something for someone who has dropped it- these everyday acts of kindness are the foundation of a compassionate life.

- **Functions of Empathy**

i. **Strengthens relationships:** Empathy allows to build social connections with others. By understanding what others are thinking and feeling, we can respond appropriately in social situations.

ii. **Regulates emotions:** Empathising with others helps learn to regulate our own emotions. Emotional regulation is important in that it allows us to manage what we are feeling, even in times of great stress, without becoming overwhelmed.

iii. **Compels us to help others:** Empathy promotes helping behaviours. Also, when we feel empathy for other people, they are also more likely to help us when they experience empathy.

iv. **Motivating prosocial behaviour:** Empathy motivates prosocial behaviour by helping people perceive others' needs for help and by making them feel a sense of relief when they help others.

v. **Conducive atmosphere:** Empathy can create a conducive atmosphere by building trust, reducing conflict, and fostering a supportive environment.

- **Philosopher's View on Empathy**

i. **David Hume:** David Hume, a Scottish Enlightenment philosopher, emphasised the role of sympathy (which we now call empathy) in moral judgements. When someone sees another person in pain, they experience a similar mental state, which is a result of psychological simulation or association. Hume believed that humans are naturally inclined to feel empathy for others, and this shared feeling forms the foundation of moral actions.

ii. **Arthur Schopenhauer:** Schopenhauer came with the theory that the source and foundation of morals had nothing to do with knowledge, but in what he called 'the great mystery of ethics'.

iii. **Confucius:** Ren is the central virtue in Confucius' teachings, often described as the feeling of compassion or kindness toward others. *"Do not do to others what you do not want done to yourself."* (*Analects* 15:24) It is the basic moral foundation of human interactions and reflects the ability to understand and care for others' feelings.

- **Roadblocks to Empathy**

i. **Pressure situation:** When our brains are under pressure we can have a hard time distinguishing between our own emotional state, and the emotional states of others.

ii. **Emotions are contagious:** An angry or short tempered response is more likely to escalate a tense situation than a more conscious measured response. Unless we are mindful of what we feel it can become easy to allow one negative interaction to infect subsequent interactions, and create an anger spiral.

iii. **Prejudices and biases:** Holding preconceived notions about certain groups of people or certain beliefs can prevent someone from empathising with individuals from those groups.

iv. **Self-centredness:** Narcissism and Egoistic tendencies create excessive focus on oneself, can block the ability to consider others' perspectives or feelings.

v. **Emotional detachment:** Some individuals protect themselves from emotional pain by detaching or avoiding emotions, which can block their ability to empathise with others.

vi. **Black-and-white thinking:** Seeing situations in extremes (e.g., right/wrong, good/bad) can hinder the nuanced understanding of others' emotions and experiences.

- **Ways to Improve Our Empathy**

i. **Active listening:** Focussing on the speaker by give our full attention. Avoiding distractions, such as phones or multitasking, and engaging fully in the conversation.

ii. **Observing non-verbal cues:** Paying attention to body languages, facial expressions, and tone of voice. Non-verbal signals often reveal more about a person's emotional state than words.

iii. **Perspective-taking:** Imagining ourselves in their shoes by deliberately imagining what it's like to be the other person, what emotions they might be feeling and what challenges they are facing.

iv. **Asking questions instead of making assumptions:** Instead of guessing at what someone else is feeling, we can directly ask them. Thoughtful questions demonstrate a level of care and curiosity to understand another person's unique experiences and point of view.

6.5 Social Skills

In emotional intelligence, the term 'social skills' refers to the skills used to effectively handle and influence other people's emotions. This may seem like manipulation, but it can be as simple as understanding that, smiling at some people makes them smile back, and can therefore make them feel more positive. In the emotional intelligence 'jigsaw', 'social skills' can therefore be considered as the final piece.

Social skills can be defined as capabilities or aptitudes employed by an individual, when interacting with others at an interpersonal level. In this way, they play a significant role, not only in socialisation, but also for individualisation, since they allow knowledge of oneself and others, which contributes to the formation of self-concept. It is the ability to use awareness of one's emotions and the emotions of others to manage emotions successfully. Clear communication, influencing and inspiring others, working well in a team, and managing conflict, all contribute to relationship management.

- **Characteristics of Social Skills**
    i. **Effective communication:** It involves clearly expressing thoughts and ideas while also understanding and interpreting what others are communicating. It is not about just verbal exchanges but also written communication, which is especially important in today's digital age.
    ii. **Conflict resolution:** Disagreements and conflicts are part of the human interactions. The ability to resolve such situations peacefully, without escalating the tension, demonstrates strong social skills. This involves compromise, negotiation, and sometimes, agreeing to disagreements respectfully.
    iii. **Adaptability:** Social situations can vary widely, and adjusting one's behaviour and approach depending upon the context is a valuable social skill. This includes navigating through different cultural norms, social settings, and diverse groups.
    iv. **Team capabilities:** A sense of respect and consideration for others' feelings, ideas, and beliefs is fundamental to social interactions.
    v. **Empathy:** The ability to understand and share another person's feelings and thoughts is paramount to building strong and meaningful relationships. Empathy involves listening carefully, showing concern, and providing support whenever needed. It enables individuals to connect on a deeper level.
    vi. **Persuasion and influencing skills:** Persuasion is the art of enthusing others, and winning them over with our ideas or proposed course of action. People who are persuasive, or have influence, read the emotional currents in a situation, and fine-tune what they are saying to appeal to those who are involved.

- **Functions of Social Skills**
    i. **Personal relationships:** The bedrock of strong personal relationships is typically found in the ability to communicate effectively, empathise, and connect with others on an emotional level. Social skills enable individuals to build and maintain rewarding personal connections and enhance their emotional well-being.
    ii. **Mental health:** There's a significant correlation between mental health and well-developed social skills. Socially content individuals often exhibit low levels of stress and high levels of happiness.
    iii. **Conflict resolution:** Social skills help people identify the issues in a conflict and find a solution that works for everyone.
    iv. **Leadership:** Having the ability to clearly express a plan and encourage others to be enthusiastic about it, while providing support and guidance.

v. **Collaboration and cooperation:** Sharing ideas and working with others to foster commitment and build a better environment for everyone.

- **Philosopher's View on Social Skills**

  i. **Aristotle:** The legendary Greek philosopher Aristotle said, *"Man is a social animal"*. He told that the very essence of being human involves living in relationships and engaging in shared activities. Aristotle also explored the concept of 'friendship' as an integral aspect of natural social human being. True friendship characterised by mutual support and shared values, reflects the deeper connections that humans seek in their social interactions.

  ii. **Confucius:** In *The Analects*, Confucius emphasises that the gentleman engages with others thoughtfully, without blindly following them, while the small man merely follows others without genuine interaction. This principle of reciprocity, known as the '*Silver Rule*' emphasises empathy in social interactions, urging individuals to consider others' feelings and desires.

  iii. **Jainism:** It encourages the principle of *Anekantavada*, which is the recognition of multiple perspectives and truths. This concept fosters tolerance, open-mindedness, and understanding in social interactions.

- **Roadblocks to Social Skills**

  i. **Lack of Confidence:** Low self-esteem or fear of rejection can make it difficult for individuals to engage in social interactions. They may feel insecure about their communication abilities, leading to social withdrawal or hesitation.

  ii. **Poor Listening Skills:** People who struggle with active listening may miss important cues in conversations, leading to misunderstandings or appearing uninterested, which can harm relationships.

  iii. **Emotional Dysregulation:** Inability to manage emotions, such as anger or frustration, during social interactions can lead to inappropriate responses, conflict, or strained relationships.

  iv. **Rigid Behaviour:** Lack of adaptability or flexibility in social settings can make it difficult to navigate various social norms or different types of people, resulting in awkward or inappropriate interactions.

  v. **Cultural or Social Differences:** Different cultural backgrounds can create misunderstandings or misinterpretations of behaviour, gestures, or communication styles, leading to difficulty in social interactions.

  vi. **Excessive Use of Technology:** Over-reliance on digital communication can limit face-to-face interactions, leading to difficulty in reading non-verbal cues, understanding tone, or maintaining real-life conversations.

- **Ways to Improve Social Skills**
  i. **Engaging with others:** Finding ways to further conversations with friends, family and close coworkers by asking open-ended questions.
  ii. **Developing listening skills:** Equally as important as being able to share our own thoughts is being an active listener. In doing so, we allow others to feel comfortable sharing their ideas and input. Practice listening skills by maintaining eye contact, using non-verbal communication like nodding when we agree and asking clarifying questions when hearing something we misunderstand.
  iii. **Finding social skills resources:** There are many classes, books, podcasts, and tools available both online and offline to help improve our social skills.
  iv. **Taking responsibility:** Taking responsibility for our actions and apologising when necessary, demonstrates emotional maturity and strengthens relationships. It shows that we are aware of how our actions affect others and are willing to make amends.
  v. **Developing emotional vocabulary:** Being able to accurately identify and express emotions is a key aspect of emotional intelligence. When we can articulate our feelings, it helps others understand our perspective and fosters more meaningful connections.
  vi. **Learning to read non-verbal cues:** Emotional intelligence involves understanding unspoken emotions. Reading non-verbal cues like body language, facial expressions, and tone of voice helps us understand what others are feeling.

7. MODELS OF EMOTIONAL INTELLIGENCE

7.1 Mayer and Salovey Model of Emotional Intelligence

This model proposes that there are four fundamental emotion-related abilities. They are:

- **Perceiving Emotions:** This is the ability to accurately perceive and recognise emotions in oneself and others, as well as in various stimuli such as facial expressions, voice tone, and body language. It involves being aware of emotional cues and understanding what they signify.
  Example: When a colleague's facial expression changes during a meeting and their eyes look tense, we perceive that they may be feeling stressed or upset.
- **Using Emotions to Facilitate Thought:** This involves using emotions to enhance cognitive processes, including problem-solving, decision-making, and creativity. It means that emotions can provide valuable information that can guide our thinking and behaviour.
  Example: After receiving positive feedback at work, we feel energised and motivated and this helps enhance our creative problem-solving abilities.

- **Understanding Emotions:** Understanding emotions involves the capacity to comprehend complex emotional relationships, such as how emotions can evolve and blend together. It also involves understanding the causes and consequences of different emotional states.
  Example: When children cry after losing a game, instead of dismissing their tears, we recognise that their distress may stem not just from the loss, but from the feeling of embarrassment in front of their friends. We offer comfort by acknowledging their emotions and encouraging them to try again.
- **Managing Emotions:** Managing emotions is the ability to regulate and control one's emotions effectively. This includes managing negative emotions, fostering positive ones, and adapting emotional responses to different situations.
  Example: After a disagreement with a friend, we might feel intense anger. Rather than sending an angry text or saying something hurtful in the heat of the moment, we choose to take a walk to cool down. Later, we have a constructive conversation, addressing the issue calmly and thoughtfully to resolve it.

7.2 Nine Layer model – The Pyramid of Emotional Intelligence

1. Emotional Stimuli: Every day we receive a lot of information/stimuli from our environment. We need to incorporate these stimuli into categories because they help us to understand the world and the people. Sensorial stimuli are received by the agent, when an event occurs. The cognitive mechanisms process these stimuli and produce the emotional stimuli for each of the sensory emotions. Emotional stimuli are then processed by a cognitive mechanism that determines what emotion to feel and subsequently produce an emotional reaction which may influence the occurrence of a behaviour. The emotional stimuli forms the base of the pyramid of EI pointing to the upper levels of it.

2. Emotion Recognition: The next level of the pyramid is the recognition of emotions simultaneously expressed at times. Emotion recognition involves the ability to accurately decode the expressions of others' feelings, usually transmitted through non-verbal channels (i.e., the face, body, and voice). This ability is positively linked to social ability and interaction, as non-verbal behaviour is a reliable source of information on the emotional states of other persons. The ability to recognise and express emotions in others is a trivial part of the daily human interactions and interpersonal relationships as it is a representation of a critical component of human socio-cognitive capacities.

3. Self-Awareness: Socrates's guiding principle was knowing oneself. It means having the ability to understand one's feelings, having an accurate self-assessment of one's own strengths and weaknesses, and showing self-confidence. Aristotle too believed that knowing oneself is the beginning of all wisdom. These two ancient Greek thoughts encompass the concept of self-awareness, a cognitive capacity, which is the following step in our pyramid after having conquered the previous two. Self-Awareness is having a clear vision of our personality, including our strengths, weaknesses, thoughts, beliefs, feelings and motives. As we develop self-awareness, we are able to change our thoughts which, in turn, allows to change our emotions and eventually change our actions. It can be defined as the realisation of oneself as an individual being. Developing self-awareness is the first step to develop EI. Daniel Goleman identified self-awareness as emotional consciousness, accurate self-esteem, and self-confidence.

4. Self-Management: Self-management allows to control our reactions so that we are not driven by impulsive behaviours and feelings. With Self-management, we become more flexible, extroverted, and receptive, and at the same time less critical on situations and less reactionary to people's attitudes. Moreover, we are aware about what to do. When we have recognised our feelings and have accepted them, we are then able to manage them much better. This does not mean that we must crush our negative emotions, but if we realise them, we can amend our behaviour and make small or big changes to the way we react and manage our feelings even if the latter is negative.

5. Social Awareness—Empathy—The Discrimination of Emotions: Since we have cultivated the ability to understand and control your own emotions, we are ready to move on to the next step of recognising and understanding the emotions of people around us. Self-Management is a prerequisite for Social-Awareness. It is an expansion of our emotional awareness. Social Awareness refers to the way people handle relationships and awareness of others' feelings, and needs. Being socially aware means that we understand how we react to different social situations, and effectively modify our interactions with other people so that we achieve the best results. Empathy is the most important and essential EQ component and is directly related to social-awareness. It is the ability to put oneself in another's place, to understand him/her as a person, to feel him/her and to take into account the perspective related to this person or with any person at a time. The net result of this is the development of social skills and a personal continuous improvement process.

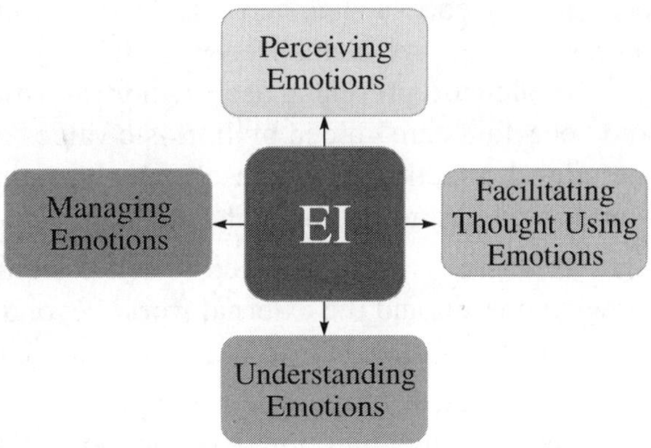

6. Social Skills—Expertise: After developing social awareness, the next step in the hierarchy of emotional intelligence (EI) is mastering social skills. In the context of EI, social skills refer to the ability to effectively influence and manage other people's emotions to navigate interactions successfully. These skills encompass the capacity to empathise with others, understand their perspectives, and align with their emotions and thoughts.

Social skills are fundamentally about bringing out the best in others—motivating, inspiring, and influencing them, as well as fostering communication, building meaningful relationships, and facilitating personal growth and conflict resolution. Key components of social skills within EI include leadership, influence, development, communication, conflict management, teamwork, and collaboration.

Expertise in emotional dynamics can be described as the ability to heighten sensitivity to emotional cues, accurately assess their relevance in interactions, and strategically engage with others' emotions. This includes both expressing one's emotions effectively and responding thoughtfully to the emotions of others during interactions, such as negotiations or collaborative efforts.

7. Self-Actualisation—Universality of Emotions: As soon as these six levels have been met, the individual has reached the top of Maslow's hierarchy of needs—Self-actualisation. Self-actualisation, according to Maslow is the realisation of personal potential, self-fulfillment, pursuing personal development, and peak experiences. It is important to note that self-actualisation is a continuous process of becoming, rather than an ideal state one reaches such as 'happy ever after'. Carl Rogers also created a theory that included a 'growth potential' whose purpose was to incorporate in the same way the 'real self' and the 'ideal self', thereby cultivating the appearance of the 'fully functioning person'. Self-actualisation is one of the most significant EI skills. It is a measure of our sense that we have a substantial personal commitment to life and that we are offering the gifts to our world that are most important for us. Self-actualisation helps feel empathy and kinship towards humanity as a whole and also cultivates the universality of emotions, so that those they have EI in one culture probably have EI in another culture too and they have the ability to understand the difference in emotions and their meanings despite the fact that sometimes emotions are culturally dependent.

8. Transcendence: Maslow proposed that individuals who achieve self-actualisation may occasionally enter a state he termed 'transcendence.' At this level, individuals focus on helping others achieve self-actualisation, attain self-fulfilment, and realise their highest potential. Transcendence represents a deeper, more holistic level of human consciousness, where interactions and behaviours are guided by intrinsic values and purposes, rather than utilitarian motives. This includes connecting with oneself, others, humanity as a whole, other species, nature, and the world in a meaningful and authentic way.

Transcendence is closely linked to self-esteem, emotional well-being, and empathy. It involves viewing oneself and the external world beyond the confines of ego, fostering a heightened sense of meaning and relevance to others and to life itself.

Plato's concept of transcendence aligned with the belief in an absolute goodness that can only be grasped through intuition. His transcendental ideas extended to divine principles, the cosmos, the human soul, and the underlying reality within material things, emphasising their higher significance.

Self-transcendence can manifest through various behaviours and perspectives, such as sharing wisdom or emotions with others, embracing the physical and natural changes of aging, accepting death as a part of life, helping others, seeking knowledge about the world, letting go of past losses, and finding spiritual meaning in life.

9. Emotional Unity: Emotional unity represents the highest level of emotional intelligence, characterised by a positive orientation toward maintaining a balanced state of emotions. This internal harmony allows individuals to feel joy, peace, prosperity, and an awareness of universal truth and interconnectedness.

In a symbiotic world, actions that benefit oneself ultimately benefit others. Emotional unity begins with self-love, enabling us to extend this feeling to everything around us. By recognising the miracle of life and embracing optimism, we strengthen our connection to others. The deeper we follow our hearts, the less likely we are to harm others or humanity as a whole.

Emotional unity fosters humility and empathy, embracing imperfections in others. As Parmenides expressed, *"Being is ungenerated and indestructible, whole, of one kind and unwavering, and complete. Nor was it, nor will it be, since now it is, all together, one, continuous."*

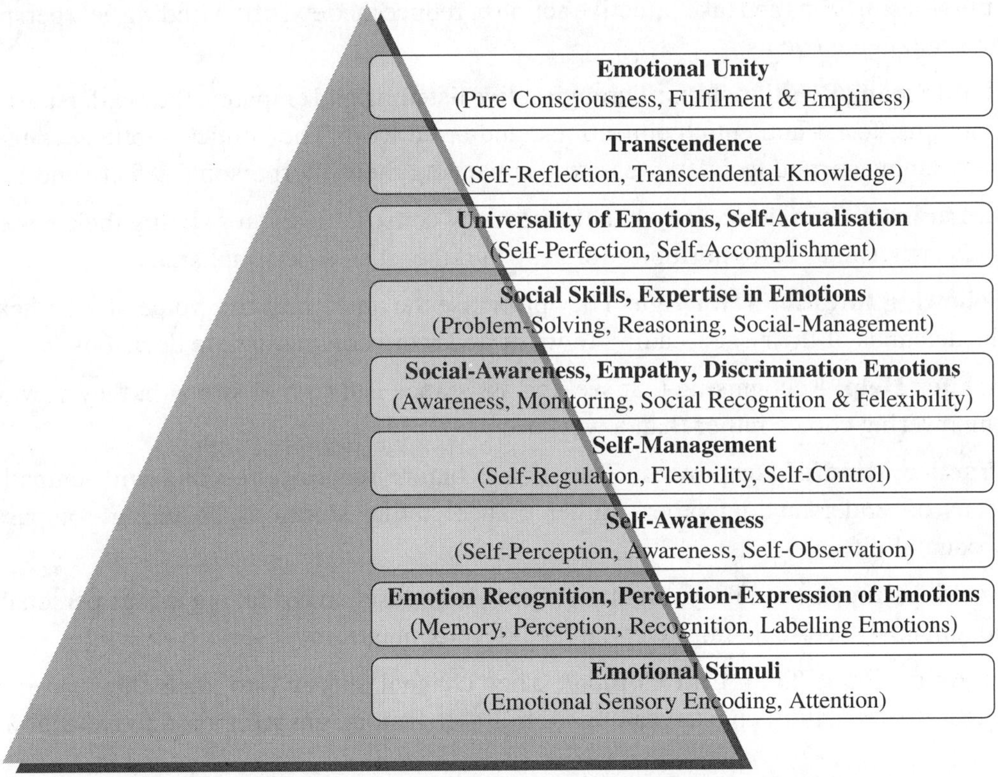

Fig. 8.1 Nine Layer model of Emotional Intelligence

8. IMPORTANCE OF EMOTIONAL INTELLIGENCE

A person with a high Emotional Intelligence is more likely to:

- **Identify and Express Feelings:** They connect with their emotions by recognising and articulating them, enabling a better understanding and management of their responses. They address root causes rather than symptoms, displaying self-awareness, assertiveness, and clear expression.
- **Clarify Goals and Purpose:** They understand their motivations, identify their values, and align their actions with their life's purpose, making plans to achieve meaningful goals.
- **Remain Calm Under Pressure:** By labelling and recognising their emotions, they maintain composure in challenging situations, preventing emotions from overwhelming rational thought.
- **Interpret Emotions:** They decipher the meaning behind emotions and, when necessary, redirect their emotional responses to be more appropriate and beneficial.
- **Manage Stress and Anxiety:** Recognising the causes and signs of stress, they reframe stressful situations and take effective action to reduce anxiety, often finding new perspectives on challenging events.
- **Build Strong Relationships:** Through active listening and empathy, they understand others' emotions, foster authentic connections, and build trust. They notice subtle cues like tone, body language, and facial expressions, enhancing their interpersonal effectiveness.
- **Learn from Criticism:** They handle feedback constructively, regulating their emotions to view criticism as an opportunity for growth rather than a personal attack.
- **Following Intuition Over Ego:** They prioritise the quiet, intuitive voice of their heart over the demands of their ego, leading to wiser and more compassionate decisions.
- **Ask for Help:** Recognising that seeking assistance is a sign of strength, they view it as an empowering choice rather than a weakness.
- **Practice Mindful Responses:** They pause before reacting, respond with empathy, and focus on understanding others rather than dictating solutions, fostering compassionate accountability.
- **Avoid Assumptions:** They maintain a growth mindset, avoid taking things personally, and continuously seek self-improvement and development.
- **Focus on What They Can Control:** They channel energy into areas they can influence rather than dwelling on external, uncontrollable factors, ensuring productive action.

9. POSITIVE AND NEGATIVE EMOTIONAL INTELLIGENCE

Positive and Negative Emotional Intelligence refers to how Emotional Intelligence (EI) is used in either constructive or harmful ways.

Positive EI	Negative EI
• Empathy	• Manipulation
• Self-awareness	• Lack of empathy
• Self-regulation	• Emotional instability
• Motivation	• Emotional suppression
• Social skills	• Emotional blackmail
• Active listening	• Insensitivity
• Compassion	• Poor communication
• Conflict resolution	• Passive-aggressiveness
• Adaptability	• Arrogance
• Emotional resilience	• Stubbornness
• Patience	• Defensive behaviour
• Positivity	• Intolerance
• Open-mindedness	• Overreacting to criticism
• Understanding nonverbal cues	• Disregarding others' feelings
• Self-confidence	• Blaming others
• Interpersonal effectiveness	• Gossiping
• Collaboration	• Holding grudges
• Leadership	• Sarcasm as a means of communication
• Persuasion	• Emotional outbursts
• Empowering others	• Seeking revenge

10. ROLE OF FAMILY IN GROOMING EMOTIONAL INTELLIGENCE

Family, as the foundational unit of a society, plays a pivotal role in shaping a child's behaviour. A child's Emotional Intelligence (EI) is profoundly influenced by parental EI, which encompasses discipline, empathy, understanding, warmth, and other key factors. Emotionally competent parents are more likely to foster healthy emotional development in their children, delivering effective and nurturing parenting.

According to EI researchers and authors, EI plays a critical role throughout life and, like any skill, can be developed in children. Daniel Goleman's introduction of the EQ concept in 1996 inspired various schools to begin teaching children how to identify and understand their own emotions as well as recognise the emotions of others.

As children grow, the emotional care they receive from their parents becomes deeply embedded in their emotional foundation. This care influences their social behaviour, ability to integrate with peers, and relationships with relatives. Effective parenting goes beyond intellect—it requires a sense of belonging, care, and affection that shapes a child's emotional well-being.

> **? Thought Box**
>
> How can families foster emotional intelligence in children through everyday interactions, and what specific parenting practices contribute most effectively to nurturing emotional resilience, empathy, and self-awareness?

Children often struggle to label their own emotions or make sense of their experiences. Non-judgemental acceptance by parents of the child's wide range of emotions creates a sense of security and deep emotional connection. This fosters confidence in children, assuring them they are cared for and can express their feelings without fear.

A healthy parent-child relationship builds trust and comfort, enabling children to express their emotions freely. Parents who guide their children at every stage of life create an environment where emotional expression is encouraged. This support promotes psychological and physical well-being, helping children navigate their emotions and develop resilience.

11. EMOTIONAL INTELLIGENCE AND CIVIL SERVICE

Emotional Intelligence (EI) is increasingly being recognised as a potential solution to the challenges that plague governance and administration, both in the country and globally. The underlying premise is that individuals with higher EI become better humans and more effective professionals, ultimately contributing to the establishment of a sustainable and functional democracy.

> **? Thought Box**
>
> What specific emotional intelligence competencies should be prioritised in civil service training to prepare officers for high-pressure situations and ethical decision-making?

This discussion highlights the significance of EI in the workplace, particularly in the context of civil services. It underscores the importance of incorporating EI as an essential component of civil servant training to enhance their emotional competence, decision-making, and ability to address complex challenges effectively.

11.1 Relevance of EI in the Current Environment of Civil Services

Civil servants in key bureaucratic roles face immense emotional demands from peers and the public while navigating an increasingly complex and challenging environment. These challenges include:

- Rapidly evolving social structures and values
- Growing regional, economic, and digital divides, coupled with rising population and unemployment
- Shortages of basic necessities like housing, drinking water, and infrastructure
- Greater public awareness alongside marginalised and voiceless populations
- The pressure of widespread IT adoption, which demands governments to appear efficient and in control
- Decentralisation through the 73rd and 74th Constitutional Amendments, creating new political dynamics
- Rising expectations for improved, transparent, and participatory governance
- Frequent politicisation of issues and increasing cynicism towards politics and administration
- Heightened public dissent, agitation, and aggression, often triggered by minor incidents
- Internal conflicts within the administration over policies, programmes, and their implementation
- Administrative issues such as political pressures, corruption, outdated laws, over-centralisation, and limited growth opportunities

This environment is more demanding and hostile than ever, leaving civil servants struggling to cope using traditional methods. While reforms have been attempted, many have failed due to neglecting crucial aspects like attitudes and emotional intelligence (EI).

The emotionally intelligent civil services can achieve a lot if they are professionally competent and positive in their approach. In fact, structural reforms need not be juxtaposed with attitudinal ones.

11.2 Role of EI in Helping Civil Servants

Emotional Intelligence can help the civil servants in three ways at the workplace:

- To achieve amicable work environment;
- Improvement in the behaviour and performance of individual workers;
- Improvement in organisational performance.

The Civil Services and the Public Administration take the inspiration from the private sector and other public sector organisation in other countries to implement and impart training for EI. This can also help understand the importance of EI in the workplace. Also, the government can devise and create environment which is compatible with day-to-day application of EI for the public servants.

Understanding EI can help the public servants understand the work environment better, they can also engage with their superiors, subordinates, and the public in an effective manner. This can lead to a positive atmosphere in the workplace and prevent unnecessary disturbances and clashes. Thus, understanding emotions and being emotionally knowledgeable and resilient improve the efficiency and effectiveness of the organisation, and thereby ultimately deliver quality services to the public concerned.

Numerous organisations in public and private sectors have used EI and reported positive results. In India, Hindustan Petroleum has used EI to create an environment that fosters emotionally intelligent leadership. As an initial measure it has trained frontline leaders and provided them with opportunities to put EI into practice.

> **? Thought Box**
>
> To what extent can emotional intelligence training transform civil service culture to be more empathetic, inclusive, and citizen-focused?

Specifically, the awareness and the application of EI helps in the following manner:

- Greater interpersonal skills (crucial for good citizen administration)
- Increased capacity to handle – Changes in work, Pressures and stress, Conflicts
- Ability to see the long-term effects of one's actions/attitudes
- Increased levels of commitment, trust, worthiness and conscientiousness
- Being able to see things in a holistic manner
- Being able to bounce back from setbacks and maintain optimism
- Finding healthy ways to handle negative/extreme feelings
- Having greater motivation – achievement drive, initiative, persistence, motivating others as well
- Better ability to communicate
- Enhanced group dynamics in terms of cooperation, collaboration, and building bonds
- Enhanced leadership traits, including the knowledge about when and how to lead, when to follow
- Ability to use win–win model for negotiations
- Ability to appreciate diversity and value of others
- Ability to perform multiple tasks due to better time and information management.
- Greater focus
- Aware of but minimally concerned with and affected by office politics
- Not prone to aggression
- Ability to be a change catalyst

In crux, Emotional Intelligence adds far more of the qualities that make us more human.

11.3 EI-in Designing Training Curriculum for Civil Servants

Ideally, teaching of emotional skills should begin at home and be reinforced in schools. However, this may not happen as is the case in India like many other countries, thus a majority who enter the civil services need to be made aware of EI. The good thing is that it can be taught and thus be inculcated in employees.

Four key issues must be addressed to incorporate Emotional Intelligence (EI) into the training curriculum effectively:

1. Target Audience: While EI training is ideally beneficial for all employees, resource and time constraints necessitate prioritisation. The focus should start with high-ranking officers and young inductees undergoing induction training, as they are future leaders. Efforts should also aim to embed EI at all levels of government, for example, through engaging documentaries or resources accessible in offices.

2. Course Content: The curriculum should be tailored to the career stage of the trainees. An introductory programme could include:

- The concept of EI, including its scientific basis
- The comparison of EI and IQ in workplace contexts
- The significance of EI in professional settings
- Measurement of EI, covering the relevance, use, and limitations of different tests

3. Training Tools and Techniques: A variety of methods can be employed, such as organisational surveys, group activities, audio-visual aids, individual coaching, case studies, workshops, and seminars. These approaches should be adapted to address the specific cultural and operational needs of the trainees.

4. Implementation into Practice: Training must equip participants with actionable strategies to apply EI concepts in their unique workplace environments. Departments and offices should develop practical initiatives to foster emotional maturity among their employees, aligning these with their specific challenges and requirements.

Training in EI may not overcome all the distortions created by inappropriate socialisation and upbringing, but it can at least make the people mature to a workable level. One also has to keep in mind that all the techniques available in psychology may not be of use in politico-administrative context. Changes would need to be made. The implication is that EI should be an integral part of organisation development and human resources development strategy. Further, EI can be part of the curriculum of courses in Public Administration in colleges and universities. The government can also use its authority to influence the educational institutions, especially schools, to introduce and use the concept and skills of EI.

12. WAYS TO RAISE YOUR EMOTIONAL INTELLIGENCE

All information reaches brain through our senses, and when this information is overwhelmingly stressful or emotional, instinct comes up and our ability to act will be limited to the fight or freeze the response. Therefore, to expose to wide range of choices and the ability to make better decisions, we need to be able to bring up our emotions into balance at our will.

Memory is also strongly associated with emotion. By learning to stay connected to the emotional part of our brain as well as the rational, we will not only expand our range of choices when it comes to responding to a new event, but we will also put up the factor of emotional memory into our decision-making process. This will help prevent us from continually repeating earlier mistakes and bitter events.

To improve our EI in decision-making abilities, we need to understand and manage our emotions. This is accomplished by developing key skills for controlling and managing overwhelming stress and becoming an effective communicator in the course of time.

EI is built by dwindling stress, staying focused, and staying connected to ourselves and others. We can do this by learning key skills. The first two skills are essential for controlling and managing overwhelming stress and the last three skills greatly improve the interpersonal communication. Each skill builds on the lessons learned in practicing the earlier skills.

13. EMOTIONAL ILLITERACY

A few years ago in Chennai, one of India's major cities, a teacher was killed by a student with a knife. The incident occurred after the teacher scolded the student for not completing his homework. The boy, filled with anger and frustration, carried out the act in a moment of irrationality. This event highlights a deficiency in Emotional Intelligence (EI).

Mental illness, particularly depression, is one of the most common challenges faced by teenagers. Children today are burdened with a heavy educational load, leading to immense pressure. In India, students come from diverse socio-economic and cultural backgrounds, each with their own level of EI. Cultivating EI in children is a vital task for parents, teachers, and the government. For example, children from disadvantaged backgrounds may struggle with anxiety and have more fragile emotional states, making them more susceptible to emotional difficulties.

Emotional illiteracy refers to the inability to understand, express, or manage one's emotions, which also prevents one from understanding or empathising with others' emotions. This disconnect limits emotional awareness and often leads to impulsive, reactive behaviour, leaving individuals emotionally trapped and unable to navigate their feelings effectively.

14. EMOTIONAL RESILIENCE

Emotional resilience is the ability to respond to stressful or unexpected situations and crises. It is the capability to perform consistently in a range of situations under pressure and to adapt behaviour appropriately. It is about how well an individual manages negative emotions when things get tough and how quickly he can take charge of himself and refocus on the needs of those around him and move forward.

The amount of emotional resilience we have is determined by a number of different things, including our age, identity, and what we have experienced in our life.

SUMMARY

- Emotions help us learn, enhance memory, and control our responses, giving meaning to situations.
- Howard Gardner identified seven types of intelligence: logical, musical, kinesthetic, spatial, linguistic, interpersonal, and intrapersonal.
- Emotional Intelligence is the ability to manage one's emotions and relationships effectively.
- EI plays a larger role than IQ in shaping personal and social progress.
- Daniel Goleman's EI framework includes self-awareness, self-regulation, motivation, empathy, and social skills.
- Mayer and Salovey's model defines four emotional abilities: perceiving, using, understanding, and managing emotions.
- The Nine Layer Pyramid of Emotional Intelligence includes stages from emotion recognition to emotional unity.
- Positive and Negative EI refers to using EI constructively or harmfully.
- Children's EI is heavily influenced by parental EI, including discipline, empathy, and warmth.
- EI in civil services is vital for accountability, governance, and improving civil servants' effectiveness.
- Emotionally intelligent civil servants contribute to a healthier democracy by treating others as humans.
- Emotional illiteracy is the inability to understand or manage emotions, limiting our actions and leading to reactive behaviour.
- Emotional resilience is the ability to handle stress, adapt to crises, and manage emotions effectively under pressure.

PRACTICE QUESTIONS

1. Intelligence is no more a one dimensional skill and now there is a radical departure from earlier approaches which conceived intelligence as a purely cerebral quality. "The term EI cannot be defined but can be explained with traits". Explain.
2. EI can be a key to success in your life especially in your career. Discuss by explaining your trait with that required in civil services.
3. What is emotional competence? How can that be acquired?
4. "Apart from intellectual intelligence and moral qualities, EI is the last step to make a bureaucrat successful in career". Discuss with examples.
5. "As the bureaucratic processes moved more and more away from the historical concepts of dehumanisation and impersonality, the notion that emotional skills are essential to job performance and customer service has gained foothold in the public administration sector". Explain.
6. What is EI? Explain the components which make up EI.
7. Bring out a training programme to develop EI among public servants.
8. How is emotional quotient different from intelligence quotient?
9. "Emotionally intelligent people scale higher reaches than others". Discuss the importance of EI among public servants with reference to the above statement.
10. Differentiate between feelings and emotions.
11. How EI plays a vital role in shaping the personality of an individual?
12. To become successful in the career, how EI enables one to achieve the same?
13. Do you think EI is much essential for becoming a successful leader? If so, elucidate it with example?
14. What is emotional resilience? How is it beneficial for an individual? Explain with example.

PREVIOUS YEARS' QUESTIONS

1. "What really matters for success, character, happiness, and lifelong achievements is a definite set of emotional skills – your EQ – not just purely cognitive abilities that are measured by conventional IQ tests." Do you agree with this view? *UPSC CSE Mains 2023*
2. Apart from intellectual competency and moral qualities, empathy and compassion are some of the other vital attributes that facilitate the civil servants to be more competent in tackling the crucial issues or taking critical decisions. Explain with suitable illustrations. *UPSC CSE Mains 2022*
3. In case of crisis of conscience does emotional intelligence help to overcome the same without compromising the ethical or moral stand that you are likely to follow? Critically examine. *UPSC CSE Mains 2021*

4. What are the main components of emotional intelligence (EI)? Can they be learned? Discuss. *UPSC CSE Mains 2020*
5. "Emotional Intelligence is the ability to make your emotions work for you instead of against you". Do you agree with this view? Discuss. *UPSC CSE Mains 2019*
6. How will you apply emotional intelligence in administrative practices? *UPSC CSE Mains 2017*
7. Anger is a harmful negative emotion. It is injurious to both personal and work life. (a) Discuss how it leads to negative emotions and undesirable behaviours. (b) How can it be managed and controlled? *UPSC CSE Mains 2016*
8. What is 'emotional intelligence' and how can it be developed in people? How does it help an individual in taking ethical decisions? *UPSC CSE Mains 2013*

Aptitude and Foundational Values for Civil Services

9

1. INTRODUCTION

LEARNING OBJECTIVES

1. Understanding the concept of bureaucracy and its importance
2. Understanding the features of bureaucracy, and their roles and functions
3. Understanding the concept of aptitude and their significance
4. Identifying the aptitudes needed in a civil servant
5. Understanding of the foundational values needed in a civil servant
6. Learning the qualities ascribed in a professional public servant
7. Understand the maladies plaguing bureaucracy
8. Learning the need for bureaucratic reforms and reforms in bureaucracy needed

The state and its administration serve as the backbone of an organised society, providing structure, governance, and the necessary mechanisms for societal progress. The significance of a well-functioning state is provided by the words of Kautilya in his *Saptanga* theory of State, which describes the elements of the state and their importance for its functioning. This intrinsic relationship between individuals and the state underscores the essential role of governance in fostering community and cooperation.

In *The Social Contract*, Jean-Jacques Rousseau eloquently argues, "*The strength of the state is in its law*." He emphasises that a fair and just legal framework is crucial for maintaining order and protecting the freedoms of its individuals. Effective administration is vital to the realisation of this legal framework, as it translates policies into practice and serves as a bridge between the government and the populace.

The importance of administration is further given by modern leaders like Sardar Vallabhbhai Patel, who emphasised that there was no alternative to the administrative system prevalent in India at the time of independence, though it required a shift in the objectives and functioning. This statement reinforces the need for an effective administrative framework that prioritizes public welfare.

In the dynamic landscape of public administration, the success of the civil servant hinges on a delicate balance of law enforcement with aptitudes and foundational values. As Mahatma Gandhi observed, "*The best way to find yourself is to lose yourself in the service of others.*" This quote captures the essence of civil service, where commitment to public welfare is paramount. Civil servants must not only possess technical skills but also embody core values such as integrity, accountability, and empathy.

The need for a civil servant with values was given by Dr B. R. Ambedkar through his words, "However good a constitution may be, if those who are implementing it are not good, it will prove to be bad. However, bad a constitution may be, if those implementing it are good, it will prove to be good". In a rapidly changing world, civil servants are called upon to navigate complex societal challenges while ensuring that the principles of integrity, accountability, and public service remain at the forefront of their actions. This chapter delves into the essential aptitudes coupled with the core values that underpin effective public administration.

2. ESSENTIALITY OF BUREAUCRACY

Bureaucracy is derived from the Latin word '*bureau*', used from the early 18th century in Western Europe not just to refer to a writing desk, but an office, i.e. a workplace, where officials worked. The word bureaucracy came into use shortly before the French revolution and then rapidly spread to other countries. The greek suffix- *kratia* (or) *kratos*- means 'Power or Rule'. Bureaucracy thus basically means the rule of the officialdom.

In the words of Pfiffner, "*bureaucracy is a systematic organisation of tasks and individuals into a pattern which can most effectively achieve the ends of collective efforts.*"

According to Paul H. Appleby, "*bureaucracy is a class of technically skilled persons, who are organized in a hierarchical way and serve the state in an impartial manner.*"

In brief, bureaucracy is a system of administration wherein there is a specialisation of functions, objectives qualifications for office, action according to the adherence to fixed rules, and a hierarchy of authority and delegated powers.

The essentiality of civil service can be studied under the following heads:

2.1 Civil Service as an Instrument of Governance

The primary role of the government is to govern by maintaining peace, law and order, and ensuring the safety and security of its citizens. This includes upholding contracts between individuals and resolving any disputes that arise. In the early stages of government evolution, these foundational duties were its main focus.

As governments developed, additional responsibilities emerged, but the core function of ensuring stability remained constant. Without peace, societal progress is impossible, and this foundational role is essential for a civilised life.

Over time, the regulatory function of public administration has grown more complex. Governments now employ new methods for equitable distribution of resources and adopt advanced technologies to improve public service delivery.

> **? Thought Box**
>
> How can the civil service balance its dual role as an impartial executor of government policies and a proactive agent of change, while ensuring accountability and public trust in a rapidly evolving socio-political landscape?

2.2 Civil Service as an Instrument of Development and Change

Public administration plays a vital role as an agent of change and development, reflecting the aspirations, intellect, and goals of the people it serves. Development efforts rely heavily on a robust public administration to provide essential manpower for institutions, infrastructure, industry, and scientific research.

While the private sector contributes, it often lacks the incentive to establish critical infrastructure, like rail networks, telecommunications, and nationwide research initiatives. Here, public administration is crucial, providing the foundational support necessary for comprehensive development. Aid agencies have emphasised that financial assistance alone is ineffective without a skilled and efficient public administration to implement development programmes.

Public administration is not only central to economic growth but also serves as a key instrument for social change in developing countries. Through welfare initiatives and legal reforms—addressing issues like dowry, caste discrimination, and rights for vulnerable groups—it drives societal progress. Although political leaders set the agenda for development, public administration is responsible for drafting, enforcing, and sustaining these changes, making it an indispensable element of progress.

2.3 Civil Service as an Instrument of Welfare State

In a modern democratic state, the government is responsible for a range of welfare services, such as education, healthcare, and social security. With the decline of joint family support systems, the government now assumes care for the elderly, orphans, widows, and unemployed youth, especially during economic downturns.

Development also brings challenges, like urban slums, pollution, and juvenile delinquency, which require the government to identify issues and implement solutions. Public administration thus plays a dual role: protecting citizens' rights and delivering essential services. The effectiveness of public administration directly impacts public welfare, underscoring why the modern state is often termed an "Administrative State." As Prof. V.V. Donham observed, the success of our civilisation largely depends on the strength of its administration.

2.4 Stabilising Role of Civil Service in Society

The main role of public administration is to stabilize social institutions and maintaining order with minimal disruption. Administrators focus on preserving continuity rather than pursuing new, untested paths, positioning themselves as society's stabilising and guardians of tradition.

This stabilising role has both positive and negative aspects. Positively, it helps uphold established principles and maintain system stability. However, it can also resist change, hindering innovation and slowing reform efforts that could improve the existing system.

2.5 Civil Service as a Key to Modern Society

Civil service is vital to modern society, transforming government policies into practical actions that impact daily life and uphold stability. It addresses complex challenges while promoting accountability and fairness, making it essential for development and social equity. By strengthening democracy and enhancing public trust, civil service serves as a cornerstone of effective and responsive governance.

2.6 Civil Service as a Mechanism for Promoting Culture in the Society

Public administration is not just an instrument of governance, it is also an important instrument used for promoting and preserving the culture of the society. The ideals and the values of the state may be high, and its impact on the lives of the people can only be measured only if these values are put in actual practice. Thus the public administration becomes an important instrument to implement the values and the ideals of the state. By becoming the part of social and cultural life of the people, it has become a permanent force in determining the character and activities of the state itself. Hence, Waldo calls administration as, "*part of the cultural complex which is not only acted upon but which also acts*."

2.7 Civil Service as a Fourth Branch of Government

Until the 19th century, the state's role was mainly regulatory, with public administration focused on control rather than public service. However, as society grew more complex, the state took on greater responsibilities for social change and development, prioritizing public welfare. This shift marked the end of **laissez-faire governance**[1] and the rise of an interventionist welfare state,

[1]**Laissez-faire governance:** Laissez-faire is an economic philosophy that advocates for minimal government intervention in the economy

increasing the importance of public administration. Scholars began to view public administration as a distinct entity, elevating it as the "fourth branch" of government alongside the executive, legislature, and judiciary.

2.8 Civil Service in Policy Making Role

Civil servants play a pivotal role in advising ministers, identifying key policy areas, analyzing various alternatives, and proposing solutions to societal challenges. They serve as intermediaries between interest groups and politicians, offering insights grounded in both internal expertise and external consultation. This ensures their recommendations are often more comprehensive and well-informed than those of other stakeholders.

3. FEATURES AND ESSENTIAL ELEMENTS OF BUREAUCRACY

Bureaucracy plays a significant, indeed pivotal role in economic and social advancement of a nation, especially a developing one. As stated by Kofi Annan, former Secretary General of the United Nations, "*Good Governance is perhaps the single most important factor in eradicating poverty and promoting development*".

Max Weber, a German sociologist helps us in understanding the reason for bureaucracy's growth, importance and its impact on the society. He created an 'Ideal-type Bureaucratic model' which has been a great contribution not only to public administration but also to other general sciences. According to Weber, '*Bureaucracy is by far the most efficient instrument of large scale administration which has ever been developed and the modern social order has become overwhelming dependent on it.*' He was of the opinion that a purely bureaucratic form of organisation had the chance and capability to attain the highest level of efficiency. Weber further said that '*This type of organisation is in principle applicable with equal facility to a wide variety of different fields. It may be applied in profit making business or in charitable organisations, or in any number of other types of private enterprises serving ideal or material ends. It is equally applicable to political and religious organisations. With varying degree of approximations to a pure type, its historical existence can be demonstrated in all these fields.*'

The following are the characteristic features of the ideal-rational type bureaucracy as elaborated by Weber:

1. **Hierarchy:** It is the basic feature in the organisation which defines the position—the ranking of various positions in a descending order from top to bottom. Each level controls a level below them. Thus, no office is left uncontr olled in the system. It serves as a line of control and also as delegation of authority.
2. **Division of Labour:** The functioning is divided, based on specialisation. Each employee is given a specific function and they thus become a master of it. The area of competence is

demarcated. This raises the overall productivity and efficiency of the organisation. Each official thus knows what his function is and what to perform and also what not to perform that is not to encroach upon the functions of others.

3. **Rules:** The official function is carried out on the basis of rules. It helps to avoid the arbitrariness, personal favour, etc. which may hinder the working of the organisation. The rules make sure the decision taken at higher levels get implemented at the lower levels and also help in maintaining the uniformity and in coordination of the efforts in the organisation. Thus, rules help in stability, continuity and probability of the system and each one knows the outcome of their action.
4. **Impersonality:** Irrational sentiments have to be avoided in any organisation and the officials should discard their personal likes and dislikes while performing their official duty. Thus, decisions should be governed by rational factors and not personal factors. And impersonality helps in dealing with people both within and outside the organisation.
5. **Official Records:** The official records of the organisation are maintained. All the decisions and activities of the organisation are recorded in writing and are preserved for future reference.
6. **Differentiation of Public and Private Ends:** Personal interests and private ends are kept separate from the public purpose and rationality should always be maintained in the organisation. Bureaucrats are paid employees of the organisation, their tenure is determined by official rules and regulations, and they should not have any exclusive interest in the organisation.

Weber describes the 'Ideal-type' organisation as a purely bureaucratic structure, which he argues is the most efficient and rational means of exercising control. He highlights its superiority in precision, stability, discipline, reliability, and calculability of results, making it suitable for a wide range of administrative tasks.

4. ROLES AND FUNCTIONS OF BUREAUCRACY

As a complex and multi-layered system, the bureaucracy plays a crucial role in sustaining the administrative structure of the country, irrespective of political shifts. The key roles and functions of bureaucracy includes:

1. **Policy Implementation:** Bureaucrats convert broad policy decisions into actionable plans that ensure these decisions have a tangible impact at the grassroots level.
2. **Advisory Role in Policymaking:** They provide data, technical expertise, and analysis to the political leaders that contribute to informed decision-making. Senior officials within ministries and departments assist in drafting bills, framing rules, and defining frameworks, thus significantly impacting policymaking by offering practical insights on feasibility, impact, and logistics.

3. **Maintaining Continuity and Stability:** Civil servants hold office irrespective of the changing political landscape, ensuring that administrative functions continue uninterrupted. This stability is pivotal to public trust, as it helps sustain government operations and maintain a balanced institutional memory, which preserves the rule of law.
4. **Public Service Delivery:** Bureaucrats play a crucial role in ensuring access to essential services, including healthcare, education, water supply, electricity, and social welfare benefits. This interface becomes particularly vital as bureaucracy is often the most direct representation of government intervention in citizens' lives.
5. **Regulatory and Supervisory Functions:** They play an essential role in regulating and supervising compliance with laws across various domains such as land revenue, environmental standards, industrial operations, and labour laws. Regulatory bodies staffed by civil servants monitor adherence to standards and take necessary action against violations.
6. **Upholding Rule of Law:** A fundamental responsibility of the bureaucracy is upholding the rule of law and enforcing the legal framework that ensures government actions align with constitutional values.
7. **Crisis Management and Disaster Response:** In the event of natural disasters, health crises, or emergencies, they lead efforts to coordinate relief operations, manage rescue missions, and ensure efficient resource distribution. Through national and state-level disaster management frameworks, bureaucrats work with multiple agencies to mitigate the impact of disasters and bring about timely recovery.
8. **Promoting Socio-Economic Development:** They implement poverty alleviation programmes, drive rural development initiatives, and promote sustainable economic policies that support inclusive growth. Civil servants at local levels work closely with communities, fostering social equity and economic inclusion, thereby contributing to nation-building efforts and reducing inequality.

5. WHY ARE VALUES NEEDED IN BUREAUCRACY?

In the 21st century, the role of bureaucracy is evolving rapidly, influenced by shifts in public expectations, technological advancements, and complex global challenges. The changing role of bureaucracy is due to:

1. **Increased Public Scrutiny and Accountability**: In the information age, bureaucracies operate under the public eye more than ever before. Citizens demand transparency, accountability, and responsiveness. This shift has transformed the bureaucratic role from a secluded administrative body to an openly accountable one.
2. **Technological Advancements**: Digital technologies have redefined bureaucratic functions, automated routine processes and enabling data-driven decision-making. As a result,

bureaucracy is shifting toward more strategic roles, where decisions are informed by complex datasets, and service delivery is increasingly digital. The bureaucrat's role now requires adaptability and technological proficiency alongside traditional expertise.

3. **Integration of Global Perspectives in Policy-Making:** In an interconnected world, bureaucratic policies are increasingly influenced by international standards and global agreements. Bureaucracies are now involved in addressing transnational issues such as climate change, human rights, and economic interdependence.

This changing landscape necessitates a renewed focus on values, as they serve as the anchor that keeps bureaucracy grounded in its foundational mission of public service. Values remain essential to ensure that this power is wielded responsibly and ethically. Values act as the moral infrastructure within which bureaucracies operate, helping officials navigate the complexities of modern governance with a clear sense of purpose and integrity. As bureaucracy transforms, values serve as the stabilising force that upholds its relevance and integrity. Values are not merely ideals but operational principles that ensure bureaucracy remains an institution committed to public welfare, justice, and sustainable progress.

Ultimately, value-driven bureaucracy is capable of meeting the demands of today's world while staying true to its core mission of serving the people.

QUOTES ON APTITUDE

"Aptitude found in the understanding and is often inherited. Genius coming from reason and imagination, rarely. **Marcus Aurelius**

Genius is nothing but a greater aptitude for patience. **Benjamin Franklin**

Most do violence to their natural aptitude, and thus attain superiority in nothing. **Baltasar Gracian**

Genius consists of equal parts of natural aptitude and hard work. **Andre Maurois**

Each man has to seek out his own special aptitude for a higher life in the midst of the humble and inevitable reality of daily existence. Than this, there can be no nobler aim in life. **Maurice Maeterlinck**"

6. APTITUDE

The term aptitude originates from the Latin word *aptos,* meaning 'fitted for.' It is defined as a natural ability or talent, reflecting an inherent capacity for excelling in a specific field, such as an art form, academic subject, or profession.

Aptitude is indicative of one's potentialities. Aptitude emerges from the interplay between inherited traits and environmental influences. An individual is born with certain potentialities and the environment helps or hinders the expression of these potentialities. The concept of aptitude is very broad which embraces any characteristic which contributes to learning, including intelligence, achievement, personality, interests and skills. It is not just confined to 'specialised learning capacities' such as music or painting. Aptitude predicts future ability. When we say, "X has scholastic aptitude", it means that X will be successful or do well in academic activities. Thus, aptitude always has a futuristic reference. Aptitudes are qualities of an individual, that can be harnessed by appropriate training.

However, aptitude cannot be directly equated with intelligence. Aptitude can be described as a specific ability of an individual, whereas intelligence is the general mental ability cutting across different types of tasks. Thus, aptitude has a defined/narrow scope compared to intelligence. Aptitude is future-oriented, reflecting the potential for learning and growth, while intelligence is present-focused, showcasing current abilities. Intelligence is what the person knows and what he can perform in different areas.

7. APTITUDE VS ATTITUDE

While attitude refers to how one feel about a particular person, thing, event, or idea, aptitude refers to one's ability to perform a particular kind of task. Both aptitude and attitude can be cultivated. Aptitude relates to competence, while attitude reflects character and virtues.

Table 9.1: Comparison of Attitude and Aptitude

Feature	Attitude	Aptitude
Definition	Attitude is a set of beliefs, emotions and ideas.	Aptitude is the ability of a person to acquire a specific skill.
Character	It is subjective and influenced by experiences, values, and norms.	It is innately developed, referring to the potential or capacity.
Formation and development	Changes over time through experiences, education, and ethical reasoning.	Normally considered inherent but can also be developed through practice and training.
Dynamics	Dynamic and mouldable – can evolve with new experiences and understanding.	Relatively stable but can be enhanced through deliberate practice and education.
Evaluation	Assessed through behavioural observations, discussions, and surveys.	Evaluated using proficiency tests, performance assessments, and problem-solving scenarios.
Influence on actions	Dictates ethical behaviour based on moral values, beliefs and emotional responses.	Determines the ease and effectiveness with which tasks are performed.

(*contd.*)

Feature	Attitude	Aptitude
Scale	It is usually good or bad, positive or negative.	It is not relative as it is a measure of competency.
Nature	Attitude is a mental construct.	Aptitude can be physical or mental.
Significance in civil service	Important for ethical decision-making, teamwork, and leadership in public administration.	Key for technical proficiency, and task execution in administrative settings.
Example	Sardar Vallabhbhai Patel, the 'Iron Man of India', known for his attitude of patriotism and his deep commitment to a unified and independent India.	Sardar Vallabhbhai Patel's aptitude in negotiation skills and pragmatic, no-nonsense approach towards complex political issues.

8. NEED FOR APTITUDE IN CIVIL SERVICES

Civil servants are tasked with the responsibilities of implementing policies, overseeing public resources, and safeguarding the welfare of citizens. As they navigate diverse and often unpredictable situations, possessing strong aptitudes enables them to make informed decisions that promote transparency, accountability, and public trust.

- The civil services form the essential, permanent structure underpinning the administration, making it crucial to have a high-caliber, professional, skilled, and dedicated workforce to uphold the standards of public administration.
- In Indian public administration, civil servants handle a wide array of responsibilities, ranging from basic administrative and clerical duties to complex decision-making and policy implementation, while also serving as a bridge between the government and citizens. To succeed in these roles, civil servants must possess varied skills, including strong analytical abilities, the capacity to grasp complex issues, and an aptitude for building collaborative networks and working effectively in teams.
- Leaders in public administration encounter diverse challenges daily, such as high unemployment, limited government funding, and rapidly shifting socio-economic landscapes. Laws and administrative rules alone cannot address every situation, and past successes may not always be replicable as circumstances evolve constantly. In these scenarios, civil servants require a high degree of critical thinking and quick decision-making skills to exercise judgment confidently.
- The push for e-governance and the motto 'Minimum Government, Maximum Governance' call for transformative changes in government structures, as well as in the approach and mindset of government officials. Given the rapidly evolving and increasingly complex roles of administrators, civil servants must be equipped with the skills and capabilities necessary to meet new challenges, including proficiency in new technologies and adapting to modernized ways of working. They must embody the role of "Agents of Change," driving reform initiatives forward.

- In India's diverse context, civil servants often confront contrasting socio-economic objectives that can lead to moral and ethical dilemmas regarding their roles and duties. This requires an aptitude for navigating contradictions, resolving dilemmas, and maintaining a resilient spirit to perform despite adverse conditions.
- Within the framework of inclusive governance, administrators need to assemble teams across various stakeholder groups. For instance, an economic development director striving to foster a business-friendly environment in a city must engage local business leaders, the Chamber of Commerce, and environmental advocates. This necessitates strong interpersonal skills to bridge gaps, foster collaboration toward common goals, and effectively receive and act on feedback.

Winston Churchill said, "*To each, there comes in their lifetime a special moment when they are figuratively tapped on the shoulder and offered the chance to do a very special thing, unique to them and fitted to their talents.*" This emphasises the crucial role that civil servants play in shaping society and the importance of aligning their aptitudes with their responsibilities.

? Thought Box

In a diverse and dynamic society like India, how can the integration of both technical aptitude and emotional intelligence in civil services enhance decision-making and ensure more inclusive governance?

9. APTITUDES NEEDED IN A CIVIL SERVANT

The effectiveness of civil servants hinges on a diverse array of aptitudes that empower them to navigate the complexities of public administration. In a role that demands not only technical proficiency but also a deep understanding of social dynamics, civil servants must cultivate aptitudes that enable them to analyse multifaceted issues, make informed decisions, and respond swiftly to the ever-evolving needs of the community.

1. **Organisational Skills:** Organisational skills ensure the smooth execution of policies, efficient use of resources, and timely delivery of public services.
2. **Critical Thinking**: It is a key aptitude for civil servants, as it enables them to navigate complex issues, evaluate options carefully, and make informed decisions in public administration.
3. **Effective Resource Utilisation**: It allows them to maximize efficiency, meet public service goals, and uphold accountability.
4. **Collaborative Networking**: It enables them to build strong alliances, coordinate across sectors, and foster partnerships that enhance public service delivery.
5. **Professionalism**: It encompasses ethical behaviour, a commitment to excellence, effective communication, and a strong dedication to public service, all of which are essential for maintaining public trust and ensuring effective governance.
6. **Innovation**: Being open to new ideas and willing to explore unconventional methods helps civil servants find effective solutions to complex problems.

7. **Negotiating Skills**: Civil servants often encounter conflicting interests among stakeholders. Strong negotiation skills can help them mediate disputes and find mutually acceptable solutions.
8. **Adaptability**: Civil servants must be able to adjust their decision-making processes in response to new information, shifting priorities, or unexpected developments.
9. **Ethical Reasoning**: It is essential for fostering a culture of ethics and integrity in public service, ensuring that civil servants act in the best interest of the community they serve.

10. FOUNDATIONAL VALUES OF CIVIL SERVICE

In a democracy, an effective civil service is defined by a unique set of values that set it apart from other professions. Key principles such as integrity, commitment to public service, impartiality, political neutrality, and anonymity are regarded as the cornerstones of an efficient civil service. In some countries, these values have been embodied in laws – e.g. in Australia, and in some countries these are enshrined in the respective constitutions. For instance, Article 153 of the Polish Constitution specifies, "A corps of civil servants shall operate in the organs of government administration in order to ensure a professional, diligent, impartial and politically neutral discharge of the State's obligations".

In India, the values of the civil service have developed through years of tradition. These values also find place in various rules, including the Code of Conduct. The current set of 'enforceable norms' for civil servants are the 'Conduct Rules', exemplified by the Central Civil Services (Conduct) Rules of 1964 and similar regulations for members of the All India Services or employees of various state governments. As previously mentioned, while the Conduct Rules include broad guidelines such as 'maintaining integrity and complete dedication to duty', and avoiding 'conduct unbecoming of a government servant,' they mainly focus on listing specific actions considered undesirable for government employees. Unlike other countries, India does not have a formal Code of Ethics for its civil servants. The foundational values of civil service form the bedrock of ethical governance, shaping the conduct, decision-making, and overall integrity of public servants. These values ensure that civil servants uphold principles that foster trust and accountability within society.

10.1 Integrity

> "Real integrity is doing the right thing, knowing that nobody's going to know whether you did it or not."
>
> **Oprah Winfrey**

As per civil services competency dictionary, Integrity is defined as "consistently behaving in an open, fair, and transparent manner and honours one's commitments, and works to uphold the public service values."

Integrity is the quality of being honest and having strong moral principles and doing the right things even when no one is watching. It is the consistency between an individual's internal values and their outward actions. People with high personal integrity act in alignment with their beliefs and principles, even in the absence of others observing.

- **Types of Integrity**

1. **Moral Integrity:** Moral integrity is about consistently choosing actions that align with values like honesty, fairness, compassion, and justice, regardless of personal gain or societal pressures. Moral integrity often requires courage, as it may involve standing up against wrongdoing, making sacrifices, or holding oneself accountable to high standards.

   Example, Mahatma Gandhi was a person of profound moral integrity. His life was a testament to his commitment to ethical principles, nonviolence, and truth, often encapsulated in his philosophy of *Satyagraha*.

2. **Intellectual Integrity:** Individuals with intellectual integrity avoid distorting facts, suppressing evidence, or yielding to biases. This integrity type is crucial in fields where the pursuit of truth is foundational, such as academia, research, and journalism. Upholding intellectual integrity leads to trustworthy information and fair interpretations, benefiting society as a whole.

   Example, Galileo Galilei upheld intellectual integrity in his pursuit of understanding the cosmos. In the early 1600s, Galileo championed the heliocentric model, which stated that the Earth revolves around the Sun, despite significant backlash from the Catholic Church, which supported the geocentric view.

1. **Professional Integrity:** Professional integrity refers to adherence to ethical standards, honesty, and accountability in one's work. It builds credibility and trust in workplaces, serving as a backbone for ethical business practices, transparent communication, and responsible decision-making. It enables professionals to uphold the reputation of their field and contribute to public trust.

   Example, Ratan Tata led the Tata Group to uphold professional integrity by repaying government loans ahead of schedule even during the 2008 financial crisis.

2. **Social Integrity:** Social integrity focuses on mutual respect, inclusiveness, and the common good, creating environments where individuals feel valued and safe. Upholding social integrity builds social trust, promotes cooperation, and strengthens the moral fabric of society by fostering relationships rooted in fairness, empathy, and accountability.

   Example, Martin Luther King's commitment to nonviolence, influenced by Gandhi, exemplified social integrity. He believed that violent responses would perpetuate a cycle of hatred and oppression. By leading peaceful demonstrations, such as the Montgomery Bus

Boycott, he demonstrated that integrity involves pursuing justice without compromising one's ethical standards and social harmony.

- **Importance of Integrity in Civil Services**

1. **Developing Conscience**: Integrity helps civil servants to act according to their moral compass rather than simply following orders. For example, a police officer with integrity might refuse an order to fire on unarmed, peaceful protestors, valuing ethics over blind obedience.
2. **Advancing Social Good**: Civil servants have extensive powers and responsibilities that impact society. By acting with integrity, they ensure that their decisions benefit the community as a whole, rather than serving personal or biased interests.
3. **Combating Corruption**: Civil servants with integrity actively resist corrupt practices, working to eliminate unethical behaviour that undermines public trust and delays progress. Example, Ashok Khemka an IAS, advocated for transparency, accountability, and land reform in India. His efforts have often resulted in controversy, multiple transfers, and legal battles, but he has remained steadfast in his commitment to ethical governance.
4. **Stewardship of Public Resources**: Civil servants are entrusted with public funds, raised through taxes, to provide essential public goods and services. Integrity ensures they manage these resources responsibly, focusing on public benefit rather than misappropriation.
5. **Preventing Abuse of Power**: Integrity acts as a safeguard against the misuse of authority, as seen when police officers refuse bribes or other unethical inducements. Ethical behaviour reinforces public confidence in the fairness and reliability of public institutions.
6. **Role Model Behaviour**: Civil servants are expected to lead by example. With integrity as a guiding principle, they inspire others within the administration and the public to adopt ethical practices, fostering a culture of trustworthiness and respect. Example, Armstrong Pame IAS is a role model for his public service, determination, and innovative approach to governance. He built a 100 km road, known as the "People's Road", without government funding. The road connects Manipur to Nagaland and Assam, and improved access to education, healthcare, and markets for around 40 villages.
7. **Core to Administrative Ethics**: Integrity is the foundation of ethics in public service, setting the tone for ethical standards across the administration. Civil servants with integrity strengthen the credibility and ethical grounding of the entire system, reinforcing the moral fabric of public service.

- **Causes for the Decline of Integrity in Civil Service**

1. **Historical causes:** Under British rule, the focus was on exploiting resources rather than developing the country. This led to low-paying administrative positions for Indians, prompting many to engage in unethical practices.

2. **Economic causes:** Rapid urbanisation and industrialisation have elevated material wealth and economic power as key indicators of status. Low salaries and persistent inflation compel civil servants to resort to unethical behaviour to maintain their social standing.
3. **Popular tolerance:** A lack of strong public outrage allows corruption to thrive. Many citizens choose to pay bribes instead of reporting corrupt officials, perpetuating the cycle of corruption.
4. **Bureaucratic Inefficiency:** Complicated and **sluggish**[2] procedures in government offices encourage corrupt practices, as individuals seek speed money to expedite processes.
5. **Outdated Legal Framework:** Current anti-corruption laws are insufficient, resulting in lengthy trials and minimal penalties. Reforming these laws to include stricter penalties and faster trials is essential to combat corruption effectively.
6. **Collusion with Business Interests:** Big businessmen, dishonest merchants, and contractors frequently bribe civil servants to gain undue advantages. In some cases, they share a portion of their ill-gotten profits with government employees, further entrenching corruption.
7. **Influence of Pressure Groups:** Organisations like the Indian Chamber of Commerce and various trade associations contribute to corruption by lobbying for favours on behalf of their members. They often influence the ruling elite through social gatherings, such as dinners and **luncheons**[3], fostering a culture of favouritism.

QUOTES ON INTEGRITY

"Let me define a leader. He must have vision and passion and not be afraid of any problem. Instead, he should know how to defeat it. Most importantly, he must work with integrity. **Abdul Kalam**

Integrity without knowledge is weak and useless, and knowledge without integrity is dangerous and dreadful. **Samuel Johnson**

Integrity means that you are the same in public as you are in private. **Joyce Meyer**

One of the truest tests of integrity is its blunt refusal to be compromised. **Chinua Achebe**

Integrity reveals beauty. **Thomas Leonard**

To me, integrity means always doing what is right and good, regardless of the immediate consequences. It means being righteous from the very depth of our soul, not only in our actions but, more importantly, in our thoughts and in our hearts. **Joseph B. Wirthlin**"

[2]**Sluggish:** moving slowly than normal
[3]**Luncheons:** plural of lunch

10.2 Impartiality

"An impartial government and an impartial administration are the very foundations of a just society." **M.K. Gandhi**

Impartiality is the principle of treating all individuals equally and fairly, without any bias or favouritism. By adhering to impartiality, decisions and judgments are made based on objective facts rather than personal preferences or prejudices, which is crucial for maintaining trust and credibility.

- **Types of Impartiality**

  1. **Political Impartiality:** It requires that public officials carry out their duties without allegiance to any political party or ideology, regardless of changes in government. This form of neutrality ensures that civil servants serve the public and the state rather than partisan interests.
     Example, T.N. Seshan, who served as the chief election commissioner from 1990 to 1996, resisted political interference and institutionalised free and fair elections in India.
  2. **Public Impartiality:** It refers to the duty of public officials to act without bias toward any individual, group, or section of society. It ensures that all people, regardless of their social, economic, religious, or cultural backgrounds, are treated fairly and equally in matters of public service, resources, and decision-making.

     Example, Former District Collector of Osmanabad, Maharashtra, Mr. Kaustubh Diwegaonkar, IAS, sat on the floor with a disabled visitor when the visitor was unable to sit in a chair.

- **Importance of Impartiality in Civil Services**

  1. **Equal Treatment under the Law:** By remaining impartial, civil servants ensure that all individuals are treated equally, regardless of caste, religion, gender, economic status, or political affiliation. This upholds the constitutional principle of equality before the law.
  2. **Promoting Social Harmony:** Impartiality enables civil servants to implement policies and programmes without religious or cultural bias, upholding the constitutional value of secularism. This helps take right action in complex situations like riots or communal violence.
  3. **Makes ethical decisions**: When civil servants approach their duties impartially, they evaluate situations based on objective criteria and established laws, ensuring that decisions are made with transparency and justice.
  4. **Fosters Public Trust**: When citizens see that civil servants make unbiased, transparent decisions, it strengthens their trust in public institutions. Trust is vital for social cohesion

and for the public to feel confident in accessing government services, engaging in civic processes, and following laws. Example, U. Sagayam, IAS of Tamil Nadu cadre, when serving as the Sub-Divisional Magistrate in Ooty, exemplified his impartiality by accusing the District Collector of favouritism towards operators of large tea estates.

5. **Reduces Corruption and Favouritism**: Impartiality helps prevent corruption and favouritism, as civil servants make decisions based on objective criteria rather than personal gains or external influences. Example, In 2009, the then Chief Election Commissioner N. Gopalaswami recommended to the President that Election Commissioner Navin Chawla be removed from office because of his ties to Congress Party.

QUOTES ON IMPARTIALITY

"I judge people by their own principles—not by my own. **Martin Luther King Jr.**

Nothing can conduce more to the order and stability of a government than the simplicity of the laws, the proper definition of rights, and their impartial and consistent administration. **Sam Houston**

Impartiality is not neutrality. It is partiality for justice, fairness, and truth. **Amin Maalouf**

Truth is a matter of fact, not of opinion. Truth is inherently impartial, and the pursuit of truth must be free of prejudice and favoritism. **Dalai Lama**"

10.3 Non-Partisanship

"True leadership is exemplified by the ability to rise above partisanship and act in the best interest of all citizens."

Non-partisanship refers to the principle of remaining neutral and not showing allegiance to any political party, ideology, or faction. It involves acting without bias or favouritism, particularly in political, governmental, or organisational contexts. In essence, non-partisanship is about prioritising the common good over partisan interests.

While both non-partisanship and impartiality emphasise neutrality and fairness, non-partisanship specifically pertains to political neutrality, ensuring that no political party is favoured in governance and public administration. Impartiality is a broader concept that applies to any decision-making process, focusing on fairness and objectivity without bias. Both principles are essential for maintaining trust and integrity in democratic systems and public service.

For example, non-partisanship will enable a District Collector to effectively fulfil the responsibilities of a Returning Officer during elections.

- **Importance of Non-partisanship in civil services**

 1. **Upholds Public Trust:** By staying non-partisan, civil servants build trust across political divides, showing that their actions are guided by objective standards and laws rather than by political influence.
 2. **Promotes Stability in Governance:** Government policies and programmes change with each political cycle. Non-partisan civil servants provide continuity and stability by ensuring the smooth implementation of new policies, regardless of their personal beliefs or the party in power.
 3. **Prevents Political Manipulation:** When civil servants remain neutral, they reduce the risk of being used as instruments of political agendas, which could lead to biased governance and undermine democratic principles. Example, Raghuram Rajan, former Governor of RBI focussed on strengthening India's financial stability by taking stances that were often politically unpopular. His fight against inflation and the increase in interest rates were seen as moves that might slow down growth in the short term. However, Rajan remained steadfast, prioritising the long-term stability of the economy over short-term political gains.
 4. **Strengthens Professionalism:** Non-partisan civil servants maintain a professional work environment focused on skills, expertise, and competence.
 5. **Promotes Meritocracy**[4]**:** Non-partisanship helps to ensure that promotions, assignments, and recognitions within civil services are based on merit rather than political connections. Here is a negative example for partisanship. Sachin Vaze, a self-styled 'encounter specialist' in the Mumbai Police, was suspended 16 years ago following a custodial death case. After his suspension, he aligned himself with the Shiv Sena, which is said to have facilitated his **reinstatement**[5] in the police force in 2020.

QUOTES ON NON-PARTISANSHIP

"To be locked into partisan politics doesn't permit you to think clearly. — **Rudy Giuliani**

To be nonpartisan doesn't mean we're nonpolitical. — **Shane Claiborne**"

---

[4]**Meritocracy:** A country or social system where people get power or money on the basis of their ability
[5]**Reinstatement:** An act or instance of being restored to a former position or state

10.4 Objectivity

"Objectivity does not mean detachment, it means respect, that is, the ability not to distort and to falsify."
Erich Fromm

Objectivity is the 'quality of being able to make a decision or judgment in a fair way that is not influenced by personal feelings or beliefs.' It is the ability to make decisions based on facts or empirical evidences.

Objectivity in ethics, also known as "moral absolutism," is the belief that actions can be judged as right or wrong regardless of the situation or consequences. It's based on the idea that there are universal moral principles that apply to everyone, regardless of their culture, religion, or personal beliefs.

- **Types of Objectivity**

  1. **Moral Objectivity:** Moral objectivity or moral absolutism is the belief that certain actions are universally right or wrong, regardless of circumstances, cultural context, or personal beliefs. It maintains that there are inherent moral truths applicable to everyone.
  2. **Procedural Objectivity:** Procedural objectivity involves following standardised and fair procedures to ensure impartiality and consistency. Procedural objectivity in civil services ensures that all individuals are treated according to the same rules and standards, avoiding favouritism or discrimination.
  3. **Political Objectivity:** Political objectivity requires political leaders and policymakers to prioritise the public interest over personal or partisan interests. This type of objectivity involves considering diverse viewpoints and making decisions that reflect an unbiased approach.
  4. **Emotional Objectivity:** Emotional objectivity involves separating personal emotions from decision-making or judgment processes, allowing for rational and unbiased evaluations.

- **Importance of objectivity of civil services**

  1. **Reduces Corruption:** Objectivity promotes accountability by creating a structured approach to decision-making, which discourages officials from acting on personal biases.
  2. **Prevents Misuse of Discretion:** Objectivity provides clear criteria and standards for decision-making, which helps to limit arbitrary or biased choices. Example, Durga Sakthi Nagpal, IAS made headlines for her objective stance against illegal sand mining in Uttar Pradesh, where her actions were guided by her commitment to the law rather than political influences.
  3. **Resolves Ethical Dilemmas:** Objectivity helps to ensure that decisions are based on facts and sound reasoning rather than subjective feelings or pressures. Example, Aruna

Sundararajan, former Telecom Secretary, exemplifies objectivity by her emphasis on advocating for open data initiatives that make government processes accessible to even rural citizens.

4. **Ensures Effective Use of Public Resources:** When public officials approach resource allocation objectively, they are more likely to prioritise projects and policies that genuinely serve the public interest over those that cater to personal, political, or biased motivations.

QUOTES ON OBJECTIVITY

"Objectivity is both a requirement and a guide for a rational mind, a mind that seeks to perceive reality as it is, not as it wishes it to be.
Ayn Rand

Objectivity doesn't mean treating all sides equally. It means giving each side a hearing.
Christiane Amanpour

Objectivity cannot be equated with mental blackness; rather, objectivity resides in recognising your preferences and then subjecting them to especially harsh scrutiny and also in a willingness to revise or abandon your theories when the testes fail.
Stephen Jay Gould"

10.5 Dedication to Public Service

"Public service must be more than doing a job efficiently and honestly. It must be a complete dedication to the people and to the nation."
Margaret Chase Smith

Dedication to public service refers to the unwavering commitment of individuals to serve the needs and interests of the community and society at large. It involves prioritising the well-being of the public above personal interests and motivations.

It is the ability to fully dedicate one's time and attention to the cause of public service. This quality embodies "commitment, passion, and an inner drive to serve the public good" without needing any external push or motivation. In essence, it means internalising the purpose of public service and embracing it as a personal calling.

- **Contribution of Dedication to Civil Services**

1. **Responsiveness to Community Needs:** Dedicated civil servants are more attuned to the needs of their communities, allowing them to develop and implement policies and programmes that effectively address local issues. Example, Armstrong Pame, a young bureaucrat, constructed the People's Road in Manipur solely using voluntary contributions.
2. **Innovative Solutions:** A commitment to public service often inspires creativity and innovation among civil servants, leading to the development of new approaches to solving

complex societal problems. Example, Sonam Wangchuk initiated *Operation New Hope*, transforming education in Ladakh.

3. **Advocacy for Marginalised Groups:** Dedicated public servants advocate for the needs of marginalised and underrepresented communities, ensuring that their voices are heard and considered in decision-making processes.
4. **Crisis Management:** Dedicated public servants remain committed during crises, such as natural disasters or public health emergencies. Their determination to serve helps ensure a swift and effective response, safeguarding public welfare. Example, IAS officer MG Rajamanickam carried rice sacks on his shoulder without hesitation during the Kerala floods.

QUOTES ON DEDICATION TO PUBLIC SERVICE

"Our nation is defined by its people, not by its borders. We count on our civil servants to uphold this spirit and serve with integrity, dedication, and empathy. **Atal Bihari Vajpayee**

The best way to find yourself is to lose yourself in the service of others. **Mahatma Gandhi**

The highest of distinctions is service to others. **King George VI**"

10.6 Tolerance

"Tolerance is the strength of a nation. It binds us together and allows us to flourish despite our differences."

A.P.J. Abdul Kalam

Tolerance is the ability or willingness to accept and respect the beliefs, opinions, practices, and characteristics of individuals or groups different from oneself, even when those differences may be in conflict with one's own values or views.

It encompasses an attitude of openness, understanding, and coexistence, promoting harmony in diverse societies and fostering peaceful relationships among people with varying backgrounds and perspectives.

Tolerance is not about concession, **condescension**[6], or indulgence. Rather, it is an active attitude grounded in the recognition of the universal human rights and fundamental freedoms of others. It cannot be used to justify violations of these core values under any circumstances. Tolerance should be upheld by individuals, groups, and governments alike.

---

[6]**Condescension:** disdainfulness

- **Importance of Tolerance in Civil services**

1. **Promoting Inclusivity:** Tolerance fosters respect for others, empowering individuals to stand up for the rights of marginalised groups, including those facing racial discrimination, the LGBTQ community, and minority populations. Example, Chanchal Rana, IAS helped transgenders live a 'life of dignity' in the Balangir district by *Sweekruti* scheme that bring the transgender community into the mainstream by taking up various livelihood activities.
2. **Outcome based on healthy debate:** Tolerance enables constructive discussions and debates among different groups, leading to more democratic outcomes. For instance, IAS officer Divya Devarajan mastered the Gondi language in just three months during her posting in Adilabad, Telangana, in 2017. This helped her to communicate in Gondi, and understand local problems, reduce inter-tribal conflicts, and make the administration more accessible to vulnerable groups.
3. **Facilitating Conflict Resolution:** Tolerance equips civil servants with the ability to navigate and resolve conflicts arising from cultural, ethnic, or ideological differences. This helps them mediate disputes and find common ground, contributing to social harmony.
4. **Supporting Cultural Competence:** Tolerance helps them to understand and appreciate the values, customs, and challenges of different groups. This understanding is crucial for providing services efficiently and fairly. Example, Rahul Kumar, the District Magistrate of Gopalganj in Bihar, joined students at a government school for mid-day meal to challenge and dispel a superstition labeling a widowed woman as a 'bad omen.'

QUOTES ON TOLERANCE

Tolerance isn't about not having beliefs. It's about how your beliefs lead you to treat people who disagree with you.
Timothy Keller

The highest result of education is tolerance.
Helen Keller

Tolerance is giving to every other human being every right that you claim for yourself.
Robert G. Ingersoll

The greatest test of tolerance is in living with those who disagree with us.
Mahatma Gandhi

A great mind is the one that can bear a multitude of ideas in its thoughts; tolerance is the greatest attribute of the great.
S. Radhakrishnan

10.7 Empathy and Compassion towards Weaker Sections

"Empathy is seeing with the eyes of another, listening with the ears of another, and feeling with the heart of another."
Alfred Adle

"True compassion is more than flinging a coin to a beggar. It comes to see that an edifice which produces beggars needs restructuring."
Martin Luther King, Jr.

Empathy is the ability to emotionally understand what other people feel, see things from their point of view, and imagine oneself in their place. At its core, compassion involves empathising with another person, understanding their emotions, and experiencing what they are going through.

It is the desire to assist those who are suffering, coupled with the actions taken to alleviate their pain. It can be defined as "the feeling that arises in witnessing another's suffering and that motivates a subsequent desire to help."

Compassion differs from empathy and altruism, though these concepts are interconnected. Empathy generally refers to our ability to understand and share the emotions of others, while compassion involves those emotions and thoughts being accompanied by a genuine desire to help. Altruism, on the other hand, is the selfless, kind behaviour often driven by compassion. However, one can experience compassion without acting on it, and altruistic actions are not always driven by compassion.

- **Importance of Empathy and Compassion for Civil Services**
  1. **Communicate better**: Empathetic civil servants are better listeners and ask the right questions to understand the needs of their constituents.
  2. **Create tailored solutions**: Civil servants can design policies and programmes that address specific needs by understanding the unique circumstances of different stakeholders.
  3. **Reduce conflict:** Empathy can help defuse potential conflicts by acknowledging the emotions and concerns of various parties.
  4. **Develop responsive policies and programmes:** Compassionate civil servants can develop policies and actions that better address societal needs. Example, Under Project 37, officers from Arunachal Pradesh Civil Service are pooling in money from their salary to repair anything from dilapidated schools and libraries to roads and signposts across the state.
  5. **Take action to help**: Compassionate civil servants go above and beyond basic empathy by desiring to lessen the suffering of the other person. Example, Jitendar Kumar Soni, an IAS of 2010 batch, stopped 1.5 lakh kids from walking barefoot to school by providing free footwear.

QUOTES ON EMPATHY AND COMPASSION

Empathy is the starting point for creating a community and taking action. It's the impetus for creating change.
Max Carver

Empathy is the only human superpower-it can shrink distance, cut through social and power hierarchies, transcend differences, and provoke political and social change. **Elizabeth Thomas**

The simplest acts of kindness are by far more powerful than a thousand heads bowing in prayer.
Mahatma Gandhi

Service to others is the rent you pay for your room here on earth. **Rabindranath Tagore**

11. OTHER GUIDING VALUES FOR PUBLIC SERVANTS

11.1 Public Office as a Position of Trust

A public office, as outlined by national law, is a position of trust that carries the responsibility to act in the public's best interest. As such, the primary loyalty of public officials should be to the welfare of the public, as represented through the country's democratic institutions.

Example, Puja Khedkar, IAS of 2022 batch Maharashtra cadre, is accused of using a red-blue beacon light and VIP number plates on her private Audi car. This is an example of misusing public office.

11.2 Efficiency and Effectiveness

Overall, society pays for the resources that civil servants use. Thus, the society expects them to make best use of the available resources, and that they work efficiently, avoiding unnecessary waste, extravagance and inappropriate use of the community's resources. They are also expected to maintain high standards of professionalism, probity and performance.

Example, S.R.Sankaran IAS, known as the 'People's IAS' officer, was known for his diligent efforts in bringing landmark policies like the 'Abolition of Bonded Labour Act' and the 'Land Distribution Act' to the fore. During his first tenure, he also pioneered the Integrated Development Schemes and Agencies, along with the Special Component Plan for SC/ST communities, earning him recognition as a champion of these marginalised groups.

11.3 Duty to Report

The officials are bound to report to their employers, any circumstances which could cause damages to employee, employer or the environment to limit any loss or damage. Such a report enables the administration to take time bound action for the same.

Example, in 2012, U Sagayam, IAS submitted a 13-page report to the TN government, showing that the state had lost Rs. 16,000 crores to illegal quarrying in Madurai.

11.4 Duty of Obedience

All the officials are duty bound to follow the rules and ethical guidelines for every activity. They also have to comply with the orders issued by the superiors, as long as these orders do not entail any illegal and unethical acts.

Example, During his tenure as District Magistrate in Uttar Pradesh, B.D. Pande IAS was faced with strong political pressure from local politicians and influential figures to bend the rules and allow illegal activities to continue. One significant incident was when he resisted attempts to influence his decisions regarding land and property allocations. Politicians tried to pressure him to favor certain individuals, but he stuck to the principles of fairness and legality, ensuring that all decisions were made transparently and in the public interest.

11.5 No Accepting or Offering of Gifts or Other Prerequisites

The officials should not, on their own behalf or on behalf of others, accept gifts or favours like hotel accommodations, travel, hospitality, discounts or loans that are intended by the donor to influence their work. They should also not use their position to gain undue advantage. This also applies in scenarios where these advantages do not have any impact on their functioning and service-capacity actions.

The public official, in no circumstance, in capacity of their duty should give or offer gifts or other perquisites that are intended to influence or change the recipient's service.

Example, In 1999-2000, Rajni Sekri Sibal, IAS refused to change the results of the Junior Basic Training (JBT) when offered a bribe by political powers. She also protected the list of results by hiding it under a cloth and bandages and getting her officers to sign the binding.

11.6 Professional Independence

The professional independence of civil servants is enabled by their adherence to rules and regulations, which are designed to keep them free from political influence. Civil servants are expected to make decisions that are legally correct and in accordance with established legal procedures.

11.7 Avoidance of Conflict of Interest

When public officials separate personal interests from official duties, they prevent undue influence on decision-making, promoting fairness and accountability. By avoiding conflicts, public servants uphold ethical standards, deter corruption, and set a high bar for professionalism.

11.8 Reasonable Skill and Care

The civil servants are duty-bound to act with reasonable skill and care at work and while performing other tasks related to work. These include:

(a) Being prompt
(b) Taking fair and just decisions
(c) Seeking advice from the superiors when the course of action is unclear
(d) Taking all measures to ensure that the fact and information based on which the decisions are taken is correct and that all relevant factors are taken into consideration
(e) Observing legal requirements
(f) Appreciating special needs of various sections of the society and of individuals in the community.

11.9 Active Duty of Disclosure

Officials are duty-bound to provide correct and adequate information to other authorities, companies, organisations or the common man. Also, they should not wait for someone to ask for information, they should disclose it on their own.

Example, Vinod Rai, former CAG of India, exemplified this value during his tenure by that exposed financial irregularities and corruption across several government departments, including the 2010 Commonwealth Games, the allocation of 2G telecom spectrum licenses, and coal mining blocks. He also took steps to make CAG reports more accessible by ensuring they were written in simple, clear language, and made available to the public through the publication of 'Noddy Books,' which offered condensed versions of the full reports.

11.10 No Outside and Second Jobs

A public official is prohibited from holding any outside or secondary employment, directorships and other paid assignments which are detrimental to the interests of the state. They should not engage in activities which undermine people's trust on public servants.

11.11 Accountability

Accountability is the duty or willingness to take responsibility for one's actions, decisions, and their consequences. While closely linked with responsibility, accountability adds depth, as it involves not only acknowledging the need to act appropriately but also being answerable for the results, whether favourable or unfavourable.

Example, Chandrakala, an IAS officer from the 2008 batch serving in the Uttar Pradesh Cadre, is widely recognised as the determined District Magistrate of Bulandshahr. She has gained popularity for her firm stance against corruption and irregularities in government operations. Known for publicly calling out government officers and politicians who misuse their power for personal gain and neglect their duties, she gained widespread attention after a Facebook video went viral. In the video, she confronted a civic contractor for using substandard materials and poor construction quality on the roads in Bulandshahr, bringing her into the spotlight.

11.12 Transparency

Transparency is the practice of openly sharing information, actions, and decision-making processes, allowing stakeholders to have clear and unobstructed insight into how decisions are made and implemented. It involves accessibility, clarity, and openness, fostering trust by ensuring that processes are visible, understandable, and free from hidden agendas.

Example, U. Sagayam IAS from Tamil Nadu stood as an example for transparency by openly declaring his assets to the public, inspiring public confidence and setting an example.

11.13 Responsiveness

Responsiveness is the quality of reacting quickly, positively, and appropriately to needs, requests, or changes. In the context of civil service, responsiveness means being attentive to the concerns and demands of the public and taking prompt action to address them. It involves active listening, understanding what others need, and showing a commitment to meet those needs in a timely and efficient manner.

Example, Dr Rajendra Bharud, IAS, District Collector of Nandurbar in Maharashtra, has managed to keep his district afloat even amid the second wave of the COVID outbreak, with adequate oxygen supply, beds, a well-planned vaccination drive, and systematic preparation beforehand.

11.14 Diligence

Diligence is the quality of being careful and persistent in one's work or duties. It involves putting consistent effort into tasks, paying attention to details, and striving to achieve high standards.

A diligent person approaches his responsibilities with dedication, often going beyond basic requirements to ensure quality and accuracy.

Example, the coastal state of Odisha has been repeatedly struck by cyclones, with the 1999 Super Cyclone being one of the most devastating natural disasters in India's history, claiming over 10,000 lives. Fast forward to 2022, when the cyclone Asani caused no fatalities, a remarkable improvement. A key figure in this significant shift is IAS officer Pradeep Kumar Jena, who has managed 10 cyclones, including seven in the past four years. Jena orchestrated a large-scale, well-coordinated evacuation, relocating more than a million people to safer areas. His proactive and meticulous planning, combined with an effective response, greatly reduced casualties and ensured the efficient distribution of relief.

11.15 Righteousness

Righteousness is the quality of being morally right and virtuous. It encompasses adherence to ethical principles, and standards of conduct. Righteousness often implies a commitment to doing what is right, not only in one's personal life but also in interactions with others and in society as a whole. This concept is often associated with integrity, honesty, and a sense of responsibility toward upholding moral values.

Example, R. Sankaran, a senior IAS officer, earned the reputation of being 'an ideal people's IAS officer' due to his proactive involvement in creating policies aimed at benefiting the poor. A lifelong bachelor, he dedicated himself to the welfare of scheduled castes and scheduled tribes. His efforts in the fight against bonded labour often brought him into direct conflict with successive chief ministers, but he steadfastly and courageously upheld his principles.

11.16 Fairness and Justice

Fairness refers to the quality of being impartial, equitable, and just in the treatment of individuals or groups. It involves making decisions or judgments without favouritism or bias, ensuring that everyone has an equal opportunity and is treated with respect. Justice is a broader concept that encompasses the principles of fairness and moral righteousness. It involves upholding the rule of law and ensuring that individuals receive their due rights and obligations.

Example, PS Krishnan, an IAS officer who dedicated his life to waging war against the caste system. He camps "only in the localities where dalits, scheduled castes and scheduled tribes lived" when he went on tour to villages. His presence infused in them a sense of self-esteem after living in the shadows of caste prejudice for centuries. However, it was not just pride, confidence or self-esteem he gave to the villagers, but also led massive state-backed drives for the distribution of agricultural land and housing to both the landless and homeless.

11.17 Commitment

Commitment is the firm dedication or pledge to a cause, goal, or course of action, often involving a willingness to invest time, energy, and resources to achieve it. It reflects a sense of responsibility, loyalty, and persistence, demonstrating an individual's resolve to uphold their promises or fulfil their duties, even in the face of challenges or competing interests.

Example, Mr. Kumaragurubaran, IAS of the TN cadre successfully promoted school education by ensuring universal access, equity, and quality from primary to higher secondary levels. He enhanced measures for students' overall development and introduced smart classrooms with broadband and high-tech labs in rural Tamil Nadu schools.

11.18 Adaptability

Adaptability is the ability to adjust and respond effectively to new condition or challenges. It involves being flexible in one's thinking and behaviour, allowing a person to cope with shifting circumstances and demands. Adaptable individuals are open to new ideas, willing to learn, and can modify their strategies or approaches as needed to achieve their goals.

Example, Dr. Adarsh Singh, IAS leading from the front when close to 800 villagers in Barabanki district had lost their jobs to the COVID pandemic. Instead of letting them suffer, he initiated a river restoration project in his district under MGNREGA.

11.19 Pragmatism[7]

Pragmatism entails focusing on effective solutions to real-world problems, rather than getting caught up in rigid ideologies or theoretical frameworks. Pragmatism as a civil service value emphasises the importance of practical, results-oriented approaches in public administration.

Example, IAS Saurabh Sonawane in Madhya Pradesh, who is a doctor by training, also started treating patients when there was shortage of doctors during the COVID emergency.

11.20 Courage of Conviction

Courage of conviction is the strength and resolve to uphold one's beliefs or principles, even when faced with challenges, opposition, or adversity. It involves staying true to one's values and decisions despite potential risks or difficulties.

Example, Anand Rai, the government doctor had exposed the massive *Vyapam* scam in 2013 but is now enduring what is known in bureaucratic circles as 'punishment postings' and death threats.

[7]**Pragmatism:** Thinking about solving problems in a practical way rather than by having fixed ideas

12. THE ESSENCE OF PUBLIC SERVICE PROFESSIONALISM

In the present era, there are so many conflicting demands that are being made on the professional public servants that they have to prioritise and choose among from several conflicting values. Thus, the pressure on the public servants is very high. Which set of values is being chosen depends on factors, such as the current political regime, the social conditions, economic pressures, cultural socialisation, institutional arrangements, organisational culture/bureaucratisation, peer group pressure and even personal conscience. After choosing the set of values, its implementation, application and which value is being applied varies between countries, states, governments, regimes, organisations, according to the conditions present at that particular point of time and the nature of activity of the organisation, the support groups, vested interests and clientele, not just its internal policy, group norms and the preferences of the individual.

1. **Providing Public Benefits:** Public service organisation does not entirely work for its redundant self-benefit. There is always a much larger and wider abiding social, and global purpose. In theory this should eliminate self-perpetuation and bureaucratic **aggrandisement**[8].
2. **Meeting an Identifiable Social Need:** All the activities performed should be based on some perceived public need. They should add value to the society from which they are based. They should advance certain standards of public welfare and their well-being.
3. **Furthering Public Interest:** Government gives enough discretion to the administrators to use authority, power and resources they have been provided, to further the public interest. This suggests that administrators, before employing discretion in such cases, should question the future direction, objectives, purposes, policies, outcomes, consequences and image that the policy takes up, whether it would improve or be of benefit for the public. Before taking a decision, one should consider the following:
   - ✓ Not just the present, but the effect of the decision on future generation.
   - ✓ Not just of human but the effect of the decision on all other living beings and environment.
4. **Advancing Universal Human Values:** Various constitutions around the world mandates the public officials to establish justice, domestic peace, provide common defence and promote general welfare, to establish an environment of liberty and equality. These values are universally accepted by governments across the globe. They imply to provide a representative and responsible government. Apart from providing these rights, some of the countries also provide for a bill of human rights. Even the United Nations has given out the Universal Declaration of Human Rights (1948) which instruct all the member states to implement these rights for the benefit of all mankind. There are also declarations condemning violence, **genocide**[9], capital punishment, narcotic substance, and organised crime, all these were for enhancing and furthering the rights of the people.

---

[8]**Aggrandisement:** The act of making something larger or greater

[9]**Genocide:** Deliberate mass killing

5. **Avoiding Harm:** The public servants should not act out of hatred or unkindness. They should not in any way impose unfair treatment. They should not cause unnecessary pain or distress, just because they have the power. They should not exploit the weaker section.
6. **Doing One's Civic Duty:** A public servant's civic duty extends beyond routine responsibilities. By setting a positive example in areas like environmental protection and community engagement, public servants serve as role models, ultimately strengthening the bond between the government and the people.
7. **Enforcing the Rule of Law:** The rule of law is the fundamental principle of democratic government, and it offers protection against the misuse of powers by the government and its administrators. Without enforcement, the law is meaningless. Presence of **arbitrariness**[10] creates condition for exploitation, abuse, discrimination, and corruption. If the situation gets out of hand, it will lead to chaos and anarchy. People may not agree with the law all the time, but they would prefer the law over arbitrariness and discretion.
8. **Following Constitutionalism:** The Constitution provides explicit safeguard and limitation on the powers of the government. Institutional mechanisms to safeguard the interests of the public and prevent excesses by the government have been clearly dealt with. The Constitution overrides all the laws, and all the laws have to satisfy the constitutional propriety. It also elaborates on the procedure to be followed and how disputes over interpretation get resolved. Explicit pledging of allegiance to the Constitution is not carried out by the public servants, but they are still expected to uphold its values.
9. **Respecting Political Subordination:** The professional public servants are subordinate to the legislators, ministers, elected officials, judges and other non-career executives. Sometimes they do convince their superiors to do their bidding, but ultimately, they cannot overstep and override their subordinate position without taking over the role of the government itself. They should adhere to this principle of political subordination. Public only acknowledges policies in the name of the political superiors and want the administrators to remain in the background. Also, rules bind them from taking part in active public political activities and to openly declare their personal opinions and beliefs.
10. **Accepting Governmental Restraints:** To prevent the administrators from usurping the power, the three branches of government, the Executive, the Legislature and the Judiciary, provide checks and balances. Thus, the government frames guidelines which state what to do and what not to do. They have their own separate and independent means of enforcement. Various departments in the bureaucracy restrain the freedom of action of one another, it is an institutionalised means of control over the turf from possible threats from intruders.
11. **Observing Official Propriety:** The public service professionals are expected to be loyal and support the existing institutional system of governance. Apart from pledging their

[10]**Arbitrariness:** A lack of restraint in the use of authority; autocracy

allegiance, they might be required to carry special insignia, or wear uniforms, or carry symbols representing the government. When public servants feel that they can no longer loyally serve the government, they should immediately resign and leave the service and should not be present inside and undermine or sabotage the government. Their willingness to extend support to the government is based on fact that they abstain themselves from political activities.

12. **Obeying Administrative Limitations:** The public servants are not granted with the power to commit on behalf of the government to any course of action without express delegation of authority to do so. This should be especially followed in cases where substantial amount of money in involved. On the contrary, they should apply the law without any reservation that is unhindered application of the law. Ineffective application, half-hearted implementation, and even worse, neglect of enforcement creates ground for an inefficient government, unfair discrimination, and increased corruption which will damage the standing of the country worldwide.
13. **Being Informed:** Ignorance of rules is no defence in the government. Being informed is not only for the people, but the public servants themselves should be aware of the intentions of the government, anything which is relevant to public decision-making and any other administrative actions which affect their work. The key indicator of professionalism is being knowledgeable, and therefore every public servant has the obligation of being informed.
14. **Being on Record:** One of the most important virtues of bureaucracy is that everything is recorded. It can always be relied upon to get and reproduce the facts when required. The documents become part of the public record. Thus, public servants do not just collect information, they disseminate information to educate, guide and report. The official reports are important documents which keep the public informed about the administration and justify its appropriateness.
15. **Setting an Example:** The public servants are always under scrutiny by the public. Every action of theirs is carefully watched. Their conduct sets a standard and example for the rest of the society to follow. What may be accepted in private might constitute offensive public behaviour. What the government tolerates becomes a practice for others to follow. So, if the government wants to change the behaviour of the people, it should set an example by practising what it preaches. By government it means not only the temporary political masters, but also the permanent civil servants on whom the former is dependent on for their effectiveness.
16. **Being Idealistic:** An idealistic public servant is one who upholds the highest ethical standards, driven by a sincere commitment to public welfare. They prioritise the needs of the people, especially those who are marginalised, over personal or political interests, acting transparently and with integrity to maintain public trust. Idealistic public servants embrace empathy, understanding the struggles of the citizens they serve, and they make

decisions that are fair and impartial. They are resilient, persevering through challenges and setbacks while continuously striving to bring positive change to society. With a vision for a better future, they advocate for sustainable development, social justice, and improved quality of life for all, embodying a balanced blend of idealism and practical dedication that fosters genuine progress and trust.

17. **Being Virtuous:** The public leaders are always expected to have high moral standards. The consequences of setting a bad example in the public service can be grave. They are expected to display all kinds of virtues of righteous like being kind, considerate, hardworking, tolerant, modest, respectful, aesthetic, and so on.
18. **Being Human and Humane:** The professional public servants are the face of the anonymous bureaucracy and a distant government. Understanding and compassion are the two important virtues which translate into being human and humane while conducting the public's business. Not just recognising weaknesses in others, these officers should also recognise their own fallibility and understand and accept their own mistakes and errors. Although they may be the **vanguard**[11] of the government, there may be some areas where even they lack the expertise, and hence they should be humble and avoid the air of superiority.
19. **Being Meritorious:** Like several other professions, public service is also grounded on the merit system. The entry is thus based on open competition among the talented. Similarly, the career progression is based on competition among the successful performers and the highest position are reached by the most professionally deserving based on the criteria which includes knowledge, competence, innovation, and contribution to profession.
20. **Being Model Employers:** Since their job is public in nature, the public service professionals act as model employers to avoid prejudice or exclusion during the selection process. This also enables them to provide decent working conditions, exhibit proper employment practice and encourage development of the professionals.
21. **Being Fit:** The public service professionals are generally expected to have high levels of physical and mental fitness. Physical fitness ensures they can handle extended hours, respond to emergencies, and operate efficiently under challenging conditions. Meanwhile, mental fitness enables resilience, emotional stability, and the capacity for clear decision-making under pressure.
22. **Expanding Public Policy-making Capacity:** Generally, better results are obtained from improving public policy-making capabilities than improving the managerial abilities. The policy-making sciences are now claiming professional status and recognition in their own right.
23. **Undertaking Continuous Legal, Regulatory and Administrative Reforms:** Much of the government's and administrator's work deals with combating daily operations. Public

[11]**Vanguard:** A group of people leading the way in new developments or ideas

service professionals rarely have an opportunity to look at them objectively. They cannot review all such arrangements made. Varied observations reveal that the shortcomings and remedial measures get distorted in the detail. Like the policy sciences, the present legal, regulatory and administrative reformers seek recognition and professional status.

24. **Adopting More Business-like Methods:** The administrators recognise that the government is not a business, but public service could benefit by adopting a more business-like approach:
    - *Lean Processes:* Adopt lean methodologies to minimise waste and optimise resource usage, just as businesses do to cut down on costs.
    - *Public as Customers:* View citizens as customers who deserve timely, effective services, and design policies and processes with a customer-centric mindset.
    - *Performance Metrics:* Set clear performance indicators and targets for bureaucratic work, mirroring business KPIs, to gauge success and areas for improvement.
    - *Long-Term Goals:* Similar to a business strategy, adopt a clear vision and set long-term goals for government initiatives, aligning day-to-day work with these objectives.
25. **Combating Bureau Pathologies:** Every large organisation suffers from some kind of shortcomings. If these are left unattended, they tend to get out of hand, eventually resulting in severe obstacles that inhibit performance improvement. The public service professionals recognise that these bureau pathologies have to be first admitted then promptly addressed with the best available resources.
26. **Promoting Democracy:** Democracy is the key for better governance. But democracy does not mean mere change in the political system and organisation. There has to be fundamental changes in the roles of social institutions, the rights of the individual have to be readjusted vis-à-vis the state, the liberalisation principles has to applied to socio-economic arrangements as well as the political set up. The organisational structure of the public administration would also undergo such changes. Public service professionals have to adopt additional set of values which also tends to come into conflict and therefore they need to reorder their priorities accordingly.
27. **Altering the 'Master–Servant' Relationship:** The public service professionals traditionally assume that they are the masters and the public is their servant, but the process of democratisation has reversed this relationship. Hence, the public is now the masters and the professionals, their servants. It can be well understood that public service professionals should promote a genuine pluralist society.
28. **Decentralising Government:** The government does not centralise all its public activities, rather it decentralises those activities which can be better handled locally and regionally, that can better adhere to the preferences of the people at the grassroots. The public service professional has the expertise to determine whether a government activity can be best decentralised or centralised. Traces of the past practices of authoritarianism should be removed or eclipsed; hence, the symbols have to be altered, nomenclature changed and

titles and places renamed. The subjects of the states are now citizens with enforceable rights and freedom.

29. **Enforcing Liberty and Individual Rights:** The state generally restricts the liberty and freedom, but dedicated public professionals have sought to enlarge its scope and thus, protect the rights of the individuals against unwarranted interference by the state.
30. **Guarding Against Corruption:** Democracy cannot be built upon rotten foundations. If the administrators demonstrate that they are not tolerant of corruption, there is very little possibility of it being practiced. Both the democratically elected government and the administrators are obliged to keep their hands clean and reprimand those who cannot.
31. **Engaging Public in Administration:** Democratic public administration necessitates bringing people into the folds of the government and various administrative arrangements, such as the criminal justice systems, volunteering, etc.

13. MALADIES OF BUREAUCRACY

"Whatever a leader does, common men generally follow. And
Whatever standards that person sets by his deeds, the society pursues."

Bhagavad Gita

The bureaucracy in India plays a pivotal role in governance, tasked with implementing policies, programmes, and laws established by the government. Indian bureaucracy has adapted over time, undergoing structural and functional changes that provide continuity in administration and serve as a safeguard against the unchecked authority of elected officials, promoting decisions based on merit. However, the system faces persistent challenges. Despite having a complex structure for administrative **adjudication**[12], the Indian bureaucracy is often criticised for being authoritarian, monopolising power, and retaining a colonial-era mind-set that fosters conservative neutrality over dynamic adaptation.

Indian bureaucracy suffers from paradoxes that hamper its effectiveness. It is often marked by an inflated sense of self-importance, rigidity in following departmental decisions and precedents, and an indifference that makes it unresponsive to the evolving needs of the public. Originating from a narrow social base, the bureaucracy frequently lacks a nuanced understanding of developmental issues, particularly at the rural level. Its top-down hierarchy is maintained by a small cadre of seasoned executives who often fail to update their approaches, limiting intellectual agility. Common issues such as red tape, corruption, insularity, and a slow pace in adapting to social, economic, and technological changes continue to impair it's functioning.

Furthermore, bureaucrats are sometimes perceived as unaccountable, operating behind layers of paperwork and maintaining a culture of secrecy that conceals public dealings. When errors or

[12]**Adjudication:** A formal judgement on a disputed matter.

misdeeds come to light, bureaucrats often evade accountability by referring matters to committees or commissions, which can delay or obscure resolutions. These factors contribute to a perception of bureaucracy as self-serving, resistant to reform, and detached from the public's needs.

13.1 Challenges and Reform Imperatives in Indian Bureaucracy

International analyses of Indian bureaucracy reveal deep-rooted inefficiencies and challenges that inhibit effective governance and public service. Key issues include overstaffing paired with insufficient capacity-building efforts, leading to unsustainable workforce expenditures and skill gaps. The absence of a performance-driven culture and outdated appraisal systems further hinder accountability, with inconsistent promotion and empanelment standards affecting professional advancement and morale.

Political interference is a critical problem, often manifesting in arbitrary transfers that compromise continuity and institutional stability. The lack of robust transparency and accountability frameworks has led to an erosion of public service values, with ethical standards declining and bureaucratic morale waning. Procedural obsolescence and an ineffective evaluation system create an environment that resists modernisation and discourages adaptability.

Indian bureaucracy is also marred by politicisation and communal biases, resulting in dereliction of duty and productivity deficits. There is a persistent inability to transcend colonial administrative legacies, which, along with wastefulness and low productivity motivation, compounds its ineffectiveness. Finally, pervasive corruption and minimal public engagement are endemic issues, underscoring an urgent need for structural reform to enhance accountability, instil ethical governance, and align the bureaucracy with India's developmental aspirations.

13.2 Indian Bureaucracy–Major Ailments

The Indian bureaucracy, often regarded as the executive arm of governance, plays a pivotal role in the country's administration. However, it is beset by several major ailments that impede its effectiveness and efficiency. As India **grapples**[13] with the demands of globalisation, the bureaucracy faces the dual challenge of adapting to evolving economic realities while addressing long-standing issues within the governance framework. These ailments not only undermine public trust but also hinder the bureaucracy's ability to effectively serve the citizenry, making it imperative to address these challenges for a more responsive and accountable administrative system. The following are the major ailments affecting Indian bureaucracy:

1. **Lack of Shared Vision:** Lack of vision and cohesion of thinking process is a major impediment in bringing the people, the government and bureaucracy to a common point that ultimately focus on the integral development of the country. The difference of interests lead to misgovernance and the values such as altruism and selflessness are undermined.

---

[13]**grapples:** (*verb*) fight to win something

2. **Lack of *Esprit de Corps*[14]:** Mutual loyalty shared by the members of an administration promotes 'integrity'. The onus is entrusted upon every individual of the bureaucratic system. Today's administrative mechanism is flooded with problems like rigid hierarchy, lack of coordination among various hierarchical levels, hostility among seniors and subordinates, etc. Absence of cordiality and lack of empathy is witnessed at the organisational level which hinders the progress as a whole.
3. **Perpetual Uncertainties**: Problems such as frequent transfers, demotions, political interventions, etc. along with corruption and red tapism in bureaucracy make the system progressively undemocratic. Infringement of politicians upon bureaucracy has thinned down the scope of bureaucratic space and undermines the rationality behind it. Such perpetual uncertainties coupled with the growing discretion of governments in this regard pave way for the deterioration of the passion towards work.
4. **Power Struggle**: Being 'apolitical' is considered as one of the important traits of a bureaucrat. But 'Political Neutrality' is no longer an accepted norm since the lure of postings, money, and prosperity is making the bureaucrats side with a political party and act in favour of them. Mired in the shades of such political scenario, uprightness is completely overlooked, and the political bias has become a common norm.
5. **Impractical Grand Agendas:** Most of the promises made and agendas set have not been met, thereby questioning the 'accountability' of the executive and the bureaucracy as well. The objectives which were set since Independence to eradicate poverty, unemployment, and assuring basic needs of the individual is still on papers as mere policies. These impractical grand agendas put the 'trustworthiness' of the government and bureaucracy into question.
6. **Personal Values:** Personal values affect the way a bureaucrat looks at things and in turn have a huge impact on their decision-making capability. Caste, religion, ethnicity, political views, etc make their way, more often than not, into the actions and decisions of bureaucrats. This puts the honour, justice, fairness, equality and integrity of the administrator into question.
7. **Seniority Matters:** It is a scenario that India faces since ages where seniority gets rewarded over sincerity. This brings a demotivating mind set to the young administrator who brings in new fascinating innovative ideas into the fold, where some of these ideas get rejected by the veteran officers and sometimes they get rewarded for it. This spoils healthy, dynamic and responsive administration. It also creates a culture of mediocrity where, in some cases, ambitious administrator leave as there is no meaningful consequence for their performance.
8. **Superhuman Status:** Bureaucrats in India wield significant power, controlling resources, personnel, and decision-making processes. This authority can create a sense of invincibility

[14]**Esprit de Corps:** An important concept in management that emphasises unity, camaraderie, and a shared sense of purpose.

or a 'God-complex,' where the individual starts believing they are superior to others. This mind set leads to a loss of humility, with bureaucrats forgetting that their privileges are meant solely to facilitate their duties. Over time, this results in pride overshadowing the essential virtue of humility, impacting their effectiveness and public trust.

9. **Hostile Environment:** An office environment becomes hostile when there is an abuse of power, unfairness in decisions, and lack of cooperation with the co-workers, which in turn leads to lack of effectiveness and decreased productivity. Bureaucrats need to act with professionalism and integrity to cope with these environments. An environment that involves people with similar ambitions and goal will lead to a stable path towards achieving the needs of the society, and also improve efficiency of the work.
10. **Lure of Perquisites:** This culture of entitlement can overshadow the core mission of public service, leading to prioritisation of personal gain over public welfare. The lure of perquisites among bureaucrats in India can negatively impact governance by shifting the focus from public service to personal gain, breed complacency and reduce motivation to implement policies effectively. Excessive attention to maintaining these privileges can erode accountability and transparency, weakening the public's trust in the administration, hindering efficient service delivery and fosters corruption.
11. **Managing Non-professional Employees:** India's administrative system is largely dominated by generalist officers from the IAS and state services, who occupy top policy-making and administrative roles, often without specialised expertise in the fields they manage. India urgently needs to move away from the generalist approach in bureaucratic recruitment. Reforms are needed to balance both generalist and specialist character of bureaucracy, promoting collaboration and integration to enhance overall effectiveness and address the complex challenges faced by the Indian administration.
12. **Hostile Leadership:** Leadership plays an important role in the way a system functions. A hostile work environment can erode employee morale, motivation, and productivity. Such leadership can stifle innovation and hinder effective communication, resulting in inefficiencies in service delivery.
13. **Delaying Tactics to Avoid Responsibility:** Bureaucrats may use various strategies, such as protracted processes, excessive paperwork, or bureaucratic jargon, to defer decision-making and accountability. This behaviour often stems from a fear of repercussions, lack of clarity in responsibilities, or a culture that discourages risk-taking.
14. **Colleague or Enemy:** Jealousness and the fear of successor getting rewarded in a department pulls down the role of the administrators. The fear of transfers also plays a major role as one yield to the pressure of the government when one resists it.
15. **Earning Hostility:** When the administrators resist doing anything in favour of his family, friends, caste groups, their immediate bosses, and colleagues, they earn hostility. This in turn leads to affect the mental aspects of the administrators, which makes them be abusive over their staffs and be rude to his co-workers. When they are abusive to their staffs, this

also may create a sense dissatisfaction and hostility from their staffs which finally leads to overall failure of the machinery.

16. **Bureaucratic Indecision and Risk Aversion**[15]**:** Bureaucratic indecision and risk aversion in India are rational self-preservation strategies employed by bureaucrats to shield themselves from various legal and extra-legal risks to their careers, reputations, and personal safety. These risks stem from organisational design issues, institutional norms, and political influences. As a result, Indian bureaucracy often focuses excessively on routine tasks, suffers from coordination failures, process overload, poor public perception, low motivation, and declining service quality.

14. BUREAUCRATIC REFORMS

Bureaucracy is central to socio-economic development and nation-building, historically serving as the backbone of India's governance system. However, it is undergoing significant transformation due to greater public participation in decision-making and the shifting role of the state. Bureaucrats now face new challenges arising from contemporary socio-economic and political dynamics, making it impractical to adhere to Weber's rigid, rule-bound, hierarchical model. Instead, the need of the hour is a transparent and accountable bureaucracy. The new resources at the disposal of the bureaucracy—such as information channels, decision-making power, and political support—must be harnessed effectively to achieve organisational and developmental goals.

To revamp bureaucracy, many developing countries have adopted a two-pronged approach: modernising the administrative system and reorganising the bureaucratic structure. Bureaucratic performance can be enhanced through measures like performance evaluation, streamlining inquiries, overhauling grievance procedures, linking performance with incentives, implementing Citizens' Charters, improving service delivery, public involvement, a clear code of conduct, decentralisation, and strengthening capacity-building. Bureaucracy must meet two key needs: **capacity**—the ability to efficiently achieve objectives—and **control**—accountability to higher authorities, particularly elected representatives in the legislative branch.

Comprehensive structural, procedural, and behavioural reforms are necessary for a bureaucracy that is participatory, responsive, and sensitive to citizens' needs. Structurally, reducing hierarchy is essential to eliminate centralised systems and interpersonal conflicts. Behaviourally, bureaucrats must be sensitised to the needs of marginalised groups, encouraged to take innovative steps toward administrative reform, and recognised for their initiative and commitment. A development-focused bureaucracy must not be insular but rather goal-driven, results-oriented, and people-centred, ensuring effective service delivery and responsiveness to citizens' needs.

[15]**Aversion:** A strong feeling of not liking somebody/something

14.1 Need for the Reform

Civil servants are crucial in shaping policies and ensuring effective on-the-ground implementation. A World Bank study of six measures of perceived quality of governance affecting per capita GDP of more than 150 countries concluded that "results show a strong positive causal relationship from improved governance to better development outcomes".

An assessment report of the World Bank says, "the civil service in India, the legendary 'steel frame' of the British Raj is today battling against onslaughts to its relevance. The strengths of the civil service in India lies in its extraordinary pool of skills and talents, its field experience, its extensive networking, its appreciation and overview of the functioning of the government at the cutting edge, its understanding of delivery systems for development, awareness of the formal and informal socio-economic networks in the field, its 'can deliver' attitude, its role in national integration, its ready adaptability to new and unfamiliar situation and tasks, and its social orientation, bolstered by intense competition among the officers."

The civil service has undoubtedly played a crucial role in preserving unity, providing stability, and maintaining order in India—a diverse country with frequent ethnic, communal, and regional tensions. However, concerns persist about its performance in achieving a results-oriented government. Critics argue that the Indian Civil Service tends to prioritise internal processes over outcomes. Systemic rigidities, unnecessary complexities, and excessive centralisation in policy and management structures often hinder its effectiveness. Hierarchical structures and numerous veto points further complicate decision-making, making the process lengthy and restrictive.

In India, civil servants are formally accountable to their respective ministers, but in practice, this accountability is often vague and generalised. Without a system of predefined accountability, the relationship between ministers and civil servants tends to be reactive, shaped by emerging issues. Senior civil servants are expected to guide ministers on the long-term social benefits of policies, ensuring that decisions are not solely driven by short-term political goals. However, the accountability framework varies significantly, depending on how each minister interprets it—ranging from comprehensive oversight to minimal involvement. This ambiguity can lead to either collusion or discord, both of which can negatively impact administrative efficiency.

The country is experiencing rapid and transformative changes, including accelerated economic growth, urbanisation, environmental challenges, technological advancements, and heightened local awareness. Civil servants, as public service agents, must be equipped to respond swiftly to these shifts. However, they are often perceived as resistant to change, prioritising their privileges and career prospects, making these an end in themselves.

In the political landscape, the 73rd and 74th Constitutional Amendments aimed to empower rural and urban local governments as true institutions of self-governance. Yet, despite over sixteen years since their enactment, progress has been slow. Local governments remain largely 'local' in form but continue to operate with significant state and central influence, highlighting the need for fundamental administrative reforms at the district level.

Profound changes in the global economy, growing interdependence, and transformative shifts in government operations have underscored the need for a skilled and effective civil service. Advances in telecommunications and computing offer vast potential for efficient service delivery, yet resistance to simplifying procedures remains a barrier to implementing e-governance. In essence, for the civil service to remain relevant and capable of addressing current and future demands, a fundamental transformation is essential.

Over time, civil society organisations have taken on a larger role in governance, reflecting growing demands for improved accountability and transparency. Similarly, the private sector is increasingly delivering services that were once solely under public sector control. Civil servants should thus regard civil society and the private sector as partners in governance. The focus must shift from the dominance of government in all spheres to fostering effective governance, with an emphasis on decentralisation and citizen-centric approaches.

The Indian Civil Service needs a shift toward data-driven, results-oriented performance assessments based on clearly defined metrics. Such reforms are essential to foster accountability, improve efficiency, and ensure that the civil service delivers measurable impact in line with contemporary governance expectations.

The following issues have tainted the current landscape of civil services capacity building and call for reform.

1. Existing training policy interventions were sporadic and largely confined to individual and intermittent innovations.
2. Stereotyped working in silos or compartments, rather than under an overall unifying vision and of national priorities.
3. Lack of a lifelong and continuous learning environment for all civil servants.
4. Barriers to exchange of knowledge preventing collaborative working.
5. Moving from a RULES-BASED to a ROLES-BASED management system.
6. Lack of professionalism and poor capacity building.
7. Inefficient incentive systems that do not appreciate upright and outstanding civil servants but reward the corrupt and the incompetent.
8. Outmoded rules and procedures that restrict a civil servant from performing effectively.
9. Systemic inconsistencies in promotion and empanelment.
10. Lack of adequate transparency and accountability procedures - there is also no safety for whistle blowers.
11. Arbitrary and whimsical transfers – insecurity in tenures impedes institutionalisation.
12. Political interference and administrative **acquiescence**.[16]
13. A gradual erosion in values and ethics.

[16]**Acquiescence:** The reluctant acceptance of something without protest

14. Patrimonialism (Patrimonialism = monopoly of power + discretion – accountability – transparency): Patrimonialism erodes civil servant independence, reducing them to subservience to the leader and preventing them from serving citizens impartially.

It is well recognised that civil service reform is broadly recognised as essential and inevitable, playing a crucial role in both governance and socio-economic development.

14.2 Key Principles of Civil Services Reform

1. **Setting right the asymmetry of power:** There is an imbalance in the exercise of power within governance. Systemic rigidities, unnecessary complexities, and excessive centralisation often render public servants ineffective and constrained, hindering their ability to achieve positive outcomes.
2. **Insulating civil servants from undue political interference:** In a democracy, the civil service must be accountable to the elected government. However, there is criticism that growing partisan intervention and **cronyism**[17] are eroding the Rule of Law, distorting incentives, and allowing corruption. The relationship between the political executive and the civil service needs transformation, grounded in mutual understanding, respect, and a clear recognition of each other's distinct roles and responsibilities.
3. **Professionalisation with stability of tenure and competition:** Modern administration faces complex challenges across various sectors, which demand both specialised expertise and extensive experience in relevant fields. However, current procedures and practices are inadequate in developing and effectively utilising domain-specific expertise. Current procedures and practices, however, fall short in developing and effectively utilising domain-specific expertise. Reforms are needed to build and leverage this expertise for improved public service delivery.
4. **Citizen-centric administration:** The civil services are currently perceived as a large, impersonal organisation, lacking commitment to human needs and values. It is crucial to address this perception, especially in the era of participative democracy, by transforming the governance system into a true instrument of service to the people.
5. **Accountability:** There is a widespread perception that current accountability mechanisms are insufficient. Often, non-performance goes unchecked, while competence and integrity lack proper recognition and reward. To address this, innovative and effective mechanisms must be established to safeguard public funds, ensure desired outcomes, and strengthen accountability across the board.
6. **Outcome orientation:** Government monitoring currently focuses mainly on tracking expenditure against budgets and, occasionally, on defined outputs. However, it's essential to shift towards measuring actual outcomes. To fully support this shift, changes are needed in attitudes, monitoring and evaluation systems, incentives, and accountability measures.

---

[17]**Cronyism:** The appointment of friends and associates to positions of authority, without regard to their qualifications

7. **Promoting public service values and ethics:** Beyond the traditional civil service values of efficiency, integrity, accountability, and patriotism, it is essential for civil servants to embrace ethical and moral values such as probity in public life, respect for human rights, compassion for the marginalised, and a dedicated commitment to their welfare.

14.3 Components of Civil Service Reform

Fig. 9.1 Components of civil service reform

1. **Size and Structure of Government:** Since independence, the government has expanded ministries, departments, and civil service positions, creating senior posts and other roles that have increased political and bureaucratic patronage. However, this growth was not balanced by reducing lower-priority tasks or addressing redundancies. Besides budgetary impacts, this expansion has overstretched implementation capacity and intensified coordination challenges. Civil servants now spend more time defending jurisdictional boundaries, navigating complex internal processes, and coordinating across numerous agencies. Additionally, vested interest groups at all levels have emerged, obstructing reform and rationalisation efforts.

2. **Recruitment:** Civil service recruitment and promotion are influenced by factors such as patronage versus merit, as well as considerations of ethnic, religious, regional, and gender preferences. Political dimensions often play a significant role, not only at the highest levels of policy and programme formulation but also in grassroots regulatory and control activities.

   The recruitment process for the Indian Civil Services is one of the most rigorous globally. However, evolving societal and economic trends necessitate greater emphasis on technological proficiency and areas like human rights. Additionally, the examination currently places limited focus on assessing managerial skills, which are vital for effective governance.

   - **Generalists vs Specialists:** With advancing technology and growing specialisation, civil service roles require expertise that generalists often lack. Allowing civil servants to transition between public and private sectors could make these roles more appealing and competitive.

     Lateral recruitment can introduce fresh ideas and expertise, encouraging civil servants to improve performance. However, challenges include attracting private sector professionals, aligning salaries, ensuring fair selection processes, and addressing union opposition to market-based pay. Transparent eligibility and assessment criteria are crucial to avoid favoritism or political bias. A phased approach can help maximise benefits, such as enhanced skills and motivation, while minimising risks like favouritism and staff demoralisation.
   - **Capacity Building and Human Resources Development:** The need for civil service reforms is driven both by global developments and by advances in technology and communication, which are shrinking distances and transforming commerce, making traditional administrative practices outdated and ineffective. To address this, key measures are required: simplifying rules and procedures, expanding authority delegation, strengthening enforcement and accountability, and ensuring prompt resolution of public grievances.
   - **Reforming and Restructuring Human Resource Management:** Building a motivated and capable civil service requires merit-based and non-discriminatory recruitment, which rests on the absence of political patronage, transparent rules and procedures, open competition and selection by an independent agency. It is important to address demotivating factors like frequent and arbitrary transfers, a poor work environment, **decrepit**[18] housing and health facilities, as well as special factors affecting women in office and field jobs.
   - **Strengthening Meritocracy in Promotion:** A statutory body, the Civil Services Board (CSB), can be established to oversee matters such as transfers and promotions of civil servants. This would help reduce political interference in their careers and allow the board to separate civil service performance issues from political influence.

[18]**Decrepit:** The state of being decrepit

3. **Performance and Promotion**: "But those who do not consume goods and increase then in just ways should be made permanent in their offices, being devoted to what is agreeable and permanent to the king." **–Arthashastra**

   A good employee performance appraisal system is a pre-requisite for an effective performance management system, and it should be more consultative and transparent. The current promotion system in civil services is based on a time-scale and guaranteed tenure, with no provisions for performance-based incentives or disincentives. This lack of accountability is a major drawback, making the Indian civil services largely unresponsive to the state. Promotions should be merit-based, with authorities implementing best practices and evaluating civil servants' performance both qualitatively and quantitatively, using a range of parameters.
4. **Professionalism and Modernity:** Civil service reform requires a strategic focus on developing professional skills across three key functional areas: implementation, programme/project preparation, and policy formulation. Additionally, it is essential for civil servants to cultivate expertise in specific domains or specialisations to address the complex demands of governance effectively.

   A critical component of these reforms is e-governance. With rising literacy rates and enhanced access to technology, information and communication technology (ICT) can significantly improve transparency and accountability in civil services. No modern civil service reform can be complete without a strong emphasis on ICT, as it enables more accessible, efficient, and accountable public service.

   In the light of evolving societal needs, civil servants must adopt a proactive stance toward development, approaching reforms with openness rather than **scepticism**[19]. By embracing reform initiatives from within, civil servants can foster a more dynamic, accountable, and responsive civil service that actively contributes to the nation's progress. This internal commitment to reform will help create a vibrant, forward-thinking, and service-oriented workforce in alignment with the changing needs of society.
5. **Civil Service Accountability:** Civil servants have long played a crucial role in balancing continuity and change within the administration. Governed by strict rules and procedures, they operate under the 'Rule of Law' rather than personal discretion. However, this reliance on rigid rules is often cited as a factor contributing to power misuse and corruption among officials. The rise of media has further exposed civil servants to greater public scrutiny, holding them accountable to a broader audience and encouraging transparency in their actions. This external oversight has become an essential check, pushing civil servants towards more ethical and responsible governance.

   While transparency and accountability are distinct concepts, transparency is essential for achieving accountability. To hold a civil servant accountable, it is crucial to have access to information regarding their decisions and actions. This underscores the need for legislation like the Right to Information (RTI) Act and protections for whistle-blowers,

[19]**Scepticism:** A sceptital attitude

empowering citizens to report misconduct without the fear of **reprisal**[20]. Such measures are vital for fostering a culture of openness and responsibility within the civil service. Some of the actions recommended for increased accountability are as follows:

- Strengthen and streamline reporting mechanisms
- Expedite and simplify departmental inquiries
- Link performance with incentives
- Overhaul employee grievance procedures
- Act promptly on audit findings
- Implement Citizen's Charters to monitor service delivery
- Enforce the Right to Information Act
- Establish a code of conduct for civil servants

These steps aim to create a more transparent, responsive, and accountable civil service.

14.4 Change in Mind-Set

To meet the evolving demands of society and the economy, the civil service must undergo a paradigm shift in mind set and approach. Here's a breakdown of the changes required to ensure more effective performance in public service:

Aspect	Traditional Approach	Evolving Approach
Commitment	Primarily to the civil service structure	Primarily to serving the public
Core Values	Integrity and neutrality	Integrity, impartiality, and efficient delivery
Role	Follower of precedent	Creator, adaptive to new challenges
Work Focus	Policy and ministerial support	Diverse roles across operations, policy, specialised skills, and ministerial support
Primary Aim	Leading the development of major policy areas	Delivering tangible outcomes of major policy initiatives
Experience	Broadens through short tenures within the public sector	Broadens through roles in both public and private sectors
Training	Fast-track training programmes	Ongoing career development and continuous learning
Orientation	Status quo, resistant to change	Embraces change and innovation
Work Structure	Monopolistic	Competitive, emphasising collaboration and efficiency

This shift encourages civil servants to be more adaptive, outcome-oriented, and open to cross-sector experiences, aligning with the dynamic needs of modern governance and public expectations.

[20]**Reprisal:** An act of retaliation

14.5 Suggested Reforms

1. **Link Compensation to Competence:** Introduce merit-based compensation to foster a culture of excellence, accountability, and high performance. A mandatory performance management system across government organisations will ensure individual contributions are measured and rewarded.
2. **Fixed Tenures for Stability:** Implement fixed tenures for bureaucrats to reduce frequent transfers caused by political alignment, enabling a stable and professional administrative system focused on long-term goals.
3. **Encourage Innovation:** Senior bureaucrats must lead by promoting innovation and flexibility, addressing the hesitation of junior officials to make bold decisions. This culture shift should cascade through all bureaucratic levels.
4. **Enhance Collaboration:** Strengthen inter-departmental coordination to tackle complex challenges more effectively, improving efficiency and policy outcomes.
5. **Uphold Integrity:** Define 'Public Service Values' to guide ethical conduct, with violations treated as misconduct. Address conflicts of interest by revising the code of ethics and restricting officials from serving on public boards.
6. **Revamp Recruitment and Promotions:** Emphasise performance-based assessments in IAS recruitment and promotions, ensuring a meritocratic and accountable system while safeguarding against political interference.

14.6 Civil Service Reforms – 2nd ARC Recommendations

The 2nd Administrative Reforms Commission (ARC) was established to address challenges in India's civil service and propose reforms to enhance its efficiency and effectiveness. Its primary goal was to revamp the civil service structure, making it more responsive, accountable, and capable of meeting the demands of governance in a rapidly evolving environment while fostering a culture of reform and innovation.

- **2nd ARC Recommendations on Civil Service Reforms**

Capacity Building

1. All civil servants should undergo mandatory training before each promotion and each officer/official should be evaluated after each training programme. Successful completion of the training programmes should be made mandatory for promotions.
2. The objective of mid-career training should be to develop domain knowledge and competence required for the changing job profile of the officer.
3. Public servants should be encouraged to obtain higher academic qualifications and to write papers for reputed and authoritative journals.

Performance Management System

A good employee performance appraisal system is a pre-requisite for an effective performance management system. The existing performance appraisal system should be strengthened on the following lines:

1. Making appraisal more consultative and transparent.
2. Performance appraisal formats to be made job specific.
3. Performance appraisal should be year-round: provisions for detailed work-plan and a mid-year review should be introduced for all services.
4. Training modules for implementing performance management systems should be designed and introduced for training programmes for civil servants.

Motivating Civil Servants

There is a need to recognise the outstanding work of serving civil servants including through national awards. Awards for recognising good performance should also be instituted at the state and district levels. It must be ensured that selection for such awards is made through a prompt, objective, and transparent mechanism because the value of such awards should not get compromised by either subjectivity or lack of transparency. Further, all organisations should evolve their own in-house mechanism for rewarding good performance from simple, verbal and written appreciation to more tangible rewards.

Relations between the Political Executive and Civil Servants

There is a need to safeguard the political neutrality and impartiality of the civil services. The onus for this lies equally on the political executive and the civil services. This aspect should be included in the Code of Ethics for ministers as well as the Code of Conduct for public servants.

It is essential to lay down norms for recruitment in government to avoid complaints of favouritism, **nepotism**[21], corruption and abuse of power.

Civil Services Code

The proposed Civil Services Bill should include Civil Services Values and the Code of Ethics. Additionally, Conduct Rules for civil servants should be revised to align with these values and ethical standards.

Civil Service Values: The civil servants shall be guided by the following values in addition to a commitment to uphold the Constitution, the discharge of their functions:

1. Absolute integrity at all times
2. Impartiality and non-partisanship
3. Objectivity
4. Dedication to public service
5. Empathy towards weaker sections

[21]**Nepotism:** Using one's power or influence to get unfair advantage

Code of Ethics: The following should be included in the Code of Ethics for civil servants:

1. **Integrity:** Civil servants should be guided solely by public interest in their official decision making and not by any financial or other consideration either in respect of themselves, their families or their friends.
2. **Impartiality:** Civil servants in carrying out their official work, including functions like procurement, recruitment, delivery of services, etc, should take decisions based on merit and free from any partisan consideration.
3. **Commitment to public service:** Civil servants should deliver services in a fair, effective, impartial and courteous manner.
4. **Open accountability:** Civil servants are accountable for their decisions and actions and should be willing to subject themselves to appropriate scrutiny for this purpose.
5. **Devotion to duty:** Civil servants should always maintain absolute and unstinting devotion towards their duties and responsibilities.
6. **Exemplary behaviour:** Civil servants should treat all members of the public with respect and courtesy and always should behave in a manner that upholds the rich traditions of the civil services.
7. **Fixation of tenures:** All senior posts should have a specified tenure. The task of fixing tenures for various posts may also be assigned to this independent agency – Central Civil Services Authority.

Constitution of the Central Civil Services Authority

The central government shall, by notification in the official gazette, constitute a body to be known as the Central Civil Services Authority to exercise the powers conferred on, and to perform the functions.

A Central Civil Services Authority should be constituted under the proposed Civil Services Bill. The Central Civil Services Authority shall be a five-member body consisting of the chairperson and four members (including the member-secretary). The authority should have a full time member-secretary of the rank of Secretary to the Government of India. The chairperson and members of the authority should be persons of eminence in public life and professionals with acknowledged contributions to society.

The Second ARC sought to modernise the civil service in India through a series of strategic reforms focused on decentralisation, training, compensation, and the dynamic roles of civil servants, all aimed at creating a more effective governance structure. The success of the ARC's recommendations depended heavily on the active participation of civil servants and the government's commitment to implementing these reforms.

Attributes of a Good Administrator

- Willingness to assume responsibility
- A steadily enlarging ability to deal with more problems

- A strong bent toward action
- A good listener
- Effective with people
- Capacity to build their own strength by building the competence of their organisation
- Capacity to use their institutional resources
- Avoiding using power or authority for their own sake
- Welcoming reports of troublesome things
- A good team-worker
- A good initiator

(*Source: Public Administration for a Welfare State, Paul H Appleby, 1961*)

14.7 Mission *Karmayogi*

Mission *Karmayogi* – the National Programme for Civil Services Capacity Building (NPCSCB) – provides civil service officers with the Karmayogi Bharat Portal, an online learning platform designed to develop a competent civil service grounded in Indian values, with a shared understanding of national priorities. The mission aims to create a future-ready civil service, equipped with the right attitude, skills, and knowledge, aligned with the vision of new India.

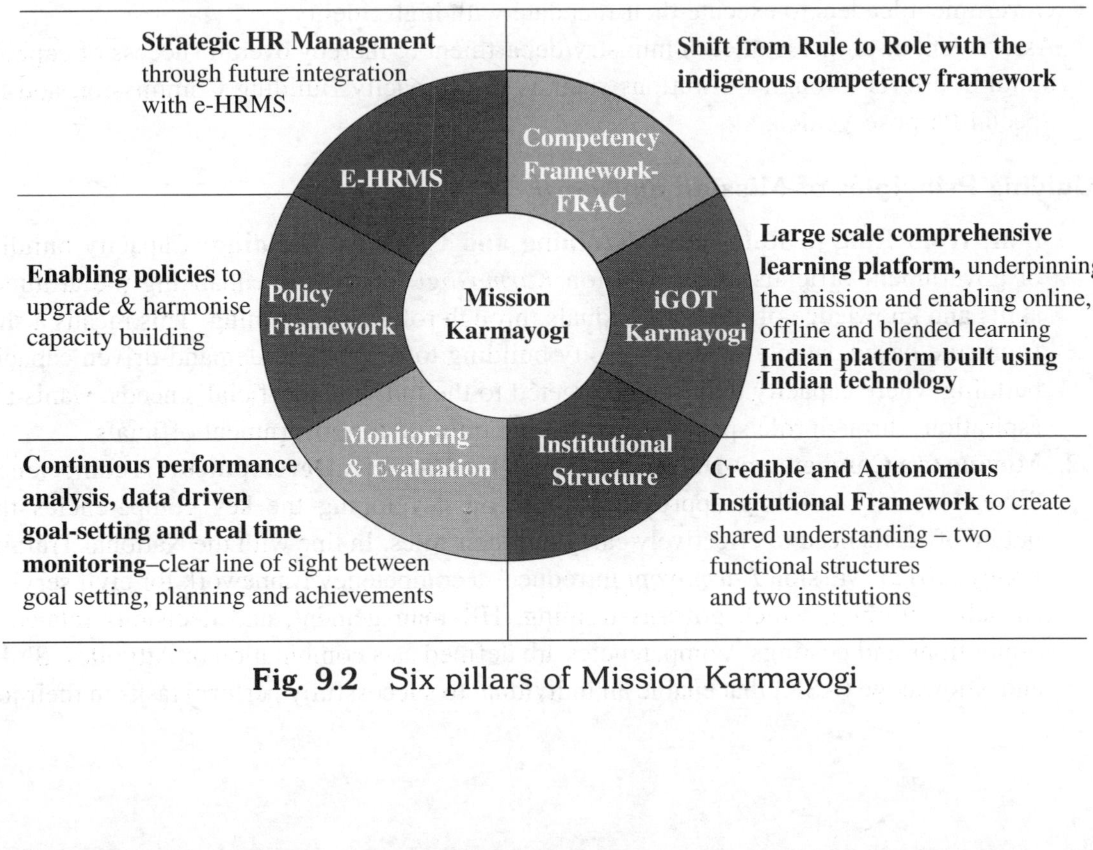

Fig. 9.2 Six pillars of Mission Karmayogi

Karmayogi Bharat seeks to transform the civil services capacity-building framework by establishing a robust digital ecosystem that enables continuous, anytime-anywhere learning, ensuring officials are prepared for the future. To achieve this vision, the mission focuses on guiding civil service officials through competency-based capacity building by offering online, face-to-face, and blended learning options, facilitating discussions through topical forums, managing career paths, and providing reliable assessments to credibly gauge officials' competencies.

CITIZEN AT THE CENTRE OF MISSION *KARMAYOGI*

Mission *Karmayogi* focuses on improving government-citizen interactions by transforming officials into enablers for citizens and businesses. It emphasises the development of behavioural, functional, and domain-specific competencies to enhance the ease of living and ease of doing business. By design, Mission *Karmayogi* adopts a citizen-centric approach to civil service reforms.

The mission aims to enhance state execution capacity by enabling:

- Government officials to learn and grow continuously.
- Government officials to collaborate across departments and regions, breaking down silos and empowering officials with access to information.
- Government leaders to execute their mandate with high fidelity.
- Assessment of progress of each ministry/department & thereby overall success of capacity building efforts through institutions such as the Capacity Building Commission and the Special Purpose Vehicle.

- **Guiding Principles of Mission *Karmayogi***

  1. **Shift from Rule to Role-Based Training and Capacity Building:** Capacity building of government officials under Mission *Karmayogi* focuses on enhancing the attitudes, skills and knowledge of these individuals through role-based training. This means a shift from rule-based, supply-driven capacity building to role-based, demand-driven capacity building where capacity building is targeted to the individual official's needs, wants and aspirations through role specific, just-in-time training for government officials.
  2. **Moving to a Competency-Driven Approach for Capacity Development:** A competency-driven capacity building approach focuses on developing the key competencies that public officials need to effectively carry out their roles. In line with the National Training Policy (2012), Mission *Karmayogi* introduces a competency framework for civil services capacity building, which governs training, HR management, and decisions related to promotions and postings. Competencies are defined as a combination of Attitudes, Skills, and Knowledge (ASK) that enable an individual to successfully perform tasks in their job.

3. **Democratising and Enabling Continuous, Lifelong Learning Opportunities:** The current civil services capacity building process is hindered by the lack of a continuous learning environment. Mission *Karmayogi* seeks to provide all government officials, regardless of hierarchy or location, with the opportunity to consistently build and strengthen the competencies required for their roles. By offering equitable access to learning materials, the initiative ensures that world-class capacity building is accessible to a wider section of civil services through the use of technology.
4. **Moving Beyond Silos in the Government:** Mission *Karmayogi* aims to break down silos across various government ministries and departments, fostering collaboration and joint efforts toward shared national goals and priorities.
5. **70:20:10 Mandate:** Mission *Karmayogi* adopts the 70:20:10 model of lifelong learning, which suggests that 70% of learning comes from on-the-job experiences and reflections, 20% from working with others, and 10% from formal training.
6. **Linking Goal Setting, Planning & Achievement:** Mission *Karmayogi* strives to align learning and capacity building with both organisational goals and the career aspirations of individual officials, while also incorporating performance measurement to track progress.
7. **Establishment of Unbiased Systems of Evaluation:** Mission *Karmayogi* will implement objective, fair, and independent assessments to evaluate the performance of civil servants, ensuring a transparent and unbiased approach to performance appraisal.

- **Significance of Mission *Karmayogi***

Right person for the right role at the right time. It is planned that Mission *Karmayogi* will transform the professional outlook and attitude of the government workforce.

A GLOBAL LEADER: Largest capacity building programme in the world, which will cover 46 lakhs employees at the centre, and eventually 1.5 crore government officials across centre, states and local bodies.

BETTER ON-TIME SERVICE DELIVERY: Citizens can be assured that their priorities are being handled by officials who are best trained to do so. This will greatly enhance public satisfaction and help eliminate grievances.

CITIZEN DELIGHT, IMPROVED SENTIMENT: Programmes for strengthening behavioural competencies of civil servants, especially for those at the cutting-edge level, especially where the citizen interacts with a public official will provide a hassle-free and enjoyable experience for the citizen.

ACCOUNTABILITY AND TRANSPARENCY BY DESIGN: The outcomes of the capacity-building efforts will be appraised by the HR Council chaired by the Hon'ble Prime Minister and shared with the citizens through comprehensive annual reports.

LOCAL PROBLEMS, GLOBAL VIEW: The focus of the programme on global learning with Indian values will enable officials to design and develop solutions for local problems using the best available knowledge.

The ultimate goal of Mission *Karmayogi* is to ensure ease of living for the common man, promote ease of doing business, and foster Citizen-Centricity by narrowing the gap between the government and its citizens.

14.8 Civil Service Reforms and Good Governance

A well-functioning civil service promotes good governance by enabling sound policymaking, efficient service delivery, and ensuring accountability and responsible use of public resources. 'Good Governance' serves as a comprehensive framework not only for administrative and civil service reform but also as a bridge connecting Civil Service Reform with a broader framework for making policy decisions effective within viable systems of accountability and citizen participation. Administrative reform aims to streamline government structures, while governance reform focuses on improving legal and policy frameworks to create an environment conducive to effective decision-making. This includes participatory systems that enable civil society's active role in policy and programme development and an effective, transparent system for oversight and accountability in government actions. Civil service reform cannot be pursued in isolation; it must be aligned with administrative reforms for impactful and effective results. It demands sustained commitment from both political and administrative leaders.

14.9 Civil Service Reforms and Socio-Economic Development

Civil service reform seeks to enhance administrative capacity for core government functions, improving the quality of services provided to citizens and supporting sustainable economic and social development. These reforms support macroeconomic stability by restoring budgetary balance, boosting revenue collection, managing aid effectively, and improving development outcomes through sound implementation of investment frameworks and public expenditure plans. Additionally, the reform aids in designing and executing equitable social development programmes. Enhancing the capacity of civil servants and improving their morale are critical to all these functions.

SUMMARY

Bureaucracy is an administrative system based on specialisation, qualifications, adherence to rules, hierarchy, and delegated authority. Its significance lies in governance, societal welfare, stability, cultural promotion, and development.

Weberian Bureaucracy: Hierarchy, division of labor, rules-based actions, impersonality, record-keeping, and separation of public/private roles.

Functions: Policy advice, implementation, continuity, public service delivery, crisis management, socio-economic development, and upholding the Rule of Law.

Values and Aptitudes for Civil Servants

Core Values: Integrity, impartiality, non-partisanship, accountability, transparency, and dedication to public service.

Essential Skills: Organisational abilities, critical thinking, collaboration, adaptability, ethical reasoning, and innovation.

Professionalism: Ensures public trust through honesty, respect, and dedication.

Challenges in Indian Bureaucracy

- Colonial-era mindset, rigid hierarchies, red tape, and resistance to change.
- Issues of corruption, political interference, lack of accountability, and risk-averse culture.
- Frequent transfers, entitlement culture, and poor coordination reduce stability and efficiency.

Civil Service Reforms

Shift from rule-based to role-based management, focus on professionalisation, tenure stability, and citizen-centric governance.

Key Actions:

- Merit-based recruitment with emphasis on technology and managerial skills.
- Mandatory training, transparent performance appraisals, and linking rewards to outcomes.
- Strengthening ethical standards, insulating from political interference, and fixed tenures.
- Establishing a Civil Services Authority and a comprehensive Code of Ethics.
- Broader Impact: Fostering good governance, socio-economic development, and efficient resource use.

Mission *Karmayogi*: A national initiative for competency-based, continuous learning for civil servants. It emphasises role-specific training, breaking silos, lifelong learning, and alignment with governance priorities to improve efficiency, service delivery, and citizen satisfaction. These reforms aim to build a modern, responsive, and accountable bureaucracy capable of addressing evolving challenges and contributing to national progress.

PREVIOUS YEARS' QUESTIONS

1. "Mindless addiction to Form, ignoring the Substance of the matter, results in rendering of injustice. A perceptive civil servant is one who ignores such literalness and carries out true intent". Examine the above statement with suitable illustrations. *UPSC CSE Mains 2024*
2. Apart from intellectual competency and moral qualities, empathy and compassion are some of the other vital attributes that facilitate the civil servants to be more competent in tackling the crucial issues or taking critical decisions. Explain with suitable illustrations. *UPSC CSE Mains 2022*
3. Write short notes on the following in 30 words each: *UPSC CSE Mains 2022*
   (i) Constitutional morality
   (ii) Conflict of interest
   (iii) Probity in public life
   (iv) Challenges of digitalisation
   (v) Devotion to duty
4. (a) Identify five ethical traits on which one can plot the performance of a civil servant. Justify their inclusion in the matrix.
   (b) Identify ten essential values that are needed to be an effective public servant. Describe the ways and means to prevent non-ethical behaviour in the pubic servants.
   UPSC CSE Mains 2021
5. Should impartial and being non-partisan be considered as indispensable qualities to make a successful civil servant? Discuss with illustrations. *UPSC CSE Mains 2021*
6. "Integrity is a value that empowers the human being." Justify with suitable illustration.
   UPSC CSE Mains 2021
7. "The best way to find yourself is to lose yourself in the service of others." —Mahatma Gandhi
   UPSC CSE Mains 2020
8. What do you understand by the term 'public servant'? Reflect on the expected role of public servant. *UPSC CSE Mains 2019*
9. "Non-performance of duty by a public servant is a form of corruption". Do you agree with this view? *UPSC CSE Mains 2019*
10. State the three basic values, universal in nature, in the context of civil services and bring out their importance. *UPSC CSE Mains 2018*
11. "In looking for people to hire, you look for three qualities: integrity, intelligence and energy. And if they do not have the first, the other two will kill you." —Warren Buffett.
    What do you understand by this statement in the present-day scenario? Explain.
    UPSC CSE Mains 2018
12. Examine the relevance of the following in the context of civil service:
    (a) Transparency
    (b) Accountability

(c) Fairness and justice
(d) Courage of conviction
(e) Spirit of service *UPSC CSE Mains 2017*

13. One of the tests of integrity is complete refusal to be compromised. Explain with reference to a real life example. *UPSC CSE Mains 2017*
14. Without commonly shared and widely entrenched moral values and obligations, neither the law, nor democratic government, nor even the market economy will function properly. What do you understand by this statement? Explain with illustration in the contemporary times. *UPSC CSE Mains 2017*
15. Why should impartiality and non-partisanship be considered as foundational values in public services, especially in the present day socio-political context? Illustrate your answer with examples. *UPSC CSE Mains 2016*
16. "Integrity without knowledge is weak and useless, but knowledge without integrity is dangerous and dreadful." What do you understand by this statement? Explain your stand with illustrations from modern day context. *UPSC CSE Mains 2014*
17. There is a heavy ethical responsibility on the public servants because they occupy positions of power, handle huge amounts of public funds, and their decisions have wide ranging impact on society and environment. What steps have you taken to improve your ethical competence to handle such responsibility? *UPSC CSE Mains 2014*
18. What do you understand by the following terms in the context of public service?
    Integrity
    Perseverance
    Spirit of service
    Commitment
    Courage of conviction.
    Indicate two more attributes which you consider important for public service. Justify your answer.
    UPSC CSE Mains 2013

Public Service Values and Ethics in Public Administration

10

1. ETHICS IN PUBLIC LIFE

LEARNING OBJECTIVES

1. Recognising the importance of integrating ethics with politics
2. Analysing the causes, impact, and remedies for criminalisation of politics
3. Exploring challenges in political funding, and identifying potential remedies for transparency
4. Examining the ethical shortcomings in the legislature and its impact
5. Recommending an ethical framework for the judiciary and civil servants to uphold impartiality
6. Differentiate between value conflicts and conflicts of interest in governance contexts
7. Addressing ethical dilemmas involved in decision-making
8. Understanding the significance of accountability in fostering ethical governance

Ethics is grounded in the notion of responsibility and accountability. In a democracy, every holder of public office is accountable ultimately to the people. Such accountability is enforced through a system of laws and rules, which the elected representatives of the people enact in their **legislatures**.[1] Ethics provides the basis for the creation of such laws and rules. It is the moral ideas of people that give rise to, and shapes the character of laws and rules. Our legal system **emanates**[2] from a shared vision of what is good and just.

The fundamental principle in a democracy is that all persons holding authority derive it from the people, in other words, all public functionaries are trustees of the people. With the expansion of the role of government, public functionaries exercise considerable influence over the lives of people. The trusteeship relationship between the public and the officials requires that the authority entrusted to the officials be exercised in the best interest of the people or in 'public interest'.

The role of ethics in public life has many dimensions. At one end, it is the expression of high moral values, and at the other, the specifics of action for which a public functionary can be held legally accountable. Any framework of ethical behaviour must include the following elements:

[1] **Legislatures:** a governing body that makes laws and can also amend or repeal them
[2] **Emanates:** to produce or show something

(a) Codifying ethical norms and practices.
(b) Disclosing personal interests to avoid conflict between public interest and personal gain.
(c) Creating a mechanism for enforcing the relevant codes.
(d) Providing norms for qualifying and disqualifying a public functionary from office.

A system of laws and rules, however elaborate, cannot provide for all situations. But the higher the echelon in public service, the greater is the ambit of discretion. And it is difficult to provide a system of laws and rules that can comprehensively cover and regulate the exercise of discretion in high places.

Indeed, any person who is privileged to guide the destiny of the people must not only be ethical, but must also be seen to practice these ethical values. Although all citizens are subject to the laws of the land, in the case of public servants, there must be standards of behaviour more stringent than those for an ordinary citizen. It is at the interface of public action and private interest that the need arises for establishing not just a code of ethics, but a code of conduct. A code of ethics would cover broad-guiding principles of good behaviour and governance, while a more specific code of conduct should, in a precise and unambiguous manner, stipulate a list of acceptable and unacceptable behaviour and action.

2. ETHICS IN POLITICS

There is a growing demand for regulating the standards of public life of those working in the public service. Many criticise that politicians are not ethical, that they are more concerned with gaining and retaining power than with ensuring the well-being of the public. Political ethics and personal morality are not always aligned. Some would argue that politicians should stick to universal principles such as justice or fairness to better rule us. On the other hand, political realists would argue that there is no room for ethics in politics, or that the ethical principle that rule citizens' behaviour should not bound politicians. In fact, political leaders throughout history very often had to make unethical decisions to advance the interests of their nation or faction. These two schools can be grouped as the Gandhian view of politics which is idealist, and the Machiavelli view of politics based on realpolitik.

2.1 Gandhian View of Politics

Mahatma Gandhi **condemned**[3] the trend of divorcing politics from ethics, and opined that the goodness of politics cannot be ensured without ethical principles. He was a blended version of saint and a politician who visualised politics as a tool to elevate mankind socially, economically, morally, and spiritually. He was a proponent of politics intrinsically imbued with values and high moral conduct. He wanted to upraise the nature of politics to sacred politics. He advocated spiritualisation of politics and made an intense bid for ethicising the political domain. Gandhi

[3]**Condemned:** Criticise, Denounce

was of the view that righteous means should be solely used for attaining political objectives. He wanted to uplift the present state of politics to sacred politics. By sacredness, he meant that it should be purged of vicious tendencies and narrow mindedness.

Gandhi discovered that the entire gamut of politics had been misguided and moving on the wrong track. But to him, as in other spheres of life, politics should be a pursuit for truth and this search must be for uplifting the general conscience of the people. Every individual must be liberated from the agony of hunger, and must avert exploitative and oppressive behaviour. He would then be in a position to work for his own development through the performance of obligations. An inclusive morality would surface which would catalyse an environment for a healthy political life. In a speech at the All-India National Education Conference on January 13, 1930, he noted that some people believed morality had no connection with politics. He expressed concern that the character of leaders was often disregarded. He emphasised that if *Swaraj* did not aim to uplift people morally and refine and stabilise their civilization, it would hold no real value. He further stressed that the foundation of their civilisation laid in prioritising morality in all aspects of life, both public and private.

For him, politics without principles would ultimately lead to violence and decadence. To him, politics itself was his religion. He wanted to uplift the present state of politics to sacred politics. On July 3, 1940, he declared that his approach to politics had always been rooted in ethics and religion, and that his strength stemmed from this foundation. He explained that his commitment to ethics and religion naturally led him to engage in politics. He further asserted that anyone who loves their country is inherently compelled to take an active interest in political matters.

2.2 Machiavelli on Politics

Unlike, Aristotle, who might have regarded politics and morality as constituting one whole science, where state power was seen as a means to a higher end conceived in moral terms, Machiavelli did not uphold the ethical purpose of the state. Rather, he believed that the power of the state is an end in itself. Consequently, he confined his attention to the means best suited to the acquisition, retention, and expansion of power.

In his best-known treatise—*The Prince*, Machiavelli condemned the moralistic perspective of authority. For that reason, he emancipated politics from religion, and morality in direct opposition to a moralistic theory of politics. Machiavelli said that the only real concern of the political ruler is the acquisition and maintenance of power.

Yet, the relationship between politics and ethics still remains a contested topic. Napoleon said that the great difficulty with politics was that there are no established principles. He noted that politics and principles have seldom gone together. If at all they did, it was generally in the nature of an exception, or that the principle itself was distorted to suit the political objective. That's why leaders like M. N. Roy and Jaya Prakash Narayan even opposed the system of party politics because in elections, political parties adopt corrupt practices. So, they suggested party-less democracy in India.

2.3 Criminalisation of Politics

'Criminalisation of Politics' refers to the participation of individuals with criminal backgrounds in politics, including their ability to contest elections and secure positions in state or federal legislatures. This phenomenon often stems from the nexus between politicians and criminals, where individuals with criminal charges are permitted to run for office.

Despite the framers of the Indian Constitution and early members of Parliament envisioning a clean and ethical political framework, concerns about the infiltration of crime into politics were voiced as early as the first general election in 1952. This fear has since grown into a significant challenge for Indian democracy. In fact, as far back as in 1922, Mr. C. Rajagopalachari had anticipated the present state of affairs, when he wrote in his prison diary: "*Elections and their corruption, injustice and tyranny of wealth, and inefficiency of administration, will make a hell of life as soon as freedom is given to us.*"

> **? Thought Box**
>
> What systemic reforms are necessary to prevent individuals with criminal backgrounds from entering politics while respecting democratic principles?

According to data from the ADR, since 2004, there have been more candidates elected to the Indian Parliament who had criminal accusations against them. In 2004, 24% of lawmakers had active criminal cases, and by 2019, that number had increased to 43%. According to a petition submitted in February 2023, since 2009, there has been a 44% increase in the number of MPs having declared with criminal cases. In the 2019 Lok Sabha elections, 159 MPs have significant criminal cases against them, including rape, murder, attempted murder, kidnapping, and crimes against women. The 2024 Lok Sabha polls were historic not only in terms of the number of voters (64.2 crore), but also for the wrong reasons. A record 251 (46 percent) of the 543 newly elected members have criminal cases registered against them, and 27 of them have been convicted, revealed an analysis done by Association of Democratic Reforms (ADR).

- **Causes of Criminalisation**

1. Money and Muscle Power: The influence of money and muscle power in Indian politics has been a longstanding issue. As early as 1977, the National Police Commission, headed by Dharam Vira, observed that political parties often rely on musclemen to influence the electorate, particularly around election time. Politicians thrive on the muscle power provided by criminal elements, which distorts the democratic process and encourages corruption and lawlessness.

2. Caste and Religion in Indian Politics: Caste and religion play a significant role in the criminalisation of politics in India. Politicians often favour individuals from their own caste or religion, leading to a biased decision-making that undermines the principles of equality and fairness. This trend is prevalent in various states, where ministers prioritise the interests of their own communities over the larger public good. Such practices foster division and inequality within the political system.

Panchayat elections, like other elections in recent times, highlight the pervasive influence of caste and religion. As long as political affiliations and strategies remain rooted in these social divisions, the integrity of India's democratic processes remains compromised.

3. Inefficient Criminal Justice System: Legal delays and the politicisation of the criminal justice system are major contributors to the criminalisation of politics. In his book *When Crime Pays*, Milan Vaishnav highlights how the **sluggish**[4] judicial process allows individuals with criminal backgrounds to exploit legal loopholes and enter politics. The lack of swift and fair legal proceedings enables criminal elements to thrive within the political system, perpetuating a cycle of corruption and crime.

4. Public opinion and the Perpetuation of Corruption: In post-independence India, there has been a notable lack of a strong public stance against corruption. While systemic corruption is widely recognised, there is a widespread tendency to accept it as an unavoidable reality rather than challenging it. This contributes to the criminalisation of politics, as corrupt practices go unopposed. Those who dare to resist or expose such practices often face **punitive**[5] actions, or are denied opportunities, further discouraging resistance and ensuring the perpetuation of corruption in politics.

- **Effect of Criminalisation of Politics**

1. Impact on Administration and Police: The criminalisation of politics has made the administration and police the first casualties, leading to a legal system that is neither fair nor impartial. As political influence over the law enforcement agencies grows, the objectivity of the police is compromised. Their role in maintaining law and order becomes skewed, making it difficult to uphold justice effectively. The politicisation of police and administrative services weakens the foundation of democratic governance.

2. Government Response and Inadequate Action: Recognising the gravity of the situation, the Government of India addressed the issue by convening a conference of chief ministers in 1992, titled 'Administration of Criminal Justice in India.' This conference underscored the critical issue of inadequate financial support for the police, judiciary, and prison system, which are the three pillars of the criminal justice system. The resolution passed during the conference highlighted that expenditures on these areas had declined over the years, further aggravating the challenges of delivering justice and maintaining law and order.

---

[4]**Sluggish:** Slow, inactive
[5]**Punitive:** Harsh

The conference also expressed concern about the increasing criminalisation of politics and the politicisation of administration. A committee under the Home Minister was recommended to address follow-up actions, but unfortunately, no substantial progress was made, leaving the system vulnerable to further degradation.

3. Economic and Social Consequences: The criminalisation of politics has had a severe impact on the nation's economy. One of the major consequences is the influx of black money into the political system, which distorts the legitimate economic processes. This undermines economic stability and fosters corruption, making it difficult for the economy to grow sustainably.

Additionally, the criminalisation of politics introduces a culture of violence, which not only erodes social harmony, but also sets a bad example for the youth. As violence and corruption become normalised, public confidence in democracy as a viable system of government diminishes, creating a sense of disillusionment among citizens.

4. Negative Effects on Key Institutions: The **repercussions**[6] of criminalisation extend beyond the economy and society. It adversely affects key institutions such as the judiciary, police, investigating agencies, the Parliament, and bureaucracy. The judiciary and investigative agencies, once seen as impartial, become vulnerable to political pressure, losing their ability to uphold justice without bias. Similarly, the Parliament and the bureaucracy suffer from corruption and inefficiency, undermining their capacity to serve the public good. Even the media, a crucial pillar of democracy, can be manipulated by criminalised politics, leading to biased reporting and diminished credibility.

5. Undermining Free and Fair Elections: Finally, the criminalisation of politics erodes the fundamental principle of free and fair elections. When money and muscle power dominate the electoral process, the integrity of elections is compromised. Candidates with criminal backgrounds are able to secure electoral victories through coercion and manipulation, distorting the democratic process and denying voters the opportunity to make informed, unbiased choices. This ultimately weakens the democratic fabric of the nation and diminishes trust in the political system.

2.4 Issues in Funding of Political Parties

One of the most pressing critiques of contemporary democracy is its struggle to regulate the overwhelming influence of money in politics. While elections are indispensable to democracy, the financial resources required for political campaigns make it difficult to imagine elections without substantial monetary involvement. Political parties require significant funds to operate effectively, contest elections, and serve as an opposition.

[6]**Repercussions:** an unpleasant effect or result of something

Traditionally, Indian political parties financed their activities through private donations and membership fees. Corporate donations were permitted under certain restrictions and had to be disclosed in company accounts. The Representation of the People Act (RPA) of 1951 introduced limits on election campaign spending, with candidates exceeding these limits facing disqualification or annulment of their elections. However, by the 1960s, concerns grew about the nexus between black money and political fundraising. Reports such as the Santhanam Committee on Prevention of Corruption (1964) and the Wanchoo Direct Taxes Enquiry Committee (1971) highlighted the infiltration of black money into politics.

A significant development occurred in 1985 when the Companies Act was amended through Section 293A to allow corporate donations to political parties under specific conditions. Recognising the growing challenges of electoral financing, the National Front government established the Dinesh Goswami Committee on Electoral Reforms in 1990. This committee recommended limited state support, such as subsidised fuel for campaign vehicles, rental costs for microphones, voter identity slips, and additional electoral roll copies.

By 1993, political funding became a concern for Indian industry. The Confederation of Indian Industry (CII) formed a task force that proposed making corporate donations tax-deductible, and requiring shareholder approval for political contributions.

In 1998, the Indrajit Gupta Committee on State Funding of Elections (Gupta Committee) recommended partial state funding, primarily in kind. It proposed providing political parties with free airtime on state-owned TV and radio channels, and suggested private broadcasters offer similar support. Additional recommendations included subsidised fuel, paper for election materials, postage stamps, electoral roll copies, loudspeakers, telephone facilities, and refreshments on counting day, all within prescribed limits.

These measures aimed to balance the financial needs of political campaigns with transparency and fairness, though challenges in implementation persist, which includes the following:

In recent times the demand for black money to finance parties and campaigns has increased. Kapur and Vaishnav sought to demonstrate the nexus between the real estate sector and election funding. Specifically, they examined the alleged relationship between politicians and builders, in which politicians invest their illegal wealth in the construction industry, and builders cooperate because they are beholden to politicians for **discretionary**[7] favours.

There is also evidence that the mounting costs of election campaigns results in circumvention of expenditure limits, parties' preference for wealthy candidates, and increase in the participation of criminals in electoral politics. Parties and candidates tend to use their term of office to accumulate war chests for future elections, and for nursing their constituencies. There is evidence that they raise these resources through any means available, including, through corrupt means such as kickbacks for regulatory and allocative favours while in office.

---

[7]**Discretionary:** To right to decide something based on one's own judgement

Further, the lack of any effective system of internal democracy within parties reinforces corrupt fund-raising and the lack of financial accountability. In this respect, India stands in contrast to Germany, which regulates the internal affairs of parties. Parties in India have evolved to be top-down and often controlled by a founding family.

Under the current system, party leadership has no incentive to raise funds through large numbers of small-sum donations, given the large sums needed and the high transaction costs involved in raising many small contributions. It is far easier to raise the large sums needed in big tranches from a relatively small number of big donors, typically in unaccounted forms. The apparent result is that parties and politicians raise funds from businesses in black money form, in return for discretionary contracts and regulatory favours, and spend more than campaign finance laws allow without disclosure. There is no incentive to break out of this corrupt equilibrium. It is simply how 'the system' works.

• POTENTIAL REMEDIES

1. Electoral Trusts: Despite two decades of economic liberalisation, India's political-economic landscape remains characterised by businesses' vulnerability to discretionary government actions at both the central and state levels. While licensing powers have been reduced, businesses continue to face numerous bureaucratic hurdles, including the need for multiple government approvals to start, operate, or expand their operations.

This bureaucratic environment has led to a risk-averse approach among industrial groups. Many businesses have turned to tax-exempt electoral trusts to make political contributions. These trusts often distribute funds to political parties across the spectrum in a formulaic manner, ensuring that no single party is favoured, thereby avoiding political disfavour.

2. Encouraging Grassroots Funding for Political Parties: One potential solution to the issue of opaque political funding is to encourage political parties to rely more on grassroots donations, particularly small-sum contributions. This would foster greater internal democracy within parties, and improve transparency. Canada's successful implementation of tax credits for small donations serves as an exemplary model. Similarly, state funding of political campaigns, based on transparent criteria, could incentivise grassroots financing, enhance party membership participation, and reduce dependence on large, opaque contributions.

3. Corporate Donations and Transparency: Raising the limits on corporate donations could improve the transparency of political financing by allowing more legal funds into the political system. Some corporate groups, such as the Tata Group, have already taken steps to comply with legal norms by establishing electoral trusts. The Tata Group, for example, allocates its political contributions based on the party strength in the Lok Sabha, ensuring a more balanced and transparent distribution.

2.5 Ethics of Coalition Politics

The term coalition has been derived from the Latin word '*coalitio*' which is the verbal substantive of "*coalescere*'-meaning together, and '*alescere*'—to grow up, which means to grow together. In the political sense, the term coalition denotes an alliance or temporary union of political forces for forming a single government.

First, all the political parties who enter into a coalition always aims to maximise their long-term influence over the decision-making process. Second, because of the awareness concerning the re-distributive consequences of a coalition, the member parties often compete against each other over the allocation of redistribution benefits. Third, the competition among the coalition partners is restricted by the degree to which each partner is willing to tolerate competitive demands on the part of the allies. Fourth, in a situation where the tolerance among the coalition partners remains at a high level, competitiveness is rewarded with disproportionally high returns in terms of political influence.

In the countries with multiparty systems, such as Belgium and the Netherlands, almost all the governments have been coalitions. However, the countries like India in the recent past have seen the coalition government being formed on the basis of as many as eighteen parties i.e., the Vajpayee-led government in 1998. The start of coalition politics in India started from the 1967 elections which witnessed the coalition politics in another form, now involving the non-Congress opposition parties. Opposition parties were able to defeat Congress in the assembly elections in six states by joining into an electoral coalition.

The second phase in the evolution of coalition politics was marked by the defeat of the Congress in 1977 parliamentary as well as the assembly elections with Janata Party forming the government. The 1989–2014 was the coalition era where two poles around NDA and UPA formed governments. 2024 elections saw the re-emergence of coalition politics in India.

Former PM Manmohan Singh had stated that India lacks coalition *dharma* whereas, Bidyut Chakrabarty, in his book *Coalition Politics in India,* talked about the lack of coalition culture in India.

The working of the coalition governments has been affected by the need to secure inter-party consensus. The heterogeneity of the coalition partners in terms of their social basis and ideologies has often resulted in disagreements between cabinet ministers on political and departmental matters. The coalition governments at the centre have been formed, not on the positive basis of ideological homogeneity, but on the negative basis of capturing power. This factor has contributed to the lack of efficacy, as well as, stability of these governments.

The governance also has suffered because of the weakened position of the Prime Minister in the coalition governments formed in recent years. The Prime Minister has been in no position to choose ministers in the council of ministers who do not belong to his own party, as they are chosen by their respective party leaders.

2.6 Ethics in Politics in the Era of Social Media

Rising political polarisation is partly fuelled by the fragmentation of the news media, and the proliferation of misinformation on social media. Initially, social media was hailed as a transformative tool for strengthening democracy and the rule of law, enabling policy changes, institutional reforms, and social movements with far-reaching political impact. Events such as the 2009 Iranian protests, the Arab Spring (2010), the Brazil Spring (2013), the #BlackLivesMatter (2013), #MeToo (2017) movements, the Gezi Park protests in Turkey (2014), and the Umbrella Movement in Hong Kong (2014) showcased the potential of digital media in addressing social injustices, discrimination, oppression, corruption, and other human rights violations.

Increasingly, politicians, political parties, and governments have adopted platforms like Twitter, Facebook, and Instagram to engage directly with constituents, and shape public opinion. While social media has democratised access to political dialogue, amplified underrepresented voices, and encouraged inclusiveness, it also raises significant concerns.

The unchecked spread of misinformation, hate speech, and propaganda has created divisions and fostered mistrust in the political discourse. Algorithms on these platforms often prioritise sensational or controversial content over accurate reporting, exacerbating the problem. The rapid dissemination of misinformation, disinformation, and conspiracy theories on social media poses a serious threat to fact-based political dialogue. Customised feeds based on user behaviour can limit exposure to diverse perspectives, reinforcing existing biases and creating echo chambers.

> **? Thought Box**
>
> How can technology be leveraged to enhance transparency and accountability while ensuring it aligns with ethical principles?

The prioritisation of data collection over user privacy by social media companies raises concerns about the misuse of personal information for targeted political advertising. Additionally, reliance on social media for political engagement can undermine traditional forms of participation, such as voting and civic activism.

Addressing these challenges requires a multifaceted approach. Key measures include promoting media literacy, supporting fact-checking organisations, encouraging diverse voices in political discourse, and holding social media companies accountable. Transparency in funding sources, ethical practices to prevent manipulation, and respecting user privacy rights are essential for responsible social media use.

Fact-checking organisations play a critical role in countering the spread of misinformation. Simultaneously, reforms in social media algorithms to prioritise truthful and balanced content over sensationalism can help restore trust and promote constructive political dialogue.

2.7 Ethics of Identity Politics

The term 'identity politics' broadly refers to the idea that an individuals' political perspectives are influenced by their social identities. In a multicultural and diverse society like India, ascriptive identities such as caste, religion, language, and ethnicity significantly shape political dynamics. These identity groups emerge naturally in any society that values freedom of association, as people tend to organise around shared characteristics. Preventing such formations would, in effect, suppress associational freedom, which is a hallmark of democracy.

While identity politics can empower marginalised groups by giving them a platform to fight for their rights, it can also foster divisions by pitting communities against one another based on differences. This dual nature of identity politics has sparked debates about its role in shaping political discourse and governance.

In India, identity politics has deep historical roots, influenced by the country's colonial past, partition, and post-independence developments. The partition of India on religious lines, aimed at creating Pakistan as a homeland for muslims, resulted in immense violence, and has left lasting scars on the nation.

Post-independence, identity politics began to manifest in various forms:

- **Caste-Based Politics:** The push for protective discrimination for oppressed caste groups, such as reservations in education and employment became a cornerstone of identity politics. While these policies empowered marginalised communities, they also intensified confrontational politics, leading to governance challenges.
- **Religion:** Religion remains a significant factor in Indian politics, influencing voter behaviour and party strategies. According to a Pew Research Centre study (2022), 84% of Indian adults consider religion to be 'very important' in their lives, and religious tolerance is viewed as central to being 'truly Indian.' However, rising political tensions have deepened divides between communities, with major religious groups perceiving stark differences from one another.
- **Linguistic Identity:** India's linguistic diversity, with over 19,500 languages or dialects (2011 Census), has also fuelled identity politics. The reorganisation of states on linguistic lines in 1956 addressed some demands but also set the stage for ongoing claims. For instance, movements for 'sons of the soil' policies and attacks on migrant workers in Maharashtra reflect the enduring relevance of linguistic identities. Unlike religion, linguistic consciousness often coexists harmoniously with national consciousness, yet it remains a persistent driver of identity politics.
- **Ethnic identity:** In the Northeastern states, identity politics revolves around ethnicity, often tied to demographic changes, relative deprivation, and uneven development. This has resulted in periodic conflicts and demands for greater autonomy or recognition.

Identity politics raises ethical dilemmas. On one hand, it provides a voice for marginalised groups and safeguards cultural diversity. On the other, it can lead to:

1. **Vote Bank Politics:** Political parties often prioritise identity-based appeasement over substantive issues like health, education, and economic development.
2. **Criminalisation of Politics:** The competition for identity-based vote banks has contributed to unethical practices in politics.
3. **Populism:** Promises like reservations for specific groups often overshadow broader developmental agendas.
4. **Community Conflicts:** Clashes, such as the recent Meitei-Kuki conflict in Manipur, underscore the potential for identity politics to inflame tensions.

Identity politics in India exemplifies the tension between individual liberties and community consciousness. Scholars like Beteille have noted that the Indian polity consistently seeks to balance liberal individualism with the concerns of collective identity. However, as Gandhi feared, politics driven by narrow identity interests can lead to a departure from principles, undermining the pursuit of the common good.

For identity politics to contribute positively, it must be rooted in ethical principles that prioritise inclusivity, justice, and equality. Addressing the challenges requires political will, strong institutions, and a focus on policies that transcend identity divides to foster national unity and development.

3. ETHICS OF LEGISLATURE

Minimising legislative misconduct requires the creation of an 'ethics regime'— a set of standards to govern member conduct and a system to administer those standards. The problem is not that legislators are inherently corrupt, or will necessarily become so. Rather, the nature of their positions requires legislators to continually face difficult ethical dilemmas. Legislators must constantly decide among competing interests—national, constituent-based, political, and personal. This difficulty is amplified by the fact that most legislators simultaneously hold positions in the private sector, and as such are perpetually "changing hats" from one position to the other.

In addition, legislators are subject to intense scrutiny by the media, non-governmental organisations, and the public at large. Given this environment, it is in the best interest of the legislators to develop a code of conduct and financial disclosure rules that guide difficult decisions and protect against false accusations. Over time, an ethics regime creates norms whereby proper conduct can become second nature. In sum, a comprehensive and successful ethics regime can serve as a map by which legislators can navigate the sometimes-treacherous waters of political life.

Legislative misconduct can occur even after an MP or minister leaves office. Problems arise because former legislators enjoy access to privileged information, and through their government connections, may be able to exert undue influence over their former colleagues.

Receiving gifts is a problematic issue for legislators. The presentation of gifts to political leaders is a time-honoured practice, and is generally perceived as an expression of respect. On occasion, however, gifts represent compensation for political favours.

Trinamool Congress MP Mahua Moitra was expelled from the Lok Sabha following a discussion on the ethics committee report regarding a 'cash for query' issue. The controversy revolved around accusations that Moitra had engaged in unethical conduct related to parliamentary queries in exchange for financial favours. The Constitution of India has listed freedom of speech as a privilege of a Member of the Indian Parliament. A violation or an abridgement of this privilege is deemed a serious infraction of legislative ethics.

Consequently, any payment of money to a member, even by way of a gift, is perceived as bribery to them, and adversely affecting their freedom to speak freely and openly on issues of public interest. The 1951 Mudgal Case, and the Import License Scandal of 1974 provide examples to support this. In 1951, after being paid by the Bombay Bullion Association, Mudgal, a Member of the Parliament, moved amendments to the Forward Contracts (Regulations) in the Parliament on behalf of the association. In 1974, another Member helped obtain seven import licenses for some bogus companies in Pondicherry in consideration of a payment made to him.

A legislative ethics is a formal framework which regulates the behaviour of legislators by establishing what is considered to be an acceptable behaviour and what is not. In other words, it is intended to promote a political culture which places considerable emphasis on the propriety, correctness, transparency, and honesty of parliamentarians' behaviour.

3.1 Best Practices

In Argentina, the criminal code directly regulates the acceptance of gifts by the Members of Parliament (MPs), prohibiting them from accepting gifts given to their position. In Australia, MPs are permitted to receive gifts, unless there is a risk of a conflict of interest arising from them.

In Germany, Ireland, and the United Kingdom, MPs are required to disclose their interests and any potential conflicts of interest, but are still allowed to participate in discussions and deliberations. In contrast, in Australia, Canada, and South Africa, MPs are prohibited from voting on issues that could present a conflict of interest.

There are three main approaches to regulating an MPs' conduct and conflicts of interest:

1. **External Oversight:** This approach involves creating an independent external body, established through legislation, to administer and enforce the code of conduct for MPs. This body oversees MPs' behaviour and reports either to the legislature or a committee. Alberta and Ontario follow this model, and New South Wales is considering a more stringent version, where a breach of the code would be treated as a legal violation. The enforcement of the code could be handled by an independent commission.

2. **Internal Oversight within the Legislature:** This model involves a body within the legislature that monitors MPs' conduct. It can take the form of a parliamentary committee (like in Japan), or an independent parliamentary commissioner established under standing orders or House resolutions (rather than by separate legislation). This body reports to the legislature or a committee. The UK and some Canadian federal legislature proposals follow this model.
3. **Internal Discipline through Ethics Committees:** The United States Congress follows a system where discipline is managed internally by each House through a detailed set of rules and guidelines. Each House has its own code of official conduct, and an ethics committee independent of the other House handles investigations and advisory rulings. These committees have jurisdiction over the members and staff, investigate misconduct allegations, and can impose sanctions.

3.2 Ethics Committee

Subsequently, an all-party meeting was held on 15 September 1995, under the chairmanship of the then Union Home Minister, Shri S.B. Chavan, to look into the whole gamut of criminal-politician nexus and the related issue of declaration of assets and liabilities by the members of Parliament and ministers. The points, which inter alia, constituted the agenda were:

1. Setting up of a Parliamentary Committee on ethics as distinct from the committee of privileges which would act as a guardian on the activities of members of Parliament.
2. Adoption of a code of conduct at the level of political parties to ensure a cleaner public life, e.g., not to give party tickets to persons having criminal record.
3. All political parties should have open audited accounts which must be published annually.
4. Giving more teeth to the nodal group set up as a consequence of the recommendations of the Vohra Committee Report.
5. Changes in the legal system, simplification of the procedure and dispensation of quick justice.

The Ethics Committee of the Rajya Sabha, the first such committee formed by any legislature in India, was constituted by the Chairman of the Rajya Sabha on March 4, 1997. Its purpose was to oversee the moral and ethical conduct of members, and to examine cases referred to it concerning ethical violations and misconduct. The procedures and rules applicable to the Committee of Privileges were adopted for the Ethics Committee, with the Chairman of the Rajya Sabha authorised to make any variations or modifications as needed. The committee was officially inaugurated on May 30, 1997, by the then Vice-President of India and Chairman of the Rajya Sabha, Shri K.R. Narayanan.

The creation of the Ethics Committee marked a significant milestone in the history of Indian parliamentary democracy. Committees like these are in operation in only a few countries, and by establishing this committee, India joined the ranks of these select nations. The Ethics Committee of the Rajya Sabha consists of ten members, including its chairman, who is nominated by the Chairman of the Rajya Sabha. The chairman is typically from the largest party in the House, and other members generally include the leaders, deputy leaders, and chief whips of the various parties or groups in the Rajya Sabha.

While inaugurating the committee, Shri K.R. Narayanan explained that by selecting the leaders of political parties as members, the aim was to enhance the committee's prestige and influence. This approach also sought to foster an indirect, yet meaningful connection with the political parties, all of which are deeply invested in upholding the highest ethical standards in parliamentary life. According to Narayanan, this initiative provided a common platform for all political groups to come together in their commitment to maintaining the integrity of the institution of Parliament.

There is a committee of ethics of the Lok Sabha to oversee the moral and ethical conduct of members of that House. Apart from the existing norms, the committee recommended that the members should abide by the following general ethical principles:

(i) Members must utilise their position to advance general well-being of the people.
(ii) In case of conflict between their personal interest and public interest, they must resolve the conflict so that personal interests are subordinate to the duty of public office.
(iii) Conflict between private financial/family interest should be resolved in a manner that the public interest is not jeopardised.
(iv) Members holding public offices should use public resources in such a manner as may lead to public good.
(v) Members must keep uppermost in their mind the fundamental duties listed in Part-IV of the Constitution.
(vi) Members should maintain high standards of morality, dignity, decency, and values in public life.

As per available information, only a few state legislatures, such as Andhra Pradesh, Odisha etc., have adopted the codes of conduct for their legislators. A resolution was unanimously adopted at the 'All-India Conference of Presiding Officers, Chief Ministers, Ministers of Parliamentary Affairs, Leaders and Whips of Parties on Discipline and Decorum in Parliament, and Legislatures of States and Union Territories' held at New Delhi on 25th November, 2001. The resolution included adoption of a code of conduct for legislators. It was also recommended that ethics committees be constituted in all legislatures where these have not already been constituted for enforcing the code of conduct.

3.3 Decline of Ethics in Legislature

In recent years, there has been growing concern that the Indian political system is under significant strain, with a noticeable decline in values within public life. This situation poses a serious threat to the future of democracy and requires urgent attention.

The Vohra Committee's 1995 report highlighted the troubling nexus between criminal gangs, the police, the bureaucracy, and politicians, which has become evident in various parts of the country. This unhealthy alliance has contributed to a gradual erosion of parliamentary values. One of the key issues is the lack of genuine commitment among parliamentarians to uphold these values. Personal gain often takes precedence over the image and integrity of Parliament, with parliamentary values being sidelined or ignored. Many members treat the institution as a given, rather than a sacred trust.

Additionally, there has been a disturbing rise in the number of parliamentarians with criminal backgrounds. This creates a paradox, where candidates with significant muscle power and financial resources, regardless of their qualifications or integrity, have a higher chance of winning parliamentary seats. Another concern is the increasing dominance of coalition politics, which has led to a tendency to bypass debate and discussion. The frequent use of ordinances to avoid negotiations with coalition partners or opposition undermines the deliberative and representative nature of the Parliament, which is detrimental to healthy democratic practices.

> **? Thought Box**
>
> How can legislative bodies restore public trust and reinforce ethical standards while balancing political pragmatism and accountability in a rapidly changing societal landscape?

Moreover, there is a growing perception that the Parliament has shifted from being a public institution to a space controlled by a few entrenched dynastic **oligarchs**.[8] In this scenario, the Parliament seems to have been privatised, with the parliamentary hall treated as a private domain for these oligarchs. Key issues such as accountability, decorum, debate, and discussion are easily sidelined, as if they were mere internal family matters rather than matters of national importance. Finally, the frequent defection and horse-trading of parliamentarians have further diminished their loyalty, reducing it to a commodity that can be bought and sold. These practices undermine the electoral process, erode public trust, and promote power politics at the expense of the people's will.

---

[8]**Oligarchs:** It is a form of government in which power rests with a small number of people/ Syndicate

3.4 Remedies

1. Promoting Clean and Skilled Leadership in Politics: Political parties must prioritise selecting candidates with clean background and demonstrate a genuine commitment to nominating skilled professionals, such as lawyers, doctors, social activists, and academicians. Their expertise, experience, and potential can significantly enhance the quality of policymaking and governance.

2. Ensuring Transparency Through the RTI Act: To increase transparency and accountability, political parties should be brought under the purview of the Right to Information (RTI) Act. This reform would enable public scrutiny of crucial aspects like fundraising, agenda-setting, ticket distribution, internal party elections, and corporate affiliations. The urgency of this measure is underscored by Transparency International's 2013 report, which rated political parties among the most corrupt institutions.

3. Introducing Mechanisms for Public Accountability: Mechanisms to recall underperforming parliamentarians should be established, empowering citizens to demand accountability. Progress in this direction includes the judiciary's directive to the Election Commission to introduce the 'Right to Reject' option—popularly known as 'None of the Above' (NOTA)—in electronic voting machines (EVMs) and ballot boxes. Additionally, a compulsory referendum for legislative matters of high national importance could strengthen public participation in decision-making.

4. Codifying Parliamentary Rules for Discipline and Decorum: Codification of parliamentary rules is essential to ensure participation in debates, discipline, and decorum. Strict penalties, including fines, should be imposed for violations. Compulsory attendance during parliamentary sessions must be mandated, with exceptions granted only through prior approval from the Speaker. Moreover, the conduct of parliamentarians outside the Parliament should be monitored to maintain public trust and uphold the dignity of their office.

5. Performance Audits and Constituency Accountability: Parliamentarians should have an annual report card that evaluates their attendance, participation in debates and discussions, and the number of questions raised in Parliament. These performance metrics should be made accessible to their constituents, ensuring transparency and informed public engagement. Furthermore, an institutional mechanism should be established to annually audit the income, wealth growth, and constituency performance of parliamentarians. Such audits would foster accountability, mitigate corruption, and rebuild trust in public representatives.

3.5 Legal Measures

Our Constitution establishes democratic institutions with independent functioning to help realise the ultimate goal of a welfare state. To regulate political activities and uphold democratic values while curbing the criminalisation of politics, various laws have been enacted.

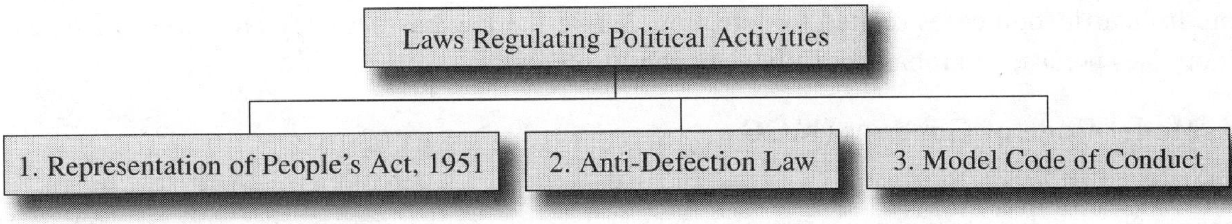

- **Representation of People's Act, 1951**

This Act outlines the qualifications and disqualifications for participation in the election process, aiming to eliminate criminal elements from politics.

- **Section 8** provides for the disqualification of individuals convicted of certain offences. If a person is sentenced to more than two years in prison, they are barred from standing for election for six years after completing their sentence. This discourages corruption, bribery, and the incitement of hatred or social evils by political figures. However, the law does not prevent individuals with pending criminal cases from contesting elections. Disqualification only occurs upon conviction.
- **Section 123(3)** prohibits the use of religion, race, caste, community, or language to sow enmity or hatred during campaigns.
- **Section 135C** bans the sale, distribution, or gifting of liquor on polling day, a measure aimed at reducing the influence of money and muscle power in politics.

In the Lily Thomas Case (2013), a two-judge bench of the Supreme Court ruled that Members of Parliament and State Legislatures convicted of crimes with a sentence of two or more years would cease to be members from the date of sentencing. Despite this, the Law Commission's 244th Report noted that disqualification based on conviction has proven ineffective in preventing the criminalisation of politics.

- **Anti-Defection Law**

This law addresses defections in Parliament or state legislatures, specifically targeting members of political parties, independents, and nominated members.

The term '*Aaya Ram, Gaya Ram*' was coined to describe frequent defections during the 1960s. Defection refers to when a member of a political party switches allegiance to another party after an election.

A member can be disqualified if they:

1. Voluntarily give up their membership of a political party or join another party after elections.
2. Vote or abstain from voting against the directive of their political party on crucial issues.
3. A nominated member joins a political party after six months of taking their seat.
4. An independent member joins a political party.

However, if two-thirds of a legislature party agree to merge with another party, they are exempt from disqualification. The Chairman or Speaker of the House has absolute authority to decide on disqualification cases related to defection. While the law has been effective to some extent, loopholes persist, and it has not fully achieved its objectives.

- **Model Code of Conduct (MCC)**

The Model Code of Conduct is a non-statutory framework issued by the Election Commission to ensure free and fair elections under Article 324 of the Constitution. The MCC provides guidelines regulating the conduct of political parties and candidates during election campaigns.

It sets standards for:

- Political meetings, campaigns, and processions before elections.
- The creation and dissemination of election manifestos.
- Monitoring the overall political conduct during elections.

Although the MCC is not legally enforceable, it has gained significant strength in recent years due to its strict enforcement by the Election Commission and the moral authority it holds among the public. Political parties have voluntarily agreed to follow the MCC, making it a widely respected framework that helps ensure fair electoral practices.

These laws collectively aim to strengthen the democratic framework by regulating political activities, curbing corruption, and maintaining the integrity of elections. However, ongoing efforts are needed to address loopholes and enhance their effectiveness in promoting transparency and accountability in the political process.

4. ETHICAL FRAMEWORK FOR THE JUDICIARY

Independence of the judiciary is **inextricably**[9] linked with judicial ethics. An independent judiciary enjoying public confidence is a basic necessity of the rule of law. Any conduct on the part of a judge, which demonstrates a lack of integrity and dignity, will undermine the trust reposed in the judiciary by the citizens. The conduct of a judge should, therefore, should always be above reproach. A mere prescription of a code of conduct is not an end in itself. Along with the code of conduct, a mechanism for enforcing the code needs to be evolved.

It would be desirable to designate a senior Judge of the Supreme Court as the 'Judicial Values Commissioner'. The Judicial Values Commissioner should be empowered to enquire into cases of violation of the code of conduct, and report the matter to the Chief Justice of India for taking action. The Judicial Values Commissioner should have jurisdiction over the judges of the Supreme Court, and members of other judicial and quasi-judicial bodies. A similar institution should also be constituted at the state level. Closely linked with this is the issue of judicial accountability.

The need for an effective mechanism for the enforcement of judicial accountability cannot be overemphasised. Judicial independence and accountability should go together. Article 235 of the

[9]**Inextricably:** inseparably

Constitution of India provides for the 'control' of the High Court over the subordinate judiciary, clearly indicating that the provision of an effective mechanism to enforce judicial accountability is a part of our constitutional philosophy.

It cannot be doubted that the independence of a subordinate judge is as important as that of a judge in a High Court or in the Supreme Court. If this is accepted, then there should be no reason not to consider an accountability mechanism for the higher judiciary. Article 124 vests the power of appointment of the Chief Justice of India (CJI) and the Judges to the Supreme Court in the President.

The system of appointments to the higher courts, as stipulated by the Constitution and as interpreted by the Supreme Court, has always placed the highest premium on judicial independence. In India, it is only a collegium of judges that recommends to the President names for elevation to the bench and there is no outside advice available for this purpose. Judicial pronouncements have made the recommendation binding. Perhaps in no other country in the world does the judiciary have a final say in its own appointments. In India, neither the executive, nor the legislature has much say in who is appointed to the Supreme Court or the High Courts.

The current system of appointments is not open to public scrutiny, and thus lacks accountability and transparency. A closely related aspect of the accountability of judges is the mechanism for the removal of judges for deviant behaviour. Other than impeachment under Articles 124(4) and 217(1), there is no mechanism to proceed against any inappropriate behaviour or misdemeanour of judges. At the time of framing the Constitution, it was felt that judicial conventions and norms would constitute strong checks. However, the impeachment provisions have turned out to be impracticable as it is virtually impossible to initiate any impeachment proceedings, let alone successfully conclude them.

There are five stages, all of them difficult to accomplish. First is a mandatory presentation of not less than hundred Lok Sabha members or fifty Rajya Sabha members for giving notice. At the second stage, the Speaker or the Chairman has to admit the motion; if they do not admit it, the matter ends there. In the third stage, if there is one, a committee is appointed to conduct an enquiry. The fourth stage is that the committee makes a report, and forwards it to the Speaker or the Chairman. The fifth and final stage is reached when the two Houses of the Parliament proceed to act in the manner prescribed by Section 6(3) of the Judges (Inquiry) Act.

Inadequacy of the existing mechanism was affirmed in the K. Veeraswami case, 1991. The issue of appointment and removal of judges was examined by the National Commission to Review the Working of the Constitution and it recommended the constitution of the National Judicial Commission for appointment of judges. The Law Commission in its 195th Report examined the draft Judges (Inquiry) Bill, 2005. It stated: Judicial independence is not absolute. Judicial independence and accountability are two sides of the same coin. They ought not to be viewed as an encroachment on Judicial independence by the Executive or by the Legislature. The Law Commission observed that the Bill of 2005, which provides for the establishment of a National

Judicial Council consisting only of judges is constitutionally valid and is consistent with the concept of independence of the judiciary, judicial accountability, and doctrine of separation of powers.

While supporting the idea of a Code of Conduct for the Judiciary, it recommended that the Code should be published in the Gazette of India, and till such time the Judicial Council publishes a Code of Conduct, the Bill must provide that the 'Restatement of Values of Judicial Life' adopted by the Supreme Court in its Resolution dated May 7th, 1997, shall be treated as the Code of Conduct for the purposes of the proposed law. It also favoured the suggestion that a breach of the Code of Conduct could be treated as misbehaviour.

While the constitution of the National Judicial Council is a positive development in the direction of ensuring greater judicial accountability, the composition of the Council needs to be broad-based, and its powers enhanced so that it can exercise the necessary oversight of the judiciary. It is necessary to ensure that only candidates of the highest integrity and ability are appointed to these courts, and that, once appointed, they perform their duties with the highest standards of integrity, honesty, dedication and competence. This requires most meticulous scrutiny at the time of appointment. Such scrutiny would be ensured if the National Judicial Council has representation from the Executive, the Legislature, and the Judiciary. As pointed out, the impeachment process for removing **errant**[10] judges has failed.

Given the vital position of higher courts in our constitutional scheme, and the critical role higher courts are playing to correct the distortions in the functioning of other institutions and organs of state, it is of paramount importance to ensure both competence and integrity in the higher judiciary. The appointment of judges in higher courts should be with the participation of the Executive, Legislature, and the Chief Justice, and it should be a bipartisan process above day-to-day politics.

Therefore, the proposed National Judicial Council should comprise representatives of all three organs of the State - the Legislature, the Judiciary and the Executive. Such a body can devise its own procedures in identifying and screening the candidates for the higher judiciary. The NJC should be entrusted with the responsibility of recommending removal of judges of higher courts. Such recommendations should be binding on the President, and Articles 124 and 217 of the Constitution should be amended accordingly. This revised procedure for the removal of judges is necessitated by the failure of the impeachment process in India.

According to Article II, Section 4 of the US Constitution, the President, Vice President and all civil officers of the United States shall be removed from office or impeachment for, and conviction of treason, bribery or other high crimes and misdemeanours. So far, 17 federal officials, including two Presidents, one Cabinet officer, one senator and 13 federal judges have faced impeachment proceedings. While the two Presidents, Andrew Johnson and Bill Clinton were acquitted, one other President, Richard Nixon chose to resign in the face of certain impeachment and removal.

[10]**Errant:** lawbreaking, offending

The preponderance of judges among those who faced impeachment is evident in the US. Out of the 13 judges who were impeached, 9 were removed from office, and 4 were acquitted. Thus, the impeachment process worked satisfactorily in the US. But the failure of the impeachment process in India, as well as the inability of the system to address serious questions of probity in the judiciary necessitate a revised, transparent, accountable, and a bipartisan process for enquiry into judicial misconduct and removal of judges.

Simultaneously, changes would also have to made in the Judges (Inquiry) Act, 1968. The creation of such a council will require changes in three places in the existing laws. Any change in the process of appointment to the Supreme Court will require that Article 124 of the Constitution be amended to provide for a National Judicial Council. A similar amendment will have to be made to Article 217. Also, since the Council is to have the authority to oversee and discipline judges, further changes will need to be made to Article 217.

4.1 Restatement of Values of Judicial Life

At the Chief Justices' Conference held in New Delhi in September 1992, it was decided that there was a need to reaffirm the pre-existing and universally accepted norms, guidelines, and conventions.

Therefore, the restatement of the pre-existing and universally accepted norms, guidelines, and conventions called 'Restatement of Values of Judicial Life' was prepared, and this serves as a guide to be observed by judges.

This is very essential for a strong and independent judiciary, indispensable in the impartial administration of justice. This has been considered in the Full Court Meeting of the Supreme Court of India on May 7, 1997, and has been adopted for due observance. The 'Restatement of Values of Judicial Life' is a comprehensive, but not exhaustive code of ethics.

- **Restatement of Values of Judicial Life**
  1. Justice must not only be done but must also appear to be done. Judges' behaviour must uphold public confidence in judicial impartiality, avoiding actions that undermine this perception.
  2. Judges should not contest or hold elective positions in clubs, societies, or associations, except those related to law.
  3. Judges must avoid close associations with individual members of the Bar, especially those practicing in their court.
  4. Judges must ensure no immediate family member, such as a spouse, children, or in-laws, who are members of the Bar, appears before them, or is involved in their cases.
  5. Judges must prohibit family members who are lawyers from using their residence or facilities for professional work.

6. Judges should maintain a level of detachment consistent with the dignity of their office.
7. Judges must not preside over matters involving their family, close relations, or friends.
8. Judges should avoid public debates or expressing opinions on political issues or pending judicial matters.
9. Judges should let their judgements speak for themselves and refrain from media interviews.
10. Judges must not accept gifts or hospitality except from close family or friends.
11. Judges should not hear cases involving companies in which they hold shares unless they disclose their interest, and no objections are raised.
12. Judges must not speculate in shares, stocks, or similar investments.
13. Judges must not engage in trade or business, directly or indirectly, except for publishing legal works or hobbies not amounting to business.
14. Judges should not solicit or associate with fundraising activities.
15. Judges must not seek financial benefits tied to their office unless clearly permissible, resolving any doubts through the Chief Justice.
16. Judges must remain conscious of public scrutiny and avoid actions that diminish the dignity of their office.

5. ETHICAL FRAMEWORK FOR CIVIL SERVANTS

The Committee on Prevention of Corruption (Santhanam Committee, 1964) had remarked: 'For a country like India, development of her material resources and raising the standards of life of all classes are, indeed imperative. At the same time, the deterioration in the standards of public life has to be arrested. Ways and means have to be found to ensure that idealism and patriotism have the proper place in the ambition of our youth. The lack of moral public service values and ethics in public administration earnestness, which has been a conspicuous feature of recent years, is perhaps the greatest single factor which hampers the growth of strong traditions of integrity and efficiency.'

The inculcation of values facilitating the subordination of the self to a larger, societal good and engendering a spirit of empathy for those in need of ameliorative state interventions are not skills which could be easily imbibed after joining the civil services. Such attitudes need nurturing over not merely individual lifetimes, but through successive generations – the 'right' ethos takes long to evolve. Nevertheless, it must be accepted that our civil service system has a tradition of attitudes and achievements which sets examples to be emulated by current and prospective civil servants. It must also be accepted that the existing framework for maintaining and promoting the norms of 'right conduct' cannot be enforced through a rigid mindless enforcement of laws and rules.

It is all a question of striking the right balance. Within the civil services there are formal, enforceable codes setting out norms of expected behaviour, with 'sanctions' prescribed for unacceptable departures from such norms. There are also inchoate conventions of propriety and acceptable behaviour without formal sanctions, but with non-observance of such practices and conventions attracting social disapproval and stigma. The current set of 'enforceable norms' are 'Conduct Rules', typified by the Central Civil Services (Conduct) Rules – 1964, and analogous rules applicable to members of the All-India Services or employees of various state governments.

The norms prescribed in such rules are much older than the rules themselves. Thus, specific acts were proscribed from time-to-time through notifications under the fundamental rules and the civil service regulations. Some examples are the disapproval of habitual lending and indiscriminate borrowing (1869), and the banning of various actions – accepting gifts (1876), buying and selling property (1881), making commercial investments (1885), promoting companies (1885), and accepting commercial employment after retirement (1920). The breach of such prohibitions entailed punitive actions like removal from service. There were, of course, provisions like 'illegal gratification' or bribery – Sections 161 to 165 of the IPC, or 'criminal breach of trust by a public servant' – Section 409 IPC, which provide terms of imprisonment.

In 1947, with the enactment of the Prevention of Corruption Act, a new set of offences was also created. In the 1930s, a compendium of instructions containing 'dos and don'ts' was issued, and was collectively called the 'Conduct Rules'. The compendium was converted in the form of distinct rules in 1955. The Santhanam Committee recommended considerable enlargement of such rules resulting in the 1964 version. These rules have subsequently been updated to include additional norms of behaviour.

Some of the additions are the requirement of observing courtesy, prohibiting demanding and accepting dowry, prohibiting sexual harassment of women employees, and, recently, prohibition to employ children below 14 years of age as domestic help. This is understandably a continuing process, and reflects the changing, often increasing expectations of society from the civil services. The code of behaviour as enunciated in the Conduct Rules, while containing some general norms like 'maintaining integrity and absolute devotion to duty' and not indulging in 'conduct unbecoming of a government servant', is generally directed towards cataloguing specific activities deemed undesirable for government servants. There is no code of ethics prescribed for civil servants in India, although such codes exist in other countries.

What we have in India are several Conduct Rules, which prohibit a set of common activities. These Conduct Rules do serve a purpose, but they do not constitute a Code of Ethics. There is, of late, a concern that more 'generic norms' need to be added to the list of accepted conduct. In this context, a conflict of interest is an important area which should be adequately addressed in these codes. It is necessary to build safeguards to prevent a conflict of interest. A draft 'Public Service Bill' under consideration of the Ministry of Personnel, Public Grievances, and Pensions seeks to lay down a number of generic expectations from civil servants, which are referred to as 'values'.

- **The salient 'values' envisaged in the Bill are:**
    - Allegiance to the various ideals enshrined in the Preamble to the Constitution,
    - Apolitical functioning,
    - Good governance for betterment of the people to be the primary goal of civil service,
    - Duty to act objectively and impartially,
    - Accountability and transparency in decision-making,
    - Maintenance of the highest ethical standards,
    - Merit to be the criteria in selection of civil servants made consistent, however, with the cultural, ethnic and other diversities of the nation,
    - Ensuring economy and avoidance of wastage in expenditure,
    - Provision of healthy and congenial work environment, and
    - Communication, consultation, and cooperation in performance of functions, i.e., participation of all levels of personnel in management.

The draft Bill also envisages a Public Service Code and a Public Service Management Code, laying down more specific duties and responsibilities. Violation of the Code would invite punishments akin to the current major and minor penalties by the heads of institutions/organisations. A Public Service Authority is also envisaged to oversee implementation of the Code and the values indicated above, and to render advice in the matter of the values and the Code. The various issues discussed above are not significant only for the civil services., but they are also important for all segments of the bureaucracy, and, equally so, for all local bodies and their employees.

After the 73rd and the 74th Amendments of the Constitution, the local bodies now have an important role to play in the nation's development and have major executive powers. It is essential that the need for relevant codes for these bodies and their employees, and for any public authority, is recognised. In 1999, the Government of Australia enacted the Australian Public Service Act, which prescribes a set of Public Service Values. These are not merely aspirational statements of intent, but all employees are expected to uphold these values and comply with the Code, even as senior executives are expected to promote these values.

Interestingly, the Public Service Commissioner is authorised to evaluate the extent to which agencies incorporate and uphold the values, and the adequacy of the systems and procedures required to ensure compliance with the Code. He has both statutory powers and policy responsibilities. These include an annual report to the Parliament on the state of the service, including an evaluation of the extent to which various agencies of the government have incorporated the values.

Therefore, there should be a set of Public Service Values which should be stipulated by law and as in the case of Australia, and there should be a mechanism to ensure that civil servants constantly aspire towards these values. The values prescribed in the draft Public Services Bill, 2006, is a step in the right direction. It has been noticed that normally codes of conduct are prescribed for a 'service'. Along with this, it would be desirable that organisations also prescribe codes of conduct. This is particularly true of organisations having public interface. The prevailing practice of nominating serving officers on the boards of public sector bodies may compromise with the desired objectivity and independence necessary for decision making in these bodies.

Also, the government is both the owner and the sovereign authority controlling the public undertaking. It would be unrealistic and imprudent for an official to sit in judgement of a decision taken by a board of which he is a member. There is a case for neither nominating nor permitting serving officers to be nominated on boards of public sector bodies since there could be a conflict of interest.

6. ETHICAL CONCERNS AND DILEMMA

6.1 Value Conflicts

Should the police be given access to the biometric information database collected through Aadhaar? Should surrogacy be banned? Should educational institutions and hospitals be banned from advertising? Should Indian railways be privatised? There is no one universal answer for such questions. The answers vary from person to person. Furthermore, for the same person trying to answer such questions does so, after considering several views within oneself. It is precisely this internal inconsistency that is called 'Value conflict'. Value conflict is a variation in opinions due to differences in long-cherished belief systems in present action scenario. Such conflicts cannot be resolved easily, as they are not based on objective facts but on individual's subjective beliefs and views.

The very nature of bureaucracy and the numerous and complicated tasks that public servants are engaged to more often result in value conflicts. Value conflicts are inevitable in a bureaucracy where multiple tasks are undertaken, involving several stakeholders. Rather than considering such conflicts as impediments to progress, they have to be seen as enriching the decision-making by bringing to table multiple values and alternative views. The real challenge to a bureaucrat is to manage conflicts and make decisions by considering different value sets and accommodating them harmoniously.

- **Reasons for Value Conflicts**

Value conflicts in public service are both historical and contemporary. The reasons for value conflicts in today's bureaucracy are:

1. The changing nature of state to a more welfare-oriented state, along with rising expectation of people towards the state leads to ushering in new values into the system.
2. Globalisation both in economical and socio-cultural terms has led to the import of multiple viewpoints, belief systems, perspectives and values.

3. All policy issues involve decision-making and judgements which are seldom value-neutral.
4. The ambiguity and open-ended nature of goals makes way for discretion in decision-making, and it is here that an individual's personal values come to play.
5. The inherent conflict to adapt to changes, and the need to maintain existing standards bring along value conflicts.
6. Value conflicts arise as a consequence of the need to respond to the growing expectations of the public, and the necessity to maintain efficient and effective service within the budget.
7. The changing nature of service delivery which includes the PPP model, engagement of NGOs and consultants leads to conflicts arising out of cooperation.
8. Religious and cultural values of individuals are not always in conformity with their professional and organisational values.
9. The demographic changes viz. the rising population, particularly the rise of aged people and the rise of working population puts enormous pressure on the state, changing the way it needs to work.
10. Introduction of new technologies leading to rise of new values of mechanisation, impersonal work culture, value neutrality, consumerism, etc.

- **Types of Value Conflicts**

The value conflicts can be broadly categorised under three types:

- Intrapersonal Value Conflicts
- Interpersonal Value Conflicts
- Individual–Organisational Value Conflicts

1. Intrapersonal Value Conflicts: Intrapersonal conflicts occur within an individual. The main reason being the competition and contradiction of multiple personal values. For example, a bureaucrat is often caught between being loyal to the boss and the organisation, and being rational in his decision-making. Resolution of such conflicts requires an extensive self-assessment of priorities and re-orientation of work towards achieving them.

2. Interpersonal Value Conflicts: Interpersonal value conflicts occur between individuals. This is due to the fact that various individuals are variously motivated, and have different objectives and ambitions. When they come together to work, they bring about a clash of values. For example, in an organisational hierarchy, the aspirations of the top-level management and the front-line employees are not the same. The former is highly concerned about the growth and development of the organisation, while the latter, occupying the base level of the organisational pyramid, is primarily focused on monetary gains.

3. Individual–Organisational Value Conflicts: Individual–organisational value conflicts occur between an individual and the organisation. The reason is divergence of values of the organisation and that of the individual. The individual does not always concur with the values of the organisation. For example, a trade union versus management conflict often surfaces when the demands of the employees are unheard, thereby leading to various strikes disrupting the functioning of the organisation/industry. Resolution of conflicts at an interpersonal level and an individual–organisational level requires a clear and unambiguous statement of values, and more importantly, a value-focused leader who would motivate and bring everyone together.

- **Typical Conflicts**

As a result of socialisation, which refers to the process of inheriting norms, customs, values, and ideologies from the family, school, peer group, society, etc., an individual develops a value system with certain skills and habits necessary for participating within their own society. Value building, though is a lifelong process, is often crystallised when a person attains a certain age, ranging between 25–26 years. This predestined value system is often immutable, and value conflict arises when the place of work demands the other way. Value conflicts occur when two values of similar force are present at the same time.

The following are few examples of values that can conflict with each other. Loyalty vs. honesty, efficiency vs. social stability, laissez-faire economy vs. accountability, competition vs. cooperation, individual responsibility vs. collective responsibility, transparency vs. privacy, freedom of speech vs. security, achievement vs. ascriptive, need to control vs. need for discretion, generosity vs. material success, equality vs. individualism, tradition vs. modernity, public servant vs. political servant, freedom of information vs. confidentiality.

1. Laissez–Faire Economy versus Accountability: The case of bitcoins, the 'virtual currency' or 'crypto currency' brought about the conflict between a laissez-faire economy and the need for accountability. It put forward the question as to whether the governments should abstain from controlling this virtual currency. While some advocated for complete freedom in the production, distribution, and management of money to end the monopoly of central banks, others called for a ban on such virtual currencies for a lack of control and accountability. The lack of accountability resulted in black marketing and money laundering of bitcoins, and emerged as a menace at the global level.

2. Freedom of Speech versus Security: The one-day ban on the famous news channel NDTV for revealing the sensitive details about the Pathankot attack is a recent example of freedom of speech (media) versus national security. This was the first time ever that a news channel was barred from broadcasting for breaching the national security laws in the country. While the government has defended the ban in the interest of national security, the Editors Guild of India has condemned it as a violation of the freedom of media.

3. Public Servant versus Political Servant: Frequent transfers (47 times in 25 years) faced by a senior IAS officer of Haryana cadre Mr. Ashok Khemka is an ideal example of such typical conflict. Mr. Khemka, whose actions has got the attention when he cancelled the mutation of a 58-crore land deal between Congress president Sonia Gandhi's son-in-law Robert Vadra and realty giant DLF, and ordered a probe into the controversial land deals done by Vadra in Haryana. He was hounded by the previous Congress government in Haryana headed by Bhupinder Singh Hooda for this action. He has received death threats for his crusade against corruption, and his frequent transfers portray the attitude of the political bosses.

4. Freedom of Information versus Confidentiality: The individual responsible for one of the most significant leaks in US political history, Edward Snowden, the former technical assistant for the Central Intelligence Agency of USA is responsible for handing over material from one of the world's most secretive organisations – the National Security Agency. Emerged as the whistleblower that does not fear the consequences of going public, he said, "*I am not afraid, because this is the choice I've made.*" He exposed the ethical and legal concerns of the sting operation, and alarmed how privacy is in peril in the present-day world.

• Challenges to Values in Public Service

Value conflicts occur at all levels of public service. However, there are specific challenges that the bureaucracy faces in contemporary governance, namely:

1. New Public Management and Pro-Market Reforms,
2. Politicisation of the Civil Services,
3. Technology Boom,
4. Decentralisation and Delegation, and
5. Changes in Personnel Administration

1. New Public Management and Pro-Market Reforms: The 1980's and early 1990's saw dramatic changes in the world order. The end of cold war brought about the disintegration of USSR, and also ended the reign of communism. This period saw the emergence of a new model of governance, which widely promoted market interest. It is this new model which came to be variously called as the New Public Management or Pro-Market Administration, or entrepreneurial government, etc.

This period saw the expansion of philosophies of capitalism by promotion of the principles of liberalisation, privatisation and globalisation. The values of efficiency, economy, and effectiveness became the cardinal values of this new model of governance. As a consequence, the interaction between the state and its citizens underwent a sea of change. There is a change from 'government to governance' which present challenges to values of public servants.

The increasing interactions and cooperation between the state and private players, rising the PPP model of governance, and engagement of NGOs has swept aside traditional values of governance, such as hierarchy of authority and control, impersonality, meritocracy, unity of command, unidirectional command structures, etc. Governance in contemporary times has grown beyond the government, and as such policymaking and implementation, which hitherto was the domain of the state, now entails private players, international organisations, civil society, NGOs and citizens. This has led to a shift from state-centred governance to networked governance to ensure control, and fix accountability. This fragmentation of the single unified structure has led to stretching of the capacity and applicability of value systems, which was the core of state-centred governance.

The last two decades saw a shift towards market-based economy. 'Consumer to customer' has been the call word for this market of rationalism-based economic reforms. The policies adopted clearly called for separation policy formulation structures from policy implementation structures. The rolling back of the state by pruning bureaucracy has been favoured to encourage greater private participation and third party involvement. This has certainly posed challenges to public service loyalty and integrity. From effectiveness and pro-public functioning, the shift is towards economy and efficiency. The state-owned commercial enterprises and duties are more than just making profit, whereas private commercial enterprises are solely profit-oriented. Such new values emerging as a result of pro-market reforms are challenging the values of public service.

2. Politicisation of Civil Services: Who should a public servant be loyal to?

(a) Public
(b) Colleagues
(c) Politicians
(d) All the above.

It is in this complicated environment that a bureaucrat constantly works. Loyalty conflicts are inherently part of the bureaucratic system, and this raises the question of applicability of values to public servants. When a situation arises where does the loyalty of a bureaucrat lie? The bureaucrat, for one reason or other, is forced to serve the political purposes at the cost of public good.

3. Technology Boom: There is a clear difference between how a person responds to another person and a computer responds to a person. An individual can differentiate between the rich and the poor, and can make a decision accordingly. In other words, a person will have compassion and will be able to empathise. On the contrary, a computer, in the name of 'value neutrality', cannot differentiate between the wealthy and the needy. The very basic value of public service – being a champion of the poor is challenged by technology today.

4. Decentralisation and Delegation: With rising workload and complexities of work, decentralisation and delegation has become the norm. This has led to the development of sub-cultures and values that are in conflict with the values of the parent organisation. Often, it is the parent organisation of the head office that formulates the policies which are mostly oriented towards public values or welfare. The lack of shared values between the field office and the head office is the biggest challenge that the contemporary administration faces.

5. Changes in Personnel Administration: Today, one sees the dependency on technocrats and specialists for governance. The challenge is inculcation of public service values among such specialists and private players. With respect to traditional public servants, the public service values are inculcated and reinforced because of their constant and long exposure to those values as part of their job. Unfortunately, the specialists and technocrats' association with the state is for a very limited amount of time, which is clearly insufficient to inculcate public service values.

Value conflict is a difference of opinion created by differences in long-held beliefs, and the conflict cannot be easily resolved with facts, because the differences are belief-based and not fact-based. It is the value system of an individual that enables better decision-making, which is considered as a very important personality trait of a bureaucrat. The manifestation of better decisions is the result of better characterisation shaped by the innate values.

Value conflict has a positive side as well. When a conflict arises different values along with different options are surfaced. Therefore, for addressing a particular issue such options are inevitable. Such value conflicts therefore help to take better decisions. Resolving value conflicts would only strengthen the values held dear by a person. Furthermore, as one moves from one conflict to another, their decision-making ability matures and allowing them to easily arrive at decisions.

6.2 Conflict of Interest

A conflict of interest involves a conflict between the public duty and the private interest of a public official, in which the official's private capacity interest could improperly influence the performance of their official duties and responsibilities. When a person, in his official capacity, is been influenced by any other considerations, which may at times reduce his efficiency, leading to conflict of interest. Conflict of interest can arise among civil servants, politicians, lawyer, physician, etc. It may exist irrespective of the consequence of it, may it be ethical or unethical. The conflict of interest in an administrative system eventually leads to abuse of the public office, thereby resulting in a breach of trust.

- **Forms of 'Conflict of Interest'**

1. Self-Dealing: When a person, who works for the government and also owns a private business, and when there is a collision between both, he would be left with this type of conflict of interest. The paradox may impact the decision of the person, making him oriented towards the actions in which the 'benefit of oneself' is preferred over the benefit of common good.

2. Outside Employment: 'Outside employment' refers to any paid activity that is performed in addition to the official responsibilities of a full-time employee. This conflict arises when the interest of a person in a private job contradicts his work for the government. A personal motive is preferred over the social motive, and material benefits gain priority, undermining the selflessness of the person.

3. Revolving Door Politics: The conflict of interest is quite common in a political scenario where the politicians and civil servants take the role of legislators and regulators. Revolving door lobbyists become politicians and vice versa, thereby framing the legislations and regulations according to their personal will, which has resulted in various scams in India over the past. Political analysts have claimed that the reciprocated privileges are always detrimental to the nation, and eventually lead to breach of law and morality.

4. Family Interests: A close relative, like a spouse or a child gets employed in a firm, or where the goods or services are purchased from such a relative, or a firm that is owned by relative, are faced with this type of conflicts. 'Blind trust' is a common problem which arises out of such interest. Abuse of this type of interest results in nepotism.

5. Favouritism:

> *'Nearly all men can stand adversity, but if you want to test a man's character give him power.'*
> **Abraham Lincoln**

It is a penchant of civil servants who are in the position to allocate or distribute state resources. It is generally practiced to extend one's position and wealth. It is a procedural problem with flawed qualification, and a lack of skill and efficiency.

It can be in the form of:

I. Clientelism,
II. Cronyism,
III. Nepotism.

I. Clientelism: It is a type of favouritism where a situation in which a public servant uses his authority to obtain favour for his own self, or his relatives, or friends, or any political party, or religious, or ethnic groups. It is a common **proclivity**[11] to favour kith and kin.

For example: In the M. C. Mehta vs. Kamal Nath case, it was observed that Kamal Nath used his power as the Minister of Environment and Forest to allot reserve forest land on the banks of river Beas to Span Motels Pvt. Ltd to build resorts. The resort was built by encroaching the forest land, and in the course of construction of the resort, the course of the river was changed, which led to flooding. The Supreme Court quashed the lease of the land to the resort, and directed the Himachal Pradesh government to reclaim and restore the forest land.

II. Cronyism: It is another type of favouritism where there is an abuse of power which in some way helps a private organisation due to partialism in the distribution of state resources.

For example: Vijay Mallya was accused of wilful default of loans that amounts to ₹7000 crore. The State Bank of India had alleged that funds were diverted several times from Kingfisher Airlines to various United Breweries Group companies and other firms. Mallya's Kingfisher is

---

[11]**Proclivity:** inclination, liking

among the top five wilful defaulters in the country, the others being Winsome Diamonds and Jewellery, Zoom Developers, Surya Vinayak Industries, and Deccan Chronicle Holdings.

The default has sent a strong message about the economic system characterised by close, mutually advantageous relationships between business leaders and government officials eventually leading to the loss of public and investor confidence, thereby affecting the nation as a whole. Raghuram Rajan, the former Governor of RBI said "*One of the greatest dangers to the growth of developing is the middle-income trap, where crony capitalism creates oligarchies that slow down growth.*"

III. Nepotism: It is a special form in which the office bearer who holds the right to make appointments favours his kinfolk family. It can also lead to a conflict in loyalties within an organisation.

For Example: The Aircel–Maxis controversy is an example of this type of favouritism. In 2006, Maxis, a Malaysian company, acquired Aircel by buying 74% of its stake. In 2011, Sivasankaran, the owner of Aircel, complained to the CBI that Dayanidi Maran had arm twisted him to sell his stakes to Maxis. The CBI report alleged that Maran received ₹549 crore for favouring Aircel, and the amount was allegedly received by a company owned by his brother Kalanithi Maran. This kind of practice, among those with power or influence, of favouring relatives or friends has resulted in various scams and corruption on a large scale, causing a huge loss to the government's exchequer.

- **Identifying a Conflict of Interest**

When work decisions come into collision with personal interests, it becomes inevitable, giving rise to a conflict of interest. Listed below are a few situations where conflict of interest may mushroom up:

1. When you start to doubt your confidence of acting impartially.
2. When you have a thought about what an honest person working with you actually thinks about you while performing your duties.
3. When you feel worried about your colleagues being aware of your personal connection with any private organisation during your decision-making processes.
4. When you feel insecure about the reputation that you have among your staff.

- **Sources of a Conflict of Interest**

1. Financial Interest: The preference to material prosperity is one of the biggest causes for financial conflict of interest. When a conflict arises over the duty for which the person is obliged to, and the work in which the person has an innate interest owing to its financial gains, it is the latter that is given priority. When there is a contradiction between a government and a private job, it is the latter that is preferred over the former in most of the cases due to its monetary benefits.

2. Professional Interest: Personal values are needed to be compromised in certain situations when the profession demands the other way. The objective vs. subjective morality is put to question when professional interests contradict with the personal interests.

For example, the physicians are subjected to take certain decisions professionally, even if they contradict with their personal interests in cases, such as euthanasia, abortion, etc. A similar situation can be seen when judges are subjected to confer a death penalty. It includes family, professional, and prejudicial interests as well. It is here that the value system of an individual determines the decisions to be made and actions to be taken by them. When there arises a conflict, it is the preference of a particular value over the other which impacts the decision-making and addresses the dilemma.

- **Principles for dealing with favouritism**
  1. Foster meritocracy by competitive and merit-based recruitment and performance appraisal-based promotion.
  2. Competition must be made transparent by ensuring that the vacancies are advertised publicly. and with all eligibility conditions and procedures of recruitment given in detail.
  3. Integrity must be upheld in case of sanctions for not complying with the procedures that are ought to be followed.
  4. It must be ensured that the qualified and unsuccessful candidates who, in their opinion, assume that proper procedure is not followed. should be given a chance to appeal to an independent authority.
  5. There must be a clear set of rules and proper regulations as to what public servant are permitted to get as gratuities or gifts during their course of employment, and the ways in which these gratuities can be recorded. The problem here is to differentiate in what constitutes a gift and a bribe. Gift is something that is offered in good faith, and when it tries to attempt to influence the official, it becomes a bribe. Bribes in general create a feeling of obligation, for example, a free meal or ticket to a sporting event or discounts on commercial purchases are sensed to create a feeling of obligation.
  6. The other method in which the integrity in public service can be maintained is by disclosing the asset and liability details of the public servant and his/her immediate relatives. This can be monitored by anti-corruption activists, media, and enforcement personnel to develop a fair regime of public officials.

There are many possible ways of creating an ethical infrastructure by the above means to control both the conflict of interest and corruption. Reform measures vary from place-to-place depending on the levels of corruption. A one size fits all approach does not apply here. The measure to be applied and an ethical regime to come up will take time. A public official can be concerned with the exercise of entrusted official power, with direct or indirect consequences for citizens.

The functional responsibilities of public officials should, therefore, be the primary focus of the organisation's conflict of interest policy, the relevant code of ethics/code of conduct, and the organisation's transparency and accountability mechanisms. Today, conflict and corruption are inevitable in an administrative setup. But combating it in the long run puts the onus on every individual to make the democracy more progressive and participative.

6.3 Ethical Dilemmas Faced by Public Servants

Public servants are confronted with many ethical dilemmas, some of the most common are:

- administrative discretion,
- corruption,
- nepotism,
- administrative secrecy,
- information leaks,
- public accountability, and
- policy dilemmas.

The above-mentioned potential areas of conflict are not necessarily ethical dilemmas in themselves. It is how the public servant reacts when he is confronted by activities pertaining to these phenomena that could prove to be the ethical dilemma:

1. How would they react when they find out that administrative discretion is abused, or that corruption or nepotism is practiced?
2. Should he blow the whistle?
3. Is actively engaging in pressure group activities because he sympathises with their views justifiable?
4. Should he actively participate in party politics?
5. Or should he endeavour only to promote the public good and uphold the high standards of the public office?

6.4 How to Solve an Ethical Dilemma?

Ethical dilemma does not offer a definite and obvious solution that would comply with all ethical norms, and it is the biggest challenge of an ethical dilemma. Throughout the history of humanity, philosophers have aimed and worked to find solutions to ethical dilemmas.

The following approaches to solve an ethical dilemma were deduced:

- **Refute the paradox (dilemma):** The situation must be carefully analysed and the existence of dilemma must be logically refuted.
- **Value theory approach:** Choose the alternative that offers the greater good or the lesser evil.
- **Find alternative solutions:** In some cases, the problem can be reconsidered, and new alternative solutions may arise.

When confronted with ethical dilemmas, such criteria should be used as to whether the public servant would be proud to tell their parents or grandparents about their decision, or whether they could sleep well at night and face themselves in the mirror in the morning. They should often rely on their own personal integrity in making ethical decisions. It is not always easy to know what to do.

The following guidelines will not tell exactly what to do, but within the context, they will help one to evaluate the situation more clearly by examining their own values and those required. Answering the following questions encourage deep reflection on the social and ethical implications of one's actions:

1. Is the problem or dilemma as it seems? If uncertain, investigate further.
2. Is the contemplated action legal and ethical? If unsure, clarify.
3. How will this action affect your self-perception?
4. Have you understood and considered the perspective of those who oppose this action? Is their stance reasonable?
5. Who will benefit or suffer from this action? To what extent and for how long?
6. Would you be comfortable if others acted in the same way?
7. Have you consulted knowledgeable and objective individuals, including experts, on this matter?
8. Would it embarrass you if your actions were revealed to friends, family, coworkers, or superiors?

Understanding ethical dilemmas are especially more significant in professional life of a public servant. Not being able to determine the optimal solution to such dilemmas in a professional setting may result in very serious consequences for the society at large. In order to solve ethical problems, strict ethical standards should be developed. In addition, public servants should be provided strong and quality ethical training to resolve ethical dilemmas efficiently.

In an era marked by global complexities and rapid changes, ethical leadership has emerged as a cornerstone for sustainable governance.

7. ACCOUNTABILITY AND ETHICAL GOVERNANCE

Values in bureaucracy, though is gaining prominence in current times, it was given due importance from ancient period itself. Kautilya's *Arthashastra* gives an elaborate and detailed instructions to the emperor-king based on implicit values which were held cardinal by the society. Kautilya by the 'Law of the Fish' or *Matsya Nyaya*, stresses the importance of welfarist and pro-social attitude, which should guide the administrators. *Arthashastra* and later *Dharmashastra* became the core of the value systems guiding the administration until the beginning of Muslim rule in India.

The beginning of Muslim rule in India brought about a shake-up in the values that guided the administrators. The highly centralised and paternalistic administration which particularly strengthened during the Mughal Empire was inward looking.

The centralisation was on account of lack of trust and insecurity of the rulers. The *Mansabdari* system bred nepotism and gave importance to unconditional and unquestioning loyalty towards the King and the State. However, the most negative impact of the Mughal administration was the importance that was given to grand ceremonies. The ceremonies were used as a tool to showcase their strength and prestige, and thereby subdue and suppress the masses. The British who came later also adopted this mechanism, and used it as a weapon in Indian administration.

The arrival of the British in India brought about a paradigm shift in the administrative setup of India. The British established the steel framework of Indian bureaucracy as we see today. Their rule led to the establishment of most of the behavioural values of Indian bureaucracy. They reinvented the Office of District Overlord, *Mansabdari* which became decadent by then. This reinvention endowed the Office with rationality and modernity. This was done by codification of laws and competitive examination-based recruitment.

British elitist and gentlemanly ethics formed the basis of Indian Civil Services values. The British never intended to permanently settle in India. The two societies were different in their race, culture, practices, and social structure. Directly ruling the natives without getting assimilated into the society proved to be a tough task. In such a scenario, they adopted the only way out—a class of professionals and regular-salaried employees in the middle and lower levels of administration. There arose a middle class, which took advantage of the opportunities presented by the new administrative system.

This newly formed middle class of civil servants were imitative in character. They imitated the customs, mannerisms, practices, principles, habits, and philosophies of the British rulers. It is through this imitation, the values such as high—handedness, paternalistic benevolence, ivory tower attitude and god complex got entrenched into the Indian Civil Services. They worked for the organisation loyally to maximise the profits of the organisation, namely the British, and to maximise their own budgets which popularly came to be called 'Bureaupathic behaviour'.

Challenges Faced by Bureaucrats

- **Unsupportive Environment:** Dealing with the difference of opinion with the co-workers often presents a challenge to the bureaucrats. An office environment becomes hostile when there is an abuse of power, unfairness in decisions and lack of cooperation with the co-workers, which in turn, leads to a lack of effectiveness and reduced productivity. Bureaucrats need to act with professionalism and integrity to cope with these environments. In situations where there is q lack of support from their co-workers, bureaucrats need to involve like-minded people in their close circles and identify possible solutions.

  Bureaucrats can involve in conversation with the senior staffs and explain the situation to them. An environment that involves people with similar ambitions and goals will lead to a stable path towards achieving the needs of the society, and also improve the efficiency of work.

- **Temptation of Rewards:** Urban postings often offer better amenities, while rural postings lack basic facilities, leading to dissatisfaction. A bureaucrat posted in an urban area will have access to first class services, such as fine-dine restaurants, club houses, top schools, and colleges for their children etc., while the ones posted at rural place would have to contend with fluorine concentrated water and locally available vegetables and grains.
  While one discharges functions from a cushioned throne, the other discharges from a thorn throne. Posting at a remote and inconvenient place acts as a demotivating factor to a bureaucrat. These inherently systemic variations make the bureaucrat less interested and unfocused in the functions he performs. He often engages in siding with political bosses, tolerating corruption, and flattering seniors with gifts to secure lucrative and desirable postings.
- **Managing Nonprofessional Employees:** The present administrative system, which is a British legacy, follows a common competitive examination to recruit IAS officers, which is conducted by the UPSC. This evaluates the candidate's general knowledge, which involves having a basic understanding of a wide range of topics. Specialised knowledge is assessed for officers in departments like health, agriculture, transport, public works, irrigation, etc., which are usually headed by generalist I.A.S. officers. This has created two categories of bureaucrats, viz.; 'Generalists' and 'Specialists', and has resulted in a kind of ill-feeling between the two. It is high time in India that we do away with the generalist character of recruitment of bureaucracy. This is considered to be one of the foremost reasons for the failure of DRDO, the government organisation which has not seen the fruits of success over years. Most often being compared with ISRO, the main difference lies in the professionalism where ISRO is dominated by specialists in its own field, and has tasted a lot of success.
- **Hostile Leadership:** Leadership plays an important role in the way a system functions. Proactive bureaucrats often lack support from their senior officers, who may view them as threats. This undermines innovation, creates a toxic environment, and hampers the overall system efficiency.
- **Everyone is Expendable:** Bureaucrats, as generalists, face constant uncertainty with promotions, transfers, and other disruptions. The fear of repercussions fosters risk-aversion and a tendency to conform, often leading to corruption and inefficiency.
- **Delaying Tactics to Avoid Responsibility:** Bureaucrats, under external and internal pressures, may procrastinate to avoid responsibility. Unrealistic promises, poor planning, inadequate resources, and favouritism demands contribute to delays, compromising accountability.
- **Colleague or Enemy:** Competition, jealousy, and fear of being replaced foster mistrust among bureaucrats. Pressure from political bosses and the fear of transfers force them to prioritise survival over collaboration.
- **Earning Hostility:** When the administrators resist doing anything in favour of his family, friends, caste groups, their immediate bosses, and colleagues, they earn hostility. This in

turn affects the mental faculties of the administrators, which causes them to be abusive with their staffs and be rude to their co-workers. When he is abusive to his staffs, this also may create a sense dissatisfaction and hostility from his staffs, which finally leads to the overall failure of the machinery.

7.1 Significance of Accountability and Ethical Governance

As there is an increasing crisis of legitimacy, ethics and accountability constitute significant elements for the government at present. Progressively, it has also been realised that this crisis will not be resolved by performance management alone, and ethical responsible behaviour is expected from politicians and public servants. The responsibility of the public officers have been enhanced through devolution and decentralisation processes.

Demands for integrity have been raised with the increasing interaction between the public and the private sector. With these developments, it is now very crucial to apprise the ethical system. Broadly speaking, accountability exists when there is an individual or body, and the performance of functions or tasks by that individual or body are subject to another's oversight, direction, or request that they provide information or justification for their actions.

In the arena of ethics, accountability is answerability, liability, and the expectation of account-giving. Answerability is considered as the obligation of the government and public officials to justify their actions and decisions to the public and to those tasked with providing oversight. For preventing the abuse of power and for ensuring that the power is directed towards efficiency, effectiveness, responsiveness, and transparency, accountability is a crucial and fundamental requirement.

Accountability is very significant for good governance. Appraising the ongoing effectiveness of public officials or public bodies ensures that they are performing to their full potential, being responsive to the community they are meant to be serving, and instilling a sense of confidence in the government.

The community must be able to trust the integrity of the civil service's decision-making process as civil servants are entrusted with special responsibilities, and take decisions that affect the citizen's life. Civil executives are expected to be responsive, impartial and uphold high standards of professionalism. Holders of public office must necessarily stay accountable for their decisions and actions to the public, and must be ready to submit themselves to whatever scrutiny is appropriate to the office they hold.

Accomplishment of ethical standards in the governance system is assisted by effective accountability as accountability and ethics are strongly related. People's representatives are provided ample opportunities to raise, among other things, issues of ethics and morality in the governance system. For instance, the Public Accounts Committee, which gives its comments on the report of the Comptroller and Auditor General, raises matters that directly or indirectly relate to ethics and good governance.

Good Governance acts as a comprehensive framework for administrative and civil service reforms. A well-functioning, efficient, and ethical governance aids in fostering good policy-making, ensuring effective service delivery, promoting accountability and responsibility in utilising public resources, which are the elements of good governance.

8. STRENGTHENING ETHICAL AND MORAL VALUES IN GOVERNANCE

Despite over 75 years since independence, there have been glaring lacunas in the effective public service delivery on part of administration. This is visible by means of being unable to achieve policy targets and the ineffective nature of policy programmes, such as poverty eradication, housing for all, etc. The most important reasons associated with these are corruption, bureaucratic lethargy, maladministration, and the such. Various committees have been formed, and administrative commissions have been appointed to bring about ethical values in to the administration. Mentioned below are some of the suggestions extracted from various committees and commissions:

1. Capacity building in the anti-corruption agencies should be assured through training, and by associating the required experts during enquiries/investigations.
2. There should be a profiling of officers. The capabilities, professional competence, integrity, and reputation of every government servant must be charted out and brought on record.
3. School awareness programmes should be introduced, highlighting the importance of ethics, and how corruption can be combated.
4. All offices having large public interfaces should have an online complaint tracking system. If possible, this task of complaint tracking should be outsourced.
5. There should be an external periodic mechanism of audit of complaints in offices having large public interfaces.
6. Each office should make an annual public statement regarding their pending audit queries.
7. Whistleblowers exposing false claims, fraud, or corruption should be protected by ensuring confidentiality and anonymity, protection from victimisation in their career and other administrative measures to prevent bodily harm and harassment.
8. In addition to imposing penalties in criminal cases, the law should hold public servants accountable for any loss they cause to the state or citizens through corrupt acts. They should be required to compensate for the loss incurred and also be liable to pay damages.
9. The Citizen's Charter must incorporate the fundamental ethical principles and specific attitudes which are to be present in every civil servant.

10. The Citizen's Charter should be made legally enforceable, which would then curtail discretion.
11. Integrity testing as a measure to check corruption and maladministration should be put in place.
12. A national database containing the details of all corruption cases at all levels should be created. This database should be in the public domain.
13. Citizens may be involved in the assessment and maintenance of ethics in important government institutions and offices.
14. Annual Property Return (APR) of all public servants be put on the website.
15. Each department of the government should develop an internal evaluation mechanism on the basis of clearly laid down parameters. The result of such evaluation should be made part of the Annual Administration Report. Departments should be held accountable for the outcomes, and there should be a sharp focus on the service delivery.
16. To provide a clean, honest, and transparent government, antiquated rules and procedures in the government must be discarded, and new simplified ones must be put in place.
17. Ethical standards for civil servants should be made clear and lucid. Civil servants are required to be familiar with the basic principles and standards that they have to apply to their work.
18. The code of ethics should enable the civil servant to distinguish between acceptable behaviour and unacceptable behaviour.
19. The legal framework should reflect ethical standards. It should contain the minimum obligatory standards and principles of behaviour for every civil servant.
20. The legal framework should state the basic values of public service, and should also provide a mechanism for guidance, investigation, disciplinary action, and prosecution.
21. Laws should be enacted in such a way that the reasons behind a bureaucrat's decision are expressly noted and revealed.
22. The ethics audit as part of the annual audit should be put in place.
23. Systemic threats that weaken the ethical values should be first identified and addressed accordingly.
24. Apart from general threats, specific threats to ethics, the standards and integrity of civil servants should be anticipated, and appropriate responses must be prepared.
25. Statutory Vigilance Commissions on the lines of the CVC should come into existence in all the states.
26. Performance appraisal and management methods which would strengthen the ethical values in civil services should be adopted.

? Thought Box

How can leaders balance ethical principles with the political realities of governance, such as competing interests and resource constraints?

27. The external and internal complaint and redressal system must be robust and swift.
28. Training and development in rational decision-making should include the code of ethics as a component.
29. Not just making and publishing the code of ethics, but there should be an enforceable code of ethics which should be harmoniously linked to practices and procedures in the organisation.
30. The code of ethics should be given a statutory status.
31. Training should be given to civil servants which increases their technical competence to identify ethical problems. Only upon identification of problems can they be redressed.
32. The code of ethics should not only set out the principles which are to be maintained, but it should also provide for how these principles are to be applied.
33. Apart from the general code of ethics, specific codes of conduct for various organisations and various circumstances should be enforced, as the problems faced by a police officer would be very different from that of a teacher.
34. To secure speedy disposal of disciplinary inquiries – both pending ones and those that will arise in future – there is a requirement of the availability of Inquiry Officers who have the background, time and willingness to take up the task. Keeping in view the spread of senior government servants, the Government of India may undertake preparations for a panel of retired officers of competence and reputation for integrity, fairness and objectivity to be appointed as Inquiry Officers or as Presenting Officers.
35. For other major cities in the country, various departments/ministries should prepare similar panels of retired officers. The Central Board of Direct Taxes, for example, could have a panel for places with large presence of senior officers, while the Department of Posts could have a panel where the Post Masters General is located. Other organisations and departments of the Central Government may act also in a similar manner to prepare panels of retired officers to act as Inquiry Officers or Presenting Officers.

9. ETHICS, SOCIAL RESPONSIBILITY, AND GOVERNANCE: THE TRIFECTA FOR SUSTAINABLE PROGRESS

These three pillars form an interdependent ecosystem in an interconnected world and shapes the trajectory of nations and organisations. They also define the essence of humanity's collective journey towards a fair, just, and equitable future.

Ethics: Ethics, as the moral compass of individuals and institutions, plays a crucial role in steering decision-making, and helps in distinguishing right from wrong. In governance, ethical considerations emphasise transparency, integrity, and the greater good by transcending political manoeuvring. To ensure that leaders and organisations remain accountable to their stakeholders and maintain public trust, upholding ethical principles is extremely crucial. Governance can become a vessel adrift in stormy seas, swayed by short-term gains and personal ambitions without ethics.

Social Responsibility: Social responsibility transcends profits and extends to the impact an entity has on the society at large as it bridges the gaps and fosters inclusion. Individuals, corporations, and governments alike bear a responsibility to address social and environmental challenges. With social responsibility, there will be more investments in education, healthcare, poverty alleviation, and environmental sustainability thereby contributing to inclusive growth. It reflects a commitment to humanity's shared welfare.

Governance: Effective governance incorporates ethics and social responsibility into its framework, ensuring that decisions serve both immediate needs and long-term goals. It requires transparent structures, efficient processes, and the cultivation of trust between leaders and the governed.

Ethics, social responsibility and governance are not merely theoretical concepts; they represent more than that, and constitute the essence of a world striving for holistic progress and development. These pillars provide the foundation upon which just societies and successful organisations are built. Nurturing this triad is not just a choice, but a responsibility that shapes the destiny of generations to come. In a world teeming with possibilities, the convergence of ethics, social responsibility and governance illuminates the path towards a brighter, more sustainable future.

SUMMARY

- A democracy relies not just on laws, but on the ethical conduct of public servants, whose accountability and morality sustain trust and governance.
- Gandhi saw politics as a moral endeavour to awaken conscience and fight exploitation. He stressed that *Swaraj* should purify civilisation, warning that politics without principles leads to decay.
- Machiavelli, in *The Prince*, separated ethics from politics, asserting that a ruler's goal is to gain and retain power, unbound by moral or religious concerns.
- Despite constitutional ideals, crime in politics has been an issue since 1952, driven by the nexus between politicians and criminals.
- Factors include money and muscle power, caste, religion, a weak justice system, corruption, and public tolerance.
- Criminalisation fosters corruption, violence, and economic harm, it erodes democracy and pressures key institutions, undermining their impartiality.
- Financial resources dominate elections. While reforms like state funding and transparency have been suggested, implementation remains a challenge.

- Transparent political funding can be achieved through electoral trusts, grassroots contributions, and corporate donations.
- Indian coalitions, often formed for power rather than a shared ideology, face conflicts, governance issues, and weakened leadership.
- Social media amplifies voices and movements, but also spreads misinformation, hate speeches, and divisive propaganda, raising concerns about privacy and political manipulation.
- Social identities like caste, religion, and ethnicity shape political dynamics, empowering marginalised groups to demand their rights.
- Conflicts arise from deeply held belief systems, which are subjective and resistant to resolution through objective facts.
- Value conflicts in bureaucracy stem from the evolving welfare-oriented role of the state, globalisation, and rising public expectations, which introduce diverse values and challenges. Factors such as policy ambiguity, personal beliefs, demographic shifts, technological advancements, and changing service delivery models further complicate decision-making and service efficiency.
- The value conflicts can be broadly categorised under three types: (a) Intrapersonal Value Conflicts (b) Interpersonal Value Conflicts (c) Individual–Organisational Value Conflicts.
- Challenges to public service values: (a) New Public Management and Pro-Market Reforms (b) Politicisation of Civil Services (c) Technology Boom (d) Decentralisation and Delegation (e) Changes in Personnel Administration.
- A clash arises when a public official's private interests risk influencing their public duties.
- Forms of conflict of interest: (a) Self-Dealing (b) Outside Employment (c) Revolving Door Politics (d) Family Interests (e) Favouritism.
- Sources of conflict of interest: (a) Financial Interest (b) Professional Interest (c) Personal Interest.
- Significance of accountability ensures officials meet their potential, respond to community needs, and bolster public confidence in governance.

PREVIOUS YEARS' QUESTIONS

1. It is believed that adherence to ethics in human actions would ensure smooth functioning of an organisation/system. If so, what does ethics seek to promote in human life? How do ethical values assist in the resolution of conflicts faced by an individual in their day-to-day functioning?
UPSC CSE Mains 2022
2. Explain the process of resolving ethical dilemmas in public administration.
UPSC CSE Mains 2018
3. What is mean by 'conflict of interest'? Illustrate with examples the difference between the actual and potential conflicts of interest. *UPSC CSE Mains 2018*
4. Young people with ethical conduct are not willing to come forward to join active politics. Suggest steps to motivate them to come forward. *UPSC CSE Mains 2017*

5. A conflict of interest in the public sector arises when(a) official duties, (b) public interests, and (c) personal interests are taking priority one above the other. How can this conflict in administration be resolved? Describe with an example. *UPSC CSE Mains 2017*
6. What do you understand by the terms 'governance', 'good governance', and 'ethical governance'? *UPSC CSE Mains 2016*
7. Public servants are likely to confront with the issues of 'Conflict of Interest.' What do you understand by the term 'Conflict of Interest' and how does it manifest in the decision-making by public servants? If faced with a conflict-of-interest situation, how would you resolve it? Explain with the help of examples. *UPSC CSE Mains 2015*
8. "A mere compliance with the law in not enough, the public servant also has to have a well-developed sensibility to ethical issues for the effective discharge of duties." Do you agree? Explain with the help of two examples, where (i) an act is ethically right, but not legally; and (ii) an act is legally right, but not ethically. *UPSC CSE Mains 2015*
9. What does 'accountability' mean in the context of public service? What measures can be adopted to ensure individual and collective accountability of public servants? *UPSC CSE Mains 2014*
10. There is a heavy ethical responsibility on public servants because they occupy positions of power, handle huge amounts of public funds, and their decisions have wide-ranging impact on the society and environment. What steps have you taken to improve your ethical competence to handle such responsibility? *UPSC CSE Mains 2014*
11. What does ethics seek to promote in human life? Why is it all the more important in public administration? *UPSC CSE Mains 2014*
12. It is often said that 'politics' and 'ethics' do not go together. What is your opinion in this regard? Justify your answer with illustrations. *UPSC CSE Mains 2013*

Laws, Rules, Regulations and Conscience as Sources of Ethical Guidance

11

1. LAW AS A SOURCE OF ETHICS

LEARNING OBJECTIVES

1. Identifying various sources of Ethics and understanding how the law acts as a source of ethics
2. Comprehending as to what is conscience and how it helps to understand one's own behaviour and assess oneself

1.1 Source of Ethics

Ethics or moral principles derive its contents from different sources. There are many factors which contribute to the moral vision of an individual or a community following can be considered as a source of ethics.

- **Parents and family**

A human being's first and foremost learning point is parents and then family. Children quickly learn what is right or wrong by their reactions of others.

- **School, friend and peers**

Vivekananda said, '*Tell me who your friend is. I will tell you who you are*'. Thus, friends are an integral part of individual's life. An individual first encounters his/her friend in school. He/she learn what is right and wrong from teachers, text books, friends and peers.

- **State**

The state becomes source of ethics, especially in terms of law. Individual will align his/her actions according to the law prescribed by the state. Most people avoid things, which are legally prohibited mainly to avoid punishments or through his/her conscience.

- **Religion**

Religion and beliefs are created mainly to bring order in the society. Individual may encounter questions like 'Who am I?', 'What is the purpose of myself?' at some point or other in his/her life. Religion gives answers for ethical conduct and prescribes way of life.

- **Moral Vision**

Moral vision is the way in which an individual views himself/herself and others. It depends on how an individual develops as a moral being. Though there are so many sources (parents, peer, society, religion, etc.) final interpreter of ethics is individual himself/herself. It influences an individual's decision making.

Though there are many sources for ethics or to decide what is right? Or wrong? Law prescribed by a state government machinery plays huge role in shaping it. It is not only the source of ethics for an individual but for a community as a whole.

1.2 Law

Law is a set of rules prescribed by a country or community to regulate the actions of its members. In other words, it is a code of conduct given by a governing authority to an individual or to a society to maintain an order in the society. It may be enforced by punishments and penalties.

In a democratic system, the law is passed by legislature. Laws are written in a specific code, to interpret when they are required. It sets out standards, procedures and principles that must be followed. It is enforceable by a judicial system or police machinery, with a view that breaking a law is a crime or unacceptable behaviour.

1.3 Ethics

Ethics are about 'what is right?' or 'what is wrong?' or 'what to do' and 'what not to do?' According to an individual or a group of community or professionals, it governs an individual's behaviour and influence his/her decision making. Different set of ethics valid for different set of professionals. Sometimes there arises a clash between ethics of different community.

For example, for an army man killing an enemy is a professional ethics. But a doctor's professional ethics encourage him/her to serve the same person.

Thus, ethics differ from person to person, community to community, religion to religion and profession to profession, etc.

1.4 Law and Ethics

Ethics and law are usually closely related to each other in some cases where law mandates the ethical conduct. After all, law and ethics are derived from society and for the society, and there is no surprise that is has common area where law and ethics meets.

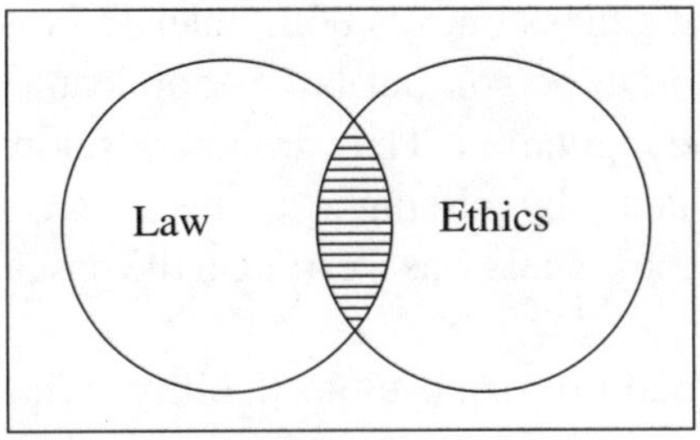

Fig. 11.1 Coincidence of Law & Ethics

For example, 'killing a person'; 'stealing things'; 'lying' are all wrong according to law and ethics. Thus, law and ethics coincide in this point.

1.5 Comparison between Law and Ethics

Though law contains ethics and ethics contains law it differs in certain areas or situations.

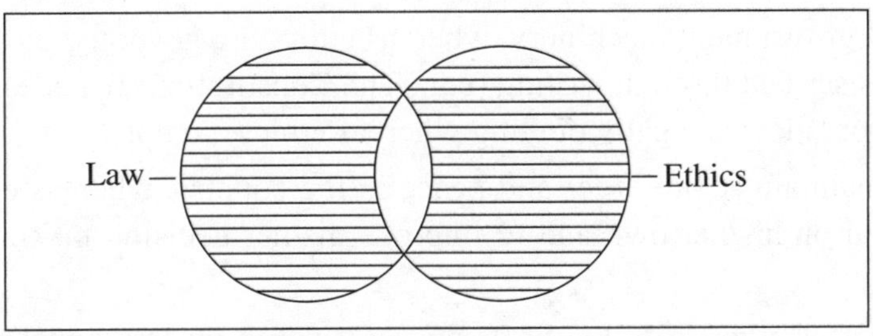

Fig. 11.2 Difference between Law & Ethics

Killing a person according to law is wrong but when a woman kills a person who is trying to rape her will be right according to her ethics.

In a certain religion, practicing non-vegetarianism might be wrong according to their ethics, but it may not be wrong, according to law. They can be enforced differently.

Ethics do not have punishments or penalties but if a person does not follow the law, he/she has to go through punishment prescribed by judiciary constitution/any law prescribed by the government. The only way to check against breach of ethics is social condemnation.

- Laws are enforced by the state, whereas ethics are imposed by a society or institution.
- Law is concerned only with external affairs of a human being, whereas ethics are concerned with both internal and external affairs of human being.
  E.g.: Law punishes a person who commits crime physically (theft, killing). Thus, law regulates and controls external human conduct. It punishes only when evil intention is translated into action. But ethics controls both inner and external motives.
- Ethics change from person to person but law is applicable uniformly to all and everyone must conform to the same regulation. They are universal in character.
- Laws can be changed instantly by passing a statute.
  E.g.: Marriage among homosexuals was a crime in the past but today, in some countries it is recognised.
- Laws can impose strict liability or absolute liability. Whereas ethics cannot be imposed through such liabilities, as it is more concerned with intentional fault of the wrong does than the outcome.
  E.g.: Killing a person will be liable to punishment according to the law but ethics recognises his/her intention or motivation behind the act.
- Some unethical behaviour is not illegal according to law but are unacceptable to morality.
  E.g.: Telling lies not helping poor may be ethically wrong but not against spirit of law.
- Similarly, there are many things which are illegal in the eyes of state are acceptable as ethics.
  E.g.: Driving license is mandatory to drive in the road according to law. But ethically, you are correct as long as it did not harm others.

Law is governed by government machinery, whereas ethics are governed by an individual or the society. Laws are prescribed through writing (e.g., The Constitution; IP code), whereas ethics are abstract (in other words law is legally binding whereas ethics are not).

Law is created to maintain social order and peace in the country, whereas ethics are created to govern an individual on his/her own and to improve his/her decision making capability in day today life.

Ethics have a choice whether to follow it or not as it based on individual's decision. But law compels a person to follow the guidelines prescribed by it.

1.6 Why Law should be Used as a Source of Ethics?

Law plays a greater role in ethical decision making. Ethics have a choice to follow or not making it legally binding can only be done by Law. Moreover, it is difficult to quote morality or ethics to punish an individual for his/her wrong doings because it differs from person to person, society to society. Law will provide common set of rules and thus help to achieve fraternity among the citizens of a nation. A country to achieve a nation state primarily follows the path of law.

Though there have been difference of opinion regarding fundamental nature of law, it is to be regarded as a source of ethics. Law is a reflection of customs of society. If moral principles and ethics to be followed effectively by the society, then there must be high, reasonable and authoritative law which should command an individual.

Each and every institution in a state might have different obligations to serve but it should be in consistence with Law, to bring uniformity in the system. This type of arrangements will strengthen the unity and integrity of a Nation State.

> **? Thought Box**
>
> Can laws alone effectively shape ethical behavior in society, or is there a risk that reliance on law as a source of ethics might limit personal moral responsibility and critical thinking?

1.7 Some Drawbacks to Follow Law

There cannot be law to regulate the very breath of life. It hinders an individual's privacy and freedom. The world is full of experience. Law restricts human beings to experiment the very nature of life. Though old India civilisation has minimum difference between Law and Ethics. It has widened over a period of time.

There is a saying that *'A genuine change must first come from within the individual, only then can he/she attempt to make a significant contribution to humanity'*. Law will dormant this evolution.

If we analyse the Laws prescribed over centuries it differs from country to country and community to community.

For example, *'An eye for an eye'* which was prescribed in the **Hammurabi code**[1] might not be relevant in the present democratic institution.

Law hinders the philosophical evolution of human beings. The great Periyar and Bharathiyar's actions during their period might be lawfully or ethically wrong but today it was portrayed.

The Law being sovereign might have some drawbacks.

1.8 Conclusion

Ethics and Law may differ in some point or coincide in some point but both are needed to bring uniformity and order in the society. Though ethics is used to check the beast embedded in human being, Law will prevent human beings to act in a beastly manner. So, laws should be used as source of ethics to avoid confusion in the society. Lastly, laws which are not based on the sentiment of ethics of a society are less effective and less permanent.

[1]It is one of the oldest and most comprehensive written legal codes, created by King Hammurabi of Babylon around 1754 BCE. It consists of 282 laws engraved on a stone stele and covers various aspects of society. It emphasises justice, accountability, and social hierarchy, with different punishments based on the offender's and victim's social status.

2. CONSCIENCE

2.1 Introduction

The knowledge about one's moral principles, the awareness to act upon those principles thereby understanding one's own behaviour and assessment of oneself is the conscience of an individual. To be precise it is the character manifestation of an individual's inward looking tendency and the vice versa. The notion of conscience is reflected in the philosophical, religious and common sense approach of a person.

In Latin, the term conscience refers to sharing 'knowledge' (*scientia*) 'with' (*con*). But it did not specify the type of knowledge involved and to whom it is shared with. It traditionally refers to the moral knowledge that is 'shared with oneself'.

The etymological relation between 'Consciousness' and 'Conscience' is that the former indicates the 'psychological and phenomenal' dimension of mind, while the latter is the 'moral' dimension of mind.

2.2 Understanding Conscience

- **Conscience as a Pluralistic, Neutral and Subjective Concept**
    1. Conscience as a pluralistic concept
       The moral values possessed by oneself need not be conscientiously accepted by others. What is morally right according to one's conscience may have a 'conscientious objection' from another person's point of view
       For example, 'abortion' according to one may be 'morally correct' when it puts a woman in peril. But someone else may have a 'conscientious objection' to abortion overlooking the woman's right and focusing on the general moral stance on taking away a life
    2. Conscience as neutral concept
       Appealing to conscience does not include any moral justification of a conduct or principle. It does not bear any connection with any substantial moral view. It is usually based on one's innate decision to take an appropriate action according to a situation rather being accustomed to a predetermined moral stand
       For example, the morality of abortion is no way related to the acceptance of it by some as right and opposition to it by some as wrong whatever may be their reasoning
    3. Conscience is subjective
       It only refers to what individuals 'believe' without externalities or justification. What is morally approved in one situation or circumstance might be morally disapproved at some other situation or circumstance

For example, even if a person objects abortion in other circumstances, he believes abortion is right when it poses a risk to a woman's health. Here, according to his value abortion is ethically wrong (objective) and morally right (subjective) in this context

- **Conscience as Understanding about Oneself, Knowing about Self (Self-knowledge) and Assessing Themselves (Self-assessment).**
  1. The role of conscience is not that of merely gaining knowledge about one's character. The knowledge in question is the 'ground' for a moral assessment by conscience.
  2. Conscience is more like an inner judge. It is an impartial spectator and a moral judgement about a man and his actions and a judgement either of acquittal or condemnation.
  3. Kant defines in the 'Metaphysics of Morals' as 'Conscience is practical reason holding the human being's duty before him for his acquittal or condemnation in every case that comes under a law'.
  4. Conscience has often been associated with negative feelings, such as shame, guilt, fear, contrition, etc.
     In this case, it again acts as an inner judge to uproot the negative feelings thereby making us more aware and escalating us on the value building scale.

- **Understanding Function of Conscience in Relation to Knowledge**
  1. In this sense, conscience bring us some form of moral knowledge or moral beliefs either in absolute sense, i.e., knowledge of divine laws or in a relative sense, i.e., knowledge of social norms.
  2. That is **epistemic**[2] function of conscience gives us a mediated knowledge and does not give us direct access to the source of knowledge.
  3. It has two dimensions. Conscience as a faculty for indirect moral knowledge and Conscience as a faculty for direct moral knowledge.
  4. The former is associated with 'witness'. Say, for an example, we cannot acquire the knowledge of moral law of God from any external source but we can only witness the presence of God's law within us. Conscience cannot directly contemplate God. Such indirect and imperfect knowledge suits religious traditions very well.
  5. But in the latter, i.e., conscience as a faculty of direct moral knowledge imparts greater understanding of the norms and make us well informed about the laws and the societal framework. Say, for example, education imparts values on the young minds and can free conscience from the corrupting influences of the society.

---

[2]**Epistemic:** Relating to knowledge or to the degree of its validation

- **Conscience as Motivation to Act Morally**
  1. The important aspect of a perfect characterisation is that an individual must be motivated entirely from within and not by any external means. That is self-motivation is an important personality trait.
  2. According to Kant, 'Conscience is a feeling of pleasure or displeasure associated with myself'.
  3. Conscience makes an individual to exercise his duties based on the moral values he possesses. The positive feelings associated with conscience act as a motivational force and drive the individuals to execute their duties.
- **Conscience Self-identifying Moral Commitments and Moral Integrity**
  1. Conscience gives every individual a private space to find his/her own sense of identity. The moral commitments one possesses enable them to stick to their conscience and act accordingly even though the social and legal obligations would demand otherwise.
  2. This scenario makes a person to take an informed decision based on his moral commitments and help to avoid the dilemma faced by him.
  3. Moral integrity means people adhering to 'identity-conferring commitments'. Lack of conscience arises when there is a gap between this moral integrity and conduct.
- **Freedom of Conscience**
  1. According to Article 18 of Universal Declaration of Human Rights, 'Everyone has the right to freedom of thought, conscience and religion.'
  2. It is not possible to compel someone to believe or to not believe something. It is one's 'inward conviction' and includes the 'freedom to act' as well as the 'freedom to refrain from acting'.
  3. Freedom of conscience involves discarding one's ignorance thereby becoming more aware of oneself and legitimising one's act by themselves and developing an authenticity that is inseparable from the notion of truth and it is justifiable.
  4. It is aligned more towards reality and situational awareness than prejudices.

2.3 Conclusion

It was the conceptualisation of conscience that brought a dramatic change in the world order during the 17th century. The then world was beware of the political changes that were taking place during these times and conscientiously decided upon their future to avoid a war like situation. The conceptual mapping demystified the Conscience and gave a psychological, moral and ethical dimension to the thought process of the world nations. Today's world demands a lot from each and every person in the nook and corner of the world and it is the conscience that makes oneself aware of the scenario and make him prepared to meet the needs of this growing world.

SUMMARY

- Various sources of Ethics include – Parents and Family, School, friend and peers, State, religion and Moral Vision
- Ethics and law are usually closely related to each other in some cases where law mandates the ethical conduct.
- Ethics change from person to person but law is applicable uniformly to all and everyone must conform to the same regulation. They are universal in character.
- Law is created to maintain social order and peace in the country, whereas ethics are created to govern individual on his/her own and to improve his/her decision making capability in day today life.
- Conscience refers to an individual's awareness and understanding of their moral principles, along with the motivation to act in accordance with them.
- It involves self-knowledge, self-assessment, and the ability to evaluate one's own behaviour. Conscience is inherently pluralistic, neutral, and subjective, reflecting personal moral commitments and integrity while guiding ethical decision-making.

PRACTICE QUESTIONS

1. What all can be the important requisites for ensuring probity in governance? Do you think these requisites are deficient in Indian scenario? If so, to what extent? Also, suggest some remedies to promote these requisites.
2. How inevitable is the law of whistle-blowers in India? What steps should be initiated to ensure the safety and well-being of whistle blowers if at all a legislation is going to be initiated on whistle blowing?
3. Is India over regulated? Are the laws/rules which create a climate which facilitate corruption?
4. An enforceable code of ethics is the need of the hour for politicians, bureaucrats and corporate managers. Comment.
5. Draft a code of Ethics or an ethical credo for:
   (i) Administrators
   (ii) Law enforcement agency
   (iii) Parliamentarians
   (iv) Corporate managers
   (Give five effective code of ethics which you think are most important rules)
6. A virtuous and courageous person can alone use the instrument of conscience. Comment.

7. Describe work culture in India. How is it different from occidental work culture? Write down some measures to improve it to facilitate growth of ethical organization.
8. Differentiate the work culture between public and private institutions in India. How has globalisation changed work culture since past 2 decades?

PREVIOUS YEARS' QUESTIONS

1. Differentiate between the following Law and ethics
2. Is conscience a more reliable guide when compared to laws, rules and regulations in the context of ethical decision-making? Discuss. *UPSC CSE Mains 2023*
3. Distinguish between laws and rules. Discuss the role of ethics in formulating them. *UPSC CSE Mains 2020*
4. What is meant by 'crisis of conscience'? How does it manifest itself in the public domain? *UPSC CSE Mains 2019*
5. "In doing a good thing, everything is permitted which is not prohibited expressly or by clear implication." Examine the statement with suitable examples in the context of a public servant discharging his/her duties. *UPSC CSE Mains 2018*
6. Law and ethics are considered to be the two tools for controlling human conduct so as to make it conducive to civilized social existence. Giving examples, show how the two differ in their approaches. *UPSC CSE Mains 2016*
7. "A mere compliance with law is not enough, the public servant also have to have a well developed sensibility to ethical issues for effective discharge of duties". Do you agree? Explain with the help of two examples where (i) an act is ethically right, but not legally and (ii) an act is legally right, but not ethically. *UPSC CSE Mains 2015*

Ethics in International Relations

12

1. INTRODUCTION

Immanuel Kant, in his concept of 'Perpetual Peace', highlighted the role of moral principles in global relations, advocating the maxim, 'Act only according to that maxim whereby you can, at the same time, will that it should become a universal law.' This underscores the idea that nations, like individuals, have an ethical duty to act in ways that uphold universal justice and harmony. In an increasingly interconnected world, where decisions made in one corner of the globe reverberate across borders, the role of ethics becomes paramount. From humanitarian crises and climate change to trade policies and conflict resolution, ethical considerations challenge the dominance of **realpolitik**,[1] urging nations to act not just with power, but with responsibility and compassion.

LEARNING OBJECTIVES

1. Understanding the relationship between morality and national interest
2. Exploring the connection between morality and international relations
3. Examining the various dimensions of 'Just War' theory
4. Comprehending about the ethical considerations by a country to avoid war
5. Knowing about humanitarian intervention and how it violates state sovereignty
6. Knowing ethical issues involved in climate change, refugee crisis etc.

2. MORALITY Vs. NATIONAL INTEREST

Morality refers to an existing code of conduct put forward by a society that applies to all beings in that society. This code of conduct determines what should be done and what should not be done by an individual. It means both motives as well as behaviours. It helps in distinguishing between right and wrong. Morals are relative to every culture which means they differ from culture to culture. But there are certain morals that are common and can be universalised. It is this morality that we apply to foreign policies and international relations.

[1]**Realpolitik:** Principles based on practical considerations, rather than moral or ideological

National interest in general means the goals and ambitions of the nation in the realms of economy, military, culture, power, and prestige. A much narrower definition would be 'survival of the state' and yet this is the most important definition. In the contemporary world, however, national interest is facing a definitional crisis. Reputation, credibility, power, money, competition, ideological challenge, etc., can be used to invoke national interest. The scope of national interest is ever expanding and accommodating. The foreign policy of each nation is formulated on the basis of its national interest and it is always at work for securing its goals. It is a universally accepted right of each state to secure its national interests.

> **? Thought Box**
>
> Can nations consistently harmonise their moral responsibilities with national interests, or are conflicts between them unavoidable in the quest for power and security?

For ages, thinkers and practitioners of international relations have taken various stands on the above issue. Broadly, the views can be categorised under four schools of thought:

- The divergent school is of the view that morality and national interest are polar opposites and are fundamentally different. It would be a cosmic occurrence if a foreign policy serves national interest together while satiating our moral impulses.
- On the contrary, the collinear school propounds that there cannot be any conflict between national interest and morality. They consider that national interest is in itself a moral concept. A statesman's highest moral duty is to ensure that welfare and security of the state is protected which is in the nature of so-called national interest. Hans Morgen Thau propounded this view.
- A third convergent viewpoint is that while morality and national interest are logically different, they do coincide in reality. A statesman at no point will frame a grossly immoral policy and say it is in the interest of the nations.
- A fourth view, subscribed by Niebur Arnold Wolfers and others, holds that a foreign policy made out in national interest will, at times, fail the test of morality. There will be times when a statesman will have to sacrifice morality for the security welfare and prosperity of his or her people.

All the schools of thought are mostly theories and descriptive. They deal with the debate between morality and national interest. However, the reality is quite different. While morality is concerned with what is right or wrong, national interest on the contrary is concerned with what is advantageous or disadvantageous in the prevailing situations for the nation.

In a foreign policy, priority is given to advantages that are in the interest of the nation. Morality takes a back seat in almost all foreign policies. However, morality altogether cannot be neglected. This is due to the fact that a policy based solely on national interest will necessarily be short lived. For long-term peace, security and prosperity of a nation, one cannot simply afford to neglect morality.

Now looking at the other way. Can national interest be sacrificed at the altar of morality? This is highly not a plausible scenario as one cannot feed a starving man with morals. In essence, the way forward is to strike a balance, a compromise, find a centre of gravity between national interest and morality. If truly we are to act in national interest, then we have to establish sustainable peace and prosperity and ensure that it is always better to do what is right.

3. MORALITY AND INTERNATIONAL AFFAIRS

Climate change, drug trafficking, terrorism, capitalism, communism are some of the aspects discussed at the international level. All the above issues and their impacts have to be seen from national and international levels. To unearth the relationship between morality and international approach, we look at three important theories namely, consequentialism, deontology, and virtue ethics. Before we understand these theories in relation to morality, we need to explore a key underlying eternal debate between moral universalists and moral relativists.

The first thing that we ought to look at is whether humans share moral values and whether morality differs spatially and temporally. If one does not believe that there are at least some values that are shared globally, then international law will not only be different to formulate but also, meaningless.

3.1 Morality—Universalists vs. Relativists

Cultural relativists hold that morality is something that is always relative to particular cultures. Moral diversity across times and places shows that there is no shared morality and thus concludes that there is no one objective moral value or set of values in the world, independent of those endorsed by particular societies or communities. They argue that the very fact that there is an eternal debate about universal morals indicates that people disagree about moral values and this disagreement **precludes**[2] the possibility of universal morals.

If one is to look into this line of argument then morality is simply a matter of following norms of the culture you happen to be born into. There can be no right or wrong, better or worse. Norms are simply the attitudes or evolved preferences of a culture or a community. This school of thought recognises the existence of diverse cultures and belief systems and tolerates their practices without judging them as right or wrong. According to the relativist perspective, practices such as child marriage and genital mutilation should be accepted as cultural facts rather than subjected to scientific or moral scrutiny.

According to international law, to hold the cultural relativists view is problematic because it dramatically limits what we can say about the rightness and wrongness of moral attitudes and practices. Given that international law is fundamentally about promoting better state of affairs, the relativist take is profoundly debilitating. Essentially what relativists put forth is a collection

[2]**Precludes:** To prevent something from happening

of different cultures with different moral codes that all exist separately. There is no universal standard or vantage point from which these moral stances can be judged, argued about or contemplated. This relativist construction of moral diversity, however, imposes silence regarding moral matters and does not permit even cross cultural, let alone global discussion.

Sometimes and in some places, people have believed that the earth is flat, even today some societies do. However, the reality is different. It is, therefore, false to claim that just because there are differences, substantive conclusions cannot be drawn. There are always chances that one side could be right.

Therefore, the simple fact of cultural differences does not prove that there is no moral truth. Of course, this does not mean that there are universal or shared values, but it is enough to show that truth is beyond differences and can be universal. The final argument against relativists is that while viewing cultures as distinct and separate entities may have been valid centuries ago, it has lost relevance in today's world.

4. CAN A WAR BE JUST?

War has had its own horrors, even when the weapon was a sling and a pebble. The bloody business of severing the carotid artery sends **jitters**[3] down one's spine. The aftermath of war is even more horrible. The aftermath of war fills the graves more than war itself. It leads to large number of orphans, widows, homeless and starving people. These horrors are not occasional human experiences. These horrors make one think what moral justification there can be for war, if only there is or was any. Three schools of thought have emerged as per this line of thinking: pacifism, realism and just war theory.

1. **Pacifism:** This theory advocates for peaceful relations over violence and conflict, emphasising methods like arbitration to resolve disputes. Surrender or migration should be used to resolve disputes and not war. The very horrors of war that we can observe or experience lay emphasis on the fact that war is immoral and has to be forbidden. War seems to allow just about everything that ethics forbids. In war there is killing, maiming, rape, torture, theft, lying, selfishness, and all these crimes, of course, at **magnanimous proportions**.[4]

   Pacifists argue that because of the immorality of war people should choose not to participate in war. Rather they could employ other methods, such as work slowdown, non-cooperation, civil disobedience, and other such passive acts. People are pacifists for one or some of these reasons: religious faith; non-religious belief in the sanctity of life and practical belief that war is wasteful and ineffective.
2. **Realism:** While war is immoral to pacifists, it is non-moral to realists. They argue that firstly, there are no significant moral relationships between nations, the way there are

---

[3]**jitters:** Feeling nervous or panic

[4]**Magnanimous proportions:** Of great magnitude

relationships between people. Promises and relationships between nations are in the nature of contracts and in a state of respect to one another.

Secondly, once the war starts moral considerations are not even considered and they are kept in the closet. Warring nations cannot be criticised for how they fight. Killing enemy soldiers, destroying enemy properties, killing prisoners of war and the like does not constitute moral mistakes.

Realists take the position that ethics and war do not mix. They consider it as an oxymoron to talk about warring ethically. Extreme form of realists say that anything is possible in war which is the other way of saying that justice and war are polar opposites. Referring specifically to war, realists believe that it is an inevitable part of an **anarchical**[5] world system; that it ought to be resorted to only if it makes sense in terms of national self-interest; and that, once war has begun, a state ought to do whatever it can, to win. While realism is a complex and often sophisticated doctrine, its core propositions express a strong suspicion about applying moral concepts, like justice, to the conduct of international affairs. Realists believe that moral concepts should be employed neither as descriptions of, nor as prescriptions for, state behaviour on the international plane.

3. **Just War Theory:** Just war theory sits in between the two extremes of pacifism and realism. It says that some wars are moral, while others are immoral. Just war theorists frame certain principles based on which one can determine where the war is morally justified. Many of the rules developed by the just war tradition have since been codified into contemporary international laws governing armed conflict, such as the United Nations Charter and the Hague and Geneva Conventions. The tradition has thus been doubly influential, dominating both moral and legal discourse surrounding war. It sets the tone, and the parameters, for the great debate.

   The principles are divided into two namely *Jus ad bellum* (Justice of the war) and *Jus in bello* (Justice in the war).

   ➢ ***Jus ad bellum*:** The justice of the war theory puts forward six criteria to determine whether starting a war is morally justified.
      - Defending in case of aggression on one's nation and going to the aid of an ally on humanitarian grounds, threats of imminent danger are some of the causes that come under the just cause criteria to justify going to war.
      - Good intention means entering a war with the intent to act in accordance with the just cause that prompted that war. Thus, when a nation aggresses, the good intention would be only to defend and not use the opportunity to gain territory.
      - The proportionality criterion means that the costs of warring should be in line with the benefits. It necessarily means that 'war means' should not outweigh 'war benefits'.

---

[5]**Anarchical:** Not being under control

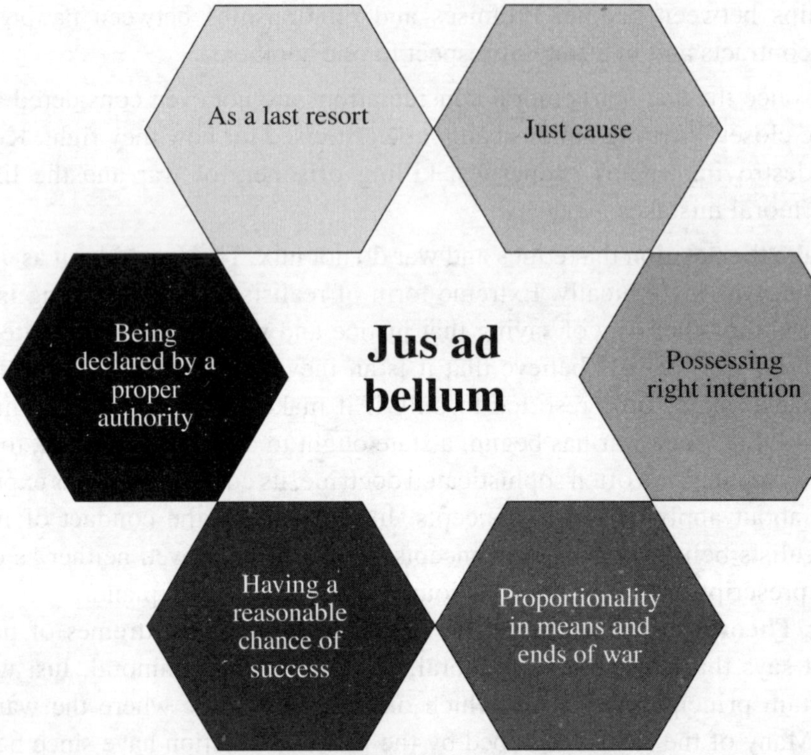

Fig. 12.1 Justice of the war

- The success criterion says that if no good is going to result from the war, then the country should not go to war. It helps guide nations in deciding whether to fight or not.
- Legitimate authority tells that only certain people are authorised to make the decision whether to wage the war or not. The authorised ones are not private citizens, NGO's and lot, rather only those governmental leaders who have legal authority to send a nation to war.
- The last resort criterion is most important that one should not urge to move to war. There is always another negotiating move sanction, political manoeuvre, boycott and such non-military actions that could be tried before firing bullets and launching missiles.

➢ **Jus in bello:** In contrast to justice of the war which talks about criteria before the beginning of the war, justice in war criteria talks about the situations which arise after the war starts. The *Jus in bello* doctrine directs how combatants are supposed to act or should act. It indulges three broad principles:

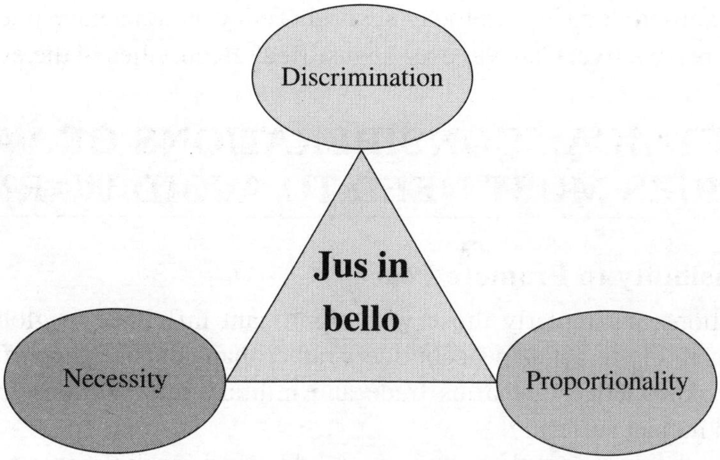

Fig. 12.2 Justice in the war

- The discrimination principle says that those in war have to discriminate between the legitimate targets of war and others. The legitimate targets to attack are supposed to be the combatants and the support staff. Non-combatants and civilians should be unharmed, wounded soldiers and prisoners of war can also be included as non-combatants. While some *collateral* civilian casualties are excusable, it is wrong to take deliberate aim at civilian targets. An example would be saturation bombing of residential areas.
- The proportionality principle concerns how much force is morally appropriate. Any offensive action should remain strictly proportional to the desired objective. This principle overlaps with the proportionality principle of *Jus ad bellum*. Proportionality in *Jus in bello* means toning down the extent and violence of warfare to minimise destruction and proportionality. This principle also condemns killing wounded enemy as the loss of life is not balanced by any significant military gain. According to this principle, soldiers may only use force proportional to the end they seek. They must restrain their force to that amount appropriate to achieving their aim or target. Weapons of mass destruction, for example, are usually seen as being out of proportion to legitimate military ends.
- The necessity principle essentially means that military action can only be taken to the extent that is absolutely necessary to achieve a legitimate military objective, implying that excessive force beyond what is required to win is not permitted; it acts as a constraint on the use of force, alongside other key principles like discrimination and proportionality.

Everything having said and done, except of pacifism, others justify war one way or the other. While realism hits it on the force, just war theory (JWT) makes a back door entry. Just war theory is one of the most abused doctrines in today's world. Today, nations have put every principle of Just war Theory to perspective. Can war ever be justified? Beauty lies in the eyes of the beholder.

5. WHAT ETHICAL CONSIDERATIONS OR VALUES COUNTRIES MUST NEED TO AVOID WAR?

1. Moral Responsibility to Promote Peace

- Powerful nations, particularly those with significant influence in global politics, bear a moral responsibility to act as peacebuilders rather than conflict **perpetuators.**[6]
- They must acknowledge that arms trade and military interventions frequently intensify violence and human suffering.
- From an ethical standpoint, these nations should prioritise diplomacy, conflict resolution, and peacebuilding efforts over economic gains from arms sales.
- Their actions should be guided by the principles of humanitarianism, prioritising the well-being of people affected by conflicts.

2. Accountability in Arms Trade

- The arms trade, particularly from developed nations, is a major factor in sustaining conflicts around the world.
- From an ethical standpoint, these nations must be held responsible for the repercussions of their arms exports.
- Providing weapons to unstable regions or authoritarian regimes often prolongs conflicts, resulting in human rights abuses, widespread displacement, and civilian casualties.
- Ethical governance necessitates stringent regulations on arms exports, ensuring that weapons are not supplied to countries or groups likely to use them to perpetuate violence or oppress vulnerable communities.

3. Avoiding Economic Self-Interest over Global Stability

- A key ethical concern is the emphasis on economic gains at the expense of global stability.
- Weapon industries generate significant profits for powerful nations, often at the expense of peace and security in conflict zones.
- Ethically, these nations must resist the temptation to prioritise short-term financial gains from arms sales over long-term peace and stability.
- This involves reforming policies that enable the arms industry to lobby for ongoing military engagements or interventions, driven by profit motives but resulting in prolonged suffering.

---

[6]**Perpetuators:** Instigators, catalysts

4. Human Rights and Justice

- Human rights should be at the forefront of international relations and conflict resolution.
- Powerful nations bear an ethical responsibility to prioritise and advocate for human rights in their foreign policies.
- Providing support or arms to groups involved in human rights violations, even for strategic purposes, **blatantly**[7] contradicts ethical principles
- Nations must act in accordance with international humanitarian law, ensuring that their actions and alliances do not contribute to war crimes, ethnic cleansing, or other forms of injustice.

5. Non-Intervention and Respect for Sovereignty

- Ethically, powerful nations should uphold the sovereignty of other countries and refrain from unnecessary involvement in their internal conflicts.
- Such interventions frequently result in power imbalances, destabilisation, and extended periods of conflict. Instead, diplomacy and multilateral cooperation through international bodies like the United Nations should be the primary tools for resolving conflicts.
- Non-intervention also means not fuelling proxy wars by supplying weapons or military support to competing factions within a nation.

6. Promoting Conflict Resolution and Peaceful Negotiation

- Influential nations should prioritise investment in diplomatic efforts and peace negotiation mechanisms over military solutions. Ethical leadership on the global stage entails fostering dialogue between conflicting parties and leveraging economic, political, and social measures to promote peace.
- This approach necessitates a transition from military interventions to strategies centred on conflict prevention and resolution, emphasising sustainable peace agreements that tackle the underlying causes of disputes.

7. Global Justice and Economic Inequality

- Many conflicts around the world are rooted in economic inequality, social injustice, and resource exploitation.
- Developed nations often benefit from these imbalances, particularly through the extraction of resources in conflict zones.
- Ethically, these nations must work to address global inequalities and ensure that their economic activities do not contribute to conflict.
- This includes fair trade practices, equitable resource distribution, and supporting development initiatives that reduce the economic disparity fuelling conflicts.

---

[7]**Blatantly:** Clear or obvious

8. Ethical Leadership in International Organisations

- Developed nations often wield considerable influence in international organisations such as the United Nations, NATO, and the World Bank. Ethically, they should leverage this power to promote peace, justice, and conflict resolution instead of advancing narrow national agendas.
- This involves backing international peacekeeping initiatives, implementing arms **embargoes**,[8] and advocating for sanctions against violators of international norms. Ethical leadership requires using their influence to reinforce global governance systems that prioritise peace over profit.

9. Climate Change and Environmental Justice

- Climate change is increasingly acknowledged as a catalyst for conflict, especially in vulnerable regions. Developed nations, being the primary contributors to climate change, have an ethical duty to address its effects, which frequently intensify resource scarcity, displacement, and conflict.
- Ethical action on climate change—such as reducing emissions, providing aid to affected regions, and supporting sustainable development—can help prevent conflicts that arise from environmental degradation and competition for resources.

10. Promoting Transparency and Reducing Corruption

- The arms industry often operates under a veil of secrecy, with deals conducted behind closed doors and minimal accountability. This opacity enables unethical practices, such as bribery and corruption, to flourish.
- Powerful nations have an ethical responsibility to advocate for transparency in the arms trade, ensuring all transactions are open to public scrutiny and decision-making processes remain free from corruption. This requires stringent oversight of arms manufacturers to prevent undue influence on government policies.

6. HUMANITARIAN INTERVENTION Vs. STATE SOVEREIGNTY

International relations scholar, Hedley Bull, said that intervention is dictatorial or coercive interference by an outside party or parties in the sphere of jurisdiction of a sovereign stateor more

[8]**Embargoes:** An official order to stop doing business with another country relating to or using force or threats

broadly of an independent political community. However, the words dictatorial and **coercive**[9] put a notion that the intervention is wrong. Therefore, this definition needs modification. It can be said that intervention is a coercive action by an outside party in the sphere of jurisdiction of a sovereign state, more broadly of an independent political unit.

1. Responsibility to protect (R2P)

Sovereign states hold the responsibility to shield their citizens from preventable catastrophes, such as mass murder, rape, and starvation. However, when a state is unwilling or unable to fulfil this duty, the broader international community must assume this responsibility. Humanitarian intervention, as defined by Simon Caney, refers to a coercive action undertaken by an external party or multiple parties within the jurisdiction of a sovereign state or an independent political community, aimed partly or entirely at safeguarding the welfare of its members. This definition is widely regarded as the most precise explanation of humanitarian intervention, with specific elements emphasised to provide a comprehensive understanding of the concept.

- Firstly, it must be noted that humanitarian intervention necessarily involves coercion and this does not necessarily mean the use of military but also non-military weapons, such as economic sanctions, trade embargoes, arresting weapons supply, arrests, and the like.
- Secondly, the intervention not necessarily has to be against the interest of the state. It could also be in favour of the state. There are cases where states themselves invite outside agencies to come to their assistance.
- Thirdly, the intervention need not be for the welfare of the members of the state rather it could be one of its core objectives. This, however, is highly debatable and for the moment let us consider it to be true.

He defines human intervention as any violation of state sovereignty taken by one or more actors that have protecting human rights as a central reason for violating state sovereignty where there is substantial evidence of this motive in the outcomes of the intervention.

2. For State Sovereignty/Against Humanitarian Intervention

The doctrine and practice of humanitarian intervention highlight a dilemma in global governance: a tension arising from the difficulty of balancing the primacy of state sovereignty with the protection of human rights. State sovereignty is regarded as a fundamental principle in international law, playing a key role in maintaining global order.

Every state is a summation of individuals which necessarily means a state is analogous to a person. And just as an individual person's independence is respected, so should be a state's. Nations are bound to each other, similarly to individuals and therefore, every nation has to allow another nation its right. The most important right for everyone is freedom which manifests into

[9]**Coercive:** Relating to or using force or threats

sovereignty. A right of one nation imposes a duty on the other nation to respect and not violate its rights.

3. International Order and Stability

Permitting humanitarian interventions will enable other interventions a back door entry and thereby destroy international order. Furthermore, small frivolous reasons shall be used to justify this under the pretext of humanitarian intervention. In all likelihood individual scores will be settled and selfish gains will be fulfilled under humanitarian intervention. This is due to the fact that humanitarian intervention is so wide a concept, all-encompassing and can accommodate all kinds of claims.

Globalisation and cosmopolitanism have interconnected different countries of the world like never before. This creates a spill-over effect, destabilising multiple regions. However, even if humanitarian intervention causes instability, this alone does not prove that it is unjustified.

4. The Ineffectiveness of Intervention

For a number of reasons, intervention does not succeed in its objectives. The efficacy of humanitarian intervention has always been a subject of grave concern. A close analysis of the UN peacekeeping activities shows that human intervention has consistently been unsuccessful in establishing peace and long-term prosperity of the state.

The external agencies have insufficient knowledge about another state and its population to make fruitful decisions. UN intervention in Somalia and Cambodia explains the cases where the human intervention was afflicted by poor information.

Another reason is that states seldom act out of **altruism**,[10] and they usually intervene for the furtherance of their national interests rather than the rights of the people aboard. To complicate things further, even if external agencies are well informed and motivated by altruism, intervention flounders due to resistance from members of the country itself that is subject to intervention. United Nations Operations in Somalia (UNOSOM), for example, encountered resistance from Somalis once when Admiral Jonathan Howe began to hunt down General Aidid.

John Stuart Mill argues that external intervention will seldom provide sustainable success. He argues that a political system will prove viable only if the people are committed to the process and for that the people should fight.

However, an inability to fight should not be confused with an unwillingness to fight. Therefore, Mill's central point though valid will need further tweaking. People might be committed to their political vision and will also be aided by outside bodies to achieve their goals when they are weak without resources and force.

---

[10]**Altruism:** unselfish concern for other people

5. For Humanitarian Intervention/Counter Restrictionists

- Whether humanitarian intervention is justifiable.
- Whether external agencies have an obligation to intervene.
- Whether external agencies have a right to intervene.

The interpretation of humanitarian intervention and international law has been a matter of dispute between both camps restrictionists and counter-restrictionists. Restrictionists base their arguments on the principle of sovereignty and the norm of non-intervention.

Counter-restrictionists argue that UN charter does not ban the use of force in cases when a state abuses human rights on a massive scale. The legal argument of humanitarian intervention goes back to the 17th century when international lawyers viewed military intervention in lines of the just war tradition.

6. Is Humanitarian Intervention Justified?

The cosmopolitans claim that every individual has moral interest or value that has to be respected. Every person has a right not to be murdered, raped, or imprisoned without trial and the like. These are universal moral rights that every person possesses and as such these moral rights have to be respected as well as protected. Also state sovereignty is generally attributed with interval power, authority, and external autonomy. However, responsibility and accessibility are also important attributes of state sovereignty. States have value only when they respect people's moral interests. They possess no right to rule regardless of the citizens' welfare. The moment they do not act in accordance to their responsibility, they lose their moral ground for sovereignty and are to be held accountable.

7. An Obligation to Humanitarian Intervention

The complementary of right is duty. When people have a right there is a duty on the external agencies not to violate people's right but also to respect and protect such rights. The presence of people's rights and interests generate obligations on the others.

8. Right to Humanitarian Intervention

Natural law gives rise to a moral duty to protect civilians from human rights abuse. This stems from the fact that right to life is an important component of natural law. All cultures, religions, and communities value the sanctity of human life. No culture, welcomingly, embraces murder, rape, drug abuse, etc. Therefore, right to life is universal and from this arises the right to protect and be protected.

As a matter of international law, humanitarian intervention remains purely a matter of political preferences of the person making the argument. It is generally accepted that the UNSC can declare anything it deems to be a threat to international peace and security subject. The leap from provisions providing for the delivery of humanitarian relief to humanitarian intervention is a long one but not too long for those politically motivated to do so.

There are complexities and challenges of humanitarian intervention in international relations. They are:

1. Fundamental human rights are vested in individuals as members of human race and not in their status as citizens of particular states.
2. Where the state has failed or collapsed, the social contract binding the subjects to the sovereign ceases to operate. In such circumstances, the privilege of sovereignty is no longer relevant and external intervention, therefore, does not derogate from state sovereignty for none exists.
3. One cannot even begin to address this issue without noting the fact that we operate in an international system where the most important political and military decisions are taken not at the international but at national level. It is, therefore, impossible to prevent considerations of national interests from intruding upon decisions regarding international intervention for ostensibly humanitarian purposes.
4. Humanitarian intervention seems to be inevitable. Decisions to intervene or not to intervene or to withdraw are made largely on the basis of strategic and economic considerations that may have little to do with humanitarian concerns even if they are justified with reference to such altruistic ideals.

7. ETHICS OF INTERNATIONAL AID

International aid refers to support offered by one nation or an international organisation to another country dealing with various challenges. The ethics of aid involve two distinct issues:

1. **Motives for Providing Aid:** This concerns the reasons behind giving aid. Is it driven by ethical considerations, such as humanitarian or charitable intentions, or a sense of global responsibility? Or is it motivated by self-interest or political agendas?
2. **Impact of Aid:** This pertains to the outcomes of aid rather than its motives. If aid effectively reduces poverty, feeds hungry children, addresses emergencies, or helps a struggling nation improve the lives of its citizens, it carries a strong moral foundation and justification. Conversely, if aid is motivated by political or self-serving reasons and ends up supporting an oppressive regime that violates human rights, such aid is **unequivocally**[11] immoral or, at the very least, non-moral.
3. **Complex Cases:** Mixed scenarios present ethical dilemmas. For example, aid may be given with genuine humanitarian intentions to assist the poor, yet its benefits might be diverted to **bolster**[12] a corrupt government or enrich an elite class in the recipient country. Another

[11]**Unequivocal:** Meaving no doubt

[12]**Bolster:** To support/encourage

instance involves aid motivated by a blend of self-interest, politics, global responsibility, charity, and humanitarianism—factors so intertwined that they defy separation and clear analysis.

However, ethical considerations are crucial in contemporary international aid to ensure that interventions are effective, respectful, and lead to long-term positive outcomes. These considerations guide donor organisations, governments, and non-governmental organisations (NGOs) in providing aid responsibly.

1. Respect for Recipient Nations' Autonomy

Aid must respect the sovereignty of recipient nations, enabling them to determine their priorities and strategies. External aid should not undermine local institutions or impose foreign ideologies but instead strengthen a nation's ability to achieve its goals.

Example: The Line of Credits given by the Indian government to partner countries for infrastructure development and improve the lives of people. These infrastructure projects are crucial for promoting economic activities and improving quality of life. One such example is Sri Lanka's 900-kilometer road network, which was funded by an Indian assistance programme.

2. Transparency and Accountability

Aid providers must be transparent about their objectives, funding sources, and expenditures. Accountability mechanisms ensure that aid reaches its intended beneficiaries and fosters trust among stakeholders.

Example: Many organisations regularly publish detailed reports about their funding, allocation of resources, and project outcomes. By maintaining transparency, they build trust and ensure resources are used effectively.

3. Avoiding Harm and Dependency

Aid should be structured to minimise harm and prevent dependency. Programmes should empower communities to become self-reliant, fostering sustainable economic and social development.

Example: China has practised lending large infrastructural loans, which many observers have called a 'debt trap', as it inevitably took control of defaulter's assets in case of failure of debt repayments, for instance in Sri Lanka.

4. Long-Term Sustainability

Aid initiatives should aim for long-lasting impact by addressing systemic challenges rather than temporary relief. Projects must be environmentally, socially, and economically sustainable to benefit future generations.

Example: The Green Climate Fund supports climate adaptation and mitigation projects globally, ensuring that countries vulnerable to climate change can build resilient infrastructure and sustainable practices to combat future challenges.

5. Humanitarian Principles

Aid provided in emergencies or conflict zones should be impartial, neutral, and focused on saving lives and alleviating suffering, without political or economic agendas.

Example: Doctors provide medical care in conflict zones and areas facing humanitarian crises, prioritising those in need regardless of the political context. Their mission is grounded in neutrality and impartiality, ensuring aid is delivered without bias.

Ethics in international aid is not merely a theoretical ideal but a necessity for achieving meaningful and sustainable impact. Ethical international aid has the potential to bridge global inequalities and foster a world where assistance uplifts rather than imposes, enabling societies to thrive on their own terms.

8. CLIMATE CHANGE AS AN INTERNATIONAL ISSUE

Why Climate Change is an Ethical Problem?

Climate change presents a severe ethical problem, forcing us to confront different questions as individual moral beings, and even more as members of larger political systems. It is genuinely global and seriously intergenerational, and crosses species boundaries. It also occurs in a place where existing institutions and theories are weak.

Ethical Issues Involved

- Greater political inertia surrounding climate action that tells, we are failing the ethical test.
- Immediate wants vs. future generation needs (intergenerational justice).
- Humankind welfare vs. sustainable management of the environment.
- Common but differentiated responsibility.
- Individual and collective responsibility.
- Tyranny of the contemporary, a collective action problem in which earlier generations exploit the future by taking modest benefits for themselves now while passing on potentially catastrophic costs later.
- Over the past 25 years, high levels of emissions have persisted, indicating a disregard for the future and the immediate interests overshadow long-term consequences.
- With the existing infrastructure, implementing a very rapid reduction in emissions would likely lead to social and economic turmoil, including humanitarian crises and significant disruptions for the current generation.

- The core challenge of climate change is ethical, with considerations of justice, rights, welfare, virtue, political legitimacy, community, and humanity's relationship with nature forming the foundation of the policy decisions required.

The climate problem cannot be truly addressed if solutions lead to catastrophic consequences for future generations or perpetuate harm and injustice, such as the marginalisation or devastation of poorer nations.

9. ETHICAL ISSUES OF REFUGEE CRISIS

Refugees are individuals escaping conflict, persecution, and human rights violations who have crossed into another country. Upon reaching a safe destination, they are often hungry, traumatised, and exhausted from enduring a long and perilous journey. The refugee crisis is one of the most pressing international issues today, involving millions of displaced persons fleeing from conflict, persecution, environmental disasters, and human rights violations. The global refugee crisis challenges international systems, humanitarian aid frameworks, and national policies on asylum, immigration, and integration

Ethical Considerations Involved

- Refugees fleeing conflict, **persecution**,[13] or disaster have an inherent right to protection under international law. The ethical question is how far states and international bodies are willing to uphold their bare minimum human rights and dignity.
- The ethical dilemma of burden-sharing arises because the burden of hosting refugees often disproportionately falls on neighbouring countries or lower-income nations that already face challenges.
- Ethical questions that arise about the balance between upholding national sovereignty and fulfilling international humanitarian obligations.
- Whether national security concerns can justify restrictive asylum policies.
- There is a need to ensure that refugees are not merely surviving but are given the opportunity to thrive in their new environments, contributing to the society as a whole.
- Should countries always uphold the principle of non-refoulement, meaning not sending refugees back to places where they face serious threats, even if it means accepting large numbers of refugees?
- Is it ethical for countries to set quotas on the number of refugees they accept, and how should these quotas be distributed based on need?

---

[13]**Persecution:** Harassment

CASE STUDIES

1. The Gulf War (1990–91)

The Persian Gulf War is an international conflict triggered by the Iraq's invasion of Kuwait. To retaliate, a strong US led coalition consisting of troops from Saudi Arabia, Egypt, etc. was formed. The operation of anti-Iraq coalition was named as 'Operation Desert Storm'. Earlier, the United Nations Security Council (UNSC) asked Iraq to withdraw from Kuwait and imposed a trade ban on it. As Iraq refused to withdraw from Kuwait, UNSC authorised the use of forces. The war ended with the victory of the US led coalition.

Ethical Issues/Questions Involved

- Was the use of military force sanctioned by UN justified as a last resort, or were there alternative diplomatic measures that could have resolved the crisis without escalating violence?
- Did the coalition forces sufficiently adhere to the principle of distinction in international humanitarian law, which requires distinguishing between combatants and civilians?
- To what extent is environmental destruction in warfare morally permissible, given its long-term impact on ecosystems and human livelihoods?
- Were the post-war sanctions ethically justifiable, given their disproportionate impact on civilians rather than the Saddam Hussein regime they aimed to target? What would have been the consequences if there was no war on Iraq?
- There are three moral challenges involved:
    a. Repressive and aggressive regime in Iraq,
    b. Proliferation of Weapons of Mass Destruction as suspected by the USA, and
    c. Global terrorism and its link with Iraq.
- Whether the pre-emptive use of forces without any concrete proof of weapons of mass destruction is ethically/morally permissible?
- Is the use of muscular unilateralism justified for just cause?
- Is the death penalty of Saddam Hussein (Iraqi leader) right during war?

2. Israel Palestine Issue

The world's only Jewish state, Israel is located east of Mediterranean Sea. Palestine, with its native Arab population, is Israel's immediate neighbour. The Israeli Palestine conflict is over the issue of controlling the territory. The social and political developments in Europe convinced

Jews that they needed their own country and their ancestral land seemed like the right place to establish it. There is an unsettled turbulent environment prevalent in the region.

Ethical Questions Involved

- The historical rationale for the birth of a Jewish state could not be the most reasonable reason. But in the context of Jewish history, over thousands of years climaxing in the Holocaust, no one could argue with Jewish fears of extinction and their need for a secured homeland.
- For Israelis, it is the establishment and maintenance of a secure Jewish state. For Palestinians, it is the creation of an independent state in territories they consider their homeland. How can the conflicting rights to self-determination be balanced in a way that respects the identities and aspirations of both groups?
- Israel had encouraged injustice by assisting settlements in Palestinian territory.
- The state uses violence as a method to bring about a change which they want. Can the use of violence against people be justified?
- Discriminatory state's solution, 55% of Palestine state was given to Jewish state, but it represents only 30% of total population. Is it justifiable?
- The United States and the other western powers which are against the nuclear technology are very much silent on the issue of nuclear technology development in Israel. Is this discrimination ethically acceptable?
- Does the Israel's blockade of Gaza restricting the movement of essential goods and people violate the ethical principle of proportionality by causing excessive harm to the civilian population in pursuit of security objectives?
- Does the use of civilian areas as military shields violate ethical norms, and how should opposing forces respond without exacerbating civilian harm?
- How can the preservation and shared access to religious and cultural heritage be ensured to respect the dignity and beliefs of all communities?

3. Afghanistan Issue

Afghanistan has historically served as a crossroads of ancient and medieval civilisations. Its modern history, however, has been marked by prolonged conflict. The Soviet-Afghan War (1979–1989) devastated the nation, as Soviet forces clashed with Afghan Mujahedeen groups. The Soviet Union's phased withdrawal, completed in 1989, left the country in turmoil, leading to a civil war that lasted until 1996.

Amid this chaos, the Taliban emerged in 1994 as a significant force. A guerrilla group advocating Muslim fundamentalism, they gained control of Afghanistan in 1996. The situation shifted dramatically following the terrorist attacks on the United States on September 11, 2001. The U.S.-led 'War on Terror' targeted both the Taliban regime and Al-Qaeda, led by Osama Bin Laden. By 2002, the Taliban had been toppled, and Al-Qaeda's networks in Afghanistan dismantled.

In August 2021, following the withdrawal of U.S. and NATO forces, the Taliban regained control of Afghanistan, ending a 20-year foreign military presence. Their strict interpretation of Islamic law has drawn global concern, particularly regarding women's rights, freedom of speech, and the inclusivity of their governance.

Ethical Issues/Considerations

- The war is justified on the basis of right to self-defence from the grave threat of terrorism. Whether an all-out military action is the last resort!
- Is the war undertaken as per 'Just War Theory' moral principles?
- With the US policy in Afghanistan, Pakistan became the sanctuary for Taliban and Al Qaeda. If the US was interested in war on terror, then was there any consistency of treatment with all other terror groups in Pakistan?
- The most enduring question with regards to not only in Afghanistan War, but also in every war is the ethics of killing, can it be right ever to use force to kill innocent people intentionally?
- To what extent should the international community intervene in Afghanistan's internal affairs? Does non-intervention amount to complicity in human rights violations?
- How can aid be delivered without strengthening an oppressive regime? Is withholding aid ethical if it punishes ordinary Afghans more than their rulers?
- Is the global community doing enough to address gender-based oppression in Afghanistan?
- Should global security take precedence over Afghanistan's internal stability?
- Do sanctions on Afghanistan achieve justice or perpetuate suffering?
- Do countries involved in Afghanistan's past conflicts have a greater ethical obligation to help rebuild?

4. Sudan Civil War

The civil war in Sudan, which began in April 2023, is rooted in a power struggle between two military factions: the Sudanese Armed Forces (SAF) led by General Abdel Fattah al-Burhan and the Rapid Support Forces (RSF) led by General Mohamed Hamdan Dagalo, also known as "Hemedti." This conflict has caused widespread destruction, mass displacement, and severe humanitarian crises.

Ethical Considerations Involved

- Should the international community intervene militarily to stop atrocities? (R2P)
- Do neighbouring countries have an ethical duty to accept refugees despite their own challenges?
- What is the morality of using civilian populations as leverage in warfare?
- Question on the responsibility of international actors in supplying arms to warring factions.
- How can journalists report on the conflict responsibly without sensationalising violence or perpetuating harmful stereotypes?

5. Russia Ukraine Conflict

Russia's annexation of Crimea and its support for separatist movements in eastern Ukraine set the stage for ongoing hostilities. Russia views NATO's expansion eastward as a security threat, while Ukraine seeks closer ties with Western institutions. Now in its third year, the Russian war of aggression against Ukraine remains at the very top of the international security agenda. Thousands of civilians have been killed, and over 8 million Ukrainians have fled the country, creating Europe's largest refugee crisis since WWII.

Ethical Issues/Considerations Involved

- The ethical question centres around whether any nation has the right to act on perceived security threats by violating another country's sovereignty.
- The use of indiscriminate weapons, such as cluster bombs or targeted missile strikes in civilian areas – these tactics may violate the principle of distinction under international humanitarian law, which demands that combatants distinguish between military targets and civilians.
- The conflict has led to millions of refugees fleeing Ukraine. This raises ethical questions about the responsibilities of neighbouring countries and the global community in providing asylum and humanitarian aid.
- Are economic sanctions and collective punishment sanctions against Russia ethical, given their impact on civilians?
- Russia has issued nuclear threats during the conflict, and this raises the ethical dilemma of whether it is ever justifiable to threaten the use of nuclear weapons or engage in nuclear posturing as a bargaining chip, given the catastrophic consequences for humanity.
- Western nations have provided Ukraine with weapons to defend itself against Russia. Does supporting a defensive war justify the extended violence and loss of life, or should efforts be focused on peace talks and diplomatic solutions?
- With NATO and Russia indirectly engaging in a proxy conflict, Ukraine can be seen as a pawn in the broader geopolitical rivalry between Russia and the West. Does this situation highlight how smaller nations are often caught in the crossfire of proxy wars?

6. World Trade Organisation (WTO)

WTO is a global international organisation that deals with the rules of trade between the nations. Its function is to regulate the international trade. The goal of this organisation is to help the producers, exporters, and importers to organise and conduct business smoothly.

Ethical Issues Involved in International Trade under World Trade Organisation

- It is good if a trade policy results in greater benefits to its stake holders. But what happens if it is at the cost of exploiting the most vulnerable people, say people of developing and under-developed countries?

- The developing countries obviously need some fairer and equitable system in world trade, so that their economies can also grow vertically.
- We have a commitment to fight injustice but that does not mean the use of military force. But equitable development is not happening. Consider the case of Africa, in 1980 its share in the global trade was 6% and in 2002 it dropped to just 2% despite the fact that it has 12% of world's population and a large amount of resources.
- Is it ethical for an international organisation such as WTO to place economic considerations superior to environmental rights or human rights?
- There is a widespread criticism at various levels that WTO is increasing inequality, the rich become richer and the poor become poorer.
- The policy of protectionism followed by certain countries also have ethical dimension. Protectionism is the policy purposefully restricting the trade between nations through methods such as increasing various tariff and non-tariff barriers.
- An organisation like WTO should play a proactive role to eliminate such protectionism.. Doesn't this mean loss to the domestic manufacturers and also increase in unemployment?

Moral Values in Indian Foreign Policy

- Principle of non-violence
- Principle of peaceful coexistence
- Mutual respect for each other's territorial integrity
- Principle of self-determination
- Moral, diplomatic, and economic support for the struggle against colonialism, racialism and apartheid
- Support for global south
- Non-alignment
- India's role in UN peace keeping
- *Vasudhaiva Kutumbakam*
- Nuclear disarmament and No First Use policy

SUMMARY

- While morality is concerned with what is right or wrong, national interest on the contrary is concerned with what is advantageous or disadvantageous in the prevailing situations for the nation.
- Three schools of thought have emerged on question of whether there can be a just war: pacifism, realism and just war theory.

- The Just War principles are divided into two, namely *Jus ad bellum* (Justice of the war) and *Jus in bello* (Justice in the war).
- Nations should prioritise peacebuilding and diplomacy over economic gains, ensuring accountability for arms trade, respecting human rights, avoiding destabilising interventions, and promoting conflict resolution for lasting peace.
- The debate between humanitarian intervention and state sovereignty centres on the 'Responsibility to Protect' (R2P), which holds states accountable for protecting citizens from severe harm, with international intervention as a last resort.
- While aimed at protecting human rights, humanitarian interventions often conflict with state sovereignty, risking ineffective outcomes, undermining international order, and serving national interests over humanitarian goals.
- Ethical concerns around international aid include motives—humanitarian or self-interested—and its impact, questioning whether it improves conditions or supports harmful regimes, complicating its moral justification.
- Climate change poses global ethical challenges, including political inaction, balancing present needs with future generations, and managing tensions between human welfare and sustainable environmental practices.
- The refugee crisis, driven by conflict and environmental disasters, raises ethical issues like burden-sharing, restrictive asylum policies, and balancing national sovereignty with international humanitarian obligations under non-refoulement principles.

PREVIOUS YEARS' QUESTIONS

1. 'International aid' is an accepted form of helping 'resource-challenged' nations. Comment on 'ethics in contemporary international aid'. Support your answer with suitable examples.
   UPSC CSE Mains 2023
2. Russia and Ukraine war has been going on for the last seven months. Different countries have taken independent stands and actions keeping in view their own national interests. We are all aware that war has its own impact on the different aspects of society, including human tragedy. What are those ethical issues that are crucial to be considered while launching the war and its continuation so far? Illustrate with justification the ethical issues involved in the given state of affair. *UPSC CSE Mains 2022*
3. "Refugees should not be turned back to the country where they would face persecution or human right violation." Examine the statement with reference to ethical dimension being violated by the nation claiming to be democratic with open society. *UPSC CSE Mains 2021*
4. Strength, peace, and security are considered to be the pillars of international relations. Elucidate.
   UPSC CSE Mains 2017
5. At the international level, bilateral relations between most nations are governed on the policy of promoting one's own national interest without any regard for the interest of other nations. This leads to conflicts and tension between the nations. How can ethical consideration help resolve such tensions? Discuss with specific examples. *UPSC CSE Mains 2015*

Corporate Governance

13

1. INTRODUCTION

LEARNING OBJECTIVES

1. Understanding the concept of corporate governance, and why it is treated as an ethical principle
2. Analysing the basic principles of corporate governance with a focus on the **OECD** guidelines
3. Critically evaluating the current state of corporate governance in India and explore its regulatory framework
4. Comprehending the Companies Act of 2013 and the Fugitive Economic Offenders Act of 2018 on corporate governance
5. Learning about business ethics in India and how it is formulated across organisations while assessing the effectiveness of the measures taken to improve ethical practices

In 1991, India embarked on a transformative journey by adopting Liberalisation, Privatisation, and Globalisation (LPG) reforms, shifting towards an open and competitive economy. These reforms triggered a period of accelerated growth, leading to an expansion of India's financial markets, particularly the stock markets, which have grown substantially in scale and significance. As businesses grow larger and more complex, the role of corporate governance becomes increasingly critical. It bridges the gap between corporate performance and stakeholder expectations, fostering trust and protecting the interests of shareholders, employees, customers, and society at large. Beyond compliance with legal and regulatory frameworks, governance embodies ethical leadership, strategic foresight, and a commitment to long-term sustainability. Corporate governance lies at the heart of modern business success, shaping the way organisations are managed and held accountable in an interconnected global economy.

2. CONCEPT OF CORPORATE GOVERNANCE

Corporate governance is defined as a structured system encompassing various systems, principles, and processes that guide how a company is directed and controlled, ensuring alignment with the interests of all **stakeholders**.[1] These stakeholders include employees, customers, management, and shareholders, each of whom plays a pivotal role in a company's ecosystem. At its core, corporate governance aims to establish a balanced approach to managing the company's resources and decision-making processes, safeguarding the interests of all parties involved.

Infosys defines it as an ethically driven process aimed at enhancing wealth generation. The OECD (Organisation of Economic Co-operation and Development) describes it as the system that directs and controls corporations, distributing rights and responsibilities among participants like the board, managers, and shareholders. Wipro emphasises values like integrity, while ITC highlights wealth generation and societal expectations. SEBI (Security and Exchange Board of India) views corporate governance as respecting shareholders' rights and ensuring ethical business conduct.

The Companies Act of 1956 and 2013 provide the legal framework for corporate governance in India. Post-1991 reforms and globalisation have increased attention on corporate governance, highlighting the need for ethical codes to navigate partnerships and capital access in today's competitive world.

3. WHY DO WE NEED CORPORATE GOVERNANCE?

1. **Changing Ownership Structure:** With globalisation, ownership structures in businesses frequently shift due to mergers, **acquisitions**,[2] and joint ventures. Corporate governance provides a structured framework to manage these transitions smoothly.

   Example: In 2008, Tata Motors acquired Jaguar Land Rover from Ford. A well-structured corporate governance framework enabled Tata Motors to manage the transition effectively and maintain business continuity.
2. **Fiduciary Relationship:** The management's relationship with shareholders is built on trust. Corporate governance ensures accountability, protecting investors' and shareholders' interests.
3. **Increasing Complexities:** As businesses grow and diversify, the risk of misusing public funds rises. Corporate governance is essential to maintain ethical standards in a complex business environment.

   Example: Amazon's rapid global expansion and diversification into sectors like healthcare, AI, and logistics have created a highly complex operational structure. Amazon's corporate

[1] **Stakeholders:** Individuals or groups impacted by a company's operations, including employees, shareholders, customers, and communities.

[2] **Acquisitions:** The act of obtaining or buying something

governance policies play a vital role in managing these complexities, ensuring compliance, ethical standards, and transparent operations across different business domains.

4. **Rising Scandals:** The increase in corporate fraud and scandals underscores the need for governance to prevent misuse of funds and uphold integrity.
5. **Passive Shareholders:** Since shareholders often play a limited role, corporate governance is crucial to prevent directors from exploiting this gap for personal gain.
6. **Risk Mitigation:** Corporate governance helps assign clear responsibilities, reducing investment, and reputational risks by ensuring accountability.

   Example: JP Morgan's 'London Whale' trading losses (2012) exposed gaps in risk management and oversight. Due to weak governance controls, the bank suffered substantial financial losses.
7. **Public Image and Trust:** Companies with strong governance are more trusted by the public, enhancing their reputation and competitiveness in a market where ethical practices are highly valued.

   Example: Tata Group is known for its ethical business practices and strong corporate governance. Tata's governance structure promotes transparency, social responsibility, and ethical standards. This reputation has helped the company build trust and maintain customer loyalty over the years.

4. BASIC PRINCIPLES OF CORPORATE GOVERNANCE

1. **Minority Recognition:** Corporate governance should ensure that **minority shareholders**'[3] voices are heard, and their concerns addressed at general meetings, preventing their interests from being overlooked by majority shareholders and board members.
2. **Stakeholder Recognition:** Beyond shareholders, non-shareholder stakeholders like employees, vendors, and the community should have their interests acknowledged to foster strong, sustainable relationships and a supportive environment for growth.
3. **Board Functions:** The board's responsibilities, authority, and roles should be clearly defined, with structures, policies, and accountability in place. Boards should empower management, oversee goal achievement, understand organisational risks, and challenge executive decisions as needed.
4. **Transparency:** Transparency in financial reports, transactions, and all written documents is key to building trust, with information presented clearly and accurately.
5. **Accountability:** The board and management should be accountable to shareholders, upholding their **fiduciary responsibility**[4] to act in the shareholders' best interests and meet organisational objectives.

---

[3]**Minority Shareholders:** Investors who own a smaller portion of a company's shares and may have limited influence over corporate decisions.

[4]**Fiduciary Responsibility:** The obligation of trust and responsibility towards stakeholders, especially shareholders.

6. **Fairness:** Fair treatment of all shareholders is essential, with the board ensuring the protection of shareholder rights and adhering to principles of equity.
7. **Sustainability:** Business operations should be conducted in a way that creates and distributes value sustainably, ensuring benefits for all stakeholders and the ability to reinvest for future growth.

4.1 OECD Principles[5] on Corporate Governance

In response to a 1998 OECD council request, and updated in 2004, the OECD established key principles that provide a global framework for corporate governance. Widely adopted by both OECD and non-OECD countries, these guidelines help set national standards and practices. The five main principles are:

1. **Shareholder Rights:** Protect and facilitate the exercise of shareholder rights, allowing their active participation in important corporate decisions.
2. **Equitable Treatment:** Ensure fair treatment for all shareholders, including minority and foreign shareholders, preventing misuse of control.
3. **Stakeholder Role:** Acknowledge the rights and roles of stakeholders in corporate governance, promoting cooperative relationships.
4. **Transparency:** Uphold transparency through timely, accurate disclosure of financial and operational information.
5. **Board Responsibility:** Define the board's duties to ensure strategic guidance, effective oversight, and accountability to stakeholders.

These principles form a foundation for countries to create fair, transparent, and accountable corporate governance frameworks.

5. MODELS OF CORPORATE GOVERNANCE

Corporate governance systems vary significantly across different regions of the world, each reflecting distinct legal, economic, and cultural contexts. Some of the prominent models include:

1. **Anglo-American Model:** This model emphasises the separation of ownership and control, meaning that shareholders (owners) are distinct from the management (controllers) of the company. In this framework, major decisions are subject to shareholder approval, and there is a strong focus on maximising shareholder value. This model is prevalent in the United States and the United Kingdom, where corporate governance practices prioritise transparency, accountability, and fiduciary duties to shareholders.

---

[5]**OECD Principles:** Guidelines developed by the Organisation for Economic Cooperation and Development to establish global standards for corporate governance.

2. **German Model:** Often referred to as the two-tier model, the German system features a clear division between the supervisory board and the management board. The supervisory board, which includes representatives from shareholders and employees, oversees the management board, which is responsible for day-to-day operations. This model is characterised by a significant influence of banks and financial institutions as major shareholders, fostering a long-term investment perspective rather than short-term profit maximisation.
3. **Indian Model:** The Indian corporate governance model represents a hybrid of the Anglo-American and German systems. It encompasses various types of corporations, including private companies, public companies, and public sector undertakings (which comprise statutory companies, government companies, banks, and other financial institutions). In private companies, for instance, control often rests with promoters and their families, who rely less on external equity capital. Public companies, on the other hand, may have a more dispersed ownership structure. Despite these variations, the effectiveness of any corporate governance model in India hinges on adherence to established principles and practices, ensuring accountability, transparency, and responsible management.

   Overall, while these models provide a framework for corporate governance, their success relies heavily on the commitment to uphold the underlying principles and functions of governance in both spirit and practice.

6. REGULATORY FRAMEWORK OF CORPORATE GOVERNANCE IN INDIA

In India, the corporate governance landscape is shaped by a robust regulatory framework aimed at promoting ethical business practices, ensuring transparency, and protecting the interests of all stakeholders. This framework consists of various laws, regulations, and institutions that work collectively to regulate corporate behaviour and foster a culture of accountability.

6.1 Key Legal Framework

1. **The Companies Act of 1956/2013:** The Companies Act is foundational legislation that governs the formation, regulation, and **dissolution**[6] of companies in India. The 2013 Act introduced significant reforms, including enhanced corporate governance provisions, stricter compliance requirements, and mechanisms for shareholder protection. Key provisions include regulations on board composition, the roles of directors, and the protection of minority shareholders' rights.

[6] **Dissolution:** The official act of ending

2. **Securities (Contracts) Regulation Act, 1956:** This act regulates the trading of securities and ensures fair practices in the securities market. It establishes the framework for the registration of stock exchanges and securities and outlines the rights and obligations of market participants.
3. **SEBI Act, 1992:** The Securities and Exchange Board of India (**SEBI**) Act established SEBI as the regulatory authority for the securities market. Its primary objectives are to protect the interests of investors, promote the development of the securities market, and regulate market participants to ensure fairness and transparency.
4. **Listing Agreements:** These are contracts between companies and stock exchanges that outline the compliance obligations for listed entities. They include requirements for disclosure, corporate governance practices, and financial reporting, ensuring that listed companies adhere to high standards of accountability.

6.2 List of Regulators

The regulatory framework for corporate governance in India comprises several key institutions, each playing a vital role in maintaining corporate integrity and protecting stakeholder interests:

1. **Ministry of Corporate Affairs (MCA):** The MCA is responsible for overseeing corporate affairs in India and enforcing compliance with the Companies Act and other related legislation. It plays a critical role in protecting investor interests, facilitating corporate development, and ensuring that companies operate within the legal framework.
2. **Serious Fraud Investigation Office (SFIO):** This multi-disciplinary organisation investigates serious financial frauds that have substantial public interest implications. It employs specialised teams to conduct thorough investigations into complex financial transactions, ensuring accountability for corporate misconduct.
3. **Company Law Board:** Established under the Companies Act, this quasi-judicial body **adjudicates**[7] disputes and ensures compliance with corporate laws. It has the authority to hear and resolve matters related to company management, governance, and shareholder rights.
4. **Registrar of Companies (RoC):** The RoC is responsible for the registration of companies and ensuring compliance with statutory requirements under the Companies Act. It acts as a key regulatory authority that monitors company operations and enforces adherence to legal standards.
5. **Securities and Exchange Board of India (SEBI)[8]:** SEBI's primary functions include protecting investor interests, regulating the securities market, and promoting fair trading

[7] **Adjudicates:** Making a formal judgement on a disputed matter

[8] **SEBI (Securities and Exchange Board of India):** Regulatory body overseeing India's securities and capital markets

practices. It has the authority to investigate and penalise violations of securities laws, ensuring a transparent market environment.

6. **Institute of Chartered Accountants of India (ICAI):** The ICAI regulates the accounting profession in India and establishes standards for auditing and financial reporting. By setting ethical standards for accountants, the ICAI contributes significantly to corporate governance and financial transparency.
7. **Stock Exchanges:** Stock exchanges serve as platforms for trading securities and are responsible for enforcing compliance with regulatory requirements. They play a crucial role in ensuring that listed companies adhere to governance standards, thereby protecting investor interests.
8. **Income Tax Department:** This department ensures compliance with taxation laws, impacting corporate governance through financial accountability and reporting. It enforces tax laws that require companies to maintain transparent financial records, contributing to overall corporate accountability.
9. **Enforcement Directorate:** Operating under the Ministry of Finance, the Enforcement Directorate is responsible for enforcing economic laws related to money laundering and foreign exchange violations. It investigates financial crimes, ensuring that companies adhere to legal standards in their financial transactions.

6.3 Principle Laws and Regulations

The regulatory framework of corporate governance in India is supported by several key laws that establish standards for corporate behaviour and accountability:

1. **The Indian Companies Act, 2013/1956:** This act governs various aspects of corporate operations, including company formation, governance structures, directors' duties, and financial reporting. The 2013 amendment introduced new provisions aimed at enhancing corporate governance, such as mandatory audits, board independence, and enhanced disclosure requirements.
2. **The Securities and Exchange Board of India Act, 1992:** This act provides SEBI with the authority to regulate the securities market, protecting investor interests and promoting fair practices. It enables SEBI to introduce regulations that enforce compliance and maintain market integrity.
3. **SEBI Regulations, 2009:** These regulations set out comprehensive guidelines for corporate governance practices for listed companies, ensuring they maintain transparency and accountability in their operations. They cover areas such as board composition, disclosure norms, and the establishment of audit committees.
4. **The Foreign Exchange Management Act, 1999:** FEMA regulates foreign exchange transactions and establishes guidelines for foreign investments in Indian companies. It

impacts corporate governance by ensuring compliance with foreign exchange laws and promoting ethical international business practices.

5. **The Chartered Accountants Act, 1949:** This act governs the accounting profession, establishing standards for auditing and financial reporting. The ICAI, under this act, plays a crucial role in maintaining the integrity of financial reporting, which is fundamental to good corporate governance.
6. **The Income Tax Act, 1961:** This act regulates taxation for companies, ensuring compliance with tax laws. It emphasises financial transparency, requiring companies to maintain accurate financial records and adhere to ethical financial practices.
7. **Revised Clause 49 of Listing Agreement:** Clause 49 sets mandatory corporate governance standards for listed companies, addressing board composition, audit committee requirements, and disclosure norms. It aims to enhance accountability and protect the interests of shareholders.

6.4 Initiatives on Corporate Governance in India

1. **Cadbury Report and Confederation of Indian Industry (CII):** The Cadbury Report, established in 1991, was a response to high-profile corporate scandals in the UK and sought to improve financial transparency and governance.

   The CII, in 1997, adopted principles from the Cadbury Report and formulated the 'Desirable Corporate Governance' code, which recommended that at least 30% of the board of directors of listed companies should comprise independent, non-executive directors, particularly in companies with significant turnover. The CII code emphasised the need for boards to disclose certain key information to enhance transparency and ensure that compliance certificates accompany annual reports, thus fostering accountability among listed companies.
2. **Kumar Mangalam Birla Committee – SEBI Initiative:** Recognising the limitations of the CII code, SEBI appointed the Kumar Mangalam Birla Committee to draft a comprehensive corporate governance framework for listed companies in India. The committee's recommendations included mandatory requirements for establishing audit committees and distinguishing the roles of the board of directors and management.

   The mandatory aspects were incorporated into Clause 49 of the **listing agreement**,[9] which mandates compliance with corporate governance standards, thereby ensuring that companies uphold ethical standards in governance.

[9]**Listing Agreement:** Contract between a company and a stock exchange outlining compliance requirements for listed companies

3. **Naresh Chandra Committee – Government of India Initiative:** Established in 2002, the Naresh Chandra Committee examined **corporate audit**[10] practices, the role of auditors, and the relationship between auditors and companies. The committee made several key recommendations regarding auditor appointments, remuneration, and the overall governance structure, many of which were incorporated into the Companies (Amendment) Bill of 2003.
4. **Narayana Murthy Committee – SEBI Initiative:** In response to the findings of the Naresh Chandra Committee, SEBI appointed the Narayana Murthy Committee to enhance corporate governance standards further. This committee focused on strengthening the definitions and roles of **independent directors,**[11] enhancing the responsibilities of audit committees, and promoting transparency in company transactions with shareholders.

   It also recommended the establishment of a **whistleblowing policy**[12] to encourage ethical reporting of misconduct, thereby fostering a culture of accountability within organisations.
5. **J. J. Irani Committee – Ministry of Corporate Affairs Initiative:** Formed in 2004, the J. J. Irani Committee was tasked with evaluating the Companies Act of 1956 and suggesting reforms. The committee proposed the introduction of the one-person company concept, as seen in other countries, to facilitate ease of doing business and improve governance. Its recommendations encompassed areas such as board governance, management practices, minority interest recognition, and investor education, emphasising the need for inclusive and participatory governance structures.
6. **CII Task Force on Corporate Governance:** Following the Satyam scandal in 2009, the CII established a task force to address the corporate governance challenges highlighted by the crisis. The task force recommended a series of voluntary measures to improve governance, including the separation of the roles of the chairman and CEO, the establishment of a formal nomination process for independent directors, and the implementation of a robust whistleblower policy. The recommendations aimed to restore investor confidence and ensure that companies adhere to best practices in corporate governance.

? Thought Box

Independent directors are considered the 'conscience of the board,' yet challenges like conflicts of interest, political influence, and limited accountability hinder their effectiveness. How can companies and regulators address these issues to strengthen their role in promoting good governance?

[10]**Corporate Audit:** A subcommittee of the board of directors focused on financial reporting, compliance, and risk management. It ensures the company has full visibility of its economic transactions, reducing errors and assisting a company in making key decisions.

[11]**Independent Directors:** Non-executive board members without financial or operational ties to the company, responsible for impartial oversight.

[12]**Whistleblowing Policy:** Procedures enabling employees to report unethical or illegal activities within the organisation without fear of retaliation.

7. COMPANIES ACT, 2013

The **Companies Act, of 2013,**[13] represents a significant overhaul of the Companies Act, of 1956, which had become outdated and needed substantial reform. The changing economic landscape, advancements in corporate practices, and the need for enhanced transparency and accountability necessitated a comprehensive update. The Act was enacted to create a more contemporary framework that addresses the needs of corporations, regulators, and various stakeholders in India.

Rationale for the Revamp of Companies Act 1956

The earlier Companies Act lacked provisions to effectively regulate modern corporate governance and practices, leading to issues related to transparency, compliance, and **corporate malfeasance**.[14]

Recognising these deficiencies, the Government of India undertook a thorough review of the existing legislation, culminating in the introduction of the Companies Act, 2013. This Act aims to foster a business-friendly environment, enhance corporate governance, and align Indian corporate laws with international standards.

Salient Features of the Companies Act, 2013

The Companies Act, of 2013, introduces several transformative features that significantly alter how companies operate in India:

1. **One Person Company (OPC):** The Act introduces the concept of a One Person Company, allowing for a new form of private company with only one director and one shareholder. This provision facilitates solo entrepreneurs to register a company, enhancing the ease of doing business.
2. **Auditor Restrictions:** Auditors are restricted to auditing a maximum of 20 companies and may serve a company for a maximum tenure of 5 years, subject to annual re-appointment. This aims to reduce conflicts of interest and improve auditor independence.
3. **Insider Trading Provisions:** The Act prohibits directors and key managerial personnel from engaging in the buying or selling of shares (call and put options) of the company, its holding company, or subsidiaries if they possess price-sensitive information. This is a proactive measure against **insider trading**[15] and ensures fair market practices.

---

[13]**Companies Act of 2013:** A parliamentary act that forms the primary source of company law and regulates the maintenance of account books and the preparing, filing, or adopting financial statements of any organisation operating in India.

[14]**Malfeasance:** An intentional action that causes injury or harm to someone.

[15] **Insider trading:** It is the illegal use of non-public information to trade a company's securities, giving insiders an unfair advantage and undermining market fairness. Global regulations enforce penalties to prevent it.

4. **Duties of Directors:** The Act explicitly defines the duties of directors, mandating that they act in good faith, exercise due diligence, and ensure the interests of the company and its stakeholders are prioritised. It also mandates **board diversity**,[16] requiring at least a woman director on the board.
5. **National Company Law Tribunal (NCLT)[17]:** The Act establishes the National Company Law Tribunal and the National Company Law Appellate Tribunal for the resolution of disputes and hearing of appeals. This aims to expedite judicial processes related to corporate matters.
6. **Mergers and Amalgamations:** The Act simplifies procedures for mergers and amalgamations, enabling companies to streamline these processes with government approval. It also facilitates cross-border mergers, thereby promoting international business collaboration.
7. **Class Action Suits[18]:** For the first time, the Act introduces class action suits, allowing a group of people to be represented by one individual in legal proceedings. This is particularly beneficial for minority shareholders seeking to protect their interests against corporate misconduct.
8. **Non-Audit Services for Auditors:** The Act prohibits auditors from providing non-audit services to the companies they audit, thereby enhancing auditor independence and minimising conflicts of interest.
9. **Shareholder Limitations:** The maximum number of shareholders in a private company has been increased from 50 to 200, thereby allowing for greater participation in private ownership. Additionally, the maximum number of partners in partnerships has been capped at 100.
10. **Timeliness in Rehabilitation and Liquidation:** The Act mandates time-bound procedures for the rehabilitation and liquidation of companies, ensuring that these processes are conducted efficiently and transparently.
11. **Corporate Social Responsibility (CSR)[19]:** Section 135 of the Act introduces mandatory Corporate Social Responsibility for certain classes of companies. Companies with a net worth of ₹500 crore or more, turnover of ₹1,000 crore or more, or net profit of ₹5 crore or more in a financial year are required to spend 2% of their average net profit of the preceding three financial years on CSR activities. This provision aims to promote corporate citizenship and social responsibility among large corporations.

---

[16]**Board Diversity:** Inclusion of individuals from varied backgrounds, including gender and expertise, on a corporate board.

[17]**NCLT (National Company Law Tribunal):** Judicial body for resolving corporate disputes in India.

[18]**Class Action Suits:** Legal actions initiated by a group of people against an organisation for similar grievances.

[19]**CSR (Corporate Social Responsibility):** A business model advocating practices focused on social and environmental benefits beyond profit maximisation focusing on blending ethical, sustainable, and self-regulatory processes to increase social responsibility.

8. FUGITIVE ECONOMIC OFFENDERS ACT, 2018

Industrial growth plays a crucial role in a country's overall development, often requiring substantial investments from banks and financial institutions. However, in recent years, a disturbing trend has emerged where affluent entrepreneurs, involved in financial scams, **abscond**[20] to foreign countries to evade legal proceedings. This practice not only leads to a rise in non-performing assets **(NPAs)** for banks but also severely erodes public confidence in the financial system.

To combat this issue, the Government of India enacted **the Fugitive Economic Offenders Act of 2018**,[21] which serves as a legislative framework to address the menace of economic offenders fleeing the country. This law aims to deter such individuals from exploiting legal loopholes, ensure they are held accountable under Indian law, and protect the integrity of the financial system.

> **? Thought Box**
>
> In 2022, the Indian aviation industry saw the acquisition of Air India by the Tata Group through its subsidiary Tallace. How do you think this merger will impact India's position in the global aviation industry?

'Fugitive economic offender' is a person against whom a special court has issued an arrest warrant in connection with a significant economic offence and who either:

- Leaves India to avoid prosecution, or
- Refuses to return to India to face legal proceedings.

Once an individual is declared an FEO, the court is empowered to **confiscate**[22] their properties, including:

- Proceeds of crime derived from unlawful activities,
- *Benami* properties (assets held in someone else's name to conceal ownership),
- Assets located both within India and abroad.

The Act's primary objectives are:

1. **Deterrence Against Economic Crimes:** It aims to deter individuals from engaging in significant financial misconduct and fleeing the country to escape accountability.
2. **Confiscation of Illegally Acquired Assets:** The Act empowers authorities to confiscate the properties and assets of fugitive economic offenders, ensuring they do not benefit from their illegal actions.
3. **Expedited Legal Processes:** By providing a streamlined legal framework, the Act seeks to address cases of fugitive offenders efficiently and ensure swift justice.

---

[20]**abscond:** Leave hurriedly or flee, usually to avoid arrest
[21]**Fugitive Economic Offenders Act of 2018:** A law targeting individuals who evade prosecution for major economic offences by fleeing the country. The law authorises the Indian government to seize and confiscate the assets of the individuals avoiding prosecution.
[22]**Confiscate:** To take something away from somebody as a punishment

4. **Reinstating Public Confidence:** It aims to restore faith in the financial system by demonstrating that individuals who defraud institutions or the public will be held accountable, regardless of their attempts to evade the law.
5. **Safeguarding the Rule of Law:** The legislation underscores the importance of adherence to legal and judicial procedures, reinforcing that no individual is above the law.
6. **Economic Stability:** By addressing the financial losses caused by such offenders and recovering assets, the Act contributes to stabilising the economy and reducing the burden of non-performing assets (NPAs) on banks and financial institutions.

Notable cases under the **Fugitive Economic Offenders Act** include individuals like Vijay Mallya, Nirav Modi, and Nitin Sandesara, who have been accused of large-scale financial crimes and fled India to evade prosecution. They were declared Fugitive Economic Offenders under the Act, enabling authorities to seize their assets in India, even while they remain overseas. Offenses covered by this Act include money laundering, cheque dishonour, counterfeiting, and major frauds involving substantial amounts of money.

While the **Fugitive Economic Offenders Act of 2018**, faces procedural challenges, such as ambiguities in timelines and international cooperation, it remains a critical tool in India's fight against financial fraud. Its deterrent effect, combined with the ability to hold offenders accountable and recover assets, underscores its importance in protecting the economy and upholding the rule of law.

9. BUSINESS ETHICS IN CORPORATE GOVERNANCE

Business ethics refers to the application of ethical principles to the complex moral dilemmas that arise in business settings. It ensures that businesses operate not only for profit but also consider their social responsibilities. A company is deemed ethical when it effectively balances its economic goals with its obligations to society, customers, employees, and the environment.

At its core, business ethics encompasses both written codes of conduct and unwritten principles that guide decision-making processes. It provides a framework for companies to conduct themselves responsibly in their daily interactions with various stakeholders, thereby promoting integrity, fairness, and transparency.

9.1 Perspectives of Ethical Decision-Making in Businesses

1. **Shareholder's Perspective:** This viewpoint emphasises maximising returns for shareholders, prioritising their financial interests above other considerations. Decisions are often guided by profitability and short-term gains, which can lead to ethical dilemmas if the shareholders' interests conflict with broader social responsibilities.

2. **Stakeholder's Perspective:** In contrast, the stakeholder perspective broadens the focus to include all parties affected by business decisions—employees, suppliers, customers, communities, and the environment. This approach advocates for a balance of interests, fostering ethical decision-making that considers the long-term impacts on all stakeholders rather than solely prioritising shareholder profit.

9.2 Why Do We Need Ethics in Business?

1. **Sustainable Growth:** Ethical practices are crucial for the long-term sustainability of businesses. While unethical behaviour may provide short-term gains, it often leads to reputational damage and eventual failure. Companies that adhere to ethical standards build trust and loyalty among customers, which is essential for sustained success.
2. **Customer Confidence:** A business rooted in ethical principles fosters customer trust. Consumers are more likely to support companies known for quality products and ethical behaviour. This trust translates into customer loyalty, repeat business, and positive word-of-mouth, all of which are vital for a company's success.
3. **Investor and Employee Protection:** Ethics go beyond codified rules; they encompass the relational trust between employees and management, as well as between companies and investors. Ethical practices help protect these relationships from exploitation, ensuring that employees are treated fairly, and investors' interests are safeguarded against management malpractice.
4. **Corporate-Societal Bonding:** Ethical behaviour strengthens the relationship between businesses and society. A single unethical act can **tarnish**[23] the reputation of an entire industry, leading to widespread distrust. Companies that prioritise ethics help cultivate a positive public perception, benefiting not just themselves but their sectors as a whole.
5. **Public Image:** A company's public image is significantly influenced by its adherence to ethical practices. Positive corporate reputations, exemplified by companies like Tata and Johnson & Johnson, stem from their commitment to ethical behaviour, which in turn enhances customer acceptance and loyalty.
6. **Smooth Growth:** Ethical principles facilitate harmonious relationships among all stakeholders, leading to a conducive environment for business operations. This results in smoother processes, promoting growth, expansion, and diversification without the disruptions often caused by unethical practices.
7. **Consumer Empowerment:** With the rise of consumer awareness, businesses are held accountable for their practices. Consumers today are knowledgeable about their

> **? Thought Box**
>
> How do you think the rise of Zomato in the food delivery industry can be used to demonstrate customer confidence and corporate-societal bonding?

[23] **Tarnish:** To spoil the good opinion people have of somebody/something

rights and expect companies to deliver quality products and services. The legal framework supporting consumer rights further compels businesses to operate honestly and fairly.

8. **Labour Welfare:** Ethical businesses recognise the importance of their employees as integral stakeholders. Ensuring fair wages, job security, and a supportive work environment leads to a motivated workforce. Companies that prioritise employee welfare benefit from enhanced loyalty and reduced turnover, ultimately contributing to their success.
9. **Social Harmony:** Ethical business practices contribute to social cohesion and stability. By fostering healthy competition and ethical dealings among businesses, society can thrive. This approach encourages mutual respect and collaboration, which are essential for a prosperous community.
10. **Employees' Productivity:** When ethical practices are embedded in workplace culture, employees experience higher morale and motivation. A positive work environment fosters a sense of belonging and commitment, leading to improved performance and productivity. Ultimately, this benefits the company's bottom line and contributes to overall success.

10. ETHICAL ISSUES IN BUSINESS

10.1 Ethical Issues of Accounting

- **Creative Accounting**[24]: This involves using accounting techniques to present a desired image of a company's financial health, which can mislead stakeholders. For example, Enron employed creative accounting practices to hide its debts and inflate profits, leading to its infamous collapse.
- **Insider Trading:** When corporate insiders buy or sell stock based on non-public information, it undermines market integrity. For instance, Raj Rajaratnam was convicted of insider trading, which involved trading on confidential information from several companies.
- **Excessive CEO Compensation:** High executive pay packages can lead to ethical concerns, especially when they are disproportionate to the company's performance. The case of Wells Fargo, where CEO John Stumpf was criticised for his high compensation amidst the bank's fake accounts scandal, highlights this issue.

10.2 Ethical Issues of Personnel Management

- **Discrimination:** Discrimination in hiring, promotions, or pay based on age, gender, race, or other factors is a significant ethical concern. For example, the case of Walmart faced

[24]**Creative Accounting:** Manipulative financial reporting to present a desired image of a company's financial status.

a gender discrimination lawsuit, alleging that women were paid less and promoted less frequently than their male counterparts.

- **Sexual Harassment:** Seeking sexual favours or creating a hostile work environment can lead to severe ethical and legal ramifications. The allegations against Harvey Weinstein exemplify how such behaviours can permeate workplace cultures and lead to significant fallout.
- **Union Busting:** Coercive actions against employees who wish to unionise can violate ethical standards. Companies like Amazon have faced accusations of using **intimidation**[25] tactics against union organisers, raising concerns about labour rights.

10.3 Ethical Issues of Sales and Marketing

- **Price Fixing: Colluding**[26] with competitors to set prices can harm consumers and violate antitrust laws. The financial crisis of 2008 revealed numerous cases where banks engaged in price-fixing related to mortgage-backed securities.
- **Manipulation of Loyalty Programmes:** Businesses may exploit consumer loyalty through deceptive marketing practices. Airlines, for instance, have been criticised for adding fees to 'free' flights obtained through loyalty points, obscuring true costs.
- **Subliminal Advertising:** The use of hidden messages to manipulate consumer behaviour raises ethical concerns. For example, the controversy over the use of subliminal messages in advertisements led to debates about consumer rights and corporate responsibility.

10.4 Ethical Issues of Production

- **Defective Products:** Companies that knowingly release defective products, like the Takata airbag scandal, which resulted in multiple fatalities, face significant ethical scrutiny.
- **Environmental Harm:** Corporations like BP faced severe backlash for the Deepwater Horizon oil spill, which highlighted the ethical obligations of companies to protect the environment and avoid pollution.
- **Animal Testing:** Ethical concerns arise regarding the use of animals in product testing, especially in the cosmetics industry, where alternatives exist. The controversy surrounding companies like L'Oréal has spurred consumer advocacy against animal testing.

10.5 Ethical Issues of Intellectual Property, Knowledge, and Skills

- **Patent Infringement:** Companies that use patented technology without permission can face legal challenges. For instance, the lawsuit between Apple and Samsung over smartphone technology patents illustrates the tension in protecting intellectual property.

---

[25]Frightening/menacing

[26]**Colluding:** Cooperate in an unlawful or secret way to deceive or gain advantage

- **Biopiracy:** The appropriation of indigenous knowledge or resources without fair compensation is an ethical issue. For example, the controversy over the use of the neem tree in pharmaceuticals highlights the need for fair recognition and remuneration of indigenous communities.
- **Industrial Espionage**[27]**:** The unethical act of stealing trade secrets, as seen in the case of Google vs. Uber over self-driving technology, underscores the importance of ethical standards in competitive business practices.

11. CAUSES OF UNETHICAL CONDUCT IN AN ORGANISATION

- **Unrealistic Goals:** When organisations set unattainable targets, it may lead employees to resort to unethical means to meet these goals. For example, the pressure on sales teams to meet quotas can lead to deceptive practices such as falsifying sales records.
- **Acute Competition:** The intense competition in the market can encourage businesses to engage in unethical behaviour to gain an advantage. For instance, companies may resort to smear campaigns against competitors, as seen in various political advertising strategies.
- **Greed:** An insatiable desire for more wealth can drive unethical conduct. The financial crisis of 2008 was partly fuelled by greed among banking executives who prioritised short-term profits over ethical considerations, leading to widespread financial misconduct.
- **Poor Leadership:** When leaders do not model ethical behaviour, it sets a poor precedent for employees. The scandal at Theranos exemplified how poor leadership and unethical practices can lead to a company's downfall.

12. BAD CORPORATE GOVERNANCE AND ITS IMPACT ON THE ECONOMY

1. **Erosion of Investor Confidence**
   - Poor governance practices, such as lack of transparency, fraud, and inadequate disclosures, deter investors from committing capital to companies.
   - *Example*: The **Enron scandal** (2001) in the US, where deceptive accounting practices caused one of the largest bankruptcies in history, led to massive investor losses and distrust in the corporate system.
2. **Increase in Non-Performing Assets (NPAs)**
   - Governance failures in corporations often result in mismanagement of loans, defaults, and bad debts.

[27] **Industrial Espionage:** Undercover work, spying

- *Example*: The **IL&FS financial crisis** (2018) in India involved mismanagement of public funds, leaving a ₹91,000 crore debt burden and aggravating India's NPA crisis.

3. **Economic Instability and Market Volatility**
    - Governance scandals can trigger significant volatility in stock markets, causing widespread financial instability.
    - *Example*: The **Satyam scandal** (2009) in India caused a stock market crash, significantly affecting the IT sector and shareholder wealth.
4. **Reduction in Employment and Economic Activity**
    - Poor governance can lead to company bankruptcies, which result in massive job losses and affect ancillary industries.
    - *Example*: The collapse of **Kingfisher Airlines** due to governance failures led to thousands of job losses and negatively impacted the aviation industry in India.
5. **Deterrence of Foreign Direct Investment (FDI)**
    - Nations with a reputation for corporate scandals and weak governance frameworks discourage foreign investors, affecting capital inflows and economic expansion.
    - *Example*: The **PNB scam** (2018) involving Nirav Modi and Mehul Choksi created a global perception of weak financial oversight in India, impacting FDI inflows into the banking and financial sectors.
6. **Creation of Unfair Markets and Monopolies**
    - Poor governance enables unethical corporations to manipulate markets, suppress competition, and exploit consumers.
    - *Example*: The **Volkswagen emissions scandal** (2015) showed how fraudulent practices allowed the company to gain a market edge by cheating emission tests, harming competitors and the environment.
7. **Corruption and Resource Misallocation**
    - Governance lapses are often tied to corruption, leading to inefficient allocation of resources.
    - Such practices weaken public trust in institutions and hinder sustainable economic development.
    - *Example*: The **Commonwealth Games scam** (2010) in India revealed massive corruption in infrastructure projects, diverting public funds and damaging the country's global reputation.

? Thought Box

How bad would you assess India's current debt problem? How has NPA affected the financial progress of India in the last decade?

13. MEASURES TO IMPROVE ETHICAL PRACTICES

1. At the Institutional Level

Ethical Code of Conduct[28]: Organisations should develop and distribute a clear ethical code that outlines expected behaviours and consequences for unethical conduct. For example, the implementation of the Sarbanes-Oxley Act led many companies to adopt comprehensive ethics training and codes of conduct.

Ethics Committee: Establishing an ethics committee can provide oversight and support for ethical behaviour within the organisation. Companies like Starbucks have implemented ethics boards to address employee concerns and ensure compliance.

Transparency: Organisations should promote transparency in their operations, making policies and procedures accessible to employees. Companies that openly communicate their ethical standards, such as Patagonia, build trust and encourage accountability.

Zero Tolerance Policy: Enforcing strict penalties for unethical behaviour can deter misconduct. Companies like Johnson & Johnson exemplify this approach by taking decisive actions against employees who violate their ethical standards.

2. At the Government Level

Clear Laws and Regulations: Governments must establish straightforward laws to govern business ethics, ensuring clarity and fairness. For example, the Dodd-Frank Act introduced measures to enhance transparency in financial institutions following the 2008 crisis.

Stringent Penalties: Enforcing strict penalties for violations can deter unethical behaviour. The Federal Sentencing Guidelines for Organizations, which outline penalties for corporate misconduct, exemplify this approach, aiming to hold companies accountable for ethical breaches.

14. INDEPENDENT DIRECTORS

Independent directors are non-executive members of a company's board who do not have any fiduciary relationships with the company. They have not served as executives in the company for at least the last three financial years. Often referred to as the 'conscience' of the board,

[28]**Ethical Code of Conduct:** A set of guidelines designed to influence ethical behaviour within an organisation.

independent directors play a crucial role in ensuring that the board functions impartially and effectively, contributing to corporate governance and accountability.

According to regulatory requirements, independent directors must comprise at least one-third of a company's board strength. They are mandated to hold at least one meeting annually without the participation of non-independent directors, ensuring they can freely discuss issues concerning governance and company performance.

Key Roles and Functions

- **Oversight:** Independent directors are responsible for monitoring and guiding the company's operations, providing an objective viewpoint that is vital for strategic decisions.
- **Conflict Resolution:** They serve as mediators in conflicts of interest between the company's management and shareholders, promoting transparency and fairness.
- **Risk Management:** Independent directors are expected to identify potential risks to the company and advise on mitigation strategies.
- **Corporate Governance:** They uphold ethical standards and ensure that the company adheres to legal and regulatory frameworks, enhancing the company's reputation and trustworthiness.

Despite their important roles, independent directors have faced significant challenges and criticisms, especially in light of recent corporate scandals.

Issues and Challenges Faced by Independent Directors

1. **Appointment-Related Issues: Political Partisanship:** The Companies Act may not be followed rigorously, leading to appointments that lack true independence. For example, there have been instances where leaders of the ruling party have been appointed as independent directors in public sector undertakings (PSUs), compromising their objectivity.

   Favouritism and Nepotism: The case of the Infrastructure Leasing & Financial Services (IL&FS) crisis highlighted how some independent directors were appointed due to personal connections with the promoters rather than their expertise. Reports indicated that individuals who were close to the company's management had a significant influence on the board appointments, which compromised their ability to provide unbiased oversight.
2. **Reliability Issues: Reliance on Resignation During Crises:** During the IL&FS crisis in 2018, several independent directors resigned in the wake of financial irregularities. Their quick exits were seen as a failure to fulfil their oversight roles, further damaging investor confidence in the company's governance and stability.

   Fear of Accountability: After the collapse of the fraud-prone construction company, Jaypee Infratech, potential independent directors were reluctant to join boards due to fears of being held accountable for decisions made during their tenure. This hesitancy highlighted the chilling effect that high-profile corporate failures can have on attracting qualified individuals to such positions.

3. **Lack of Board Evaluations:** A 2016 report by InGovern highlighted that, under its rating system, only five of the top 100 companies received high scores for effective board evaluations. This indicates a significant gap in accountability and performance assessment among independent directors.
4. **Compensation Concerns:** The average remuneration for independent directors increased by 21% in the fiscal year 2015–16, raising concerns that higher pay might compromise their objectivity. This trend suggests that the provisions aimed at ensuring their impartiality may be undermined.
5. **Conflicts of Interest:** A notable case occurred with the independent directors of the company Fortis Healthcare, who were found to have substantial financial interests in the company, leading to conflicts of interest in their decision-making processes. Such situations highlight the need for stringent regulations that prevent independent directors from holding financial stakes that could compromise their objectivity.

15. CORPORATE SOCIAL RESPONSIBILITY (CSR)

Corporate Social Responsibility (CSR) refers to the processes and practices adopted by businesses to incorporate social and environmental considerations into their operations. CSR aims to go beyond profit maximisation, promoting social good and ensuring accountability to stakeholders, including employees, consumers, and the broader community. CSR has gained global recognition as corporations increasingly engage in initiatives that promote social well-being alongside their business interests.

The necessity for CSR arises from the limitations of government resources, especially in developing countries. CSR enables organisations to fill gaps in social welfare and contribute positively to societal needs.

The benefits of CSR include

- **Creating a Favourable Public Image:** Companies that demonstrate social responsibility often enjoy a strong reputation, as exemplified by Tata, which is associated with trust and integrity.
- **Encouraging Employee Involvement:** Employees feel a sense of pride and ownership in their company's contributions to society, leading to increased morale and productivity.
- **Aligning Societal and Organisational Goals:** Companies benefit from improved community relations and a more supportive workforce, enhancing their operational success.

- **Enhancing Decision-Making Freedom:** By engaging in CSR, companies may face less regulatory scrutiny, allowing for more agile decision-making processes.
- **Promoting Healthy Competition:** Organisations that actively engage in social responsibility can inspire others to follow suit, fostering a culture of accountability and community support.

Issues with CSR

- **Profit-Driven Motives:** Many companies view CSR as a marketing tool to enhance their image rather than a genuine commitment to social issues, diluting its impact.
- **Lack of Expertise:** Many organisations do not employ dedicated CSR professionals, leading to inefficiencies in planning and executing CSR initiatives.
- **Transparency Concerns:** The effectiveness of CSR is undermined by NGOs and local agencies failing to disclose information about their programmes and financial utilisation, affecting trust and cooperation.
- **Imbalanced Spending:** CSR funds are often concentrated in popular areas like education and health, neglecting other critical sectors such as sanitation and infrastructure.
- **Geographic Disparities:** CSR funding is heavily skewed towards certain states, with less funding directed to underdeveloped regions, particularly in the Northeast of India.
- **Inherent Contradictions:** The legal framework around CSR can be contradictory, as legislation cannot inspire genuine corporate accountability. Companies may meet legal requirements superficially without effecting meaningful change.

Way Forward

- **Encouraging Two-Way Communication:** Regular dialogue between companies and NGOs can strengthen partnerships. Companies can participate in steering committees to align efforts with NGOs, as seen in initiatives like the Village Transformation mission in Maharashtra.
- **Collaboration and Co-Creation:** Organisations should actively involve NGOs in a partnership approach, attending joint meetings and contributing valuable insights to improve **CSR** initiatives.
- **Establishing Accountability Regimes:** Companies should define clear objectives for CSR activities and ensure stringent monitoring and due diligence of implementation partners.
- **Moving from CSR to CSV:** Companies should transition from simply fulfilling CSR mandates to Creating Shared Value (CSV), where business success and social progress are intertwined.
- **Enhancing Legal Frameworks:** Implementing stricter laws and transparency requirements can hold companies accountable and improve CSR effectiveness.
- **Diversifying CSR Spending:** Organisations should expand their CSR focus beyond a few areas to promote equitable development across various sectors.

16. CORPORATE SUSTAINABILITY

Corporate sustainability encompasses strategies and practices aimed at meeting stakeholder needs today while safeguarding human and natural resources for the future. It integrates economic, environmental, and social dimensions into corporate decision-making, ensuring long-term viability and ethical responsibility.

Key Drivers to Ensure Sustainability

- **Internal Capacity Building Strength:** This involves enhancing the organisation's ability to identify and manage risks effectively. By developing skills, processes, and systems, companies can transform potential risks—such as market volatility, regulatory changes, and environmental challenges into opportunities for competitive advantage.
  This proactive approach not only boosts resilience but also fosters innovation and adaptability.
- **Social Impact Assessment:** Companies must evaluate how their operations affect communities and social structures. By conducting thorough assessments, organisations can become more aware of cultural shifts, changes in consumer behaviour, and social needs. This sensitivity enables businesses to engage positively with stakeholders, promote social well-being, and align their strategies with societal expectations.
- **Repositioning Capability:** To remain relevant in a rapidly changing business environment, organisations must be willing to innovate and develop new strategies. This repositioning involves embracing new technologies, exploring alternative business models, and continually adapting to market demands. By fostering a culture of innovation, companies can create sustainable products and services that resonate with consumers while driving growth.
- **Crystallisation of Activities:** Ensuring consistency in all business activities is crucial for sustainable growth. Organisations should aim to align their missions, goals, and operational practices across all levels. This crystallisation process not only enhances efficiency but also strengthens the company's brand identity and stakeholder trust, contributing to a more sustainable and cohesive approach to business.

17. RECENT STEPS TAKEN TO IMPROVE CORPORATE GOVERNANCE

17.1 Uday Kotak Committee

The Uday Kotak Committee was constituted by the Securities and Exchange Board of India (SEBI) to address the issues surrounding corporate governance in India. Some of the important recommendations include:

- **Enhanced Role of Independent Directors:** The committee emphasised the need for **independent directors** to play a more active role in corporate governance. This includes ensuring that they have the necessary expertise and time to fulfil their duties effectively.
- **Strengthening the Audit Committee:** Recommendations were made to enhance the powers and responsibilities of the audit committee to ensure better oversight of financial reporting and compliance.
- **Minimum Number of Independent Directors:** The committee proposed increasing the minimum number of **independent directors** required on the boards of listed companies, especially for larger firms.
- **Regular Performance Evaluation:** The report suggested that boards should conduct regular performance evaluations of **independent directors** and the board, ensuring accountability and continuous improvement.
- **Disclosure Norms:** The committee called for improved disclosure requirements for related party transactions to enhance transparency and **mitigate**[29] conflicts of interest.

> **? Thought Box**
>
> How does a healthy CSR system lead to a greater brand image as well as a positive social impact? Justify your answer by comparing and contrasting the CSR approaches followed by Tata Group and Infosys in India.

17.2 Additional Steps to Improve Corporate Governance

1. **Punitive Action and Accountability: SEBI** has initiated punitive actions in various high-profile cases involving alleged corporate governance failures. Cases under scrutiny include those related to **Raymond Ltd**, **InterGlobe Aviation Ltd**, fund diversion at **CG Power and Industrial Solutions Ltd**, and the **NSE's algorithmic trading and co-location case**. These actions signify a commitment to holding companies accountable for governance lapses.
2. **Amendments to the Companies Act, 2013:** To build trust and simplify compliance, the government amended the Companies Act, reclassifying 16 '**compoundable offences**' as '**civil defaults**.' This change aims to reduce the burden on companies and encourage

[29]**Mitigate:** Reduce/Alleviate

compliance rather than penalisation. Furthermore, the **Company Law Committee** has recommended further reclassification of 46 offences, streamlining regulatory oversight.

3. **Independent Director Database: SEBI** has established an **independent director database** to register qualified experts. This initiative aims to enhance the availability of competent **independent directors** for corporate boards, improving governance standards.
4. **Strengthening Norms for Related Party Transactions: SEBI** is in the process of tightening regulations surrounding related party transactions to prevent conflicts of interest and ensure greater transparency in corporate dealings.

18. MOVING TOWARDS GOOD CORPORATE GOVERNANCE

To achieve Good Corporate Governance, a combination of global best practices, existing legal frameworks, and forward-looking concepts is essential.

1. **Right Board Leadership:** Establishing strong leadership at the board level is crucial for fostering a culture of integrity, fairness, transparency, and ethical conduct. This culture should be communicated to all employees through training programmes.
2. **Clear Anti-Corruption Policies:** Companies must implement clear policies for zero tolerance toward bribery and corruption. This includes measures to prevent market manipulation and money laundering.
3. **Integrity of Financial Statements:** The accuracy and integrity of financial statements are fundamental for stakeholder trust. Audit committees must be functional, ensuring all necessary information is accessible to auditors and facilitating direct communication between them.
4. **De-criminalisation of Business Laws:** The process of de-criminalising business laws should continue to reduce unnecessary legal burdens on companies.
5. **Inclusive Governance Principles:** Corporate governance should encompass all stakeholders, including the government, creditors, employees, customers, vendors, and the community.
6. **OECD Recommendations:** The OECD has provided valuable suggestions, such as:
   - Training for independent directors on the company's business.
   - Enhancing investor education to promote better participation in general meetings.
   - Improving the selection process for independent directors.

Good corporate governance, beyond mere compliance with laws, facilitates ease of doing business and contributes to overall growth.

SUMMARY

- Corporate governance is defined as a structured system encompassing various systems, principles, and processes that guide how a company is directed and controlled, ensuring alignment with the interests of all stakeholders.
- The **OECD principles** provide a global framework emphasising shareholder rights, equitable treatment, stakeholder engagement, transparency, and responsible board oversight.
- Corporate governance models vary globally. India's model combines American and German features, tailored for private, public, and government entities, with success relying on transparency, accountability, and ethical practices.
- Key regulators, including **SEBI**, MCA, RoC, and ICAI, oversee compliance, investigate fraud, and maintain financial and governance standards.
- Laws like FEMA and the Income Tax Act ensure transparency in foreign investments and financial reporting. Initiatives like the CII Code (1997), inspired by the UK's Cadbury Report, promoted transparency, independent directors, and board disclosures.
- The Kumar Mangalam Birla Committee (1999), the Naresh Chandra Committee (2002), the Narayana Murthy Committee (2003), the J.J. Irani Committee (2004) and the CII Task Force (2009) have played key roles in rebuilding trust.
- Key features of the **Companies Act of 2013** and the **Fugitive Economic Offenders Act of 2018** have helped expedite legal processes, and restore public confidence in the financial system.
- Business ethics are vital for long-term success, fostering growth, trust, and satisfaction. Issues include creative accounting, insider trading, discrimination, harassment, and unethical practices driven by competition or unrealistic targets.
- Independent directors ensure oversight, conflict resolution, and transparency in governance. CSR involves businesses supporting society and the environment, aiding social welfare, especially in resource-limited developing countries.
- Efforts to improve corporate governance include recommendations from the Uday Kotak Committee, such as strengthening the role of independent directors and enhancing audit committees.

PREVIOUS YEARS' QUESTIONS

1. In the contemporary world, the corporate sector's contribution to generating wealth and employment is increasing. In doing so, they are bringing an unprecedented onslaught on the climate, environmental sustainability, and living conditions of human beings. In this background, are Corporate Social Responsibility (CSR) efficient and sufficient enough to fulfil the social roles and responsibilities needed in the corporate work mandated? Critically examine.

   UPSC CSE Mains 2022

2. Corporate social responsibility makes companies more profitable and sustainable. Analyse.

   UPSC CSE Mains 2017

Probity in Governance: The Code of Conduct and the Code of Ethics

14

LEARNING OBJECTIVES

1. Understanding the codes of conduct, morality, and standards in governance
2. Grasping the concept of public service and exploring various governance philosophies
3. Appreciating the significance of a code of ethics in public administration
4. Differentiating between the codes of conduct and the code of ethics
5. Comprehending professional ethics for doctors, lawyers, and engineers
6. Comparing international codes of conduct and their application in governance
7. Understanding the role of work culture and its impact on organisational success

Ethics is a set of principles or moral guidelines of right conduct. It is also defined as the set of values and related principles which helps guide the thoughts, behaviour, attitude, choice and actions of individuals. Ethics helps us to understand and decide whether one's thought and actions go together or not, and to identify whether the actions are right or wrong. Both individuals and organisations have ethical standards. These standards act as guidelines and help individuals belonging to an organisation and organisations belonging to the society maintain a consistent approach in carrying out their duties and making decisions. Moreover, these guidelines also help ensure that the stakeholders of an organisation maintain a consistent and appropriate behaviour towards insiders and also towards the clients and the persons outside the organisation.

Morals, values, standards, codes and norms help lead a better intrinsic and extrinsic life for both individuals and organisations. Codes and norms will directly enhance the standard and quality of life. The code of ethics also acts as the guideline and documentation for the future generations for their welfare and better livelihood. This will also help the young society prevent irreparable moral damages by rectifying their mistakes and also to enhance the capability to face any unpredicted and unforeseen nature of future situations.

Each and every organisation is expected to maintain its morals and values. Governments have sole responsibilities towards its citizens. Civil servants take important decisions that affect the entire aspect of a community's life and livelihood. They are responsible for managing resources entrusted to them by the community and hence, they have special obligations towards social upliftment. Because of this, the society expects the civil servants to function fairly, impartially and efficiently. The community at large should hold trust and confidence in the integrity of the civil services in resource augmentation and in decision-making process.

In a democracy, civil service must have a separate set of values and principles that distinguishes it from other professions so that it is efficient in its functions. The following values are considered to be the hallmarks of an efficient civil service.

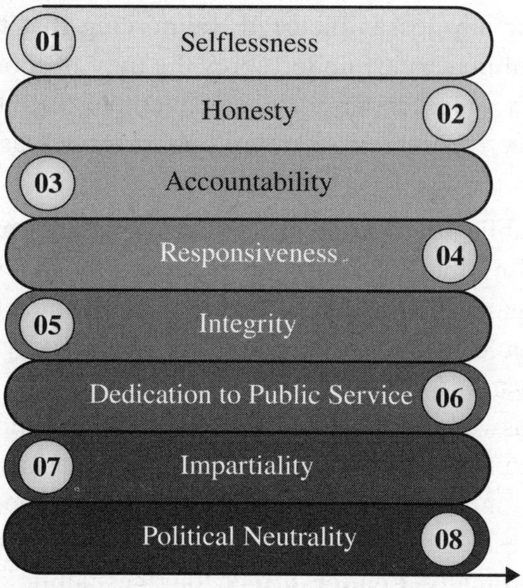

Fig. 14.1 Qualities of a Civil Services Officer

Countries like India, Australia and Poland have embodied these values in their laws and constitutions. As the backbone of any democratic society, the civil service must uphold its standards by ensuring that the decisions and actions of the civil servants align with the policies and principles of the government in power. Values like professionalism, responsiveness and impartiality of civil servants in serving successive governments are the key elements that help to maintain the highest standards of our democratic political system.

1. CONCEPT OF PUBLIC SERVICE

Concept of public service refers to essential activities that are crucial for the well-being and development of society. These services are so vital that those in authority are obligated to ensure their continuous operation, even if it requires the use of force to maintain them. This responsibility arises from the principle that government officials, bound by the rule of law, must act in accordance with their duty to serve the public, with their power being derived not from sovereignty but from their role in advancing the collective interest. Public services address social needs that, if disrupted, could threaten the survival and progress of the society, requiring authorities to consistently deploy resources to meet these needs. The significance of public services lies in their contribution to social stability and development, with the state being responsible for organising and ensuring their delivery. Furthermore, the state is seen as liable for any harm caused by the failure of public services, shifting the role of the state towards an insurer of social risks. Public services are also rooted in social solidarity, where the collective treasury compensates individuals for any losses incurred, reinforcing that they benefit all citizens. In summary, the concept of public service underscores the duty of those in authority to guarantee the uninterrupted provision of essential services. It emphasises legal accountability, social responsibility, and the collective interest, framing public service as a fundamental duty of the state and its officials.

The seven principles of public life outline the ethical standards expected from public office holders. **Selflessness** requires that decisions be made solely in the public interest, avoiding any personal or financial gains. **Integrity** mandates that public officials avoid any financial or other obligations that could influence their actions. **Objectivity** emphasises that decisions, such as appointments or awarding contracts, should be based on merit. **Accountability** ensures that public officials are answerable for their actions to the public and are open to scrutiny. **Openness** calls for transparency, where decisions and their reasons are clearly communicated, with information restricted only when necessary for the public good. **Honesty** necessitates the declaration of private interests and the resolution of any conflicts of interest in a manner that protects the public interest. Finally, **Leadership** encourages public officials to lead by example, promoting these principles through their actions. Together, these principles aim to ensure that public office holders act with integrity, transparency, and accountability, fostering public trust and contributing to effective governance.

2. PHILOSOPHICAL BASIS OF GOVERNANCE

2.1 Social Contract Theory: Foundations of Society and Governance

Social contract theory is a foundational concept in political philosophy that explores the origins of society and the legitimacy of governmental authority. It asserts that individual's consent, explicitly or implicitly, to establish a society and government to maintain order and protect their rights. By examining human behaviour in a hypothetical 'State of Nature', theorists have sought to understand why societies form and how authority derives its legitimacy. Thomas Hobbes, in his work *Leviathan*, describes the State of Nature as a brutal condition of chaos where life is "solitary, poor, nasty, brutish, and short." To escape such an existence, individuals surrender their natural rights to a sovereign authority in exchange for security and order. This sovereign, or 'Leviathan', must wield absolute power to ensure stability and prevent a return to anarchy.

John Locke offers a contrasting perspective in *Two Treatises of Government*. He envisions the State of Nature as a more cooperative environment where individuals, governed by natural law, possess inherent rights to life, liberty, and property. For Locke, the social contract creates a government whose primary role is to protect these natural rights. Unlike Hobbes, Locke argues that citizens have the right to revolt if their government fails to uphold its obligations, an idea that deeply influenced democratic thought and revolutions in the 18th century. Jean-Jacques Rousseau critiques the inequalities of modern society in *The Social Contract*, famously stating, "Man is born free, and everywhere he is in chains." He introduces the concept of the 'general will', which represents the collective interests of the community. According to Rousseau, true freedom arises when individuals align their personal interests with the general will, fostering equality and unity within society.

In the 20th century, John Rawls revitalised social contract theory in *A Theory of Justice*. Rawls proposes a thought experiment known as the 'Original Position', where individuals design a just society without knowing their social status or personal circumstances. Through this 'Veil of Ignorance', Rawls argues for principles of justice that ensure equal basic liberties and allow inequalities only if they benefit the least advantaged members of society.

Social contract theory provides a framework for understanding governance, emphasising that legitimate authority arises from the consent of the governed. It underscores the balance between individual rights and collective responsibilities, urging citizens to uphold their role in the social contract. Beyond political systems, it raises ethical questions about justice, equality, and the role of government in promoting the common good. Despite its enduring relevance, the theory has faced critiques. Feminist and race-conscious scholars have argued that traditional frameworks often overlook the experiences and rights of marginalised groups. These critiques have prompted modern reinterpretations, expanding the theory to address contemporary issues such as global justice, environmental sustainability, and systemic inequalities.

Social contract theory continues to shape political thought, offering timeless insights into the dynamics of governance and the moral imperatives of collective life. Its evolution reflects humanity's ongoing pursuit of a just and equitable society.

2.2 The Philosophical Basis of Utilitarianism in Governance

Utilitarianism provides a compelling framework for governance, emphasising the ethical evaluation of actions and policies based on their consequences. Rooted in the principle of maximising overall happiness, it offers a systematic approach to decision-making that seeks to promote well-being and minimise suffering. At the core of utilitarianism is consequentialism, the idea that the moral worth of an action is determined solely by its outcomes. In governance, this means policies are evaluated not on intentions or adherence to rules but on their ability to deliver positive results, such as increased happiness or reduced suffering. This contrasts with deontological ethics, which prioritises duties and principles irrespective of outcomes.

A central tenet of utilitarianism is the 'Greatest Happiness Principle', which holds that the best actions are those that generate the greatest happiness for the greatest number. Applied to governance, this principle demands that decisions maximise overall well-being, ensuring that the happiness of all affected individuals is considered rather than privileging specific groups or interests. Impartiality is another key element of utilitarian thought, emphasising that everyone's happiness matters equally. In governance, this means that policymakers must weigh the welfare of all citizens without bias or favouritism. This agent-neutral perspective reinforces the idea that promoting the greater good is a universal moral responsibility, not limited to personal or localised concerns.

Historically, utilitarianism has been associated with a drive for moral and social reform. Thinkers like Jeremy Bentham and John Stuart Mill criticised unjust laws and harmful practices, advocating for changes that would promote greater utility. This reformist ethos aligns with governance practices aimed at rectifying societal injustices, reducing suffering, and improving collective well-being. The utilitarian framework also introduces a rational, systematic approach to decision-making in governance. Policymakers are encouraged to assess the potential benefits and harms of various actions, considering both immediate and long-term consequences. This analytical method helps ensure that decisions are guided by evidence and reason, prioritising actions with the most positive overall impact.

Finally, utilitarianism challenges the notion of psychological egoism, which claims that individuals act purely out of self-interest. Instead, it advocates for a broader moral obligation to prioritise the common good. This principle underscores the responsibility of governments and individuals to act in ways that enhance collective welfare, rather than merely pursuing personal or political gain.

In summary, utilitarianism in governance is grounded in its focus on outcomes, the maximisation of overall happiness, and an impartial, reformist approach to policy evaluation. These principles offer a robust ethical foundation for creating a more just and beneficial society, guiding leaders toward decisions that serve the greater good.

2.3 Gandhian Model of Governance

The Gandhian model of governance, rooted in the vision of *Ramarajya*, emphasises grassroots empowerment, self-reliance, moral authority, and harmony. By *Ramarajya*, Gandhi referred to a state of governance that embodies peace, equality, and universal well-being—where every individual, irrespective of status, lives in harmony with others and the environment. Politically, it translates to *Swaraj* or self-rule, a concept Gandhi equated with both individual autonomy and collective self-governance. At its core, the Gandhian governance model seeks to empower people at the grassroots level, envisioning villages as self-sufficient republics (*Gram Swaraj*). Each village would function autonomously, combining legislative, executive, and judicial responsibilities, and fostering participatory democracy. Gandhi saw this decentralization as essential for revitalising villages, where the majority of Indians lived, and considered their development the cornerstone of a truly independent India.

Gandhi's *Swaraj* goes beyond political independence; it encompasses individual, social, and economic dimensions. For Gandhi, true self-rule required individuals to practice self-discipline, self-assessment, and self-purification, fostering *swadeshi* or self-reliance. Politically, it emphasised self-government rather than reliance on external authorities, even national ones. Gandhi believed in the sovereignty of the people, governed by moral authority rather than coercion. He argued that *swaraj* would emerge only when people were educated to resist the misuse of power through constructive and voluntary action. In *Hind Swaraj* (1909), Gandhi laid out a blueprint for his governance model, rejecting the exploitative, industrialised framework of colonial rule. He called for an integral revolution, addressing all spheres of life—economic, social, and spiritual. Political independence, he maintained, was merely a precursor to achieving *Poorna Swaraj* or complete independence through non-violent and truthful means.

Gandhi's approach sharply contrasted with other leaders of the Indian National Congress, including Nehru, who dismissed his model as unrealistic. Gandhi, however, believed in slow, voluntary progress through constructive work rather than relying on centralised, top-down policies. His emphasis was on values rather than shortcuts or rapid industrialisation, advocating for sustainable development rooted in social justice. Critics have often labelled Gandhi's vision of *Ramarajya* and *Gram Swaraj* as utopian, arguing that it remains impractical in modern governance. However, Gandhi himself acknowledged the aspirational nature of his ideals, emphasising that they represent a distant but necessary goal. In the face of persistent poverty, inequality, and social unrest, his philosophy offers an alternative pathway to sustainable and inclusive development, prioritising moral, social, and economic freedoms alongside political independence.

The Gandhian model of governance, therefore, calls for a reimagining of development based on values of self-reliance, equity, and harmony, rejecting exploitative systems in favour of a decentralised, participatory, and non-violent order. It remains a relevant framework for addressing modern challenges of governance and social justice.

2.4 Good Governance as in Kautilya's Arthashastra

Kautilya's concept of good governance, as articulated in the *Arthashastra*, outlines fundamental principles designed to ensure the welfare of the state and its citizens. At its core is the belief that a ruler's success is intrinsically tied to the well-being of the people. He famously stated, *'In the happiness of his subjects lies his happiness; in their welfare, his welfare,'* emphasising that the primary goal of governance should be the happiness and welfare of the subjects. Kautilya identified three primary objectives of good governance. First, ensuring national security and developing infrastructure, such as roads and trade networks, to support commerce and economic growth. Second, formulating and implementing effective policies to eliminate barriers to economic development and encourage capital formation. Third, fostering a transparent, fair, and compassionate administration that prioritises the common good. These objectives highlight the interdependence of economic stability, security, and ethical administration.

Ethical leadership was a cornerstone of Kautilya's vision. He believed that rulers should embody moral duty (*dharma*), material well-being (*artha*), and aesthetic fulfilment, rising above ordinary morality to govern effectively and safeguard the state's interests. This ethical foundation was complemented by the emphasis on knowledge and intelligence, which Kautilya deemed essential for political stability, economic growth, and national security. Accountability and anti-corruption measures were critical elements of Kautilya's governance framework. He advocated for strict rules of conduct and the fair enforcement of punitive measures to maintain order and curb corruption. Impartial punishment, he argued, was vital to uphold societal righteousness. Additionally, Kautilya highlighted the importance of administrative efficiency, urging the appointment of competent ministers and officials to ensure effective governance.

Finally, Kautilya stressed the interdependence of governance, ethical conduct, and economic growth. He believed that robust institutions and sound administration were vital for sustained prosperity. His insights into governance—blending ethical leadership, administrative efficiency, and policy-driven economic development—continue to resonate in contemporary discussions on public administration and governance.

2.5 Weber on Governance

Max Weber's theories on governance, particularly his concept of bureaucracy, are foundational to modern public administration. He emphasised rational-legal authority, where governance is based on formal rules and laws, ensuring legitimacy through legal frameworks rather than personal traits or traditions. His model of bureaucracy highlighted key features: hierarchical organisation, specialisation of labour, rule-based operations, merit-based recruitment, and impersonal administration to ensure efficiency, consistency, and impartiality. Weber also stressed rationalisation, replacing traditional decision-making with logical, systematic processes for stability and predictability. While advocating professionalism and accountability, he warned against over-bureaucratisation, which could lead to rigidity and inefficiency.

2.6 Karl Marx on Governance

Karl Marx's views on governance are deeply rooted in his broader theories of society, economics, and class struggle. He argued that the political structures of a society are not independent entities but are shaped by its economic base. For Marx, the state arises from, and serves the interests of the ruling class—the bourgeoisie—who control the means of production. Governance under capitalism, he contended, is inherently exploitative, reinforcing class divisions and economic inequalities. This exploitation is perpetuated not only through coercion but also through dominant ideologies that legitimise the status quo.

Marx envisioned a radically different form of governance in a socialist society, characterised by collective ownership of the means of production and equitable distribution of resources. He proposed a system governed by the principle, *"from each according to his ability, to each according to his needs,"* emphasising participatory governance and the collective nature of labour. In this framework, governance would no longer serve the interests of a ruling class but prioritise human freedom and the elimination of alienation.

Marx also critiqued the state as an apparatus designed to maintain existing power structures and suppress revolutionary change. He argued that true human emancipation requires transforming the social and economic conditions that underpin these systems. For Marx, governance should ultimately aim at collective self-rule by the proletariat, leading to a society where power is democratised, and human potential is fully realised. In summary, Marx's perspective links governance to economic structures, critiques the capitalist state, and advocates for a socialist model that fosters equality and collective well-being.

2.7 Hegel on Governance

Hegel's philosophy of governance is deeply rooted in his broader philosophical system, particularly his concepts of the state, freedom, and ethical life (*Sittlichkeit*). His views on governance highlight the interplay between individual freedom, ethical development, and the role of the state as a rational and unifying force. For Hegel, the state represents the highest realisation of freedom, not as a mechanism of control, but as the embodiment of ethical life where individual and collective interests are harmonised. True freedom, in his view, is actualised within the context of the state, which serves as the rational will of the people and the ultimate form of social organisation. Good governance, therefore, is characterised by the promotion of ethical life through laws and institutions that reflect this rational will. The state mediates between individual desires and the universal good, fostering both social order and the moral development of its citizens.

Hegel differentiates between the state and civil society, where civil society represents the realm of individual economic and social interests. Good governance involves balancing these two spheres by integrating the interests of civil society into the broader framework of the state. This balance prevents societal fragmentation and ensures social cohesion, with the state overseeing civil society to promote the common good. Hegel places significant emphasis on the legislative process, advocating for laws that are universal and promote the welfare of all citizens. He argues that governance should not rely on unqualified universal suffrage, which risks apathy and uninformed decision-making. Instead, he supports a more educated electorate capable of meaningful participation in governance, ensuring that legislative functions are rational and aligned with the state's unity.

Another key feature of Hegel's governance model is the inclusion of estates —social classes or groups with political recognition. These estates act as intermediaries between the government and the people, ensuring representation of diverse interests while maintaining state cohesion. Their participation in the legislative process strengthens public engagement and creates a system where governance reflects the complexities of the society. Hegel also advocates for gradual reform rather than radical change. He emphasises the importance of continuity with existing institutions, where reforms are aligned with the ethical and rational development of society. Good governance, in this sense, focuses on achieving legal equality, public welfare, and societal stability without undermining established frameworks.

Hegel's philosophy of governance envisions the state as a rational and ethical entity that reconciles individual freedoms with the common good. Good governance, according to Hegel, requires a balance between state authority and civil society, effective representation of societal interests, and a commitment to gradual, rational reform that respects the continuity of social institutions.

2.8 New Public Management

The 1992 World Bank report *Governance and Development* introduced a pivotal shift in the understanding of governance, emphasising its central role in achieving sustainable development. The report highlighted key principles such as accountability, transparency, the rule of law, and public sector efficiency, arguing that weak governance—marked by corruption, inefficiency, and a lack of participation—hinders economic growth and development. This perspective linked the quality of governance directly to developmental outcomes, adding a new dimension to public management.

Coinciding with this, the emergence of New Public Management (NPM) sought to reform traditional bureaucratic systems by integrating market-oriented practices, decentralisation, and performance measurement. NPM focused on efficiency, accountability, and results, introducing features such as managerial autonomy, where public organisations operate as self-contained units, and a customer-oriented approach that prioritises citizen needs. This shift was influenced by global economic changes in the 1980s and 1990s, which emphasised deregulation, privatisation, and the transformation of states into "competition states." Furthermore, dissatisfaction with bureaucratic inefficiencies led to the adoption of market-driven governance, supported by economic theories like Public Choice Theory, which advocated for reducing the government size and fostering competition.

Together, the World Bank's governance framework and NPM's principles created a paradigm shift that encouraged governments to focus on efficiency, citizen engagement, and institutional integrity. While NPM aims for greater public sector efficiency, it must also align with the core values of good governance—such as accountability, transparency, equity, and participation—to ensure that public services are inclusive, equitable, and responsive to the needs of society.

3. PROBITY

Probity refers to the quality of having strong moral principles, integrity, and honesty, especially in public life and governance. It represents the ethical standards that public officials are expected to uphold while performing their duties. Probity emphasises ethical conduct, where decisions prioritise public interest over personal gain. It requires transparency, accountability, and the avoidance of conflicts of interest, ensuring that officials act in ways that inspire confidence and trust. A core aspect of probity is accountability, which mandates that public officials take responsibility for their actions and decisions. This accountability ensures adherence to the rule of law and encourages scrutiny from the public and oversight bodies, fostering trust in governance. Integrity, another key element, demands that officials avoid corrupt practices and resist external pressures that could compromise their responsibilities, further strengthening public faith in institutional systems.

Maintaining probity is critical for building and sustaining public trust in government. When citizens perceive their leaders as ethical and transparent, they are more likely to support and engage with governmental initiatives. Probity also plays a pivotal role in reducing corruption by promoting ethical behaviour and discouraging practices that undermine governance. This, in turn, creates an environment conducive to economic growth and equitable development. Additionally, probity underpins effective governance by ensuring that decisions are based on merit and public interest, resulting in better public service delivery. It also contributes to social justice by ensuring that resources and opportunities are distributed fairly without favouritism or bias. A robust legal framework further enforces probity, with mechanisms to report and address corruption while promoting transparency.

Probity is a cornerstone of good governance. It fosters trust, accountability, and integrity, thereby building a transparent, equitable, and accountable system that serves the public effectively and upholds the principles of democracy.

4. CODES OF CONDUCT

Every organisation/institution has its own standards or codes of conduct through which it communicates its values, missions and visions, ethical codes for decision-making and rules of behaviour. It is a part of every organisation's effort to infuse organisational values to its employees, essential aspects of business ethics, regulating their behaviour within the organisation and with the wider community in the course of building an organisation to reach higher standards.

In order to bring about efficiency in the organisation, codes of conduct or codes of behaviour are formulated by each organisation. Codes of conduct tries to prevent certain specific types of behaviour like

- Emotional disturbances
- Conflict of interest
- Self-dealing
- Bribery
- Corruption
- Political neutrality
- Inappropriate actions

Failure of many of the corporate companies, and the emergence of corporate scandals, and their impact on a country's capital market, investor sentiment and its economy is largely attributed to the failure of practicing the codes of conduct. More often, the individuals and groups in corporates are demanding more transparency from their leaders than profit maximisation. Since 2014, India has taken various efforts to promote and enforce standards of conduct for business, as well as governmental and non-governmental organisations, e.g., legislation on corporate social responsibility.

- **Good Conduct is Good Business**

For a successful venture in business, it is essential that the businesspeople recognise and practice good conduct and integrity. 'Good Conduct is Good Business' is the mantra that is believed and practiced by management experts and business legends for their better performance and to scale high levels. The successful functioning of multinational corporate companies which have operational facilities at various locations across the world is attributed to the enforcement of code of conducts in their facilities. Apart from this, these corporates also bring about a change in the value transformation among corporate companies in the developing world, e.g., implementation of corporate governance by Indian corporates.

For multinational companies, it is the code of conduct that acts as a reference or real document for effective decision-making. Since these organisations are spread across various locations, the codes of conduct help to bind:

1. Employees with the leaders in the management level,
2. Among employees themselves, and
3. Corporates' ideals with that of the government's social vision.

The failure of corporate companies is attributed to their failure to practice these codes in true spirit. In this case, it is the senior level management team which is accused of failing to provide leadership for the enforcement of these codes. An effective code would result in better controls and regulations in an organisation, which is directly linked to its financial performance.

- **Morality and Standards**

Morality is yet another component which is not only linked with the performance of an organisation, but the standards set in morality would lead to overall performance of the economy. It is a mandatory obligation on the part of the organisation and its employees to comply with the applicable laws and guidelines of the government and regulatory authorities. Any organisation should not support or encourage the employees who use unlawful means to achieve the desired results. These activities may include:

1. Misconduct
2. Unlawful activities
3. Payments for illegal activities
4. Political conspiracy
5. Indirect contributions
6. Rebates
7. Bribery
8. Threat and physical assault
9. Misuse of official position
10. Misuse of company's records

It is the utmost duty of the organisation not to permit any activity that fails to stand the closest possible public scrutiny and expectations. A code of conduct prescribed in a company for its employees should have the standards that are well above the minimum standards fixed. Hence, all employees must ensure that their actions should in no way contravene to the existing rules and regulations that govern the organisation's operations. If an employee is uncertain about the implications of any legal requirement, then he/she should, at once, refer the matter to the higher authorities who can seek appropriate legal advice and regulate the behaviour pattern.

Adherence to the code of conduct prescribed by the government and regulatory bodies is mandatory for public servants. Public servants should always be reminded of the dictum that the government machinery is not for profit or financial benefits, rather it is a system established to provide the basic amenities to the people, and to promote their standard of living. Thus, public servants should realise their responsibility and act with dignity and integrity in performing their official functions.

4.1 Code of Conduct for Civil Servants

- **Origin of Civil Servants Code**

"I would advise you to maintain to the utmost the impartiality and incorruptibility of administration. A civil servant cannot afford to, and must not, take part in politics. Nor must he involve himself in communal wrangles. To depart from the path of rectitude in either of these respects is to debase public service and to lower its dignity. Similarly, no service worth the name can claim to exist if it does not have in view the achievement of the highest standard of integrity. Unhappily, India today cannot boast of an incorruptible service, but I hope that you, who are now starting, as it were, a new generation of civil servants, will not be misled by black sheep in the fold, but render your service without fear or favour and without any expectation of extraneous rewards.

You are the pioneers in the Indian Service, and the future of this service will depend much upon the foundation and traditions that will be laid down by you, by your character and abilities and by your spirit of service. You can look forward to your future with trust and confidence, and if you serve in the true spirit of service, I am sure you will have your best reward. I shall ask you, therefore, to devote yourselves to your studies, fully conscious of the responsibilities and opportunities that await you and seek from what you hear instruction with a humble mind. I wish all of you Godspeed."

Sardar Vallabhai Patel

Note: Text of a speech delivered to the probationers at the All-India Administrative Service Training School, Delhi, April 1947. Originally published in *Bombay Chronicle*, April 21, 1947. This extract was circulated at the Civil Services Day function at Vigyan Bhawan, New Delhi, on April 21, 2007. This extract is taken from The Collected Works of Sardar Vallabhbhai Patel. Volume XII (1 January 1947–31 December 1947).

4.2 Morals and Values of Civil Servants as Contained in Civil Services (Conduct) Rules, 1964

Based on the recommendations of the Committee on Prevention of Corruption headed by Late Shri K. Santhanam, the conduct rules for the government servants were revised with a view to maintaining integrity in public services. The Central Civil Services (Conduct) Rules, 1964, were notified laying down the code of conduct for central government employees. The public service and the public servants shall be guided by the following values in the discharge of their functions.

Every government servant shall, at all times:

(i) Maintain absolute integrity
(ii) Maintain devotion to duty
(iii) Do nothing which is unbecoming of a government servant

(iv) Patriotism and upholding national pride
(v) Allegiance to the Constitution and the law of the nation
(vi) Objectivity, impartiality, honesty, diligence, courtesy, and transparency
(vii) Every government servant holding a supervisory post shall take all possible steps to ensure the integrity and devotion to duty of all government servants for the time being under his control and authority
(viii) No government servant shall, in the performance of his official duties, or in the exercise of powers conferred on him, act otherwise than in his best judgement except when he is acting under the direction of his official superior
(ix) The direction of the official superior shall ordinarily be in writing. Oral direction to subordinates shall be avoided, as far as possible. Where the issue of oral direction becomes unavoidable, the official superior shall confirm it in writing immediately thereafter
(x) A government servant who has received oral direction from his official superior shall seek confirmation of the same in writing as early as possible, whereupon it shall be the duty of the official superior to confirm the direction in writing
(xi) No government servant shall:
  (a) In the performance of his official duties, act in a discourteous manner
  (b) In his official dealings with the public or otherwise, adopt dilatory tactics or wilfully cause delays in disposal of the work assigned to him
(xii) Every government servant shall, at all times:
  (a) Act in accordance with the government's policies regarding the age of marriage, preservation of the environment, protection of wildlife and cultural heritage
  (b) Observe the government's policies regarding prevention of crime against women
(xiii) Prohibition of sexual harassment of working women

4.3 Latest Amendment in Central Services (Conduct) Rules, 1964

In India, the current set of ethical norms are the conduct rules, contained in the Central Services (Conduct) Rules, 1964, and rules applicable to members of the All-India Services or employees of various state governments. The code of behaviour as enunciated in the conduct rules, while containing some general norms like 'maintaining integrity and absolute devotion to duty' and not indulging in 'conduct unbecoming of a government servant' is generally directed towards cataloguing specific activities deemed undesirable for government servants. These conduct rules do not constitute a code of ethics.

The centre, based on consultations with the state governments, issued the All-India Services (Conduct) Amendment Rules, 2014, stating, among other things, that every member of the service shall take decisions solely based on merit and in public interest, and use public resources efficiently, effectively, and economically. The new commandments prevent a bureaucrat from misusing his position to take decisions that seek to derive financial or material benefit for himself, his family, or friends. 'Every member of the service shall make choices, take decisions and make recommendations on merit alone,' say the rules. Another rule cautions civil servants against placing themselves under any financial or other obligations to any individual or organisation which may influence the performance of their official duties.

Stressing on the need for confidentiality in key government matters, the rules make civil servants liable to maintain confidentiality in performance of their duties as required by the laws, particularly where the information or disclosure may prejudicially affect the security of the state, strategic, scientific, or economic interests of the state, friendly relations with foreign countries, or lead to incitement of an offence, or illegal or unlawful gains to any person.

Other amendments require civil servants to perform their duties with a high degree of professionalism, uphold supremacy of the Constitution, uphold the sovereignty and integrity of India, the security of the state, public order, decency and morality, maintain integrity in public service, act with fairness and impartiality and not discriminate against anyone, particularly the poor and under-privileged sections, and maintain discipline in discharge of duties and be liable to implement lawful orders duly communicated to them.

4.4 Public Services Bill, 2007

The Draft Public Services Bill, 2007, proposes the necessary first step towards evolving a code of ethics.

It states in Chapter III,

1. Values of Public Service: The public service and the public servants shall be guided by the following values in the discharge of their functions:
   (1) Patriotism and upholding national pride,
   (2) Allegiance to the Constitution and the law of the nation,
   (3) Objectivity, impartiality, honesty, diligence, courtesy, and transparency, and
   (4) Maintain absolute integrity.
2. Without prejudice to the provisions of this Act, the central government may, on the recommendations of, or in consultation with the central authority, notify from time-to-time other values in this section.
3. Review of Public Service Values: The central authority may from time-to-time review the adoption, adherence to, and implementation of the public service values in the departments or organisations under the central government, and send reports to the central government.
4. Public Services Code:
   (1) The government shall promote the public service values and a standard of ethics in the public service operations, requiring and facilitating every public service employee:
      i. to discharge official duties with competence and accountability, care and diligence, responsibility, honesty, objectivity, and impartiality, without discrimination and in accordance with the law,

ii. To ensure effective management, professional growth, and leadership development,
iii. To avoid misuse of official position or information, and using the public money with utmost care and autonomy, and,
iv. Function with the objective that the public services and the public servants are to serve as instruments of good governance and to provide services for the betterment of the public at large, foster socio-economic development, with due regard to the diversity of the nation, but without discrimination on the ground of caste, community, religion, gender, or class, and duly protecting the interest of poor, underprivileged, and weaker sections.

(2) The government shall, in consultation with the central authority, prepare a public services code of ethics for guiding the public service employees within 1 year from the commencement of this Act.

4.5 Consolidation of Values Expected from Civil Servants as Contained in Draft Public Services Bill, 2007

Generic expectations from civil servants, which are referred to as 'values' are as under:

1. Allegiance to the various ideals enshrined in the Preamble to the Constitution,
2. Apolitical functioning,
3. Good governance for the betterment of the people to be the primary goal of civil service,
4. Duty to act objectively and impartially,
5. Accountability and transparency in decision-making,
6. Maintenance of the highest ethical standards,
7. Merit to be the criteria in the selection of civil servants being consistent, however, with the cultural, ethnic, and other diversities of the nation.
8. Ensuring economy and avoidance of wastage in expenditure.
9. Provision of healthy and congenial work environment.
10. Communication, consultation, and cooperation in performance of functions, i.e., participation of all levels of personnel in management.

4.6 Importance of Ethical Code of Conduct

First, the codes of ethics increase the probability that people will behave in certain ways. They do this partially by focusing on the character of their actions, and partly by focusing on the sanctions/punishments for violations. Second, good ethics codes can help public servants focus on actions that result in doing the right things for the right reasons. Ethical behaviour should become a habit, and effective codes allow both bureaucrats, and elected officials to test their actions against the expected standards. Transparency and responsiveness can be achieved through effective implementation of the ethical code of conduct.

Third, the codes of ethics do not take away one's own moral autonomy or absolve the public servant from the obligation to reason. The codes of ethics provide a strong prima facie reason to act in a certain moral way. Public servants' duties are converted into responsibility.

Fourth, the codes of ethics can function as a professional statement that it expresses the public service's commitments to a specific set of moral standards. This has both cognitive and emotive value.

Ethics is grounded in the principle of responsibility and accountability. In a democracy, every holder of public office is accountable ultimately to the people. Such an accountability is enforced through a system of laws and rules, which the elected representatives of the people enact in their legislatures. Ethics provides the basis for the creation of such laws and rules. It is the moral ideas of people that give rise to and shapes the character of laws and rules. Our legal system emanates from a shared vision of what is good and just.

The fundamental principle in a democracy is that all persons holding authority derive it from the people; in other words, all public functionaries are trustees of the people. With the expansion of the role of the government, public functionaries exercise considerable influence over the lives of the people. The trusteeship relationship between the public and the officials requires that the authority entrusted to the officials be exercised in the best interest of the people, or in 'public interest'.

> **? Thought Box**
>
> How can the implementation of a strong ethical code of conduct in public service influence the trust and accountability of government institutions?

A system of laws and rules, however elaborate, cannot provide for all situations and predictions. It is no doubt desirable, and perhaps possible, to govern the conduct of those who occupy positions in the lower places and exercise limited or no discretion. But the higher the level in public service, the greater is the ambit of discretion. And it is difficult to provide for a system of laws and rules that can comprehensively cover and regulate the exercise of discretion in high places.

4.7 Nolan Committee on Standards in Public Life

One of the most comprehensive statements of what constitutes ethical standards for holders of public office came from the Committee on Standards in Public Life in the United Kingdom, popularly known as the Nolan Committee, which outlined the following seven principles of public life:

1. **Selflessness:** Holders of public office should take decisions solely and primarily in terms of public interest. They should not do so in order to gain financial or other material benefits for themselves, their family or their friends.
2. **Integrity:** Holders of public office should not place themselves under any financial or other obligation to outside individuals or organisations that might influence them in the performance of their official duties.

3. **Objectivity:** In carrying out public businesses, including making public appointments, awarding contracts, or recommending individuals for rewards and benefits, holders of public office should make choices on merit.
4. **Accountability:** Holders of public office are accountable for their decisions and actions to the public and must submit themselves to whatever scrutiny is appropriate to their office.
5. **Openness:** Holders of public office should be as open as possible about all the decisions and actions they take. They should give reasons for their decisions and restrict information only when the wider public interest clearly demands.
6. **Honesty:** Holders of public office have a duty to declare any private interests relating to their public duties, and to take steps to resolve any conflicts arising in a way that protects the public interest.
7. **Leadership:** Holders of public office should promote and support these principles by leadership and example.

These principles of public life are of general applicability in every democracy. Arising out of such ethical principles, a set of guidelines of public behaviour in the nature of a code of conduct becomes essential for public functionaries. Indeed, any person who is privileged to guide the destiny of the people must not only be ethical but must be seen to practice these ethical values.

Although all citizens are subject to the laws of the land, in the case of public servants, there must be standards of behaviour more stringent than those for an ordinary citizen. It is at the interface of public action and private interest that the need arises for establishing not just a code of ethics, but a code of conduct. A code of ethics would cover broad-guiding principles of good behaviour and governance, while a more specific code of conduct should, in a precise and unambiguous manner, stipulate a list of acceptable and unacceptable behaviour and action.

5. CODE OF ETHICS

The code of ethics is nothing but a set of moral values, which is evolved by the social, cultural, and other traditional establishments. Unlike a law which is enacted by the legislature, the code of ethics comes out of social, cultural, moral guidelines and norms which is noticed directly or indirectly in our day to day life, e.g., code of ethics in culture, governance, business and profession, religion, etc.

Code of Ethics in various spheres of life:

In Culture	In Public life	In Governance	In Religion
E.g., Preserving the uniqueness of our primitive culture and tradition, ensuring that customs, traditions, and rituals are followed.	E.g., Responsibility, accountability, transparency, integrity, impartiality, and empathy towards the weaker sections.	E.g., Good governance, resource utilisation, welfare of citizens, citizens' charters, right to information, e-governance, etc.	E.g., Recognising and respecting the individuality, freedom of belief, thoughts, and religious practices, secularism, etc.

Everyone is expected to follow ethical and moral codes in whatever walks of life they are. The ultimate aim of ethics is promoting social harmony through integrity, and responsiveness, and at the same time recognising individual freedom and values. Almost all the corporate forms which employ large number of people adopt code of ethics and the individuals are supposed to follow these regulations. All the individuals occupying important posts in private organisations or with the government are supposed to be driven by the moral codes. It is these people who would drive the company or government to achieve the desired results. Any organisation lacking these individuals would ultimately fail in their venture.

Given below are some of the values that could be included in code of ethics.

1. Operating the business/corporate environment in an ethical manner that is higher than the enacted law and rules.
2. Organisation's functionaries should ensure customer satisfaction, as well as be equally committed to stand with the organisation's integrity.
3. Employers and employees should be committed to improve both professionally and personally. This can happen only when both the parties accept full responsibility for their work and actions.
4. Respect the rights of customers and consumers to retain their confidence with the company, and at the same time maintain confidence of all information that is required by the organisation.

As an individual, apply the golden rule: 'Do unto others as you would have them do unto you.'

Ethics can be a dilemma because thoughts and value systems of individuals or groups are different from each other. What a few or a particular society considers ethical may be unethical to another individual or society.

6. CODE OF CONDUCT Vs. CODE OF ETHICS

The terms 'Code of Ethics' and 'Code of Conduct' are often mistakenly used to mean the same. But they are different as the code of ethics govern decision-making process, while the code of conduct govern actions of an organisation. They both act as the two most common ways by which companies self-regulate, and hold them responsible to themselves and to the society as well. With the emergence of globalisation and the presence of multinational companies worldwide, these two terms have gained more importance. These codes not only provide direction, but also guidelines for employees to establish a public image of good behaviour that benefits the business, the organisation's integrity, and the government's accountability and responsibility towards its citizens.

There has been a lot of information and philosophies about the code of ethics and the code of conduct. As their names suggest, the code of ethics have a weighing upon the decisions made by individuals and companies, whereas the code of conduct have a bearing upon the actions taken by individuals, as well as organisations. The confusion between the two is because of the similarities in conduct that are deemed acceptable by law, and ethics that are acceptable to the society.

Every organisation has its own code of conduct, i.e., written rules and regulations about how employees should behave in different situations so that the organisational values are respected and adhered to. For example, most of the companies do not allow their employees to smoke inside the working area of the company. But if an employee, being a habitual smoker, finds himself in a situation when there is no one is around, and there is no chance of him being caught by any sensor or camera, it is his decision of not smoking that comes within the purview of the code of ethics and not the code of conduct.

Code of Conduct	Code of Ethics
• The codes of conduct are largely concerned with governing actions.	• The codes of ethics are largely concerned with decision-making.
• The codes of conduct are rules and regulations that must be strictly followed by the employees of an organisation, and failure to follow would attract penal actions that could lead to their removal from the company.	• The codes of ethics are behaviour patterns, or actions that are unwritten rules and regulations, and their violation is usually frowned upon by the company, though not prohibited under law.
• Conduct standards generally require little judgement; you obey, or incur a penalty and face the consequences. The code provides a fairly clear set of expectations of the company from its employees about the actions that are required, acceptable, or prohibited.	• Ethical standards generally are wide-ranging and non-specific; they are designed to provide a set of values or decision-making approaches that could help the employees to make independent judgements about the most appropriate course of action.
• It generally highlights an individual's behaviours and attitude, rather than a community or society.	• Code of ethics visualises society or community thoughts and expressions. It is a documentation for individual actions within societal values and morals.
• Since the code is created by organisations/ companies, violation of the code of conduct leads to severe penalties and punishments.	• As the code of ethics is not created or enacted by legislature, in many cases, violations may not lead to penalties and punishments. But it will have severe impact on the company's goodwill, and also act as the cause for moral failure of personalities.
• It is artificially architected by groups of individuals or organisations. It takes less time to get structure and an implementation.	• The code of ethics is not architected, but it is the result of the evolution of morals and traditional codes.
• Violation of the code of conduct leads to failure of business, or loss of revenue to the organisation.	• Even though in most of the cases, a violation of the code of ethics does not lead to measurable or visual effects in organisations, it causes the failure in the moral values of the organisation machinery. Sometimes it leads to a collapse in entire social and moral practices.

Both the codes are similar in some form as they attempt to encourage specific forms of behaviour and actions by employees. Ethics guidelines attempt to provide guidance about values, morals, and choices to influence decision-making, whereas conduct regulations assert whether some specific actions are appropriate or inappropriate.

The code of ethics for an organisation or for a profession are developed more in the form of statement of morals, values, and beliefs that defines an organisation or a group. Moral statements are inspirational and motivational, while the rules or principles are the beliefs that individual members of an organisation should consider in order to continue as members of the organisation.

The code of conduct, on the contrary, translates the values (documented in the code of ethics) into specific behavioural standards, keeping in mind the possible reflection on the stakeholders' interest.

7. ARC RECOMMENDATIONS FOR THE CODES OF CONDUCT

The Second Administration Reforms Commission has studied the issue of ethics in public life in other countries, and in its report on 'Ethics in Governance', it has highlighted the seven principles of public life enunciated by the Nolan Committee in UK. Drawing from these, the commission also would suggest the inclusion of the following principles in the Code of Ethics for civil servants in India:

Integrity: Civil servants should be guided solely by public interest in their official decision-making and not by any financial or other consideration, either in respect of themselves, their families, or their friends.

Impartiality: Civil servants in carrying out their official work, including functions like procurement, recruitment, delivery of services, etc., should take decisions based on merit alone.

Commitment to Public Service: Civil servants should deliver services in a fair, effective, impartial, and courteous manner.

Open Accountability: Civil servants are accountable for their decisions and actions, and should be willing to subject themselves to appropriate scrutiny for this purpose.

Devotion to Duty: Civil servants shall maintain absolute and unstinting devotion towards their duties and responsibilities at all times.

Exemplary Behaviour: Civil servants shall treat all members of the public with respect and courtesy, and, at all times, should behave in a manner that upholds the rich traditions of the civil services.

? Thought Box

How can the recommendations of the Administrative Reforms Commission (ARC) for a code of conduct enhance the integrity and efficiency of civil services, and what challenges might arise in their effective implementation?

8. INTERNATIONAL COMPARISON

By its Resolution 58/4 of 31 October 2003, the General Assembly adopted the United Nations Convention against Corruption. Article 8 of the Resolution states:

1. To fight corruption, each state party shall promote, inter alia, integrity, honesty, and responsibility among its public officials, in accordance with the fundamental principles of its legal system.
2. In particular, each state party shall endeavour to apply, within its own institutional and legal systems, codes or standards of conduct for the correct, honourable and proper performance of public functions.
3. For the purposes of implementing the provisions of this article, each state party shall, where appropriate and in accordance with the fundamental principles of its legal system, take note of the relevant initiatives of regional, interregional and multilateral organisations, such as the International Code of Conduct for Public Officials contained in the annex to General Assembly resolution 51/59 of 12 December 1996.
4. Each state party shall also consider, in accordance with the fundamental principles of its domestic law, establishing measures and systems to facilitate the reporting by public officials of acts of corruption to appropriate authorities, when such acts come to their notice in the performance of their functions.
5. Each state party shall endeavour, where appropriate and in accordance with the fundamental principles of its domestic law, to establish measures and systems requiring public officials to make declarations to appropriate authorities regarding, inter alia, their outside activities, employment, investments, assets, and substantial gifts or benefits from which a conflict of interest may result with respect to their functions as public officials.
6. Each state party shall consider taking, in accordance with the fundamental principles of its domestic law, disciplinary or other measures against public officials who violate the codes or standards established in accordance with this article.

8.1 Civil Service Values in the United Kingdom

The civil service is an integral and key part of the government of the United Kingdom. It supports the government of the day in developing and implementing its policies, and in delivering public services. Civil servants are accountable to ministers who, in turn, are accountable to the Parliament.

As a civil servant, you are appointed on merit based on fair and open competition and are expected to carry out your role with dedication and a commitment to the civil service and its core values: integrity, honesty, objectivity, and impartiality.

In this code:

- 'Integrity' puts obligations of public service above your own personal interests;
- 'Honesty' is being truthful and open;
- 'Objectivity' is based on advice and decisions on rigorous analysis of the evidence; and
- 'Impartiality' is acting solely according to the merits of the case, and is serving equally well under governments of different political persuasions.

These core values support good government and ensure the achievement of the highest possible standards in all that the civil service does. This in turn, helps the civil service to gain and retain the respect of ministers, the Parliament, the public, and its customers.

8.2 Civil Service Values in Australia's Public Service Act

Section 13 of Australia's Public Service Act outlines the code of conduct for the nation's civil service, establishing clear expectations for employee behaviour and responsibilities. The code mandates that the civil servants must:

- Act with honesty, integrity, care, and diligence in their duties.
- Treat everyone with respect, courtesy, and without harassment during their work.
- Comply with all applicable Australian laws, and follow lawful and reasonable instructions from authorised individuals within their agency.
- Maintain confidentiality in dealings with ministers or their staff.
- Disclose and take reasonable steps to avoid conflicts of interest, whether real or apparent.
- Use commonwealth resources responsibly and appropriately.
- Avoid providing false or misleading information in response to official requests.
- Refrain from improper use of insider information, position, or authority for personal or external benefit.
- Consistently uphold the values, integrity, and reputation of the Australian Public Service (APS).
- Behave in a manner that enhances Australia's reputation while serving overseas.
- Avoid sharing or disclosing public business or official information without authorisation, except as required by their duties.

8.3 Civil Service Values from an Extract of the Code of Good Governance of Spain

Spain's Code of Good Governance emphasises that senior public officers must adhere not only to legal obligations, but also to ethical principles. These principles, though not explicitly stated in regulations, guide conduct, and include objectivity, integrity, neutrality, responsibility, impartiality, transparency, efficiency, honesty, and equality. Public service should be dedicated to the welfare of the citizens, ensuring confidentiality, credibility, and exemplary conduct.

8.4 Conclusion

Ethics codes, once considered luxuries, are now integral to preventing corruption and ensuring effective governance. They are essential to modern public administration, as integrity is key to the success and fairness of public programs. Developing effective codes of ethics is crucial for combating corruption and advancing societal progress. However, these codes must be supported by the actions of individuals, public servants, and institutions, emphasising the need for internal responsibility and the promotion of social harmony.

9. WORK CULTURE

Introduction

> "No company, small or large, can win over the long run without energised employees who believe in the mission and understand how to achieve it." **Jack Welch**

The success of an organisation is purely dependent on the 'degree of cohesion' among its members to meet the goal of the organisation. Work culture can be defined as the 'values, norms and guiding beliefs that are shared by the members of an organisation.' To be precise, it is the synergy between the technical skills and the behavioural skills of the members of the organisation.

Workplace culture is a distinctive sociological construct. It works in a much similar way compared to other types of cultures in a community, but varies in one significant aspect: it is intrinsically multicultural. The result of an organisational culture is based on the type of organisation, the staff, the principles, policies, and values of the workplace. There is a large variety of organisational cultures that appear in different environments; some occur naturally, and some are implemented by the executive management in the company.

9.1 Importance of Work Culture

(a) Creating a positive work culture will foster an environment conducive for employee retention and work satisfaction.

(b) It paves the way for achieving the two critical functions of an organisation, namely,

  (i) Internal integration – which is the collective identity of the individuals of an organisational set up, and knowing how to work together.

  (ii) External adaptation – how the organisation meets the goals and deals with outsiders.

(c) A strong organisational culture makes the workplace more attractive to potential employees.

(d) It also helps in the retention of the existing talents or employees. This would help the organisation avoid investments made on new hire searches and their respective set-up costs.

Considering in mind the costs of hiring, training, and impact on team productivity, it is ideal to create an environment where people are less likely to leave.

(e) It also contributes greatly towards improving the brand value of a company. It helps in synchronising the employees' perceptions with that of the customers', thereby establishing a positive public perception of the company as a whole. A happy employee is the best brand ambassador for the organisation.

9.2 Types of Organisational Culture

Most companies fall into two major predominant models: strong culture and weak culture. Employees have a sense of empowerment and understanding of the company goals, regulations, and philosophy in a strong culture. On the contrary, in an organisation with a weak culture, employees are apathetic, unmotivated, lazy, uninterested, and function under a rule of fear. Specific types of organisational culture are as follows:

(a) Academy Culture: Academy culture comprises of employees who are studious and highly skilled, and are forthcoming when it comes to training and advancements. Intense training for new employees and improvement training for existing employees are the key elements of success of this workplace. Employees for this type of organisations are hired based on their existing skill sets and their willingness to learn and grow. Turn-over rates are low, and the employees are willing to do their job to the best of their capability. Academic culture is used widely in hospitals, universities, educational institutions, and research facilities to catch up with the current information and technology.

(b) Normative Culture: Normative culture is widespread in corporate workplace. It involves following strict regulations and guidelines that maintain the policies of the organisation. The rate of creativity and freedom is low in this type of organisation, and the employees would seldom deviate from their specific job role or break rules. These types of organisations run slender, and are not suitable for every type of employee.

(c) Pragmatic Culture: The first and only focus of a pragmatic culture workplace are 'customers'. The customer or client comes before anything or anyone else. Since every customer is different, these types of workplaces are directly opposite to a normative culture environment. Employees don't stick to strict and rigid rules. The rate of flexibility is high depending on the needs and requirements of the customer.

(d) Club Culture: Employees that are highly skilled and competent in their functional area are mostly likely be hired in a club cultured organisation. Wide areas are taken into consideration before hiring an employee, like educational qualifications, special skill sets, prior work experience, and even personal interests. This can be seen in organisations like the CBI, commercial pilots, and specialist branches of the defence forces. Hard work often pays off in a club culture type of organisation. These types of employers often reward hard work with promotions and frequent appraisals.

(e) Baseball Team Culture: Baseball team culture is one of the highly attractive organisational structures from an employee's perspective. This type of environment is all about the employees first. They believe that the work will get done accurately as long as the workers are happy, which in turn makes the employees to stick around the company for a long time. A good example of a baseball team culture is Google. The employees get to do pretty much what they wish for. Social events and company outings are a regular thing, and incentives are a big factor in this type of culture. Today, more and more organisations are moving to this type of work culture.

(f) Fortress Culture: Fortress culture could be the worst, or the best depending on how good you are at what you do. It is all about performance and numbers. The employees are a part of the organisation only as long as their contribution helps in the success of the organisation. For example, a salesman seeks out contacts, secures, and retains businesses. The company will replace the salesman if he does not fulfil their quota. The time and money spent on training and development of these employees are another downside to this type of work culture due to the high termination rates of these companies.

(g) Tough Guy Culture: Micro-management is the key factor of a tough guy culture. Every step of the employee is monitored, scrutinised, and guided when something does not meet the expected standards of the company. People with creative minds and independent working styles would find this a difficult place to work. The customer service sector is a real good example of this. In all organisations, the customer service representatives must follow the given set of scripts religiously when answering calls in a call centre. Any deviation from the script, even by a word or two will be taken seriously by the management.

(h) Process Culture: Process culture is based off on a set of regulations and procedures that the employees follow willingly. It is more in the form of an ideology, rather than a bulleted list of dos and don'ts used in a normative culture. Employees know why they are there, and are often self-starters. The employees in a process culture are very unlikely to be micro-managed when compared to a tough guy culture, and are rarely given performance reviews. Large scale assessing of work is done in most cases, with an annual review based on the employee's aspirations and goals within the organisation. NGO's, civil society organisations and such are examples of this kind of organisation.

9.3 Characteristics of a Negative Work Culture

Negativity is quite common in a working environment, which is a major impediment in achieving the organisational goals. Negative work culture gets reflected in every aspect of an organisation, such as values, vision, and attitude of the employees. A negative work culture affects human interactions, and eventually destroys the entire organisational setup. The following are the characteristics of negative work culture:

(a) Authoritarian Leadership: The nature of a leader is vital for an organisation to succeed. Enforcing the instructions and imposing the decisions unilaterally make the employees rebellious to instructions, thereby hampering the work culture.

(b) Strict Rules and Rigid Policies: A highly formalised organisational setup, accompanied with hyper competitiveness infringe an employee's freedom to work, resulting in work pressure.

(c) Personal Motive and Self Interest: This leads to conflict of individual and organisational interests and provides chances for disputes.

(d) Lack of Morality and Discipline: Unethical behavior at the top of the organisation trickles down to front-line employees, impacting the entire organisation. It is because of the lack of morality, corruption has become an accepted norm in many organisations. Also, it is the responsibility of the organisation to sue the unethical employees despite their hierarchy.

(e) Favouritism: The practice of giving unfair preferential treatment to one person or group at the expense of another is quite common in most of the organisations. Favouritism to an individual or a group promotes unhealthy interpersonal relationship among workers.

(f) Gossips and Speculation: Damaging the credibility of co-workers is commonly seen at workplaces. Gossip is as old as communications, and no workplace is immune from it. Taking it to the heart leads to distractions, affecting the quality of work.

9.4 Characteristics of a Positive Work Culture

(a) Value-based Leadership: A good leader influences his followers in a positive way to achieve the desired objectives. Occupying the top level of the organisational pyramid, the CEOs and heads of the organisations have the responsibility of orienting their employees to attain the mission and vision of the organisation.

(b) Positive Thinking and Positive Attitude: Maintaining a positive relationship and imbibing positive thinking in the minds of the employees are important to building a positive work culture. A positive attitude makes the employees love their work, thereby contributing to the efficiency of the organisation.

(c) Individualism vs. Collectivism: Performance appraisal, awards, and recognition motivate employees to work better. Each employee should be treated as unique. Assuring a dignified work ambience is very important for yielding better performance among the employees. At the same time promoting group interests through team orientation, group discussions, training programs, proper disclosure methods, employee-friendly policies, and grievance redressal promotes professionalism and a healthy work environment. *Esprit de corps* developed by the workers help to meet out the ethical challenges and avoid disputes.

(d) Interpersonal Trust: Trust is vital for better coordination and cooperation among employees. Developing such interpersonal trust results in loyalty to each other, and loyalty to organisation as well.

(e) Stress Management: Creating a stress-free environment enhances the output of the employees. Stress management can be taught through training sessions, workshops, etc. Also, space for recreation within the office environment, and activities including sports, leisure rooms, and picnics can help the employees to manage stress.

(f) Innovation: Encouraging innovation makes the organisational structure more participative and dynamic. It can be either internal. For example, innovation carried out in projects, or innovation in the organisational symbols like logo, etc., or creating space for innovative ideas can make the system progressive and updated.

(g) Code of Ethics: Organisational ethics, coupled with social responsibility within an organisation ensure better corporate governance, which is the need of the hour in most of the organisations. Corporate social responsibility has fostered societal concern and shifted the perception that corporations are solely profit-driven.

9.5 Steps to Overcome a Negative Work Culture

i. Identifying the root of the negativity.
ii. Improving the communication.
iii. Personal interactions with employees.
iv. SWOT analysis.
v. Devising an efficient hiring process.
vi. Making the office environment more participative.
vii. Bringing down dominance.
viii. Recognising and rewarding the employees.

An efficient organisation is the reflection of an efficient work culture with strong underlying values. Policy reforms envisaging an effective and secure environment is vital for the overall progress of organisations. Engaging employees' hearts, minds, and hands is the most lasting source of competitive advantage. Assuring a positive working environment helps in weeding out unethical practices and to ensure better corporate governance.

9.6 Indian Perspective of the Administrative Work Culture

The administrative work culture of India is unique given its history. The British rule played a dominant role in shaping the administrative work culture of India, and also for the ills of the same. The administrative work culture that we see and experience today is not something that one can feel proud about.

I. Causes for poor administrative work culture

(a) Colonial Legacy: During the British regime, there was a strong correlation between the Indian political system and the administrative system. The Indian administrative system was influenced by the political system, and vice versa. That is why the exploitative and authoritarian nature of the political system is reflected on today's administrative set up as well. Though India became progressively democratic after independence, the legacy of the colonial administrative system continues to exist till date.

(b) Archaic System and Laws: The laws that are governing the Indian administration are mostly the laws laid down by the British. The same laws continue with little or no modification at all. Those laws created an administrative structure and put in place rules that suited the needs of an imperialistic power. The needs of a democratic and a welfare state are quite different from that of an imperialistic state. Very little attention is paid in framing new laws and restructuring archaic laws. This paves the way for a democratic setup to become imperialistic. These laws are simply fitted into the Indian system without analysing the requirement of the system.

(c) Strict and Rigid Hierarchy: The Indian administrative work culture is characterised with too many hierarchical levels and rigid framework. The rigid hierarchy leads to a unidirectional command structure and unidirectional communication. The lack of flexibility in the system results in unilateral decision making, strict superior sub-ordinate relationship, etc., hampering the functioning of the entire system.

(d) Political Interventions: It is a well-known fact that our administrative system is plagued by political interferences and interventions. The administration is not allowed to function independently. Such interventions are the root cause for corruption and nepotism. Furthermore, constant interference brings down the morale of the administration.

(e) Influence of Societal Set up on Administration: In a diverse country like India, the societal hurdles like casteism, religious superstitions, along with customary and cultural prejudices largely impact the administrative system. People strongly accustomed to traditional beliefs are reluctant to change according to the growing needs of the society, causing hindrance in implementing the objectives at the workplace.

> **? Thought Box**
>
> In India, how can the administrative work culture be transformed to align with the values of accountability, transparency, and efficiency, and what role do political will and institutional reforms play in this transformation?

(f) Arbitrariness: The size of the administration has grown exponentially since independence. Together with this has grown delegated legislation. This has led to vesting a lot of discretionary powers into the hands of administration. As a result, arbitrariness in decision-making has become the norm of administration. Corruption, favouritism and nepotism are outcomes of arbitrary exercise of power.

II. How to bring about a make-over of the Indian administrative work culture?

Reforms in the Indian administrative work culture must be holistic to ensure a meaningful and lasting impact. This requires changes at three levels: structural, procedural, and behavioural. Among these, behavioural reform is the most challenging, yet vital. Transforming the behaviour and attitudes of administrators is essential for achieving sustainable improvements in governance. A critical driver of behavioural reform is political will. The absence of a strong political resolve continues to hinder progress. The elected representatives should step in and wholeheartedly commit to implementing reforms that resonate with genuine intent and dedication.

SUMMARY

- Civil service, as the backbone of democracy, must reflect government policies in its decisions. Civil servants must maintain confidentiality as per legal requirements.
- Public service embodies accountability and collective responsibility, guided by ethical principles like selflessness, integrity, and transparency. Public servants should remember their duty is to serve, not for personal profit.
- Various governance models, including Gandhian, Kautilyan, Weberian, and Marxist, emphasise ethical leadership and societal welfare.
- New Public Management (NPM) promotes efficiency, decentralisation, and citizen-focused reforms, while probity ensures governance transparency.
- Organisations must avoid activities that fail public scrutiny and expectations.
- The codes of ethics guide decision-making, while the codes of conduct govern actions. They help employees maintain a positive public image and organisational integrity.
- Professional ethics balances public and private interests.
- The codes of conduct organise duties, while the codes of ethics regulate values and responsibilities.
- Ethical conflicts arise at the intersection of public duty and private interest, necessitating both the codes of ethics and conduct.
- Integrity is key to the success of public programs.
- A positive work culture fosters employee retention, satisfaction, and alignment with organisational goals. It further enhances employee attraction and retention, reducing recruitment costs.
- Different types of organisational cultures include academy, normative, pragmatic, club, baseball team, fortress, and process cultures.

- A negative work culture can stem from authoritarian leadership, strict rules, and favouritism. To improve a negative culture, organisations should focus on communication, interaction, and employee recognition.
- Poor administrative culture in India results from colonial legacy, rigid hierarchies, and political influences.

PREVIOUS YEARS' QUESTIONS

1. The 'Code of Conduct' and 'Code of Ethics' are the sources of guidance in public administration. There is the code of conduct already in operation, whereas the code of ethics is not yet put in place. Suggest a suitable model for the code of ethics to maintain integrity, probity and transparency in governance. *UPSC CSE Mains 2024*
2. 'Probity is essential for an effective system of government and socio-economic development.' Discuss. *UPSC CSE Mains 2023*
3. What do you understand by term 'good governance'? How far have the recent initiatives, in terms of e-Governance steps taken by the state, helped the beneficiaries? Discuss with suitable examples. *UPSC CSE Mains 2022*
4. What do you understand by the term 'public servant'? Reflect on the expected role of a public servant. *UPSC CSE Mains 2019*
5. What do you understand by 'probity' in governance? Based on your understanding of the term, suggest measures for ensuring probity in government. *UPSC CSE Mains 2019*
6. 'Non-performance of duty by a public servant is a form of corruption.' Do you agree with this view? Justify your answer. *UPSC CSE Mains 2019*
7. Effective utilisation of public funds is crucial to meet development goals. Critically examine the reasons for the under-utilisation and mis-utilisation of public funds and their implications. *UPSC CSE Mains 2019*
8. What is meant by public interest? What are the principles and procedures to be followed by the civil servants in public interest? *UPSC CSE Mains 2018*
9. Distinguish between "Code of Ethics" and "Code of Conduct" with suitable examples. *UPSC CSE Mains 2018*
10. Discuss the Public Services Code as recommended by the 2nd Administrative Reforms Commission. *UPSC CSE Mains 2016*

Probity in Governance: Utilisation of Public Funds and Challenges of Corruption

15

1. INTRODUCTION

> "Whether one wishes or not, honey or poison kept on tongue gets tasted eventually. So it is, corruption and wealth accumulation by government officials. It is highly likely that they do accumulate more or less wealth by corruption in their tenure."
>
> **Chanakya Niti**

According to Kautilya, human nature poses corruption. It is human psyche. He argued that it is virtually impossible for a government servant to refrain from taking even a small portion of the king's revenue.

Just as it is impossible to tell when a fish in water is drinking, it is equally difficult to determine when a government official is **embezzling**[1] funds.

Kautilya was well-versed with the characteristics of bureaucrats and statesmen. However, he also laid down rules to prevent misuse of power.

Efficient utilisation of public funds lies at the heart of governance and development, serving as a critical tool for delivering public goods, infrastructure, and welfare schemes. However, the mismanagement and misappropriation of these funds due to corruption undermine the very foundation of public trust and hinder socio-economic progress. Corruption distorts resource allocation, perpetuates inequality, and erodes institutional integrity, leading to inefficiencies in achieving developmental goals.

LEARNING OBJECTIVES

1. Understanding reasons and impacts of ineffective utilisation of public financial resources
2. Learning about the ways to effectively utilise public funds
3. To gain a comprehensive understanding of corruption, including its definition, causes, consequences, and the systemic reforms required to address it effectively
4. Understanding the social audit system in India and how it is used as a tool to fight corruption
5. Learn about the role of media in combating corruption
6. Learn about the key institutional framework in place to combat corruption

---

[1]**Embezzling:** Stealing, misusing fund

2. UTILISATION OF PUBLIC FUNDS

"Public money ought to be touched with the most scrupulous conscientiousness of honour. It is not the produce of riches only, but of the hard earnings of labour and poverty."

Thomas Paine

Public funds represent the financial resources belonging to the public, which are managed by the state as a custodian. The term 'public fund management' refers to the influence of how governments handle these resources on economic growth and the well-being of citizens. Effective management of public funds involves overseeing both the government's revenue generation and expenditure processes. The government's revenue includes taxes, income generated by state-owned enterprises (PSUs), foreign aid, and other financial sources.

2.1 Ineffective Utilisation of Public Funds

Ineffective utilisation of public funds occurs when government resources are mismanaged, leading to wastage and failure to meet objectives. It can be classified as:

- **Misutilisation of Public Funds**

Misuse of public funds refers to expenditures made without proper authorisation or in violation of relevant laws, regulations, policies, or procedures. It also includes unnecessary or wasteful purchases that do not align with the organisation's business or operational needs. Misuse of public assets involves the unauthorised or inappropriate use of government property and the failure to ensure its proper safeguarding.

- **Underutilisation of Public Funds**

The underutilisation of planned expenditures by states stems from institutional and procedural hurdles in implementing schemes and deficiencies in the district level planning process. Key issues include insufficient staff for planning, inadequate capacity building, limited community involvement, and centralised decision making.

Budgetary bottlenecks such as delays in fund disbursal, sanction orders, and limited financial delegation to district-level authorities exacerbate the problem. Additionally, uniform norms for Centrally Sponsored Schemes across states and top-down, unrealistic budgeting practices, often without ground-level cost analysis, hinder effective resource allocation and utilisation.

- **Misappropriation of Public Funds**

Misappropriation of funds involves the unlawful use of someone else's money. Although the individual committing the act had legal access to the funds, using them for personal gain or for any unauthorised purpose constitutes the crime. For example, misappropriation of public funds occurs when Members of Parliament misuse MPLAD funds by directing them to private trusts or societies they have established. It also includes recommending prohibited projects, influencing the selection of implementing agencies, directly handling payments to contractors, and resisting measures to ensure transparency and accountability.

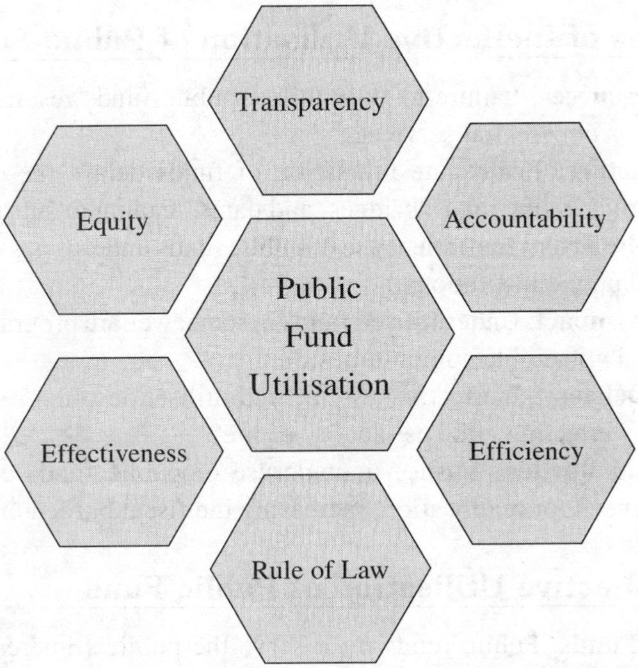

Fig. 15.1 Principles of Public Fund utilisation

2.2 Reasons for Ineffective Utilisation of Public Funds

There are several reasons why the utilisation of public funds can be ineffective:

- **Bureaucratic Inefficiencies**: Delays in approvals and red tape can hinder the timely implementation of projects.
- **Lack of Capacity**: Insufficient technical and administrative expertise can lead to poor planning and execution.
- **Political Interference**: Decisions may be influenced by political considerations rather than financial prudence.
- **Corruption**: Mismanagement and embezzlement of funds can divert resources away from their intended purposes.

- **Incomplete Planning**: Poorly designed projects can lead to cost overruns and delays.
- **Resource Constraints**: Inadequate budget allocation can limit the scope and effectiveness of projects.
- **Lack of Accountability**: Weak oversight mechanisms can result in unchecked spending and misuse of funds.

2.3 Implications of Ineffective Utilisation of Public Funds

- **Wastage of Resources**: Failure to fully utilise public funds results in resource wastage, depriving citizens of essential services.
- **Poor Infrastructure**: Inadequate utilisation of funds delays the completion of critical infrastructure projects like roads, bridges, and dams, leading to substandard infrastructure.
- **Erosion of Public Trust**: Inefficient use of public funds undermines citizens' confidence in government and public institutions.
- **Negative Social Impact**: Underutilised funds in social welfare programmes adversely affect marginalised and vulnerable communities.
- **Poor Service Delivery**: Ineffectiveness in fund utilisation often results in subpar public services, directly affecting citizens' quality of life.
- **Increased Fiscal Burden**: Misuse or underuse of public funds can lead to unplanned expenses or the need for reallocation, increasing the fiscal burden on the government.

2.4 Ways for Effective Utilisation of Public Fund

- **Use of Public Funds**: Public funds must serve the public's interests and align with the organisation's strategic and business goals.
- **Adherence to Law**: Funding decisions must follow the rules set by the Parliament through appropriations.
- **Budget Alignment**: Funding must stay within the entity's budget and have clear, justified costs.
- **Keep it Simple**: Funding requirements should be practical, straightforward, and proportionate to the amount, complexity, and risk involved. Reduce compliance costs wherever possible.
- **Authority Delegation**: Decisions must be made by authorised individuals as per the entity's delegation system.
- **Policies and Procedures**: Funding should follow established policies unless a documented decision is made to do otherwise.
- **Ethical Conduct**: Decision-makers must adhere to ethical standards outlined in the state sector code of conduct or equivalent guidelines.

- **Conflict of Interest**: Systems must be in place to identify, manage, and record conflicts of interest effectively.
- **Record-Keeping**: Maintain proper records to support decisions, ensure accountability, and facilitate monitoring and management.
- **Manage Risks**: Identify and manage risks in the funding arrangement, striking a balanced approach that weighs risks against expected benefits without being overly cautious.

3. CORRUPTION – DEFINITION

> "Corruption is an improbity or decay in the decision-making process in which a decision-maker consents to deviate or demands deviation from the criterion, which should rule his or her decision-making, in exchange for a reward or for the promise or expectation of a reward, while these motives influencing his or her decision." **Dr. Petrus van Duyne**

Prevention of Corruption Act, 1988 describes 'Corruption' basically in terms 'of taking gratification other than legal renumeration in respect of an Official act'.

Central Vigilance Corruption (CVC) defined corruption as "behaviour by officials in the public sector, whether politicians or civil servants, in which they improperly and illegally enrich themselves or those close to them or induce others to do so by misusing their position."

Corruption is a complex phenomenon to be understood fully. The roots of corruption lie deep in the political and bureaucratic institutions of the nation. Though the term corruption cannot be defined precisely, the World Bank has sought for a simple and straightforward definition of corruption i.e., 'the abuse of public office for private gain'.

When a public official accepts, solicits or extorts bribe, we can term it as abuse of public office. Public office can also be abused for personal benefit even if no bribe is offered, through patronage and nepotism. It is also exploited when private agents actively offer bribes to bypass public policies and procedures in order to gain a competitive edge and make a profit.

Thus, it would be proper to define corruption from a moral standpoint as – 'Corruption is the use of a position of trust for dishonest gain'.

From the above definition about corruption, we can derive the following basic postulates about corruption:

1. Corruption involves deliberate deviation from one's duty.
2. It can be direct or indirect but needs to be conscious.
3. It is done for personal aggrandisement or gain.
4. It is done by violating some commonly accepted norms of behaviours.

QUOTATIONS ON CORRUPTION

"Be the Change you want to see in the World. **Mahatma Gandhi**

Power does not corrupt. Fear corrupts... perhaps the fear of a loss of power. **John Steinbeck**

Where do the evils like corruption arise from? It comes from the never-ending greed. The fight for corruption-free ethical society will have to be fought against this greed and replace it with 'what can I give' spirit. **A. P. J. Abdul Kalam**

It is not the young people that degenerate; they are not spoiled till those of mature age are already sunk into corruption. **Montesquieu**

The corruption of the best things gives rise to the worst. **David Hume**

The negligence of a few could easily send a ship to the bottom, but with the help of a few righteous men, the ship can be brought back to the shore. **Sardar Vallabhai Patel**

No man who is corrupt, no man who condones corruption in others, can possibly do his duty to the community. **Theodore Roosevelt.**"

3.1 Forms of Corruption

Administrative malpractices may take many forms, and they are understood around the world with the subject of numerous legal or academic definitions. Governments believe that certain types of corruption are more effectively addressed through regulatory or civil law measures. Various forms of corruption can be broadly classified under the following heads:

1. **Bribery**
   - Bribery involves offering or requesting an incentive to affect the way someone in a position of authority performs their duties. These incentives can take various forms, such as money, gifts, loans, fees, rewards, or other benefits. Bribery exists in two forms:
     1. Active – Offering, promising, or paying a bribe
     2. Passive – Soliciting, agreeing to receive, or accepting a bribe
2. **Grease payments**
   A grease payment, also known as a facilitation payment, is a sum given to a foreign official to speed up a routine task, such as processing paperwork or issuing licenses and permits. These payments are meant to accelerate the timing of an official's actions, rather than to influence the decisions they make.

3. **Graft**
   Graft is a form of political corruption in which a politician uses their power and influence unscrupulously for personal gain. For instance, a politician might misappropriate government funds for personal gain or exploit insider knowledge of forthcoming government decisions to advance their own private economic interests.
4. **Trading of information**
   Trading of information occurs when an employee gives or receives a bribe in return for confidential information. This offence is referred to as insider trading when such information is used to trade an organisation's stocks, bonds, or other securities.
5. **Trading in influence**
   Trading in influence, which is also referred to as influence peddling, is the practice of using a person's influence in government or connections with authorities to obtain an undue advantage for another, usually in return for payment.
6. **Gifts and hospitality**
   Almost every organisation participates in some form of hospitality with current or potential business partners, which is seen as a common and crucial aspect of conducting business. However, gifts and hospitality can be viewed as bribes if they lack transparency or are excessively extravagant.

   The Central Vigilance Commission has identified the following modes of corruption:
   - Misappropriation of public money and stores
   - Possession of disproportionate assets
   - Abuse of official position/powers
   - Acceptance of illegal gratification in recruitments, postings, transfers and promotions
   - Acceptance of gifts
   - Misuse of imported and allotted quotas by various firms with the connivance of public servants
   - Moral turpitude
   - Unauthorised occupation and subletting of government quarters
   - Under-assessment of income tax and estate duty for pecuniary gain
   - Showing favours to contractors and firms
   - Claiming of false travelling allowance and house rent
   - Purchase of immovable property without prior permission or intimation
   - Misuse of government employees for personal work
   - Production of forged certificates of age of birth or community
   - Acceptance of substandard stores/work
   - Borrowing money from contractors/firms having official dealings with officers
   - Incurring pecuniary obligations of persons with whom the public servants have official dealings

- Causing loss to government by negligence or otherwise
- Irregularities in the reservation of seats by rail and by air
- Non-delivery of money orders, insured covers and value payable parcels
- Irregularity in the grant of import and export licences
- Irregularity in the grant of the telephone connections
- Misuse of advance sanctioned for purchase of scooters and cars
- Abnormal delay in settlement of compensation claims to displaced persons
- Wrong assessment of claims of displaced persons and
- Cheating in connection with the sale and purchase of plots for residential purpose.

3.2 Causes of Corruption

The causes of corruption are many and complex. Following are some of the causes of corruption:

1. **Social causes**
   - Accepting corruption as normal part of life which results in a morally vitiated atmosphere, i.e., social acceptance of corruption.
   - The growing value of consumerism and its resultant impact on everyone in the society.
   - General degradation of social values and changing pattern of education and reduction in the importance of value education.
   - Nepotism which has been in vogue since ancient period has its impact on recruitment even today. Nepotism breeds corruption.
   - Lack of vigilant civil society and local level community mechanisms which can act as effective accountability mechanisms.
   - Group embeddedness.
2. **Economic Causes**
   - Rise in the cost of living due to privatisation, liberalisation and globalisation.
   - Rising inflation and its cascading effects on essential commodities.
   - Poverty syndrome which means problems arising out of financial crises especially in middle class population because of rising prices, inflation, etc.
   - Inadequate remuneration of officials.
   - Mismatch in pay structure between various sectors of economy.
   - License and permit concepts though reduced in paper and procedures are still prevalent in bureaucratic culture.
   - The political and bureaucratic control on the economic system.
   - Breeding black money because of the tougher tax regime acts as oxygen for corruption.
3. **Political Causes**
   - Corrupt practices in the institution of election are a prime source of corruption.

- Political parties which capture power by corrupt practice set a vicious cycle where the seed for bureaucratic corruption gets sown followed by corruption in business.
- Emergence of coalition politics and resultant coalition compulsions, such as lucrative ministries, huge contracts, etc.
- Political corruption protects those who indulge in corruption.
- Personal funding of elections and fund raising by parties for election.
- Politicisation of criminals resulting in criminalisation of politics.
- Politicisation of civil services.

4. Administrative Causes

- Culture of secrecy and red tapism.
- High degree of centralisation.
- The security of tenure results in no accountability; this lack of accountability and control nurtures corruption.
- British legacy on administrative culture, which was marked by discretion coupled with secrecy, resulted in lack of accountability of the bureaucratic machinery.
- Amateur political boss and their dependence on the bureaucracy.
- Intellectual corruption of officials resulting in favouring a particular section, group or individuals.
- Excessive regulation and administrative delay.
- Absence of whistleblowers protection mechanism.

5. Judicial Factors

- Judicial delay in disposal of cases.
- Expensive judicial system makes a common man not to venture into litigations.
- Corruption in judiciary, especially at lower levels.
- Judicial abstinence to consider discretionary cases of administration.

6. Legal Factors

- Laws such as Official Secrets Act that promote secrecy.
- Loopholes in Anti-Corruption Laws.
- Constitutional Safeguard (Article 311).

7. Historical Causes

- Ancient India – Kautilya highlighted the concept of corruption in *Arthasastra*.
- Mughal period – Huge corruption due to *mansabdari* system and auction of public offices.
- British India – Bureaucracy possessed huge discretion without any accountability; corruption pervaded all levels of administration.

Corruption has become self-sustaining and self-reinforcing system. Corruption has set a vicious cycle involving five players—politics, bureaucracy, businessmen, goons and lastly the society in general by remaining tolerant, resulting in multi-organ failure.

3.3 Consequences of Corruption

Corruption can have a range of negative impacts on society including political, social, and economic consequences. Here are some of the consequences of corruption:

1. **Economic consequences**
   - Corruption is a major global economic issue, costing 5% of the world's GDP and over $1 trillion annually in bribes, as per the World Economic Forum and World Bank. It hinders economic development, disrupts resource allocation, and poses serious threats to national security and sustainable development.
   - Corruption undermines investments, slows economic growth, distorts government spending, and strengthens the underground economy. It widens income inequality, concentrating wealth among a few elites while reducing the size of the middle class. This uneven wealth distribution exacerbates poverty and economic disparity.
   - Additionally, corruption deters foreign investment by increasing business risks and reducing trust in government institutions. It creates uncertainty in the business environment, further impacting economic growth and development.
   - Corruption fosters monopolies or oligopolies, enabling influential businesses to bribe officials, manipulate policies, and dominate markets unfairly. In the public sector, corruption redirects investments toward projects offering more opportunities for bribes, often at the expense of public welfare. It distorts government spending priorities, reduces regulatory compliance, lowers the quality of services and infrastructure, and increases fiscal pressures on governments.
2. **Social consequences**
   - **Poverty and Inequality:** Corruption deepens inequality by limiting access to public services for disadvantaged groups and concentrating wealth and power among a few. Corruption also fuels organised crime, terrorism, state incapacity, polarisation, unrest, and human rights violations.
   - **Effects on Education:** Corruption in education undermines meritocracy. Practices like capitation fees erode quality, inflate education costs, and harm international standards. Bribery in teacher recruitment and promotion further degrades the education system.
   - **Impunity and Partial Justice:** When corruption infiltrates the justice system, the powerful can escape accountability while marginalised groups face wrongful accusations and unfair treatment. This undermines trust in prosecutors and judges, leading to partial or denied justice.
3. **Political consequences**
   - **Undermines Democratic Institutions**: Corruption weakens the legitimacy of democratic systems by reducing accountability in elections and policymaking.

- **Reduces Transparency**: It obscures government actions, eroding citizens' trust in officials and institutions.
- **Diminishes Public Trust**: Corruption breaks the social contract between citizens and the state, leading to widespread distrust in governance.
- **Increases Political Instability**: Loss of trust in government fuels social unrest and weakens political stability.
- **Encourages Authoritarianism**: Corruption empowers leaders who rely on bribery and patronage to maintain control, promoting authoritarian rule.

> **? Thought Box**
>
> How do the multifaceted consequences of corruption—economic, social, and political—undermine sustainable development, and what strategies can be implemented to mitigate these impacts?

3.4 Measures to Tackle Corruption

1. **Institutional measures**
   - **Enhancing Law Enforcement:** The government should allocate adequate resources, focus on capacity building for law enforcement agencies, and ensure judicial independence.
   - **Improving Media Accountability:** Strengthen regulatory frameworks like the Press Council of India, promote self-regulation within the media, and establish mechanisms to prevent the spread of misinformation.
   - **Key ARC Recommendations:**
     - ✓ Place Anti-Corruption Bureaus under the control of the State Vigilance Commission.
     - ✓ Empower state economic offences units for better investigations and coordination among agencies.
     - ✓ Develop a code of ethics for public officials and employees to uphold ethical standards.
2. **Policy measures:**
   - **Strengthening Governance:** India must address corporate secrecy, foreign bribery, and the role of complicit enablers such as bankers and lawyers.
   - A **National Anti-Corruption Strategy (NACS)** similar to South Africa's can be developed to enhance governance and effectively combat corruption.
   - **Stakeholder Engagement:** Building trust and fostering collective action requires the active involvement of stakeholders, including government institutions, public servants, citizens, and the business community.
   - **Promoting Transparency:** Provide the public with timely, accessible, and meaningful information, particularly on public spending and resource allocation.

3. **Economic measures**
   - **Political Funding Reforms:** There is an urgent need to regulate political party funding by enhancing transparency, capping campaign expenditures, and disclosing funding sources. State funding of elections can be considered to reduce the influence of money and muscle power in electoral processes.
   - **Strengthening International Collaboration:** Global efforts should focus on seizing, confiscating, and repatriating criminal proceeds to victims and states, in compliance with international obligations and domestic laws. Support for initiatives like the FATF and the implementation of the GlobE Network (Global Operational Network of Anti-Corruption Law Enforcement Authorities) is crucial.
4. **Social measures**
   - **Public Engagement:** Promote public participation through awareness campaigns and by ensuring whistleblower protection. Establish mandatory public registers of lobbyists, enable public scrutiny of lobbying activities, and enforce strict conflict-of-interest regulations.
   - **Education and Awareness:** Incorporate digital education and literacy into school curricula while fostering ethical values such as honesty and integrity from an early age.
   - **Women Empowerment:** Increasing women's representation in leadership roles can help dismantle entrenched networks of corruption, including sexual bribery, and enhance the delivery of public and social services.

3.5 Systemic Reforms for Ending Corruption

Reform is a continuous process required to be done in every domain. Legacy has been an important reason for enrichment of corruption in every sphere of the governance. To weed out the maladies from corrupt practices and rejuvenate administration, systemic reforms are a mandate. As, stagnation amount to ruination, reformation leads to effective development.

The following are different means of reformation to fight the evil of corruption:

1. **Bringing in Competition and Eliminating Monopoly**: Demonopolising improves competition thereby reducing opportunities for corruption. But a competitive field should be ensured through price regulatory mechanism in order to deliver the performance and protect public interest.
2. **Reviewing Existing Procedures, Rules and Acts Thereby Simplifying Them:** Most of our administrative procedures and rules were evolved in pre-independence period which could not be relevant in today's context. Moreover, they had enough room for discretion and arbitrary action which are the standing pillars of corruption. A review of all those

existing manuals, conduct codes and acts is required to simplify and also to make them easily accessible and understandable to the citizens, thereby putting a check on red tapism, excessive discretion and improve speedy service delivery. The method of single window clearance is a good example of simplification of procedures.

3. **Infrastructure Development:** To reform the system, the basic necessity is to develop the required infrastructure that could help in simplification of processes, effective delivery of services within stipulated time frame, easy access of required information, etc. Development of the required infrastructure, such as computerisation, digitisation, documentation, communication through the use of information technology, creation of integrated database of government departments, single window access, creation of kiosks, etc., is of primary importance.
4. **Service Delivery:** The service provided by government to various stakeholders should be targeted and be delivered within stipulated time frame and such could be attained through e-governances mechanism. There are multiple examples that exist to prove that e-governance has resulted in effective service delivery and reduced level of corruption, e.g., e-sugam, e-seva, gyandoot, e-cops, etc. Also e-governance initiative provides for the involvement of civil society, NGOs, common public, etc., in the process of decision making, thereby providing for attainment of good governance.
5. **Redress Mechanism:** This is an important area which needs to be given greater impetus to eliminate corruption. Effective grievances redressal mechanism should be established in every government department that could be easily accessed by the common public. Also, the complaints should be sorted out and addressed effectively within a stipulated time. Complaints on erring officials should be viewed seriously after making proper investigation on the genuineness of the complaints.
6. **Promote Transparency:** In the era of RTI, it is the right of every citizen to know about the function of his/her government except those that are sensitive information. Therefore, voluntary disclosure of every activity of administration is required to make the system transparent. A transparent system would result in fixing responsibility and ensuring accountability, which would help in elimination of corruption.
   - **Preventive and Punitive Measures:** To weed out corruption there should be established preventive and punitive measures. The rules and procedures of governance and administration should be such that they inherently prevent corruption, such as
     - ➢ Fixing of responsibility
     - ➢ Efficient and effective supervision
     - ➢ Proper vigilance mechanism
     - ➢ Reducing discretion
     - ➢ Periodic evaluation of officials
     - ➢ Improving citizen's accessibility and responsiveness of the system

On determination of frauds there should be such punitive measures to ensure that the erring officials are punished and also the punishment awarded should act as a deterrent on other officials from involving in corrupt practices.

- Monitoring complaints
- Proper investigative mechanism
- Identifying the corrupt officials
- Disciplinary proceedings—timely action and finalisation
- Risk profiling of officers and placing them in non-sensitive posts
- Criminal proceedings: invoking PCA and PML where required
- Confiscation of property, etc., are such punitive actions that should form part of the system.

Corruption is rooted so deep into our system that to remove it from root level requires reformation from that level. Once the root is cleaned the branches will follow. E-governance, use of ICT, involvement of civil society, citizens, NGOs, media, etc., in decision making would make the system transparent and accountable. But to sustain a corruption free system every individual should lead an ethical life and ethics should be made the culture of the nation.

4. SOCIAL AUDIT

"Do more than belong: participate." **William Arthur Ward**

Social audit is based on the principle that democratic local governance should be conducted with the consent and understanding of all stakeholders, as much as possible. It is, therefore, a continuous process rather than a one-time event. Social audit involves measuring, understanding, reporting, and improving an organisation's social and ethical performance, serving as a crucial tool for evaluating its social accountability.

However, social audit is often mistakenly seen as a form of audit focused on verifying the accuracy of financial or statistical statements, similar to a traditional audit. While a conventional financial audit examines financial records based on accounting principles, a social audit is broader in scope, focusing on assessing and enhancing an organisation's social performance and impact. Social auditing is again distinct from evaluation in that it is an internally generated process whereby the organisation itself shapes the social audit process according to its stated objectives.

4.1 Key Steps in Conducting a Social Audit

1. Agreeing on parameters of audit and defining the scope of audit.
2. Accessing official records from the government regarding the status of implementation.

3. Identifying and training local youth, children of beneficiaries and volunteers on the audit practice
4. Proactive dissemination of records in the local community.
5. Verification of official records with actual realities.
6. Facilitating eligible beneficiaries and registration of grievances.
7. Documenting findings and sharing it in a public collective platform i.e. Social Audit Public. Hearing which is attended by the local community, implementing agencies and facilitated by the social audit teams. This is a forum where implementing agencies announce the action to be taken on findings individually
8. Social Audit reports shared with implementing agency and in the public domain for action to be taken within a stipulated time period

4.2 Social Audit System in India

- Tata Iron and Steel Company (TISCO), based in Jamshedpur, introduced social audits in 1979 as part of its operations.
- The Mazdoor Kisan Shakti Sangathan (MKSS), a grassroots organisation in Rajasthan, India, pioneered the concept of social audits in the mid-1990s.
- Social audits gained constitutional recognition in India through the 73rd and 74th Amendments in 1992.
- On May 8, 2002, the Supreme Court of India issued directives establishing clear lines of accountability related to social audits.
- Social Accounting and Audit (SAA) was first adopted in India in 2003 by Sambhav, a social enterprise.
- The Right to Information Act, 2005, significantly strengthened the social audit system in the country.
- The social audit process gained traction with the enactment of the National Rural Employment Guarantee Act (NREGA) in 2005, later renamed the Mahatma Gandhi National Rural Employment Guarantee Act (MGNREGA).
- The Centre for Social Initiative and Management (CSIM) began promoting social audits in India in 2008.
- In 2014, the Government of India mandated social audits under the National Rural Livelihoods Mission (NRLM).

4.3 Social Audit as a Tool for Fighting Corruption

Social audits can engage populations directly in the fight against corruption where:

- The audit uncovers instances of corruption, such as the embezzlement of programme funds, demands for bribes to release funds, or the outright denial of funds to participants who are entitled to them.

- The auditors are able to communicate their findings in a clear and understandable manner to the affected individuals or groups.
- Those impacted by the findings are informed about the violations of law or policy that led to their losses and are made to understand the implications.
- A third party, such as a government agency or civil society organisation, organises a public forum where government officials and elected representatives discuss the audit results in a non-threatening environment, allowing the affected individuals to participate and confirm the accuracy of the findings.

Social audits are important because they have potential to bridge the gap between anti-corruption constituencies in government and society.

4.4 Status of Social Audit in India

CASE STUDIES: MGNREGA

Launched in 2005 by the Ministry of Rural Development, the Mahatma Gandhi National Rural Employment Guarantee Scheme (MGNREGS) is one of the world's largest work guarantee programmes, providing the rural poor with the right to employment. Social audit serves as the built-in anti-corruption mechanism under the MGNREGA Act of 2005. Section 17 of the Mahatma Gandhi National Rural Employment Guarantee Act (MGNREGA) empowers the Gram Sabha to oversee the implementation of works, establishing a legal framework for conducting social audits. The Mahatma Gandhi National Rural Employment Guarantee Audit of Schemes Rules, 2011, prescribe the procedures for conducting social audits and define the responsibilities of various stakeholders, including the Social Audit Unit (SAU), state governments, and MGNREGA field workers, for uniform implementation across the country. To maintain the independence of Social Audit Units, they are allocated funds amounting to 0.5% of the MGNREGA expenditure incurred by the state in the preceding year. Additionally, the Central Government holds the authority to withhold MGNREGS funds if states fail to conduct regular social audits.

Evaluation

- As on November 2023, only six states have exceeded 50% completion of social audits for works undertaken under MGNREGS in gram panchayats. Kerala stands out as the only state to achieve 100% social audit coverage in gram panchayats.

- After years of introduction not many states have incorporated it. Those that have done so are also found with lacunae. Lack of political will and bureaucratic acceptance has been a major impediment in bearing its real fruit.
- Lack of transparency in maintenance of records, unwillingness on part of the administrative officials in production of records, lack of proper auditing knowledge on part of people are some of the reasons for the process to remain slow in many parts of the country.
- Also, there is no clear statute and power to fix responsibility on the erring officials and to penalise them. It is because of this attitude, it turns toothless and remains mostly a namesake process. The Andhra Pradesh example of social audit also shows similar trend, less than 1% action was taken on erring officials by the departments. Lack of cooperation on part of bureaucracy and politicians is ruining the whole vision and mission of process.

The purpose of conducting a social audit is not to assign blame to individuals, but to evaluate the organisation's performance in relation to its social, environmental, and community objectives. The audit findings need to be owned up and internalised by the respective departments/organisations. To ensure the follow-up for social audit, the departments should develop an action plan with respect to the recommendations outlined in the report. Following this, the departments should establish a dedicated task force to ensure the prompt implementation of the action plan, in accordance with the guidelines outlined in the social audit report. Social audit, a powerful weapon of citizen empowerment is made to remain blunt. It needs to be sharpened to attain its zenith and also should be mandated in almost every sphere of governance thereby arresting corruption right from the grassroots level.

5. ROLE OF MEDIA IN COMBATING CORRUPTION

Media being the fourth pillar of democracy has an important role to perform in the fight against corruption. In today's world its presence can be felt in every walk of life around the world. World's worst corruption scandals are brought to public through media, e.g., Watergate. Therefore, a vigil media is the wealth of the democracy.

The media, including social media, plays a crucial role in combating corruption by holding both the public and private sectors accountable and demanding transparency. Numerous studies have shown a link between press freedom and lower levels of corruption. The media exposes corruption in the public sector, especially in areas where government activities are intentionally or unintentionally kept opaque. Media plays a crucial role to curb corruption by following ways:

1. **Investigative Journalism:** Investigative journalists dig deep into irregularities in governance, business practices, and public sector dealings, often revealing systemic corruption.

   Examples: The Bofors Scandal (1980s), 2G Spectrum Scam (2010) and Adarsh Housing Society Scam was uncovered largely due to persistent media investigations.

2. **Creating Transparency in Governance:** By broadcasting parliamentary debates, public audits, and citizen engagement initiatives, media reduces the scope for malpractices. Transparency discourages corrupt practices by increasing the risk of exposure.
3. **Empowering Citizens through Awareness**: Media acts as a bridge between the government and the people, educating citizens about their rights and the consequences of corruption. Campaigns like *Jaago Re* (Wake Up) and India Against Corruption have empowered citizens to take an active stand against unethical practices. An informed citizenry becomes a potent force for accountability and reform.
4. **Amplifying Anti-Corruption Movements:** Media platforms have been instrumental in mobilising public opinion against corruption. Coverage of protests, social movements, and public hearings helps **galvanise**[2] support and build pressure on authorities.
   Examples: The Anna Hazare-led Lokpal Movement (2011) gained nationwide traction due to extensive media coverage. Social media platforms amplified campaigns like *#CorruptionFreeIndia*, making them accessible to a global audience.
5. **Acting as a Watchdog and Pressure Group:** Reports on discrepancies and delays in investigations, trials, and policy implementation create public pressure for swift action.
   Example: The Nirav Modi PNB Scam coverage intensified public demand for reform in banking governance.
6. **Leveraging Digital Media for Accountability**: Social media platforms like Twitter, Facebook, and Instagram have democratised information dissemination. Digital campaigns and hashtags often spotlight corruption cases and mobilise public outrage. Example: The Vyapam Scam in Madhya Pradesh gained traction due to relentless coverage on digital platforms. Crowdsourced data on platforms like 'I Paid a Bribe' empower individuals to report instances of corruption anonymously.

A vigil media should continuously monitor and report important government and corporate/private activities that could have major implications on people's life. But ethical conduct is required in such circumstances too, just as reporting and bringing out a scandal is an ethical duty, in the same way it is the duty of the media to avoid working for ratings and clickbaits to gain over their competitors. They should be cautious before reporting allegations and informations accessed by them. The usage of such critical information for the sake of business could ruin the life of individuals involved or even spoil the process of investigation by leaking confidential details.

> **? Thought Box**
>
> How can traditional and social media effectively collaborate to expose corruption, promote transparency, and foster accountability in governance and society?

Therefore, Press Information Bureau of India has evolved a code of conduct for the print media, similarly defines the code of conduct for the IT Act electronic and communication media. But these norms should promote and not suppress the freedom of speech and expression.

---

[2] **Galvanise:** Arouse, Energise

6. KEY FRAMEWORKS AND INSTITUTIONS ADDRESSING CORRUPTION IN INDIA

Corruption is a significant challenge that undermines governance, erodes public trust, and hampers economic development. To address this pervasive issue, India has established a comprehensive framework of laws, institutions, and guidelines aimed at ensuring accountability, transparency, and integrity in public administration.

1. **Prevention of Corruption Act, 1988**: The primary legislation for combating corruption, prescribing punishments for public servants involved in corrupt practices.
2. **Central Bureau of Investigation (CBI)**: The principal agency tasked with investigating corruption cases involving public officials.
3. **Central Vigilance Commission (CVC) and State Vigilance Commissions**: Responsible for addressing citizens' grievances concerning corruption.
4. **National Human Rights Commission (NHRC)**: Provides a platform for citizens to lodge complaints if their rights are violated.
5. **All-India Services (Conduct) Rules, 1968**: Prohibit government employees from activities that may undermine their integrity or impartiality, such as accepting bribes, engaging in partisan politics, or disclosing confidential information.
6. **Central Civil Services (Conduct) Rules, 1964**: Restrict central government employees from engaging in actions that compromise their integrity or impartiality.
7. **Administrative Tribunals**: Bodies like the Central Administrative Tribunal (CAT) act as specialised courts to resolve disputes arising from government administrative actions, including corruption-related issues.

6.1 Whistleblowers Protection Act, 2014

Whistleblowing can be defined as an act of disclosing/making public something that is illegal or unethical which happened/happening in an organisation or public office. Whistleblowers are individuals who reveal information about illegal, unethical, or improper activities within an organisation. Often insiders with direct knowledge or evidence of wrongdoing, such as fraud, corruption, safety violations, or other misconduct, whistleblowers can be employees, former employees, contractors, or even external parties who observe or discover these activities. It is the responsibility of every government to provide legal safeguard for whistleblowing by permitting and protecting the act of disclosure. Provisions and protection for whistleblowing is an important aspect of United Nations Convention Against Corruption (UNCAC), 2005. As signatory, India complied with UNCAC by enacting the Whistleblowing Protection Act of 2011. Prior to the passage of the Act, the CVC was allowed to act on such complaints (whistleblowing) by a resolution passed by the government in 2004.

1. **Important Features of the Act**
    - **Protection Against Victimisation**: The Act includes robust measures to shield whistleblowers from any form of victimisation or **retaliation**[3] for reporting wrongdoing.
    - **Nature of disclosure:** Complaints can be made against an act of corruption, misuse of power, a criminal offence by a public servant. Any person, a public servant, an NGO, etc., can make such disclosure but with sufficient documents and records to establish the allegations.
    - **Competent Authorities**: Specific authorities are designated to handle public interest disclosures, with roles defined according to the nature of the complaint. For example, complaints against Union Ministers are directed to the Prime Minister as the competent authority.
    - **Identity Verification and Timeframe**: Complainants must disclose their identity as anonymous submissions are not accepted. Complaints must be filed within a maximum period of seven years.
    - **Mechanism of proceeding**: On enquiry if the allegations are found to be true the CVC recommends for action such as initiating disciplinary proceedings against the public servant, step to redress loss to the government and also to initiate criminal proceedings where needed, to the respective public authority. A mechanism to conduct enquiry should form part of every public authority.
    - **Exemptions and Appeals:** The disclosure of cabinet proceedings related to sovereignty, peace, security and international relations are exempted from disclosure. Certain categories, such as Special Protection Group personnel, are exempt from the Act's purview. Aggrieved individuals may appeal the decisions of the Competent Authority to the respective High Court within 60 days.
    - **Penalties for Breaching Confidentiality**: Disclosing a complainant's identity can result in imprisonment for up to three years and a fine of ₹50,000. Submitting false or misleading information knowingly may attract a penalty of up to two years of imprisonment and a fine of ₹30,000.
    - **Annual Reporting**: The Competent Authority must prepare an annual report detailing its activities, which is submitted to the Central or State Government and subsequently presented before the Parliament or State Legislature.
    - **Overriding Clause**: The Whistleblower Protection Act takes precedence over the Official Secrets Act of 1923, permitting disclosures as long as they do not compromise national sovereignty.

2. **Issues in Whistleblower's Protection Act, 2014**
    - It is important to note that the Act does not define or establish standards for the concept of victimisation. As a result, whistleblowers are not adequately protected, and in many

[3] **Retaliation:** Retaliate: Counterattack

cases, they choose to remain anonymous out of fear of potential retaliation against themselves or their families.

- According to the Act, any whistleblower complaint must be submitted to the Competent Authority, as defined in the legislation. The Competent Authority varies depending on the individual against whom the complaint is made. Typically, the Competent Authority is a senior official within the same hierarchy as the person being accused. This undermines the neutrality of the investigation, often leading to biased findings.
- The Act does not offer any rewards to whistleblowers following the successful resolution of their claims. However, the Securities and Exchange Board of India (SEBI) Prohibition of Insider Trading Regulations, 2015, allows for the discretionary payment of rewards, set at 10% of the monetary penalties imposed. These rewards are capped at a maximum of Rs. 10 crores.

However, 10 years have passed since the enactment without any amendments having been made to the Act. There has been a rampant cry for strengthening various features of the Act to make it whistleblower-friendly and for providing adequate protection to whistleblowers under the same.

6.2 Lokpal and Lokayukta Act, 2013

1. **Background**

   In the 1960s, India's Administrative Reforms Commission recommended establishing two specialised bodies, the Lokpal and Lokayukta, to address citizens' grievances and complaints related to corruption. On the pattern of Scandinavian ombudsman, machinery for the redressal of citizen's grievances was created in India. A legislation for establishment and appointment of the office of Lokpal and Lokayuktas was enacted by our Parliament. "Lokpal and Lokayuktas are considered to be bulwarks of democratic government against the tyranny of officialdom".

   The Act paves the way for setting up of the institution of Lokpal at the centre and Lokayuktas at states by law enacted by the respective state legislatures within one year of coming into force. It provides for a mechanism for dealing with complaints of corruption against public functionaries, including those in high offices.

2. **Significant provisions in the Act**
   - **Lokpal and Lokayuktas:** The establishment of the Lokpal at the national level and Lokayuktas at the state level creates a consistent framework for vigilance and anti-corruption efforts across the country, at both the central and state levels.
   - **The Selection Committee** comprises the Prime Minister as the Chairperson, the Speaker of the Lok Sabha, the Leader of the Opposition in the Lok Sabha, the Chief Justice of India or a judge nominated by them, and an eminent jurist appointed by the President.

- Upon receipt of a complaint against any public official in relation to the offences committed under the Prevention of Corruption Act, Lokpal may pass an order directing its own inquiry wing or any other agency to conduct a preliminary inquiry.
- Lokpal shall supervise such investigation by the concerned agency.
- Upon filing of such report by the investigative agency, Lokpal may either grant sanction for the prosecution of such public official or in the alternative direct such agency to file a closure report before the concerned jurisdictional court.
- Further, to ensure transparency, Lokpal shall maintain a repository of all complaints indicating the status of such complaints.
- Lokpal has jurisdiction over the following functionaries:
  - ✓ Prime Minister (including a former one)
  - ✓ Union Ministers
  - ✓ Members of Parliament
  - ✓ Groups A, B, C and D officers of the Central Government
  - ✓ Any member or employee of any organisation or trust established by an Act of Parliament or partly financed by the Central Government
  - ✓ Any officer of a society or association or trust, which is in receipt of any donation from any foreign source under the Foreign Contribution (Regulation) Act, 2010 in excess of ₹10 Lakh in a year or such higher amount as the Central Government may notify
- Lokpal is empowered with all powers vested in a civil court, under the Code of Civil Procedure, 1908. Further, the Lokpal, during the investigation / inquiry, has the power to summon / inquire into the conduct of any person in the following cases:
  - ✓ Any person involved in the act of abetting, bribe giving or bribe taking.
  - ✓ Any person who would assist the inquiry / investigation process, and the Lokpal can call upon such person to furnish such information
  - ✓ Any person, in the opinion of Lokpal, whose reputation is prejudicially going to be affected by the investigation / inquiry in respect of the complaint
- Lokpal has been given power to search and seize any document which, in its opinion, could be used as evidence for the purpose of the proceedings.
- Lokpal has supervision over the functioning of the CBI in respect of all complaints, which is in consonance with the intention of the legislature to create an ombudsman to supervise the anti-corruption investigation framework at the federal level.
- Clear time lines are given:
  - ✓ Preliminary enquiry – 3 months extendable by 3 months.
  - ✓ Investigation – 6 months, which may be extended by 6 months at a time.
  - ✓ Trial – 1 year extendable by 1 year and, to achieve this, special courts to be set up.

  - ✓ Enhancement of maximum punishment under the Prevention of Corruption Act from 7 years to 10 years. The minimum punishment under sections 7, 8, 9 and 12 of the Prevention of Corruption Act will now be 3 years and the minimum punishment under section 15 (punishment for attempt) will now be 2 years.
- To add teeth to the above powers of the Lokpal, the Lokpal Act has also empowered the Lokpal to grant sanction for initiating prosecution in respect of any public official under Section 20(7)(a) of the Lokpal Act, which overrides the requirement given in the PC Act and the CrPC in relation to procuring sanctions from the respective governments with which the public servant is employed.
- **Lokpal and Lokayukta (Amendment) Act, 2016:** The amendment revises the Lokpal and Lokayuktas Act, 2013, particularly regarding the declaration of assets and liabilities by public officials.
  - ✓ It allows the leader of the largest opposition party in the Lok Sabha to be part of the selection committee for choosing the ombudsman if there is no recognised Leader of Opposition.
  - ✓ It modifies Section 44 of the Act, which previously required public officials to declare their assets and liabilities within 30 days of assuming office.
  - ✓ The amendment removes the 30-day deadline, instead allowing public officials to report their assets and liabilities according to timelines prescribed by the government.
- **Changes in the Functions of the CVC:** The implementation of the Lokpal and Lokayuktas Act strengthens the Central Vigilance Commission (CVC), enabling it to function more independently and assertively:
  - ✓ **New Sections Added**: Sections 8A and 8B were introduced in the CVC Act, 2003, granting the CVC authority to investigate matters referred by the Lokpal concerning Group 'B', 'C', and 'D' central government employees, as well as officials and staff of corporations, companies, societies, and local authorities owned by the central government.
  - ✓ **Supervisory Powers over CBI**: The CVC is now empowered to supervise the Central Bureau of Investigation (CBI) in cases related to offences under the Prevention of Corruption Act, 1988, ensuring greater objectivity and accountability in its operations.

The Lokpal has therefore effectively been constituted as an anti-corruption ombudsman with supervisory powers, with the aim to ensure that the investigation / inquiry proceedings in respect of a complaint against a public official is undertaken with fairness, transparency and promptness.

3. **Limitations**

The Lokpal Act has faced criticism for several limitations, including government influence over its appointment and functioning, which undermines its independence. The prohibition of anonymous complaints discourages whistleblowers, while the 7-year limitation period for filing complaints may exclude some cases. Severe penalties for false complaints could deter genuine grievances, and the lack of transparency in handling complaints against the higher-level public servants raise concerns. Additionally, the Lokpal cannot independently initiate investigations, and excessive focus on the form of complaints over their content further weakens its effectiveness.

SUMMARY

- Public fund management refers to how governments handle resources, impacting economic growth and citizen well-being. Effective management oversees revenue generation and expenditure.
- Misuse of public funds involves unauthorised spending or violations of laws and policies.
- Underutilisation of planned expenditures arises from procedural hurdles and deficiencies in district-level planning.
- Misappropriation of funds is the unlawful use of legally accessed money for personal or unauthorised purposes.
- Factors causing ineffective public fund utilisation include bureaucratic inefficiencies, corruption, political interference, poor planning, and resource constraints.
- Implications of ineffective fund utilisation include poor infrastructure, loss of public trust, reduced service delivery, and increased fiscal burden.
- Corruption is the dishonest use of a position of trust for personal gain, including bribery, graft, and trading in influence.
- Causes of corruption stem from social, economic, political, legal, and administrative factors.
- Impacts of corruption:
  - *Economic*: Slows growth, distorts spending, widens inequality, and deters investment.
  - *Social*: Fuels poverty, damages public services, and worsens crime and rights violations.
  - *Political*: Undermines democracy, reduces transparency, and erodes public trust.
- Combatting corruption requires:
  - *Institutional measures*: Stronger law enforcement, media accountability, anti-corruption reforms.
  - *Policy measures*: Strengthened governance and stakeholder involvement.
  - *Economic measures*: Political funding regulation and international cooperation.
  - *Social measures*: Public awareness, education, and empowerment, especially for women.
- Social audits evaluate organisations' social accountability and empower citizens in combating corruption.
- Media's role, including social media, is to ensure transparency and hold sectors accountable.
- India's anti-corruption framework includes laws like the Prevention of Corruption Act (1988), institutions such as the CBI and CVC, and tribunals like CAT to address corruption disputes.

PREVIOUS YEARS' QUESTIONS

1. "Corruption is the manifestation of the failure of core values in the society." In your opinion, what measures can be adopted to uplift the core values in the society? *UPSC CSE Mains 2023*
2. Whistleblower, who reports corruption and illegal activities, wrongdoing and misconduct to the concerned authorities, runs the risk of being exposed to grave danger, physical harm and victimisation by the vested interests, accused persons and his team. What policy measures would you suggest to strengthen protection mechanism to safeguard the whistleblower? *UPSC CSE Mains 2022*
3. An independent and empowered social audit mechanism is an absolute must in every sphere of public service, including judiciary, to ensure performance, accountability and ethical conduct. Elaborate. *UPSC CSE Mains 2021*
4. Effective utilisation of public funds is crucial to meet development goals. Critically examine the reasons for underutilisation and misutilisation of public funds and their implications. *UPSC CSE Mains 2019*
5. "Non-performance of duty by a public servant is a form of corruption". Do you agree with this view? Justify your answer. *UPSC CSE Mains 2019*
6. "Corruption causes misuse of government treasury, administrative inefficiency and obstruction in the path of national development." Discuss Kautilya's views. *UPSC CSE Mains 2016*
7. Today we find that inspite of various measures of prescribing codes of conduct, setting up vigilance cells/commissions, RTI, active media and strengthening of legal mechanism, corrupt practices are not coming under control. (a) Evaluate the effectiveness of these measures with justifications. (b) Suggest more effective strategies to tackle this menace. *UPSC CSE Mains 2015*
8. There is a heavy ethical responsibility on the public servants because they occupy positions of power, handle huge amounts of public funds, and their decisions have wide ranging impact on society and environment. What steps have you taken to improve your ethical competence to handle such responsibility? *UPSC CSE Mains 2014*
9. It is often said that poverty leads to corruption. However there is no dearth of instances where affluent and powerful people indulge in corruption in a big way. What are the basic causes of corruption among people? Support your answer with examples. *UPSC CSE Mains 2014*
10. Given below are quotations of great moral thinkers/philosophers. For each of these quotations, bring out what it means to you in the present context:
    "There is enough on this earth for every one's need but for no one's greed."
    —Mahatma Gandhi.
    UPSC CSE Mains 2013
11. Given below are quotations of great moral thinkers/philosophers. For each of these quotations, bring out what it means to you in the present context:
    "Nearly all men can withstand adversity, but if you want to test a man's character, give him power."
    —Abraham Lincoln.
    UPSC CSE Mains 2013

Information Sharing and Transparency in Government: Right to Information

16

According to the Second Administrative Reforms Commission, 'The Right to Information Law of 2005 signals a radical shift in our governance culture and permanently impacts all state agencies. The effective implementation of this law depends on three fundamental shifts: from the prevailing culture of secrecy to a new culture of openness; from personalised **despotism**[1] to authority coupled with accountability; and from unilateral decision-making to participative governance.'

LEARNING OBJECTIVES

1. Understanding the concept and significance of the Right to Information (RTI) Act in promoting accountability and combating corruption
2. Understanding how the RTI Act came into existence
3. Deducing the relationship between RTI and administrative reforms
4. Critically examining the constitutional underpinnings of the RTI Act and analysing the limitations posed by laws
5. Understanding the exemptions and exclusions
6. Case studies to developing insight into how citizens can use RTI effectively
7. Understand the ARC–II recommendations

1. MARTYRS IN THE FIGHT AGAINST CORRUPTION

During the last few years, some common people have laid down their lives fighting against corruption in public life.

Satyendra Kumar Dubey: Project Director Technical, National Highways Department, was murdered for exposing corruption in the Golden Quadrilateral Project in Gaya, Bihar.

Amit Jethwa: A prominent RTI activist and 'Green Crusader' was campaigning against alleged illegal mining in the Gir Sanctuary areas of Gujarat, which some politicians backed. Unidentified assailants shot at him.

---

[1]**Despotism:** Tyranny/Dictatorship

Satish Shetty: Famous in Pune for boldly invoking the RTI Act to bring to light corruption in land dealings was killed while he was out for his morning walk.

Arun Sawant: Shot dead for exposing corruption in Badalpur Municipality.

Sola Ranga Rao: Paid through his life for using the RTI Act to ask for information from Mandal Parishad Development Office on funds disbursement.

Venkatesh Nayak: Died in his fight against the encroachment of government lands.

Shanmugam Manjunath: An IIM graduate who was murdered for exposing the sale of adulterated petrol. He was a marketing manager (grade-A officer) for the Indian Oil Corporation (IOC), who was murdered for sealing a corrupt petrol station in Lakhimpur Kheri, UP. This incident inspired several students at IIM, IIT, and other institutes culminating with the IIM students setting up the 'Manjunath Shanmugam Trust' to improve governance in Indian public life.

2. THE STRUGGLE FOR RIGHT TO INFORMATION: THE BACKGROUND

Of all the Right to Information Acts, enacted in more than seventy countries in the world today, the Indian Act is reported to be the best-drafted one. The United Nations Development Programme in its appeal 'Eliminate Corruption, Enable Better Living' has hailed India's RTI Act as the best in practice.

This act did not come about easily but it was achieved as the first and only after a protracted and hard-fought struggle by thousands of activists and various civil society members. It started with the relentless fight by civil society groups for People's Rights in Rajasthan that finally, in 1997, resulted in the enactment of the RTI Act in that state. In Rajasthan, it was alleged that during the 1990s there was widespread corruption and malpractices in the implementation of poverty alleviation schemes.

The *Mazdoor Kisan Sakthi Sangathan* (MKSS) in Rajasthan made great groundwork to unearth the malpractices in the poverty alleviation schemes and after having got the prima facie facts, MKSS set up a public inquiry. This public inquiry revealed that a few public servants had indulged in large-scale corruption and malpractices. The affected public themselves came out boldly, averred that records had been manipulated for the works that were still undone such as for road works, desilting of lakes, etc., and that thousands of public servants had been benefited by these. This bold act of the public brought home the realisation to keep the public informed about the government's plans, policies, etc. It is equally fundamental right on the part of the public to demand information on such public schemes.

The struggle that began for copies of bills, vouchers, and muster rolls of development works has compelled the state government to bring out state RTI. Even though the act was not the best of its kind on RTI, it has laid the foundation for a nationwide demand for comprehensive laws in RTI.

Aruna Roy, Nikhil Dey, and *Sarpanch* Changan Singh of MKSS, backed by the public, launched a series of struggles for RTI. Their persistent efforts led to Rajasthan's proclamation in 1995, declaring it would be the first state in India to grant citizens access to government records. However, the announcement remained unimplemented for nearly a year. In April 1996, MKSS resumed its struggle, organising a massive demonstration urging the government to act. Despite another announcement, the government did not follow through. In May 1997, MKSS intensified its agitation with the slogan 'Do or Die,' causing a significant impact. As a result, Rajasthan enacted its RTI law, and MKSS expanded its efforts nationwide, leading to the formation of the National Campaign for People's Right to Information (NCPRI). This movement gained support from numerous organisations and human rights groups to establish the RTI Act across India.

In 2002, the NDA Government headed by Sri Atal Bihari Vajpayee passed a bill on the Freedom of Information Act, 2002, in the Parliament. But it did not become an Act. In 2004, the UPA government headed by Shri Manmohan Singh included the RTI Act in its election manifesto; and when it formed the government, started taking steps to fulfil its promise. In August 2004, the National Advisory Council, the NCPRI, and the Commonwealth Human Rights Initiative (CHRI) together made some changes to the 2002 RTI Bill and submitted its core document. Based on this core document, in December the new bill on the RTI Act was introduced in the Parliament. The bill was approved by the Lok Sabha on 11 May 2005, and by the Rajya Sabha on 12 May. The Indian President's approval was obtained on 15 May and the bill formally became an Act. It was published in the Government Gazette on 22 June and from 12 October 2005, it has been in implementation.

3. EVOLUTION OF RIGHT TO INFORMATION (INDIA)

- The Constitution does not explicitly provide the Right to Information as a fundamental right, but it is inherent in Article 19(1)(a) and Article 21 of the Constitution of India.
- In India, RTI is based on Article 19(1)(a) of the Constitution, which guarantees the freedom of speech and expression.
- India has also ratified the Universal Declaration on Human Rights. Article 19 of the declaration provides for the right to receive and impart Information.
- Supreme Court in various cases, such as State of UP vs. Raj Narain, S.P. Gupta vs. UOI, Dinesh Trivedi vs. UOI, Bhopal gas leak case, etc., has asserted the idea of 'Right to Know' as a fundamental right.
- Mathew Commission (1982) emphasised on Right to Know.

- Fifth Pay Commission (1994–97) recommended the abolition of the Official Secrets Act and the introduction of the Right to Information.
- 1995: The Press Council of India brought out the first blueprint of model RTI.
- 1997: Tamil Nadu enacted the first Right to Information Act followed by Goa.
- 1997: Shourie Committee – Another draft on RTI.
- 2000: Rajasthan and Karnataka enacted their Right to Information Acts.
- 2001: Delhi enacted its Right to Information Act.
- 2002: Maharashtra and Assam enacted their Right to Information Acts.
- 2002: Freedom of Information Act introduced and enacted but never notified.
- 2005: The right to Information was finally enacted and got notified and came into force.

4. SIGNIFICANCE OF RTI

1. Promotes the idea of popular sovereignty.
2. Promotes openness, transparency, and **accountability**[2] in administration.
3. Empowers citizens to combat corruption.
4. Prevents administrative arbitrariness or high-handedness.
5. Bridges the gap between providers and recipients of public service.
6. Makes citizens part of the decision-making process in the government.
7. Strengthens grassroots democracy through people's participation.
8. Empower people to have access to other rights.
9. Promotes good governance through transparency, accountability, predictability and participation.
10. Provides transparency in government organisations by making them function more objectively thereby enhancing predictability.
11. Enables citizens to participate in the governance process effectively by providing information about the functioning of government.
12. Access to information can empower the poor and the weaker sections of the society to demand and get information about public policies and actions, thereby leading to their welfare.
13. Right to Information has been seen as the key to strengthening **participatory democracy**[3] and ushering in people-centred governance.
14. Promotes administrative reforms by exposing the weaknesses and gaps in the system.
15. Exempts certain intelligence and security organisations from its purview. However, information on corruption and human rights violations is not excluded from this act.

---

[2] **Accountability:** Liability/responsibility

[3] **Participatory Democracy:** A system where citizens actively engage in decision-making processes

5. RTI AND ADMINISTRATIVE REFORMS

RTI and administrative reforms have a mutually reinforcing symbiotic relation:

1. RTI ensures transparency, accountability, and efficiency which are the goals of the administrative reforms as well.
2. RTI helps in exposing the shortcomings of the system which leads to further administrative reforms.
3. RTI cannot succeed in its implementation until and unless supported by structural and procedural reforms. Thus, administrative reforms are a necessity for RTI's success.

6. RIGHT TO INFORMATION ACT, 2005

The Right to Information Act, 2005 (RTI Act) is a landmark legislation enacted by the Indian Parliament to promote transparency and accountability in government and public institutions. It enables citizens to know how the government functions, how decisions are made, and how public resources are utilised.

The Act specifies that citizens have a right to:

- Request any information (as defined). This information can be requested in various formats, including copies of records, documents, and electronic media.
- Inspect documents, works, and records maintained by government bodies.
- Take certified samples of materials of work.

6.1 Information: The Concept

Information refers to any material in any form – including records, documents, memos, emails, opinions, advice, press releases, circulars, orders, reports, papers, samples, models, data in electronic formats, and details about private entities accessible by public authorities under existing laws. Requests for information under RTI can help make the civil servants aware of the problems and thus lead to corrective action.

6.2 How to Procure Information: the Process

Under the RTI Act, all covered authorities must appoint a Public Information Officer (PIO) to handle information requests. Citizens can submit written requests to the PIO, who is obligated to provide the requested information. If the request pertains to another public authority, the PIO must transfer the relevant portion of the request to the appropriate PIO within 5 days. Additionally, public authorities must appoint Assistant Public Information Officers (APIOs) to receive and forward RTI requests and appeals.

Key Provisions

Requester's details: The applicant needs to provide only their name and contact details—no additional personal information is required.

Time Limits for Response:

PIO: Reply within 30 days of receiving the request.

APIO: Reply within 35 days of receiving the request.

Transferred Requests: If transferred to another PIO, the response must be provided within 30 days from when the new PIO receives it.

Corruption/Human Rights Issues: Requests involving corruption or human rights violations by scheduled security agencies (Second Schedule) must be addressed within 45 days, with prior approval from the Central Information Commission.

Life or Liberty Cases: If the request involves life or liberty, the PIO must respond within 48 hours.

6.3 Exemptions of RTI

The following types of information are exempted from disclosure under the RTI Act:

1. Information that would prejudicially affect the sovereignty, security, and integrity of India.
2. Information that would affect the strategic, scientific, or economic interests of the state or the relation with foreign state.
3. Information that has been expressly forbidden to be published by any court of law or tribunal or the disclosure of which may constitute contempt of court.
4. Information that would cause a breach of privilege of the Parliament or the State Legislature.
5. Information including commercial confidence, trade secrets, or intellectual property.
6. Information that could endanger someone's life, physical safety, or reveal confidential sources assisting law enforcement or security.
7. Information that would impede the process of investigation, apprehension, or prosecution of offenders.
8. Information that relates to personal information, the disclosure of which has no relationship to any public activity or interest, or which would cause unwarranted invasion of the privacy of the individual.

Thought Box

What steps can be taken to ensure the RTI framework remains robust against political and bureaucratic interference? Do you think the role of political parties plays a significant role in improving these processes? If yes, how?

Notwithstanding any of the exemptions listed above, a public authority may allow access to information, if the public interest in disclosure outweighs the harm to the protected interests.

6.4 Exclusions of RTI

Central Intelligence and security agencies specified in the Second Schedule, such as IB, RAW, Central Bureau of Investigation (CBI), Directorate of Revenue Intelligence, Central Economic Intelligence Bureau, Directorate of Enforcement, Narcotics Control Bureau, Aviation Research Centre, Special Frontier Force, BSF, CRPF, ITBP, CISF, NSG, Assam Rifles, Special Service Bureau, Special Branch (CID), Andaman and Nicobar, The Crime Branch – CID-CB, Dadra and Nagar Haveli and Special Branch, Lakshadweep Police, and agencies specified by the state governments through a notification will also be excluded.

The exclusion, however, is not absolute and these organisations must provide information about allegations of corruption and human rights violations.

6.5 Implementing Issues of the Act

The implementation of RTI faces several challenges that hinder its effectiveness and full realisation of its objective. Some of the key issues include:

1. **Lack of Awareness:** Many citizens, particularly in rural and marginalised areas, are unaware of their rights under the RTI. The lack of knowledge about the existence of the law or how to use it, and also the digital illiteracy prevents individuals from accessing information.
2. **Reluctance and Hostility:** Some government officials may resist providing information due to the fear of exposing corruption, inefficiency, or errors in governance. This reluctance can result in delayed responses or denial of information.
3. **Inadequate Training:** Many public servants lack proper training on the RTI Act, resulting in incorrect or inadequate responses, non-compliance, and in some cases, refusal to provide information.
4. **Frivolous Requests:** Some individuals may misuse RTI by submitting frivolous or excessive requests. While the law does not prohibit such requests, they can overload the system, causing delays for those with genuine concerns.
5. **Lack of Monitoring:** There is often inadequate monitoring of RTI implementation, which allows public authorities to ignore or delay requests without facing any serious consequences. This problem is **exacerbated**[4] by the lack of a dedicated body or oversight mechanism to ensure the proper functioning of the RTI system.
6. **Corruption and Bribery:** In some cases, public officials may demand bribes to provide the requested information or to expedite the process. This corrupt practice undermines the fundamental purpose of the RTI Act and erodes public trust in the system.

[4]**Exacerbated:** Make a situation/problem/feeling worse

7. **Vague Exemptions:** Many RTI laws allow for information to be withheld under broad exemptions such as national security, trade secrets, and personal privacy. These exemptions are often used excessively or arbitrarily, preventing access to important public information.
8. **Balancing Public Interest and Privacy:** A fundamental challenge in RTI implementation is balancing the need for transparency with the protection of individual privacy. Public authorities sometimes misuse the notion of privacy to withhold information that is legitimately in the public interest.
9. **Political Interference:** Political leaders or parties may exert undue influence over public authorities, preventing the disclosure of information that could reflect poorly on them or their policies. This leads to selective transparency and undermines the principle of equal access to information.
10. **Inadequate Digital Infrastructure:** While many RTI systems have moved online, not all government institutions have the necessary technological infrastructure to support an efficient digital RTI process. This may lead to issues such as non-functioning websites, slow response times, or a lack of access to e-services.

Addressing these issues requires systematic reforms such as improving awareness campaigns, training public officials, simplifying procedures, strengthening enforcement mechanisms, enhancing the scope of application and ensuring the independence of the RTI process. Appointment of Central Information Commissioners and State Information Commissioners should be done in a **bipartisan**[5] manner involving the leader of the opposition, and Chief Justices of the Supreme Court and High Court.

Only by tackling these barriers can the RTI law achieve its potential to enhance transparency and hold public authorities accountable.

7. RECOMMENDATIONS OF SECOND ADMINISTRATIVE REFORMS

1. The Official Secrets Act, 1923 should be repealed and substituted by a chapter in the National Security Act, containing provisions relating to official secrets.
2. Relevant provisions of the Indian Evidence Act, 1872, civil procedure code needs to be amended.
3. (a) As an affirmation of the importance of transparency in public affairs, ministers on assumption of office may take an oath of transparency along with the oath of office, and the requirement of administering the oath of secrecy should be dispensed with. Articles 75(4) and 164 (3) and the Third Schedule should be suitably amended.

[5]**Bipartisan:** Supported by or involving two political parties

(b) Safeguard against disclosure of information against the national interest may be provided through written undertaking by incorporation of a clause in the national security law dealing with official secrets.

4. Civil services rules of all states may be reworded in such a manner that disclosure of full and accurate information under the RTI is a duty in good faith.
5. (a) Section 12 of the Act may be amended to constitute the Selection Committee of CIC with the Prime Minister, Leader of the Opposition, and the Chief Justice of India. Section 15 may be similarly amended to constitute the Selection Committee at the State level with the Chief Minister, Leader of the Opposition, and the Chief Justice of the High Court.
   (b) The Government of India should ensure the constitution of SICs in all states within three months.
   (c) The CIC should establish four regional offices of CIC with a Commissioner heading each. Similarly, regional offices of SICs should be established in larger states.
   (d) At least half of the members of the Information Commissions should be drawn from non-civil services backgrounds. Such a provision may be made in the rules under the Act, by the Union Government, applicable to both CIC and SICs.
   (e) All Ministries/Departments/Agencies/Offices with more than one PIO have to designate a nodal Assistant Public Information Officer with the authority to receive requests for information on behalf of all PIOs. Such a provision should be incorporated into the rules by the appropriate governments.

   All public authorities may be advised by the Government of India that along with the PIOs they should also designate the appellate authority and publish both, together.
6. **Suo-moto disclosures**[6] should also be available in the form of printed, priced publication in the official languages, revised periodically (at least once a year).
7. All government functionaries should be imparted at least one day of training on the Right to Information within a year.
8. Awareness campaigns may be entrusted to credible non-profit organisations at the state level.
9. The CIC and the SICs may be entrusted with the task of monitoring the effective implementation of the Right to Information Act in all public authorities. (An appropriate provision could be made under Section 30 by way of removal of difficulties.)
10. NCC may be set up under the chairpersonship of the Chief Information Commissioner with the nodal Union Ministry, the SICs, and representatives of states as members. The NCC would:
    (a) Serve as a national platform for effective implementation of the Act,

[6]**Suo-moto Disclosure:** The term 'suo-moto' is a Latin phrase meaning 'on its own motion.' It is a proactive disclosure of information by public authorities under the Right to Information Act of 2005

(b) Document and **disseminate**[7] best practices in India and elsewhere,
(c) Monitor the creation and functioning of the national portal for the Right to Information,
(d) Review the rules and executive orders issued by the appropriate governments under the Act,
(e) Carry out impact evaluation of the implementation of the Act, and
(f) Perform such other relevant functions as may be deemed necessary.

11. States may be advised to set up independent **public grievances**[8] redressal authorities to deal with complaints of delay, harassment, or corruption.
12. (a) Organisations that perform functions of a public nature that are ordinarily performed by the government or its agencies, and those that enjoy **natural monopoly**[9] may be brought within the purview of the Act.
    (b) Norms should be laid down that any institution or body that has received 50% of its annual operating costs, or a sum equal to or greater than 1 crore during any of the preceding three years should be understood to have obtained 'substantial funding' from the government for the period and purpose of such funding.
    (c) Any information which, if it were held by the government, would be subject to disclosure under the law, must remain subject to such disclosure even when it is transferred to a non-government body or institution.

8. RIGHT TO INFORMATION ACT—KEY TO GOOD GOVERNANCE

1. Change in archaic laws, procedures and practices.
2. The Official Secrets Act should be repealed and substituted by a chapter in the National Security Act.
3. Indian Evidence Act, 1872 should be amended to aid disclosure of officially classified information.
4. Civil Service Rules of all states should be reworded—civil servants shall communicate all information applicable under the RTI to the public.
5. Manual of official procedure to be reworded on the same lines.

---

[7] **Disseminate:** To spread information, knowledge, ideas etc. so that it reaches as many people as possible

[8] **Public Grievances:** This is a complaint, or a representation made by individuals or groups of people in a court of law against a decision or action taken by the government or an organisation

[9] **Natural Monopoly:** It occurs when a single firm can supply a good or service to an entire market at a lower cost than multiple competing firms due to economies of scale

9. RIGHT TO INFORMATION— SUCCESS STORIES

Strategic use of the RTI Act can help overcome bureaucratic delays, empower individuals to overcome corruption and claim their rightful entitlements. A few examples are as follows:

CASE STUDIES

CASE STUDY 1

R. Chandran, a retired assistant engineer from TNEB in Tiruvallikkeni, Chennai, has been freelancing as a house wiring professional. When he decided to apply for a license, he realised he had lost his educational certificates. He applied to the Directorate of Technical Education, paying the necessary fees for a duplicate certificate. However, after eight months, he still hadn't received it.

Following advice, he filed a request under the RTI Act, 2005, to expedite action on his earlier application. Shortly after, he received a duplicate of his Degree Certificate, signed by the relevant authorities.

? Thought Box

What do success stories of RTI applications reveal about its power to bring justice to marginalised groups?

CASE STUDY 2

Vijayakumar from Ambattur, Chennai, registered for his PhD through correspondence with a deemed university in Salem in 2006. Despite paying full fees, he received neither study materials nor his identity card, and no guide was assigned for his PhD. After a year, when he inquired, the management demanded payment of the second-year fees before sending the materials.

Following advice, Vijayakumar requested an explanation for not receiving his first-year materials. The university responded that it was not covered by the RTI Act and was not obligated to reply, citing a court injunction in Salem.

Vijayakumar appealed to the UGC, which pointed out that the university, receiving UGC grants, was required to provide the requested materials. The UGC sent a letter to both the university and Vijayakumar.

The day after receiving the UGC's letter, Vijayakumar was contacted by the university, informing him that his identity card, study materials, and guide details were ready for collection. He traveled to Salem and received everything he had requested.

CASE STUDY 3

Mazloom Nadaf, a 70-year-old rickshaw puller in Bihar, struggled for five years to get his house under the Indira *Awas Yojana*. When authorities demanded a bribe of ₹5000 to process his application, he refused and sought help from an NGO's legal aid centre. With their assistance, Nadaf filed an RTI application along with requesting the progress report on his application. The Circle Officer forwarded the RTI to the Block Development Officer (BDO), who responded promptly by treating Nadaf with respect, handing him ₹15,000 as the first instalment, and assuring him that his other requests would be addressed.

CASE STUDY 4

Laxmi, a 70-year-old woman from Haryana's Bhiwani district, used the Right to Information Act to access files related to her late son's pension and benefits. Her son, a Delhi Traffic Police constable, had died in a road accident five years earlier. Despite delays, Laxmi appealed to the Central Information Commission (CIC), which granted her access to file noting regarding terminal benefits of ₹4 lakh and the family pension. Armed with this information, Laxmi filed an application that successfully secured her daughter-in-law Mamta's rightful monthly pension.

CASE STUDY 5

Arif shared his experience of using the Right to Information (RTI) Act to resolve a prolonged issue with his flat's paperwork. After purchasing a flat in his wife's name two and a half years ago, he received only the registry paper from the builder and later discovered he also needed a transfer copy and blueprint. Despite multiple visits to the bank, officials claimed all necessary documents had already been provided.

Having prior knowledge of RTI, Arif filed an application in his wife's name with an RBI officer. Within five days, the bank contacted him, addressed his concerns, and assured him the paperwork would be completed by the next day. True to their word, he received all the required documents by the next morning.

Arif emphasised how RTI empowered him to expose the nexus between bankers and builders, urging citizens to recognise the power of RTI in holding government officials accountable. The RTI Act continues to be celebrated as a vital tool for ensuring transparency and accountability in governance.

CASE STUDY 6

Khetramani Samantrai, who bought a small piece of land near Dhauli, Bhubaneswar, faced a 1.5-year delay in receiving her land deed documents from the District Sub-Registrar Office (DSO), despite repeated visits with notary Karunakar Swain.

On July 13, 2006, Khetramani sought help at an RTI camp run by CYSD Bhubaneswar. With guidance from volunteers, she filed an RTI application under Section 6(1) and approached the DSO with support. After intervention by the Public Information Officer (PIO) and insistence on accountability, the head clerk produced the documents within 15 minutes.

RTI empowered Khetramani to resolve the issue, demonstrating its effectiveness in ensuring justice and accountability.

CASE STUDY 7

The Right to Information (RTI) Act helped expose a massive rural development scam in Rajasthan's Janawad *panchayat*, where over 70% of ₹1 crore in annual funds was siphoned off by a corrupt nexus of officials and the *sarpanch.* Villagers used RTI to uncover fraudulent claims, such as ₹2 lakhs for a dispensary allegedly built in 1995, which had existed since the 1960s.

By accessing *panchayat* records, villagers discovered 49 out of 146 development projects, including wells, roads, and schools, existed only on paper. Their collective action led to the *sarpanch's* imprisonment, suspension of 13 officials, and mandatory annual social audits for *panchayat* funds.

This case demonstrates RTI's power to hold officials accountable, fight corruption, and ensure development funds reach the intended beneficiaries.

RTI has once again come to the rescue of the people of Rajasthan by nailing those responsible for the 'mother of all rural development scams' in Rajasthan.

CASE STUDY 8

Eighty-year-old Laxmi Devi finally received her old-age pension, thanks to the Right to Information (RTI) Act.

Living with her daughter, who works as a domestic help in Khirki village, Laxmi Devi applied for a pension in May 2005, but saw no progress despite repeated visits to the office. Frustrated, she sought help at an RTI camp organised by the NGO *Satark Nagarik Sanghathan.*

She discovered her application was missing and reapplied. By December, her pension was approved, entitling her to ₹350 per month and a ₹1,750 cheque for the five-month delay. RTI brought Laxmi the justice she had almost given up on.

CASE STUDY 9

After repeated complaints from his wife and neighbours about irregular gas cylinder deliveries by M/s Kankria Gas Agency, Mr. Vijay Kumar took action. He filed a detailed requisition with Hindustan Petroleum Corporation Ltd. (HPCL) under the RTI Act, requesting information on the agency's LPG distribution practices, including:

1. The number of domestic and commercial customers served by the agency.
2. Details of customers with one or multiple cylinders.
3. Cylinder procurement figures by the agency from HPCL.
4. Demand and supply records of gas cylinders, including booking and delivery details.
5. Actions taken by HPCL against gas agencies in Pune for erratic distribution, if any.

Mr. Kumar submitted the application at 1 PM, and by 2:45 PM, his wife informed him that the dealer had promptly delivered the gas cylinder. The swift response highlights the power of RTI in ensuring accountability and resolving grievances effectively.

CASE STUDY 10

In the village of Someshwar, ration cards were collected after the *panchayat* elections, two years ago to issue the new ones. However, the cards were never returned, leaving villagers, especially those with **BPL**[10] and *Antyodaya* cards, in distress. The delay also affected ration shop owners.

Frustrated, Devendra Singh Rawat of Josh Bal Panchayat sought help from the village *pradhan* but received no support. Determined, he filed an RTI application at the Block Development Office, inquiring about the delay.

Within two days, the *pradhan* and the Village Development Officer visited Devendra, admitting, "If we knew you would file an RTI, we would have issued the cards earlier." What had been pending for two years was resolved in just two days, showcasing the RTI's power to ensure accountability and prompt action.

CASE STUDY 11

In Bageshwar, Tara Dutt discovered his name had been removed from the BPL list during a survey without any explanation. This removal also stalled benefits like the '*Kanya Dhan*' scheme, which provides financial aid for girl children.

After learning about the RTI Act through his children, who attended an NGO-sponsored workshop, Tara filed an RTI application to inquire about the removal. When he received no

[10]**BPL (Below Poverty Line):** It is a metric implemented by the Indian government to identify households or individuals who require government assistance. BPL varies from state to state and has a wide range of parameters

response, he appealed to the Block Development Officer with support from Bhuvan Chandra Pandey, a SIMAR facilitator.

Following the appeal, it was decided that Tara's BPL status would be restored within two months, and the stalled *'Kanya Dhan'* payments would resume immediately. This highlights the RTI Act's effectiveness in addressing grievances and ensuring access to rightful benefits.

CASE STUDY 12

Jeya Sheela, a resident of Ramanathapuram, Tamil Nadu, tragically lost her son in a road accident on July 29, 2016, near Thirupullani. In October 2016, she applied for compensation under the Victim Compensation Fund at the local police station. However, she faced repeated requests for proof of the accident, and to her frustration, the documents she submitted were misplaced by the authorities.

Determined to secure justice, Jeya filed an RTI application, which ultimately helped her receive the compensation she was entitled to, ensuring accountability in the process.

CASE STUDY 13

Leena Ahuja, a Delhi resident, sought details about a property in Noida from the Greater Noida Industrial Development Authority. Despite several weeks of waiting, her request was ignored. Frustrated by the delay, Leena leveraged the online RTI portal of the Noida Authority. Through this, she successfully obtained information about the current property owner and relevant documentation. Her persistence demonstrated how the RTI Act empowers citizens to demand accountability and transparency from public office.

CASE STUDY 14

The infamous 2G spectrum scam, which occurred during the UPA regime, involved the auctioning of telecom frequencies at grossly undervalued rates. Allegations surfaced that the top minister colluded with certain mobile companies, accepting bribes in exchange for favourable allocations. This malpractice reportedly cost the national exchequer an estimated ₹1.76 lakh crore. The scandal came to light due to an RTI filed by activist Subhash Chandra Agrawal, showcasing the power of information in uncovering large-scale corruption.

Thought Box

There are still over 4 lakhs pending RTI cases in India as of 2024. How effective do you think the RTI system has been over the decades?

CASE STUDY 15

An RTI filed by the non-profit organisation Housing and Land Rights Network unveiled a shocking misuse of funds by the Delhi government. Approximately ₹744 crore, initially allocated for dalit welfare, was diverted to the Commonwealth Games. The investigation revealed that a significant portion of these funds was spent on amenities that existed only on paper, pointing to corruption and money laundering. This case highlighted the critical role of RTI in exposing unethical practices in governance.

10. RTI AND YOUNG GENERATION

***Jan Chetna Kendra* (Pauri)** – In Beena Bisht's village, illegal sand mining for profit was harming the environment, and officials often ignored the issue. Despite facing threats, Beena filed an RTI request for information on uncontrolled sand **quarrying.**[11] With her family's support, the *panchayat* passed a resolution that only villagers could mine sand, and permission would be required before quarrying.

***ARPAN* (Pithoragarh)** – In villages plagued by low electricity voltage, Vimala Basera filed an RTI for details on the power supply. Though she received no response, the electricity situation improved. Similarly, children in the village filed an RTI to inquire about crackdowns on illegal alcohol, leading to a significant reduction in illegal liquor.

***Bal Panchayat* Horrawalla (Dehradun)** – Devrat, a 16-year-old, filed an RTI about hazardous cement pipes blocking the road. Within days, the pipes were removed, resolving the safety issue.

Vimarsh (Nainital) – After learning about RTI, children in Mangoli filed a request about birth registrations. As a result, the *panchayat* secretary registered several births and distributed birth certificates.

Phaguniakhet, Khurpatal – Himani, Ganesh, and Deepa filed an RTI about the prolonged power outage in their village. While they did not receive a response, the electricity department changed the transformer within a week.

Saral (Nainital) – Meena Arya filed an RTI about the lack of computer education in her school. Despite threats from teachers, the computers were returned, and computer classes resumed.

---

[11] **Quarrying:** Sand digging

School Toilets – In another school, children could not use the locked toilets. After a complaint by student Sapna Arya and an RTI request, the locks were removed permanently.

SBMA (Uttarkashi) – Jaideep Negi filed an RTI about the irregular visits of the Auxiliary Nurse Midwife (ANM). Initially, the ANM tried to intimidate Jaideep, but after multiple RTI requests from other villages, the ANM began visiting the village regularly, improving local healthcare services.

These cases demonstrate the power of RTI in addressing community issues, from environmental concerns to access to basic services.

11. RTI AMENDMENT ACT, 2019

The Right to Information (Amendment) Act, 2019 was passed by the Lok Sabha and Rajya Sabha with President Ram Nath Kovind's consent. This amendment introduced key changes, particularly in Section 13, which governs the tenure and service conditions of the Chief Information Commissioner (CIC) and Information Commissioners (ICs). Prior to the amendment, subsections (1) and (2) set a fixed five-year term for these positions. The amendment grants the Central Government the discretion to determine their tenure.

Additionally, subsection (5), which previously aligned the salaries and allowances of the CIC with the Chief Election Commissioner and ICs with Election Commissioners, was changed. Post-amendment, the government now determines their salaries and allowances. The amendment also empowers the government to make rules regarding the tenure and compensation of the CIC and ICs, as well as the functioning of state information commissions.

> **? Thought Box**
>
> How can society prevent the misuse of RTI for personal gains or harassment while preserving its core purpose?

Critics argue that these changes are arbitrary and authoritative, granting the central government more control and undermining the independence of both central and state information commissions. In defense, the government stated that the amendment clarifies the distinction between the Information Commission, a **statutory body**,[12] and the Election Commission, a constitutional body under Article 324. The government contended that equating the two was inappropriate due to their differing legal and institutional frameworks.

---

[12]**Statutory Body:** A statutory body is an organisation, or an entity established by the governing law to implement, enforce, and regulate certain public and private activities

SUMMARY

- RTI promotes popular sovereignty, bridging the gap between public service providers and recipients, strengthening grassroots democracy, and driving **administrative reforms** by exposing system weaknesses.
- RTI and administrative reforms support each other. The appointment of Information Commissioners should be bipartisan, involving the leader of the opposition and the Chief Justices of the SC and HC.
- Five states—Jharkhand, Manipur, Sikkim, Andhra Pradesh, and Mizoram—have yet to establish State Information Commissions. The Commission has recommended their formation within three months. These commissions should ensure diverse societal representation, with at least half of the members being non-Civil Servants.
- The RTI Act is vital for promoting transparency, fighting corruption, and enhancing citizen participation in governance. However, its full potential is underutilised due to implementation challenges and inefficiencies.
- Key challenges to RTI include low public awareness, inefficient record management, bureaucratic resistance, inaccessibility of official documents, and lack of data automation, which need to be addressed by emerging civil servants.
- Recommendations for improving the state-citizen relationship include repealing the Official Secrets Act, raising public awareness, and ensuring bipartisan and inclusive appointments to the Information Commissions.

PREVIOUS YEARS' QUESTIONS

1. There is a view that the Official Secrets Act is an obstacle to the implementation of the Rights to Information Act. Do you agree with the view? *UPSC CSE Mains 2019*
2. 'The Right to Information Act is not all about citizens' empowerment alone; it essentially redefines the concept of accountability.' *UPSC CSE Mains 2018*
3. Some recent developments such as the introduction of the RTI Act, media and judicial activism, etc., are proving helpful in bringing about greater transparency and accountability in the functioning of the government. However, it is also being observed that at times the mechanisms are misused. Another negative effect is that the officers are now afraid to make prompt decisions. Analyse this situation in detail and suggest how this dichotomy can be resolved. Suggest how these negative impacts can be minimised. *UPSC CSE Mains 2015*
4. Today we find that despite various measures like prescribing codes of conduct, setting up vigilance cells/commissions, RTI, active media, and strengthening legal mechanisms, corrupt practices are not coming under control.
   (a) Evaluate the effectiveness of these measures with justifications.
   (b) Suggest more effective strategies to tackle this menace. *UPSC CSE Mains 2015*

Information Sharing and Transparency in Government: Citizens' Charter

17

1. CONCEPT, ORIGIN, AND PRINCIPLES

Good governance is essential for both social and economic sustainable development. The three essential aspects emphasised in good governance are transparency, accountability and responsiveness of the administration. The Citizens' Charter Acts as one of the most valuable tools in ensuring good governance.

A Citizens' Charter is a document of commitments, generally made by a government agency to a citizen with respect to the services being provided to them (citizens). The Citizens' Charter, in addition to outlining the service commitment of organisations or service providers towards providing quality, high standard services, also includes mechanisms for re-addressing grievances.

LEARNING OBJECTIVES

1. Understanding the fundamental Concept of Citizen's Charter
2. Understanding its origin and rationale
3. Comprehending its objectives
4. Recognising the factors contributing towards its growth
5. Appreciating the significance of this charter in Indian context
6. Learning about charter's implementation process
7. Exploring the recommendations of the 2nd Administrative Reforms Commission (ARC) regarding the Citizens' Charter
8. Understanding the ARC's seven-step model for a citizen-centric governance

The 'Citizens' Charters Initiative' is a response to the quest for solving the problems which a citizen encounters, day in and day out, while dealing with organisations providing public services. The concept of the Citizens' Charter enshrines the trust between the service provider and its users. The Citizen's charter is a written agreement between the service delivery agencies and citizens regarding the services. The Citizen's Charter empowers the citizens to demand the committed standards of services. Furthermore, the Citizen's Charter is expected to indicate WHERE TO GO and HOW TO PROCEED.

The concept was initially introduced and put into practice in the United Kingdom, by the then Prime Minister John Major's Conservative Government, in 1991. Its aim was to continuously improve the quality of public services for the people of the country so that these services respond to the needs and wishes of the users. The programme was relaunched in 1998 by the Labour Government of Tony Blair which rechristened it as 'Services First'.

The basic objective of the Citizens' Charter is to empower the citizen in relation to public service delivery.

2. OBJECTIVES BEHIND THE CITIZENS' CHARTER

1. Appropriately laying down service standard accounts as per public expectations and popularising them so that people become better aware.
2. Simplification of rules, regulations, and working norms for the better delivery of services.
3. Time-bound grievance redressal of people.
4. Establish network with functionaries promoting service groups and their participation.
5. Bringing transparency in the organisation.
6. Wide publicity of the standards of the organisation.
7. More independent and impartial grievance redressal.
8. Consistent and continued improvement in the quality of services aced to the service groups.
9. Clarifications of the objectives of organisation functionaries.
10. Developing better responsiveness and reciprocity of the organisation.
11. Modification in services account as per the changing needs of the people or service groups.

3. SIX PRINCIPLES OF THE CITIZENS' CHARTER

The six principles of the Citizens' Charter movement as originally framed were:

1. **Quality:** Improving the quality of services;
2. **Choice:** Wherever possible;
3. **Standards:** Specifying what to expect and how to act if standards are not met;
4. **Value:** For the taxpayers' money;
5. **Accountability:** Individuals and Organisations; and
6. **Transparency:** Rules/Procedures/Schemes/Grievances.

4. REASONS FOR THE GROWTH OF THE CITIZENS' CHARTER

1. Globalisation, privatisation and liberalisation;
2. Internal market orientation;
3. State from only provider to one of the providers;
4. Consumerism—consumer accountability;

5. RTI—the Citizens' Charter is a part of it, though not a legal binding;
6. From beneficiary public to customer public;
7. Part of internal management reforms to improve service quality and service delivery;
8. Part of good governance and corporate governance to involve all the stakeholders.

5. RATIONALE OF THE CITIZENS' CHARTER

The Citizens' Charter is an expression of understanding between the citizens and the provider of a public service with respect to the quantity and quality of service the former receives. It is essentially about the rights of the public and the obligations of the public servants. As public services are funded by citizens, either directly or indirectly through taxes, citizens have the right to expect a particular quality of service that is responsive to their needs and is provided efficiently at a reasonable cost. The Citizens' Charter is a written, voluntary declaration by service providers about service standards, choice, accessibility, non-discrimination, transparency and accountability.

It should be in accordance with the expectations of the citizens. Therefore, it is a useful way of defining for the customers, the nature of service provision, and the explicit standards of service delivery. A further rationale for the Charter is to help change the mindset of the public official from someone with power over the public, to someone with the right sense of duty in spending the public money collected through taxes and in providing the citizens with necessary services. However, the Citizens' Charter should not simply be a document of assurances or a formula which imposes a uniform pattern on every service. It is meant to be a tool kit of initiatives and ideas to raise the level of standards and service delivery and increase public participation, in the most appropriate way.

If successfully implemented, the charter can enable the following:

- Improved service delivery;
- Greater responsiveness of officials towards the public; and
- Greater public satisfaction with services.

6. THE INTERNATIONAL SCENE

The United Kingdom was the first country to introduce the Citizens' Charter initiative, following which many countries started implementing similar programmes, for example,

1. Australia – Service Charter, 1997;
2. Belgium – Public Service Users' Charter 1992;
3. Canada – Service Standards Initiative, 1995;
4. France – Service Charter, 1992;
5. India – Citizens' Charter, 1997;

6. Malaysia – Client's Charter, 1993;
7. Portugal – The Quality Charter in Public Services, 1993; and
8. Spain – The Quality Observatory, 1992.

Also, the Government of Malaysia issued Guidelines on the Client's Charter in 1993 to assist government agencies to prepare and implement the Client's Charter, which is "a written commitment by an agency to deliver outputs or services according to specified standards of quality." (Government of Malaysia, 1998).

7. THE INDIAN SCENARIO

It was at a conference of the chief ministers of various states and union territories held in 1997 in New Delhi, presided over by the Prime Minister of India, that an "Action Plan for Effective and Responsive Government" at the centre and state levels was adopted. One of the major decisions taken during the conference was that the central and state governments would formulate the Citizens' Charters, starting with those sectors that have a large public interface (e.g., Railways, Telecom, Posts, Public Distribution Systems, and the like).

The Charter was expected to incorporate the following elements:

1. Vision and Mission Statements;
2. Details of business transacted by the organisation;
3. Details of clients;
4. Details of services provided to each client group;
5. Details of grievance redressal mechanism, and how to access it; and
6. Expectations from the clients.

By March 2005, several Citizens' Charters had been formulated by the Central Government Ministries/Departments/Organisations and various agencies of State Governments and Administrations of Union Territories.

8. IMPLEMENTATION OF THE CITIZENS' CHARTER

In India, the Department of Administrative Reforms and Public Grievances in Government of India (DARPG) initiated the task of coordinating, formulating and operationalising the Citizens' Charters. Guidelines for formulating the Charters, as well as a list of dos and don'ts were communicated to various government departments/organisations to enable them to bring out focused and effective charters. For the formulation of the Charters, the government agencies at the Centre and State levels were advised to constitute a task force with representation from users, senior management, and cutting-edge staff.

Initially, the banking sector was identified for the purpose of implementing the Citizens' Charter due to its customer service orientation. The banking sector also had the advantage of information technology to speed up various processes. The primary objective of this exercise was to develop the banking sector as a model of excellence in the implementation of the Citizens' Charter. To begin with, three major national level banks were selected for implementing Citizens' Charter, namely, (a) Punjab National Bank, (b) Punjab and Sind Bank, and (c) Oriental Bank of Commerce.

The following key issues were highlighted for exemplary implementation of the Citizens' Charter:

(i) Stakeholder involvement in the formulation of the Citizens' Charters;
(ii) Deployment of the Citizens' Charters in the banks by full involvement of the staff, especially the employees at the cutting-edge level;
(iii) Creation of awareness about the Charter amongst the customers of the banks; and
(iv) Special training for employees at all levels about the concept and implementation of the Citizens' Charter.

9. EVALUATION OF THE CITIZENS' CHARTER

After the implementation of the charter's elements on a pilot basis, an external agency by the name The National Institute of Bank Management (NIBM) was engaged to reassess and re-evaluate the implementation of the Citizens' Charter of these banks.

The major findings of the evaluation carried out by the agency, as stated in its report were:

(i) In majority of the cases, the Charters were not formulated through a consultative process;
(ii) By and large, the service providers are not familiar with the philosophy, goals, and the main features of the charter;
(iii) In none of the departments evaluated, had adequate publicity been given to the charters. In most departments, the charters were only in the early stages of implementation;
(iv) No funds were specifically earmarked for awareness generation on the Citizens' Charter.

10. INADEQUACIES AND GROUND REALITIES UNDERMINING THE CITIZENS' CHARTER'S EFFECTIVENESS

1. At times, not **pragmatic**[1] because of field functionaries and their lack of awareness.
2. Inadequacies in capacity-building among functionaries.
3. Lack of education and changed orientation even among the service groups.
4. Inadequacies in bringing the cultural changes in the organisation.
5. Rigidity of law and some legal hurdles.

[1]**Pragmatic:** Dealing with problems in a practical way rather than by following ideas or principles

6. Gap between field and headquarters, and the lack of effective participation on field.
7. Lack of impartial and independent or effective ombudsman system.
8. Prevailing culture of corruption, opaque, procedural and bureaucratic control.
9. Poor design and content.
10. Inadequate groundwork in terms of assessment and reforming its processes to deliver the promises made in the Charters.
11. Lack of public awareness of the concept of the Citizens' Charter.
12. The Charters are rarely updated, revised, or reviewed.
13. There is a lack of precision on the standards and commitments in several cases.
14. On the commitment front, the charter programme has been throttled on account of poor planning and resource commitment for publicity.
15. The Citizens' Charters have still not been adopted by all ministries/departments.

11. RECOMMENDATIONS FOR STRENGTHENING THE CITIZENS' CHARTER FOR BETTER GOVERANCE

1. Involving stakeholders in fixing standards.
2. Creating awareness among the people.
3. Wide publicity about the Citizens' Charter.
4. Clear channel of hierarchy to be mentioned for effective grievance redressal.
5. Independent and impartial ombudsman for grievance redressal.
6. Appropriate modification with the passage of time.
7. Changing legal procedures.
8. To change the culture of organisation to train them in client orientation and participatory management.
9. Performance audit with the Citizens' Charter.
10. Active HRD in organisation, effective personnel policies to get rid of incompetency.
11. Linking performance and service delivery with performance appraisal.
12. The need for citizens and staff to be consulted at every stage of formulation of the Charter.
13. Orientation of staff about the salient features and goals/objectives of the Charter; vision and mission statement of the departments, and skills such as team building, problem solving, handling of grievances, and communication skills.
14. The need for the creation of a database on consumer grievances and redress.
15. The need for wider publicity of the Charter through print media, posters, banners, leaflets, handbills, brochures, local newspapers, etc., and also through electronic media.
16. Earmarking of specific budgets for awareness generation and orientation of staff.
17. Replication of the best practices in this field.

12. HOW TO MAKE THE CITIZEN'S CHARTER EFFECTIVE?

In its Fourth Report on 'Ethics in Governance', the Commission briefly addressed the issue of Citizens' Charters. The Commission stressed the value of focusing on a concise set of realistic and achievable commitments rather than an extensive list of ambitious but impractical goals like:

12.1 Internal Restructuring Should Precede Charter Formulation

A meaningful Citizens' Charter aims to enhance service quality and for that it requires a thorough analysis of the organisation's existing systems and processes. The systems must be redesigned, and new initiatives should be implemented as necessary.

Charters developed after such internal reforms are far more credible and effective than those created as superficial exercises without addressing systemic improvements.

12.2 Universal Approach Doesn't Fit Everyone

The challenge becomes even more complex as the capabilities and resources that governments and departments need to implement the Citizens' Charter vary significantly across the country. Added to these are differing local conditions. The highly uneven distribution of the Citizens' Charters across states is a clear evidence of this ground reality. For example, some agencies may need more time to specify and agree upon realistic standards of service. For others, additional effort might be required to motivate and equip the staff to participate in this reform exercise.

Such organisations could be given time and resources to experiment with the standards, grievances redressal mechanisms or training. They may also need more time for internal restructuring of the service delivery chain or introducing new systems. Therefore, the Commission is of the view that the formulation of the Citizens' Charter should be a decentralised activity with the head office providing broad guidelines.

12.3 Elaborate Consultation Process

The Citizens' Charters should be formulated after extensive consultations within the organisation followed by a meaningful dialogue with the civil society. Inputs from experts should also be considered at this stage.

12.4 Constructive Commitments to be Brought

The Citizens' Charters must be precise and make firm commitments of service delivery standards to the citizens/consumers in quantifiable terms, wherever possible. With the passage of time, an effort should be made for more **stringent**[2] standards of service delivery.

Redressal Mechanism in case of the default Citizens' Charter should clearly lay down the relief which the organisation is bound to provide if it has defaulted on the promised standards of delivery. In addition, wherever there is a default in the service delivery by the organisation, citizens must also have recourse to a grievances redressal mechanism.

12.5 Periodic Evaluation of the Citizens' Charters

Every organisation must conduct periodic evaluation of its Citizens' Charter preferably through an external agency. This agency while evaluating the Charter of the organisation should also make an objective analysis of whether the promises made therein are being delivered within the defined parameters. The result of such evaluations must be used to improve upon the Charter. This is necessary because a Citizens' Charter is a dynamic document which must keep pace with the changing needs of the citizens as well as the changes in underlying processes and technology.

Systematic monitoring and review of the Citizens' Charters is necessary even after they are approved and placed in the public domain. Performance and accountability tend to suffer when officials are not held responsible for the quality of a charter's design and implementation.

In this context, end-user feedback can be a timely aid to assess the progress and outcomes of an agency that has implemented a Citizens' Charter. This is a standard practice for Charters implemented in the UK.

12.6 Ensuring Accountability of Officers

For all aforementioned points, senior officials or heads of agencies or other designated officers should be held accountable for their respective Citizens' Charters. The monitoring mechanism should fix specific responsibility in all cases where there is a default in adhering to the Citizens' Charter.

12.7 Including Civil Society in the Process

Organisations need to recognise and support the efforts of civil society groups in preparation of the Charters, their dissemination and facilitating information disclosures. There have been a number of states where the involvement of civil society in this entire process has resulted in vast improvement in the contents of the Charter, its adherence as well as educating the citizens about the importance of this vital mechanism.

[2]**Stringent:** Tight, constricted

13. LESSONS LEARNT IN QUALITY ASSURANCE

1. Involve customers in the creation of guarantees, standards, redress policies, complaint systems and customer service agreements.
2. Educate customers about the services that an organisation provides, so they will have realistic notions of what is possible and will understand their own responsibilities.
3. Keep pressure on from outside the organisation to create meaningful guarantees, standards, redress policies and complaint systems.
4. Create an outside review process to approve guarantees, standards, redress policies, complaint systems, and performance measurement processes associated with them.
5. Publicise your standards, guarantees, redress policies, complaint systems and results.
6. Involve frontline employees in creating standards and other tools—and in figuring out how to meet them—to help them buy in.
7. Empower frontline staff to make decisions.
8. Use standards, guarantees, complaints and customer councils to redesign, reengineer and restructure.
9. Study other organisations including private companies, to see how you might rethink, redesign, and reengineer.
10. Back up your quality assurance approach with training, mentoring, learning, networking, and other support for employees.
11. Do not create a separate unit to do this; integrate customer quality assurance into your strategic and performance management systems.
12. Make sure that leadership is seriously committed.

14. THE SEVOTTAM MODEL

Sevottam is a Service Delivery Excellence Model which provides an assessment-improvement framework to bring about excellence in public service delivery. The need for a tool such as Sevottam arose from the fact that the Citizens' Charters by themselves could not achieve the desired results in improving the quality of public services. Besides, the absence of a credible grievances redressal mechanism within the organisations also became a major impediment in improving the service delivery standards. Thus, it seemed necessary that unless there is a mechanism to assess the outcomes of various measures, the reform initiatives would not yield the desired results.

? Thought Box

How can the Sevottam model be effectively implemented to bridge the gap between policy intent and actual service delivery, ensuring accountability and citizen satisfaction in public services?

The Sevottam model works as an evaluation mechanism to assess the quality of internal processes and their impact on the quality of service delivery. The Sevottam model has three modules:

1. The first component of the model requires effective Charter implementation, thereby opening up a channel for receiving citizens' inputs, a way in which organisations determine service delivery requirements. The Citizens' Charters publicly declare the information on citizens' entitlements thereby making citizens better informed and hence empowering them to demand better services.
2. The second component of the model, "Public Grievance Redress" requires a good grievance redressal system operating in a manner that leaves citizens more satisfied with how the organisation responds to complaints/grievances, irrespective of the final decision.
3. The third component, "Excellence in Service Delivery", postulates that an organisation can have an excellent performance in service delivery only if it is efficiently managing well the key ingredients for good service delivery and building its own capacity to continuously improve service delivery.

15. THE ARC SEVEN STEP MODEL FOR CITIZEN CENTRICITY

This model draws from the principles of the IS 15700:2005, the Sevottam model, and the Customer Service Excellence Model of the UK. Each organisation should follow a step-by-step approach which would help it in becoming increasingly more citizen centric. This approach should be followed not only by the top management, but also by each unit of the organisation that has a public interface, i.e., top management has the dual responsibility of setting standards for itself as well as guiding the subordinate offices in setting their own standards.

(a) Define all services which you provide and identify your clients.
(b) Set standards and norms for each service.
(c) Develop capability to meet the set standards.
(d) Perform to achieve the standards.
(e) Monitor performance against the set standards.
(f) Evaluate the impact through an independent mechanism.
(g) Continuous improvement based on monitoring and evaluation results.

SUMMARY

- The Citizens' Charter is an initiative to solve the problems which a citizen encounters day to day.
- It is an understanding between citizens and the provider of a public service.
- Objectives behind the Citizens' Charter are quality; choice; standards; value; accountability; and transparency.
- It is meant to be a tool kit for initiatives and ideas to raise the level of the standard and service delivery and increase public participation.
- Initially, the banking sector was selected for implementing the Citizen's Charter.
- Key issues affecting the effectiveness of the Citizen's Charter include a lack of field-level awareness, inadequate capacity building, resistance to change, rigid laws, absence of effective ombudsman systems, limited consultation during formulation, bureaucratic rigidity, funding shortages, poor design, insufficient public awareness, and infrequent updates.
- Sevottam Model helps greatly in enhancing service delivery.
- Suggestions for strengthening the Citizens' Charter include internal restructuring; wide consultation; decentralised charter formulation; firm commitments; clear redressal mechanism; periodic evaluation; end-user feedback; and accountability of officers.

PREVIOUS YEARS' QUESTIONS

1. Explain the basic principles of the Citizens' Charter movement and bring out its importance.
   UPSC CSE Mains 2019
2. The Citizens' Charter is an ideal instrument of the organisational transparency and accountability, but it has its own limitations. Identify the limitations and suggest measures for greater effectiveness of the Citizens' Charter. *UPSC CSE Mains 2018*

Quality of Service Delivery: e-Governance

18

1. INTRODUCTION

LEARNING OBJECTIVES

1. Understanding e-governance and the types of interactions in e-governance affecting Indian administration and governance
2. E-governance and SMART governance
3. Limitations and best practices in e-governance
4. The role of civil servants in digital transformation

According to the World Bank, e-governance refers to the use, by government agencies, of information technologies (such as Wide Area Networks, the internet and mobile computing) that can transform relations with citizens, businesses and other arms of government. These technologies can serve a variety of different ends: better delivery of government services to citizens, improved interactions with business and industry, citizen empowerment through access to information, or more efficient government management.

The resulting benefits can be less corruption, increased transparency, greater convenience, revenue growth, and/or cost reductions. E-Governance is the public sector's use of information and communication technologies with the aim of improving information and service delivery, encouraging citizen participation in the decision-making process and making government more accountable, transparent and effective.

United Nations Educational, Scientific and Cultural Organisation (UNESCO) defines e-governance as, 'e-governance is the application of information and communication technology (ICT) for delivering government services, exchange of information, communication transactions, integration of various stand-alone systems and services between government-to-customer (G2C), government-to-business (G2B), government-to-government (G2G) as well as back office processes and interactions within the entire government framework.'

2. TYPES OF INTERACTIONS IN e-GOVERNANCE

The report on the e-governance of the Second Administrative Reforms Commission states that e-governance facilitates interaction among different stakeholders within government. The four main types of interactions in e-governance are as follows:

i. Government to Citizen (G2C)
ii. Government to Business (G2B)
iii. Government to Government (G2G) and
iv. Government to Employees (G2E)

These interactions may be described as follows:

(i) G2C (Government to Citizens): An interface is established between the government and the citizens, facilitating the efficient delivery of a wide range of public services. This interface not only enhances the accessibility and availability of these services but also improves their overall quality. The core objective is to make governance more citizen friendly.

It empowers citizens with the flexibility to:

1. Choose **when** to interact with the government (e.g., 24/7 access),
2. Decide **where** to access services (e.g., service centres, kiosks, or from home/workplace), and
3. Select **how** to engage with the government (e.g., via the internet, fax, telephone, email, or in person).

(ii) G2B (Government to Business): E-governance tools are employed to streamline interactions between the government and the business community, which provides goods and services. The aim is to reduce bureaucracy, save time, lower operational costs, and foster a transparent and efficient business environment.

G2B initiatives can be both transactional and facilitative:

1. **Transactional**: Licensing, permits, procurement, and revenue collection.
2. **Promotional and Facilitative**: Encouraging trade, tourism, and investment.

These measures create a conducive environment for businesses, enabling them to operate more effectively and efficiently.

(iii) G2G (Government to Government): This type of interaction leverages information and communications technology to not only reorganise the processes within government entities but also to enhance the flow of information and services both within and between these entities. Such interactions occur exclusively within the governmental sphere and can be either horizontal (between departments) or vertical (across different levels of government). The primary goal is to improve efficiency, performance, and overall output.

(iv) G2E (Government to Employees): Government is by far the biggest employer and like any organisation, it has to interact with its employees regularly. This interaction is a two-way process between the organisation and the employee. The use of ICT tools helps make these interactions fast and efficient on the one hand and increases the satisfaction levels of employees on the other.

3. e-GOVERNANCE — SMART GOVERNANCE

The world over governments have adopted the e-governance master plans intending to leverage the full potential of ICT to improve the efficiency as well as the capability of government processes and services, with a specific focus on e-services that will enable increased citizen participation and attempt to create an open, transparent environment, through the integration of different government information systems and services.

E-governance takes governance to another level. It has the potential to transform traditional governance into **SMART governance**. The acronym SMART stands for Simple, Moral, Accountable, Responsible, and Transparent governance.

(a) **S implies Simple:** Simplification of various rules, regulations, and government processes through the use of ICT by providing the user with a friendly experience.

(b) **M implies Moral:** Morality refers to the emergence of an entirely new system of ethical values in the political and administrative machinery. The infusion of the latest technology has improved the efficiency of anti-corruption agencies, police, judiciary, etc.

(c) **A implies Accountable:** Accountability of public service functionaries is ensured by facilitating proper design, development, and implementation of effective management information systems and performance measurement mechanisms.

(d) **R implies Responsible:** By streamlining the process to speed up service delivery, the system will become more responsive.

(e) **T implies Transparent:** Bringing information to the public domain which was hitherto confined to government departments. This will make the process and functioning more transparent.

4. BENEFITS OF e-GOVERNANCE

There are various benefits to implementing an e-government. The main advantage would be that e-governance would improve the efficiency of the current governing system. It would in turn save money and time. There are some other benefits as well. Let us have a look at them:

1. Improved access to information and high-quality services for citizens.
2. Ensures the availability of timely and reliable information on various aspects of governance.
3. Saves time, effort, and money for target groups by offering one-stop online access to public services, supported by automated back-end processes.
4. Simplifies complex procedures by eliminating redundant processes, streamlining structures, and introducing necessary changes to statutes and regulations, resulting in a more efficient, accountable, and straightforward government.
5. Brings government services directly to the citizens' doorsteps.
6. Enhances interaction between the government and citizens, strengthens democracy, and ensures public services are consumer oriented.
7. Promotes better access to information and government agencies, efficient service delivery, and greater transparency in government interactions.
8. Aids in improving internal efficiency, reorganising administrative processes, and enhancing the quality of services provided.
9. Reduces bureaucratic hurdles, delays, and inconveniences by leveraging modern technology and tools through e-governance interventions.
10. Facilitates knowledge sharing to drive continuous improvement in governance quality.
11. Redefines the internal structure of organisations, introducing enhanced control systems for improved management.
12. Encourages greater public participation in administrative processes.
13. Expands the government's reach, both geographically and demographically.
14. Empowers citizens by increasing their access to governance and decision-making processes.
15. Introduces innovation in the delivery of services.
16. Enhances the flexibility of service usage, offering more adaptable solutions for citizens.
17. Internally, within governmental organisations, it provides the following advantages:
    (a) Eliminates duplication of efforts,
    (b) Reduces transaction costs,

? Thought Box

How would you evaluate the Citizenship Amendment Act (CAA) of 2019 upholding the government's responsibility of ensuring and safeguarding the democracy of Indian citizens?

(c) Simplifies procedures,
(d) Improves communication and coordination, and
(e) Strengthens information security and management.

5. LIMITATIONS OF e-GOVERNANCE

E-governance in LMLI (Lower-Middle or Lower-Income) countries like India suffers from the following limitations:

1. Insufficient institutional and physical infrastructure, hindering the speedy and effective implementation of e-governance initiatives.
2. Lack of a standardised and universal framework for implementation.
3. States adopting diverse models in a **piecemeal**[1] manner, rather than a holistic approach, making integration across users and institutions challenging.
4. Inadequate training for officials in 'change management' strategies.
5. Employee resistance and reluctance to embrace change.
6. Predominantly 'process-centric' models instead of being 'citizen-centric.'
7. A significant rural population (64%) faces challenges in connectivity and communication despite efforts to improve accessibility to modern technology. Limited focused development, lack of effective implementation strategies, insufficient education, and training leave room for improvement. Many small public offices and village panchayats remain unequipped to utilise digital communication effectively.
8. The success of e-governance lies in increasing meaningful electronic interactions between citizens and the government, not merely in building infrastructure.
9. A conducive environment is essential for the successful implementation of e-governance initiatives, which is often lacking in developing countries.
10. Effective e-governance requires comprehensive business process re-engineering, involving a step-by-step examination and redesign of processes, with no shortcuts.
11. Investments in overcoming infrastructural challenges are fraught with risks.
12. The knowledge and resources required for e-governance have not fully trickled down to local levels. Smaller towns and village panchayats lack the financial and technical capacity to initiate and develop e-governance systems.
13. Low utilisation of e-portals for public services due to limited internet access for a significant portion of the population.
14. Scarce and untimely resources, coupled with vulnerabilities to cyberattacks, expose e-governance platforms to potential threats. Without robust security measures, personal data like addresses and bank information remain at risk.

[1]**Piecemeal:** (*adv.*) not done according to the plan but in different ways through a period of time.

6. BEST SCHEMES OF e-GOVERNANCE IN INDIA

6.1 National e-Governance Plan

Over the years, both State Governments and Central Ministries in India have launched numerous initiatives to advance e-governance, aiming to enhance the delivery and accessibility of public services. These efforts reflect a gradual evolution, transitioning from the mere computerisation of government departments to more sophisticated initiatives focused on citizen-centricity, service orientation, and transparency.

The lessons learned from earlier e-governance projects have significantly influenced the development of the country's progressive e-governance strategy.

Recognising the importance of accelerating e-governance implementation across national, state, and local government sectors, it was clear that a programmatic approach, driven by a unified vision and strategy, is essential. This approach holds the potential to generate substantial cost savings through the sharing of core and support infrastructure, facilitate **interoperability**[2] through standardised frameworks, and provide citizens with a seamless view of Government services.

The National e-Governance Plan (NeGP) offers a comprehensive framework for e-governance initiatives nationwide, aligning them towards a common vision and shared goals. This plan is progressively building a vast infrastructure that reaches even the most remote villages, accompanied by large-scale digitisation of records, making them easily and reliably accessible online. The ultimate goal is to bring public services closer to citizens, as highlighted in NeGP's Vision Statement:

'Make all Government services accessible to the common man in his locality through common service delivery outlets, ensuring efficiency, transparency, and reliability of these services at affordable costs to meet the basic needs of the common man.'

6.2 Digital India Mission

Digital India Mission was Launched in 2015. This initiative aims to digitally empower the nation by creating secure and stable digital infrastructure, providing government services digitally, and achieving universal **digital literacy**[3].

Here are some of the key e-governance initiatives among various sectors:

---

[2]**Interoperability:** The ability of different systems, devices, or organisations to work together and exchange information effectively.

[3]**Digital Literacy:** The ability to use digital tools and technologies effectively to access, evaluate, and communicate information.

- **Sector: Governance and Public Administration**

E-Governance initiatives related to Governance and Public Administration aim to leverage digital technologies to promote efficient and timely delivery of public services. These initiatives enable better data collection, monitoring, and policy enforcement while ensuring transparency and accountability. Below are some examples of e-governance initiatives in the fields of Governance and Public Administration:

1. Unified Mobile Application for New-age Governance (UMANG)

Main Objective: To provide a one-stop gateway to all government schemes and services.

An initiative by the National e-Governance Division (NeGD), Ministry of Electronics and Information Technology (MeitY), UMANG strives to be the one-stop gateway to all government schemes and services through different channels like Mobile Application (iOS, Android), Chatbot, Voice Bot and Website. It provides access to more than 1,570 government services and over 22,000 bill payment services.

2. DigiLocker

Main Objective: To provide access to authentic digital documents to citizen's digital document wallets.

This platform supports the paperless availability of public documents. DigiLocker is a flagship initiative of the Ministry of Electronics & IT (MeitY) under the Digital India programme. DigiLocker aims at 'Digital Empowerment' of citizens by providing access to authentic digital documents to citizen's digital document wallets. DigiLocker is a secure cloud-based platform for the storage, sharing, and verification of documents & certificates. DigiLocker has over 11.7 crore users, with more than 532 crore documents made available from 2,167 issuing organisations.

3. MyGov

Main Objective: To facilitate an efficient citizen engagement platform.

MyGov platform builds partnerships between citizens and the government. It is the citizen engagement platform of the Government of India. It is an Independent Business Division under Digital India Corporation, a Section 8 company under the Ministry of Electronics & Information Technology. A citizen engagement platform designed to enable participatory governance. More than 2.48 crore users actively engage with MyGov.

4. MeriPehchaan

Main Objective: To provide a single sign-on platform to citizens.

Launched in July 2022, this National Single Sign-on platform provides citizens with easy access to government portals. MeriPehchaan, a Single Sign-On platform authenticates citizens easily and securely. It is an extensive collaboration of the three mainstream SSO platforms Jan

Parichay, e-Pramaan, and DigiLocker. MeriPehchaan authenticates the user based on multiple authentication parameters like username, mobile number, Aadhaar, PAN, etc.

5. MyScheme

Main Objective: To offer one-stop search and discovery of government schemes.

Launched in July 2022, MyScheme is a National Platform that aims to offer one-stop search and discovery of government schemes. It provides an innovative, technology-based solution to discover scheme information based on the eligibility of the citizen.

The platform helps the citizen to find the right government schemes for them. It also guides on how to apply for different government schemes. Thus, no need to visit multiple government websites.

6. E-SANCHAR

Main Objective: To provide required crucial information to citizens.

E-SANCHAR is a system that disseminates important information to citizens through automated voice calls, targeting deprived citizens and ensuring they are informed about government initiatives for **SMART governance**.

- **Legislature**

E-Governance initiatives in the legislative sector focus on improving transparency, accountability, and efficiency in the functioning of legislative bodies. These initiatives help digitise legislative processes, enhancing communication between lawmakers and citizens, and improving public access to legislative information. Below are some prominent examples of e-governance initiatives designed to improve the functioning of legislatures in India:

1. e-Vidhan (Digital Legislative Process)

Main Objective: To transform the legislative process into a paperless efficient system.

The e-Vidhan project is a significant initiative aimed at transforming the legislative process into a paperless, efficient system. It involves the digitalisation of the functioning of legislative assemblies, including the preparation and presentation of bills, debates, discussions, and voting.

2. Lok Sabha and Rajya Sabha Websites

Main Objective: To ensure transparency in the legislative process.

The websites of the Lok Sabha (Lower House) and Rajya Sabha (Upper House) provide a platform for citizens to access detailed information about parliamentary sessions, debates, bills, and members of parliament. These websites are key to ensuring transparency in the legislative process.

4. e-Bill System

Main Objective: To facilitate electronic presentation and tracking of bills.

The e-bill system is a digital platform that facilitates the electronic presentation and tracking of bills in the Indian Parliament and state legislatures. This system allows MPs and MLAs to access and review bills, suggest amendments, and track their progress. It efficiently streamlines the processing of bills.

5. Integrated Parliamentary Data Management System (IPDMS)

Main Objective: To streamline the process of managing parliamentary data.

The Integrated Parliamentary Data Management System is an initiative that helps streamline the management of parliamentary data. It integrates data from various sources, including bills, questions, motions, and other legislative activities, into one centralised digital platform.

6. Parliamentary Research and Reference Services

Main Objective: To provide timely information to lawmakers.

The Parliamentary Research and Reference Services provide lawmakers with timely information and analysis related to bills, policies, and legislative issues. These services are available digitally and help legislators make informed decisions.

7. Online Question Management System

Main Objective: To enable legislators to submit and track questions.

The Online Question Management System (QMS) enables MPs and MLAs to submit and track questions to be raised in legislative sessions. It automates the process of submitting questions, providing answers, and tracking the status of questions raised in the legislature.

- **Judiciary**

E-Governance initiatives in the judiciary aim to modernise court systems, enhance access to justice, improve transparency, and increase the efficiency of judicial processes. These digital initiatives help streamline case management, reduce delays, and improve citizen engagement with the judiciary. Here are some prominent examples of e-governance initiatives that have improved the functioning of the judiciary in India:

1. e-Courts Project

Main Objective: To digitalise court proceedings.

The e-Courts Project is one of the largest e-governance initiatives in the Indian judicial system, aimed at digitising court proceedings and providing e-services to both the public and the judiciary. The initiative connects district courts across India, enabling seamless case management and faster delivery of justice. It also aims for the digitalisation of court records, case files, and judgements. It facilitates the online filing of cases and automated scheduling and tracking of hearings.

2. National Judicial Data Grid (NJDG)

Main Objective: To provide a centralised database of all case details.

The National Judicial Data Grid is a real-time platform that provides a centralised database of case details across all district and subordinate courts in India. It offers a comprehensive view of pending cases, their status, and timelines, helping in better case management and tracking. In this way, it facilitates the identification of trends and bottlenecks in the judicial system thereby helping in better allocation of judicial resources to clear case backlogs.

3. Justice e-Access Portal

Main Objective: To make legal information easily available.

The Justice e-Access Portal is a public-facing platform that allows citizens to access details about ongoing cases, court judgements, orders, and more. It ensures transparency by making legal information readily available online.

4. e-Filing System

Main Objective: To enable the online filing of cases, petitions, and documents.

The e-Filing System allows litigants, lawyers, and other stakeholders to file cases, petitions, and documents electronically through a secure online platform. This system is integrated with the overall e-court infrastructure. It helps in the reduction of physical visits to court premises, making the process more efficient.

5. Legal Aid Mobile Apps (e.g., Nyaya Bandhu)

Main objective: To provide free legal aid.

Nyaya Bandhu is a mobile app launched by the Ministry of Law and Justice to provide free legal aid to those who cannot afford it. The app allows users to connect with legal professionals for guidance and assistance in legal matters.

6. Case Information System (CIS)

Main Objective: To efficiently track and manage cases.

The Case Information System (CIS) is a digital tool implemented in courts across India for case tracking and management. It provides information on the status of cases, upcoming hearings, judgements, and other case-related details. It also provides e-mail and SMS notifications for hearing updates.

7. SUPACE

Main Objective: To assist judges with legal research.

The Supreme Court has launched 'SUPACE,' an AI-based portal to assist judges with legal research, enhancing the efficiency of the judicial system.

8. FASTER Digital Platform

Main Objective: To facilitate communication of various court orders.

This platform facilitates the secure electronic communication of interim orders, stay orders, and bail orders from the Supreme Court to the relevant authorities.

- **Finance**

E-Governance initiatives for the utilisation of public funds in India aim to enhance transparency, accountability, and efficiency in the management and distribution of government resources. These initiatives leverage digital platforms to track, monitor, and streamline public expenditure, ensuring that funds are used effectively for various development programmes and services. Below are some notable examples of e-governance initiatives for the utilisation of public funds in India:

1. PFMS (Public Financial Management System)

Main Objective: To enable real-time tracking of funds across various government schemes.

PFMS is an integrated platform developed by the Ministry of Finance to monitor and track the utilisation of public funds across various government schemes and programmes. It enables real-time tracking of funds from the central government to the implementing agencies and end **beneficiaries**.

2. M-Governance for Fund Disbursement

Main Objective: To make use of mobile applications for efficient and timely disbursement of funds.

Various state and central government initiatives leverage mobile governance (m-Governance) to facilitate the disbursement of public funds. For example, mobile applications provide farmers with timely subsidies, disaster relief funds, or other financial assistance directly to their mobile wallets.

3. Audit and Accounting Automation[4] (e-Accountability)

Main Objective: To facilitate automatic auditing of financial transactions.

The e-Accountability initiative ensures that the financial transactions of government departments are automatically audited and tracked using digital platforms. This initiative helps in the efficient utilisation of funds by automating audits and enabling transparent fund allocation.

4. GSTN (Goods and Services Tax Network)

Main Objective: To track revenue generation and integrate with other financial systems.

---

[4]**Automation:** The process by which machines and computers are used to carry menial or highly specialised tasks without human interference or reliance.

The Goods and Services Tax (GST) system in India integrates tax collections and expenditure tracking to ensure efficient public fund utilisation. The GSTN platform enables the government to track tax revenue generation, and its seamless integration with other financial systems ensures accountability.

5. SWIFT (Society for Worldwide Interbank Financial Telecommunications)

Main Objective: To monitor investments and financial flows.

SWIFT is a system introduced to monitor investments and financial flows related to state and central government schemes. It helps track the investment of public funds in long-term infrastructure projects, ensuring transparency and reducing financial mismanagement.

6. Government e-Marketplace (GeM)

Main Objective: To facilitate effective procurement of goods and services by various government departments.

GeM is an online platform to facilitate transparent and efficient procurement of goods and services for government departments, thereby ensuring the proper utilisation of public funds in purchasing goods and services.

7. IFMIS (Integrated Financial Management Information System)

Main Objective: To ensure accountability at every stage of public fund utilisation.

IFMIS is a system that integrates the financial management of government departments, including budgeting, accounting, and expenditure control. It helps ensure that public funds are used for their intended purposes and that there is accountability at every stage of fund utilisation. Improves financial reporting and helps prevent financial mismanagement by centralising financial management across ministries and state departments.

8. Bharat Interface for Money (BHIM) and Unified Payments Interface (UPI) for Subsidies

Main Objective: To enable direct benefit transfer of subsidies and welfare benefits.

BHIM and UPI facilitate the direct transfer of subsidies and welfare benefits to the beneficiaries. This initiative ensures that public funds are used effectively, and subsidies are transferred directly to the bank accounts of eligible individuals, removing intermediaries. They improve efficiency as they facilitate instant payments through mobile-based apps.

These e-governance initiatives help streamline the allocation, utilisation, and monitoring of public funds, thereby reducing corruption, increasing transparency, and ensuring that funds reach the intended beneficiaries in an efficient and timely manner.

- **Agriculture**

E-Governance initiatives in the agriculture sector leverage digital tools, technology, and platforms to improve governance, efficiency, transparency, and service delivery to farmers, agricultural businesses, and stakeholders. These initiatives aim to enhance productivity, address farmer challenges, and promote sustainable agricultural practices. Here are some notable examples of e-governance initiatives in agriculture:

1. eNAM (National Agricultural Market)

Main Objective: To Integrate mandis and provide real-time information.

eNAM is a pan-India electronic trading platform developed by the Government of India to enable farmers, traders, and buyers to trade in agricultural commodities online. The platform integrates mandis (markets) across India and provides farmers with real-time information on market prices, enabling them to make informed decisions.

2. Kisan Call Centers (KCC)

Main Objective: To provide expert advice and guidance to farmers.

The Kisan Call Centers are a part of the e-governance framework, where farmers can call a toll-free number to seek guidance on agricultural practices, government schemes, weather, pest management, and more. It provides 24/7 access to expert advice on agriculture and multilingual support to cater to diverse regions.

3. Soil Health Management Systems (e.g., Soil Health Cards)

Main Objective: To digitally record soil health data and provide recommendations.

The Soil Health Card Scheme facilitates the online issuance of soil health cards and provides farmers with personalised soil health reports based on soil samples, which helps in the appropriate use of fertilisers. The scheme is supported by a digital platform that records soil health data and provides recommendations for soil health improvement and balanced fertiliser use.

4. Agri-Tech Platforms (e.g., Digital Green)

Main Objective: To provide video-based training to farmers.

Digital Green is an e-governance initiative that uses technology to improve agricultural practices by providing farmers with video-based training. This initiative is designed to offer content in local languages and based on local practices.

5. Farming Input Delivery Platforms (e.g. eKrishi Yantra)

Main Objective: To digitally connect farmers with the required inputs.

These platforms connect farmers with inputs like fertilisers, seeds, and agricultural machinery through e-commerce and digital applications. For example, eKrishi Yantra helps farmers access modern machinery for farm operations through an online platform. These platforms provide access to agricultural machinery on rent and provide real-time updates on available services and equipment. They also facilitate online purchase of farming inputs.

6. mKisan Portal

Main Objective: To provide SMS-based updates to farmers.

The M-Kisan portal is a government initiative that provides farmers with SMS-based updates on agricultural news, weather forecasts, pest attacks, market prices, and agricultural tips. It also provides information on crop management, market trends, government schemes, and policies for farmers.

7. National Mission on Agricultural Extension and Technology (NMAET)

Main Objective: To digitally deliver agricultural extension service.

NMAET promotes the use of digital platforms for the dissemination of agricultural extension services. It leverages e-governance to deliver technology, training, and knowledge resources to farmers.

8. PM-KISAN (Pradhan Mantri Kisan Samman Nidhi)

Main Objective: To use digital platforms for facilitating registrations and Direct Benefit Transfers.

PM-KISAN is a government scheme that provides direct income support to farmers. Through e-governance, farmers are registered on a digital platform, and funds are transferred directly to their bank accounts.

These e-governance initiatives help improve the efficiency of agricultural practices, enhance farmers' access to essential services, and promote transparency in the sector.

- **Health**

E-Governance initiatives in the health sector aim to improve the accessibility, efficiency, and quality of healthcare services. By leveraging digital technologies, these initiatives streamline health services, enhance transparency, and improve patient outcomes. Below are some examples of e-governance initiatives that have significantly improved health systems:

1. National Health Mission (NHM) and Health Management Information System (HMIS)

Main Objective: To enable real-time data collection, monitoring, and management of health services.

The National Health Mission (NHM) is a government initiative to provide accessible, affordable, and quality healthcare services, particularly in rural areas. The Health Management Information System (HMIS) is part of this mission, enabling real-time data collection, monitoring, and management of health services. It facilitates digital tracking of healthcare services, including immunisation, maternal health, and disease control programmes. It integrates health data from primary health centres, district hospitals, and health programmes. It provides a dashboard for monitoring key health indicators and programme performance.

2. Ayushman Bharat (PM-JAY) – Pradhan Mantri Jan Arogya Yojana

Main Objective: To facilitate online registration and identification of eligible **beneficiaries**.

Ayushman Bharat is a flagship health insurance scheme that provides financial protection to low-income families for secondary and tertiary healthcare. The Pradhan Mantri Jan Arogya Yojana (PM-JAY) is a major component of this scheme that uses e-governance tools facilitating online registration and identification of eligible beneficiaries to deliver healthcare services to citizens.

3. eSanjeevani (Telemedicine Services)

Main Objective: To provide remote consultations to patients.

eSanjeevani is the Indian government's telemedicine service aimed at providing remote consultations to patients. It is an initiative to bridge the gap in healthcare access, especially in rural and underserved areas, using digital technologies. It facilitates online consultations with doctors using video conferencing and provides real-time health advice, prescriptions, and follow-up consultations.

4. Digitisation of Health Records (eHealth Record System)

Main Objective: To digitally record and store medical records of patients.

The eHealth Record (EHR) system is designed to digitise and store medical records for patients, making it easier to access and update health information across healthcare providers and institutions.

5. National Digital Health Mission (NDHM)

Main Objective: To digitally integrate the health ecosystem.

The National Digital Health Mission (NDHM) aims to build an integrated digital health ecosystem that enables the exchange of health data between hospitals, health providers, and patients. It facilitates the creation of a digital health ID for every citizen.

6. Integrated Disease Surveillance Programme (IDSP)

Main Objective: To enable real-time monitoring of disease outbreaks.

The Integrated Disease Surveillance Programme (IDSP) uses digital platforms to collect, analyse, and disseminate information about infectious diseases across India. The system enables real-time monitoring of disease outbreaks and health emergencies. These e-governance initiatives have significantly contributed to strengthening health systems across India, improving accessibility, quality of care, and overall efficiency in the delivery of healthcare services.

? Thought Box

How would you critically evaluate the performance of IDSP in responding to the nationwide threat of COVID-19?

- **Urban Development**

E-Governance initiatives in urban development aim to enhance the quality of life in cities by improving the delivery of public services, ensuring transparency, and promoting citizen engagement. By leveraging technology, these initiatives streamline urban management processes, improve infrastructure, and make urban governance more efficient and accessible. Here are some prominent examples of e-governance initiatives in urban development:

1. Smart Cities Mission

Main Objective: To make use of technology for sustainable urban development.

The Smart Cities Mission is one of the largest initiatives by the Government of India to promote sustainable urban development using technology. The mission aims to make cities more liveable, sustainable, and resilient by integrating smart technology into urban infrastructure and services. It provides for the development of smart infrastructure like smart roads, smart lighting, and intelligent traffic management systems. It facilitates the use of sensors and data analytics for efficient resource management (e.g., water, electricity).

2. Swachh Bharat Mission (SBM) – Urban Component

Main Objective: To achieve clean and open defecation-free cities.

The Swachh Bharat Mission aims to achieve a clean and open-defecation-free India by improving urban sanitation. The urban component leverages e-governance tools to monitor sanitation activities, waste management, and cleanliness in cities. It facilitates citizen participation through mobile apps for reporting issues like garbage dumping and unclean public spaces.

3. e-Municipality (e-Governance in Municipal Services)

Main Objective: To effectively digitalise municipal services.

e-Municipality is an initiative that involves the digitisation of municipal services such as property tax payment, water supply management, building plan approvals, and more. It aims to bring transparency and ease to municipal governance.

4. Unified Metropolitan Transport Authority (UMTA)

Main Objective: To establish efficient urban transport systems in metropolitan cities.

The Unified Metropolitan Transport Authority (UMTA) is a framework established to plan and implement efficient urban transport systems in metropolitan cities. UMTA uses e-governance solutions for integrated transportation management. It integrates digital ticketing for buses, metro, and other public transport services. It provides for real-time tracking of buses, trains, and other modes of transport using GPS and mobile apps.

5. City-wide GIS Mapping for Urban Planning

Main Objective: To create digital maps for urban planning and development.

Geographic Information System (GIS) mapping is used to create digital maps for urban planning and development. By integrating GIS technology, cities can manage land use, monitor infrastructure, and plan for future growth more efficiently.

6. Online Building Approval System

Main Objective: To obtain building approvals digitally.

Many urban local bodies have digitised the process of obtaining building approvals and permits. The Online Building Approval System allows developers and property owners to apply for permissions, track their applications, and obtain approvals digitally.

7. Integrated Control and Command Centres (ICCC)

Main Objective: To use data analytics for monitoring various aspects of urban life.

Integrated Control and Command Centres are set up in cities to manage urban infrastructure and services using data analytics and real-time monitoring. These centres use e-governance tools to monitor various aspects of urban life, from traffic management to disaster response.

- **Rural Development**

E-Governance initiatives in rural development focus on improving the quality of life in rural areas by enhancing access to services, promoting transparency, ensuring better resource management, and fostering community participation. Digital technologies are used to bridge the gap between rural citizens and government services, making them more accessible and efficient. Below are some key examples of e-governance initiatives in rural development:

1. Mahatma Gandhi National Rural Employment Guarantee Act (MGNREGA) – e-MGNREGA

Main Objective: To use technology to streamline work allocation and wage payments.

e-MGNREGA is the digital platform for the Mahatma Gandhi National Rural Employment Guarantee Act (MGNREGA), which guarantees 100 days of wage employment per year to rural households. The initiative uses technology to streamline the management of the programme, ensuring transparency and accountability in wage payments and work allocation.

2. Digital India Land Records Modernisation Programme (DILRMP)

Main Objective: To ensure transparency and efficiency in land administration.

The Digital India Land Records Modernisation Programme (DILRMP) aims to digitise land records to ensure transparency and efficiency in land administration. This initiative helps rural farmers and landowners access land-related information easily. It also provides e-filing of land disputes and automated land record updates.

4. e-District Project

Main Objective: To reduce the need for citizens to physically visit government offices.

The e-District Project is an initiative to provide government services to rural citizens through digital platforms, aiming to reduce the need for physical visits to government offices. It provides online applications for various government services like income certificates, caste certificates, and ration cards. It also provides for e-authentication and e-signature for document processing.

5. National e-Governance Plan (NeGP) – Rural Development

Main Objective: To enhance rural governance and service delivery.

The National e-Governance Plan (NeGP) aims to provide affordable and accessible online government services in rural areas. Under NeGP, several initiatives have been implemented to enhance rural governance and service delivery. Common Services Centres (CSCs) are digital kiosks in rural areas offering services such as government forms, utility bill payments, and online education.

6. e-Panchayat

Main Objective: To enhance the functionality of grass-level governance bodies in rural India.

E-Panchayat is a digital initiative aimed at enhancing the functionality of Panchayati Raj Institutions (PRIs), which are the grassroots-level governance bodies in rural India. The initiative seeks to improve the delivery of services and transparency in local governance. It facilitates online management of Panchayat records, including financial management, planning, and implementation of rural development schemes. It also provides online monitoring of the progress of rural development projects.

7. Rural Road Development – e-Road Monitoring

Main Objective: To effectively monitor rural road development projects.

e-Road Monitoring Systems are used for monitoring the progress of rural road development projects, especially under schemes like the Pradhan Mantri Gram Sadak Yojana (PMGSY).

- **Employment and Skill Development**

E-Governance initiatives in employment and skill development aim to improve the efficiency and accessibility of job opportunities, training programmes, and skill development services. By leveraging digital platforms and technologies, these initiatives connect job seekers with employment opportunities, provide online training, and ensure better management of employment schemes. Below are some prominent examples of e-governance initiatives in employment and skill development:

1. National Career Service (NCS) Portal

Main Objective: To bridge the gap between job seekers and employers.

The National Career Service (NCS) is an initiative by the Ministry of Labour and Employment aimed at bridging the gap between job seekers and employers across India. It provides for online registration for job seekers and employers. It effectively does job matching based on skills, qualifications, and location.

2. Skill India and Pradhan Mantri Kaushal Vikas Yojana (PMKVY)

Main Objective: To efficiently provide skill training to the youth in India.

The Skill India initiative, including the Pradhan Mantri Kaushal Vikas Yojana (PMKVY), aims to provide skill training to the youth in India. The initiative uses e-governance tools to register, monitor, and certify candidates undergoing skill training programmes.

3. e-Shram Portal

Main Objective: To create a national database of unorganised workers.

The e-Shram Portal is an initiative by the Ministry of Labour and Employment to create a national database of unorganised workers, including daily wage workers, construction workers, and migrant workers. The portal also provides access to various social security schemes and employment-related benefits.

4. Atmanirbhar Skilled Employee Employer Mapping (ASEEM) Portal

Main Objective: To provide analytics for tracking the labour market and skills in demand.

The ASEEM Portal is designed to bridge the demand and supply of skilled labour by mapping employers with skilled workers. It is a part of the Skill India Mission and enables the tracking of skilled workforce availability. It is an online platform for employers to register their skill requirements. Skilled workers can create profiles and connect with potential employers. It then provides real-time matching of job seekers with available job opportunities. It provides analytics to track labour market trends and demands for specific skills.

5. Swayam and Swayam Prabha

Main Objective: To provide free online courses from top institutions.

Swayam is an online education platform launched by the Government of India to provide free online courses in various subjects, including skill development. Swayam Prabha offers TV-based educational content to rural areas. Free online courses are offered by top universities and institutions and also provide certification for successful course completion.

6. Diksha

Main Objective: To create a common space for achieving large-scale learning goals.

Diksha is a national-level educational platform designed to help students and teachers collaborate and contribute, leveraging a common space to achieve large-scale learning goals across the country.

7. Skill Development Information Management System (SDMS)

Main Objective: To enable digital tracking of training programmes and outcomes.

The Skill Development Information Management System (SDMS) is a digital platform that facilitates the monitoring, evaluation, and management of skill development initiatives and training programmes in India. It provides for digital tracking of training programmes and outcomes. It facilitates data analytics to evaluate the effectiveness of skill development initiatives. It also provides real-time updates on enrolment, certification, and placement of trainees.

These e-governance initiatives in employment and skill development are transforming the landscape of workforce training and job opportunities, especially for India's growing population.

- **Environment and Energy**

E-Governance initiatives related to environment and energy aim to leverage digital technologies to promote sustainability, streamline regulatory processes, and enhance environmental protection and energy management. These initiatives enable better data collection, monitoring, and policy enforcement while ensuring transparency and efficient resource management. Below are some examples of e-governance initiatives in the fields of environment and energy:

1. National Clean Energy Fund (NCEF)

Main Objective: To facilitate online tracking and monitoring of **fund allocations** for clean energy projects.

The National Clean Energy Fund (NCEF) is a government initiative to promote clean energy technologies. The funds are collected through a cess on coal and are used to finance projects related to clean energy, energy efficiency, and renewable energy development. There is online tracking and monitoring of fund allocations for clean energy projects. There are also digital approval processes for proposals and disbursement of funds. Digital tools are used to evaluate the environmental impact of funded projects.

2. Green Rating for Integrated Habitat Assessment (GRIHA)

Main Objective: To evaluate the environmental performance of buildings.

GRIHA is a national rating system for green buildings, developed by the Ministry of New and Renewable Energy (MNRE) and implemented through digital platforms. It evaluates the environmental performance of buildings and encourages sustainable building practices. It facilitates online registration and assessment of green building projects. It also provides for integration with an environmental impact assessment tool and provides real-time data collection on energy consumption, water usage, and waste management.

3. Energy Conservation Building Code (ECBC)

Main Objective: To facilitate architects and builders to assess and improve the energy efficiency of their designs.

The Energy Conservation Building Code (ECBC) is a framework that sets the minimum energy performance standards for commercial buildings. It encourages the adoption of energy-efficient technologies and practices in the building sector. It provides for online registration and certification of buildings complying with ECBC standards and facilitates the use of digital tools for architects and builders to assess and improve the energy efficiency of their designs.

4. National Action Plan on Climate Change (NAPCC) – e-Governance for Monitoring and Reporting

Main Objective: To facilitate tracking the progress of climate action programmes.

The National Action Plan on Climate Change (NAPCC) includes eight national missions focused on various aspects of climate change. The government has established e-governance platforms to monitor the implementation of these missions and assess their impact on environmental sustainability. Climate Action Dashboard is a digital platform for tracking the progress of climate action programmes. There is online data reporting and monitoring of emissions reductions.

5. Central Pollution Control Board (CPCB) – Online Monitoring of Air and Water Quality

Main Objective: To provide real-time data collection and reporting on pollution levels.

The Central Pollution Control Board (CPCB) monitors air, water, and noise pollution across India. It uses e-governance tools to collect and analyse environmental data, and to issue environmental clearances and permits for industries. Online Air Quality Monitoring System is used for real-time data collection and reporting on air pollution levels in various cities. Water Quality Monitoring system uses digital platforms for monitoring river and groundwater quality.

6. State-Wise Solar Rooftop Portal

Main Objective: To provide digital mapping of potential solar rooftops.

Various states in India have launched solar rooftop portals to promote and track the installation of solar power systems in residential, commercial, and institutional buildings. These portals provide a platform for users to apply for incentives, subsidies, and approvals for solar installations. It also provides for digital mapping of potential solar rooftops based on location and weather data.

? Thought Box

How can emerging civil servants integrate Solarpunk ideas to innovate and explore new approaches for utilising solar energy in advancing sustainable governance in India?

7. Perform, Achieve, and Trade (PAT) Scheme

Main Objective: To facilitate efficient digital tracking of energy consumption reductions by industries.

The PAT Scheme is part of India's National Mission on Enhanced Energy Efficiency. It targets energy-intensive industries and incentivises them to reduce energy consumption through a market-based mechanism. It facilitates efficient digital tracking of energy consumption reductions by industries. Energy Efficiency Certificates (EECs) are issued for energy savings and can be traded on a digital platform.

8. Green India Mission – e-Governance for Forest and Biodiversity Conservation

Main Objective: To monitor forest cover, track biodiversity, and improve forest management.

The Green India Mission is one of the eight national missions under the National Action Plan on Climate Change (NAPCC). e-governance initiatives have been used to monitor forest cover, track biodiversity, and improve forest management.

Best practice e-governance schemes of various states:

- **iMine**—an IT Intervention for Managing Integrated Networked Enterprise designed to enhance operational efficiency by optimum utilisation of its resources.
- **MAGIC**—Mineral Administration and Governance through ICT to achieve 'Zero Visit Office' of Gujarat minerals department.
- **SPARSH**—A special project for assistance, rehabilitation, and strengthening of the handicapped and a healing touch for disabled, old age,destitute, and a projcct conceived and developed by the Madhya Pradesh government.
- **E-Sevai**—Tamil Nadu e-Governance Agency (TNeGA) has developed an e-Sevai application for the online delivery of various **citizen-centric** services of government departments to the public through Common Service Centres (CSCs).
- **Lokvani**—an initiative taken by the Uttar Pradesh government to bridge the **digital divide**[5] and 'connect' the common man to the strategy makers in a seamless fashion.
- **PROOF**—a coalition of community service organisations for the quarterly public disclosure of Bangalore City Corporation's financial records aimed to enhance accountability to the citizens through transparency.
- **Nemmadi Rural Telecentre Project** in Karnataka—a part of the PPP model was formed to emphasise the goals of responsive governance by developing an effective, efficient, transparent, and accountable system of public service delivery in the entire state of Karnataka.
- **Pancha Tantra Online System**—improves the functioning of gram panchayats in the state of Karnataka.

[5]**Digital Divide:** The gap between individuals or regions with access to modern ICT and those without.

- **Model e-villages**—for bridging the **digital divide** in Northeast India
- **e-SLA**—Monitoring System by the Government of NCT of Delhi has developed an online monitoring system for recording and tracking the delivery of services guaranteed under its Public Service Guarantee Act.
- The Greater Hyderabad Municipal Corporation has launched an offsite real-time monitoring system that leverages information and communication technologies to streamline and monitor the progress of waste management.
- **FAMS**—in Madhya Pradesh has leveraged satellite technology and a computer-based communication network to protect the state's natural reserves, wildlife, and livelihoods of its tribal population.
- **Maha-e-Biz**—provides a single window clearance portal by Maharashtra.

MeitY has developed the draft National Data Governance Framework Policy, which aims to unlock the full potential of India's digital government vision. The policy focuses on enhancing the efficiency of data-driven governance and public service delivery while promoting data-based research and innovation.

The adoption of e-governance brings significant benefits for both governments and citizens, such as improved efficiency, transparency, and accessibility. However, it also introduces considerable challenges related to security and privacy that must be addressed to protect sensitive data, maintain public trust, and ensure the success of digital transformation initiatives.

The government is taking necessary steps to address challenges related to **data privacy**[6] and security by enforcing provisions under the Information Technology (IT) Act, 2000, which includes measures for both data privacy and data security. By implementing robust cybersecurity protocols, enforcing strict data protection regulations, and conducting ongoing risk assessments, governments can mitigate the risks associated with e-governance and fully leverage the advantages of digital governance.

7. KEY BUREAUCRATS INSTRUMENTAL IN DRIVING VARIOUS e-GOVERNANCE INITIATIVES

1. Kumaragurubaran Jayabalan, IAS

Mr. Kumaragurubaran, an IAS officer from Tamil Nadu, has significantly contributed to advancing e-governance and improving public service delivery through digital platforms.

- **E-Sevai Centre Initiative:** He played a pivotal role in enhancing accessibility, efficiency, transparency, and accountability in government services.

[6]**Data Privacy:** Protecting personal data from unauthorised access or misuse, ensuring that individuals' information remains confidential.

- **Registration Reforms:** As Inspector General of Registration, he leveraged IT to streamline property deed registration.
- **Temple Land Protection:** In the Hindu Religious and **Charitable Endowments** Department, he utilised modern technology to survey and reclaim large parcels of temple land from encroachments.
- **School Education Initiatives:** During his tenure in the School Education Department, he promoted universal access, equity, and quality education. He introduced measures for holistic child development and established smart classrooms with broadband connectivity and high-tech labs in rural schools across Tamil Nadu.

2. T Bhoobalan, IAS

Tumakuru became the first district in Karnataka to offer doorstep tax collection, thanks to IAS officer T. Bhoobalan, known as the Taxman of Tumakuru. He revamped the tax collection system, starting with computerising the department and introducing a digital database to eliminate accounting loopholes. He also launched the SPARC (Smart Public Axial Revenue Collection) Android app integrated with EDC machines. Within a year, the initiative boosted the tax payment rate from 25% to 85%, with projections exceeding 90% soon.

3. Jitendra Kumar Soni, IAS

Jitendra Kumar Soni, an IAS officer of the Rajasthan cadre, is renowned for leveraging technology to enhance governance. His initiatives include integrating technology into daily administrative functions, such as the Poll Day SMS Monitoring System, the Biometric Attendance System in government schools, and Sampark, a WhatsApp-based grievance collection and redressal platform. Soni is also recognised for his contributions to disaster management and was honoured with the State e-Governance Award in 2014–15.

4. Ritu Maheshwari, IAS

At Kanpur Electricity Supply Company Ltd (KESCo), Ritu Maheshwari implemented digital solutions to reduce losses and combat electricity theft. After assuming office in 2011, she oversaw the installation of advanced meters for one-third of the company's customer base. These meters digitally track electricity consumption and detect distribution system leaks in real time. Under her leadership, the company's losses decreased significantly from 30% to 15%.

5. A.K. Viswanathan, IPS

A.K. Viswanathan was the Greater Chennai City Police Commissioner who was instrumental in bringing the city under complete CCTV surveillance through the 'Third Eye Programme.'

This programme was part of the police's crime prevention and detection efforts. The programme involved the installation of over 2.5 lakh cameras with the participation of both the public and private sectors.

6. Dr Abdul Qayum, IFS

Abdul Qayum devised a mobile app named E-Forest Fire for predicting forest fires. The app has helped in reducing forest fires in Arunachal Pradesh by 31% in comparison to five-year data collected from 2015–2020.

7. Ashish Tiwari, IPS

Mr Ashish Tiwari is an IIT-Kanpur alumnus and an ex-investment banker. He is an IPS officer from Uttar Pradesh cadre. He developed an app to digitally handle cop deployment, leave management, community policing, and other tasks. This brought greater efficiency in the functioning of the department.

8. B Raghu Kiran, IRS

Techie-turned-IRS officer B Raghu Kiran decided to put his software skills to good use by developing an app (called GST Verify) to verify whether or not a seller/service provider is authorised to collect the tax.

9. Dr. Rajendra Bharud, IAS

Dr Rajendra Bharud, being the District Collector of Nandurbar, Maharashtra made a significant technology contribution. He successfully implemented GIS-based planning for COVID-19 management, ensuring effective healthcare delivery in tribal areas. He also made use of mobile apps and data analytics for real-time monitoring of vaccination drives.

10. Smita Sabharwal, IAS

Smita Sabharwal, widely known as 'The People's Officer' in Telangana, has earned recognition for leveraging digital tools to enhance service delivery. She implemented effective citizen feedback mechanisms and promoted mobile-based grievance redressal systems, ensuring efficient and responsive governance.

11. Aruna Sundararajan, IAS

Aruna Sundararajan has been instrumental in advancing e-governance in Kerala. Recognised for her innovative approach, Forbes described her as an 'IAS officer who thinks like a businesswoman,' reflecting her commitment to public welfare through strategic and impactful initiatives.

8. CRITICAL CONDITIONS FOR THE SUCCESS OF e-GOVERNANCE

(a) Adequate Infrastructure

To fully realise the benefits of e-governance, more e-governance projects have to be implemented by building adequate e-infrastructure, particularly in rural and backward regions. Dependence on ICT has increased as compared to other instruments of service delivery for the obvious reasons of cost-effectiveness, equity, participation, and increased responsiveness and accountability of the service providers.

As dependence has increased, we need to have 'e-readiness' for promoting effective e-governance. World Economic Forum Consultation Report on e-readiness defines it as the ability of the ICT networks to effectively adapt themselves to social and economic advancement which can be achieved through building adequate e-infrastructure and bringing awareness among the leaders of government, civil society, and market organisations.

By building adequate e-infrastructure and initiating more rural-centric e-governance projects, keeping in mind the requirements of the larger section of the population, e-governance can be promoted more effectively in India.

(b) Sound Policy and Legal Framework

New regulations and laws are essential with regard to the application of ICT in promoting governance to ensure accountability and supply of quality goods and services by the private and public sectors without harming the larger society. Removal of obsolete laws and discretionary powers, simplification of procedures to avoid administrative bottlenecks and constitution of single windows ensure speedy disposal of cases.

For the successful application of electronic governance, a range of legislative regulations is required covering the aspects of electronic signatures, electronic **archiving,** data matching, freedom of information, data protection, computer crime, and intellectual property rights. Already the Government of India has an IT Act and Convergence Bill.

The following policy and legal initiatives are to be taken to strengthen e-governance in India:

- Accountability law for making public servants accountable and responsive for non-performance and malfunctioning of their departments.
- Law for privacy ensuring that the information about the citizens is not misused.
- A law in line with the US Government Paper Elimination Act (GPEA) to promote the use of electronic media.
- Amendments to Consumers Protection Law, Tariffs and Taxation Laws, Intellectual Property Regulations, etc., are required.

- Preparing guidelines for content, technological standards, and electronic payments.
- Setting standards for electronic publishing, **archiving**, e-mails, etc.

(c) Socially Relevant Technologies and Integrated Management

Lack of people participation, fractured relationship between government agencies and citizens, lack of availability of local resources, limited integration with local CSOs, and exogenous social and economic environment are the reasons that failed ICT to deliver the full range of services in governance matters. Updating of data in local languages, standardisation in all areas, such as encoding, application logic for common applications, user interfaces, preparing data dictionaries, making appropriate cyber laws, procedural and legal changes in the decision and delivery-making processes as well as in the institutions encouraging public–private partnerships can facilitate the successful application of the e-governance projects in India.

Efforts are needed to incorporate local languages and local content into the internet in a massive way. Accessing the internet using a keyboard may limit the use of the internet. So, there is a need to develop voice-enabled internet service in Indian languages and applications should emerge out of the Indian way of life.

(d) Public–Private Partnership (PPP model)

It is a fact that India needs a huge amount of funds for the implementation of e-governance projects. The government does not have that. In this regard, encouraging private investment seems to be the possible answer. PPP model can be encouraged to initiate the projects to meet the needs of the rising population. The Gujarat Check–Post Project is an example of a PPP model for promoting e-governance in India.

(e) Political and Administrative Leadership

State governments with committed political and administrative leadership are mainly responsible for promoting e-governance in their states in spite of poor communication infrastructure facilities. State governments such as Telangana, Andhra Pradesh, and Karnataka have taken major initiatives in popularising e-governance to improve the quality of administration.

They were able to overcome many barriers in the implementation of e-governance projects through a focused and strategic approach aiming at specified targets and allowing a reasonable time frame for attaining them. Specialised agencies have also come up within the government to initiate innovative experiments. It is sometimes argued that given the low level of development of communication infrastructure in most Indian states, the prospects of e-governance are bleak.

Even in situations where the initial conditions for trying out e-governance appear to be non-existent in terms of inadequate skilled personnel or weak infrastructure, a gradual, flexible, and reflective approach can bring about drastic positive changes.

(f) Role of Civil Society

The civil society bodies, such as citizen groups, associations, and social activists are playing an active role in extending ICT for the empowerment of citizens and effective delivery. In a project, Cyber Grameen, a non-profit organisation set up by Krishna Prasad Tripuraneni, a telecom entrepreneur in Chennai, wireless technology was used to offer digital entertainment, distance learning, telemedicine, and government services. NGOs are also making officials responsive and accountable through e-governance projects.

The Online Complaint Monitoring System (OCMS) in Mumbai Municipal Corporation (BMC) with the active involvement of an NGO, named Praja Foundation, to redress citizens' grievances can be mentioned in this regard. It enables the citizens to register complaints and receive information on the complaint status quickly and easily, without the need to visit or call the ward offices at restricted times.

Civil society and its representatives have been kept out of most of the programmes. Even in cases where such participation is sought, the linkages are either weak or notional. The CARD experience of Andhra Pradesh suggests that until and unless civil society bodies are made active in the delivery of services, the situation will not improve.

(g) Human Resources Development and Capacity Building

The lack of skilled human resources and a cohesive strategy are major obstacles to using ICT in governance. A fragmented approach to e-governance programs has led to high costs without achieving desired outcomes. Organisational, technical, and human factors have hindered ICT's effectiveness in governance.

Information systems are social, not just technical, and require a focus on their social aspects at the operational level. Studies highlight mismanagement, unfavorable attitudes, and a lack of orientation among officials as barriers to progress. Many projects have suffered due to insufficient skills and motivation among administrative staff.

Training to build technical skills and enhance motivation is crucial. For example, senior officers in Andhra Pradesh underwent a four-month training program at IIM Ahmedabad, covering hardware, software, and IT implementation challenges with a practical focus.

9. ARTIFICIAL INTELLIGENCE AND DIGITAL TRANSFORMATION – COMPETENCIES FOR CIVIL SERVANTS

The rise of digital technologies, particularly Artificial Intelligence (AI), is transforming how societies function, and fundamentally changing the way governments operate. Digital transformation has become a key priority for public administrations around the world, driven by the need to improve efficiency, enhance citizen services, and address increasingly complex governance challenges. As the public sector increasingly integrates digital solutions, equipping civil servants with the necessary competencies has become critical to achieving successful digital transformation and efficient e-governance. These competencies empower civil servants to navigate technological changes and lead effective, citizen-centric governance.

9.1 Core Digital Competencies for Civil Servants

Civil servants must possess a diverse set of digital competencies to manage and implement digital transformation effectively. The required key competencies include:

1. **Digital Leadership:** Civil servants must be able to lead digital change by setting clear visions, guiding teams, and fostering innovation across public sector organisations. Digital leadership is essential for embedding digital transformation within governance structures.
2. **Problem Identification:** The ability to identify governance issues that can be addressed through digital solutions is critical for driving effective policy and service delivery in the digital age.
3. **Digital Literacy:** A basic understanding of digital technologies is foundational for all civil servants. Digital literacy enables employees to navigate modern tools and platforms, ensuring that they can work effectively in a digital environment.
4. **Open Data:** Promoting transparency through open data practices enhances decision-making processes and fosters public trust in government institutions.
5. **Data-Driven Approaches:** Civil servants must be adept at using data to inform policies, optimise public services, and deliver evidence-based decisions, making data central to the governance process.

? Thought Box

How would government involvement in the ed-tech sector influence upskilling and skill specialisation, given the growing popularity of technical and digital courses offered online by prominent private institutions?

6. **Artificial Intelligence (AI):** Understanding the potential of AI in public administration is critical. Civil servants should know how AI can be used to improve efficiency, enhance service delivery, and drive innovation in governance.
7. **People-Centricity:** Digital transformation should always prioritise the need of citizens. Civil servants must ensure that technology is used to enhance the user experience and improve accessibility to public services.
8. **Iteration-Enabled Improvements:** Civil servants must be committed to continuous improvement, refining policies and services based on feedback and evolving citizen needs.

9.2 Key Attitudes for Digital Transformation Success

Alongside technical competencies, civil servants must adopt key attitudes to drive successful digital transformation. These include:

Trust: Building trust among colleagues and citizens is crucial for sharing information and collaborating effectively. Civil servants must communicate transparently, show respect for others, and admit mistakes when necessary.

Creativity: Creativity helps civil servants greatly in overcoming challenges, generating new ideas, and finding solutions that improve the quality of service delivery. It fosters an environment of innovation within the public sector.

Adaptability: Digital transformation is dynamic, requiring civil servants to be flexible and willing to challenge established practices. Adaptability helps civil servants navigate the complexities of digital projccts and recover from setbacks.

Curiosity: A curious mindset encourages civil servants to explore new ideas, engage with external stakeholders, and adapt solutions from other contexts to improve governance.

Experimentation: Civil servants must be willing to experiment and take calculated risks in developing digital solutions. Experimentation fosters innovation, and the acceptance of failure is crucial for continuous improvement in digital transformation.

10. NAVIGATING LEGAL, ETHICAL, AND REGULATORY CHALLENGES

With the increasing use of digital technologies and data in public governance, there are significant concerns regarding privacy, security, and the potential misuse of personal data. To ensure responsible use of digital technologies, governments must revise legal, regulatory, and ethical frameworks. Civil servants must be equipped to navigate these challenges, ensuring that digital transformation aligns with human rights and upholds public trust.

Digital transformation requires governments to rethink the ways in which they have functioned so far and to take into consideration a new set of digital principles and standards. Digital transformation can accelerate the achievement of the Sustainable Development Goals (SDGs) by enabling digital government to drive sustainability, equity, and social inclusion.

By fostering these digital competencies and attitudes among civil servants, governments can ensure that their digital transformation efforts are effective, citizen-focused, and resilient to emerging technological challenges. The integration of AI and other digital tools into governance requires a robust foundation of skills, leadership, and ethical considerations, enabling public sector organisations to meet the expectations of an increasingly digital world.

> **? Thought Box**
>
> What role does digital literacy play when it comes to India's response to global conflicts such as the Russian-Ukraine War and the Israel-Palestine War?

- **General Recommendations**
  1. Proper Awareness should be created about the competencies required by civil servants to implement digital transformation in government and to ensure improved digital governance.
  2. Capacity building should be enabled by making learning resources and training content openly accessible. This can be used, tailored, and adapted at the national level to train civil servants on relevant competencies.
  3. Cooperation must be fostered between international, regional, and national organisations including civil society organisations, supporting the training of civil servants, to facilitate knowledge exchange and mutual learning.
  4. A holistic approach should be taken by the government towards digital transformation. Firstly, the focus should be on developing a national digital transformation and AI strategy, and then a digital action plan on strengthening digital competencies, which are included in this framework.

11. CIVIL SERVANTS AND DIGITAL MEDIA

The shift from 'Desk to Digital' reflects the evolving role of civil servants in India's bureaucracy as it goes beyond traditional offices towards e-governance and active engagement on social media. This change mandates government agencies to leverage digital platforms for improved communication with citizens, offering timely updates about government programmes and services. Social media, in particular, enhances transparency by enabling direct interaction between the government and the public, which in turn fosters accountability. Moreover, digital engagement encourages civic participation, inviting feedback on policies and promoting citizen involvement in the democratic process. Social media also helps streamline service delivery and provide citizens with convenient access to government services and support.

11.1 Concerns Regarding Social Media Use by Civil Servants

- **Self-Promotion:** Bureaucrats may selectively showcase achievements, which can resemble personal branding rather than public service.
- **Ethical Issues:** Using social media during office hours may appear unprofessional, particularly when citizens awaiting assistance are neglected.
- **Accountability Pressure:** Social media increases demand for responsiveness, challenging the hierarchical, anonymous, and formal nature of Indian bureaucracy.
- **Compromised Neutrality:** Engaging in opinions or addressing criticism online may blur the impartiality expected of civil servants.
- **Fake News and Propaganda:** The spread of misinformation can complicate public policy discussions, requiring careful navigation of the digital space.

Despite these issues, social media remains a powerful tool for government outreach, increasing the accessibility and accountability of civil servants to the public. It fosters a positive perception of institutions by promoting openness, transparency, and flexibility in government. Social media engagement allows civil servants to help shape public discourse while remaining politically neutral.

This shift has even contributed to improvements in public policy, as societal values have become more prominent and the tendency toward blind obedience to political directives has lessened. Furthermore, social media has raised public awareness about government policies and programs, empowering citizens with knowledge and the means to engage.

Former Chief Election Commissioner of India, Dr S.Y. Quraishi noted, 'There is a fine line between being a charismatic public official, who is liked by the public and constantly seeking attention.' Thus, the use of social media by civil servants should remain authentic, responsive, transparent, and respectful, maintaining a balance between public engagement and professional integrity. Social media, indeed, serves as a double-edged sword, offering opportunities for positive transformation while demanding responsible and ethical usage.

? Thought Box

How can India address the misuse of digital platforms like Telegram while upholding digital rights and fostering a robust digital economy?

SUMMARY

- UNESCO defines e-governance as the public sector's use of ICT to enhance information and service delivery, promote citizen participation in decision-making, and ensure accountability, transparency, and efficiency in governance.
- Types of interactions in e-governance: Government to Citizens (G2C); Government to Business (G2B); Government to Government (G2G); Government to Employees (G2E). E-governance takes governance from one level to the next level. It has the potential to transform traditional governance into **SMART governance**—Simple, Moral, Accountable, Responsible, and Transparent governance.
- Benefits of e-governance: Avoids duplication and reduces costs, simplifies procedures and speeds up service delivery, enhances efficacy, flexibility, and innovation, empowers citizens and fosters greater participation
- Challenges include being process-centric, resistance to change, high costs, lack of training, and inconsistent patterns. Success demands:
  - Timely responses from civil servants
  - Improved communication and online accessibility to administrative resources
  - Citizen engagement in decision-making and transparency in budgets and reports
- The rise of digital technologies like AI is reshaping public administration. Civil servants need competencies in digital leadership, data-driven decision-making, and AI, along with ethical considerations, to balance professionalism, transparency, and neutrality in a digital era.

PREVIOUS YEARS' QUESTION

1. What do you understand by the term 'good governance'? How far recent initiatives in terms of e-governance steps taken by the State have helped the beneficiaries? Discuss with suitable examples. *UPSC CSE Mains 2022*

Case Studies

CASE STUDY 1

You are the commissioner of Vijayawada municipality. You noticed that even after 6 months of releasing funds for widening roads in a locality, the work has not been done. Upon investigation, you discovered that your subordinate had redirected the funds to improve the drainage system in a nearby slum area, instead of using them for the road widening project for which they were originally allocated. When you asked for an explanation, your subordinate responded by highlighting the poor hygienic conditions in the slum, where many residents, along with those in nearby colonies, have been falling sick frequently. Given the severity and urgency of the situation, your subordinate decided to allocate the funds for improving the drainage system.

Questions

1. As the responsible head of the municipality, what action would you take regarding your subordinate's decision to use the funds for an unsanctioned purpose?
2. Given that the funds were allocated for a different project, how will the council proceed with the roadwork?

Answer

The given situation underscores a dilemma between adhering to established procedures and responding to an urgent public health crisis. While the subordinate's decision to divert funds to improve drainage in a slum reflects a genuine commitment to public welfare, bypassing due process raises significant concerns about financial accountability and governance integrity.

Stakeholders	Role/Impact in the Case
Municipal Commissioner (You)	Responsible for ensuring transparency, accountability, and timely resolution of the fund diversion issue.
Subordinate Officer	Took initiative to address a health crisis but violated procedural norms, raising concerns over governance ethics.

Stakeholders	Role/Impact in the Case
Municipal Council	The approving body for fund allocation, whose authority was bypassed, leading to potential governance conflict.
Residents of the Slum Area	Beneficiaries of improved drainage and hygiene, addressing a pressing public health concern.
Residents Awaiting Road Work	Affected by delays in road widening, which impacts transportation, safety, and local development.
Public Health Authorities	Indirectly benefited by the reduced health risks in the slum area due to improved sanitation.
General Public and Taxpayers	Expect proper utilisation of public funds, adherence to procedures, and delivery of sanctioned projects.
Contractors/Vendors	Faced delays in project execution due to the diversion of funds for a non-sanctioned purpose.
Government Oversight Bodies	Concerned with ensuring compliance with financial norms and addressing fund misuse efficiently.
Media and Civil Society	Act as watchdogs by scrutinising municipal actions and influencing public opinion on governance practices.

a. Appropriate Action on the Subordinate

As a responsible municipal head, my response will ensure accountability, uphold ethical governance, and recognise the positive intent behind the subordinate's actions. The steps are as follows:

Acknowledge the Intent and Ethical Responsibility: Recognise the subordinate's action as an ethically motivated decision to address a critical public health issue in the slum area, despite the procedural lapse. This reflects a commitment to public welfare but must align with established protocols.

Issue a Formal Warning for Accountability: Provide a written warning to emphasise the importance of compliance with financial guidelines and approval processes. This reinforces the ethical principle of integrity in public administration.

Establish Clear Expectations for Transparency: Mandate that all similar decisions in the future be documented and reported through proper channels to ensure transparency and procedural correctness.

Promote Capacity Building and Ethical Awareness: Conduct targeted training programmes for municipal staff on ethical decision-making, financial accountability, and crisis management. This will instil a culture of responsibility and foresight in handling public resources.

Recognise and Advocate Proactive Action: Publicly highlight the positive impact of the drainage improvement on public health during council and public meetings, reinforcing the ethical principle of beneficence. Emphasise the importance of balancing proactive measures with adherence to procedural norms.

b. Resolution for the Road Work through the Council

1. Present a detailed report to the council highlighting the urgent hygienic conditions in the slum area that necessitated immediate intervention, the positive public health outcomes from the drainage improvement, and the unauthorised fund diversion along with the corrective actions taken to ensure accountability.
2. Seek retrospective approval from the council to regularise the use of funds for the drainage improvement project, emphasising the public health urgency and the benefits achieved.
3. Submit a proposal for additional funding or request reallocation of unutilised or surplus budgets to ensure the completion of the road-widening project, clearly outlining its importance for traffic management and urban development.
4. Engage local representatives, residents, and relevant stakeholders to build consensus and prioritise the timely completion of the road-widening project.
5. Propose policy reforms to streamline the process of fund reallocation for emergency needs, ensuring transparency, efficiency, and accountability in municipal governance.

Addressing the unauthorized fund diversion ensures accountability while effectively responding to urgent public health needs. Seeking retrospective approval and securing additional funding will enable the timely completion of vital infrastructure projects. Engaging stakeholders and implementing governance reforms will foster transparency, efficiency, and strengthen future decision-making processes.

CASE STUDY 2

As a senior officer in the Finance Ministry, you have access to some confidential and crucial information about policy decisions that the government is about to announce. These decisions are likely to have far-reaching impact on the housing and construction industry. If the builders have access to this information beforehand, they can make huge profit. One of the builders has done a lot of quality work for the government and is known to be close to your immediate superior, who asks you to disclose this information to the said builder.

Questions

1. Under tremendous pressure from your boss, would you disclose the confidential information to the private individual? Why or why not?
2. The builder is offering you a flat in a prime locality in exchange for the information. Presently, you do not own a house, and your boss is also urging you to accept the offer. How would you handle this situation?

Answer

In this scenario, where pressure and a bribe are offered to disclose sensitive information, the officer's decision tests their commitment to these values. The situation underscores the importance of moral courage and making choices that serve the public good, rather than yielding to personal or external influences.

Stakeholder	Interest	Impact
Public Servant (Officer)	Responsible for upholding confidentiality, ethical standards, and legal obligations in public service.	Must make decisions based on public interest and legal frameworks, avoiding unethical influence.
Superior (Immediate)	Exerts pressure on the officer to disclose sensitive information.	Represents potential conflict of interest, could influence the officer's decision towards unethical action.
Builder	Seeks confidential information to gain a competitive advantage and personal benefit.	Can profit unfairly from insider information, potentially distorting market competition and public policy.
Government (Public)	Relies on ethical public servants to ensure fair, transparent policy implementation.	Affected by the integrity of decision-making processes, could lose trust if unethical behaviour occurs.
Legal Authorities	Responsible for enforcing laws related to confidentiality, corruption, and unethical conduct.	Impacted by breaches of confidentiality, which could lead to legal consequences for both the officer and superior.
Housing and Construction Industry	Faces market dynamics shaped by government policies.	Will be affected by the fairness or unfair advantage created by insider information being disclosed.
Citizens/ Public	The ultimate beneficiaries or victims of fair and transparent governance.	Will experience the consequences of any decision that undermines fairness, leading to unequal opportunities.

(a) As a senior officer in the Finance Ministry, I am entrusted with a fiduciary duty to maintain the highest standards of integrity and ethical behaviour. Disclosing confidential information, especially regarding government policies with significant long-term effects, would constitute a breach of both legal and ethical obligations.

In spite of the pressure from my superior, I would steadfastly refuse to share the sensitive information with the builder.

1. **Legal and Ethical Duty**: As a senior officer, I am bound by confidentiality laws and ethical standards. Sharing sensitive information without authorization, is illegal and undermines fairness and justice. This is in direct contradiction to Kant's Categorical Imperative, which asserts that actions must adhere to universally applicable moral standards, ensuring fairness and impartiality.

2. **Duty to the Public Welfare**: My duty is to serve the public, not private interests. Disclosing confidential details would compromise government transparency and decision-making, benefiting a few at the expense of many.
3. **Mill's Harm Principle and Non-Maleficence**: According to **Mill's Harm Principle**, actions are morally justifiable only if they do not harm others. Leaking information would create market distortions, giving some an unfair edge while harming the integrity of the housing sector. Ethical governance requires fairness for all.
4. **Conflict of Interest and Professional Integrity**: The builder's connection to my superior makes this a clear conflict of interest. Upholding justice and fairness means refusing to engage in unethical practices that damage public trust. The request to disclose sensitive information creates a clear conflict of interest, given the builder's connection to my superior.
5. **Principle of Beneficence**: Public officials must work for the common good, not personal or private gain. Keeping information confidential ensures fair policies that benefit society.
6. **Ethical Leadership and Long-Term Governance**: Ethical leadership demands setting the right example. Sharing confidential details would encourage corruption and weaken trust in governance. Upholding transparency and accountability strengthen ethical governance for the long term.

(b) In this situation, where a builder offers a flat in exchange for confidential government information, and under pressure from my superior to accept, I would take the following course of action:

1. As a senior officer in the Finance Ministry, I have a fiduciary responsibility to uphold integrity and ethical standards. Accepting a bribe, in any form, would undermine public trust and violate the core principles of public service ethics.
2. Accepting the offer of a flat would directly breach anti-corruption laws and codes of conduct, leading to severe legal consequences such as charges of corruption and potential dismissal from office.
3. The conflict of interest posed by my superior's connection to the builder would impair my ability to make impartial decisions, violating the principles of justice, equity, and fair competition in government dealings.
4. By rejecting the bribe, I preserve my accountability and personal integrity, which are central to maintaining professional reputation and public confidence in government institutions.
5. I would report the incident to the relevant authorities, such as the Anti-Corruption Bureau, to ensure transparency and safeguard the integrity of the public service, preventing future instances of corruption.
6. Rejecting the bribe would reaffirm my commitment to ethical governance, ensuring decisions are made in the best interest of the public good and reinforcing the importance of moral courage in public service.

Rejecting the bribe and reporting the incident would be a steadfast commitment to upholding **ethical integrity**, **legal compliance**, and **accountability** in public service. By doing so, I ensure that my actions align with the greater **public interest**, promote **transparency**, and reinforce trust in government institutions, setting a strong example of ethical leadership for others.

CASE STUDY 3

You were allocated ₹3 lakh to organise the launch of a pilot programmes for a special central government scheme by the Prime Minister. Your team worked diligently, and the event was a huge success in your locality. The project's objectives were well-highlighted, and even the Prime Minister personally congratulated you and your team for the successful event. However, upon reviewing the expenses, you discovered that some of your team members had forged bills amounting to ₹45,000 and pocketed the money. You are also required to submit a detailed report of the expenses for the amount that was initially sanctioned.

Questions

1. What action will you take against the employees involved in forging the bill? Since, your team has won the laurels, few employees request you not to take any disciplinary action. Will you accept their request or not? Explain.
2. What mechanisms would you adopt to bring about transparency in government spending?

Answer

This case presents an ethical dilemma involving **financial misconduct** during the successful launch of a central government scheme. While the event earned praise, including from the Prime Minister, the discovery of **forged bills** raises critical concerns about **accountability**, **transparency**, and **integrity** in public spending. Addressing this situation requires a balanced approach that upholds ethical standards while reinforcing trust in governance.

Stakeholder	Role/Interest in the Case	Ethical Principles and Concerns
Prime Minister	Represents the central government and symbolises the success of the scheme's launch.	**Accountability**: Expects ethical conduct in fund utilisation to reflect transparency and integrity in governance
Officer in Charge (You)	Accountable for fund management, ensuring ethical and lawful use of resources while maintaining the programme's success	**Integrity, Responsibility**: Ensuring transparency, taking corrective actions, and adhering to professional ethics
Team Members	Played a crucial role in programme execution; some indulged in financial misconduct by forging bills	**Trust, Justice**: Trust has been breached; corrective measures must align with justice and fairness

Stakeholder	Role/Interest in the Case	Ethical Principles and Concerns
Government and Funding Agency	Funded the project and relies on accurate reporting to ensure the success and credibility of government schemes	**Transparency, Accountability**: Ensuring public funds are used effectively and reported honestly
Beneficiaries of the Scheme	Citizens benefiting from the scheme, who rely on the government for ethical, effective, and impartial governance	**Public Interest, Equity**: Misuse of funds erodes trust and undermines public confidence in governance
General Public	Observers of government ethics, efficiency, and fairness in implementing welfare initiatives	**Public Trust, Ethical Governance**: Expect adherence to ethical norms in public spending to preserve societal trust
Auditing Agencies	Tasked with ensuring financial compliance and detecting fraud in government expenditures	**Compliance, Objectivity**: Depend on accurate reporting and ethical practices to uphold financial probity

(a) Despite the event's success and the accolades received, I would firmly decline the request to forgo disciplinary action. Overlooking ethical violations, regardless of achievements, sets a harmful precedent, implying that success can justify breaches of integrity. This undermines accountability, erodes public trust, and compromises the ethical foundations of public service. While the team's efforts and dedication are commendable, it is essential to uphold ethical standards and ensure accountability. The personal congratulations from the Prime Minister are a recognition of the programme's success, not a license to ignore misconduct or bypass legal compliance. By addressing the issue transparently and impartially, I reinforce the values of integrity and fairness, which are indispensable in public service.

Action Against Employees Involved in Forging Bill:

1. **Accountability:** Strong action must be taken against those who forged bills, as this violates moral principles and is unacceptable in public service.
2. **Waiving Action:** Letting the misconduct go unpunished undermines justice and fairness, damages public trust, and encourages unethical behaviour.
3. **Investigation:** A fair and transparent inquiry will identify those involved, helping restore integrity and ensure ethical governance.
4. **Restitution:** The misappropriated funds must be returned to maintain fairness.
5. **Recognising Efforts:** While addressing the wrongdoing, we should acknowledge the honest efforts of other team members who contributed to the event's success.
6. **Transparency:** Financial reports showing the event's success and the steps taken to correct the issue must be submitted to ensure transparency and accountability.
7. **Prevention:** Regular audits, digital payments, and strict expense tracking should be put in place to prevent future fraud.

8. **Ethical Standards:** Taking ethical action reinforces fairness, justice, and responsibility, ensuring public servants maintain trust and integrity.

Actions Taken:

1. Conduct a thorough internal investigation to determine the full scope of the forgery and identify the individuals involved.
2. Hold the responsible employees accountable, as forgery violates both legal and ethical standards, damaging trust and integrity.
3. Initiate formal disciplinary action as per service rules, which may include suspension, termination, or other measures based on the severity.
4. Report the incident to law enforcement, ensuring legal consequences for criminal actions like forgery.
5. Communicate the actions taken transparently to relevant authorities and maintain the integrity of the process.
6. Strengthen internal controls and processes to prevent future instances of fraud, along with additional training on ethics and compliance for employees.

(b) Mechanisms for Transparency in Government Spending

1. **Digital Record Keeping**: Implement a digital platform to log all expenditures with timestamps, descriptions, and approvals for easy auditing.
2. **Public Disclosure**: Publish detailed expense reports on official platforms to allow public scrutiny and prevent fraudulent activities.
3. **Audit Trails and Independent Audits**: Ensure transactions have clear audit trails, with regular and surprise audits by independent bodies to verify expenditures.
4. **Whistleblower Protections**: Strengthen policies to protect whistleblowers and encourage internal reporting of corruption or mismanagement.
5. **E-Procurement Systems**: Introduce e-procurement to reduce manipulation and enable real-time tracking of bids, purchases, and payments.
6. **Training and Cultural Change**: Invest in training on ethics and financial management, fostering a culture where integrity and transparency are prioritised.
7. **Third-Party Oversight**: Engage civil society, media, and independent bodies for external monitoring to ensure proper fund usage.
8. **Feedback Mechanisms**: Create channels for public and stakeholder feedback on the use of public funds to enhance oversight and accountability.

Examples:

1. **PFMS (Public Financial Management System):** Ensures transparency by tracking government funds and providing real-time updates on their utilisation, allowing for better accountability.

2. **RTI (Right to Information) Act, 2005:** Promotes transparency by allowing citizens to request information about government spending, ensuring accountability in public service.
3. **E-Procurement System:** Provides a transparent platform for government procurement, ensuring fair bidding processes and reducing opportunities for corruption.

Addressing financial mismanagement and ensuring transparency in government spending requires strict ethical adherence, accountability, and proactive mechanisms. Recognising team success is important, but integrity must remain intact. Implementing systems like digital records, public disclosures, and audits can protect public funds and maintain trust in government processes.

CASE STUDY 4

You are pursuing a Postgraduate degree in medicine at AIIMS. One of your close friends was also preparing for the postgraduate entrance exam but, despite trying for the past two years, was unable to clear it. Frustrated and disheartened, he becomes increasingly desperate as most of his friends have already secured admission.

In his desperation, he starts exploring unethical ways to pass the exam and is approached by unscrupulous individuals who exploit wireless technology and gadgets to help candidates cheat—for a hefty sum. They even provide references to others who have used this method to secure top ranks. Your friend, convinced by their promises, shares this proposal with you and requests that you speak to his parents to help him arrange the required money.

Understanding the grave consequences of such actions, you strongly warn him against this unethical approach, explaining how it could ruin his career. However, blinded by his desperation, he ignores your advice and proceeds with the malpractice. Unfortunately, he gets caught during the exam along with several others. As a result, the Medical Council of India revokes his eligibility to practice as a registered medical professional in the country, bringing a tragic end to his medical aspirations.

Questions

1. How could you have saved your friend from going to the extent to taking extreme unfair practices?
2. What are the emotional stress and strains faced by the candidates preparing for high level competitive exams? How can they balance their emotions for success?

Answer

The above case involves 'unfair exam practices', which is not just a procedural breach but a moral impairment. The stress of lagging behind peers, combined with societal expectations, pushed the latter (my friend) to resort to unethical practices.

Stakeholders and Ethical issues involved:

S. No	Stakeholder	Ethical issue
1	Myself	• **Empathy** towards my friend's emotional struggles and offering compassionate support. • **Courage** to speak out against the unethical plan, even if it risks straining the friendship. • **Responsibility** to prevent the friend from making poor choices.
2	My friend	• **Strain of moral integrity** when resorting to cheating or unethical practices. • **Disregard** for rules by failing to adhere to the examination guidelines and ethical standards. • **Professional black mark** of a person in medical field, who is expected to possess a high level of ethical value. • **Unfairness** to honest candidates by granting an undue advantage to those who cheat. • **Loss of self-dignity:** Cheating undermines the drive to work hard, weakening qualities like dedication and perseverance while eroding one's dignity and self-respect • **Harm to the common good:** It destroys meritocracy, leading to a loss of public trust in the system. • **Revocation of medical license:** Engaging in malpractice results in the loss of the right to practice as a medical professional.
3	My friend's parents	• **Question of good parenting** as children inherit their values from parents. • **Shattering** parents' hopes of seeing their son become a postgraduate in medicine.
4	Other friends who cleared	• Should have lent **emotional and moral support** to the one who is tirelessly preparing for the medical entrance.
5	Unscrupulous people/group	• **Corrupting society:** Encouraging unfair exam practices undermines integrity and promotes dishonesty. • **Eroding fairness:** The continued use of such unethical means allows non-meritorious candidates to enter the system, compromising its credibility.
6	Institutions	• **Loss of public trust** on the system

1. To prevent my friend from resorting to such extreme measures, I could have taken a more proactive and empathetic approach

1. **Listen to his feelings**: I could have listened to his concerns, allowing him to share his frustration and fear without any judgment. Sometimes, simply having someone to talk to, can ease the pressure and make a person feel less alone.

2. **Provide clarity in thinking**: I would have reminded him that his value as a person is not tied to clearing a single exam. Everyone's journey is different, and setbacks are a part of growth.
3. **Revealing the risks and consequences**: I would be honest with him about the consequences of cheating, not just the legal and professional risks but also how it could permanently damage his career, reputation, and self-respect. Hearing about these consequences might have made him think twice before resorting to unfair practices.
4. **Suggest alternatives:** To keep his spirits up, I could have shared real stories of people who succeeded after multiple attempts or even found fulfilment by taking a different path. I would have encouraged him to explore other opportunities while he prepared, like gaining experience in a healthcare-related field or considering a different specialisation, so he wouldn't feel stuck or hopeless.
5. **Counselling help:** Professional help, like a counsellor or mentor, could also have made a difference. Someone with expertise in guiding students under stress could have offered him new strategies and emotional support.
6. **Parental involvement:** I would have encouraged an open dialogue with his parents about his struggle and the pressure he is facing. Their support and understanding might make a significant difference in his decision-making.

2. Emotional stress and strain faced by candidates

1. **Pressure to meet high expectations**: Higher level of expectations brings anxiety.
2. **Family and societal pressure**: The pressure to meet the aspirations of family and society can feel unbearable at times, making the entire process even more stressful.
3. **Comparison**: Observing peers succeed in career and life, while lagging behind fosters self-doubt.
4. **Fear of failure**: The thought of not succeeding after months or even years of hard work can be overwhelming. It's a weight that many students carry silently, and it can really take a toll on their confidence.
5. **Isolation from the surrounding world**: Preparing for such exams often means long hours of studying alone, which can lead to feelings of loneliness and being cut off from family and friends. This lack of connection can amplify stress and anxiety.
6. **Exhaustion:** When candidates push themselves relentlessly without taking breaks, it can result in complete physical and mental drain out. It's difficult to stay motivated or productive in that state, which only adds to the frustration.

3. Ways to balance emotions and handle stress

Managing the stress of exam preparation requires a balanced approach that focuses on both mental and physical well-being.

- **Mental calmness:** To combat stress and anxiety, students can practice mindfulness through meditation, or yoga. These techniques help improve focus and bring a sense of calm.
- **Quality lifestyle**: Getting adequate sleep, eating nutritious meals, and avoiding excessive stimulants like caffeine can do wonders for both physical and mental health.
- **Physical fitness routine:** Exercise not only keeps the body fit but also helps regulate stress hormones, making it easier to handle pressure.
- **Trusting the process:** One should embrace and celebrate small wins. Acknowledging even the smallest progress can boost morale and keep motivation in good line during the long journey.
- **Proper study plan:** Having a structured study plan is another effective way to stay on track. Breaking the syllabus into smaller, manageable goals with scheduled breaks can prevent burnout and enhance productivity.
- **Peer and social connect:** Seeking support from friends, family, or mentors provides emotional reassurance and can help students feel less isolated. Talking through challenges often brings clarity and practical advice.
- **Optimistic mindset:** Finally, positive affirmations can make a big difference. Focusing on personal strengths and maintaining an optimistic mindset builds confidence and helps students stay resilient in the face of challenges.

Restoring trust, fairness, and merit in the examination system requires a multi-faceted approach. Incorporating ethical education into the preparation process, utilising technology to prevent malpractice, encouraging and protecting whistleblowers, and conducting transparent investigations are critical steps. A unified commitment to integrity by all stakeholders will safeguard meritocracy and ensure that every candidate, irrespective of their socio-economic background, has equal opportunities to succeed.

CASE STUDY 5

Mr. Subham, a respected and admired bureaucrat, serves as the secretary in the Ministry of Defence. Trusted by the defence minister, he has been given significant autonomy in handling ministry affairs. However, he is nearing the end of his career and is personally struggling with a deep tragedy—having recently lost his elder son and wife in an accident. Since then, he has maintained a low profile and grown increasingly attached to his younger son, who has just completed his graduation from an average institution in the capital.

Subham is currently responsible for expediting and finalising a direct government-to-government arms contract with a major supplier. The manufacturer, who stands to gain significantly if the process moves faster, has repeatedly reached out to Subham, expressing frustration over bureaucratic delays. Subtle hints have also been made about fulfilling any personal expectations in exchange for accelerating the deal.

Meanwhile, Subham's younger son aspires to study at one of the world's most prestigious universities, which requires substantial financial support and strong references. Subham himself is considering relocating with his son, but financial constraints make it difficult. The company's spokesperson, aware of his situation, offers to cover all expenses for his son's education—including admission, tuition, and placement in a well-paying job—on the condition that Subham expedites the deal's approval.

However, due to unexpected political developments, the defence minister has decided to scrap the deal. Based on his experience, Subham believes this controversy is temporary and that the agreement will likely be signed at a later stage. Now, with only a few months left in service, he finds himself in a moral and professional dilemma. He does not want to disappoint his son, nor does he wish to fall out of favour with the minister. The deal itself does not compromise national interests, as the products are of world-class quality and would enhance the country's defense capabilities. Faced with conflicting responsibilities, Subham must decide between ethical integrity and personal obligations.

Questions

1. What are the different values involved in this situation? What values should Subham practice to keep his conscience clean and maintain his reputation?
2. What could have been the ethical consequences involved if Subham had continued to convince the minister and get the deal signed in favour of the private company for his personal benefits?

Answer

The case study deals with the ethical dilemma faced by Mr. Subham, a senior bureaucrat in the Ministry of Defence, who is entrusted with expediting a critical government arms contract. The case explores the conflict between personal interests, professional responsibility, and ethical values.

1. Values involved in the situation

S. No	Stakeholder	Values involved
1	Mr Subham	• **Professional integrity** in his long career • Accepting personal benefits for official duties can lead to a **conflict of interest.** • **Trust** of the defence minister **in his official capacity.** • **Responsibility** to make decisions that are in the best interest of **national security and public welfare.** • Personal losses in family and **responsibility as a father**.

S. No	Stakeholder	Values involved
2	Mr Subham's son	• **Aspiration vs. Ethics:** Recognising the consequences of gaining personal benefits through potentially unethical means. • **Compromising personal values:** Gaining advantages at the expense of one's integrity and ethical standards.
3	Ministry of defence	• Maintaining the confidence of the **public** in the integrity of governmental actions. • Making choices that prioritise the nation's and the public's best interests.
4	The Private Arms company	• **Professionalism** in company deals. • Offering financial support for Mr. Subham's son in exchange for speeding up the deal is **unethical.** • **Competition should be based on the merit** of its products rather than resorting to undue influence.

1. Values Subham should practice keeping his conscience clean and maintain his reputation:

1. **Maintain his highest standards of professional conduct**: Ensuring all actions comply with legal and regulatory frameworks.
2. **Work life balance**: Shubam should set boundaries and ensure work does not encroach on personal life.
3. **Parental responsibility of value inculcation on his son**: Mr. Shubam should lead by example by demonstrating ethical behaviour in his own actions, showing his son the importance of integrity and honesty. He should engage in open discussions about ethical dilemmas and the importance of making principled decisions.
4. **Seek ways to support his son without compromising his principles**: Encourage critical thinking by helping his son understand and analyse different perspectives and the consequences of actions.
5. **Responsibility as a public servant to implement government's decision:** He should follow directives and adhere to the decisions and policies set by the government and the ministry.
6. **Courage to stand against illegal offers from company:** Firmly decline any offers of personal gain in exchange for favourable decisions. If necessary, report any unethical approaches to the appropriate authorities.
7. **Transparency in company deals**: Fair processes ensuring that the deal-making process is fair and free from undue influence.

2. The ethical consequences if Subham had persisted in convincing the minister to approve the deal in favour of the private company for his personal gain would include:

1. **Erosion of Public Trust:** If Subham's actions are perceived as being influenced by personal gains rather than national interest, the public may lose trust in the ministry and the government as a whole.
2. **Legal and Departmental Repercussions:** Engaging in corrupt practices, such as accepting personal favour could lead to criminal charges, fines, or even imprisonment for Subham. Subham might face disciplinary actions, including dismissal from service, forfeiture of pension, and other professional consequences.
3. **Compromise of public service values:** Subham's actions would violate the ethical standards expected of a public servant. His action might be setting a negative precedent fostering a culture of corruption.
4. **Personal consequences:** The emotional burden of unethical actions could weigh heavily on Subham, affecting his mental and emotional well-being.
5. **Corporate Accountability:** Such incidents could lead to tighter regulations and oversight in the defense procurement industry, affecting the overall business environment.

While his personal circumstances evoke empathy, they cannot justify actions that compromise integrity, accountability, and the public trust. By making decisions grounded in professional integrity, Mr. Shubham can safeguard his reputation, contribute to the credibility of the ministry, and set a positive precedent for other public servants and his son. Ultimately, ethical conduct ensures not just thc success of an individual but the strength and trustworthiness of institutions they serve.

CASE STUDY 6

As the District Educational Officer (DEO) of Chikmagalur, you have identified a significant dropout rate among students in government schools, which has become a serious concern in the state. Many students are shifting to private schools in the same locality despite efforts to enhance infrastructure and facilities in government schools.

Despite these initiatives, the issue remains unresolved, and pressure is mounting from both the education minister, who frequently requests reports, and the media, which continues to highlight the problem.

This calls for a strategic and innovative approach to address the root causes behind the dropouts and restore confidence in government schools.

Questions

1. What will you do to improve the strength of the government schools as well as to stop the further dropouts from the school?
2. How will you find out the solution to it using Emotional intelligence?
3. Given that the student's dropout rates are an issue in government schools a local private school association approaches you with a hefty amount, to remain indifferent to the problem. You are also in a situation of severe financial crisis. Moreover, accepting the money would not significantly impact on government schools. How would you respond to this situation?

Answer

The above case describes the growing concern of **HALLOWING OUT** of government schools which could affect the enrollment rate of children from marginalised society.

1. Steps to Improve Strength in Government Schools and Prevent Dropouts

To address the dropout issue effectively, a multifaceted approach is essential:

- **Stakeholder Engagement**: Conduct community meetings with parents, teachers, and students to understand the reasons behind the shift to private schools.

- **Quality of Education**: Focus on improving teaching quality by organising regular teacher training programmes and introducing innovative teaching methodologies.
- **Curriculum Enhancement**: Introduce skill-based learning, extracurricular activities, and digital education to make government schools more appealing.
- **Improving the Infrastructure**: By integrating PPP methods to avail modern and quality structures.
- **Awareness Campaigns**: Highlight the achievements of government schools through campaigns, showcasing success stories of alumni and free facilities like mid-day meals, uniforms, and books.
- **Incentives for Attendance**: Provide scholarships or attendance-linked incentives to students, ensuring active participation.

- **Partnerships with NGOs**: Collaborate with NGOs for community outreach and additional support in enhancing facilities and promoting education.

2. Using Emotional Intelligence to Solve the Issue

- **Empathy**: Understand the concerns of parents and students, whether it's the perception of quality, peer pressure, or specific grievances. Hold empathetic discussions to address their issues effectively.
- **Self-awareness**: Be mindful of your biases and frustrations, ensuring your decisions are fair and free of personal emotions.
- **Social Skills**: Engage with community leaders, teachers, and local influencers to create a supportive network for promoting government schools.
- **Motivation**: Inspire your team of teachers and staff by recognising their efforts and aligning them with the shared goal of improving student retention.
- **Problem-Solving**: Use emotional intelligence to mediate between various stakeholders, encouraging collaboration and innovative solutions to improve education quality.

3. Refusing the Bribe

Despite financial difficulties, accepting a bribe is unethical, and it undermines the trust placed in you as a public servant. Here's how to handle the situation:

- **Reject the Offer Firmly**: Refuse the bribe and remind the private school association of the legal and moral implications of such actions.
- **Report the Incident**: File a report to the appropriate authorities about the bribery attempt, ensuring transparency and accountability.
- **Strengthen Oversight**: Increase vigilance over private schools to ensure they do not engage in unethical practices that might harm government schools.
- **Seek Support**: Address your financial crisis through legitimate means, such as availing welfare schemes, loans, or seeking advice from financial experts.
- **Showing Leadership Qualities**: By maintaining your integrity, you inspire your colleagues and the community to uphold ethical standards in governance.

In the face of moral dilemmas, the true measure of integrity lies in choosing the path of righteousness over the lure of personal gain. Upholding ethical principles not only preserves one's character but also strengthens the collective faith in just governance. By following Gandhi's talisman of striving towards the benefit of the deprived will make one to follow the path of public service.

CASE STUDY 7

You recently joined a company and, after completing your training and induction, were assigned to Mr. Mathews' team. Despite being highly qualified, sincere, dedicated and hardworking, you find yourself subjected to constant bullying from Mr. Mathews. He frequently teases you in front of others, intimidates you at every point, raises his voice, and even calls you names. His complaints often revolve around your work not being done correctly or quickly enough. However, you believe most of his criticism is unjustified, as it naturally takes time for a newcomer to adjust to the company and build rapport with colleagues.

Questions

1. What are the emotional dilemmas you would have experienced in this case. How will you overcome this?
2. You are paid a good salary in the present company and possess strong skills and talent. However, Mr. Mathews' constant belittling and mistreatment create a hostile work environment. Will you choose to resign and seek a position elsewhere? Explain your course of action, considering factors such as workplace culture, career growth, and potential solutions to address the issue before making a decision.

Answer

The above case depicts the issue of poor workplace culture where insensitive comments and remarks from senior level managers could affect not only the morale of workers but also the efficiency of the organisation itself.

1. Emotional Dilemmas and Overcoming Them

Emotional Dilemmas:

Self-Doubt: Feeling inadequate or questioning your capabilities due to constant criticism

Helplessness: Feeling powerless to improve the situation or address the issue effectively

Anger and Frustration: Experiencing resentment towards Mr. Mathews for his unjust treatment

Fear and Anxiety: Worrying about further bullying or its impact on your reputation

Overcoming Emotional Dilemmas:

1. **Self-Awareness**: Recognise that your emotions are valid but avoid letting them cloud your judgment. Remind yourself of your capabilities and qualifications.
2. **Empathy**: Try to understand if Mr. Mathews' behaviour stems from stress, insecurity, or unrealistic expectations.
3. **Assertive Communication**: Politely but firmly address specific instances of unfair treatment with Mr. Mathews, explaining how it affects your morale and productivity.
4. **Seek Mentorship**: Approach a senior colleague or HR for guidance on handling such situations effectively.
5. **Stress Management**: Practice mindfulness, exercise, or pursue hobbies to maintain emotional well-being.

2. Course of Action: Stay or Quit?

Staying in the Job:

1. **Evaluate the Situation**: Reflect on whether Mr. Mathews' behaviour is a temporary adjustment issue or a persistent toxic pattern.
2. **Try Engaging in Direct Dialogues**: Discuss with Mr. Mathew and reason with him for his actions.
3. **Focus on Growth**: Utilise the job to gain experience, prove your capabilities, and build a strong professional network.
4. **Escalate if Necessary**: If bullying persists despite polite confrontation, report the matter to HR, adhering to company policies.
5. **Develop Resilience**: View challenges as opportunities to grow stronger and navigate workplace dynamics effectively.

Quitting the Job:

1. **Assess Opportunities**: If the toxic environment outweighs the benefits and no resolution seems possible, begin exploring other job options.
2. **Strategic Exit**: Resign once you have secured another role that aligns with your career aspirations and values.

Quitting immediately might not be prudent as the situation may improve with time and proper action. However, staying should not come at the cost of your mental health or self-respect. Strive to address the issue constructively, but keep alternative plans ready in case the environment remains unsupportive. Balancing emotional intelligence with practical judgment is a key to navigating this challenge effectively.

CASE STUDY 8

You are a mid-level manager in a fast-growing organisation in Mumbai. You have applied for a one-week leave well in advance to go on a tour with your family. and it was duly approved by the HR department. However, just a day before your departure, your immediate boss assigns you an urgent task that requires at least three days to complete. This task is crucial, as it could secure projects worth ₹3 crores for the company, and you are being considered to lead the project if it succeeds.

At the same time, your family is eagerly looking forward to the trip and insists that you accompany them. They express that without you, they would rather cancel the trip altogether.

Questions

1. Discuss the various emotional dilemmas involved here and what course of action will you take in this situation.
2. Your entire family is excited and eagerly preparing for the trip, insisting that you join them. You don't want to disappoint them or hurt their feelings. At the same time, you have been given a critical task at work that could impact your career. How will you handle this situation while balancing your professional responsibilities and family commitments?

Answer

The above case depicts a critical decision-making scenario where work-life balance gets jeopardised due to unexpected work-related emergencies.

1. Emotional Dilemmas

1. **Professional Commitment vs. Personal Responsibility**: Balancing your loyalty to the organisation and its growth with your obligation to your family's expectations.
2. **Career Growth vs. Family Bonding**: The opportunity to lead a high-value project could be pivotal for your career, but missing the trip may strain family relationships.
3. **Guilt and Anxiety**: Feeling guilty about disappointing either your boss or your family, coupled with anxiety about the long-term consequences of your choice.

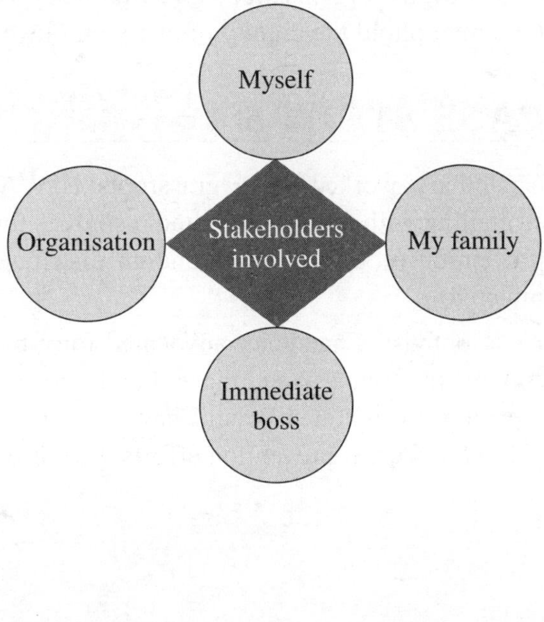

Course of Action:

1. **Communicate with Your Boss**: Explain the situation to your boss, emphasising the importance of the pre-approved leave. Offer to initiate the task, delegate parts to your team, or work remotely during the trip if feasible.
2. **Involve Your Team**: Delegate parts of the task to capable team members under your supervision, ensuring progress continues even in your absence.
3. **Reschedule or Adjust**: Negotiate with your family to reschedule the trip or explore a shorter version of the task timeline if possible.
4. **Seek a Middle Ground**: If the project's importance is critical and delegation is not an option, consider postponing the trip while planning a compensatory outing with your family soon after.

2. Handling the Family's Expectations

1. **Empathy and Assurance**: I will try to acknowledge my family's excitement and feelings. I will take efforts to share the importance of the task and how it could contribute to long-term benefits for the family.
2. **Propose a Compromise**: I will suggest a shorter trip or delay the trip by a few days. Also, will offer an enhanced experience later as compensation for their understanding.
3. **Involve Them in the Decision**: By discussing the situation openly with my family, seeking their input. This demonstrates respect for their emotions and builds mutual understanding.
4. **Make It up to Them**: If the trip is postponed or cancelled, I will plan a special outing or event to make them feel valued.

By addressing the issue with immediate corrective actions and implementing long-term preventive measures, the organisation can foster a respectful, ethical, and inclusive work culture. This will not only uphold the dignity of every employee but also enhance overall morale and productivity.

CASE STUDY 9

Chaudhary worked for a grassroots HIV/AIDS programme in Mumbai, a small non-profit struggling with funding. Limited resources forced the organisation to decide whether to prioritise prevention (education and condom distribution) or treatment (medical care for those already infected).

As a lobbyist, Chaudhary advocated for a balanced approach, allocating funds to both areas to support those at risk and those diagnosed. However, the leadership disagreed. They argued that focusing on treatment would have a greater impact since the affected population was clearly defined, whereas prevention efforts were broader and harder to measure.

Despite opposition, some believed prevention should take precedence, as reducing new infections would be more beneficial in the long run. However, the organisation ultimately shifted its funding to treatment, leaving prevention efforts largely symbolic. This decision changed Chaudhary's role—his advocacy now focused solely on treatment, sidelining prevention in practice.

After six months of struggling with this decision, Chaudhary left the organisation. He reflected on how even well-intentioned non-profits face ethical dilemmas driven by financial constraints.

Questions

1. What should be the goal of a nonprofit HIV/AIDS organisation– Prevention or Treatment or both? Give a reasoned opinion.
2. Do you think Chaudhary should have resigned once the upper management made its decision to favour treatment? Do you think Chaudhary's decision was fair to the community served?

Answer

The case of Chaudhary highlights the complex ethical and operational dilemmas faced by grassroots non-profit organisations working in resource-constrained environments. The struggle is to balance competing priorities: addressing immediate medical needs versus investing in long-term prevention efforts.

Stakeholders involved:

1. Mr. Chaudhary
2. The Non-Profit Organisation
3. Upper management of Non-Profit Organisation
4. People affected with AIDS/HIV
5. Population vulnerable to AIDS/HIV

1\. The goal of a nonprofit HIV/AIDS organization should ideally encompass both prevention and treatment to address the crisis holistically. While resource constraints often necessitate prioritisation, **a balanced approach is essential for long-term impact**.

Prevention: The Key to Reducing Future Cases

1. **Proactive approach**: Prevention efforts, such as education, awareness campaigns, and condom distribution, directly address the root cause of HIV/AIDS spread. They target at-risk populations and aim to curb new infections.
2. **Comparatively economical**: Prevention programmes are often less expensive compared to lifelong treatment, making them a financially sustainable way to reduce future treatment burdens.

Treatment: A Lifeline for Those Already Affected

1. **Moral Imperative**: People living with HIV/AIDS have an immediate need for care, making treatment an ethical priority. Providing antiretroviral therapy (ART) not only improves their quality of life but also reduces their viral load, lowering the risk of transmission.
2. **Way for a dignified life**: Effective treatment can help manage the disease and prevent it from advancing to more severe stages.
3. **National Strategy Alignment**: Many governments and global health organisations prioritise treatment in their HIV/AIDS strategies, making it a viable avenue for securing funding and support.

Why Both are Essential?

1. **Interdependency:** Prevention and treatment are inherently linked. Effective treatment reduces the viral load in patients, curbing the spread of the virus (treatment as prevention). Simultaneously, prevention efforts reduce the incidence of new cases, eventually lessening the demand for treatment.
2. **Comprehensive Support:** A dual focus ensures the organization serves the community equitably, addressing the needs of both those at risk and those already affected.

2. Chaudhary's decision to resign after upper management chose to prioritise treatment over prevention can be evaluated:

Arguments for Chaudhary's Resignation

1. **Conflict of Values:** Chaudhary strongly believed in a balanced approach to tackling HIV/AIDS through both prevention and treatment. By resigning, he demonstrated his commitment to his personal and professional values, thus avoiding value conflict.
2. **Passive in work:** Once upper management decided to focus solely on treatment, Chaudhary's ability to advocate for prevention will be significantly reduced. Staying in a role where he could no longer make an impact on prevention might have left him frustrated and ineffective. This might lower his professional enthusiasm.
3. **Advocacy for treatment:** His resignation could act as a statement highlighting the importance of prevention, potentially influencing discussions and decisions within the HIV/AIDS non-profit sector.

Arguments Against Chaudhary's Resignation

- **Impact on the Community:** The community served by the non-profit depended on both prevention and treatment efforts. By resigning, Chaudhary may have left the community without a strong advocate for prevention, potentially weakening those efforts.

- **Influence from Within:** Staying within the organisation might have given Chaudhary the opportunity to advocate for prevention incrementally and push for a more balanced approach over time.
- **Commitment to Responsibility:** Chaudhary had a duty to support those affected by HIV/AIDS. His departure could be seen as stepping away from this responsibility, particularly since his skills in grant writing and lobbying could have continued to benefit the organisation, even within its treatment-focused approach.

Hence, I don't think Chaudhary should have resigned, but influence from within the organisation to serve the larger interests of the vulnerable community he is serving.

Was the Decision Fair to the Community?

- **Ethical perspective:** Chaudhary's resignation aligned with his personal values but may not have been entirely fair to the community. The community needed both prevention and treatment programmes, and his departure likely weakened advocacy for prevention.
- **Pragmatic perspective:** If Chaudhary felt that he could no longer serve the community effectively within the constraints imposed by management, his resignation was justified. An ineffective advocate within the organisation might have achieved less than someone working from outside or in a different capacity.

Chaudhary's decision to resign was consistent with his ethical beliefs but its fairness to the community is debatable. A more balanced option might have been to stay and continue advocating for prevention while working within the system. However, if his resignation brings attention to the importance of prevention and sparks meaningful dialogue, it could still be considered a fair and impactful decision in the long run. It's essential for nonprofit organisations to navigate these ethical dilemmas carefully, balancing limited resources while striving to make the most significant impact possible.

CASE STUDY 10

You and your brother are studying in the same college. One day a group of seniors along with your brother confronts a group of your classmates. Though you have been left out, your class mates were ragged by your seniors. As a result of it, your friends suffered emotional stress.

Questions

1. What kind of emotional stress any one would undergo during ragging in colleges?
2. If you are asked by the college authorities to list the names of the students who indulged in ragging, will you disclose your brother's name also.

Answer

Ragging in colleges is a harmful and unethical practice that has severe emotional, psychological, and sometimes physical impacts on students. It creates a toxic environment that hampers trust and well-being. The situation presents a moral dilemma when one has to choose between family loyalty and justice for the affected students.

Stakeholders	Principles involved
Myself	Justice and Accountability
My brother	Empathy and Compassion
The seniors	Integrity and Honesty
Classmates	Respect for Human Dignity
College administration	Fairness and Impartiality

Emotional Stress from Ragging:

- **Anxiety and Fear**: Humiliation due to ragging can often lead to persistent anxiety or fear of being singled out.
- **Depression**: The feeling of helplessness can lead to symptoms of depression, including sadness and loss of interest in everyday activities
- **Low Self-Esteem**: Being subjected to degrading acts can significantly impact one's self-worth, leading to doubts about one's capabilities and self-image.
- **Post-Traumatic Stress Disorder (PTSD)**: Victims may develop PTSD, experiencing symptoms such as flashbacks, intense anxiety, and avoidance of triggering situations.
- **Isolation**: Victims might withdraw from social interactions to avoid further incidents, leading to social isolation.
- **Anger and Aggression**: Some individuals might respond with anger or aggressive behaviour either towards themselves or others as a way to cope with or express their distress.
- **Guilt and Shame**: Especially if the ragging involved personal revelations or acts that the victim feels ashamed of, leading to self-blame or guilt over perceived weaknesses.

Ethical Consideration in Naming the Raggers:

- **Integrity and Truthfulness**: Ethically, one should uphold the truth. Not disclosing brother's name could be seen as protecting him at the expense of justice for the victims. This could compromise your integrity and the fairness of the disciplinary process.
- **Fairness and Equality**: All participants in such acts should face the consequences equally. Protecting one individual from accountability undermines the principle of equality under rules and regulations.

- **Moral Responsibility**: There's a moral duty to prevent further harm. Revealing all participants might help in ensuring that no one else suffers from similar experiences, promoting a safer environment for everyone.
- **Family Loyalty vs. Broader Loyalty**: While there might be a personal conflict due to familial bonds, the broader loyalty should often be to the community and the institution's values of safety, respect, and anti-bullying.
- **Potential for Change**: By including the brother's name, it might also offer him a chance for personal growth, reflection, and change. This could lead to him acknowledging his mistakes and understanding the impact of his actions.
- **Personal Impact**: Despite the personal impact, it also provides an opportunity to stand for what's right, which might teach both a valuable lessons about ethics and responsibility.

The ethical course of action would be to disclose your brother's involvement if you are certain of his participation. This upholds integrity, promotes accountability, and serves the greater good of the community. However, it is also important to support your brother through the consequences, helping him learn from the experience and encouraging personal growth.

CASE STUDY 11

You are the team lead in a project of a reputed software company. One of your team members, Mr. Asish, is known for his efficiency and timely completion of any tasks assigned to him. He has been working in this organisation and on the same project for close to 5 years. However, you noticed recently that Mr. Asish has been misbehaving with one of his team members, Ms. Aparna, who is junior in the team. Ms. Aparna joined the team a year ago and is known to be a dedicated and hardworking employee. As the team lead, Ms. Aparna approaches you and shares her concerns about feeling uncomfortable in the team due to Mr. Asish's behaviour. She describes how his inappropriate comments have caused her embarrassment on multiple occasions. Now, as she is on the verge of finalising a marriage proposal, she wants to put an end to this mental distress. Ms. Aparna demands immediate action against Mr. Asish.

Question

How will you proceed and what actions will you take to resolve the situation?

Answer

As a team lead, I am responsible for maintaining a professional and respectful work environment for all the team members. Inappropriate behaviour, harassment, or misconduct are unacceptable and must be addressed promptly and impartially to ensure the well-being of all employees while upholding the organisation's values.

Stakeholders:

- Mr. Asish
- Ms. Aparna
- Team leader (myself)
- Software company's reputation

Initial Steps:

Confidential Hearing: *Empathy and Respect*—Create a safe and private space for Ms. Aparna to share her experiences openly. Assure her that her conversation is confidential, and she is heard and valued. This demonstrates respect for her dignity and acknowledges her emotional state.

Documentation: *Accountability and Fairness*—Encourage Ms. Aparna to keep a clear record of specific incidents, including dates, times, and any witnesses. This ensures that her concerns are supported by concrete facts and allows for a fair and transparent process.

Review Company Policies: *Integrity and Compliance*—Review the company's harassment policies, code of conduct, and grievance procedures to ensure that every step aligns with the organization's values and legal requirements. This shows a commitment to doing what's right.

Further Actions:

Investigation: *Impartiality and Due Process*—Conduct a fair and unbiased investigation. Consider involving HR or an external mediator to gather perspectives from witnesses. This helps maintain fairness and ensures everyone involved is treated with respect.

Interim Measures: *Protection and Welfare*—Make temporary changes to Ms. Aparna's work environment or team setup to prioritise her safety and peace of mind during the investigation. This demonstrates care for her well-being and the organisation's commitment to protecting its employees.

Confrontation and Dialogue: *Fairness and Dialogue*—Meet with Mr. Asish to discuss the allegations, ensuring he has the opportunity to share his side of the story. Conduct the conversation without judgment and document every detail carefully to maintain transparency and fairness.

If the allegations are substantiated:

Justice and Accountability: Take appropriate disciplinary action, whether it's a warning or termination, based on the severity of the findings. This shows accountability and a commitment to justice.

Restorative Justice: Where appropriate, encourage a genuine apology or a process of reconciliation to support healing and closure for all parties involved.

If the allegations are unsubstantiated:

Team Harmony and Respect: Use this as an opportunity to reaffirm standards of respectful behaviour and foster a stronger teamwork.

Vigilance: Monitor workplace interactions to ensure no retaliation or similar concerns arise in the future, promoting a culture of care and respect.

Support for Ms. Aparna: *Compassion and Support*—Offer her access to counselling or a break from work if needed. Showing genuine concern for her mental health and recovery reinforces that the organisation values her well-being.

Preventive Measures:

Education and Culture: Strengthen training programmes on ethics, inclusivity, and workplace respect. This creates a positive work environment where everyone feels safe and valued.

Policy Enhancement: Review and refine company policies to address any gaps and ensure the organisation uphold the highest ethical standards.

Follow-Up: *Responsibility and Closure*—Check in with both Ms. Aparna and Mr. Asish after the process is complete to ensure the matter is fully resolved. Stay vigilant against any lingering tensions or retaliation. This follow-up not only closes the loop but also reassures every one of the organisation's commitment to fairness and well-being.

By reframing these steps through ethical values, you not only address the immediate issue but also build a culture of respect, justice, and support within the workplace.

CASE STUDY 12

You are the principal of a reputed college in Kanpur. One day, a faculty comes to you and says, "I am not able to do justice to students by teaching the subject". He is considered to be one of the most successful teachers in your college. He appears to be emotionally disturbed.

Questions

1. What are the common stresses a teacher would face in his career?
2. What kind of stress is your faculty member undergoing in this situation, and how will you help him return to a normal state?

Answer

Teachers hold a pivotal role in shaping students' futures, but their responsibilities often come with significant emotional and professional challenges. As principal, it is both an ethical duty and a moral responsibility to address the well-being of faculty members. Providing support in such moments not only facilitates their recovery but also upholds the values of empathy, respect, and integrity within the institution.

Stakeholders	Principles involved
The faculty member	Emotional wellbeing, professional confidence
The principal	Ethical Responsibility and decision-making
Students	Quality education
The Institution	Healthy work environment, reputation
Fellow faculty members	Teamwork and mutual respect

Common Stresses Faced by Teachers:

1. **Workload Pressure:** Extensive lesson planning, grading, administrative duties, and extracurricular activities can lead to both mental and physical fatigue.
2. **Performance Expectations:** Constant pressure to achieve high academic standards can challenge a teacher's emotional stability.
3. **Student Behavior:** Addressing diverse learning needs requires patience and adaptability, which can become stressful over time.
4. **Personal vs. Professional Life:** Teachers often struggle to balance their professional obligations with their personal lives, leading to emotional strain.
5. **Emotional Investment:** Deep care for students' success can result in emotional exhaustion, especially when faced with underperformance.
6. **Adaptation to Change:** Frequent updates in curriculum, technology or teaching strategies require adaptability, which may feel overwhelming for some educators.

Stress Specific to the Current Situation:

In this instance, the faculty member appears emotionally unsettled and expresses self-doubt about his ability to teach. The ethical considerations and possible stressors include:

- **Burnout:** Overcommitment to duties without proper rest can lead to emotional exhaustion.
- **Self-Doubt:** Even a successful teacher may experience a crisis of confidence, questioning his ability to fulfil his responsibilities.
- **Personal Issues:** He might be dealing with personal challenges that affect his professional mindset.
- **Impostor Syndrome:** Despite being highly regarded, the teacher may feel unworthy of their success, highlighting a need for support.

Steps to Help Him Return to Normalcy

1. **Private Conversation:** Create a safe space for him to share his thoughts openly. Listen with empathy and reassure him of his value to the college and to his students.
2. **Identify the Stressor:** Gently explore the root cause of his distress. Encourage him to seek professional help if needed.
3. **Provide Support:** Provide Support: Offer resources like counselling to help him cope with stress. Temporarily lighten his workload to give him time to recover and regain confidence.
4. **Explore Long-term Solutions:** Consider teaching a different subject or taking a short break. Encourage collaboration with colleagues to ease his burden and provide fresh perspectives.
5. **Regular Follow-up:** Stay in touch through periodic check-ins to monitor his progress. By addressing this teacher's concerns with fairness and compassion, the principal can fulfil his ethical obligation to ensure their well-being while upholding the college's values of respect and care. Empowering the teacher during this period not only restores their confidence but also fosters a culture of trust and support throughout the institution.

CASE STUDY 13

Sarla is the Superintendent of Police (Law and Order) in Rajnagar. One day, she learned that her husband, a senior VP at a corporate firm, was having an affair with his colleague. Consequently, she decided to end her marriage. This left her with the responsibility of raising two children. Soon, her new life became challenging as she found it difficult to balance her professional commitments with the proper upbringing of her children during such an emotionally distressing time. One day, a woman approached her seeking police protection. The woman had been threatened by the wife of a local businessman, with whom she was having an affair. The wife of the businessman is the daughter of a powerful local politician with a criminal record.

Questions

1. What are the various ethical issues involved here?
2. How should Sarla overcome it?

Answer

This scenario highlights several critical ethical issues, including conflicts of interest, personal bias, professional responsibility, and the influence of power and politics in law enforcement. It also emphasizes the delicate balance between personal responsibilities and professional duties.

Key Stakeholders:

Stakeholder	Role
Sarla (SP)	Upholds moral integrity, balances personal responsibilities with professional duties, and faces ethical dilemmas.
Sarla's Children	Impacted emotionally, dealing with the consequences of family instability, and adapting socially.
The Woman	Vulnerable and seeking protection from psychological harm and social ostracism.
Local Businessman	Engaged in infidelity, causing disruption in familial and social roles.
Businessman's Wife	Engages in coercion and threats, leveraging power dynamics and social influence.
Politician (Father of Businessman's Wife)	Holds patriarchal authority and influences outcomes through political power and social hierarchy.
Police Colleagues	Share responsibility in maintaining institutional integrity and managing workplace ethics under pressure.
Local Community/ Public	Impacted by public perceptions of justice, social norms, and potential community polarization.
Judiciary	Ensures fairness and justice, upholding legal integrity and equity despite external pressures.

(a) Ethical Issues Involved:

1. **Impartiality and Professional Integrity (Kantian Duty Ethics):** Sarla must uphold her moral duty and act according to deontological (Kantian) ethics, ensuring that her decisions remain impartial even while she deals with personal emotional distress from her marital issues. Her commitment to fairness and justice should not be influenced by personal biases or external pressures.
2. **Justice and Power Dynamics (Teleological Ethics):** Sarla's role requires following teleological ethics, meaning her actions should aim for the greater good by protecting the vulnerable and promoting social justice. She must carefully handle the power dynamics posed by the businessman's wife, who is linked to a powerful political family, ensuring her actions prioritize equity over influence.
3. **Non-Maleficence and Beneficence:** Sarla must practice non-maleficence by preventing any further harm or coercion to the woman seeking protection, making sure her actions do not cause additional victimization. At the same time, beneficence requires her to actively promote the woman's well-being by ensuring her safety, emotional stability, and legal protection from threats.
4. **Conflict of Interest and Personal Bias (Virtue Ethics):** Sarla's personal distress from her divorce could lead to bias and affect her judgment. To uphold virtue ethics, she must

show emotional resilience, wisdom, and moral courage so that her professional decisions remain unaffected by her personal issues.

5. **Social Influence and Abuse of Power (Social Role Theory and Power Dynamics):** The power and privilege of the businessman's wife, who is the daughter of a politician with a criminal record, creates ethical tension. Sarla must resist coercive power and ensure the law is applied equally and fairly to everyone, regardless of influence. Social role theory shows how hierarchies can affect ethical behavior in positions of authority.
6. **Duty of Care (Ethics of Care):** Sarla's duty goes beyond legal enforcement. Ethics of care emphasizes her responsibility to protect the woman's well-being by addressing her emotional trauma, ensuring her safety, and providing support when she is vulnerable.
7. **Transparency and Accountability (Ethical Accountability):** Sarla must ensure transparency in her decision-making while maintaining ethical accountability in her actions. This includes providing clear justification for her decisions, particularly when they might be scrutinized due to the involvement of political and social power. Her integrity is crucial for maintaining public trust in law enforcement.
8. **Social Responsibility and Public Welfare (Social Justice):** Sarla's decisions should show a strong commitment to social justice by ensuring that justice is applied equally, no matter one's social status. Her actions must prioritize the public good by protecting the vulnerable and ensuring equal treatment under the law.
9. **No Harm Principle (Utilitarian Ethics):** Following utilitarian ethics, Sarla's actions should aim for the greatest good for the greatest number. She must ensure that her decisions minimise harm to both the woman and the community while promoting the long-term welfare of society—ensuring justice without compromising public safety.

(b) How should Sarla overcome the Ethical Dilemmas?

1. **Uphold Professional Integrity and Ethical Duty:** Sarla should prioritise her professional responsibilities and follow Kantian deontological ethics by acting with moral consistency. By separating her personal emotional distress from her work, she can remain objective and apply justice impartially, free from personal bias.
2. **Seek Emotional and Professional Support:** Sarla should seek emotional and professional support—such as peer guidance, mentorship, or counselling—to help manage her personal challenges. This support will help her process her emotions in a healthy way and make rational, ethical decisions while keeping her professional conduct unaffected.
3. **Apply Ethical Decision-Making Frameworks:** Sarla should use ethical decision-making frameworks by applying teleological and utilitarian principles that prioritise the greatest good. She can uphold the law and protect the community while minimising harm by focusing on the woman's well-being and safety and ensuring social justice and public welfare.

4. **Ensure Impartiality and Eliminate Personal Bias:** Sarla should reflect on her own biases and work to eliminate them. By practicing cognitive neutrality and moral vigilance, she must ensure that everyone is treated equally and fairly, regardless of social or political status.
5. **Strengthen Accountability and Transparency:** To maintain public trust and ethical credibility, Sarla should document all decisions and actions related to the case. Being transparent in her decision-making process will protect her from accusations of corruption or favouritism and affirm her commitment to ethical governance.
6. **Engage with Legal and Institutional Support Systems:** Given the involvement of powerful political figures, Sarla should collaborate with senior law enforcement authorities and legal experts. This will help her maintain ethical autonomy and ensure that the case is handled impartially, with the necessary support and resources.
7. **Prioritize the Ethics of Care:** Sarla should adopt the ethics of care by offering both physical protection and emotional support to the woman. Addressing her psychological trauma and ensuring her safety will show Sarla's commitment to helping vulnerable individuals.
8. **Promote Social Justice and Resist Political Influence:** Sarla must stay committed to social justice and resist attempts by powerful figures to sway her decisions. She should ensure that every case is handled according to the rule of law, promoting equality and fair treatment for all, while maintaining public trust in law enforcement's integrity.
9. **Follow Utilitarian Principles for Greater Good:** Sarla should view her actions from a utilitarian perspective, ensuring that her decisions benefit the community as a whole. By following the no harm principle, she should minimise harm to both the woman and society, promoting long-term stability and community welfare.

   Sarla must navigate both her personal and professional challenges by following ethical principles such as justice, integrity, and public welfare. By applying frameworks like Kantian ethics and the ethics of care, and by ensuring impartiality, transparency, and social justice, she can make fair decisions despite external pressures. Seeking professional support and focusing on the greater good will help Sarla balance her responsibilities and personal struggles, ultimately strengthening the integrity of law enforcement and building public trust.

CASE STUDY 14

While India's celebrated demographic dividend has driven rapid economic progress for decades, a growing challenge now threatens these gains: the rapid ageing of its population's upper end. This issue is a deep concern for policymakers, as India already has the world's second-largest population of elderly individuals—those aged 60 and above. As this 104-million-strong group continues to grow quickly, it will create significant socio-economic pressures. The demand for healthcare services and specialised housing is expected to spike to levels never seen before. Projections indicate that by 2050, about 20% of Indians will be elderly, up from the current 8%. So far, efforts to create a comprehensive health and social care system that meets the population's changing needs have been insufficient. Campaigns to change social attitudes toward ageing may be needed, as current views do not help the elderly live with stability and dignity. The ground realities for many elderly include abandonment by family, poverty and homelessness, limited access to quality healthcare, low levels of institutional support, and the loneliness and depression that come from being separated from their families. Traditionally, elderly care in Indian families has relied on children. According to the National Sample Survey Organisation, nearly 3% of people over 60 live alone, 9.3% live only with their spouses, and 35.6% live with their children. However, as many in the younger workforce have less time, energy, and willingness to care for their parents—or emigrate abroad—senior citizens increasingly must turn to alternative support systems. In the private sector, an estimated demand for 300,000 senior housing units—valued at over $1 billion—has spurred the development of various retirement communities and innovative healthcare delivery options for seniors. Yet, the most vulnerable elderly still depend on the government to develop creative solutions and provide the necessary resources and support.

A global study has found that the way society treats senior citizens plays a major role in improving their mental, physical, and financial health. Based on the above study,

Questions

1. What, according to you, are the factors that have led to the change in the social attitude of the present-day youth towards the elderly?
2. How can the present-day youngsters be sensitised to render honourable treatment towards the elderly?

Answer

Modern societal changes in India have diminished the traditional respect and care for the elderly, leading to increased social isolation and financial insecurity. Rapid urbanisation and evolving lifestyles have contributed to these challenges. To restore dignity and support for seniors, it is crucial to raise awareness among young people about their responsibilities toward the elderly.

(a) Factors Leading to Change in Social Attitudes of Present-Day Youth Towards the Elderly:

1. **Urbanisation and Migration**: Increased urbanisation has led to the rise of nuclear families, replacing the traditional joint family system where elderly care was an inherent responsibility. Migration for better career opportunities has left many elderly parents geographically separated from their children.

2. **Work and Time Constraint**: Long working hours and demanding professional lives leave younger individuals with limited time and energy to care for elderly family members.
3. **Changing Socioeconomic Dynamics**: Rising aspirations for individualistic lifestyles and financial independence often cause youth to prioritise personal goals over family responsibilities.
4. **Erosion of Traditional Values**: The influence of Western culture and the fading of traditional Indian values, such as 'seva' (service) and respect for elders, have led to a decline in emotional and social support for the elderly.
5. **Generational Gap**: Differences in outlook, values, and communication styles between older and younger generations create misunderstandings and reduce empathy.
6. **Financial Constraints**: The rising cost of living and economic pressures make it challenging for youth to support elderly parents financially, especially with high healthcare expenses.

(b) How to Sensitise Present-Day Youth to Treat the Elderly with Respect and Dignity?

1. **Educational Campaigns**: Implement awareness programmes in schools and colleges that highlight the importance of respecting and caring for the elderly, and recognise their valuable contributions to society.
2. **Community Engagement Programmes**: Encourage youth participation in initiatives such as volunteering at old-age homes and senior care centers to gain first-hand exposure to the challenges faced by the elderly.
3. **Strengthen Family Values**: Promote open discussions within families about the needs and roles of the elderly, fostering mutual understanding and respect across generations.
4. **Media and Advocacy Campaigns**: Utilise television, social media, and advertisements to showcase positive stories of elderly care and emphasise the benefits of building meaningful relationships with seniors.
5. **Government and Institutional Support**: Develop youth–elder mentorship programmes where seniors share their experiences and wisdom, thereby encouraging mutual respect. Additionally, offer incentives—such as tax benefits—to families that provide care for their elderly members.
6. **Integration of Technology**: Leverage technology to connect the elderly with their families through video calls and social platforms, especially when geographical distance is an issue. Create apps and platforms that facilitate elder care by providing access to healthcare services or companionship programmes.
7. **Role Models and Influencers**: Promote public figures and influencers who emphasise the importance of caring for and respecting the elderly.

Addressing the changing attitudes of youth towards the elderly requires a multi-pronged approach that combines education, community involvement, and reinforced family values. By fostering respect and empathy through these initiatives, society can build stronger intergenerational bonds and ensure a dignified, supportive environment for senior citizens.

CASE STUDY 15

The horrific gang rape and murder of a 23-year-old woman in Haryana's Rohtak serves as a stark reminder that tough legislation alone cannot eradicate sex crimes. Drawing parallels to the brutal Nirbhaya gang rape case that shook the nation, the perpetrators in Rohtak brutally smashed the victim's head and face with bricks to prevent her identification. The fact that such brutal sexual crimes continue even after the enactment of the Criminal Law (Amendment) Act, 2013—which redefined rape and imposed harsher punishments—underscores how weak policing and investigations are undermining the intent of legal provisions. To illustrate this point, consider that when the Rohtak victim's mutilated body was brought in for post-mortem, the police mistakenly described the corpse as that of an unknown male. Bafflingly, starvation was recorded as the probable cause of death. Furthermore, a lack of coordination between the forensic experts at the crime scene and the doctors conducting the post-mortem prevented the issuance of a detailed report. These systemic failings in policing and investigation significantly reduce the chances of identifying and prosecuting the guilty. The truth is that establishing effective procedures and systems is a far more challenging task, requiring substantial resources to address deficiencies in our policing structures. Consequently, lawmakers often opt for the easier route of legislating tougher laws. However, without accompanying systemic reforms, such laws fail to achieve their primary objectives. Moreover, by being overly strict, these laws become susceptible to misuse. This is precisely what has occurred with the Criminal Law (Amendment) Act, as cases are on the rise where complainants exploit the new anti-rape law to harass innocent individuals. Coupled with a prevailing climate that conflates consensual sex, elopement, or romance with rape—as evidenced by the misguided labelling of the so-called anti-Romeo squads—we now face a situation where genuine rape cases slip through the cracks while innocent people are punished. In this context of ongoing brutal crimes against women, as an administrator, it is imperative to implement systemic reforms that address these shortcomings in policing and investigation, ensuring that justice is both served and seen to be served.

Questions

1. Do you think there needs to be an attitudinal change in the mindset of the people? If so, what kind of changes would you suggest and how can these changes be brought about?
2. What are the lacunae in the policy-making process in India? How can this process be made more effective?

Answer

Immanuel Kant emphasised that we should act out of a sense of duty and respect the intrinsic worth of every individual. This case raises serious ethical concerns about the responsibilities of institutions, the mindset of society, and the role of administrators in ensuring safety, justice, and equality.

1. Attitudinal Change in the Mind-set of People

Yes, there is an urgent need to change people's mindsets to address the deep-rooted issues of gender bias and violence against women. Key measures to bring about this change include:

Suggested Changes

- **Respect for Gender Equality**: Cultivate respect for women as equals in all spheres of life.
- **Eliminating Victim Blaming**: Shift the focus from questioning a victim's character or behaviour to holding the perpetrator accountable for their actions.
- **Sexuality Education**: Introduce comprehensive sexuality education in schools to normalize discussions about consent, relationships, and the importance of respecting personal boundaries.
- **Breaking Stereotypes**: Challenge traditional gender roles that reinforce male dominance and female subservience.

How to Bring About These Changes?

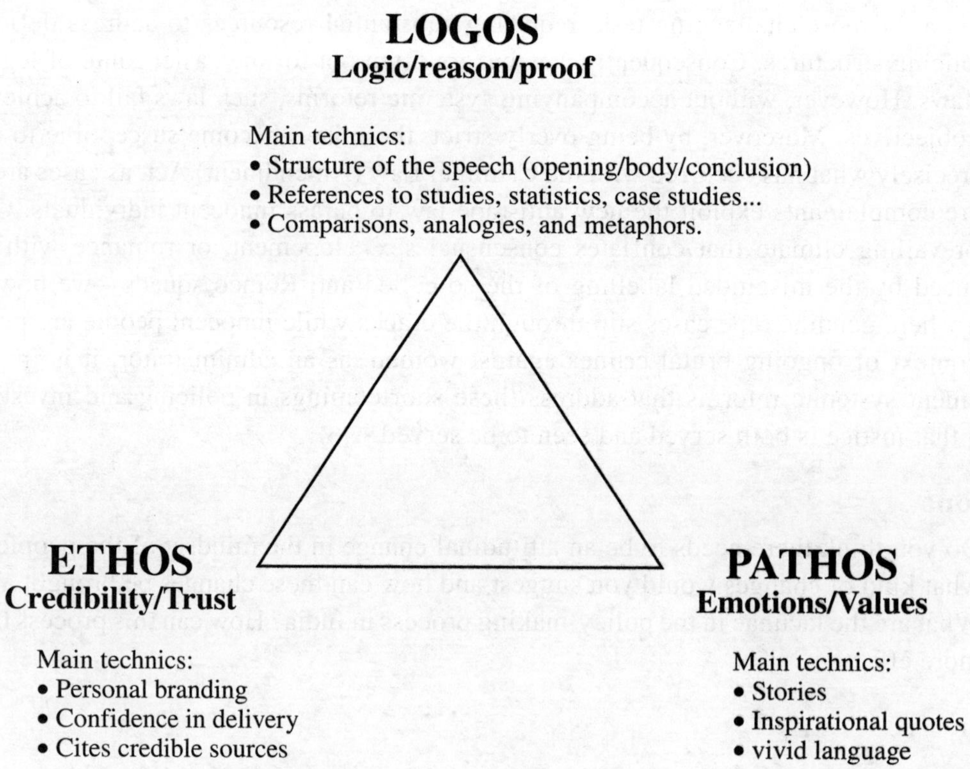

- **Nationwide Education Campaigns:** Launch widespread campaigns using mass media, social media, and community outreach to educate the public about gender equality and the importance of respecting women.
- **Role of Schools**: Integrate gender sensitisation workshops and courses into school and college curriculums.
- **Parental Guidance**: Urge parents to instil respect and empathy in their children, thereby challenging outdated societal norms.
- **Community Programmes**: Organise community events, engage religious organizations, and empower local bodies to facilitate discussions on gender issues and promote collective action.
- **Media Representation**: Encourage the responsible portrayal of women in films, TV shows, and advertisements to diminish objectification and combat stereotypes.

2. Lacunae in the Policymaking Process in India:

Identified Gaps

1. **Reactive Rather Than Proactive Approach**: Policies are frequently reactive to incidents rather than being preventive.
2. **Weak Implementation**: Inefficient enforcement mechanisms and insufficient accountability diminish the effectiveness of policies.
3. **Lack of Consultation**: During the policymaking process, there is inadequate stakeholder engagement—including civil society, experts, and affected communities.
4. **Overcentralisation**: Policies are often overly centralised, lacking the flexibility to address regional or local socio-cultural differences.
5. **Inadequate Resource Allocation**: Insufficient funding for implementation and personnel training undermines the systemic effectiveness of policies.

Making the Process More Effective

1. **Evidence-Based Policymaking**: Employ data and research to identify root causes and develop targeted interventions.
2. **Inclusive Policymaking**: Actively engage all stakeholders, including marginalized communities, in the decision-making process.
3. **Capacity Building**: Invest in comprehensive training for the police, judiciary, and other enforcement agencies to enhance law implementation.
4. **Technology Integration**: Utilize technology to streamline investigations, ensure transparency, and monitor policy implementation.

5. **Periodic Reviews**: Regularly evaluate laws and policies to identify and address loopholes through necessary amendments.
6. **Grassroots Involvement**: Empower local governance structures to adapt and effectively implement policies at the community level.

Aristotle emphasises the importance of moral education and habituation in the development of virtuous character. He argues that virtues are not innate but are acquired through repeated actions and choices. A combination of attitudinal shifts and systemic reforms is essential to address these issues comprehensively and create a safer and more equitable society.

CASE STUDY 16

Concerned by the alarming rise in student suicides in Kota, the district collector has written a heartfelt letter to parents who send their children to the city for coaching. Over the years, Kota, a small city in Rajasthan, has become India's leading coaching hub, attracting lakhs of students aspiring to secure seats in the country's top medical and engineering colleges.

Each year, over 1.5 lakh students from across the country enrol in Kota's coaching institutes, with many joining as early as the 6th grade and continuing until the 12th. These institutions have grown into a massive industry, generating an annual turnover of over ₹5,000 crore. However, despite their academic reputation, these coaching centers place immense pressure on students, subjecting them to gruelling 18-hour study schedules and often poor living conditions. As a result, many students experience severe mental, physical, and emotional exhaustion, leading to a distressingly high suicide rate.

The district collector has urged parents to grant their children the freedom to explore alternative career paths rather than forcing them into rigid academic pursuits. He expressed deep sorrow over reading numerous suicide notes from students—some pleading with parents not to impose the same burden on their younger siblings, others apologising for failing to meet expectations, and many simply admitting that science was never their true passion.

Research suggests that many students perceive suicide as the only escape from the overwhelming academic pressure imposed by their families. The collector's message is a call for greater awareness and compassion, emphasising that a child's well-being must come before societal expectations.

Questions

1. As the District Collector of Kota, what measures would you implement to help students manage their emotional well-being? Additionally, what regulations would you introduce to ensure that coaching centers operate in a way that prioritises students' mental health and overall development?

2. Should parenting be about imposing 'your dreams' on a child at any cost, or about fostering an environment where the child can discover and pursue 'their own' dreams? In light of this perspective, how can parents play a constructive role in ensuring their child's emotional well-being and balanced growth?

Answer

The increasing student suicides in Kota expose a deep ethical conflict between parental expectations, societal pressure, and children's mental well-being. This crisis emphasises the moral duty of parents, educators, and authorities to prioritise students' emotional health and overall development over the relentless pursuit of academic achievement.

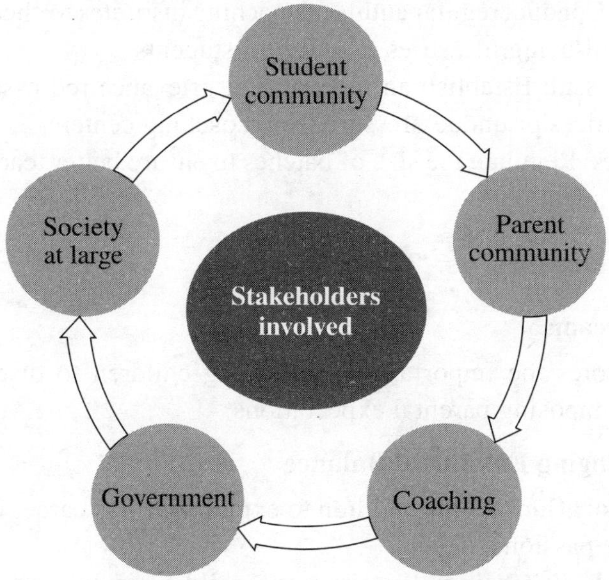

1. Steps to Help Young Children Balance Their Emotions and Regulate Coaching Centres in Kota

Steps to Help Students Balance Their Emotions

1. **Counselling Services**: Establish dedicated counselling centres in schools and coaching institutes with trained psychologists to help students manage stress, anxiety, and depression.
2. **Regular Interaction**: Organise regular open-house discussions where students can voice their concerns to mentors, teachers, and administrators.
3. **Recreational Activities**: Mandate sports, cultural programmes, and relaxation techniques like yoga and meditation in the daily routine of coaching centres.

4. **Peer Support Groups**: Create platforms for students to form peer support groups, where they can share their experiences and challenges.
5. **Helplines**: Set up 24/7 confidential helplines for students in distress to seek immediate psychological support.

Steps to Regulate Coaching Centres

- **Strict Monitoring**: Introduce licensing requirements for coaching centers with mandatory compliance to specific standards of student welfare, such as limiting study hours and ensuring safe living conditions.
- **Transparency in Admissions**: Ensure that the coaching centers provide realistic success rates and avoid creating undue pressure through exaggerated claims of results.
- **Periodic Audits**: Conduct regular audits of coaching institutes to check the physical, mental, and emotional well-being measures in place for students.
- **Grievance Redressal**: Establish an independent grievance redressal body for students to report unfair practices or undue pressure from coaching centers.
- **Limit Batch Sizes**: Regulate the size of batches to ensure better teacher-student interaction and personalised attention.

2. Balancing 'Your Dreams' vs. 'Their Dreams'

Realising 'His/Her Dreams'

The statement underscores the importance of enabling children to discover and pursue their aspirations rather than imposing parental expectations.

Role of Parents in Bringing Emotional Balance

- **Encourage Exploration**: Allow children to explore various career options and interests to identify their true passions.
- **Value Emotional Well-being**: Prioritise the child's mental and emotional health over academic or career success.
- **Set Realistic Expectations**: Understand the child's capabilities and avoid setting unrealistic goals that may overwhelm them.
- **Foster Open Communication**: Maintain an open, non-judgmental dialogue where children feel safe to share their concerns and aspirations.
- **Appreciate Efforts**: Focus on appreciating the child's efforts rather than solely emphasizing outcomes.

How to Create Supportive Situations

- **Participatory Decision-Making**: Involve the child in decision making about their education and career path, respecting their opinions and interests.

- **Provide Exposure**: Encourage children to attend workshops, internships, or extracurricular activities that help them understand different fields.
- **Celebrate Individuality**: Educate children that success comes in many forms and isn't limited to conventional definitions like IITs or medical colleges.

The Concept of Existentialism: Stresses individual freedom, choice, and responsibility in creating one's meaning and purpose in life. Encouraging students to explore their passions and make their own career choices helps them find authentic meaning rather than conforming to impose paths.